DATABASE DESIGN, APPLICATION DEVELOPMENT, AND ADMINISTRATION

InformationTechnology

INFORMATION TECHNOLOGY AT McGraw-Hill/Irwin

At McGraw-Hill Higher Education, we publish instructional materials for the higher education market. In order to expand the tools of higher learning, we publish everything you may need: texts, lab manuals, study guides, testing materials, software, and multimedia products—the Total Solution.

We realize that technology has created and will continue to create new mediums for professors and students to use in managing resources and communicating information to one another. McGraw-Hill/Irwin continues to provide the most flexible and complete teaching and learning tools available as well as offer solutions to the changing world of teaching and learning. McGraw-Hill/Irwin is dedicated to providing the tools for today's instructors and students, which will enable them to successfully navigate the world of Information Technology.

- Seminar Series and Focus Groups—McGraw-Hill/Irwin's seminar series and focus groups are offered across the country every year. At the seminar series we provide you with the latest technology products and encourage collaboration among teaching professionals. We conduct many focus groups year round where we can hear from you what we need to publish.

- ITAP–Information Technology Advisory Panel—This is a "super focus group," where we gather many of the country's top IT educators for three days to tell us how to publish the best IT texts possible. ITAPs are very instrumental in driving our publishing plans.

- McGraw-Hill/Osborne—This leading trade division company of the family of McGraw-Hill Companies is known for its best-selling Internet titles, Harley Hahn's Internet & Web yellow pages, and the Internet Complete Reference. If we don't have it in our CIT/MIS, you can find it at Osborne. For more information, visit Osborne at **www.osborne.com.**

- Digital Solutions—Whether you want to teach a class online or just post your "bricks-n-mortar" class syllabus, McGraw-Hill/Irwin is committed to publishing digital solutions. Taking your course online doesn't have to be a solitary adventure, nor does it have to be a difficult one. We offer several solutions that will allow you to enjoy all the benefits of having your course material online.

- Packaging Options—For more information about our discount options, contact your McGraw-Hill/Irwin sales representative at 1-800-338-3987 or visit our website at **www.mhhe.com/it.**

DATABASE DESIGN, APPLICATION DEVELOPMENT, AND ADMINISTRATION

SECOND EDITION

Michael V. Mannino
University of Colorado at Denver

Boston   Burr Ridge, IL   Dubuque, IA   Madison, WI   New York   San Francisco   St. Louis
Bangkok   Bogotá   Caracas   Kuala Lumpur   Lisbon   London   Madrid   Mexico City
Milan   Montreal   New Delhi   Santiago   Seoul   Singapore   Sydney   Taipei   Toronto

Irwin

DATABASE DESIGN, APPLICATION DEVELOPMENT, AND ADMINISTRATION Published by McGraw-Hill/Irwin, a business unit of The McGraw-Hill Companies, Inc., 1221 Avenue of the Americas, New York, NY, 10020. Copyright © 2004, 2001 by The McGraw-Hill Companies, Inc. All rights reserved. No part of this publication may be reproduced or distributed in any form or by any means, or stored in a database or retrieval system, without the prior written consent of The McGraw-Hill Companies, Inc., including, but not limited to, in any network or other electronic storage or transmission, or broadcast for distance learning.

Some ancillaries, including electronic and print components, may not be available to customers outside the United States.

This book is printed on acid-free paper.

domestic 1 2 3 4 5 6 7 8 9 0 DOW/DOW 0 9 8 7 6 5 4 3
international 1 2 3 4 5 6 7 8 9 0 DOW/DOW 0 9 8 7 6 5 4 3

ISBN 0-07-282350-X

Publisher: *George Werthman*
Senior sponsoring editor: *Paul Ducham*
Developmental editor: *Kelly L. Delso*
Manager, Marketing and Sales: *Paul Murphy*
Media producer: *Greg Bates*
Project manager: *Jim Labeots*
Senior production supervisor: *Michael R. McCormick*
Designer: *Kami Carter*
Senior supplement producer: *Rose M. Range*
Senior digital content specialist: *Brian Nacik*
Cover image: *The Stock Illustration Source*
Typeface: *10/12 Times New Roman*
Compositor: *Carlisle Communications, Ltd.*
Printer: *R. R. Donnelley*

Library of Congress Cataloging-in-Publication Data

Mannino, Michael V.
    Database design, application development, and administration / Michael V. Mannino–2nd ed.
        p.cm.
    Includes bibliographical references and index.
    ISBN 0-07-282350-X (alk. paper)–ISBN 0-07-121489-5 (international : alk. paper)
    1. Database design. 2. Application software–Development. 3. Database management.
    I. Title.
    QA76.9.D26 M374 2004
    005.74–dc21

                                                                    2002040967

INTERNATIONAL EDITION ISBN 0-07-121489-5
Copyright © 2004. Exclusive rights by The McGraw-Hill Companies, Inc. for manufacture and export. This book cannot be re-exported from the country to which it is sold by McGraw-Hill. The International Edition is not available in North America.

www.mhhe.com

ABOUT THE AUTHOR

Michael V. Mannino has been involved in the database field since 1980. He has taught database management since 1983 at several major universities (University of Florida, University of Texas at Austin, University of Washington, and University of Colorado at Denver). His audiences have included undergraduate MIS students, graduate MIS students, MBA students, and doctoral students as well as corporate employees in retraining programs. He has also been active in database research as evidenced by publications in major journals of the IEEE (*Transactions on Knowledge and Data Engineering* and *Transactions on Software Engineering*), ACM (*Communications* and *Computing Surveys*), and INFORMS (*Informs Journal on Computing* and *Information Systems Research*). His research includes several popular survey and tutorial articles as well as many papers describing original research. Practical results of his research on a form-driven approach to database design are incorporated into Chapter 12.

I wish to dedicate this book to my daughters, Julia and Aimee.
Your smiles inspire me every day.

PREFACE

MOTIVATING EXAMPLE   Paul Hong, the owner of International Industrial Glue, Inc., is anxious about the future of his business. Although his company has been very successful as an early adopter of Web technology, he is concerned about managing the growth of his business and continued utilization of Web technology. His business has grown rapidly as he embraced Web technology. Now he is unsure about which new directions to take to ensure the future growth of his business.

Paul Hong's main concern is updating the information technology infrastructure to support future expansion. He believes that the current infrastructure has reached its capacity to handle online order processing. Recent unavailability of the order entry website for one product line has resulted in a substantial lost sales opportunity. As his business has expanded into new markets, he has become concerned about the inability to track key business indicators across product lines. He is also concerned about management of nontraditional digital data such as product images and promotion videos as well as integrating XML product data with his order entry databases. For all of these concerns, he is unsure about proprietary versus nonproprietary technologies and standards.

All of these concerns involve significant usage of database technology as part of an enterprise computing infrastructure. Transaction processing features in enterprise DBMSs provide a foundation to increase online order processing performance as well as to improve website reliability. Data warehouse features in enterprise DBMSs provide the foundation to support small data marts as well as large data warehouses. Object database features provide the ability to manage nontraditional data as well as integrate XML product data with order entry data.

However, the solutions to Paul Hong's concerns are found not just in technology. Utilization of the appropriate level of technology involves a vision for an organization's future, a deep understanding of technology, and traditional management skills to manage risk. Paul Hong realizes that his largest challenge is to blend these skills so that effective solutions can be developed for International Industrial Glue, Inc.

INTRODUCTION   This textbook provides a foundation to understand the database technology supporting enterprise computing concerns such as those faced by Paul Hong. As a new student of database management, you need to first understand the fundamental concepts of database management and the relational data model. Then you need to master

vii

skills in database design and database application development. This textbook provides tools to help you understand relational databases and acquire skills to solve basic and advanced problems in query formulation, data modeling, normalization, application data requirements, and customization of database applications.

After establishing these skills, you are ready to study the role of database specialists and the processing environments in which databases are used. This textbook presents the fundamental database technologies in each processing environment and relates these technologies to new advances in electronic commerce and enterprise computing. You will learn the vocabulary, architectures, and design issues that provide a background for advanced study of individual database management systems, electronic commerce applications, and enterprise computing.

WHAT'S NEW IN THE SECOND EDITION

The second edition goes beyond mere refinements to the first edition. The second edition provides a considerable amount of new material and presents material from the first edition in a significantly new manner. The relentless expansion of database technology motivates most of the new material. Database technology continues to evolve rapidly in areas such as data warehouses, object-oriented databases, transaction management, and storage/optimization technologies. The second edition reflects these trends with new material about SQL:1999 and Oracle 9i, relational database technologies for data warehouses, data warehouse population processes, object-relational features in Oracle 9i, and optimization features including bitmap indexes and star joins.

The other motivation for making changes to this second edition is classroom experience with the first edition. Experience gained from my own instruction of undergraduate and graduate students along with feedback from adopters of the first edition have led to the development of new material and refinements to existing material. The most significant refinement involves data modeling coverage. Frustration with student difficulties in data modeling motivated the separation of data modeling coverage between mastering the notation (Chapter 5) and applying the notation to business problems (Chapter 6). The most significant new material is in Chapter 11 on stored procedures and triggers. This chapter was motivated by my instruction of triggers and stored procedures in an advanced database course. Additional new and refined material motivated by classroom usage of the first edition include revised coverage of normalization, the management of stored procedures and triggers, nested queries in the FROM clause, database benchmarks, refinements to transaction processing coverage, and updated coverage of SQL:1999.

In addition to new material and refinements to existing material, the second edition extends the chapter supplements. The second edition contains many new end-of-chapter questions and problems as well as SQL:1999 syntax summaries. In addition, the ER Assistant, the bundled data modeling tool, has been significantly revised, especially to support the diagram rules presented in Chapter 5.

The second edition also has a revised chapter organization to reflect the progression of topics in database design, application development, and database administration. Part 1 covers just foundation knowledge instead of details about application development. Part 2 still covers database design except for the chapters about view integration and the case study. Part 3 covers database application development, including the new chapter on stored procedures and triggers. The coverage of view integration and the case study has been moved to Part 3 to integrate database design with application development. Part 4 covers database administration and processing environments for DBMSs, material that was presented in Part 3 of the first edition.

COMPETITIVE ADVANTAGES   This textbook provides outstanding features unmatched in competing textbooks. The unique features include detailed SQL coverage for both Access and Oracle, problem-solving guidelines to aid acquisition of key skills, carefully designed sample databases and examples, a comprehensive case study, advanced topic coverage, integrated lab material, and the bundled ER Assistant. These features provide a complete package for an introductory database course. Each of these features is described in more detail in the list below whereas Table P.1 summarizes the competitive advantages by chapter.

- **SQL Coverage:** The breadth and depth of the SQL coverage in this text is unmatched by competing textbooks. Table P.2 summarizes SQL coverage by chapter. Parts 1 and 3 provide a thorough coverage of the CREATE TABLE, SELECT, UPDATE, INSERT, DELETE, CREATE VIEW, and CREATE TRIGGER statements. Numerous examples of basic, intermediate, and advanced problems are presented. The chapters in Part 4 cover statements useful for database administrators as well as statements used in specific processing environments.
- **Access and Oracle Coverage:** The chapters in Parts 1 and 3 provide detailed coverage of both Access and Oracle SQL. Each example for the SELECT, INSERT, UPDATE, DELETE, and CREATE VIEW statements are shown for both database management systems. Significant coverage of new Oracle 9i

TABLE P.1	Summary of Competitive Advantages by Chapter

Chapter	Unique Features
2	Visual representation of relational algebra operators
3	Query formulation guidelines; Oracle, Access, and SQL:1999 SQL coverage
4	Unique chapter providing a conceptual introduction to the database development process
5	Emphasis on ERD notation; diagram rules with support in the ER Assistant
6	Emphasis on the practice of data modeling; data modeling guidelines and transformations
7	Normalization guidelines and procedures
8	Index selection rules; SQL tuning guidelines; integrated coverage of query optimization, file structures, and index selection
9	Query formulation guidelines; Oracle (8i and 9i), Access, and SQL:1999 SQL coverage; advanced topic coverage of nested queries, division problems, and null value handling
10	Updatable view rules; data requirement guidelines for forms and reports
11	Unique chapter covering concepts and practices of database programming languages, stored procedures, and triggers
12	Unique chapter covering concepts and practices of view integration and design
13	Unique chapter providing a comprehensive case study on student loan processing
14	Guidelines for important processes used by database administrators
15	Transaction design guidelines and advanced topic coverage
16	Advanced topic coverage of relational database features for data warehouse processing and the data warehouse refresh process; extensive Oracle 9i data warehouse coverage
17	Integrated coverage of distributed processing and distributed databases
18	Advanced topic coverage of object-relational features in SQL:1999 and Oracle 9i

TABLE P.2	SQL Statement Coverage by Chapter

Chapter	SQL Statements
2	CREATE TABLE
3	SELECT, INSERT, UPDATE, DELETE
9	SELECT (nested queries, outer joins, null value handling); Access, Oracle (8i and 9i), and SQL:1999 coverage
10	CREATE VIEW; queries and manipulation statements using views
11	CREATE PROCEDURE (Oracle), CREATE TRIGGER (Oracle)
14	GRANT, REVOKE, CREATE ROLE, CREATE ASSERTION, CHECK clause of the CREATE TABLE statement, CREATE DOMAIN
15	BEGIN TRANSACTION, COMMIT, SET TRANSACTION, SET CONSTRAINTS, SAVEPOINT
16	CREATE MATERIALIZED VIEW (Oracle), GROUP BY clause extensions, CREATE DIMENSION (Oracle)
18	CREATE TYPE, CREATE TABLE (typed tables), SELECT (object identifiers, path expressions, dereference operator); SQL:1999 and Oracle 9i coverage

SQL features appears in Chapters 9, 11, 16, and 18. In addition, the chapters in Parts 1 and 3 cover SQL:1999 syntax to support instruction with other prominent database management systems.

- **Problem-Solving Guidelines:** Students need more than explanations of concepts and examples to solve problems. Students need guidelines to help structure their thinking process to tackle problems in a systematic manner. The guidelines provide mental models to help students apply the concepts to solve basic and advanced problems. Table P.3 summarizes the unique problem-solving guidelines by chapter.

- **Sample Databases and Examples:** Two sample databases are used throughout the chapters of Parts 1 and 3 to provide consistency and continuity. The University database is used in the chapter examples, while the Order

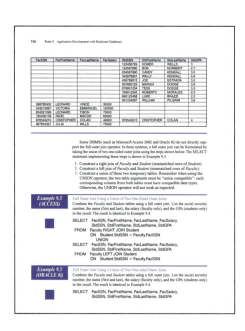

TABLE P.3	Problem-Solving Guidelines by Chapter

Chapter	Problem-Solving Guidelines
2	Visual representation of relationships and relational algebra operators
3	Conceptual evaluation process; query formulation questions
5	Diagram rules
6	Design transformations; common design errors; conversion rules
7	Combined definition of 2NF/3NF; simple synthesis procedure
8	Index selection rules; SQL tuning guidelines
9	Nested query evaluation; count method for division problems
10	Rules for updatable join queries; steps for analyzing data requirements in forms and reports
11	Trigger execution procedure
12	Form analysis steps; view integration strategies
14	Guidelines to manage stored procedures and triggers; data planning process; DBMS selection process
15	Transaction timeline; transaction design guidelines
16	Guidelines for relational database representations of multidimensional data; guidelines for refreshing a data warehouse
17	Progression of transparency levels for distributed databases
18	Object database architectures; comparison between relational and object-relational representations

Entry database is used in the end-of-chapter problems. Numerous examples and problems with these databases depict the fundamental skills of query formulation and application data requirements. Revised versions of the databases provide separation between basic and advanced examples. The website contains CREATE TABLE statements, sample data, data manipulation statements, and Access database files for both databases. Icons for the University and Order Entry databases are placed in the margins of the text to call out to students when an example begins.

Chapters in Parts 2 and 4 use additional databases to broaden exposure to more diverse business situations. Students need exposure to a variety of business situations to acquire database design skills and understand concepts important to database specialists. Other databases covering water utility operations, patient visits, academic paper reviews, personal financial tracking, airline reservations, placement office operations, automobile insurance, store sales tracking, and real estate sales supplement the University and Order Entry databases in the chapter examples and end-of-chapter problems.

- **Comprehensive Case Study:** The Student Loan, Unlimited Case is found at the end of Part 3. The case description along with its solution integrates the concepts students learned in the preceding 12 chapters on application development and database design. The follow-up problems at the end of the chapter provide additional opportunities for students to apply their knowledge on a realistic case.
- **Optional Integrated Labs:** Database management is best taught when concepts are closely linked to the practice of designing and implementing databases using a commercial DBMS. To help students apply the concepts described in the textbook, optional supplementary lab materials are available

on CD-ROM and the text's website. The CD-ROM contains labs for three Microsoft Access versions (97, 2000, and 2002) as well as practice databases and practice exercises. The Microsoft Access labs integrate a detailed coverage of Access with the application development concepts covered in Parts 1 and 3.

- **Free Data Modeling Tool:** The ER Assistant provides a simple interface for drawing and analyzing entity relationship diagrams as presented in the Part 2 chapters on database development. This unique, DBMS-independent program is packaged free with each student copy of the text. Students can quickly become productive with this program, enabling them to focus on the concepts of data modeling rather than the details of a complex CASE tool. To help students avoid diagram errors, the ER Assistant supports the diagram rules presented in Chapter 5.

- **Current and Cutting-Edge Topics:** This book covers some topics that are missing from competing textbooks: advanced query formulation, updatable views, development and management of stored procedures and triggers, data requirements for data entry forms and reports, view integration, population process for data warehouses, Web database connectivity architectures, object database architectures, data warehouse features in SQL:1999 and Oracle 9i, object-relational features in SQL:1999 and Oracle 9i, and transaction design principles. These topics can help motivated students obtain a deeper understanding of database management.

- **Complete Package for Course:** Depending on the course criteria, some students may need to purchase as many as five books for an introductory database course: a textbook covering principles, laboratory books covering details of a DBMS and a CASE tool, a supplemental SQL book, and a casebook with realistic practice problems. This textbook and supplemental material provide one complete and less expensive source for the student. In addition to the expense of using many separate books and lab manuals, the separate books lack an integrated approach.

TEXT AUDIENCE

This book is intended for a first undergraduate or graduate course in database management. At the undergraduate level, students should have a concentration (major or minor) or active interest in information systems. For two-year institutions, the instructor may want to skip the advanced topics and place more emphasis on the optional Access lab book. Undergraduate students should have a first course covering general information systems concepts, spreadsheets, word processing, and possibly a brief introduction to databases. Except for Chapter 11, a previous course in computer programming can be useful background but is not mandatory. The chapters reference computer programming concepts, but writing code is not covered. For a complete understanding of Chapter 11, computer programming background is essential. However, the basic concepts in Chapter 11 can be covered even if students do not have computer programming background.

At the graduate level, this book is suitable in either MBA or Master of Science (in information systems) programs. The advanced material in this book should be especially suitable for Master of Science students.

ORGANIZATION

As the title suggests, *Database Design, Application Development, and Administration* emphasizes three sets of skills. Before acquiring these skills, students need a foundation about basic concepts. Part 1 provides background for subsequent detailed study of database design, database application development, and database administration. The chapters in Part 1 present the principles of database management, the relational data model, and query formulation.

Part 2 provides a foundation for database design. Students desiring a career as a database administrator should be able to perform each step of the database development process. Students should learn skills of data modeling, schema conversion, normalization, and physical database design.

The chapters in Part 2 emphasize practical skills and design processes for the database development process. Chapter 4 introduces the context, objectives, phases, and tools of the database development process. Chapters 5 and 6 cover data modeling using the Entity Relationship Model. Chapter 7 covers the motivation, functional dependencies, normal forms, and practical considerations of data normalization. Chapter 8 contains broad coverage of physical database design including the objectives, inputs, file structure and query optimization background, and important design choices.

Part 3 provides a foundation for building database applications by helping students acquire skills in advanced query formulation, specification of data requirements for data entry forms and reports, coding triggers and stored procedures, and using views in the design of complex databases. Chapter 9 presents additional examples of intermediate and advanced SQL, along with corresponding query formulation skills. Chapter 10 describes the motivation, definition, and usage of relational views along with specification of view definitions for data entry forms and reports. Chapter 11 presents concepts and coding practices of database programming languages, stored procedures, and triggers for customization of database applications. Chapter 12 describes view design and view integration, which are data modeling concepts for large database development efforts. Chapter 13 provides a comprehensive case study that enables students to gain insights about the difficulties of applying database design and application development skills to a realistic business database.

Beyond the database design and application development skills, this textbook prepares students for careers as database specialists. Students need to understand the responsibilities, tools, and processes employed by data administrators and database administrators as well as the various environments in which databases operate.

The chapters in Part 4 emphasize the role of database specialists and the details of managing databases in various operating environments. Chapter 14 provides a context for the other chapters through coverage of the responsibilities, tools, and processes used by database administrators and data administrators. The other chapters in Part 4 provide a foundation for managing databases in important environments: Chapter 15 on transaction processing, Chapter 16 on data warehouses, Chapter 17 on distributed processing and data, and Chapter 18 on object database management. These chapters emphasize concepts, architectures, and design choices important for database specialists.

TEXT APPROACH AND THEME

To support acquisition of the necessary skills for learning and understanding application development, database design, and managing databases, this book adheres to three guiding principles:

1. *Combine concepts and practice.* Database management is more easily learned when concepts are closely linked to the practice of designing and implementing databases using a commercial DBMS. The textbook and the

accompanying supplements have been designed to provide close integration between concepts and practice through the following features:

- SQL examples for both Access and Oracle as well as SQL:1999 coverage.
- Emphasis of the relationship between application development and query formulation.
- Usage of a data modeling notation supported by professional CASE tools and an easy-to-use academic tool (ER Assistant).
- Supplemental laboratory practice chapters that combine textbook concepts with details of commercial DBMSs.

2. *Emphasize problem-solving skills.* This book features problem-solving guidelines to help students master the fundamental skills of data modeling, normalization, query formulation, and application development. The textbook and associated supplements provide a wealth of questions, problems, case studies, and laboratory practices in which students can apply their skills. With mastery of the fundamental skills, students will be poised for future learning about databases and change the way they think about computing, in general.

3. *Provide introductory and advanced material.* Business students who use this book may have a variety of backgrounds. This book provides enough depth to satisfy the most eager students. However, the advanced parts are placed so that they can be skipped by the less inclined.

PEDAGOGICAL FEATURES

This book contains the following pedagogical features to help students work their way through chapter content in a sensible and organized fashion:

- **Learning Objectives** focus on the knowledge and skills students will acquire from studying the chapter.
- **Overviews** provide a snapshot or preview of chapter contents.
- **Key Terms** are highlighted and defined in the margins as they appear in the chapter.

- **Examples** are clearly separated from the rest of the chapter material for easier review and studying purposes.

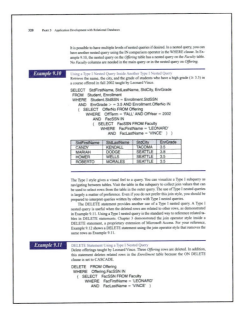

- **Running Database Examples**—University and Order Entry with icons in margins to draw student attention to examples.
- **Closing Thoughts** summarize what students have learned in the chapter.
- **Review Concepts** are the important conceptual highlights from the chapter, not just a list of terminology.
- **Questions** are provided to review the chapter concepts.
- **Problems** are included to help students practice and implement what they have learned.
- **References for Further Study** point students to additional sources on chapter content.
- **Chapter Appendixes** provide more in-depth treatment of certain principles or practices.

At the end of the text, students will find the following additional resources:

- **Glossary:** Provides a complete list of terms and definitions used throughout the text.
- **Bibliography:** A list of helpful industry, academic, and other printed material for further research or study.

In addition, a list of Web resources can be found in the Online Learning Center, www.mhhe.com/mannino.

ACCESS LAB ON CD-ROM

Lab books for both Microsoft Access 97, 2000, and 2002 are available on CD-ROM as packaging options with this text. The lab books provide detailed coverage of features important to beginning database students as well as many advanced features. The lab chapters provide a mixture of guided practice and reference material organized into the following chapters:

1. An Introduction to Microsoft Access
2. Database Creation Lab
3. Query Lab
4. Single Table Form Lab
5. Hierarchical Form Lab
6. Report Lab
7. Pivot Tables and Data Access Pages (Access 2002 only)
8. User Interface Lab

Each lab chapter follows the pedagogy of the textbook with Learning Objectives, Overview, Closing Thoughts, Additional Practice exercises, and Appendixes of helpful tips. Most lab chapters reference concepts from the textbook for close integration with corresponding textbook chapters. Each lab book also includes a glossary of terms and an index.

INSTRUCTOR RESOURCES

A comprehensive set of supplements for the text and lab manuals is available to adopters. These include:

- Instructor CD-ROM to contain Instructor's Manual, PowerPoint slides, Test Bank, and Computerized Test Bank. The test data bank provides problems for assignments, midterm exams, and final exams, in addition to questions to test basic understanding.
- Website/Online Learning Center, www.mhhe.com/mannino. The instructor center contains problem solutions, an exam and assignment data bank, PowerPoint lecture notes, case study solutions, and laboratory assignment solutions.

TEACHING PATHS

The textbook can be covered in several orders in a one- or a two-semester sequence.

The author has taught a one-semester course with the ordering of application development, database development, and database processing environments. This ordering has the advantage of covering the more concrete material (application development) before the more abstract material (database development). Lab chapters and assignments are used for practice beyond the textbook chapters. To fit into one semester, advanced topics in Chapters 8, 9, 11, 12, 15, 16, 17, and 18 may be skipped.

A second ordering is to cover database development before application development. For this ordering, the author recommends following the textbook ordering. This ordering supports a more thorough coverage of database development while not neglecting application development. To fit into one semester, advanced topics in Chapters 8, 9, 11, 12, 15, 16, 17, and 18 may be skipped.

A third possible ordering is to use the textbook in a two-course sequence. The first course covers database management fundamentals from Part 1, data modeling and normalization from Part 2, and advanced query formulation, application development with views, and view integration from Part 3. Because of the second course, the material on database design can be covered in more depth than one course alone permits. The second course emphasizes database administration skills with physical database design from Part 2, triggers and stored procedures from Part 3, and the processing environments from Part 4 along with additional material on managing enterprise databases. A comprehensive project can be used in the second course to integrate application development, database development, and database administration.

STUDENT RESOURCES

- **ER Assistant:** Packaged free with each student text, this easy-to-use data modeling tool can be used to draw and analyze ERDs.
- **Integrated Access Labs:** Available as a packaging option, these Access 97, 2000, and 2002 labs are available on CD-ROM and include additional sample databases and practice exercises not found in the text.
- **Website/Online Learning Center, www.mhhe.com/mannino:** The student center contains study outlines that include learning objectives, chapter overviews, summaries and key terms from the text, self-assessment quizzes, and other helpful online resources.

ACKNOWLEDGMENTS

The second edition of this textbook is the culmination of many years of work. Before beginning the first edition, I wrote tutorials, laboratory practices, and case studies. This material was first used to supplement other textbooks. After encouragement from students, this material was used without a textbook. This material, revised many times through student comments, was the foundation for the first edition. During the development of the first edition, the material was classroom tested for three years with hundreds of undergraduate and graduate students, along with careful review through four drafts by many outside reviewers. The second edition was developed through classroom usage of the first edition for three years, along with teaching an advanced database course for several years.

I wish to acknowledge the excellent support that I have received in completing this project. First, I thank my many database students, especially those in ISMG6080 and ISMG4500 at the University of Colorado at Denver and in the U.S. West IT Professional Program. Your comments and reaction to the draft textbook have been invaluable to its improvement.

Second, I thank the many fine reviewers who provided feedback on the various drafts of this textbook:

Rob Anson, *Boise State University*

Kirk P. Arnett, *Mississippi State University*

Robert M. Ballenger, *Wake Forest University*

Reza Barkhi, *Virginia Polytechnic Institute and State University*

Jack D. Becker, *University of North Texas*

Nabil Bedewi, *George Mason University*

France Belanger, *Virginia Polytechnic Institute and State University*

Douglas B. Bock, *Southern Illinois University—Edwardsville*

John Bradley, *East Carolina University*

Susan Brown, *Indiana University—Bloomington*

Amita G. Chin, *Virginia Commonwealth University*

Russell Ching, *California State University—Sacramento*

P. C. Chu, *The Ohio State University*

Connie W. Crook, *University of North Carolina—Charlotte*
Donald L. Dawley, *Miami University*
Robert Louis Gilson, *Washington State University*
Kingsley Gnanadran, *University of Scranton*
Sanjay Gosain, *University of Maryland*
Mark Hwang, *Central Michigan University*
Nenad Jukic, *Loyola University—Chicago*
Douglas M. Kline, *University of North Carolina*
Constance Knapp, *Pace University*
Alexis Koster, *San Diego State University*
Jean-Pierre Kuilboer, *University of Massachusetts—Boston*
Sophie Lee, *California State University—Long Beach*
Anita Lee-Post, *University of Kentucky*
John D. (Skip) Lees, *California State University—Chico*
William Leigh, *University of Central Florida*
Mary Malliaris, *Loyola University—Chicago*
Bruce McLaren, *Indiana State University*
Nirup M. Menon, *University of Texas at Dallas*
Karen S. Nantz, *Eastern Illinois University*
M. Pamela Neely, *Marist College*
Hamid Nemati, *University of North Carolina—Greensboro*
Robert Phillips, *Radford University*
Young U. Ryu, *University of Texas—Dallas*
Hsueh-Chi Joshua Shih, *National Yunlin University of Science and Technology*
Erick Slazinski, *Purdue University*
Goh Tiong, *Victoria University—Wellington*
Santosh S. Venkatraman, *University of Arkansas—Little Rock*
Peter Wolcott, *University of Nebraska—Omaha*

Your comments, especially the critical ones, have helped me tremendously in refining the textbook.

Third, I thank my Irwin McGraw-Hill editors, Rick Williamson, Paul Ducham, and Kelly Delso, for their guidance in this process as well as Jim Labeots, Kami Carter, and the other McGraw-Hill folks who helped in the production and publication of this text. Finally, I thank my wife, Monique, for her help with the textbook and supplements, along with her moral support for my effort.

Michael V. Mannino

BRIEF CONTENTS

CONTENTS

10

APPLICATION DEVELOPMENT WITH VIEWS   353

11

STORED PROCEDURES AND TRIGGERS   389

12

VIEW DESIGN AND INTEGRATION   439

FOUNDATIONS OF RELATIONAL DATABASES

Part 1 provides a background for the subsequent detailed study of database design, database application development, and database administration. The chapters in Part 1 present the principles of database management, the relational data model, and query formulation. Chapter 1 covers the basic concepts of database management including database characteristics, features and architectures of database management systems, the market for database management systems, and organizational impacts of database technology. Chapter 2 provides some background on the relational data model including data definition concepts and relational algebra operators. Chapter 3 shows numerous examples of basic and intermediate SQL along with fundamental query formulation skills.

CHAPTER 1

Introduction to Database Management

LEARNING OBJECTIVES

This chapter provides an introduction to database technology and the impact of this technology on organizations. After this chapter the student should have acquired the following knowledge and skills:

■ Describe the characteristics of business databases and the features of database management systems.

■ Understand the importance of nonprocedural access for software productivity.

■ Appreciate the advances in database technology and the contribution of database technology to modern society.

■ Understand the impact of database management system architectures on distributed processing and software maintenance.

■ Perceive career opportunities related to database application development and database administration.

OVERVIEW

You may not be aware of it, but your life is dramatically affected by database technology. Computerized databases are vital to the functioning of modern organizations. You come into contact with databases on a daily basis through activities such as shopping at a supermarket, going to an automated teller machine, ordering a book online, and registering for classes. The convenience of your daily life is partly due to proliferation of computerized databases and supporting database technology.

Database technology is not only improving the daily operations of organizations but also the quality of decisions that affect our lives. Databases contain a flood of data about many aspects of our lives: consumer preferences, telecommunications usage, credit history, television viewing habits, and so on. Database technology helps to summarize this mass of data into useful information for decision making. Management uses information gleaned from databases to make long-range decisions such as investing in plants and equipment, locating stores, adding new items to inventory, and entering new businesses.

This first chapter provides a starting point for your exploration of database technology. It surveys database characteristics, database management system features, system architectures, and human roles in managing and using databases. The other chapters in Part 1 provide details about relational databases, the most widely used kind of commercial database. This chapter provides a broad picture of database technology and shares the excitement about the journey ahead.

1.1 Database Characteristics

Database a collection of persistent data that can be shared and interrelated.

Every day, businesses collect mountains of facts about persons, things, and events such as credit card numbers, bank balances, and purchase amounts. Databases contain these sorts of simple facts as well as nonconventional information such as photographs, fingerprints, product videos, and book abstracts. With the proliferation of the Internet and the means to capture data in computerized form, a vast amount of data is available at the click of a mouse button. Organizing these data for ease of retrieval and maintenance is paramount. Thus, managing databases has become a vital task in most organizations.

Before learning about managing databases, you must first understand some important properties of databases, as discussed in the following list:

- Persistent means that data reside on stable storage such as a magnetic disk. For example, organizations need to retain data about customers, suppliers, and inventory on stable storage because these data are repetitively used. A variable in a computer program is not persistent because it resides in main memory and disappears after the program terminates. Persistency does not mean that data last forever. When data are no longer relevant (such as a supplier going out of business), they are removed or archived.

  Persistency depends on relevance of intended usage. For example, the mileage you drive for work is important to maintain if you are self-employed. Likewise, the amount of your medical expenses is important if you can itemize your deductions. Because storing and maintaining data are costly, only data likely to be relevant to decisions should be stored.

- Shared means that a database can have multiple uses and users. A database provides a common memory for multiple functions in an organization. For example, a personnel database can support payroll calculations, performance evaluations, government reporting requirements, and so on. Many users can use a database at the same time. For example, many customers can simultaneously make airline reservations. Unless two users are trying to change the same part of the database at the same time, they can proceed without waiting on each other.

- Interrelated means that data stored as separate units can be connected to provide a whole picture. For example, a customer database relates customer data (name, address, . . .) to order data (order number, order date, . . .) to facilitate order

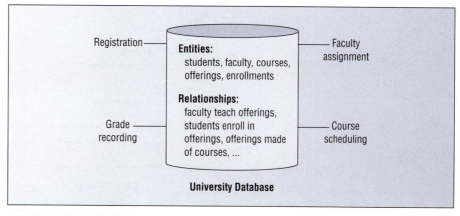

Figure 1.1

Depiction of a simplified university database.
Note: Words surrounding the database denote procedures that use the database.

processing. Databases contain both entities and relationships among entities. An <u>entity</u> is a cluster of data usually about a single topic that can be accessed together. An entity can denote a person, place, thing, or event. For example, a personnel database contains entities such as employees, departments, and skills as well as relationships showing employee assignments to departments, skills possessed by employees, and salary history of employees. A typical business database may have hundreds of entities and relationships.

To depict these characteristics, let us consider a number of databases. We begin with a simple university database (Figure 1.1) since you have some familiarity with the workings of a university. A simplified university database contains data about students, faculty, courses, course offerings, and enrollments. The database supports procedures such as registering for classes, assigning faculty to course offerings, recording grades, and scheduling course offerings. Relationships in the university database support answers to questions such as

- What offerings are available for a course in a given academic period?
- Who is the instructor for an offering of a course?
- What students are enrolled in an offering of a course?

Next, let us consider a water utility database as depicted in Figure 1.2. The primary function of a water utility database is billing customers for water usage. Periodically, a customer's water consumption is measured from a meter and a bill is prepared. Many aspects can influence the preparation of a bill such as a customer's payment history, meter characteristics, type of customer (low income, renter, homeowner, small business, large business, etc.), and billing cycle. Relationships in the water utility database support answers to questions such as

- What is the date of the last bill sent to a customer?
- How much water usage was recorded when a customer's meter was last read?
- When did a customer make his/her last payment?

Finally, let us consider a hospital database as depicted in Figure 1.3. The hospital database supports treatment of patients by physicians. Physicians make diagnoses and prescribe treatments based on symptoms. Many different health providers read and

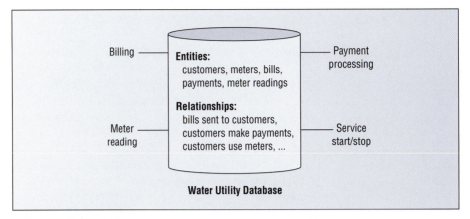

Figure 1.2   Depiction of a simplified water utility database.

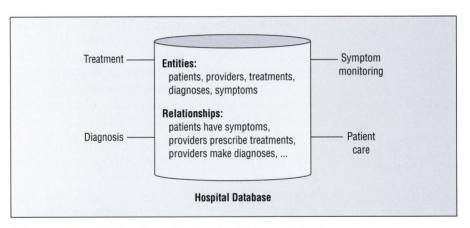

Figure 1.3   Depiction of a simplified hospital database.

contribute to a patient's record. Nurses are responsible for monitoring symptoms and providing medication. Food staff prepare meals according to a treatment plan. Physicians prescribe new treatments based on the results of previous treatments and patient symptoms. Relationships in the database support answers to questions such as

- What are the most recent symptoms of a patient?
- Who prescribed a given treatment of a patient?
- What diagnosis did a doctor make for a patient?

These simplified databases lack many kinds of data found in real databases. For example, the simplified university database does not contain data about course prerequisites and classroom capacities and locations. Real versions of these databases would have many more entities and additional uses. Nevertheless, these simple databases have the essential characteristics of business databases: persistent data, multiple users and uses, and multiple entities connected by relationships.

1.2 FEATURES OF DATABASE MANAGEMENT SYSTEMS

Database Management System (DBMS) a collection of components that support data acquisition, dissemination, maintenance, retrieval, and formatting.

A database management system (DBMS) is a collection of software that supports the creation, use, and maintenance of databases. Initially, DBMSs provided efficient storage and retrieval of data. Due to marketplace demands and product innovation, DBMSs have evolved to provide a broad range of features for data acquisition, storage, dissemination, maintenance, retrieval, and formatting. The evolution of these features has made DBMSs rather complex. It can take years of study and use to master a particular DBMS. Because DBMSs continue to evolve, you must continually update your knowledge.

To provide insight about features that you will encounter in commercial DBMSs, Table 1.1 summarizes a common set of features. The remainder of this section presents examples of these features. Some examples are drawn from Microsoft Access, a popular desktop DBMS. Later chapters expand upon the introduction provided here.

1.2.1 Database Definition

Table a named, two-dimensional arrangement of data. A table consists of a heading part and a body part.

To define a database, the entities and relationships must be specified. In most commercial DBMSs, tables store collections of entities. A table (Figure 1.4) has a heading row (first row) showing the column names and a body (other rows) showing the contents of

TABLE 1.1	Summary of Common Features of DBMSs

Feature	Description
Database definition	Language and graphical tools to define entities, relationships, integrity constraints, and authorization rights
Nonprocedural access	Language and graphical tools to access data without complicated coding
Application development	Graphical tools to develop menus, data entry forms, and reports; data requirements for forms and reports are specified using nonprocedural access.
Procedural language interface	Language that combines nonprocedural access with full capabilities of a programming language
Transaction processing	Control mechanisms to prevent interference from simultaneous users and recover lost data after a failure
Database tuning	Tools to monitor and improve database performance

StdFirstName	StdLastName	StdCity	StdState	StdZip	StdMajor	StdClass	StdGPA
HOMER	WELLS	SEATTLE	WA	98121-1111	IS	FR	3.00
BOB	NORBERT	BOTHELL	WA	98011-2121	FIN	JR	2.70
CANDY	KENDALL	TACOMA	WA	99042-3321	ACCT	JR	3.50
WALLY	KENDALL	SEATTLE	WA	98123-1141	IS	SR	2.80
JOE	ESTRADA	SEATTLE	WA	98121-2333	FIN	SR	3.20
MARIAH	DODGE	SEATTLE	WA	98114-0021	IS	JR	3.60
TESS	DODGE	REDMOND	WA	98116-2344	ACCT	SO	3.30

Figure 1.4   Display of student table in Microsoft Access.

the table. Relationships indicate connections among tables. For example, the relationship connecting the student table to the enrollment table shows the course offerings taken by each student.

Most DBMSs provide several tools to define databases. The Structured Query Language (SQL) is an industry standard language supported by most DBMSs. SQL can be used to define tables, relationships among tables, integrity constraints (rules that define allowable data), and authorization rights (rules that restrict access to data). Chapter 2 describes SQL statements to define tables and relationships.

In addition to SQL, many DBMSs provide graphical, window-oriented tools. Figures 1.5 and 1.6 depict graphical tools for defining tables and relationships. Using the Table Definition window in Figure 1.5, the user can define properties of columns such

SQL an industry standard database language that includes statements for database definition, database manipulation, and database control.

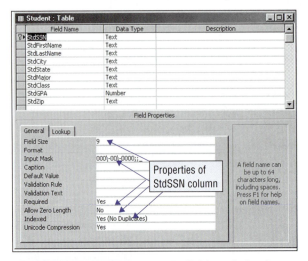

Figure 1.5   Table Definition window in Microsoft Access.

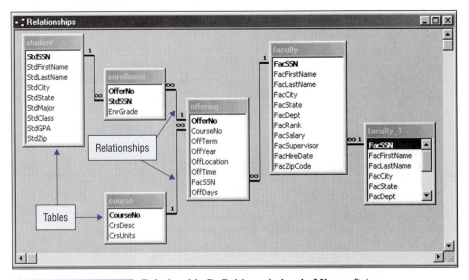

Figure 1.6   Relationship Definition window in Microsoft Access.

as the data type and field size. Using the Relationship Definition window in Figure 1.6, relationships among tables can be defined. After defining the structure, a database can be populated. The data in Figure 1.4 should be added after the Table Definition window and Relationship Definition window are complete.

1.2.2 Nonprocedural Access

The most important feature of a DBMS is the ability to answer queries. A query is a request for data to answer a question. For example, the user may want to know customers having large balances or products with strong sales in a particular region. Nonprocedural access allows users with limited computing skills to submit queries. The user specifies what parts of a database to retrieve, not the details of how retrieval occurs. The "how" part involves coding complex procedures with loops. Nonprocedural languages do not have looping statements (for, while, and so on) because only the "what" part is specified.

Nonprocedural access can reduce the number of lines of code by a factor of 100 as compared to procedural access. Because a large part of business software involves data access, nonprocedural access can provide a dramatic improvement in software productivity.

To appreciate the significance of nonprocedural access, consider an analogy to planning a vacation. You specify your destination, travel budget, length of stay, and departure date. These facts indicate the "what" of your trip. To specify the "how" of your trip, you need to indicate many more details such as the best route to your destination, the most desirable hotel, ground transportation, and so on. Your planning process is much easier if you have a professional to help with these additional details. Like a planning professional, a DBMS performs the detailed planning process to answer queries expressed in a nonprocedural language.

Most DBMSs provide more than one tool for nonprocedural access. The SELECT statement of SQL, described in Chapter 3, provides a nonprocedural way to access a database. Most DBMSs also provide graphical tools to access databases. Figure 1.7

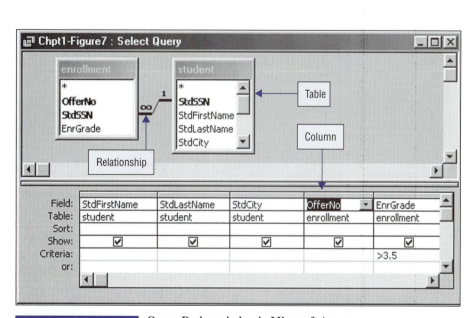

Figure 1.7   **Query Design window in Microsoft Access.**

StdFirstName	StdLastName	StdCity	OfferNo	EnrGrade
MARIAH	DODGE	SEATTLE	1234	3.8
BOB	NORBERT	BOTHELL	5679	3.7
ROBERTO	MORALES	SEATTLE	5679	3.8
MARIAH	DODGE	SEATTLE	6666	3.6
LUKE	BRAZZI	SEATTLE	7777	3.7
WILLIAM	PILGRIM	BOTHELL	9876	4

Figure 1.8   **Result of executing query in Figure 1.7.**

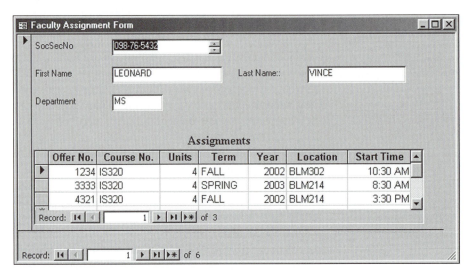

Figure 1.9   **Microsoft Access form for assigning courses to faculty.**

depicts a graphical tool available in Microsoft Access. To pose a query to the database, a user only has to indicate the required tables, relationships, and columns. Access is responsible for knowing how to retrieve the requested data. Figure 1.8 shows the result of executing the query in Figure 1.7.

1.2.3 Application Development and Procedural Language Interface

Most DBMSs go well beyond simply accessing data. Graphical tools are provided for building complete applications using forms and reports. Data entry <u>forms</u> provide a convenient way to enter and edit data, while <u>reports</u> enhance the appearance of data that are displayed or printed. The form in Figure 1.9 can be used to add new course assignments for a professor and to change existing assignments. The report in Figure 1.10 uses indentation to show courses taught by faculty in various departments. The indentation style can be easier to view than the tabular style shown in Figure 1.8. Many forms and reports can be developed with a graphical tool without detailed coding. For example, Figures 1.9 and 1.10 were developed without coding. Chapter 10 describes concepts underlying form and report development.

Faculty Work Load Report for the 2002–2003 Academic Year

Department	Name	Term	Offer Number	Units	Limit	Enrollment	Percent Full	Low Enrollment
FIN								
	JULIA MILLS							
		WINTER	5678	4	20	1	5.00%	☑

Summary for 'term' = WINTER (1 detail record)

		Sum		4		1		
		Avg					5.00%	

Summary for JULIA MILLS

	Sum			4		1		
	Avg						5.00%	

Summary for 'department' = FIN (1 detail record)

Figure 1.10   **Microsoft Access report of faculty workload.**

Nonprocedural access makes form and report creation possible without extensive coding. As part of creating a form or report, the user indicates the data requirements using a nonprocedural language (SQL) or graphical tool. To complete a form or report definition, the user indicates formatting of data, user interaction, and other details.

In addition to application development tools, a procedural language interface adds the full capabilities of a computer programming language. Nonprocedural access and application development tools, though convenient and powerful, are sometimes not efficient enough or do not provide the level of control necessary for application development. When these tools are not adequate, DBMSs provide the full capabilities of a programming language. For example, Visual Basic for Applications (VBA) is a programming language that is integrated with Microsoft Access. VBA allows full customization of database access, form processing, and report generation. Most commercial DBMSs have a procedural language interface comparable to VBA. For example, Oracle has the language PL/SQL and Microsoft SQL Server has the language Transact-SQL. Chapter 11 describes procedural language interfaces and the PL/SQL language.

Procedural Language Interface a method to combine a nonprocedural language such as SQL with a programming language such as COBOL or Visual Basic.

1.2.4 Other Features

Transaction processing enables a DBMS to process large volumes of repetitive work. A transaction is a unit of work that should be processed reliably without interference from other users and without loss of data due to failures. Examples of transactions are withdrawing cash at an ATM, making an airline reservation, and registering for a course. A DBMS ensures that transactions are free of interference from other users, parts of a transaction are not lost due to a failure, and transactions do not make the database inconsistent. Transaction processing is largely a "behind the scenes" affair. The user does not know the details about transaction processing other than the assurances about reliability.

Transaction Processing reliable and efficient processing of large volumes of repetitive work. DBMSs ensure that simultaneous users do not interfere with each other and that failures do not cause lost work.

Database tuning includes a number of monitors and utility programs to improve performance. Some DBMSs can monitor how a database is used, the distribution of various parts of a database, and the growth of the database. Utility programs can be provided to reorganize a database, select physical structures for better performance, and repair damaged parts of a database.

| **Figure 1.11** | Entity relationship diagram (ERD) created with Visio Professional. |

Transaction processing and database tuning are most prominent on DBMSs that support large databases with many simultaneous users. These DBMSs are known as enterprise DBMSs because the databases they support are often critical to the functioning of an organization. Enterprise DBMSs usually run on powerful servers and have a high cost. In contrast, desktop DBMSs running on personal computers and small servers support limited transaction processing features but have a much lower cost. Desktop DBMSs support databases used by work teams and small businesses. Embedded DBMSs are an emerging category of database software. As its name implies, an embedded DBMS resides in a larger system, either an application or a device such as a personal digital assistant (PDA) or a smart card. Embedded DBMSs provide limited transaction processing features but have low memory, processing, and storage requirements.

In addition to features provided directly by vendors of DBMSs, third-party software is also available for many DBMSs. In most cases, third-party software extends the features available with the database software. For example, many third-party vendors provide advanced database design tools that extend the database definition and tuning capabilities provided by DBMSs. Figure 1.11 shows a database diagram (an entity relationship diagram) created with Visio Professional, a tool for database design. The ERD in Figure 1.11 can be converted into the tables supported by most commercial DBMSs. In some cases, third-party software competes directly with the database product. For example, third-party vendors provide application development tools that can be used in place of the ones provided with the database product.

1.3 DEVELOPMENT OF DATABASE TECHNOLOGY AND MARKET STRUCTURE

The previous section provided a quick tour of the features found in typical DBMSs. The features in today's products are a significant improvement over just a few years ago. Database management, like many other areas of computing, has undergone tremendous technological

TABLE 1.2		Brief Evolution of Database Technology	
Era	*Generation*	*Orientation*	*Major Features*
1960s	1st generation	File	File structures and proprietary program interfaces
1970s	2nd generation	Network navigation	Networks and hierarchies of related records, standard program interfaces
1980s	3rd generation	Relational	Nonprocedural languages, optimization, transaction processing
1990s	4th generation	Object	Multimedia, active, distributed processing, more powerful operators, data warehouse processing

growth. To provide you a context to appreciate today's DBMSs, this section reviews past changes in technology and suggests future trends. After this review, the current market for database software is presented.

1.3.1 Evolution of Database Technology

Table 1.2 depicts a brief history of database technology through four generations of systems.[1] The first generation supported sequential and random searching, but the user was required to write a computer program to obtain access. For example, a program could be written to retrieve all customer records or to just find the customer record with a specified customer number. Because first-generation systems did not offer much support for relating data, they are usually regarded as file processing systems rather than DBMSs. File processing systems can manage only one entity rather than many entities and relationships managed by a DBMS.

The second-generation products were the first true DBMSs as they could manage multiple entity types and relationships. However, to obtain access to data, a computer program still had to be written. Second-generation systems are referred to as "navigational" because the programmer had to write code to navigate among a network of linked records. Some of the second-generation products adhered to a standard database definition and manipulation language developed by the Committee on Data Systems Languages (CODASYL), a standards organization. The CODASYL standard had only limited market acceptance partly because IBM, the dominant computer company during this time, ignored the standard. IBM supported a different approach known as the hierarchical data model.

Rather than focusing on the second-generation standard, research labs at IBM and academic institutions developed the foundations for a new generation of DBMSs. The most important development involved nonprocedural languages for database access. Third-generation systems are known as relational DBMSs because of the foundation based on mathematical relations and associated operators. Optimization technology was developed so that access using nonprocedural languages would be efficient. Because nonprocedural access provided such an improvement over navigational access, third-generation systems supplanted the second generation. Since the technology was

---

[1]The generations of DBMSs should not be confused with the generations of programming languages. In particular, fourth-generation language refers to programming language features, not DBMS features.

so different, most of the new systems were founded by start-up companies rather than by vendors of previous generation products. IBM was the major exception. It was IBM's weight that led to adoption of SQL as a widely accepted standard.

Fourth-generation DBMSs are extending the boundaries of database technology to unconventional data, the Internet, and data warehouse processing. Fourth-generation systems can store and manipulate unconventional data types such as images, videos, maps, sounds, and animations. Because these systems view any kind of data as an object to manage, fourth-generation systems are sometimes called "object-oriented" or "object-relational." Chapter 18 presents details about object features in DBMSs. In addition to the emphasis on objects, the Internet is pushing DBMSs to develop new forms of distributed processing. Most DBMSs now feature convenient ways to publish static and dynamic data on the Internet. Chapter 17 presents details about client–server processing features in DBMSs to support Web access to databases.

A recent development in fourth-generation DBMSs is support for data warehouse processing. A data warehouse is a database that supports mid-range and long-range decision making in organizations. The retrieval of summarized data dominates data warehouse processing, whereas a mixture of updating and retrieving data occurs for databases that support the daily operations of an organization. Chapter 16 presents details about DBMS features to support data warehouse processing.

The market for fourth-generation systems is a battle between vendors of third-generation systems who are upgrading their products against a new group of systems developed by startup companies. So far, the existing companies seem to have the upper hand.

1.3.2 Current Market for Database Software

According to Gartner Dataquest, sales of enterprise database software reached $8.8 billion in 2001, a 20.8 percent increase since 1998 but only a 1.4 percent increase since 2000. Enterprise DBMSs use mainframe servers running IBM's MVS operating system and midrange servers running Unix (Linux, Solaris, AIX, and other variations) and Microsoft Windows 2000 operating systems. Electronic commerce on the Internet and data warehouse processing have rejuvenated the market for enterprise database software. Before the advent of electronic commerce and data warehouses, enterprise DBMSs were becoming commodities and sales growth was stagnant. After the Internet and telecom slowdowns, database software sales have slowed again as business capital spending has decreased. For future sales, IDC projects sales of enterprise DBMSs to reach $20 billion by 2006.

According to Gartner Dataquest, four products dominate the market for enterprise database software as shown in Table 1.3. Although IBM holds the largest market share, Oracle dominates the faster growing Unix market. IBM's total market share is partially due to its acquisition of Informix in 2001. The overall market is very competitive with the major companies and smaller companies introducing many new features with each release.

In the market for desktop database software, Microsoft Access dominates at least in part because of the dominance of Microsoft Office. Desktop database software is primarily sold as part of office productivity software. With Microsoft Office holding about 90 percent of the office productivity market, Access holds a comparable share of the desktop database software market. Other significant products in the desktop database software market are Paradox, Approach, FoxPro, and FileMaker Pro.

To provide coverage of both enterprise and desktop database software, this book provides significant coverage of Oracle and Microsoft Access. In addition, the emphasis on the SQL standard in Parts 1 and 3 provides database language coverage for the other major products.

TABLE 1.3	2001 Market Shares by Revenue of Enterprise Database Software[2]		
Product	*Total Market Share*	*Relational DBMS Market Share*	*Comments*
IBM DB2, Informix	34.6%	34.1%	Dominates the MVS and AS/400 environments; acquired Informix in 2001; 25% share of the Unix market
Oracle 8i, 9i	32.0%	39.8%	Dominates the Unix environment (63%); strong performance in the Windows market (34%)
Microsoft SQL Server	16.3%	14.4%	40% share of the Windows market; no presence in other environments
Sybase SQL Server	2.6%	unspecified	
Other	14.5%	unspecified	Includes Computer Associates, NCR, Progress Software, MySQL, and others

Because of the potential growth of personal computing devices, most major DBMS vendors have now entered the embedded DBMS market. However, the embedded DBMS market still is dominated by smaller software companies such as Progress Software, Intersystems, and Ardent Software.

1.4 ARCHITECTURES OF DATABASE MANAGEMENT SYSTEMS

To provide insight about the internal organization of DBMSs, this section describes two architectures or organizing frameworks. The first architecture describes an organization of database definitions to reduce the cost of software maintenance. The second architecture describes an organization of data and software to support remote access. These architectures promote a conceptual understanding rather than indicate how an actual DBMS is organized.

1.4.1 Data Independence and the Three Schema Architecture

In early DBMSs, there was a close connection between a database and computer programs that accessed the database. Essentially, the DBMS was considered part of a programming language. As a result, the database definition was part of the computer programs that accessed the database. In addition, the conceptual meaning of a database was not separate from its physical implementation on magnetic disk. The definitions about the structure of a database and its physical implementation were mixed inside computer programs.

The close association between a database and related programs led to problems in software maintenance. Software maintenance encompassing requirement changes, corrections, and enhancements can consume a large fraction of computer budgets. In early DBMSs, most changes to the database definition caused changes to computer programs. In many cases, changes to computer programs involved detailed inspection of the code, a labor-intensive process. This code inspection work is similar to year 2000 compliance where date formats were changed to four digits. Performance tuning of a database was

---

[2]Market shares according to a 2002 study by Gartner Dataquest, a division of the Gartner Group.

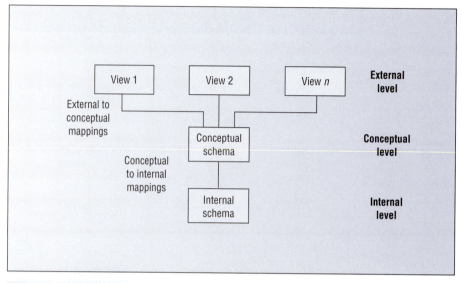

Figure 1.12 **Three Schema Architecture.**

difficult because sometimes hundreds of computer programs had to be recompiled for every change. Because database definition changes are common, a large fraction of software maintenance resources were devoted to database changes. Some studies have estimated the percentage as high as 50 percent of software maintenance resources.

The concept of <u>data independence</u> emerged to alleviate problems with program maintenance. Data independence means that a database should have an identity separate from the applications (computer programs, forms, and reports) that use it. The separate identity allows the database definition to be changed without affecting related applications. For example, if a new column is added to a table, applications not using the new column should not be affected. Likewise if a new table is added, only applications that need the new table should be affected. This separation should be even more pronounced if a change only affects physical implementation of a database. Database specialists should be free to experiment with performance tuning without concern about computer program changes.

In the mid 1970s, the concept of data independence led to the proposal of the <u>Three Schema Architecture</u> depicted in Figure 1.12. The word <u>schema</u> as applied to databases means database description. The Three Schema Architecture includes three levels of database description. The <u>external</u> level is the user level. Each group of users can have a separate external view (or view for short) of a database tailored to the group's specific needs.

In contrast, the conceptual and internal schemas represent the entire database. The <u>conceptual schema</u> defines the entities and relationships. For a business database, the conceptual schema can be quite large, perhaps hundreds of entity types and relationships. Like the conceptual schema, the internal schema represents the entire database. However, the <u>internal schema</u> represents the storage view of the database whereas the conceptual schema represents the logical meaning of the database. The internal schema defines files, collections of data on a storage device such as a hard disk. A file can store one or more entities described in the conceptual schema.

Data Independence a database should have an identity separate from the applications (computer programs, forms, and reports) that use it. The separate identity allows the database definition to be changed without affecting related applications.

....

Three Schema Architecture an architecture for compartmentalizing database descriptions. The Three Schema Architecture was proposed as a way to achieve data independence.

....

TABLE 1.4	University Database Example Depicting Differences among Schema Levels

Schema Level	Description
External	HighGPAView: data required for the query in Figure 1.7
	FacultyAssignmentFormView: data required for the form in Figure 1.9
	FacultyWorkLoadReportView: data required for the report in Figure 1.10
Conceptual	Student, Enrollment, Course, Faculty, and Enrollment tables and relationships (Figure 1.6)
Internal	Files needed to store the tables; extra files (indexed property in Figure 1.5) to improve performance

To make the three schema levels clearer, Table 1.4 shows differences among database definition at the three schema levels using examples from the features described in Section 1.2. Even in a simplified university database, the differences among the schema levels is clear. With a more complex database, the differences would be even more pronounced with many more views, a much larger conceptual schema, and a more complex internal schema.

The schema mappings describe how a schema at a higher level is derived from a schema at a lower level. For example, the external views in Table 1.4 are derived from the tables in the conceptual schema. The mapping provides the knowledge to convert a request using an external view (for example, HighGPAView) into a request using the tables in the conceptual schema. The mapping between conceptual and internal levels shows how entities are stored in files.

DBMSs, using schemas and mappings, ensure data independence. Typically, applications access a database using a view. The DBMS converts an application's request into a request using the conceptual schema rather than the view. The DBMS then transforms the conceptual schema request into a request using the internal schema. Most changes to the conceptual or internal schema do not affect applications because applications do not use the lower schema levels. The DBMS, not the user, is responsible for using the mappings to make the transformations. For more details about mappings and transformations, Chapter 10 describes views and transformations between the external and conceptual levels.

The Three Schema Architecture is an official standard of the American National Standards Institute (ANSI). However, the specific details of the standard were never widely adopted. Rather the standard serves as a guideline about how data independence can be achieved. The spirit of the Three Schema Architecture is widely implemented in third- and fourth-generation DBMSs.

1.4.2 Distributed Processing and the Client–Server Architecture

With the growing importance of network computing and the Internet, distributed processing is becoming a crucial function of DBMSs. Distributed processing allows geographically dispersed computers to cooperate when providing data access. A large part of electronic commerce on the Internet involves accessing and updating remote databases. Many databases in retail, banking, and security trading are now available through the Internet. DBMSs use available network capacity and local processing capabilities to provide efficient remote database access.

Many DBMSs support distributed processing using a client–server architecture. A client is a program that submits requests to a server. A server processes requests on behalf of a client. For example, a client may request a server to retrieve product data. The server locates the data and sends them back to the client. The client may perform additional processing on the data before displaying the results to the user. As another example, a client submits a completed order to a server. The server validates the order, updates a database, and sends an acknowledgement to the client. The client informs the user that the order has been processed.

Client–Server Architecture
an arrangement of
components (clients and
servers) and data among
computers connected by a
network. The client–server
architecture supports efficient
processing of messages
(requests for service)
between clients and servers.

To improve performance and availability of data, the client–server architecture supports many ways to distribute software and data in a computer network. The simplest scheme is just to place both software and data on the same computer (Figure 1.13(a)). To take advantage of a network, both software and data can be distributed. In Figure 1.13(b), the server software and the database are located on a remote computer. In Figure 1.13(c), the server software and the database are located on multiple remote computers.

The DBMS has a number of responsibilities in a client–server architecture. The DBMS provides software that can execute on both the client and the server. The client software is typically responsible for accepting user input, displaying results, and performing

Figure 1.13   **Typical client–server arrangements of database and software.**

some processing of data. The server software validates client requests, locates remote databases, updates remote databases (if needed), and sends the data in a format that the client understands.

Client–server architectures provide a flexible way for DBMSs to interact with computer networks. The distribution of work among clients and servers and the possible choices to locate data and software are much more complex than described here. You will learn more details about client–server architectures in Chapter 17.

1.5 ORGANIZATIONAL IMPACTS OF DATABASE TECHNOLOGY

This section completes your introduction to database technology by discussing the effects of database technology on organizations. The first section describes possible interactions that you may have with a database in an organization. The second section describes information resource management, an effort to control the data produced and used by an organization. Special attention is given to management roles that you may play as part of an effort to control information resources. Chapter 14 provides more detail about the tools and processes used in these management roles.

1.5.1 Interacting with Databases

Because databases are pervasive, there are a variety of ways in which you may interact with databases. The classification in Figure 1.14 distinguishes between functional users who interact with databases as part of their work and information systems professionals who participate in designing and implementing databases. Each box in the hierarchy represents a role that you can play. You may simultaneously play more than one role. For example, a functional user in a job such as financial analysis may play all three roles in different databases. In some organizations, the distinction between functional users and information systems professionals is blurred. In these organizations, functional users may participate in designing and using databases.

Functional users can play a passive or an active role when interacting with databases. Indirect usage of a database is a passive role. An indirect user is given a report or some data extracted from a database. A parametric user is more active than an

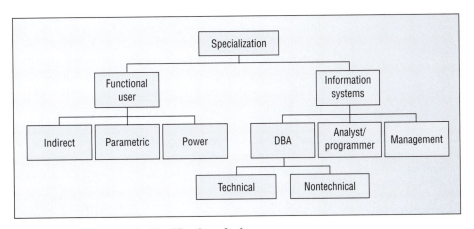

Figure 1.14   **Classification of roles.**

TABLE 1.5	Responsibilities of the Database Administrator

Technical	Nontechnical
Designing conceptual schemas	Setting database standards
Designing internal schemas	Devising training materials
Monitoring database performance	Promoting benefits of databases
Selecting and evaluating database software	Consulting with users
Designing client–server databases	
Troubleshooting database problems	

indirect user. A <u>parametric user</u> requests existing forms or reports using parameters, input values that change from usage to usage. For example, a parameter may indicate a date range, sales territory, or department name. The <u>power user</u> is the most active. Because decision-making needs can be difficult to predict, ad hoc or unplanned usage of a database is important. A power user is skilled enough to build a form or report when needed. Power users should have a good understanding of nonprocedural access, a skill described in the first part of this book.

Information systems professionals interact with databases as part of developing an information system. <u>Analyst/programmers</u> are responsible for collecting requirements, designing applications, and implementing information systems. They create and use external views to develop forms, reports, and other parts of an information system. Management has an oversight role in the development of databases and information systems.

Database Administrator a support position that specializes in managing individual databases and DBMSs.

<u>Database administrators</u> assist both information systems professionals and functional users. Database administrators have a variety of both technical and nontechnical responsibilities (Table 1.5). Technical skills are more detail-oriented; nontechnical responsibilities are more people-oriented. The primary technical responsibility is database design. On the nontechnical side, the database administrator's time is split among a number of activities. Database administrators can also have responsibilities in planning databases and evaluating DBMSs.

1.5.2 Information Resource Management

Information resource management is a response to the challenge of effectively utilizing information technology. The goal of <u>information resource management</u> is to use information technology as a tool for processing, distributing, and integrating information throughout an organization. Management of information resources has many similarities with managing physical resources such as inventory. Inventory management involves activities such as safeguarding inventory from theft and deterioration, storing it for efficient usage, choosing suppliers, handling waste, coordinating movement, and reducing holding costs. Information resource management involves similar activities: planning databases, acquiring data, protecting data from unauthorized access, ensuring reliability, coordinating flow among information systems, and eliminating duplication.

Data Administrator a management position that performs planning and policy setting for the information resources of an entire organization.

As part of controlling information resources, new management responsibilities have arisen. The <u>data administrator</u> is a management role with many of these responsibilities, the major responsibility being planning the development of new databases. The

Figure 1.15   **Organizational placement of data and database administration.**

data administrator maintains an enterprise data architecture that describes existing databases and new databases and also evaluates new information technologies and determines standards for managing databases.

The data administrator typically has broader responsibilities than the database administrator. The data administrator has primarily a planning role, while the database administrator has a more technical role focused on individual databases and DBMSs. The data administrator also views the information resource in a broader context and considers all kinds of data, both computerized and noncomputerized. A major effort in many organizations is to computerize nontraditional data such as video, training materials, images, and correspondence. The data administrator develops long-range plans for nontraditional data, while the database administrator implements the plans using appropriate database technology.

Because of broader responsibilities, the data administrator typically is higher in an organization chart. Figure 1.15 depicts two possible placements of data administrators and database administrators. In a small organization, both roles may be combined in systems administration.

CLOSING THOUGHTS

Chapter 1 has provided a broad introduction to DBMSs. You should use this background as a context for the skills you will acquire in subsequent chapters. You learned that databases contain interrelated data that can be shared across multiple parts of an organization. DBMSs support transformation of data for decision making. To support this transformation, database technology has evolved from simple file access to powerful systems that support database definition, nonprocedural access, application development, transaction processing, and performance tuning. Nonprocedural access is the most vital element because it allows access without detailed coding. You learned about two architectures that provide organizing principles for DBMSs. The Three Schema Architecture supports data independence, an important concept for reducing the cost of software maintenance. Client–server architectures allow databases to be accessed over computer networks, a feature vital in today's networked world.

The skills emphasized in later chapters should enable you to work as an active functional user or analyst. Both kinds of users need to understand the skills taught in the first part of this book. The third part of the book provides skills for analysts/programmers. This book also provides the foundation of skills to obtain a specialist position as a database or data administrator. The skills in the second and fourth parts of this book are most useful for a position as a database administrator. However, you probably will need to take additional courses, learn details of popular DBMSs, and acquire management experience before obtaining a specialist role. A position as a database specialist can be an exciting and lucrative career opportunity that you should consider.

REVIEW CONCEPTS

- Database characteristics: persistent, interrelated, and shared.
- Features of database management systems (DBMSs).
- Nonprocedural access: a key to software productivity.
- Transaction: a unit of work that should be processed reliably.
- Application development using nonprocedural access to specify the data requirements of forms and reports.
- Procedural language interface for combining nonprocedural access with a programming language such as COBOL or Visual Basic.
- Evolution of database software over four generations of technological improvement.
- Current emphasis on database software for multimedia support, distributed processing, more powerful operators, and data warehouses.
- Types of DBMSs: enterprise, desktop, embedded.
- Data independence to alleviate problems with maintenance of computer programs.
- Three Schema Architecture for reducing the impact of database definition changes.
- Client–server architecture for using databases over computer networks.
- Database specialist roles: database administrator and data administrator.
- Information resource management for utilizing information technology.

QUESTIONS

1. Describe a database that you have used on a job or as a consumer. List the entities and relationships that the database contains. If you are not sure, imagine the entities and relationships that are contained in the database.

2. For the database in question 1, list different user groups that can use the database.

3. For one of the groups in question 2, describe an application (form or report) that the group uses.

4. Explain the persistent property for databases.

5. Explain the interrelated property for databases.

6. Explain the shared property for databases.

7. What is a DBMS?

8. What is SQL?

9. Describe the difference between a procedural and a nonprocedural language. What statements belong in a procedural language but not in a nonprocedural language?

10. Why is nonprocedural access an important feature of DBMSs?

11. What is the connection between nonprocedural access and application (form or report) development? Can nonprocedural access be used in application development?

12. What is the difference between a form and a report?

13. What is a procedural language interface?

14. What is a transaction?

15. What features does a DBMS provide to support transaction processing?

16. For the database in question 1, describe a transaction that uses the database. How often do you think that the transaction is submitted to the database? How many users submit transactions at the same time? Make guesses for the last two parts if you are unsure.

17. What is an enterprise DBMS?

18. What is a desktop DBMS?

19. What is an embedded DBMS?

20. What were the prominent features of first-generation DBMSs?

21. What were the prominent features of second-generation DBMSs?

22. What were the prominent features of third-generation DBMSs?

23. What are the prominent features of fourth-generation DBMSs?

24. For the database you described in question 1, make a table to depict differences among schema levels. Use Table 1.4 as a guide.

25. What is the purpose of the mappings in the Three Schema Architecture? Is the user or DBMS responsible for using the mappings?

26. Explain how the Three Schema Architecture supports data independence.

27. In a client–server architecture, why are processing capabilities divided between a client and a server? In other words, why not have the server do all the processing?

28. In a client–server architecture, why are data sometimes stored on several computers rather than on a single computer?

29. For the database in question 1, describe how functional users may interact with the database. Try to identify indirect, parametric, and power uses of the database.

30. Explain the differences in responsibilities between an active functional user of a database and an analyst. What schema level is used by both kinds of users?

31. Which role, database administrator or data administrator, is more appealing to you as a long-term career goal? Briefly explain your preference.

PROBLEMS

Because of the introductory nature of this chapter, there are no problems in this chapter. Problems appear at the end of most other chapters.

REFERENCES FOR FURTHER STUDY

The *DBAZine* (www.dbazine.com), the *Intelligent Enterprise* magazine (www.iemagazine.com/), and the *Advisor.com* (http://www.advisor.com/) websites provide detailed technical information about commercial DBMSs, database design, and database application development. To learn more about the role of database specialists and information resource management, consult Davydov 1993; Guimaraes 1988; and Weldon 1981.

The Relational Data Model

LEARNING OBJECTIVES

This chapter provides the foundation for using relational databases.
After this chapter the student should have acquired the following
knowledge and skills:

- Recognize relational database terminology.

- Understand the meaning of the integrity rules for relational databases.

- Understand the impact of referenced rows on maintaining relational databases.

- Understand the meaning of each relational algebra operator.

- List tables that must be combined to obtain desired results for simple retrieval requests.

OVERVIEW

Chapter 1 provided a starting point for your exploration of database technology. You broadly learned about database characteristics, DBMS features, system architectures, and human roles. This chapter narrows your focus to the relational data model. Relational DBMSs dominate the market for business DBMSs. You will undoubtedly use relational DBMSs throughout your career as an information systems professional. This chapter provides the background so that you may become proficient in designing databases and developing applications for relational databases in later chapters.

To effectively use a relational database, you need two kinds of knowledge. First, you need to understand the structure and contents of the database tables. Understanding the connections among tables is especially critical because many database retrievals involve multiple tables. To help you understand relational databases, this chapter presents the basic terminology, the integrity rules, and a notation to visualize connections among tables. Second, you need to understand the operators of relational algebra as they are the building blocks of most commercial query languages. Understanding the operators will improve your knowledge of query languages such as SQL. To help you understand the meaning of each operator, this chapter provides a visual representation of each operator and several convenient summaries.

2.1 BASIC ELEMENTS

Relational database systems were originally developed because of familiarity and simplicity. Because tables are used to communicate ideas in many fields, the terminology of tables, rows, and columns is not intimidating to most users. During the early years of relational databases (1970s), the simplicity and familiarity of relational databases had strong appeal especially as compared to the procedural orientation of other data models that existed at the time. Despite the familiarity and simplicity of relational databases, there is a strong mathematical basis also. The mathematics of relational databases involves thinking about tables as sets. The combination of familiarity and simplicity with a mathematical foundation is so powerful that relational DBMSs are commercially dominant.

This section presents the basic terminology of relational databases and introduces the CREATE TABLE statement of the Structured Query Language (SQL). Sections 2.2 through 2.4 provide more detail on the elements defined in this section.

2.1.1 Tables

Table a two-dimensional arrangement of data. A table consists of a heading defining the table name and column names and a body containing rows of data.

A relational database consists of a collection of tables. Each table has a heading or definition part and a body or content part. The <u>heading</u> part consists of the table name and the column names. For example, a student table may have columns for social security number, name, street address, city, state, zip, class (freshman, sophomore, etc.), major, and cumulative grade point average (GPA). The <u>body</u> shows the rows of the table. Each row in a student table represents a student enrolled at a university. A student table for a major university may have more than 30,000 rows, too many to view at one time.

To understand a table, it is also useful to view some of its rows. A table listing or datasheet shows the column names in the first row and the body in the other rows. Table 2.1 shows a table listing for the *Student* table. Three sample rows representing university students are displayed. In this book, the naming convention for column names includes a table abbreviation (Std) followed by a descriptive name. Because column names often are used without identifying the associated tables, the abbreviation supports easy table association. Mixed case highlights the different parts of a column name.

TABLE 2.1   **Sample Table Listing of the Student Table**

StdSSN	StdFirstName	StdLastName	StdCity	StdState	StdZip	StdMajor	StdClass	StdGPA
123-45-6789	HOMER	WELLS	SEATTLE	WA	98121-1111	IS	FR	3.00
124-56-7890	BOB	NORBERT	BOTHELL	WA	98011-2121	FIN	JR	2.70
234-56-7890	CANDY	KENDALL	TACOMA	WA	99042-3321	ACCT	JR	3.50

A CREATE TABLE statement can be used to define the heading part of a table. CREATE TABLE is a statement in the Structured Query Language (SQL). Because SQL is an industry standard language, the CREATE TABLE statement can be used to create tables in most DBMSs. The CREATE TABLE statement that follows creates the *Student* table.[1] For each column, the column name and the data type are specified. Data types indicate the kind of data (character, numeric, Yes/No, etc.) and permissible operations (numeric operations, string operations, etc.) for the column. Each data type has a name (for example, CHAR for character) and usually a length specification. Table 2.2 lists common data types used in relational DBMSs.[2]

> **Data Type** defines a set of values and permissible operations on the values. Each column of a table is associated with a data type.

CREATE TABLE Student

```
(    StdSSN            CHAR(11),
     StdFirstName      VARCHAR(50),
     StdLastName       VARCHAR(50),
     StdCity           VARCHAR(50),
     StdState          CHAR(2),
     StdZip            CHAR(10),
     StdMajor          CHAR(6),
     StdClass          CHAR(6),
     STDGPA            DECIMAL(3,2)     )
```

TABLE 2.2	Brief Description of Common SQL Data Types

Data Type	Description
CHAR(L)	For fixed-length text entries such as state abbreviations and social security numbers. Each column value using CHAR contains the maximum number of characters (*L*) even if the actual length is shorter. Most DBMSs have an upper limit on the length (*L*) such as 255.
VARCHAR(L)	For variable-length text such as names and street addresses. Column values using VARCHAR contain only the actual number of characters, not the maximum length as for CHAR columns. Most DBMSs have an upper limit on the length such as 255.
FLOAT(P)	For columns containing numeric data with a floating precision such as interest rate calculations and scientific calculations. The precision parameter *P* indicates the number of significant digits. Most DBMSs have an upper limit on *P* such as 38. Some DBMSs have two data types, REAL and DOUBLE PRECISION, for low- and high-precision floating point numbers instead of the variable precision with the FLOAT data type.
DATE/TIME	For columns containing dates and times such as an order date. These data types are not standard across DBMSs. Some systems support three data types (DATE, TIME, and TIMESTAMP) while other systems support a combined data type (DATE) storing both the date and time.
DECIMAL(W,R)	For columns containing numeric data with a fixed precision such as monetary amounts. The *W* value indicates the total number of digits and the *R* value indicates the number of digits to the right of the decimal point. This data type is also called NUMERIC in some systems.
INTEGER	For columns containing whole numbers (i.e., numbers without a decimal point). Some DBMSs have the SMALLINT data type for very small whole numbers and the LONG data type for very large integers.
BOOLEAN	For columns containing data with two values such as true/false or yes/no.

---

[1]The CREATE TABLE statements in this chapter conform to the standard SQL syntax. There are slight syntax differences for most relational DBMSs.

[2]Data types are not standard across relational DBMSs. The data types used in this chapter are specified in the latest SQL standard. Most DBMSs support these data types although the data type names may differ.

TABLE 2.3	Sample Enrollment Table

OfferNo	StdSSN	EnrGrade
1234	123-45-6789	3.3
1234	234-56-7890	3.5
4321	123-45-6789	3.5
4321	124-56-7890	3.2

TABLE 2.4	Sample Offering Table

OfferNo	CourseNo	OffTerm	OffYear	OffLocation	OffTime	FacSSN	OffDays
1111	IS320	SUMMER	2003	BLM302	10:30 AM		MW
1234	IS320	FALL	2002	BLM302	10:30 AM	098-76-5432	MW
2222	IS460	SUMMER	2002	BLM412	1:30 PM		TTH
3333	IS320	SPRING	2003	BLM214	8:30 AM	098-76-5432	MW
4321	IS320	FALL	2002	BLM214	3:30 PM	098-76-5432	TTH
4444	IS320	SPRING	2003	BLM302	3:30 PM	543-21-0987	TTH
5678	IS480	SPRING	2003	BLM302	10:30 AM	987-65-4321	MW
5679	IS480	SPRING	2003	BLM412	3:30 PM	876-54-3210	TTH
9876	IS460	SPRING	2003	BLM307	1:30 PM	654-32-1098	TTH

2.1.2 Connections among Tables

Relationship connection between rows in two tables. Relationships are shown by column values in one table that match column values in another table.

It is not enough to understand each table individually. To understand a relational database, connections or relationships among tables also must be understood. The rows in a table are usually related to rows in other tables. Matching (identical) values show relationships between tables. Consider the sample *Enrollment* table (Table 2.3) in which each row represents a student enrolled in an offering of a course. The values in the *StdSSN* column of the *Enrollment* table match the *StdSSN* values in the sample *Student* table (Table 2.1). For example, the first and third rows of the *Enrollment* table have the same *StdSSN* value (123-45-6789) as the first row of the *Student* table. Likewise, the values in the *OfferNo* column of the *Enrollment* table match the *OfferNo* column in the *Offering* table (Table 2.4). Figure 2.1 shows a graphical depiction of the matching values.

The concept of matching values is crucial in relational databases. As you will see, relational databases typically contain many tables. Even a modest-size database can have 10 to 15 tables. Large databases can have hundreds of tables. To extract meaningful information, it is often necessary to combine multiple tables using matching values. By matching on *Student.StdSSN* and *Enrollment.StdSSN,* you could combine the *Student* and *Enrollment* tables.[3] Similarly, by matching on *Enrollment.OfferNo* and *Offering.OfferNo,* you could combine the *Enrollment* and *Offering* tables. As you will see later in this chapter, the operation of combining tables on matching values is known as a join. Understanding the connections between tables (or ways that tables can be combined) is crucial for extracting useful data.

[3]When columns have identical names in two tables, it is customary to precede the column name with the table name and a period as *Student.StdSSN* and *Enrollment.StdSSN.*

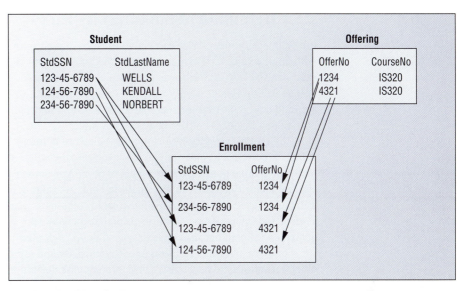

Figure 2.1 Matching values among the Enrollment, Offering, and Student tables.

TABLE 2.5	Alternative Terminology for Relational Databases

Table-Oriented	Set-Oriented	Record-Oriented
Table	Relation	Record type, file
Row	Tuple	Record
Column	Attribute	Field

2.1.3 Alternative Terminology

You should be aware that other terminology is used besides table, row, and column. Table 2.5 shows three roughly equivalent terminologies. The divergence in terminology is due to the different groups that use databases. The *table-oriented* terminology appeals to end users; the *set-oriented* terminology appeals to academic researchers; and the *record-oriented* terminology appeals to information systems professionals. In practice, these terms may be mixed. For example, in the same sentence you might hear both "tables" and "fields." You should expect to see a mix of terminology in your career.

2.2 INTEGRITY RULES

In the previous section, you learned that a relational database consists of a collection of interrelated tables. To ensure that a database provides meaningful information, integrity rules are necessary. This section describes two important integrity rules (entity integrity and referential integrity), examples of their usage, and a notation to visualize referential integrity.

2.2.1 Definition of the Integrity Rules

Entity integrity means that each table must have a column or combination of columns with unique values.[4] Unique means that no two rows of a table have the same value. For example, *StdSSN* in *Student* is unique and the combination of *StdSSN* and *OfferNo* is unique in *Enrollment*. Entity integrity ensures that entities (people, things, and events) are uniquely identified in a database. For auditing and security reasons, it is often important that business entities be easily traceable.

Referential integrity means that the values of columns in one table must match the values of columns in other tables. For example, the value of *StdSSN* in each row of the *Enrollment* table must match the value of *StdSSN* in some row of the *Student* table. Referential integrity ensures that a database contains valid connections. For example, it is critical that each row of the *Enrollment* table contains a social security number of a valid student. Otherwise, some enrollments can be meaningless, possibly resulting in students denied enrollment because nonexisting students took their places.

For more precise definitions of entity integrity and referential integrity, a number of other definitions are necessary. These prerequisite definitions and the more precise definitions are presented below.

Definitions

- Superkey: a column or combination of columns containing unique values for each row. The combination of every column in a table is always a superkey because rows in a table must be unique.[5]
- Candidate key: a minimal superkey. A superkey is minimal if removing any columns makes it no longer unique.
- Null value: a special value that represents the absence of an actual value. A null value can mean that the actual value is unknown or does not apply to the given row.
- Primary key: a specially designated candidate key. The primary key for a table cannot contain null values.
- Foreign key: a column or combination of columns in which the values must match those of a candidate key. A foreign key must have the same data type as its associated candidate key. In the CREATE TABLE statement of SQL, a foreign key must be associated with a primary key rather than merely a candidate key.

Integrity Rules

- **Entity integrity rule:** No two rows of a table can contain the same value for the primary key. In addition, no row can contain a null value for any columns of a primary key.
- **Referential integrity rule:** Only two kinds of values can be stored in a foreign key:
  > a value matching a candidate key value in some row of the table containing the associated candidate key or
  > a null value.

---

[4]Entity integrity is also known as uniqueness integrity.
[5]The uniqueness of rows is a feature of the relational model that SQL does not require.

2.2.2 Applying the Integrity Rules

To extend your understanding, let us apply the integrity rules to several tables in the university database. The primary key of *Student* is *StdSSN*. A primary key can be designated as part of the CREATE TABLE statement. To designate *StdSSN* as the primary key of *Student,* use a CONSTRAINT clause for the primary key at the end of the CREATE TABLE statement as shown below. The word *PKStudent* following the CONSTRAINT keyword is the name of the constraint. The advantage of using a constraint name is that the constraint is easy to identify when a violation occurs.

```
CREATE TABLE Student
             (      StdSSN              CHAR(11),
                    StdFirstName        VARCHAR(50),
                    StdLastName         VARCHAR(50),
                    StdCity             VARCHAR(50),
                    StdState            CHAR(2),
                    StdZip              CHAR(10),
                    StdMajor            CHAR(6),
                    StdClass            CHAR(2),
                    StdGPA              DECIMAL(3,2),
CONSTRAINT PKStudent PRIMARY KEY (StdSSN)          )
```

Candidate keys that are not primary keys are declared with the UNIQUE keyword. The *Course* table (see Table 2.6) contains two candidate keys: *CourseNo* and *CrsDesc* (course description). The *CourseNo* column is the primary key because it is more stable than the *CrsDesc* column. Course descriptions may change over time, but the course numbers remain the same. In the CREATE TABLE statement, a constraint with the keyword UNIQUE follows the primary key constraint.

```
CREATE TABLE Course
             (      CourseNo            CHAR(6),
                    CrsDesc             VARCHAR(250),
                    CrsUnits            SMALLINT,
             CONSTRAINT PKCourse PRIMARY KEY(CourseNo),
             CONSTRAINT UniqueCrsDesc UNIQUE (CrsDesc)  )
```

Some tables need more than one column in the primary key. In the *Enrollment* table, the combination of *StdSSN* and *OfferNo* is the only candidate key. Both columns are needed to identify a row. A primary key consisting of more than one column is known as a <u>composite</u> or a <u>combined primary key.</u>

TABLE 2.6	Sample Course Table

CourseNo	CrsDesc	CrsUnits
IS320	FUNDAMENTALS OF BUSINESS	4
IS460	SYSTEMS ANALYSIS	4
IS470	BUSINESS DATA COMMUNICATIONS	4
IS480	FUNDAMENTALS OF DATABASE	4

Superkeys are usually not important to identify because they are common and contain columns that do not contribute to the uniqueness property. For example, the combination of *StdSSN* and *StdLastName* is unique. However, if *StdLastName* is removed, *StdSSN* is still unique.

For referential integrity, the columns *StdSSN* and *OfferNo* are foreign keys in the *Enrollment* table. The *StdSSN* column refers to *Student* and the *OfferNo* column refers to the *Offering* table (Table 2.4). An *Offering* row represents a course given in an academic period (summer, winter, etc.), year, time, location, and days of the week. The primary key of *Offering* is *OfferNo*. A course such as IS480 will have different offer numbers each time it is offered.

Referential integrity constraints can be defined similarly to the way of defining primary keys. For example, to define the foreign keys in *Enrollment*, use CONSTRAINT clauses for foreign keys at the end of the CREATE TABLE statement:

```
CREATE TABLE Enrollment
        (       OfferNo         INTEGER,
                StdSSN          CHAR(11),
                EnrGrade        DECIMAL(3, 2),
CONSTRAINT PKEnrollment PRIMARY KEY (OfferNo, StdSSN),
CONSTRAINT FKOfferNo FOREIGN KEY (OfferNo)
                REFERENCES Offering,
CONSTRAINT FKStdSSN FOREIGN KEY (StdSSN) REFERENCES Student          )
```

Allowing Null Values in Foreign Keys

Although referential integrity permits foreign keys to have null values, it is not common for foreign keys to have null values. When a foreign key is part of a primary key, null values are not permitted because of the entity integrity rule. For example, null values are not permitted for either *Enrollment.StdSSN* or *Enrollment.OfferNo* because each is part of the primary key.

When a foreign key is not part of a primary key, usage dictates whether null values should be permitted. For example, *Offering.CourseNo*, a foreign key referring to *Course* (Table 2.4), is not part of a primary key yet null values are not permitted. In most universities, a course cannot be offered before it is approved. Thus, an offering should not be inserted without having a related course.

In contrast, the *Offering.FacSSN* column referring to the faculty member teaching the offering may be null. The *Faculty* table (Table 2.7) stores data about instructors of courses. A null value for *Offering.FacSSN* means that a faculty member is not yet as-

TABLE 2.7	Sample *Faculty* Table				
FacSSN	FacFirstName	FacLastName	FacCity	FacState	FacDept
098-76-5432	LEONARD	VINCE	SEATTLE	WA	MS
543-21-0987	VICTORIA	EMMANUEL	BOTHELL	WA	MS
654-32-1098	LEONARD	FIBON	SEATTLE	WA	MS
765-43-2109	NICKI	MACON	BELLEVUE	WA	FIN
876-54-3210	CRISTOPHER	COLAN	SEATTLE	WA	MS
987-65-4321	JULIA	MILLS	SEATTLE	WA	FIN

signed to teach the offering. For example, an instructor is not assigned in the first and third rows of Table 2.4. Because offerings must be scheduled perhaps a year in advance, it is likely that instructors for some offerings will not be known until after the offering row is initially stored. Therefore, permitting null values in the *Offering* table is prudent.

In the CREATE TABLE statement, the NOT NULL clause indicates that a column cannot have null values. You indicate that nulls are not permitted by appending the NOT NULL clause after the data type specification. You also can specify the NOT NULL clause in a CONSTRAINT clause.

```
CREATE TABLE Student
            (    StdSSN          CHAR(11) NOT NULL,
                 StdFirstName    VARCHAR(50) NOT NULL,
                 StdLastName     VARCHAR(50) NOT NULL,
                 StdCity         VARCHAR(50) NOT NULL,
                 StdState        CHAR(2) NOT NULL,
                 StdZip          CHAR(10) NOT NULL,
                 StdMajor        CHAR(6),
                 StdClass        CHAR(2),
                 StdGPA          DECIMAL(3,2),
CONSTRAINT PKStudent PRIMARY KEY (StdSSN)  )
```

Referential Integrity for Self-Referencing (Unary) Relationships

Self-Referencing Relationship a relationship in which a foreign key refers to the same table. Self-referencing relationships represent associations among members of the same set.

This section finishes with a discussion of self-referencing relationships, a special kind of referential integrity constraint. Self-referencing or unary relationships involve a single table. Self-referencing relationships are not common, but they are important when they occur. In the university database, a faculty member can supervise other faculty members and be supervised by a faculty member. For example, Victoria Emmanuel (second row) supervises Leonard Fibon (third row). The *FacSupervisor* column shows this relationship: the *FacSupervisor* value in the third row (543-21-0987) matches the *Fac-SSN* value in the second row. A referential integrity constraint involving the *FacSupervisor* column represents the self-referencing relationship. In the CREATE TABLE statement, the referential integrity constraint for a self-referencing relationship can be written the same way as other referential integrity constraints:

```
CREATE TABLE Faculty
            (    FacSSN          CHAR(11) NOT NULL,
                 FacFirstName    VARCHAR(50) NOT NULL,
```

FacRank	FacSalary	FacSuperviso	FacHireDate	FacZipCode
ASST	$35,000	654-32-1098	01-Apr-90	98111-9921
PROF	$120,000		01-Apr-91	98011-2242
ASSC	$70,000	543-21-0987	01-Apr-89	98121-0094
PROF	$65,000		01-Apr-92	98015-9945
ASST	$40,000	654-32-1098	01-Apr-94	98114-1332
ASSC	$75,000	765-43-2109	01-Apr-95	98114-9954

```
              FacLastName              VARCHAR(50) NOT NULL,
              FacCity                  VARCHAR(50) NOT NULL,
              FacState                 CHAR(2) NOT NULL,
              FacZipCode               CHAR(10) NOT NULL,
              FacHireDate              DATE,
              FacDept                  CHAR(6),
              FacRank                  CHAR(4),
              FacSalary                DECIMAL(10,2),
              FacSupervisor            CHAR(11),
CONSTRAINT PKFaculty PRIMARY KEY (FacSSN),
CONSTRAINT FKFacSupervisor FOREIGN KEY (FacSupervisor)
              REFERENCES Faculty          )
```

2.2.3 Graphical Representation of Referential Integrity

In recent years, commercial DBMSs have provided graphical representations for referential integrity constraints. The graphical representation makes referential integrity easier to define and understand than the text representation in the CREATE TABLE statement. In addition, a graphical representation supports nonprocedural data access.

To depict a graphical representation, let us study the Relationship window in Microsoft Access. Access provides the Relationship window to visually define and display referential integrity constraints. Figure 2.2 shows the Relationship window for the tables of the university database. Each line represents a referential integrity constraint or relationship. In a relationship, the primary key table is known as the parent or "1" table (for example, *Student*) and the foreign key table (for example, *Enrollment*) is known as the child or "M" (many) table.

The relationship from *Student* to *Enrollment* is called "1-M" (one to many) because a student can be related to many enrollments but an enrollment can be related to only one student. Similarly, the relationship from the *Offering* table to the *Enrollment* table means that an offering can be related to many enrollments but an enrollment can be related to only one offering. You should practice by writing similar sentences for the other relationships in Figure 2.2.

M-N (many to many) relationships are not directly represented in the Relational Model. An M-N relationship means that rows from each table can be related to many rows of the other table. For example, a student enrolls in many course offerings and a course offering contains many students. In the Relational Model, a pair of 1-M relationships and a linking or associative table represents an M-N relationship. In Figure 2.2, the linking table *Enrollment* and its relationships with *Offering* and *Student* represent an M-N relationship between the *Student* and *Offering* tables.

Self-referencing relationships are represented indirectly in the Relationship window. The self-referencing relationship involving *Faculty* is represented as a relationship between the *Faculty* and *Faculty_1* tables. *Faculty_1* is not a real table as it is created only inside the Access Relationship window. Access can only indirectly show self-referencing relationships.

A graphical representation such as the Relationship window makes it easy to identify tables that should be combined to fulfill a retrieval request. For example, assume that you want to find instructors who teach courses with "database" in the course description. Clearly, you need the *Course* table to find "database" courses. You also need the *Faculty* table to display instructor data. Figure 2.2 shows that you also need the *Offering*

1-M Relationship a connection between two tables in which one row of a table can be referenced by many rows of a second table. 1-M relationships are the most common kind of relationship.

M-N Relationship a connection between two tables in which rows of each table can be related to many rows of the other table. M-N relationships cannot be directly represented in the Relational Model. Two 1-M relationships and a linking or associative table represent an M-N relationship.

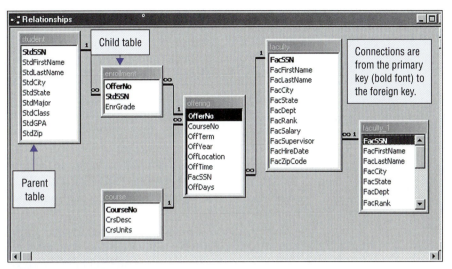

| **Figure 2.2** | **Relationship window for the university database.** |

table because *Course* and *Faculty* are not directly connected. Rather, *Course* and *Faculty* are connected through *Offering*. Thus, visualizing relationships helps to identify tables needed to fulfill retrieval requests. Before attempting the retrieval problems in later chapters, you should carefully study a graphical representation of the relationships. You should construct your own diagram if one is not available.

2.3 DELETE AND UPDATE ACTIONS FOR REFERENCED ROWS

For each referential integrityconstraint, you should carefully consider actions on <u>referenced rows</u> in parent tables of 1-M relationships. A row is referenced if there are rows in a child table with foreign key values identical to the primary key value of the parent table row. For example, the first row of the *Course* table (Table 2.6) with *CourseNo* "IS320" is referenced by the first row of the *Offering* table (Table 2.4). It is natural to consider what happens to related *Offering* rows when the referenced *Course* row is deleted or the *CourseNo* is updated. More generally, these concerns can be stated as

> **Deleting a referenced row:** What happens to related rows (that is, rows in the child table with the identical foreign key value) when the referenced row in the parent table is deleted?
>
> **Updating the primary key of a referenced row:** What happens to related rows when the primary key of the referenced row in the parent table is updated?

Actions on referenced rows are important when changing the rows of a database. When developing data entry forms (discussed in Chapter 10), actions on referenced rows can be especially important. For example, if a data entry form permits deletion of rows in the *Course* table, actions on related rows in the *Offering* table must be carefully planned. Otherwise, the database can become inconsistent or difficult to use.

Possible Actions

There are several possible actions in response to the deletion of a referenced row or the update of the primary key of a referenced row. The appropriate action depends on the tables involved. The following list describes the actions and provides examples of usage.

- **Restrict:**[6] Do not allow the action on the referenced row. For example, do not permit a *Student* row to be deleted if there are any related *Enrollment* rows. Similarly, do not allow *Student.StdSSN* to be changed if there are related *Enrollment* rows.

- **Cascade:** Perform the same action (cascade the action) to related rows. For example, if a *Student* is deleted, then delete the related *Enrollment* rows. Likewise, if *Student.StdSSN* is changed in some row, update *StdSSN* in the related *Enrollment* rows.

- **Nullify:** Set the foreign key of related rows to null. For example, if a *Faculty* row is deleted, then set *FacSSN* to NULL in related *Offering* rows. Likewise, if *Faculty.FacSSN* is updated, then set *FacSSN* to NULL in related *Offering* rows. The nullify action is not permitted if the foreign key does not allow null values. For example, the nullify option is not valid when deleting rows of the *Student* table because *Enrollment.StdSSN* is part of the primary key.

- **Default:** Set the foreign key of related rows to its default value. For example, if a *Faculty* row is deleted, then set *FacSSN* to a default faculty in related *Offering* rows. The default faculty might have an interpretation such as "to be announced." Likewise, if *Faculty.FacSSN* is updated, then set *FacSSN* to its default value in related *Offering* rows. The default action is an alternative to the null action as the default action avoids null values.

The delete and update actions can be specified in SQL using the ON DELETE and ON UPDATE clauses. These clauses are added as part of foreign key constraints. For example, the revised CREATE TABLE statement for the *Enrollment* table shows ON DELETE and ON UPDATE clauses for the *Enrollment* table. The RESTRICT keyword means restrict (the first possible action). The keywords CASCADE, SET NULL, and SET DEFAULT can be used to specify the second through fourth options, respectively.

```
CREATE TABLE Enrollment
        (       OfferNo          INTEGER NOT NULL,
                StdSSN           CHAR(11) NOT NULL,
                EnrGrade         DECIMAL(3,2),
        CONSTRAINT PKEnrollment PRIMARY KEY (OfferNo, StdSSN),
        CONSTRAINT FKOfferNo FOREIGN KEY (OfferNo) REFERENCES Offering
                ON DELETE RESTRICT
                ON UPDATE CASCADE,
        CONSTRAINT FKStdSSN FOREIGN KEY (StdSSN) REFERENCES Student
                ON DELETE RESTRICT
                ON UPDATE CASCADE   )
```

---

[6] There is a related action designated by the keywords NO ACTION. The difference between RESTRICT and NO ACTION involves the concept of deferred integrity constraints, discussed in Chapter 15.

Before finishing this section, you should understand the impact of referenced rows on insert operations. A referenced row must be inserted before its related rows. For example, before inserting a row in the *Enrollment* table, the referenced rows in the *Student* and *Offering* tables must exist. Referential integrity places an ordering on adding rows from different tables. When designing data entry forms, you should carefully consider the impact of referential integrity on the order that users complete forms.

2.4 OPERATORS OF RELATIONAL ALGEBRA

In previous sections of this chapter, you have studied the terminology and integrity rules of relational databases with the goal of understanding existing relational databases. In particular, understanding connections among tables was emphasized as a prerequisite to retrieving useful information. This section describes some fundamental operators that can be used to retrieve useful information from a relational database.

You can think of relational algebra similarly to the algebra of numbers except that the objects are different: algebra applies to numbers and relational algebra applies to tables. In algebra, each operator transforms one or more numbers into another number. Similarly, each operator of relational algebra *transforms a table (or two tables) into a new table.*

This section emphasizes the study of each relational algebra operator in isolation. For each operator, you should understand its purpose and inputs. While it is possible to combine operators to make complicated formulas, this level of understanding is not important for developing query formulation skills. Using relational algebra by itself to write queries can be awkward because of details such as ordering of operations and parentheses. Therefore, you should seek only to understand the meaning of each operator, not how to combine operators to write expressions.

The coverage of relational algebra groups the operators into three categories. The most widely used operators (restrict, project, and join) are presented first. The extended cross product operator is also presented to provide background for the join operator. Knowledge of these operators will help you to formulate a large percentage of queries. More specialized operators are covered in latter parts of the section. The more specialized operators include the traditional set operators (union, intersection, and difference) and advanced operators (summarize and divide). Knowledge of these operators will help you formulate more difficult queries.

2.4.1 Restrict (Select) and Project Operators

Restrict an operator that retrieves a subset of the rows of the input table that satisfy a given condition.

The restrict (also known as select) and project operators produce subsets of a table.[7] Because users often want to see a subset rather than an entire table, these operators are widely used. These operators are also popular because they are easy to understand.

The restrict and project operators produce an output table that is a subset of an input table (Figure 2.3). Restrict produces a subset of the rows, while project produces a subset of the columns. Restrict uses a condition or logical expression to indicate what rows should be retained in the output. Project uses a list of column names to indicate what columns to retain in the output. Restrict and project are often used together because tables can have many rows and columns. It is rare that a user wants to see all rows and columns.

Project an operator that retrieves a specified subset of the columns of the input table.

---

[7]In this book, the operator name restrict is used to avoid confusion with the SQL SELECT statement. The operator is more widely known as select.

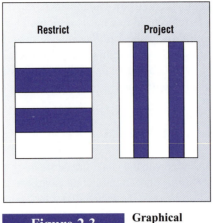

Figure 2.3   Graphical representation of restrict and project operators.

TABLE 2.8   Result of Restrict Operation on the Sample Offering Table (Table 2.4)

OfferNo	CourseNo	OffTerm	OffYear	OffLocation	OffTime	FacSSN	OffDays
3333	IS320	SPRING	2003	BLM214	8:30 AM	098-76-5432	MW
5678	IS480	SPRING	2003	BLM302	10:30 AM	987-65-4321	MW

TABLE 2.9   Result of a Project Operation on *Offering.CourseNo*

CourseNo
IS320
IS460
IS480

The logical expression used in the restrict operator can include comparisons involving columns and constants. Complex logical expressions can be formed using the logical operators AND, OR, and NOT. For example, Table 2.8 shows the result of a restrict operation on Table 2.4 where the logical expression is: OffDays = 'MW' AND OffTerm = 'SPRING' AND OffYear = 2003.

A project operation can have a side effect. Sometimes after a subset of columns is retrieved, there are duplicate rows. When this occurs, the project operator removes the duplicate rows. For example, if *Offering.CourseNo* is the only column used in a project operation, only three rows are in the result (Table 2.9) even though the *Offering* table (Table 2.4) has nine rows. The column *Offering.CourseNo* contains only three unique values in Table 2.4. Note that if the primary key or a candidate key is included in the list of columns, the resulting table has no duplicates. For example, if *OfferNo* was included in the list of columns, the result table would have nine rows with no duplicate removal necessary.

Faculty	
FacSSN	
111-11-1111	
222-22-2222	
333-33-3333	

Faculty PRODUCT Student	
FacSSN	**StdSSN**
111-11-1111	111-11-1111
111-11-1111	444-44-4444
111-11-1111	555-55-5555
222-22-2222	111-11-1111
222-22-2222	444-44-4444
222-22-2222	555-55-5555
333-33-3333	111-11-1111
333-33-3333	444-44-4444
333-33-3333	555-55-5555

Student	
StdSSN	
111-11-1111	
444-44-4444	
555-55-5555	

Figure 2.4   **Cross product example.**

This side effect is due to the "pure" nature of relational algebra. In relational algebra, tables are considered sets. Because sets do not have duplicates, duplicate removal is a possible side effect of the project operator. Commercial languages such as SQL usually take a more pragmatic view. Because duplicate removal can be computationally expensive, duplicates are not removed unless the user specifically requests it.

2.4.2 Extended Cross Product Operator

The extended cross product operator can combine any two tables. Other table combining operators have conditions about the tables to combine. Because of its unrestricted nature, the extended cross product operator can produce tables with excessive data. The extended cross product operator is important because it is a building block for the join operator. When you initially learn the join operator, knowledge of the extended cross product operator can be useful. After you gain experience with the join operator, you will not need to rely on the extended cross product operator.

Extended Cross Product an operator that builds a table consisting of all combinations of rows from each of the two input tables.

The extended cross product (product for short) operator shows everything possible from two tables.[8] The product of two tables is a new table consisting of all possible combinations of rows from the two input tables. Figure 2.4 depicts a product of two single column tables. Each result row consists of the columns of the *Faculty* table (only *FacSSN*) and the columns of the *Student* table (only *StdSSN*). The name of the operator (product) derives from the number of rows in the result. The number of rows in the resulting table is the product of the number of rows of the two input tables. In contrast, the number of result columns is the sum of the columns of the two input tables. In Figure 2.4, the result table has nine rows and two columns.

---

[8]The extended cross product operator is also known as the Cartesian product after French mathematician René Descartes.

TABLE 2.10	Sample *Student* Table

StdSSN	StdLastName	StdMajor	StdClass
123-45-6789	WELLS	IS	FR
124-56-7890	NORBERT	FIN	JR
234-56-7890	KENDALL	ACCT	JR

TABLE 2.11	Sample *Enrollment* Table

OfferNo	StdSSN	EnrGrade
1234	123-45-6789	3.3
1234	234-56-7890	3.5
4321	124-56-7890	3.2

TABLE 2.12	*Student* PRODUCT *Enrollment*

Student StdSSN	StdLastName	StdMajor	StdClass	OfferNo	Enrollment StdSSN	EnrGrade
123-45-6789	WELLS	IS	FR	1234	123-45-6789	3.3
123-45-6789	WELLS	IS	FR	1234	234-56-7890	3.5
123-45-6789	WELLS	IS	FR	4321	124-56-7890	3.2
124-56-7890	NORBERT	FIN	JR	1234	123-45-6789	3.3
124-56-7890	NORBERT	FIN	JR	1234	234-56-7890	3.5
124-56-7890	NORBERT	FIN	JR	4321	124-56-7890	3.2
234-56-7890	KENDALL	ACCT	JR	1234	123-45-6789	3.3
234-56-7890	KENDALL	ACCT	JR	1234	234-56-7890	3.5
234-56-7890	KENDALL	ACCT	JR	4321	124-56-7890	3.2

As another example, consider the product of the sample *Student* (Table 2.10) and *Enrollment* (Table 2.11) tables. The resulting table (Table 2.12) has 9 rows (3 × 3) and 7 columns (4 + 3). Note that most rows in the result are not meaningful as only three rows have the same value for *StdSSN*.

As these examples show, the extended cross product operator often generates excessive data. Excessive data are as bad as lack of data. For example, the product of a student table of 30,000 rows and an enrollment table of 300,000 rows is a table of nine billion rows! Most of these rows would be meaningless combinations. So it is rare that a cross product operation by itself is needed. Rather, the importance of the cross product operator is as a building block for other operators such as the join operator.

2.4.3 Join Operator

Join an operator that produces a table containing rows that match on a condition involving a column from each input table.

Join is the most widely used operator for combining tables. Because most databases have many tables, combining tables is important. Join differs from cross product because join requires a matching condition on rows of two tables. Most tables are combined in this way. To a large extent, your skill in retrieving useful data will depend on your ability to use the join operator.

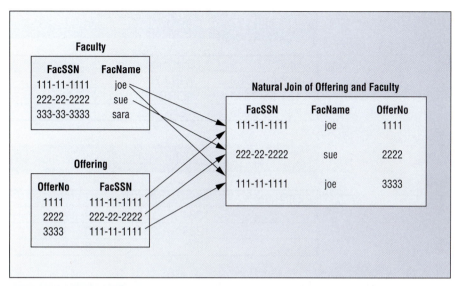

| **Figure 2.5** | **Sample natural join operation.** |

The join operator builds a new table by combining rows from two tables that match on a join condition. Typically, the join condition specifies that two rows have an identical value in one or more columns. When the join condition involves equality, the join is known as an equi-join, for equality join. Figure 2.5 shows a join of sample *Faculty* and *Offering* tables where the join condition is that the *FacSSN* columns are equal. Note that only a few columns are shown to simplify the illustration. The arrows indicate how rows from the input tables combine to form rows in the result table. For example, the first row of the *Faculty* table combines with the first and third rows of the *Offering* table to yield two rows in the result table.

The natural join operator, a specialized kind of join, is the most common join operation. In a natural join operation, the join condition is equality (equi-join), one of the join columns is removed, and the join columns have the same unqualified name.[9] In Figure 2.5, the result table contains only three columns because the natural join removes one of the *FacSSN* columns. The particular column (*Faculty.FacSSN* or *Offering.FacSSN*) removed does not matter.

Natural Join a commonly used join operator where the matching condition is equality (equi-join), one of the matching columns is discarded in the result table, and the join columns have the same unqualified names.

As another example, consider the natural join of *Student* (Table 2.13) and *Enrollment* (Table 2.14) shown in Table 2.15. In each row of the result, *Student.StdSSN* matches *Enrollment.StdSSN*. Only one of the join columns is included in the result. Arbitrarily, *Student.StdSSN* is shown although *Enrollment.StdSSN* could be included without changing the result.

[9]An "unqualified" name is the column name without the table name. The full name of a column includes the table name. Thus, the full names of the join columns in Figure 2.5 are *Faculty.FacSSN* and *Offering.FacSSN*.

TABLE 2.13	Sample *Student* Table

StdSSN	StdLastName	StdMajor	StdClass
123-45-6789	WELLS	IS	FR
124-56-7890	NORBERT	FIN	JR
234-56-7890	KENDALL	ACCT	JR

TABLE 2.14	Sample *Enrollment* Table

OfferNo	StdSSN	EnrGrade
1234	123-45-6789	3.3
1234	234-56-7890	3.5
4321	124-56-7890	3.2

TABLE 2.15	Natural Join of *Student* and *Enrollment*

Student.StdSSN	StdLastName	StdMajor	StdClass	OfferNo	EnrGrade
123-45-6789	WELLS	IS	FR	1234	3.3
124-56-7890	NORBERT	FIN	JR	4321	3.2
234-56-7890	KENDALL	ACCT	JR	1234	3.5

Derivation of the Natural Join

The natural join operator is not primitive because it can be derived from other operators. The natural join operator consists of three steps:

1. A product operation to combine the rows.
2. A restrict operation to remove rows not satisfying the join condition.
3. A project operation to remove one of the join columns.

To depict these steps, the first step to produce the natural join in Table 2.15 is the product result shown in Table 2.12. The second step is to retain only the matching rows (rows 1, 6, and 8 of Table 2.12). A restrict operation is used with Student.StdSSN = Enrollment.StdSSN as the restriction condition. The final step is to eliminate one of the join columns (*Enrollment.StdSSN*). The project operation includes all columns except for *Enrollment.StdSSN*.

Although the join operator is not primitive, it can be conceptualized directly without its primitive operations. When you are initially learning the join operator, it can be helpful to derive the results using the underlying operations. As an exercise, you are encouraged to derive the result in Figure 2.5. After learning the join operator, you should not need to use the underlying operations.

Visual Formulation of Join Operations

As a query formulation aid, many DBMSs provide a visual way to formulate joins. Microsoft Access provides a visual representation of the join operator using the Query Design window. Figure 2.6 depicts a join between *Student* and *Enrollment* on *StdSSN* using

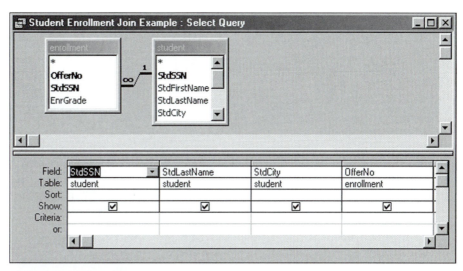

Figure 2.6   Query Design window showing a join between *Student* and *Enrollment.*

the Query Design window. To form this join, you need only to select the tables. Access determines that you should join over the *StdSSN* column. Access assumes that most joins involve a primary key and foreign key combination. If Access chooses the join condition incorrectly, you can choose other join columns.

2.4.4 Outer Join Operator

The result of a join operation includes the rows matching on the join condition. Sometimes it is useful to include both matching and nonmatching rows. For example, sometimes you want to know offerings that have an assigned instructor as well as offerings without an assigned instructor. In these situations, the outer join operator is useful.

The <u>outer join</u> operator provides the ability to preserve <u>nonmatching rows</u> in the result as well as to include the matching rows. Figure 2.7 depicts an outer join between sample *Faculty* and *Offering* tables. Note that each table has one row that does not match any row in the other table. The third row of *Faculty* and the fourth row of *Offering* do not have matching rows in the other table. For nonmatching rows, null values are used to complete the column values in the other table. In Figure 2.7, blanks (no values) represent null values. The fourth result row is the nonmatched row of *Faculty* with a null value for the *OfferNo* column. Likewise, the fifth result row contains a null value for the first two columns because it is a nonmatched row of *Offering*.

Full Outer Join an operator that produces the matching rows (the join part) as well as the nonmatching rows from both input tables.

One-Sided Outer Join an operator that produces the matching rows (the join part) as well as the nonmatching rows from the designated input table.

Full versus One-Sided Outer Join Operators

The outer join operator has two variations. The <u>full outer join</u> preserves nonmatching rows from both input tables. Figure 2.7 shows a full outer join because the nonmatching rows from both tables are preserved in the result. Because it is sometimes useful to preserve the nonmatching rows from just one input table, the <u>one-sided outer join</u> operator has been devised. In Figure 2.7, only the first four rows of the result would appear for a one-sided outer join that preserves the rows of the *Faculty* table. The last row would not

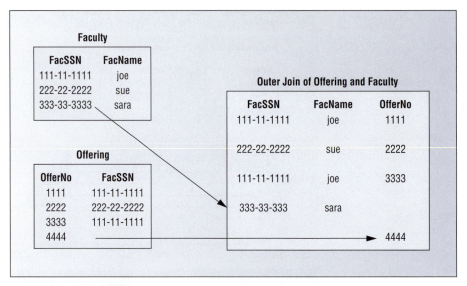

Faculty

FacSSN	FacName
111-11-1111	joe
222-22-2222	sue
333-33-3333	sara

Offering

OfferNo	FacSSN
1111	111-11-1111
2222	222-22-2222
3333	111-11-1111
4444	

Outer Join of Offering and Faculty

FacSSN	FacName	OfferNo
111-11-1111	joe	1111
222-22-2222	sue	2222
111-11-1111	joe	3333
333-33-333	sara	
		4444

Figure 2.7   Sample outer join operation.

appear in the result because it is an unmatched row of the *Offering* table. Similarly, only the first three rows and the last row would appear in the result for a one-sided outer join that preserves the rows of the *Offering* table.

The outer join is useful in two situations. A full outer join can be used to combine two tables with some common columns and some unique columns. For example, to combine the *Student* and *Faculty* tables, a full outer join can be used to show all columns about all university people. In Table 2.18, the first two rows are only from the sample *Student* table (Table 2.16), while the last two rows are only from the sample *Faculty* table (Table 2.17). Note the use of null values for the columns from the other table. The third row in Table 2.18 is the row common to the sample *Faculty* and *Student* tables.

A one-sided outer join can be useful when a table has null values in a foreign key. For example, the *Offering* table (Table 2.19) can have null values in the *FacSSN* column representing course offerings without an assigned professor. A one-sided outer join between *Offering* and *Faculty* preserves the rows of *Offering* that do not have an assigned *Faculty* as shown in Table 2.20. With a natural join, the first and third rows of Table 2.20 would not appear. As you will see in Chapter 10, one-sided joins can be useful in data entry forms.

Visual Formulation of Outer Join Operations

As a query formulation aid, many DBMSs provide a visual way to formulate outer joins. Microsoft Access provides a visual representation of the one-sided join operator in the Query Design window. Figure 2.8 depicts a one-sided outer join that preserves the rows of the *Offering* table. The arrow from *Offering* to *Faculty* means that the nonmatched rows of *Offering* are preserved in the result. When combining the *Faculty* and *Offering* tables, Microsoft Access provides three choices: (1) show only the matched rows (a join); (2) show matched rows and nonmatched rows of *Faculty;*

TABLE 2.16	Sample *Student* Table

StdSSN	StdLastName	StdMajor	StdClass
123-45-6789	WELLS	IS	FR
124-56-7890	NORBERT	FIN	JR
876-54-3210	COLAN	MS	SR

TABLE 2.17	Sample *Faculty* Table

FacSSN	FacLastName	FacDept	FacRank
098-76-5432	VINCE	MS	ASST
543-21-0987	EMMANUEL	MS	PROF
876-54-3210	COLAN	MS	ASST

TABLE 2.18	Result of Full Outer Join of Sample *Student* and *Faculty* Tables

StdSSN	StdLastName	StdMajor	StdClass	FacSSN	FacLastName	FacDept	FacRank
123-45-6789	WELLS	IS	FR				
124-56-7890	NORBERT	FIN	JR				
876-54-3210	COLAN	MS	SR	876-54-3210	COLAN	MS	ASST
				098-76-5432	VINCE	MS	ASST
				543-21-0987	EMMANUEL	MS	PROF

TABLE 2.19	Sample *Offering* Table

OfferNo	CourseNo	OffTerm	FacSSN
1111	IS320	SUMMER	
1234	IS320	FALL	098-76-5432
2222	IS460	SUMMER	
3333	IS320	SPRING	098-76-5432
4444	IS320	SPRING	543-21-0987

TABLE 2.20	Result of a One-Sided Outer Join between *Offering* (Table 2.19) and *Faculty* (Table 2.17)

OfferNo	CourseNo	OffTerm	Offering.FacSSN	Faculty.FacSSN	FacLastName	FacDept	FacRank
1111	IS320	SUMMER					
1234	IS320	FALL	098-76-5432	098-76-5432	VINCE	MS	ASST
2222	IS460	SUMMER					
3333	IS320	SPRING	098-76-5432	098-76-5432	VINCE	MS	ASST
4444	IS320	SPRING	543-21-0987	543-21-0987	EMMANUEL	MS	PROF

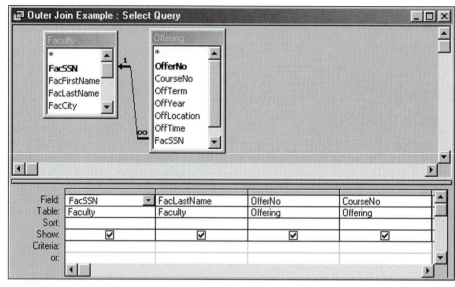

Figure 2.8   Query Design window showing a one-sided outer join preserving the *Offering* table.

and (3) show matched rows and nonmatched rows of *Offering*. Choice (3) is shown in Figure 2.8. Choice (1) would appear similar to Figure 2.6. Choice (2) would have the arrow from *Faculty* to *Offering*.

2.4.5 Union, Intersection, and Difference Operators

Traditional Set Operators the union operator produces a table containing rows from either input table. The intersection operator produces a table containing rows common to both input tables. The difference operator produces a table containing rows from the first input table but not in the second input table.

The union, intersection, and difference table operators are similar to the traditional set operators. The traditional set operators are used to determine all members of two sets (union), common members of two sets (intersection), and members unique to only one set (difference), as depicted in Figure 2.9.

The union, intersection, and difference operators for tables apply to rows of a table but otherwise operate in the same way as the traditional set operators. A union operation retrieves all the rows in either table. For example, a union operator applied to two student tables at different universities can find all student rows. An intersection operation retrieves just the common rows. For example, an intersection operation can determine the students attending both universities. A difference operation retrieves the rows in the first table but not in the second table. For example, a difference operation can determine the students attending only one university.

Union Compatibility

Union Compatibility a requirement on the input tables for the traditional set operators. Each table must have the same number of columns and each corresponding column must have a compatible data type.

Compatibility is a new concept for the table operators as compared to the traditional set operators. With the table operators, both tables must be union compatible because all columns are compared. Union compatibility means that each table must have the same number of columns and each corresponding column must have the same data type. Union compatibility can be confusing because it involves positional correspondence of the columns. That is, the first columns of the two tables must have the same data type, the second columns must have the same data type, and so on.

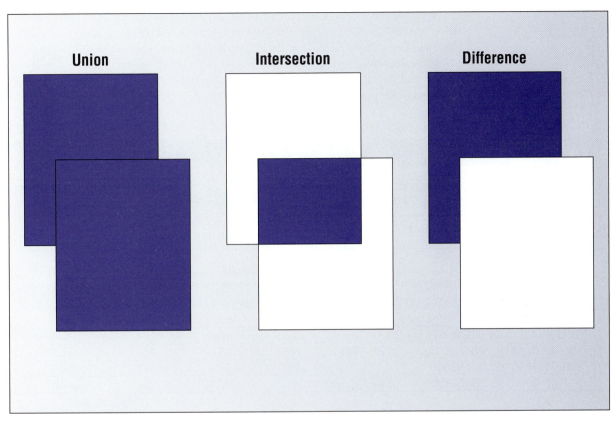

| **Figure 2.9** | Venn diagrams for traditional set operators. |

To depict the union, intersection, and difference operators, let us apply them to the *Student1* and *Student2* tables (Tables 2.21 and 2.22). These tables are union compatible because they have identical columns listed in the same order. The results of union, intersection, and difference operators are shown in Tables 2.23 through 2.25, respectively. Even though we can determine that two rows are identical from looking only at *StdSSN*, all columns are compared due to the way that the operators are designed.

Note that the result of *Student1* DIFFERENCE *Student2* would not be the same as *Student2* DIFFERENCE *Student1*. The result of the latter (*Student2* DIFFERENCE *Student1*) is the second and third rows of *Student2* (rows in *Student2* but not in *Student1*).

Because of the union compatibility requirement, the union, intersection, and difference operators are not as widely used as other operators. However, these operators do have some important, specialized uses. One use is to combine tables distributed over multiple locations. For example, suppose there is a student table at Big State University (*BSUStudent*) and a student table at University of Big State (*UBSStudent*). Because these tables have identical columns, the traditional set operators are applicable. To find students attending either university, use *UBSStudent* UNION *BSUStudent*. To find students only attending Big State, use *BSUStudent* DIFFERENCE *UBSStudent*. To find students attending both universities, use *UBSStudent* INTERSECT *BSUStudent*. Note that the resulting table in each operation has the same number of columns as the two input tables.

The traditional operators are also useful if there are tables that are similar but not union compatible. For example, the *Student* and *Faculty* tables have some compatible columns (*StdSSN* with *FacSSN*, *StdLastName* with *FacLastName,* and *StdCity* with *FacCity*), but other columns are different. The union compatible operators can be used if the *Student* and *Faculty* tables are first made union compatible using the project operator discussed in Section 2.4.1.

TABLE 2.21   *Student1* **Table**

StdSSN	StdLastName	StdCity	StdState	StdMajor	StdClass	StdGPA
123-45-6789	WELLS	SEATTLE	WA	IS	FR	3.00
124-56-7890	NORBERT	BOTHELL	WA	FIN	JR	2.70
234-56-7890	KENDALL	TACOMA	WA	ACCT	JR	3.50

TABLE 2.22   *Student2* **Table**

StdSSN	StdLastName	StdCity	StdState	StdMajor	StdClass	StdGPA
123-45-6789	WELLS	SEATTLE	WA	IS	FR	3.00
995-56-3490	BAGGINS	AUSTIN	TX	FIN	JR	2.90
111-56-4490	WILLIAMS	SEATTLE	WA	ACCT	JR	3.40

TABLE 2.23   *Student1* **UNION** *Student2*

StdSSN	StdLastName	StdCity	StdState	StdMajor	StdClass	StdGPA
123-45-6789	WELLS	SEATTLE	WA	IS	FR	3.00
124-56-7890	NORBERT	BOTHELL	WA	FIN	JR	2.70
234-56-7890	KENDALL	TACOMA	WA	ACCT	JR	3.50
995-56-3490	BAGGINS	AUSTIN	TX	FIN	JR	2.90
111-56-4490	WILLIAMS	SEATTLE	WA	ACCT	JR	3.40

TABLE 2.24   *Student1* **INTERSECT** *Student2*

StdSSN	StdLastName	StdCity	StdState	StdMajor	StdClass	StdGPA
123-45-6789	WELLS	SEATTLE	WA	IS	FR	3.00

TABLE 2.25   *Student1* **DIFFERENCE** *Student2*

StdSSN	StdLastName	StdCity	StdState	StdMajor	StdClass	StdGPA
124-56-7890	NORBERT	BOTHELL	WA	FIN	JR	2.70
234-56-7890	KENDALL	TACOMA	WA	ACCT	JR	3.50

2.4.6 Summarize Operator

Summarize an operator that produces a table with rows that summarize the rows of the input table. Aggregate functions are used to summarize the rows of the input table.

Summarize is a powerful operator for decision making. Because tables can contain many rows, it is often useful to see statistics about groups of rows rather than individual rows. The <u>summarize</u> operator allows groups of rows to be compressed or summarized by a calculated value. Almost any kind of statistical function can be used to summarize groups of rows. Because this is not a statistics book, we will use only simple functions such as count, min, max, average, and sum.

The summarize operator compresses a table by replacing groups of rows with individual rows containing calculated values. A statistical or <u>aggregate function</u> is used for the calculated values. Figure 2.10 depicts a summarize operation for a sample enrollment table. The input table is grouped on the *StdSSN* column. Each group of rows is replaced by the average of the grade column.

As another example, Table 2.27 shows the result of a summarize operation on the sample *Faculty* table in Table 2.26. Note that the result contains one row per value of the grouping column, *FacDept*.

Figure 2.10   **Sample summarize operation.**

TABLE 2.26	Sample *Faculty* Table					
FacSSN	FacLastName	FacDept	FacRank	FacSalary	FacSupervisor	FacHireDate
098-76-5432	VINCE	MS	ASST	$35,000	654-32-1098	01-Apr-90
543-21-0987	EMMANUEL	MS	PROF	$120,000		01-Apr-91
654-32-1098	FIBON	MS	ASSC	$70,000	543-21-0987	01-Apr-89
765-43-2109	MACON	FIN	PROF	$65,000		01-Apr-92
876-54-3210	COLAN	MS	ASST	$40,000	654-32-1098	01-Apr-94
987-65-4321	MILLS	FIN	ASSC	$75,000	765-43-2109	01-Apr-95

TABLE 2.27	Result Table for SUMMARIZE *Faculty* ADD AVG(*FacSalary*) GROUP BY *FacDept*

FacDept	FacSalary
MS	$66,250
FIN	$70,000

The summarize operator can include additional calculated values (also showing the minimum salary, for example) and additional grouping columns (also grouping on *FacRank,* for example). When grouping on multiple columns, each result row shows one combination of values for the grouping columns.

2.4.7 Divide Operator

Divide an operator that produces a table in which the values of a column from one input table are associated with all the values from a column of a second input table.

The divide operator is a more specialized and difficult operator than join because the matching requirement in divide is more stringent than join. For example, a join operator is used to retrieve offerings taken by *any* student. A <u>divide</u> operator is required to retrieve offerings taken by *all* (or every) students. Because divide has more stringent matching conditions, it is not as widely used as join, and it can be more difficult to understand. When appropriate, the divide operator provides a powerful way to combine tables.

The divide operator for tables is somewhat analogous to the divide operator for numbers. In numerical division, the objective is to find how many times one number contains another number. In table division, the objective is to find values of one column that contain *every* value in another column. Stated another way, the divide operator finds values of one column that are associated with *every* value in another column.

To understand more concretely how the divide operator works, consider an example with sample *Part* and *SuppPart* (supplier-part) tables as depicted in Figure 2.11. The divide operator uses two input tables. The first table (*SuppPart*) has two columns (a binary table) and the second table (*Part*) has one column (a unary table).[10] The result table has one column where the values come from the first column of the binary table. The result table in Figure 2.11 shows the suppliers who supply every part. The value s3 appears in the output because it is associated with *every* value in the *Part* table. Stated another way, the set of values associated with s3 contains the set of values in the *Part* table.

To understand the divide operator in another way, rewrite the *SuppPart* table as three rows using the angle brackets < > to surround a row: <s3, {p1, p2, p3}>, <s0, {p1}>, <s1, {p2}>. Rewrite the *Part* table as a set: {p1, p2, p3}. The value s3 is in the result table because its set of second column values {p1, p2, p3} contains the values in the second table {p1, p2, p3}. The other *SuppNo* values (s0 and s1) are not in the result because they are not associated with all values in the *Part* table.

As an example using the university database tables, Table 2.30 shows the result of a divide operation involving the sample *Enrollment* (Table 2.28) and *Student* tables (Table 2.29). The result shows offerings in which every student is enrolled. Only *OfferNo* 4235 has all three students enrolled.

---

[10]The divide by operator can be generalized to work with input tables containing more columns. However, the details are not important in this book.

Figure 2.11 Sample divide operation.

| TABLE 2.28 | Sample *Enrollment* Table |

OfferNo	StdSSN
1234	123-45-6789
1234	234-56-7890
4235	123-45-6789
4235	234-56-7890
4235	124-56-7890
6321	124-56-7890

| TABLE 2.29 | Sample *Student* Table |

StdSSN
123-45-6789
124-56-7890
234-56-7890

| TABLE 2.30 | Result of *Enrollment* DIVIDEBY *Student* |

OfferNo
4235

2.4.8 Summary of Operators

To help you recall the relational algebra operators, Tables 2.31 and 2.32 provide a convenient summary of the meaning and usage of each operator. You might want to refer to these tables when studying query formulation in later chapters.

TABLE 2.31	Summary of Meanings of the Relational Algebra Operators
Operator	*Meaning*
Restrict (Select)	Extracts rows that satisfy a specified condition.
Project	Extracts specified columns.
Product	Builds a table from two tables consisting of all possible combinations of rows, one from each of the two tables.
Union	Builds a table consisting of all rows appearing in either of two tables.
Intersect	Builds a table consisting of all rows appearing in both of two specified tables.
Difference	Builds a table consisting of all rows appearing in the first table but not in the second table.
Join	Extracts rows from a product of two tables such that two input rows contributing to any output row satisfy some specified condition.
Outer Join	Extracts the matching rows (the join part) of two tables and the unmatched rows from both tables.
Divide	Builds a table consisting of all values of one column of a binary (two-column) table that match (in the other column) all values in a unary (one-column) table.
Summarize	Organizes a table on specified grouping columns. Specified aggregate computations are made on each value of the grouping columns.

TABLE 2.32	Summary of Usage of the Relational Algebra Operators
Operator	*Notes*
Union	Input tables must be union compatible.
Difference	Input tables must be union compatible.
Intersection	Input tables must be union compatible.
Product	Conceptually underlies join operator.
Restrict (Select)	Uses a logical expression.
Project	Eliminates duplicate rows if necessary.
Join	Only matched rows are in the result. Natural join eliminates one join column.
Outer Join	Retains both matched and unmatched rows in the result. Uses null values for some columns of the unmatched rows.
Divide	Stronger operator than join, but less frequently used.
Summarize	Specify grouping column(s) if any and aggregate function(s).

CLOSING THOUGHTS

Chapter 2 has introduced the Relational Data Model as a prelude to developing queries, forms, and reports with relational databases. As a first step to work with relational databases, you should understand the basic terminology and integrity rules. You should be conversant reading table definitions in SQL and in other proprietary formats. To effectively query a relational database, you must understand the connections among tables. Most queries involve multiple tables using relationships defined by referential integrity constraints. A graphical representation such as the Relationship window in Microsoft Access provides a powerful tool to conceptualize referential integrity constraints. When applications can change a database, it is important to respect the action rules for referenced rows.

The final part of this chapter described the operators of relational algebra. At this point, you should understand the purpose of each operator, the number of input tables, and other inputs used. You do not need to write complicated formulas that combine operators. Eventually, you should be comfortable understanding statements such as "write an SQL SELECT statement to join three tables." The SELECT statement will be discussed in Chapters 3 and 9, but the basic idea of a join is important to learn now. As you learn to extract data using the SQL SELECT statement in Chapter 3, you may want to review this chapter again. To help you remember the major points about the operators, the last section of this chapter presented several convenient summaries.

Understanding the operators will improve your knowledge of SQL and your query formulation skills. The meaning of SQL queries can be understood as relational algebra operations. Chapter 3 provides a flowchart demonstrating this correspondence. For this reason, relational algebra provides a yardstick to measure commercial languages: the commercial languages should provide at least the same retrieval ability as the operators of relational algebra.

REVIEW CONCEPTS

- Tables: heading and body.
- Primary keys and entity integrity rule.
- Foreign keys, referential integrity rule, and matching values.
- Visualizing referential integrity constraints.
- Relational Model representation of 1-M relationships, M-N relationships, and self-referencing relationships.
- Actions on referenced rows: cascade, nullify, restrict, default.
- Traditional set operators: union, intersection, difference, extended cross product.
- Union compatibility.
- Subset operators: restrict (select) and project.
- Matching value operators for combining tables: join, full outer join, one-sided outer join, divide.
- Most widely used operator for combining tables: join.
- Extension of join operator for nonmatching rows: outer join operator.
- One-sided outer join preserving the nonmatching rows of one input table.
- Full outer join preserving the nonmatching rows of both input tables.
- Complex matching operator: divide operator for matching on a subset of rows.
- Operator that replaces groups of rows with row summaries: summarize operator.

QUESTIONS

1. How is creating a table similar to writing a chapter of a book?

2. With what terminology for relational databases are you most comfortable? Why?

3. What is the difference between a primary key and a candidate key?

4. What is the difference between a candidate key and a superkey?

5. What is a null value?

6. What is the motivation for the entity integrity rule?

7. What is the motivation for the referential integrity rule?

8. What is the relationship between the referential integrity rule and foreign keys?

9. How are candidate keys that are not primary keys indicated in the CREATE TABLE statement?

10. What is the advantage of using constraint names when defining primary key, candidate key, or referential constraints in CREATE TABLE statements?

11. When is it not permissible for foreign keys to store null values?

12. What is the purpose of a database diagram such as the Access Relationship window?

13. How is a 1-M relationship represented in the Relational Model?

14. How is an M-N relationship represented in the Relational Model?

15. What is a self-referencing relationship?

16. How is a self-referencing relationship represented in the Relational Model?

17. What is a referenced row?

18. What two actions on referenced rows can affect related rows in a child table?

19. What are the possible actions on related rows after a referenced row is deleted or its primary key is updated?

20. Why is the restrict action for referenced rows more common than the cascade action?

21. When is the nullify action not allowed?

22. Why study the operators of relational algebra?

23. Why are the restrict and the project operators widely used?

24. Explain how the union, intersection, and difference operators for tables differ from the traditional operators for sets.

25. Why is the join operator so important for retrieving useful information?

26. What is the relationship between the join and the extended cross product operators?

27. Why is the extended cross product operator used sparingly?

28. What happens to unmatched rows with the join operator?

29. What happens to unmatched rows with the full outer join operator?

30. What is the difference between the full outer join and the one-sided outer join?

31. Define a decision-making situation that might require the summarize operator.

32. What is an aggregate function?

33. How are grouping columns used in the summarize operator?

34. Why is the divide operator not as widely used as the join operator?

PROBLEMS

ORDER

The problems use the *Customer, OrderTbl,* and *Employee* tables of the simplified Order Entry database. Other chapters of Part 1 extend the database to increase its usefulness. The *Customer* table records clients who have placed orders. The *OrderTbl* contains the basic facts about customer orders. The *Employee* table contains facts about employees who take orders. The primary keys of the tables are *CustNo* for *Customer, EmpNo* for *Employee,* and *OrdNo* for *OrderTbl.*

1. Write a CREATE TABLE statement for the *Customer* table. Choose data types appropriate for the DBMS used in your course. Note that the *CustBal* column contains numeric data. The currency symbols are not stored in the database. The *CustFirstName* and *CustLastName* columns are required (not null).

Customer

CustNo	CustFirstName	CustLastName	CustCity	CustState	CustZip	CustBal
C0954327	Sheri	Gordon	Littleton	CO	80129-5543	$230.00
C1010398	Jim	Glussman	Denver	CO	80111-0033	$200.00
C2388597	Beth	Taylor	Seattle	WA	98103-1121	$500.00
C3340959	Betty	Wise	Seattle	WA	98178-3311	$200.00
C3499503	Bob	Mann	Monroe	WA	98013-1095	$0.00
C8543321	Ron	Thompson	Renton	WA	98666-1289	$85.00

Employee

EmpNo	EmpFirstName	EmpLastName	EmpPhone
E1329594	Landi	Santos	(303) 789-1234
E8544399	Joe	Jenkins	(303) 221-9875
E8843211	Amy	Tang	(303) 556-4321
E9345771	Colin	White	(303) 221-4453
E9884325	Thomas	Johnson	(303) 556-9987
E9954302	Mary	Hill	(303) 556-9871

OrderTbl

OrdNo	OrdDate	CustNo	EmpNo
O1116324	01/23/2004	C0954327	E8544399
O2334661	01/14/2004	C0954327	E1329594
O3331222	01/13/2004	C1010398	
O2233457	01/12/2004	C2388597	E9884325
O4714645	01/11/2004	C2388597	E1329594
O5511365	01/22/2004	C3340959	E9884325
O7989497	01/16/2004	C3499503	E9345771
O1656777	02/11/2004	C8543321	
O7959898	02/19/2004	C8543321	E8544399

2. Write a CREATE TABLE statement for the *Employee* table. Choose data types appropriate for the DBMS used in your course. The *OrdDate* column is required (not null).

3. Write a CREATE TABLE statement for the *OrderTbl* table. Choose data types appropriate for the DBMS used in your course.

4. Identify the foreign keys and draw a relationship diagram for the simplified Order Entry database. The *CustNo* column references the *Customer* table and the *EmpNo* column references the *Employee* table. For each relationship, identify the parent table and the child table.

5. Extend your CREATE TABLE statement from problem 3 with referential integrity constraints. Updates and deletes on related rows are restricted.

6. From examination of the sample data and your common understanding of order entry businesses, are null values allowed for the foreign keys in the *OrderTbl* table? Why or why not? Extend the CREATE TABLE statement in problem 5 to enforce the null value restrictions if any.

7. Show the result of a restrict operation that lists the orders in February 2004.

8. Show the result of a project operation that lists the *CustNo, CustFirstName,* and *CustLastName* columns of the *Customer* table.

9. Show the result of a project operation that lists the *CustCity* and *CustState* columns of the *Customer* table.

10. Show the result of a natural join that combines the *Customer* and *OrderTbl* tables.

11. Show the steps to derive the natural join for problem 10. How many rows and columns are in the extended cross product step?

12. Show the result of a natural join of the *Employee* and *OrderTbl* tables.

13. Show the result of a one-sided outer join between the *Employee* and *OrderTbl* tables. Preserve the rows of the *OrderTbl* table in the result.

14. Show the result of a full outer join between the *Employee* and *OrderTbl* tables.

15. Show the result of the restrict operation on *Customer* where the condition is *CustCity* equals "Denver" or "Seattle" followed by a project operation to retain the *CustNo, CustFirstName, CustLastName,* and *CustCity* columns.

16. Show the result of a summarize operation on *Customer.* The grouping column is *CustState* and the aggregate calculation is COUNT. COUNT shows the number of rows with the same value for the grouping column.

17. Show the result of a summarize operation on *Customer.* The grouping column is *CustState* and the aggregate calculations are the minimum and maximum *CustBal* values.

18. What tables are required to show the *CustLastName, EmpLastName,* and *OrdNo* columns in the result table?

19. Extend your relationship diagram from problem 4 by adding two tables (*OrdLine* and *Product*). Partial CREATE TABLE statements for the primary keys and referential integrity constraints are shown below:

```
CREATE TABLE Product . . . PRIMARY KEY (ProdNo)
CREATE TABLE OrdLine . . . PRIMARY KEY (OrdNo, ProdNo)
    FOREIGN KEY (OrdNo) REFERENCES Order
    FOREIGN KEY (ProdNo) REFERENCES Product
```

20. Extend your relationship diagram from problem 19 by adding another foreign key in the *Employee* table. The foreign key *SupEmpNo* is the employee number of the supervising employee. Thus, the *SupEmpNo* column references the *Employee* table.

21. What relational algebra operator do you use to find products contained in *every* order? What relational algebra operator do you use to find products contained in *any* order?

22. Are the *Customer* and *Employee* tables union compatible? Why or why not?

23. Using the database after problem 20, what tables must be combined to list the product names on order number O1116324?

24. Using the database after problem 20, what tables must be combined to list the product names ordered by customer number C0954327?

25. Using the database after problem 20, what tables must be combined to list the product names ordered by the customer named Sheri Gordon?

REFERENCES FOR FURTHER STUDY

Codd defined the Relational Model in a seminal paper in 1970. His paper inspired research projects at the IBM research laboratories and the University of California at Berkeley that led to commercial relational DBMSs. C. J. Date (1995) provides a syntax for the relational algebra. Ullman (1988) and Elmasri and Navathe (2002) provide a more theoretical treatment of the Relational Model, especially the relational algebra.

Appendix 2.A   **CREATE TABLE Statements for the University Database Tables**

The following are the CREATE TABLE statements for the university database tables (Tables 2.1, 2.3, 2.4, 2.6, and 2.7). The names of the standard data types can vary by DBMS. For example, Microsoft Access SQL supports the TEXT data type instead of CHAR and VARCHAR. In Oracle, you should use VARCHAR2 instead of VARCHAR.

```
CREATE TABLE Student
            ( StdSSN        CHAR(11)        NOT NULL,
              StdFirstName  VARCHAR(50)     NOT NULL,
              StdLastName   VARCHAR(50)     NOT NULL,
              StdCity       VARCHAR(50)     NOT NULL,
              StdState      CHAR(2)         NOT NULL,
              StdZip        CHAR(10)        NOT NULL,
              StdMajor      CHAR(6),
              StdClass      CHAR(2),
              StdGPA        DECIMAL(3,2),
CONSTRAINT PKStudent PRIMARY KEY (StdSSN) )

CREATE TABLE Course
            ( CourseNo      CHAR(6)         NOT NULL,
              CrsDesc       VARCHAR(250)    NOT NULL,
              CrsUnits      INTEGER,
CONSTRAINT PKCourse PRIMARY KEY (CourseNo),
CONSTRAINT UniqueCrsDesc UNIQUE (CrsDesc) )

CREATE TABLE Faculty
            ( FacSSN        CHAR(11)        NOT NULL,
              FacFirstName  VARCHAR(50)     NOT NULL,
              FacLastName   VARCHAR(50)     NOT NULL,
              FacCity       VARCHAR(50)     NOT NULL,
              FacState      CHAR(2)         NOT NULL,
              FacZipCode    CHAR(10)        NOT NULL,
              FacHireDate   DATE,
              FacDept       CHAR(6),
              FacRank       CHAR(4),
              FacSalary     DECIMAL(10,2),
              FacSupervisor CHAR(11),
CONSTRAINT PKFaculty PRIMARY KEY (FacSSN),
CONSTRAINT FKFacSupervisor FOREIGN KEY (FacSupervisor)
              REFERENCES Faculty
              ON DELETE SET NULL
              ON UPDATE CASCADE )
```

```
CREATE TABLE Offering
                    (  OfferNo      INTEGER        NOT NULL,
                       CourseNo     CHAR(6)        NOT NULL,
                       OffLocation  VARCHAR(50),
                       OffDays      CHAR(6),
                       OffTerm      CHAR(6)        NOT NULL,
                       OffYear      INTEGER        NOT NULL,
                       FacSSN       CHAR(11),
                       OffTime      DATE,
CONSTRAINT PKOffering PRIMARY KEY (OfferNo),
CONSTRAINT FKCourseNo FOREIGN KEY (CourseNo) REFERENCES Course
              ON DELETE NO ACTION
              ON UPDATE NO ACTION,
CONSTRAINT FKFacSSN FOREIGN KEY (FacSSN) REFERENCES Faculty
              ON DELETE SET NULL
              ON UPDATE CASCADE  )


CREATE TABLE Enrollment
                    (  OfferNo      INTEGER        NOT NULL,
                       StdSSN       CHAR(11)       NOT NULL,
                       EnrGrade     DECIMAL(3,2),
CONSTRAINT PKEnrollment PRIMARY KEY (OfferNo, StdSSN),
CONSTRAINT FKOfferNo FOREIGN KEY (OfferNo) REFERENCES Offering
              ON DELETE CASCADE
              ON UPDATE CASCADE,
CONSTRAINT FKStdSSN FOREIGN KEY (StdSSN) REFERENCES Student
              ON DELETE CASCADE
              ON UPDATE CASCADE  )
```

Appendix 2.B   SQL:1999 Syntax Summary

This appendix provides a convenient summary of the SQL:1999 syntax for the CREATE TABLE statement along with several related statements. For brevity, only the syntax of the most common parts of the statements is described. SQL:1999 is the current version of the SQL standard. The syntax in SQL:1999 for the statements described in this appendix is identical to the syntax in the previous SQL standard, SQL-92. For the complete syntax, refer to a SQL:1999 or a SQL-92 reference book such as Groff and Weinberg (1999). The conventions used in the syntax notation are listed before the statement syntax:

- Uppercase words denote reserved words.
- Mixed-case words without hyphens denote names that the user substitutes.
- The asterisk * after a syntax element indicates that a comma-separated list can be used.
- Names enclosed in angle brackets < > denote definitions defined later in the syntax. The definitions occur on a new line with the element and colon followed by the syntax.
- Square brackets [ ] enclose optional elements.
- Curly brackets {} enclose choice elements. One element must be chosen among the elements separated by the vertical bars |.
- The parentheses ( ) denote themselves.
- Double hyphens -- denote comments that are not part of the syntax.

CREATE TABLE SYNTAX[11]

```
CREATE TABLE TableName
( <Column-Definition>* [ , <Table-Constraint>* ] )

                   <Column-Definition>: ColumnName DataType
                   [   DEFAULT { DefaultValue | USER | NULL } ]
                   [ [  CONSTRAINT ConstraintName ] NOT NULL ]
                   [ [  CONSTRAINT ConstraintName ] UNIQUE ]
                   [ [  CONSTRAINT ConstraintName ] PRIMARY KEY ]
                   [ [  CONSTRAINT ConstraintName ] FOREIGN KEY
                        REFERENCES TableName [ ( ColumnName ) ]
                        [ ON DELETE <Action-Specification> ]
                        [ ON UPDATE <Action-Specification> ] ]
```

---

[11]The CHECK constraint, an important kind of table constraint, is described in Chapter 14.

```
<Table-Constraint>: [ CONSTRAINT ConstraintName ]
                     { <Primary-Key-Constraint> |
                       <Foreign-Key-Constraint> |
                       <Uniqueness-Constraint> }

<Primary-Key-Constraint>: PRIMARY KEY ( ColumnName* )

<Foreign-Key-Constraint>: FOREIGN KEY ( ColumnName* )
                          REFERENCES TableName [ ( ColumnName* ) ]
                          [ ON DELETE <Action-Specification> ]
                          [ ON UPDATE <Action-Specification> ]

<Action-Specification>: { CASCADE | SET NULL | SET DEFAULT | RESTRICT }

<Uniqueness-Constraint>: UNIQUE ( ColumnName* )
```

Other Related Statements

The ALTER TABLE and DROP TABLE statements support modification of a table definition and deleting a table definition. The ALTER TABLE statement is particularly useful because table definitions often change over time. In both statements, the keyword RESTRICT means that the statement cannot be performed if related tables exist. The keyword CASCADE means that the same action will be performed on related tables.

```
ALTER TABLE TableName
            { ADD { <Column-Definition> | <Table-Constraint> } |
              ALTER ColumnName { SET DEFAULT DefaultValue |
                    DROP DEFAULT } |
              DROP ColumnName { CASCADE | RESTRICT } |
              DROP CONSTRAINT ConstraintName {CASCADE | RESTRICT } }

DROP TABLE TableName { CASCADE | RESTRICT }
```

Notes on Oracle Syntax

The CREATE TABLE statement in Oracle 9i SQL conforms closely to the SQL:1999 standard. Here is a list of the most significant syntax differences:

- Oracle SQL does not support the ON UPDATE clause for referential integrity constraints.
- Oracle SQL only supports CASCADE and SET NULL as the action specifications of the ON DELETE clause. If an ON DELETE clause is not specified, the deletion is not allowed (restricted) if related rows exist.
- Oracle SQL does not support dropping columns in the ALTER statement.
- Oracle SQL supports the MODIFY keyword in place of the ALTER keyword in the ALTER TABLE statement (use MODIFY ColumnName instead of ALTER ColumnName).
- Oracle SQL supports data type changes using the MODIFY keyword in the ALTER TABLE statement.

CHAPTER 3

Query Formulation with SQL

LEARNING OBJECTIVES

This chapter provides the foundation for query formulation using the industry standard Structured Query Language (SQL). Query formulation is the process of converting a request for data into a statement of a database language such as SQL. After this chapter the student should have acquired the following knowledge and skills:

- Reason through the query formulation process using the three critical questions.

- Write SQL SELECT statements for queries involving restriction, projection, join, and summarization operators.

- Write SELECT statements for difficult joins involving three or more tables, self joins, and multiple joins between tables.

- Understand the meaning of grouping queries using the conceptual evaluation process.

- Write English descriptions to document SQL statements.

- Write INSERT, UPDATE, and DELETE statements to change the contents of a database.

OVERVIEW

Chapter 2 provided a foundation for using relational databases. Most importantly, you learned about connections among tables and fundamental operators to extract useful data. This chapter shows you how to apply this knowledge in using the data manipulation statements of SQL.

Much of your skill with SQL or other computer languages is derived from imitating examples. This chapter provides many examples to facilitate your learning process. Initially you are presented with some easy examples so that you can plunge into SQL. To prime you for more difficult examples, two mental tools (conceptual evaluation process and critical questions) are presented. The conceptual evaluation process explains the meaning of the SELECT statement through the sequence of operations and intermediate tables that produce the result. The critical questions help you transform a problem statement into a relational database representation in a language such as SQL. These tools are used to help formulate and explain the advanced problems presented in the last part of this chapter.

3.1 BACKGROUND

Before using SQL, it is informative to understand its history and scope. The history reveals the origin of the name and the efforts to standardize the language. The scope puts the various parts of SQL into perspective. We have already seen the CREATE TABLE statement. The SELECT, UPDATE, DELETE, and INSERT statements are the subject of this chapter and Chapter 9. To broaden your understanding, you should be aware of other parts of the language and different usage contexts.

3.1.1 Brief History of SQL

The Structured Query Language (SQL) has a short but colorful history. Table 3.1 depicts the highlights of SQL's development. SQL began life as the SQUARE language in IBM's System R project. The System R project was a response to the interest in relational databases sparked by Dr. Ted Codd, an IBM fellow who wrote a famous paper in 1970 about relational databases. The SQUARE language was somewhat mathematical in nature. After conducting human factors experiments, the IBM research team revised the language and renamed it SEQUEL (a follow-up to SQUARE). After another revision, the language

TABLE 3.1	SQL Timeline

Year	Event
1972	System R project at IBM Research Labs
1974	SQUARE
1975	Language revision and name change to SEQUEL
1976	Language revision and name change to SEQUEL 2
1977	Name change to SQL
1978	First commercial implementation by Oracle Corporation
1981	IBM product SQL/DS featuring SQL
1986	SQL-86 (SQL1) standard approved
1989	SQL-89 standard approved (revision to SQL-86)
1992	SQL-92 (SQL2) standard approved
1999	SQL:1999 (SQL3) standard approved

was dubbed SEQUEL 2. Its current name, SQL, resulted from legal issues surrounding the name SEQUEL. Because of this naming history, a number of database professionals, particularly those working during the 1970s, pronounce the name as "sequel" rather than SQL.

SQL is now an international standard although it was not always so.[1] With the force of IBM behind SQL, many imitators used some variant of SQL. Such was the old order of the computer industry when IBM was dominant. It may seem surprising, but IBM was not the first company to commercialize SQL. Until a standards effort developed in the 1980s, SQL was in a state of confusion. Many vendors implemented different subsets of SQL with unique extensions. The standards efforts by the American National Standards Institute (ANSI), the International Organization for Standards (ISO), and the International Electrotechnical Commission (IEC) have restored some order. Although SQL was not initially the best database language developed, the standards efforts have improved the language as well as standardized its specification. The current standard (SQL:1999) was just approved in late 1999.

Because of the size of the previous (SQL-92) and the current (SQL:1999) standards, multiple levels can be supported. The original standard (SQL-86) contained about 150 pages, while the previous standard contains more than 600 pages. In contrast, the current standard (SQL:1999) contains more than 2,100 pages. The SQL-92 specification contained three levels: Entry SQL, Intermediate SQL, and Full SQL. Unfortunately, no vendor claimed conformance beyond Entry SQL although most vendors implemented some features in the higher SQL levels and provided proprietary SQL extensions. Thus, most vendors supported a super/subset of the SQL-92 standard as they conformed to some levels of the standard and added their own extensions.

The SQL:1999 standard contains a single level of conformance called Core SQL. At the time this chapter was written, no vendor claims conformance to Core SQL, although some vendors seem close to conformance. SQL:1999 contains many features outside of Core SQL grouped into packages. The presentation in this chapter is limited to a subset of Core SQL:1999. Most features presented in this chapter were part of SQL-92 as well as Core SQL:1999. Other chapters present other parts of Core SQL as well as important features from SQL:1999 packages.

3.1.2 Scope of SQL

SQL was designed as a language for database definition, manipulation, and control. Table 3.2 shows a quick summary of important SQL statements. Only database administrators use most of the database definition and database control statements. You have already seen the CREATE TABLE statement in Chapter 2. This chapter and Chapter 9 cover the database manipulation statements. Power users and analysts use the database manipulation statements. Chapter 10 covers the CREATE VIEW statement. The CREATE VIEW statement can be used by either database administrators or analysts. Chapter 11 covers the CREATE TRIGGER statement used by both database administrators and analysts. Chapter 14 covers the GRANT, REVOKE, and CREATE ASSERTION statements used primarily by database administrators. The transaction control statements (COMMIT and ROLLBACK) are used by analysts. Chapter 15 covers COMMIT and ROLLBACK along with other aspects of transaction processing.

---

[1] Dr. Michael Stonebraker, an early database pioneer, has even referred to SQL as "intergalactic data speak."

TABLE 3.2	Selected SQL Statements	
Statement Type	*Statements*	*Purpose*
Database definition	CREATE SCHEMA, TABLE, VIEW	Define a new database, table, and view
	ALTER TABLE	Modify table definition
Database manipulation	SELECT	Retrieve contents of tables
	UPDATE, DELETE, INSERT	Modify, remove, and add rows
Database control	COMMIT, ROLLBACK	Complete, undo transaction
	GRANT, REVOKE	Add and remove access rights
	CREATE ASSERTION	Define integrity constraint
	CREATE TRIGGER	Define database rule

SQL Usage Contexts SQL statements can be used stand-alone with a specialized editor or embedded inside a computer program.

SQL can be used in two contexts: stand-alone and embedded. In the stand-alone context, the user submits SQL statements with the use of a specialized editor. The editor alerts the user to syntax errors and sends the statements to the DBMS. In this chapter, we assume stand-alone usage. In the embedded context, an executing program submits SQL statements, and the DBMS sends results back to the program. The program includes SQL statements along with statements of the host programming language such as COBOL or Visual Basic. Additional statements allow other SQL statements (such as SELECT) to be used inside a computer program. Chapter 11 covers embedded SQL.

3.2 GETTING STARTED WITH SELECT

The SELECT statement supports data retrieval from one or more tables. This section describes a simplified format of the SELECT statement. More complex formats are presented in Chapter 9. The SELECT statement described here has the following format:

```
SELECT <list of columns and expressions usually involving columns>
    FROM <list of tables and join operations>
    WHERE <list of row conditions connected by AND, OR, NOT>
    GROUP BY <list of grouping columns>
    HAVING <list of group conditions connected by AND, OR, NOT>
    ORDER BY <list of sorting specifications>
```

Expression a combination of constants, column names, functions, and operators that produces a value. In conditions and result columns, expressions can be used in any place that column names can appear.

In the preceding format, the uppercase words are keywords. You replace the angle brackets < > with information to make a meaningful statement. For example, after the keyword SELECT, type the list of columns that should appear in the result, but do not type the angle brackets. The list can include a column such as *StdFirstName* or an expression involving constants, column names, and functions. Example expressions are Price * Qty and 1.1 * FacSalary. To make meaningful names for computed columns, you can rename a column in the result table using the AS keyword. For example, SELECT Price * Qty AS Amount renames the expression Price * Qty to Amount in the result table.

To depict this SELECT format and show the meaning of statements, this chapter shows numerous examples. Examples are provided for both Microsoft Access, a popular desktop DBMS, and Oracle, a prominent enterprise DBMS. Most examples execute on both systems. Unless noted, the examples run on the 1997, 2000, and 2002 versions of Access and versions 8i and 9i of Oracle. Examples that only execute on one product are marked. In addition to the examples, Appendix 3.B summarizes syntax differences among major DBMSs.

The examples use the university database tables introduced in Chapter 2. Tables 3.3 through 3.7 list the contents of the tables. CREATE TABLE statements are listed in Appendix 2.A. For your reference, the relationship diagram showing the primary and foreign keys is repeated in Figure 3.1. Recall that the *Faculty1* table with relationship to the *Faculty* table represents a self-referencing relationship with *FacSupervisor* as the foreign key.

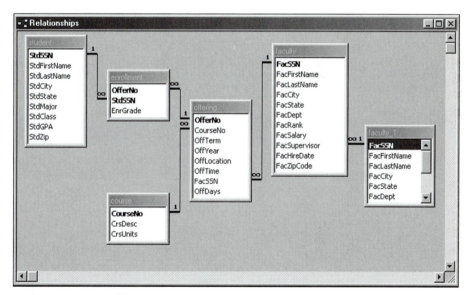

| **Figure 3.1** | **Relationship window for the university database.** |

| TABLE 3.3 | Sample *Student* Table |

StdSSN	StdFirstName	StdLastName	StdCity	StdState	StdZip	StdMajor	StdClass	StdGPA
123-45-6789	HOMER	WELLS	SEATTLE	WA	98121-1111	IS	FR	3.00
124-56-7890	BOB	NORBERT	BOTHELL	WA	98011-2121	FIN	JR	2.70
234-56-7890	CANDY	KENDALL	TACOMA	WA	99042-3321	ACCT	JR	3.50
345-67-8901	WALLY	KENDALL	SEATTLE	WA	98123-1141	IS	SR	2.80
456-78-9012	JOE	ESTRADA	SEATTLE	WA	98121-2333	FIN	SR	3.20
567-89-0123	MARIAH	DODGE	SEATTLE	WA	98114-0021	IS	JR	3.60
678-90-1234	TESS	DODGE	REDMOND	WA	98116-2344	ACCT	SO	3.30
789-01-2345	ROBERTO	MORALES	SEATTLE	WA	98121-2212	FIN	JR	2.50
876-54-3210	CRISTOPHER	COLAN	SEATTLE	WA	98114-1332	IS	SR	4.00
890-12-3456	LUKE	BRAZZI	SEATTLE	WA	98116-0021	IS	SR	2.20
901-23-4567	WILLIAM	PILGRIM	BOTHELL	WA	98113-1885	IS	SO	3.80

TABLE 3.4A   **Sample *Faculty* Table (first part)**

FacSSN	FacFirstName	FacLastName	FacCity	FacState	FacDept	FacRank	FacSalary
098-76-5432	LEONARD	VINCE	SEATTLE	WA	MS	ASST	$35,000
543-21-0987	VICTORIA	EMMANUEL	BOTHELL	WA	MS	PROF	$120,000
654-32-1098	LEONARD	FIBON	SEATTLE	WA	MS	ASSC	$70,000
765-43-2109	NICKI	MACON	BELLEVUE	WA	FIN	PROF	$65,000
876-54-3210	CRISTOPHER	COLAN	SEATTLE	WA	MS	ASST	$40,000
987-65-4321	JULIA	MILLS	SEATTLE	WA	FIN	ASSC	$75,000

TABLE 3.4B   **Sample *Faculty* Table (second part)**

FacSSN	FacSupervisor	FacHireDate	FacZipCode
098-76-5432	654-32-1098	01-Apr-1990	98111-9921
543-21-0987		01-Apr-1991	98011-2242
654-32-1098	543-21-0987	01-Apr-1989	98121-0094
765-43-2109		01-Apr-1992	98015-9945
876-54-3210	654-32-1098	01-Apr-1994	98114-1332
987-65-4321	765-43-2109	01-Apr-1995	98114-9954

TABLE 3.5   **Sample *Offering* Table**

OfferNo	CourseNo	OffTerm	OffYear	OffLocation	OffTime	FacSSN	OffDays
1111	IS320	SUMMER	2003	BLM302	10:30 AM		MW
1234	IS320	FALL	2002	BLM302	10:30 AM	098-76-5432	MW
2222	IS460	SUMMER	2002	BLM412	1:30 PM		TTH
3333	IS320	SPRING	2003	BLM214	8:30 AM	098-76-5432	MW
4321	IS320	FALL	2002	BLM214	3:30 PM	098-76-5432	TTH
4444	IS320	WINTER	2003	BLM302	3:30 PM	543-21-0987	TTH
5555	FIN300	WINTER	2003	BLM207	8:30 AM	765-43-2109	MW
5678	IS480	WINTER	2003	BLM302	10:30 AM	987-65-4321	MW
5679	IS480	SPRING	2003	BLM412	3:30 PM	876-54-3210	TTH
6666	FIN450	WINTER	2003	BLM212	10:30 AM	987-65-4321	TTH
7777	FIN480	SPRING	2003	BLM305	1:30 PM	765-43-2109	MW
8888	IS320	SUMMER	2003	BLM405	1:30 PM	654-32-1098	MW
9876	IS460	SPRING	2003	BLM307	1:30 PM	654-32-1098	TTH

TABLE 3.6   **Sample *Course* Table**

CourseNo	CrsDesc	CrsUnits
FIN300	FUNDAMENTALS OF FINANCE	4
FIN450	PRINCIPLES OF INVESTMENTS	4
FIN480	CORPORATE FINANCE	4
IS320	FUNDAMENTALS OF BUSINESS PROGRAMMING	4
IS460	SYSTEMS ANALYSIS	4
IS470	BUSINESS DATA COMMUNICATIONS	4
IS480	FUNDAMENTALS OF DATABASE MANAGEMENT	4

TABLE 3.7	Sample *Enrollment* Table

OfferNo	StdSSN	EnrGrade
1234	123-45-6789	3.3
1234	234-56-7890	3.5
1234	345-67-8901	3.2
1234	456-78-9012	3.1
1234	567-89-0123	3.8
1234	678-90-1234	3.4
4321	123-45-6789	3.5
4321	124-56-7890	3.2
4321	789-01-2345	3.5
4321	876-54-3210	3.1
4321	890-12-3456	3.4
4321	901-23-4567	3.1
5555	123-45-6789	3.2
5555	124-56-7890	2.7
5678	123-45-6789	3.2
5678	234-56-7890	2.8
5678	345-67-8901	3.3
5678	456-78-9012	3.4
5678	567-89-0123	2.6
5679	123-45-6789	2
5679	124-56-7890	3.7
5679	678-90-1234	3.3
5679	789-01-2345	3.8
5679	890-12-3456	2.9
5679	901-23-4567	3.1
6666	234-56-7890	3.1
6666	567-89-0123	3.6
7777	876-54-3210	3.4
7777	890-12-3456	3.7
7777	901-23-4567	3.4
9876	124-56-7890	3.5
9876	234-56-7890	3.2
9876	345-67-8901	3.2
9876	456-78-9012	3.4
9876	567-89-0123	2.6
9876	678-90-1234	3.3
9876	901-23-4567	4

3.2.1 Single Table Problems

Let us begin with the simple SQL statement in Example 3.1. In all the examples, keywords appear in uppercase while information specific to the query appears in mixed case. In Example 3.1, only the *Student* table is listed in the FROM clause because the conditions in the WHERE clause and columns after the SELECT keyword involve only the *Student* table. In Oracle, a semicolon or / (on a separate line) terminates a statement.

Table 3.8 depicts the standard comparison operators. Note that the symbol for some operators depends on the DBMS.

Example 3.2 is even simpler than Example 3.1. The result is identical to the original *Faculty* table in Table 3.4. Example 3.2 uses a shortcut to list all columns. The asterisk * in the column list means to list all columns of the tables appearing in the FROM clause. The asterisk serves as a wildcard character matching all column names.

Example 3.1   Testing Rows Using the WHERE Clause

Retrieve the name, city, and grade point average (GPA) of students with a high GPA (greater than or equal to 3.7). The result follows the SELECT statement.

SELECT StdFirstName, StdLastName, StdCity, StdGPA
  FROM Student
  WHERE StdGPA >= 3.7

StdFirstName	StdLastName	StdCity	StdGPA
CRISTOPHER	COLAN	SEATTLE	4.00
WILLIAM	PILGRIM	BOTHELL	3.80

TABLE 3.8   **Standard Comparison Operators**

Comparison Operator	Meaning
=	equal to
<	less than
>	greater than
<=	less than or equal to
>=	greater than or equal to
< > or !=	not equal (check your DBMS)

Example 3.2   Show All Columns

List all columns and rows of the *Faculty* table. The resulting table is shown in two parts.

SELECT * FROM Faculty

FacSSN	FacFirstName	FacLastName	FacCity	FacState	FacDept	FacRank	FacSalary
098-76-5432	LEONARD	VINCE	SEATTLE	WA	MS	ASST	$35,000
543-21-0987	VICTORIA	EMMANUEL	BOTHELL	WA	MS	PROF	$120,000
654-32-1098	LEONARD	FIBON	SEATTLE	WA	MS	ASSC	$70,000
765-43-2109	NICKI	MACON	BELLEVUE	WA	FIN	PROF	$65,000
876-54-3210	CRISTOPHER	COLAN	SEATTLE	WA	MS	ASST	$40,000
987-65-4321	JULIA	MILLS	SEATTLE	WA	FIN	ASSC	$75,000

FacSSN	FacSupervisor	FacHireDate	FacZipCode
098-76-5432	654-32-1098	01_Apr-90	98111-9921
543-21-0987		01-Apr-91	98011-2242
654-32-1098	543-21-0987	01-Apr-89	98121-0094
765-43-2109		01-Apr-92	98015-9945
876-54-3210	654-32-1098	01-Apr-94	98114-1332
987-65-4321	765-43-2109	01-Apr-95	98114-9954

Example 3.3 depicts expressions in the SELECT and WHERE clauses. The expression in the SELECT clause increases the salary by 10 percent. The AS keyword is used to rename the computed column. Without renaming, most DBMSs will generate a meaningless name such as Expr001. The expression in the WHERE clause extracts the year from the hiring date. Because functions for the date data type are not standard, Access and Oracle formulations are provided. To become proficient with SQL on a particular DBMS, you will need to study the available functions especially with date columns.

Example 3.3 (Access)

Expressions in SELECT and WHERE Clauses
List the name, city, and increased salary of faculty hired after 1991. The **year** function extracts the year part of a column with a date data type.

```
SELECT FacFirstName, FacLastName, FacCity,
        FacSalary*1.1 AS IncreasedSalary, FacHireDate
FROM Faculty
WHERE year(FacHireDate) > 1991
```

FacFirstName	FacLastName	FacCity	IncreasedSalary	FacHireDate
NICKI	MACON	BELLEVUE	71500	01-Apr-1992
CRISTOPHER	COLAN	SEATTLE	44000	01-Apr-1994
JULIA	MILLS	SEATTLE	82500	01-Apr-1995

Example 3.3 (Oracle)

Expressions in SELECT and WHERE Clauses
The **to_char** function extracts the four-digit year from the *FacHireDate* column and the **to_number** function converts the character representation of the year into a number.

```
SELECT FacFirstName, FacLastName, FacCity,
        FacSalary*1.1 AS IncreasedSalary, FacHireDate
FROM Faculty
WHERE to_number(to_char(FacHireDate, 'YYYY')   ) > 1991
```

Inexact matching supports conditions that match some pattern rather than matching an identical string. One of the most common types of inexact matching is to find values having a common prefix such as 'IS4' (400 level IS Courses). Example 3.4 uses the LIKE operator along with a pattern-matching character * to perform prefix matching.[2] The string 'IS4*' means match strings beginning with 'IS4' and ending with anything. The wildcard character * matches any string. The Oracle formulation of Example 3.4 uses the percent symbol %, the SQL:1999 standard for the wildcard character. Note that string constants must be enclosed in quotation marks.[3]

Example 3.4 (Access)	Inexact Matching with LIKE

List the senior-level IS courses.

```
SELECT *
FROM Course
WHERE CourseNo LIKE 'IS4*'
```

CourseNo	CrsDesc	CrsUnits
IS460	SYSTEMS ANALYSIS	4
IS470	BUSINESS DATA COMMUNICATIONS	4
IS480	FUNDAMENTALS OF DATABASE MANAGEMENT	4

Example 3.4 (Oracle)	Inexact Matching with LIKE

List the senior-level IS courses.

```
SELECT *
FROM Course
WHERE CourseNo LIKE 'IS4%'
```

Another common type of inexact matching is to match strings containing a substring. To perform this kind of matching, a wildcard character should be used before and after the substring. For example, to find courses containing the word DATABASE anywhere in the course description, write the condition CrsDesc LIKE '*DATABASE*' in Access or CrsDesc LIKE '%DATABASE%' in Oracle.

The wildcard character is not the only pattern-matching character. SQL:1999 specifies the underscore character _ to match any single character. Some DBMSs such as Access use the question mark ? to match any single character. In addition, most DBMSs have pattern-matching characters for matching a range of characters (for example, the digits 0 to 9) and any character from a list of characters. The symbols used for these other pattern-matching characters are not standard. To become proficient at writing inexact matching conditions, you should study the pattern-matching characters available with your DBMS.

---

[2]In Access 2002, the SQL:1999 pattern-matching characters can be used by specifying ANSI 92 query mode in the Options window. Since earlier Access versions do not support this option and this option is not default in Access 2002, the textbook uses the * and ? pattern-matching characters for Access SQL statements.
[3]Most DBMSs require single quotes, the SQL:1999 standard. Microsoft Access allows either single or double quotes for string constants.

In addition to performing pattern matching with strings, you can use <u>exact matching</u> with the equality = comparison operator. For example, the condition CourseNo = 'IS480' matches a single row in the *Course* table. For both exact and inexact matching, case sensitivity is an important issue. Some DBMSs such as Microsoft Access are not case sensitive. In Access SQL, the previous condition matches 'is480', 'Is480', and 'iS480' in addition to 'IS480'. Other DBMSs such as Oracle are case sensitive. In Oracle SQL, the previous condition matches only 'IS480', not 'is480', 'Is480', and 'iS480'. To alleviate confusion, you can use the Oracle **upper** or **lower** functions to convert strings to upper- or lowercase, respectively.

BETWEEN-AND Operator a shortcut operator to test a numeric or date column against a range of values. The BETWEEN-AND operator returns true if the column is greater than or equal to the first value and less than or equal to the second value.

Example 3.5 depicts range matching on a column with a DATE data type. In Access SQL, pound symbols enclose date constants, while in Oracle SQL, single quotation marks enclose date constants. Date columns can be compared just like numbers with the usual comparison operators (=, <, etc.). The BETWEEN-AND operator defines a closed interval (includes end points). In Access Example 3.5, the BETWEEN-AND condition is a shortcut for FacHireDate >= #1/1/94# AND FacHireDate <= #12/31/95#.

Example 3.5 (Access)

Conditions on Date Columns
List the name and hiring date of faculty hired in 1994 or 1995.

SELECT FacFirstName, FacLastName, FacHireDate
 FROM Faculty
 WHERE FacHireDate BETWEEN #1/1/1994# AND #12/31/1995#

FacFirstName	FacLastName	FacHireDate
CRISTOPHER	COLAN	01-Apr-94
JULIA	MILLS	01-Apr-95

Example 3.5 (Oracle)

Conditions on Date Columns
In Oracle SQL, the standard format for dates is DD-Mon-YYYY where DD is the day number, Mon is the month abbreviation, and YYYY is the four-digit year.

SELECT FacFirstName, FacLastName, FacHireDate
 FROM Faculty
 WHERE FacHireDate BETWEEN '1-Jan-1994' AND '31-Dec-1995'

Besides testing columns for specified values, you sometimes need to test for the lack of a value. Null values are used when there is no normal value for a column. A null can mean that the value is unknown or the value is not applicable to the row. For the *Offering* table, a null value for *FacSSN* means that the instructor is not yet assigned. Testing for null values is done with the IS NULL comparison operator as shown in Example 3.6. You also can test for a normal value using IS NOT NULL.

Example 3.6

Testing for Nulls

List the offering number and course number of summer 2003 offerings without an assigned instructor.

```
SELECT OfferNo, CourseNo
  FROM Offering
  WHERE FacSSN IS NULL AND OffTerm = 'SUMMER'
    AND OffYear = 2003
```

OfferNo	CourseNo
1111	IS320

Mixing AND and OR
always use parentheses to make the grouping of conditions explicit.

Example 3.7 depicts a complex logical expression involving both logical operators AND and OR. When mixing AND and OR in a logical expression, it is a good idea to use parentheses. Otherwise, the reader of the SELECT statement may not understand how the AND and OR conditions are grouped. Without parentheses, you must depend on the default way that AND and OR conditions are grouped.

Example 3.7

Complex Logical Expression

List the offer number, course number, and faculty social security number for course offerings scheduled in fall 2002 or winter 2003.

```
SELECT OfferNo, CourseNo, FacSSN
  FROM Offering
  WHERE (OffTerm = 'FALL' AND OffYear = 2002)
    OR (OffTerm = 'WINTER' AND OffYear = 2003)
```

OfferNo	CourseNo	FacSSN
1234	IS320	098-76-5432
4321	IS320	098-76-5432
4444	IS320	543-21-0987
5555	FIN300	765-43-2109
5678	IS480	987-65-4321
6666	FIN450	987-65-4321

3.2.2 Joining Tables

Example 3.8 demonstrates a join of the *Course* and *Offering* tables. The join condition Course.CourseNo = Offering.CourseNo is specified in the WHERE clause.

Example 3.8 (Access)

Join Tables but Show Columns from One Table Only

List the offering number, course number, days, and time of offerings containing the words *database* or *programming* in the course description and taught in spring 2003. The Oracle version of this example uses the % instead of the * as the wildcard character.

```
SELECT OfferNo, Offering.CourseNo, OffDays, OffTime
  FROM Offering, Course
  WHERE OffTerm = 'SPRING' AND OffYear = 2003
      AND (CrsDesc LIKE '*DATABASE*'
      OR CrsDesc LIKE '*PROGRAMMING*')
      AND Course.CourseNo = Offering.CourseNo
```

OfferNo	CourseNo	OffDays	OffTime
3333	IS320	MW	8:30 AM
5679	IS480	TTH	3:30 PM

There are two additional points of interest about Example 3.8. First, the *CourseNo* column names must be *qualified* (prefixed) with a table name (*Course* or *Offering*). Otherwise, the SQL statement is ambiguous because *CourseNo* can refer to a column in either the *Course* or *Offering* tables. Second, both tables must be listed in the FROM clause even though the result columns come from only the *Offering* table. The *Course* table is needed in the FROM clause because conditions in the WHERE clause reference *CrsDesc,* a column of the *Course* table.

Example 3.9 demonstrates another join, but this time the result columns come from both tables. There are conditions on each table in addition to the join conditions. The Oracle formulation uses the % instead of the * as the wildcard character.

Example 3.9 (Access)

Join Tables and Show Columns from Both Tables

List the offer number, course number, and name of the instructor of IS course offerings scheduled in fall 2002 taught by assistant professors.

```
SELECT OfferNo, CourseNo, FacFirstName, FacLastName
  FROM Offering, Faculty
  WHERE OffTerm = 'FALL' AND OffYear = 2002
      AND FacRank = 'ASST' AND CourseNo LIKE 'IS*'
      AND Faculty.FacSSN = Offering.FacSSN
```

OfferNo	CourseNo	FacFirstName	FacLastName
1234	IS320	LEONARD	VINCE
4321	IS320	LEONARD	VINCE

Example 3.9 (Oracle)

Join Tables and Show Columns from Both Tables

List the offer number, course number, and name of the instructor of IS course offerings scheduled in fall 2002 taught by assistant professors.

```
SELECT OfferNo, CourseNo, FacFirstName, FacLastName
  FROM Offering, Faculty
  WHERE OffTerm = 'FALL' AND OffYear = 2002
      AND FacRank = 'ASST' AND CourseNo LIKE 'IS%'
      AND Faculty.FacSSN = Offering.FacSSN
```

In the SQL:1999 standard, the join operation can be expressed directly in the FROM clause rather than being expressed in both the FROM and WHERE clauses as shown in Examples 3.8 and 3.9. Note that Oracle 9i supports join operations in the FROM clause, but Oracle 8i does not support join operations in the FROM clause. To make a join operation in the FROM clause, use the keywords INNER JOIN as shown in Example 3.10. The join conditions are indicated by the ON keyword inside the FROM clause. Notice that the join condition no longer appears in the WHERE clause.

**Example 3.10
(Access)**

Join Tables Using a Join Operation in the FROM Clause

List the offer number, course number, and name of the instructor of IS course offerings scheduled in fall 2002 that are taught by assistant professors (result is identical to Example 3.9). In Oracle 9i, you should use % instead of *.

```
SELECT OfferNo, CourseNo, FacFirstName, FacLastName
  FROM Offering INNER JOIN Faculty
    ON Faculty.FacSSN = Offering.FacSSN
  WHERE OffTerm = 'FALL' AND OffYear = 2002
    AND FacRank = 'ASST' AND CourseNo LIKE 'IS*'
```

3.2.3 Summarizing Tables with GROUP BY and HAVING

GROUP BY Reminder the columns in the SELECT clause must either be in the GROUP BY clause or be part of a summary calculation with an aggregate function.

So far, the results of all examples in this section relate to individual rows. Even Example 3.9 relates to a combination of columns from individual *Offering* and *Faculty* rows. As mentioned in Chapter 2, it is sometimes important to show summaries of rows. The GROUP BY and HAVING clauses are used to show results about groups of rows rather than individual rows.

Example 3.11 depicts the GROUP BY clause to summarize groups of rows. Each result row contains a value of the grouping column (*StdMajor*) along with the aggregate calculation summarizing rows with the same value for the grouping column. The GROUP BY clause must contain every column in the SELECT clause except for aggregate expressions. For example, adding the *StdClass* column in the SELECT clause would make Example 3.11 invalid unless *StdClass* was also added to the GROUP BY clause.

Example 3.11

Grouping on a Single Column

Summarize the average GPA of students by major.

```
SELECT StdMajor, AVG(StdGPA) AS AvgGPA
  FROM Student
  GROUP BY StdMajor
```

StdMajor	AvgGPA
ACCT	3.39999997615814
FIN	2.80000003178914
IS	3.23333330949148

TABLE 3.9	Standard Aggregate Functions

Aggregate Function	Meaning and Comments
COUNT(*)	Computes the number of rows.
COUNT(column)	Computes the number of non-null values in column; DISTINCT can be used to compute the number of unique column values.
AVG	Computes the average of a numeric column or expression excluding null values; DISTINCT can be used to compute the average of unique column values.
SUM	Computes the sum of a numeric column or expression excluding null values; DISTINCT can be used to compute the sum of unique column values.
MIN	Computes the smallest value. For string columns, the collating sequence is used to compare strings.
MAX	Computes the largest value. For string columns, the collating sequence is used to compare strings.

COUNT Function Usage COUNT(*) and COUNT(column) produce identical results except when "column" contains null values. See Chapter 9 for more details about the effect of null values on aggregate functions.

Table 3.9 shows the standard aggregate functions. If you have a statistical calculation that cannot be performed with these functions, check your DBMS. Most DBMSs feature many functions beyond these standard ones.

The COUNT, AVG, and SUM functions support the DISTINCT keyword to restrict the computation to unique column values. Example 3.12 demonstrates the DISTINCT keyword for the COUNT function. This example retrieves the number of offerings in a year as well as the number of distinct courses taught. Some DBMSs such as Microsoft Access do not support the DISTINCT keyword inside of aggregate functions. Chapter 9 presents an alternative formulation in Access SQL to compensate for the inability to use the DISTINCT keyword inside the COUNT function.

Example 3.12 (Oracle)

Counting Rows and Unique Column Values
Summarize the number of offerings and unique courses by year.

```
SELECT OffYear, COUNT(*) AS NumOfferings,
       COUNT (DISTINCT CourseNo) AS NumCourses
FROM Offering
GROUP BY OffYear
```

OffYear	NumOfferings	NumCourses
2002	3	2
2003	10	6

WHERE vs. HAVING use the WHERE clause for conditions that can be tested on individual rows. Use the HAVING clause for conditions that can be tested only on groups. Conditions in the HAVING clause should involve aggregate functions, whereas conditions in the WHERE clause cannot involve aggregate functions.

Examples 3.13 and 3.14 contrast the WHERE and HAVING clauses. In Example 3.13, the WHERE clause selects upper division (juniors or seniors) before grouping on major. Because the WHERE clause eliminates students before grouping occurs, only upper-division students are grouped. In Example 3.14, a HAVING condition retains groups with an average GPA greater than 3.1. The HAVING clause applies to groups of rows, whereas the WHERE clause applies to individual rows. To use a HAVING clause, there must be a GROUP BY clause.

Example 3.13

Grouping with Row Conditions

Summarize the average GPA of upper-division (junior or senior) students by major.

```
SELECT StdMajor, AVG(StdGPA) AS AvgGpa
  FROM Student
  WHERE StdClass = 'JR' OR StdClass = 'SR'
  GROUP BY StdMajor
```

HAVING Reminder the HAVING clause must be preceded by the GROUP BY clause.

StdMajor	AvgGPA
ACCT	3.5
FIN	2.800000031789
IS	3.149999976158

Example 3.14

Grouping with Row and Group Conditions

Summarize the average GPA of upper-division (junior or senior) students by major. Only list the majors with average GPA greater than 3.1.

```
SELECT StdMajor, AVG(StdGPA) AS AvgGpa
  FROM Student
  WHERE StdClass IN ('JR', 'SR')
  GROUP BY StdMajor
  HAVING AVG(StdGPA) > 3.1
```

StdMajor	AvgGPA
ACCT	3.5
IS	3.149999976158

One other point about Examples 3.13 and 3.14 is the use of the OR operator as compared to the IN operator (set element of operator). The WHERE condition in Examples 3.13 and 3.14 retains the same rows. The IN condition is true if *StdClass* matches any value in the parenthesized list. Chapter 9 provides additional explanation about the IN operator for nested queries.

To summarize all rows, aggregate functions can be used in SELECT without a GROUP BY clause as demonstrated in Example 3.15. The result is always a single row containing just the aggregate calculations.

Example 3.15

Grouping All Rows

List the number of upper-division students and their average GPA.

```
SELECT COUNT(*) AS StdCnt, AVG(StdGPA) AS AvgGPA
  FROM Student
  WHERE StdClass = 'JR' OR StdClass = 'SR'
```

StdCnt	AvgGPA
8	3.0625

Sometimes it is useful to group on more than one column as demonstrated by Example 3.16. The result shows one row for each combination of *StdMajor* and *StdClass*. Some rows have the same value for both aggregate calculations because there is only one associated row in the *Student* table. For example, there is only one row for the combination ('ACCT', 'JR').

Example 3.16

Grouping on Two Columns
Summarize the minimum and maximum GPA of students by major and class.

SELECT StdMajor, StdClass, MIN(StdGPA) AS MinGPA, MAX(StdGPA) AS
        MaxGPA
  FROM Student
  GROUP BY StdMajor, StdClass

StdMajor	StdClas	MinGPA	MaxGPA
ACCT	JR	3.5	3.5
ACCT	SO	3.3	3.3
FIN	JR	2.5	2.7
FIN	SR	3.2	3.2
IS	FR	3	3
IS	JR	3.6	3.6
IS	SO	3.8	3.8
IS	SR	2.2	4

A powerful combination is to use grouping with joins. There is no reason to restrict grouping to just one table. Often, more useful information is obtained by summarizing rows that result from a join. Example 3.17 demonstrates grouping applied to a join between *Course* and *Offering*. It is important to note that the join is performed before the grouping occurs. For example, after the join, there are six rows for BUSINESS PROGRAMMING. Because queries combining joins and grouping can be difficult to understand, Section 3.3 gives a more detailed explanation.

**Example 3.17
(Access)**

Combining Grouping and Joins
Summarize the number of IS course offerings by course description.

SELECT CrsDesc, COUNT(*) AS OfferCount
  FROM Course, Offering
  WHERE Course.CourseNo = Offering.CourseNo
      AND Course.CourseNo LIKE 'IS*'
  GROUP BY CrsDesc

CrsDesc	OfferCount
FUNDAMENTALS OF BUSINESS PROGRAMMING	6
FUNDAMENTALS OF DATABASE MANAGEMENT	2
SYSTEMS ANALYSIS	2

Example 3.17 (Oracle)

Combining Grouping and Joins

Summarize the number of IS course offerings by course description.

```
SELECT CrsDesc, COUNT(*) AS OfferCount
  FROM Course, Offering
  WHERE Course.CourseNo = Offering.CourseNo
    AND Course.CourseNo LIKE 'IS%'
  GROUP BY CrsDesc
```

3.2.4 Improving the Appearance of Results

We finish this section with two parts of the SELECT statement that can improve the appearance of results. Examples 3.18 and 3.19 demonstrate sorting using the ORDER BY clause. The sort sequence depends on the data type of the sorted field (numeric for numeric data types, ASCII collating sequence for string fields, and calendar sequence for data fields). By default, sorting occurs in ascending order. The keyword DESC can be used after a column name to sort in descending order as demonstrated in Example 3.19.

Example 3.18

Sorting on a Single Column

List the GPA, name, city, and state of juniors. Order the result by GPA in ascending order.

```
SELECT StdGPA, StdFirstName, StdLastName, StdCity, StdState
  FROM Student
  WHERE StdClass = 'JR'
  ORDER BY StdGPA
```

StdGPA	StdFirstName	StdLastName	StdCity	StdState
2.50	ROBERTO	MORALES	SEATTLE	WA
2.70	BOB	NORBERT	BOTHELL	WA
3.50	CANDY	KENDALL	TACOMA	WA
3.60	MARIAH	DODGE	SEATTLE	WA

Example 3.19

Sorting on Two Columns with Descending Order

List the rank, salary, name, and department of faculty. Order the result by ascending (alphabetic) rank and descending salary.

```
SELECT FacRank, FacSalary, FacFirstName, FacLastName, FacDept
  FROM Faculty
  ORDER BY FacRank, FacSalary DESC
```

FacRank	FacSalary	FacFirstName	FacLastName	FacDept
ASSC	75000.00	JULIA	MILLS	FIN
ASSC	70000.00	LEONARD	FIBON	MS
ASST	40000.00	CRISTOPHER	COLAN	MS
ASST	35000.00	LEONARD	VINCE	MS
PROF	120000.00	VICTORIA	EMMANUEL	MS
PROF	65000.00	NICKI	MACON	FIN

ORDER BY vs. DISTINCT
use the ORDER BY clause to sort a result table on one or more columns. Use the DISTINCT keyword to remove duplicates in the result.

Some students confuse ORDER BY and GROUP BY. In most systems, GROUP BY has the side effect of sorting by the grouping columns. You should not depend on this side effect. If you just want to sort, use ORDER BY rather than GROUP BY. If you want to sort and group, use both ORDER BY and GROUP BY.

Another way to improve the appearance of the result is to remove duplicate rows. By default, SQL does not remove duplicate rows. Duplicate rows are not possible when the primary keys of the result tables are included. There are a number of situations in which the primary key does not appear in the result. Example 3.21 demonstrates the DISTINCT keyword to remove duplicates that appear in the result of Example 3.20.

Example 3.20   Result with Duplicates
List the city and state of faculty members.

SELECT FacCity, FacState
    FROM Faculty

FacCity	FacState
SEATTLE	WA
BOTHELL	WA
SEATTLE	WA
BELLEVUE	WA
SEATTLE	WA
SEATTLE	WA

Example 3.21   Eliminating Duplicates with DISTINCT
List the unique city and state combinations in the *Faculty* table.

SELECT DISTINCT FacCity, FacState
  FROM Faculty

FacCity	FacState
BELLEVUE	WA
BOTHELL	WA
SEATTLE	WA

3.3 CONCEPTUAL EVALUATION PROCESS FOR SELECT STATEMENTS

Conceptual Evaluation Process the sequence of operations and intermediate tables used to derive the result of a SELECT statement. The conceptual evaluation process may help you gain an initial understanding of the SELECT statement as well as help you to understand more difficult problems.

To develop a clearer understanding of the SELECT statement, it is useful to understand the conceptual evaluation process or sequence of steps to produce the desired result. The conceptual evaluation process describes operations (mostly relational algebra operations) that produce intermediate tables leading to the result table. You may find it useful to refer to the conceptual evaluation process when first learning to write SELECT statements. After you gain initial competence with SELECT, you should not need to refer to the conceptual evaluation process except to gain insight about difficult problems.

To demonstrate the conceptual evaluation process, consider Example 3.22 involving many parts of the SELECT statement. It involves multiple tables (*Enrollment* and *Offering* in the FROM clause), row conditions (following WHERE), aggregate functions (COUNT and AVG) over groups of rows (GROUP BY), a group condition (following HAVING), and sorting of the final result (ORDER BY).

Example 3.22 (Access)	**Depict Many Parts of the SELECT Statement** List the course number, offer number, and average grade of students enrolled in fall 2002, IS course offerings in which more than one student is enrolled. Sort the result by course number in ascending order and average grade in descending order. The Oracle version of Example 3.22 is identical except for the % instead of the * as the wildcard character.

```
SELECT CourseNo, Offering.OfferNo, AVG(EnrGrade) AS AvgGrade
  FROM Enrollment, Offering
  WHERE CourseNo LIKE 'IS*' AND OffYear = 2002
    AND OffTerm = 'FALL'
    AND Enrollment.OfferNo = Offering.OfferNo
  GROUP BY CourseNo, Offering.OfferNo
  HAVING COUNT(*) > 1
  ORDER BY CourseNo, 3 DESC
```

In the ORDER BY clause, note the number 3 as the second column to sort. The number 3 means sort by the third column (*AvgGrade*) in SELECT. Some DBMSs do not allow aggregate expressions or alias names (*AvgGrade*) in the ORDER BY clause.

Tables 3.10 to 3.12 show the input tables and the result. Only small input and result tables have been used so that you can understand more clearly the process to derive the result. It does not take large tables to depict the conceptual evaluation process well.

TABLE 3.10	Sample *Offering* Table		
OfferNo	*CourseNo*	*OffYear*	*OffTerm*
1111	IS480	2002	FALL
2222	IS480	2002	FALL
3333	IS320	2002	FALL
5555	IS480	2003	WINTER
6666	IS320	2003	SPRING

The conceptual evaluation process is a sequence of operations as indicated in Figure 3.2. This process is conceptual rather than actual because most SQL compilers can produce the same output using many shortcuts. Because the shortcuts are system specific, rather mathematical, or performance oriented, we will not review them. The conceptual evaluation process provides a foundation for understanding the meaning of SQL statements that is independent of system and performance issues. The remainder of this section applies the conceptual evaluation process to Example 3.22.

1. The first step in the conceptual process combines the tables in the FROM clause with the cross product and join operators. In Example 3.22, a cross product operation is necessary because two tables are listed. A join operation is not necessary because the INNER JOIN keyword does not appear in the FROM statement. Recall that the cross product operator shows all possible rows by combining two tables. The resulting table contains the product of the number of rows and the sum of the columns. In this case, the cross product contains 35 rows (5 × 7) and 7 columns (3 + 4). Table 3.13 shows a partial result. As an exercise, you are encouraged to derive the entire result. As a notational shortcut here, the table name (abbreviated as E and O) is prefixed before the column name for *OfferNo*.

2. The second step uses a restriction operation to retrieve rows that satisfy the conditions in the WHERE clause from the result of step 1. We have four conditions: a join condition over *OfferNo*, a condition on *CourseNo*, a condition on *OffYear*, and a condition on *OffTerm*. Note that the condition on

TABLE 3.11	Sample *Enrollment* Table		
	StdSSN	*OfferNo*	*EnrGrade*
	111–11–1111	1111	3.1
	111–11–1111	2222	3.5
	111–11–1111	3333	3.3
	111–11–1111	5555	3.8
	222–22–2222	1111	3.2
	222–22–2222	2222	3.3
	333–33–3333	1111	3.6

TABLE 3.12	Example 3.22 Result		
	CourseNo	*OfferNo*	*AvgGrade*
	IS480	2222	3.4
	IS480	1111	3.3

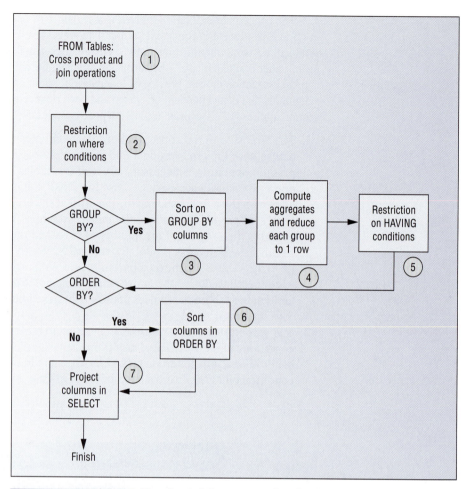

Figure 3.2   **Flowchart of the conceptual evaluation process.**

CourseNo includes the wildcard character *. Any course numbers beginning with IS match this condition. Table 3.14 shows that the result of the cross product (35 rows) is reduced to six rows.

3. The third step sorts the result of step 2 by the columns specified in the GROUP BY clause. The GROUP BY clause indicates that the output should relate to groups of rows rather than individual rows. If the output relates to individual rows rather than groups of rows, the GROUP BY clause is omitted. When using the GROUP BY clause, you must include *every* column from the SELECT clause except for expressions that involve an aggregrate function.[4] Table 3.15 shows the result of step 2 sorted by *CourseNo* and *O.OfferNo*. Note that the columns have been rearranged to make the result easier to read.

---

[4]In other words, when using the GROUP BY clause, every column in the SELECT clause should either be in the GROUP BY clause or be part of an expression with an aggregate function.

TABLE 3.13	**Partial Result of Step 1 for First Two *Offering* Rows (1111 and 2222)**

O.OfferNo	CourseNo	OffYear	OffTerm	StdSSN	E.OfferNo	EnrGrade
1111	IS480	2002	FALL	111–11–1111	1111	3.1
1111	IS480	2002	FALL	111–11–1111	2222	3.5
1111	IS480	2002	FALL	111–11–1111	3333	3.3
1111	IS480	2002	FALL	111–11–1111	5555	3.8
1111	IS480	2002	FALL	222–22–2222	1111	3.2
1111	IS480	2002	FALL	222–22–2222	2222	3.3
1111	IS480	2002	FALL	333–33–3333	1111	3.6
2222	IS480	2002	FALL	111–11–1111	1111	3.1
2222	IS480	2002	FALL	111–11–1111	2222	3.5
2222	IS480	2002	FALL	111–11–1111	3333	3.3
2222	IS480	2002	FALL	111–11–1111	5555	3.8
2222	IS480	2002	FALL	222–22–2222	1111	3.2
2222	IS480	2002	FALL	222–22–2222	2222	3.3
2222	IS480	2002	FALL	333–33–3333	1111	3.6

TABLE 3.14	**Result of Step 2**

O.OfferNo	CourseNo	OffYear	OffTerm	StdSSN	E.OfferNo	EnrGrade
1111	IS480	2002	FALL	111–11–1111	1111	3.1
2222	IS480	2002	FALL	111–11–1111	2222	3.5
1111	IS480	2002	FALL	222–22–2222	1111	3.2
2222	IS480	2002	FALL	222–22–2222	2222	3.3
1111	IS480	2002	FALL	333–33–3333	1111	3.6
3333	IS320	2002	FALL	111–11–1111	3333	3.3

TABLE 3.15	**Result of Step 3**

CourseNo	O.OfferNo	OffYear	OffTerm	StdSSN	E.OfferNo	EnrGrade
IS320	3333	2002	FALL	111–11–1111	3333	3.3
IS480	1111	2002	FALL	111–11–1111	1111	3.1
IS480	1111	2002	FALL	222–22–2222	1111	3.2
IS480	1111	2002	FALL	333–33–3333	1111	3.6
IS480	2222	2002	FALL	111–11–1111	2222	3.5
IS480	2222	2002	FALL	222–22–2222	2222	3.3

TABLE 3.16   **Result of Step 4**

CourseNo	O.OfferNo	AvgGrade	Count(*)
IS320	3333	3.3	1
IS480	1111	3.3	3
IS480	2222	3.4	2

TABLE 3.17   **Result of Step 5**

CourseNo	O.OfferNo	AvgGrade	Count(*)
IS480	1111	3.3	3
IS480	2222	3.4	2

TABLE 3.18   **Result of Step 6**

CourseNo	O.OfferNo	AvgGrade	Count(*)
IS480	2222	3.4	3
IS480	1111	3.3	2

4. The fourth step is only necessary if there is a GROUP BY clause. The fourth step computes aggregate function(s) for each group of rows and reduces each group to a single row. All rows in a group have the same values for the GROUP BY columns. In Table 3.16, there are three groups {<IS320, 3333>, <IS480, 1111>, <IS480, 2222>}. Computed columns are added for aggregate functions in the SELECT and HAVING clauses. Table 3.16 shows two new columns for the AVG function in the SELECT clause and the COUNT function in the HAVING clause. Note that remaining columns are eliminated at this point because they are not needed in the remaining steps.
5. The fifth step eliminates rows that do not satisfy the HAVING condition. Table 3.17 shows that the first row in Table 3.16 is removed because it fails the HAVING condition. Note that the HAVING clause specifies a restriction operation for groups of rows. The HAVING clause cannot be present without a preceding GROUP BY clause. The conditions in the HAVING clause always relate to groups of rows, not to individual rows. Typically, conditions in the HAVING clause involve aggregate functions.
6. The sixth step sorts the results according to the ORDER BY clause. Note that the ORDER BY clause is optional. Table 3.18 shows the result table after sorting.
7. The seventh step performs a final projection. Columns appearing in the result of step 6 are eliminated if they do not appear in the SELECT clause. Table 3.19 (identical to Table 3.12) shows the result after the projection of step 6. The

TABLE 3.19	Result of Step 7	
CourseNo	*O.OfferNo*	*AvgGrade*
IS480	2222	3.4
IS480	1111	3.3

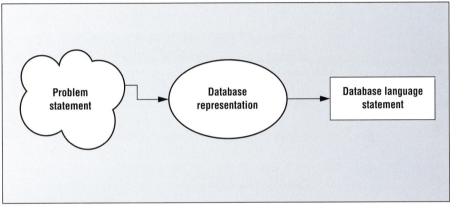

Figure 3.3   **Query formulation process.**

Count(*) column is eliminated because it does not appear in SELECT. The seventh step (projection) occurs after the sixth step (sorting) because the ORDER BY clause can contain columns that do not appear in the SELECT list.

This section finishes by discussing three major lessons about the conceptual evaluation process. These lessons are more important to remember than the specific details about the conceptual process.

- GROUP BY conceptually occurs after WHERE. If you have an error in a SELECT statement involving WHERE or GROUP BY, the problem is most likely in the WHERE clause. You can check the intermediate results after the WHERE clause by submitting a SELECT statement without the GROUP BY clause.
- Grouping occurs only one time in the evaluation process. If your problem involves more than one independent aggregate calculation, you may need more than one SELECT statement.
- Using sample tables can help you analyze difficult problems. It is often not necessary to go through the entire evaluation process. Rather, use sample tables to understand only the difficult part. Section 3.5 and Chapter 9 depict the use of sample tables to help analyze some difficult problems.

3.4 CRITICAL QUESTIONS FOR QUERY FORMULATION

The conceptual evaluation process depicted in Figure 3.2 should help you understand the meaning of most SELECT statements, but it will probably not help you to formulate queries. Query formulation involves a mapping from a problem statement into a statement of a database language such as SQL as shown in Figure 3.3. In between the problem statement and the database language statement, you convert the problem statement into a database representation. Typically, the difficult part is to convert the problem statement into a database representation. This conversion involves a detailed knowledge of the tables and relationships and careful attention to possible ambiguities in the problem statement.

In converting from the problem statement into a database representation, you should answer three critical questions:

- What tables are needed?
- How are the tables combined?
- Does the output relate to individual rows or groups of rows?

For the first question, match the columns listed in the problem to be solved with columns from various tables. Include columns that are needed for output as well as for conditions. You also should include tables that are needed only to connect other tables. For example, if you want to join the *Student* and *Offering* tables, the *Enrollment* table should be included because it provides a connection to these tables. The *Student* and *Offering* tables cannot be combined directly. All tables needed in the query should be listed in the FROM clause.

For the second question, most tables are combined by a join operation. In Chapter 9, you will use the outer join, difference, and division operators to combine tables. For now, just concentrate on combining tables with joins. You need to identify the matching columns for each join. In most joins, the primary key of one table is matched with a foreign key of another table. Occasionally, the primary key of both tables contains multiple columns. In this case, you need to match on both columns. In some situations, the matching columns do not involve a primary key/foreign key combination. You can perform a join as long as the matching columns have compatible data types. For example, when joining customer tables from different databases, there may not be a common primary key. Joining on other fields such as name, address, and so on may be necessary.

For the third question, look for computations involving aggregate functions. For example, the problem "list the name and average grade of students" contains an aggregate computation. Problems referencing an aggregate function indicate that the output relates to groups of rows. Hence the formulation requires a GROUP BY clause. If the problem contains conditions with aggregate functions, a HAVING clause should accompany the GROUP BY clause. For example, the problem "list the offer number of course offerings with more than 30 students" needs a HAVING clause with a condition involving the count function.

After answering these questions, you are ready to convert the database representation into a database language statement. To help in this process, you should develop a collection of statements for each kind of relational algebra operator using a database that you understand well. For example, you should have statements for problems that involve join operations, outer join operations, and other operators of relational algebra. As you increase your understanding of the database language, this conversion will become easy for most problems. For difficult problems such as those discussed in Section 3.5 and Chapter 9, relying on similar problems still may be useful because difficult problems are not common.

3.5 REFINING QUERY FORMULATION SKILLS WITH EXAMPLES

Let's apply your query formulation skills and knowledge of the SELECT statement to more difficult problems. All problems in this section involve the parts of SELECT discussed in Sections 3.2 and 3.3. The problems involve more difficult aspects such as joining more than two tables, grouping after joins of several tables, joining a table to itself, and traditional set operators.

3.5.1 Joining Multiple Tables with the Cross Product Style

Cross Product Style lists tables in the FROM clause and join conditions in the WHERE clause. The cross product style is easy to read but does not support outer join operations.

We begin with a number of join problems that are formulated using cross product operations in the FROM clause. This way to formulate joins is known as the <u>cross product style</u> because of the implied cross product operations. The next subsection uses join operations in the FROM clause to contrast the ways that joins can be expressed. In Example 3.23, some student rows appear more than once in the result. For example, Roberto Morales appears twice. Because of the 1-M relationship between the *Student* and *Enrollment* tables, a *Student* row can match multiple *Enrollment* rows.

Example 3.23

Joining Two Tables

List the student name, offering number, and grade of students who have a grade ≥ 3.5 in a course offering.

SELECT StdFirstName, StdLastName, OfferNo, EnrGrade
 FROM Student, Enrollment
 WHERE EnrGrade > = 3.5
    AND Student.StdSSN = Enrollment.StdSSN

StdFirstName	StdLastName	OfferNo	EnrGrade
CANDY	KENDALL	1234	3.5
MARIAH	DODGE	1234	3.8
HOMER	WELLS	4321	3.5
ROBERTO	MORALES	4321	3.5
BOB	NORBERT	5679	3.7
ROBERTO	MORALES	5679	3.8
MARIAH	DODGE	6666	3.6
LUKE	BRAZZI	7777	3.7
BOB	NORBERT	9876	3.5
WILLIAM	PILGRIM	9876	4

Examples 3.24 and 3.25 depict duplicate elimination after a join. In Example 3.24, some students appear more than once as in Example 3.23. Because only student name appears in the output, duplicate rows appear. Example 3.25 uses the DISTINCT keyword to remove the duplicate rows.

Example 3.24

Join with Duplicates

List the names of students who have a grade ≥ 3.5 in a course offering.

SELECT StdFirstName, StdLastName
 FROM Student, Enrollment
 WHERE EnrGrade > = 3.5
    AND Student.StdSSN = Enrollment.StdSSN

StdFirstName	StdLastName
CANDY	KENDALL
MARIAH	DODGE
HOMER	WELLS
ROBERTO	MORALES
BOB	NORBERT
ROBERTO	MORALES
MARIAH	DODGE
LUKE	BRAZZI
BOB	NORBERT
WILLIAM	PILGRIM

Example 3.25

Join with Duplicates Removed

List the student names (without duplicates) who have a grade $\geq$ 3.5 in a course offering.

```
SELECT DISTINCT StdFirstName, StdLastName
  FROM Student, Enrollment
 WHERE EnrGrade >= 3.5
     AND Student.StdSSN = Enrollment.StdSSN
```

StdFirstName	StdLastName
BOB	NORBERT
CANDY	KENDALL
HOMER	WELLS
LUKE	BRAZZI
MARIAH	DODGE
ROBERTO	MORALES
WILLIAM	PILGRIM

Examples 3.26 through 3.29 depict problems involving more than two tables. In these problems, it is important to identify the tables in the FROM clause. Make sure that you examine conditions to test as well as columns in the result. In Example 3.28, the *Enrollment* table is needed even though it does not supply columns in the result or conditions to test. The *Enrollment* table is needed to connect the *Student* table with the *Offering* table. Example 3.29 extends Example 3.28 with details from the *Course* table. All five tables are needed to supply outputs, to test conditions, or to connect other tables.

Example 3.26

Joining Three Tables with Columns from Only Two Tables

List the student name and the offering number in which the grade is greater than 3.7 and the offering is given in fall 2002.

```
SELECT StdFirstName, StdLastName, Enrollment.OfferNo
  FROM Student, Enrollment, Offering
 WHERE Student.StdSSN = Enrollment.StdSSN
     AND Offering.OfferNo = Enrollment.OfferNo
     AND OffYear = 2002 AND OffTerm = 'FALL'
     AND EnrGrade >= 3.7
```

StdFirstName	StdLastName	OfferNo
MARIAH	DODGE	1234

Example 3.27

Joining Three Tables with Columns from Only Two Tables

List Leonard Vince's teaching schedule in fall 2002. For each course, list the offering number, course number, number of units, days, location, and time.

```
SELECT OfferNo, Offering.CourseNo, CrsUnits, OffDays, OffLocation, OffTime
  FROM Faculty, Course, Offering
  WHERE Faculty.FacSSN = Offering.FacSSN
      AND Offering.CourseNo = Course.CourseNo
      AND OffYear = 2002 AND OffTerm = 'FALL'
      AND FacFirstName = 'LEONARD'
      AND FacLastName = 'VINCE'
```

OfferNo	CourseNo	CrsUnits	OffDays	OffLocation	OffTime
1234	IS320	4	MW	BLM302	10:30 AM
4321	IS320	4	TTH	BLM214	3:30 PM

Example 3.28

Joining Four Tables

List Bob Norbert's course schedule in spring 2003. For each course, list the offering number, course number, days, location, time, and faculty name.

```
SELECT Offering.OfferNo, Offering.CourseNo, OffDays, OffLocation, OffTime,
            FacFirstName, FacLastName
  FROM Faculty, Offering, Enrollment, Student
  WHERE Offering.OfferNo = Enrollment.OfferNo
      AND Student.StdSSN = Enrollment.StdSSN
      AND Faculty.FacSSN = Offering.FacSSN
      AND OffYear = 2003 AND OffTerm = 'SPRING'
      AND StdFirstName = 'BOB'
      AND StdLastName = 'NORBERT'
```

OfferNo	CourseNo	OffDays	OffLocation	OffTime	FacFirstName	FacLastName
5679	IS480	TTH	BLM412	3:30 PM	CRISTOPHER	COLAN
9876	IS460	TTH	BLM307	1:30 PM	LEONARD	FIBON

Example 3.29

Joining Five Tables

List Bob Norbert's course schedule in spring 2003. For each course, list the offering number, course number, days, location, time, course units, and faculty name.

```
SELECT Offering.OfferNo, Offering.CourseNo, OffDays, OffLocation, OffTime,
            CrsUnits, FacFirstName, FacLastName
  FROM Faculty, Offering, Enrollment, Student, Course
```

WHERE Faculty.FacSSN = Offering.FacSSN
  AND Offering.OfferNo = Enrollment.OfferNo
  AND Student.StdSSN = Enrollment.StdSSN
  AND Offering.CourseNo = Course.CourseNo
  AND OffYear = 2003 AND OffTerm = 'SPRING'
  AND StdFirstName = 'BOB'
  AND StdLastName = 'NORBERT'

OfferNo	CourseNo	OffDays	OffLocation	OffTime	CrsUnits	FacFirstName	FacLastName
5679	IS480	TTH	BLM412	3:30 PM	4	CRISTOPHER	COLAN
9876	IS460	TTH	BLM307	1:30 PM	4	LEONARD	FIBON

Example 3.30 demonstrates another way to combine the *Student* and *Faculty* tables. In Example 3.28, you saw it was necessary to combine the *Student, Enrollment, Offering,* and *Faculty* tables to find faculty teaching a specified student. To find students who are on the faculty (perhaps teaching assistants), the tables can be joined directly. Combining the *Student* and *Faculty* tables in this way is similar to an intersection operation. However, intersection cannot actually be performed here because the *Student* and *Faculty* tables are not union compatible.

Example 3.30	Joining Two Tables without Matching on a Primary and Foreign Key

List students who are on the faculty. Include all student columns in the result.

SELECT Student.*
  FROM Student, Faculty
  WHERE StdSSN = FacSSN

StdSSN	StdFirstName	StdLastName	StdCity	StdState	StdMajor	StdClass	StdGPA	StdZip
876-54-3210	CRISTOPHER	COLAN	SEATTLE	WA	IS	SR	4.00	98114-1332

A minor point about Example 3.30 is the use of the * after the SELECT keyword. Prefixing the * with a table name and period indicates all columns of the specified table are in the result. Using an * without a table prefix indicates that all columns from all FROM tables are in the result.

3.5.2 Joining Multiple Tables with the Join Operator Style

Join Operator Style lists join operations in the FROM clause using the INNER JOIN and ON keywords. The join operator style can be somewhat difficult to read for many join operations but it supports outer join operations as shown in Chapter 9.

As demonstrated in Section 3.2, join operations can be expressed directly in the FROM clause using the INNER JOIN and ON keywords. This join operator style can be used to combine any number of tables. To ensure that you are comfortable using this style, this subsection presents examples of multiple table joins beginning with a two-table join in Example 3.31. Note that these examples execute in Oracle 9i, but not in Oracle 8i.

Example 3.31 (Access and Oracle 9i)

Join Two Tables Using the Join Operator Style

Retrieve the name, city, and grade of students who have a high grade (greater than or equal to 3.5) in a course offering.

SELECT StdFirstName, StdLastName, StdCity, EnrGrade
 FROM Student INNER JOIN Enrollment
    ON Student.StdSSN = Enrollment.StdSSN
 WHERE EnrGrade >= 3.5

StdFirstName	StdLastName	StdCity	EnrGrade
CANDY	KENDALL	TACOMA	3.5
MARIAH	DODGE	SEATTLE	3.8
HOMER	WELLS	SEATTLE	3.5
ROBERTO	MORALES	SEATTLE	3.5
BOB	NORBERT	BOTHELL	3.7
ROBERTO	MORALES	SEATTLE	3.8
MARIAH	DODGE	SEATTLE	3.6
LUKE	BRAZZI	SEATTLE	3.7
BOB	NORBERT	BOTHELL	3.5
WILLIAM	PILGRIM	BOTHELL	4

The join operator style can be extended for any number of tables. Think of the join operator style as writing a complicated formula with lots of parentheses. To add another part to the formula, you need to add the arguments, operator, and another level of parentheses. For example, with the formula $(X + Y) * Z$, you can add another operation as $((X + Y) * Z)/W$. This same principle can be applied with the join operator style. Examples 3.32 and 3.33 extend Example 3.31 with additional conditions that need other tables. In both examples, another INNER JOIN is added to the end of the previous INNER JOIN operations. The INNER JOIN could also have been added at the beginning or middle if desired. The ordering of INNER JOIN operations is not important.

Example 3.32 (Access and Oracle 9i)

Join Three Tables Using the Join Operator Style

Retrieve the name, city, and grade of students who have a high grade (greater than or equal 3.5) in a course offered in fall 2002.

SELECT StdFirstName, StdLastName, StdCity, EnrGrade
 FROM (Student INNER JOIN Enrollment
       ON Student.StdSSN = Enrollment.StdSSN)
   INNER JOIN Offering
     ON Offering.OfferNo = Enrollment.OfferNo
 WHERE EnrGrade >= 3.5 AND OffTerm = 'FALL'
   AND OffYear = 2002

StdFirstName	StdLastName	StdCity	EnrGrade
CANDY	KENDALL	TACOMA	3.5
MARIAH	DODGE	SEATTLE	3.8
HOMER	WELLS	SEATTLE	3.5
ROBERTO	MORALES	SEATTLE	3.5

Example 3.33 (Access and Oracle 9i)

Join Four Tables Using the Join Operator Style

Retrieve the name, city, and grade of students who have a high grade (greater than or equal to 3.5) in a course offered in fall 2002 taught by Leonard Vince.

```
SELECT StdFirstName, StdLastName, StdCity, EnrGrade
 FROM ( (Student INNER JOIN Enrollment
        ON Student.StdSSN = Enrollment.StdSSN )
    INNER JOIN Offering
      ON Offering.OfferNo = Enrollment.OfferNo )
    INNER JOIN Faculty ON Faculty.FacSSN = Offering.FacSSN
    WHERE EnrGrade >= 3.5 AND OffTerm = 'FALL'
      AND OffYear = 2002 AND FacFirstName = 'LEONARD'
      AND FacLastName = 'VINCE'
```

StdFirstName	StdLastName	StdCity	EnrGrade
CANDY	KENDALL	TACOMA	3.5
MARIAH	DODGE	SEATTLE	3.8
HOMER	WELLS	SEATTLE	3.5
ROBERTO	MORALES	SEATTLE	3.5

The cross product and join operator styles can be mixed as demonstrated in Example 3.34. In most cases, it is preferable to use one style or the other, however.

Example 3.34 (Access and Oracle 9i)

Combine the Cross Product and Join Operator Styles

Retrieve the name, city, and grade of students who have a high grade (greater than or equal to 3.5) in a course offered in fall 2002 taught by Leonard Vince (same result as Example 3.33).

```
SELECT StdFirstName, StdLastName, StdCity, EnrGrade
 FROM ( (Student INNER JOIN Enrollment
      ON Student.StdSSN = Enrollment.StdSSN )
    INNER JOIN Offering
      ON Offering.OfferNo = Enrollment.OfferNo ),
    Faculty
  WHERE EnrGrade >= 3.5 AND OffTerm = 'FALL'
    AND OffYear = 2002 AND FacFirstName = 'LEONARD'
    AND FacLastName = 'VINCE'
    AND Faculty.FacSSN = Offering.FacSSN
```

The choice between the cross product and the join operator styles is largely a matter of preference. In the cross product style, it is easy to see the tables in the query. For multiple joins, the join operator style can be difficult to read because of nested parentheses. The primary advantage of the join operator style is that you can formulate queries involving outer joins as described in Chapter 9.

You should be conversant reading both join styles even if you only write queries using one style. You may need to maintain queries written with both styles. In addition, some visual query languages generate code in one of the styles. For example, Query Design, the visual query language of Microsoft Access, generates code in the join operator style.

3.5.3 Self-Joins and Multiple Joins between Two Tables

Self-Join a join between a table and itself (two copies of the same table). Self-joins are useful for finding relationships among rows of the same table.

Example 3.35 demonstrates a self-join, a join involving a table with itself. A self-join is necessary to find relationships among rows of the same table. The foreign key, *FacSupervisor,* shows relationships among *Faculty* rows. To find the supervisor name of a faculty member, match on the *FacSupervisor* column with the *FacSSN* column. The trick is to imagine that you are working with two copies of the *Faculty* table. One copy plays the role of the subordinate, while the other copy plays the role of the superior. In SQL, a self-join requires alias names (*Subr* and *Supr*) in the FROM clause to distinguish between the two roles or copies.

Example 3.35   Self-Join

List faculty members who have a higher salary than their supervisor. List the social security number, name, and salary of the faculty and supervisor.

```
SELECT Subr.FacSSN, Subr.FacLastName, Subr.FacSalary,
        Supr.FacSSN, Supr.FacLastName, Supr.FacSalary
 FROM Faculty Subr, Faculty Supr
 WHERE Subr.FacSupervisor = Supr.FacSSN
   AND Subr.FacSalary > Supr.FacSalary
```

Subr.FacSSN	Subr.FacLastName	Subr.FacSalary	Supr.FacSSN	Supr.FacLastName	Supr.FacSalary
987-65-4321	MILLS	75000.00	765-43-2109	MACON	65000.00

Problems involving self-joins can be difficult to understand. If you are having trouble understanding Example 3.35, use the conceptual evaluation process to help. Start with a small *Faculty* table. Copy this table and use the names *Subr* and *Supr* to distinguish between the two copies. Join the two tables over *Subr.FacSupervisor* and *Supr.FacSSN*. If you need, derive the join using a cross product operation. You should be able to see that each result row in the join shows a subordinate and supervisor pair.

Problems involving self-referencing (unary) relationships are part of tree-structured queries. In tree-structured queries, a table can be visualized as a structure such as a tree or hierarchy. For example, the *Faculty* table has a structure showing an organization hierarchy. At the top, the college dean resides. At the bottom, faculty members without subordinates reside. Similar structures apply to the chart of accounts in accounting systems, part structures in manufacturing systems, and route networks in transportation systems.

A more difficult problem than a self-join is to find all subordinates (direct or indirect) in an organization hierarchy. This problem can be solved in SQL if the number of subordinate levels is known. One join for each subordinate level is needed. Without knowing the number of subordinate levels, this problem cannot be done in SQL-92 although it can be solved in SQL:1999 using the WITH RECURSIVE clause and in proprietary SQL extensions. In SQL-92, tree-structured queries can be solved by using SQL inside a programming language.

Example 3.36 shows another difficult join problem. This problem involves two joins between the same two tables (*Offering* and *Faculty*). Alias table names (*O1* and *O2*) are needed to distinguish between the two copies of the *Offering* table used in the statement.

| **Example 3.36** | More Than One Join between Tables Using Alias Table Names |

List the names of faculty members and the course number for which the faculty member teaches the same course number as his or her supervisor in 2003.

```
SELECT FacFirstName, FacLastName, O1.CourseNo
  FROM Faculty, Offering O1, Offering O2
  WHERE Faculty.FacSSN = O1.FacSSN
      AND Faculty.FacSupervisor = O2.FacSSN
      AND O1.OffYear = 2003 AND O2.OffYear = 2003
      AND O1.CourseNo = O2.CourseNo
```

FacFirstName	FacLastName	CourseNo
LEONARD	VINCE	IS320
LEONARD	FIBON	IS320

If this problem is too difficult, use the conceptual evaluation process (Figure 3.2) with sample tables to gain insight. Perform a join between the sample *Faculty* and *Offering* tables, then join this result to another copy of *Offering (O2)* matching *FacSupervisor* with *O2.FacSSN*. In the resulting table, select the rows that have matching course numbers and year equal to 2003.

3.5.4 Combining Joins and Grouping

Example 3.37 demonstrates why it is sometimes necessary to group on multiple columns. After studying Example 3.37, you might be confused about the necessity to group on both *OfferNo* and *CourseNo*. One simple explanation is that any columns appearing in SELECT must be either a grouping column or an aggregrate expression. However, this explanation does not quite tell the entire story. Grouping on *OfferNo* alone produces the same values for the computed column (*NumStudents*) because *OfferNo* is the primary key. Including nonunique columns such as *CourseNo* adds information to each result row but does not change the aggregate calculations. If you do not understand this point, use sample tables to demonstrate it. When evaluating your sample tables, remember that joins occur before grouping.

| **Example 3.37** | Join with Grouping on Multiple Columns |

List the course number, the offering number, and the number of students enrolled. Only include courses offered in spring 2003.

```
SELECT CourseNo, Enrollment.OfferNo, Count(*) AS NumStudents
  FROM Offering, Enrollment
  WHERE Offering.OfferNo = Enrollment.OfferNo
      AND OffYear = 2003 AND OffTerm = 'SPRING'
  GROUP BY Enrollment.OfferNo, CourseNo
```

CourseNo	OfferNo	NumStudents
FIN480	7777	3
IS460	9876	7
IS480	5679	6

Example 3.38 demonstrates another problem involving joins and grouping. An important part of this problem is to recognize the need for the *Student* table and the HAVING condition. They are needed because the problem statement refers to an aggregate function involving the *Student* table.

Example 3.38

Joins, Grouping, and Group Conditions

List the course number, the offering number, and the average GPA of students enrolled. Only include courses offered in fall 2002 in which the average GPA of enrolled students is greater than 3.0.

```
SELECT CourseNo, Enrollment.OfferNo, Avg(StdGPA) AS AvgGPA
  FROM Student, Offering, Enrollment
  WHERE Offering.OfferNo = Enrollment.OfferNo
    AND Enrollment.StdSSN = Student.StdSSN
    AND OffYear = 2002 AND OffTerm = 'FALL'
  GROUP BY CourseNo, Enrollment.OfferNo
  HAVING Avg (StdGPA) > 3.0
```

CourseNo	OfferNo	AvgGPA
IS320	1234	3.23333330949148
IS320	4321	3.03333334128062

3.5.5 Traditional Set Operators in SQL

In SQL, you can directly use the traditional set operators with the UNION, INTERSECT, and EXCEPT keywords. Some DBMSs including Microsoft Access do not support the INTERSECT and EXCEPT keywords. As with relational algebra, the problem is always to make sure that the tables are union compatible. In SQL, you can use a SELECT statement to make tables compatible. Examples 3.39 through 3.41 demonstrate set operations on column subsets of the *Faculty* and *Student* tables. The columns have been renamed to avoid confusion.

Example 3.39

UNION Query

Show all faculty and students. Only show the common columns in the result.

```
SELECT FacSSN AS SSN, FacFirstName AS FirstName, FacLastName AS
          LastName, FacCity AS City, FacState AS State
  FROM Faculty
          UNION
SELECT StdSSN AS SSN, StdFirstName AS FirstName, StdLastName AS
          LastName, StdCity AS City, StdState AS State
  FROM Student
```

SSN	FirstName	LastName	City	State
098765432	LEONARD	VINCE	SEATTLE	WA
123456789	HOMER	WELLS	SEATTLE	WA
124567890	BOB	NORBERT	BOTHELL	WA
234567890	CANDY	KENDALL	TACOMA	WA
345678901	WALLY	KENDALL	SEATTLE	WA
456789012	JOE	ESTRADA	SEATTLE	WA
543210987	VICTORIA	EMMANUEL	BOTHELL	WA
567890123	MARIAH	DODGE	SEATTLE	WA
654321098	LEONARD	FIBON	SEATTLE	WA
678901234	TESS	DODGE	REDMOND	WA
765432109	NICKI	MACON	BELLEVUE	WA
789012345	ROBERTO	MORALES	SEATTLE	WA
876543210	CRISTOPHER	COLAN	SEATTLE	WA
890123456	LUKE	BRAZZI	SEATTLE	WA
901234567	WILLIAM	PILGRIM	BOTHELL	WA
987654321	JULIA	MILLS	SEATTLE	WA

Example 3.40 (Oracle)

INTERSECT Query

Show teaching assistants, faculty who are students. Only show the common columns in the result.

```
SELECT FacSSN AS SSN, FacFirstName AS FirstName, FacLastName AS
        LastName, FacCity AS City, FacState AS State
 FROM Faculty
      INTERSECT
SELECT StdSSN AS SSN, StdFirstName AS FirstName, StdLastName AS
        LastName, StdCity AS City, StdState AS State
FROM Student
```

SSN	FirstName	LastName	City	State
876543210	CRISTOPHER	COLAN	SEATTLE	WA

Example 3.41 (Oracle)

Difference Query

Show faculty who are *not* students (pure faculty). Only show the common columns in the result. Oracle uses the MINUS keyword instead of the EXCEPT keyword used in SQL:1999.

```
SELECT FacSSN AS SSN, FacFirstName AS FirstName, FacLastName AS
        LastName, FacCity AS City, FacState AS State
 FROM Faculty
      MINUS
SELECT StdSSN AS SSN, StdFirstName AS FirstName, StdLastName AS
        LastName, StdCity AS City, StdState AS State
 FROM Student
```

SSN	FirstName	LastName	City	State
098765432	LEONARD	VINCE	SEATTLE	WA
543210987	VICTORIA	EMMANUEL	BOTHELL	WA
654321098	LEONARD	FIBON	SEATTLE	WA
765432109	NICKI	MACON	BELLEVUE	WA
987654321	JULIA	MILLS	SEATTLE	WA

By default, duplicate rows are removed in the results of SQL statements with the UNION, INTERSECT, and EXCEPT (MINUS) keywords. If you want to retain duplicate rows, use the ALL keyword after the operator. For example, the UNION ALL keyword performs a union operation but does not remove duplicate rows.

3.6 SQL MODIFICATION STATEMENTS

The modification statements support entering new rows (INSERT), changing columns in one or more rows (UPDATE), and deleting one or more rows (DELETE). Although well designed and powerful, they are not as widely used as the SELECT statement because data entry forms are easier to use for end users.

The INSERT statement has two formats as demonstrated in Examples 3.42 and 3.43. In the first format, one row at a time can be added. You specify values for each column with the VALUES clause. You must format the constant values appropriate for each column. Refer to the documentation of your DBMS for details about specifying constants, especially string and date constants. Specifying a null value for a column is also not standard across DBMSs. In some systems, you simply omit the column name and the value. In other systems, you specify a particular symbol for a null value. Of course, you must be careful that the table definition permits null values for the column of interest. Otherwise, the INSERT statement will be rejected.

Example 3.42

Single Row Insert
Insert a row into the *Student* table supplying values for all columns.

```
INSERT INTO Student
    (StdSSN, StdFirstName, StdLastName, StdCity, StdState, StdZip, StdClass,
    StdMajor, StdGPA)
VALUES ('999999999', 'JOE', 'STUDENT', 'SEATAC', 'WA', '98042-1121', 'FR',
    'IS', 0.0)
```

The second format of the INSERT statement supports addition of a set of records as shown in Example 3.43. Using the SELECT statement inside the INSERT statement, you can specify any derived set of rows. You can use the second format when you want to create temporary tables for specialized processing.

Example 3.43

Multiple Row Insert

Assume a new table *ISStudent* has been created previously. *ISStudent* has the same columns as *Student*. This INSERT statement adds rows from *Student* into *ISStudent*.

```
INSERT INTO ISStudent
  SELECT * FROM Student WHERE StdMajor = 'IS'
```

The UPDATE statement allows one or more rows to be changed, as shown in Examples 3.44 and 3.45. Any number of columns can be changed, although typically only one column at a time is changed. When changing the primary key, update rules on referenced rows may not allow the operation.

Example 3.44

Single Column Update

Give faculty members in the MS department a 10 percent raise. Four rows are updated.

```
UPDATE Faculty
  SET FacSalary = FacSalary * 1.1
  WHERE FacDept = 'MS'
```

Example 3.45

Update Multiple Columns

Change the major and class of Homer Wells. One row is updated.

```
UPDATE Student
  SET StdMajor = 'ACCT', StdClass = 'SO'
  WHERE StdFirstName = 'HOMER'
    AND StdLastName = 'WELLS'
```

The DELETE statement allows one or more rows to be removed, as shown in Examples 3.46 and 3.47. DELETE is subject to the rules on referenced rows. For example, a *Student* row cannot be deleted if related *Enrollment* rows exist and the deletion action is restrict.

Example 3.46

Delete Selected Rows

Delete all IS majors who are seniors. Three rows are deleted.

```
DELETE FROM Student
  WHERE StdMajor = 'IS' AND StdClass = 'SR'
```

Example 3.47

Delete All Rows in a Table

Delete all rows in the *ISStudent* table.

```
DELETE FROM ISStudent
```

Sometimes it is useful for the condition inside the WHERE clause of the DELETE statement to reference rows from other tables. Microsoft Access supports the join operator style to combine tables as shown in Example 3.48. You cannot use the cross product style inside a DELETE statement. Chapter 9 shows another way to reference other tables in a DELETE statement that most DBMSs (including Access and Oracle) support.

Example 3.48 (Access)

DELETE Statement Using the Join Operator Style

Delete offerings taught by Leonard Vince. Three *Offering* rows are deleted. In addition, this statement deletes related rows in the *Enrollment* table because the ON DELETE clause is set to CASCADE.

```
DELETE Offering.*
 FROM Offering INNER JOIN Faculty
    ON Offering.FacSSN = Faculty.FacSSN
 WHERE FacFirstName = 'LEONARD'
    AND FacLastName = 'VINCE'
```

CLOSING THOUGHTS

Chapter 3 has introduced the fundamental parts of the industry standard Structured Query Language (SQL). SQL has a wide scope covering database definition, manipulation, and control. As a result of careful analysis and compromise, standards groups have produced a well-designed language. SQL has become the common glue that binds the database industry. You will no doubt continually encounter SQL throughout your career.

This chapter has focused on the most widely used parts of the SELECT statement. Numerous examples were shown to demonstrate conditions on different data types, complex logical expressions, multiple table joins, summarization of tables with GROUP BY and HAVING, sorting of tables, and the traditional set operators. The subset of SELECT described in this chapter allows you to formulate problems involving the project, restrict, join, summarize, union, intersection, and difference operators of relational algebra. This chapter also briefly described the modification statements INSERT, UPDATE, and DELETE. These statements are not as complex and widely used as SELECT.

This chapter has emphasized several ways to help you formulate queries. A seven-step process using sample tables was introduced to help you see how a result is derived. You may find this evaluation process helps in your initial learning of SELECT as well as provides insight on more challenging problems. To help formulate queries, three questions were provided to guide you. You should explicitly or implicitly answer these questions before writing a SELECT statement to solve a problem. An understanding of both the critical questions and the conceptual evaluation process will provide you a solid foundation for using relational databases. Even with these formulation aids, you need to work many problems to learn query formulation and SELECT well.

This chapter covered an important subset of SELECT. Other parts of SELECT not covered in this chapter are outer joins, nested queries, and division problems. Chapter 9 covers advanced query formulation and additional parts of the SELECT statement so that you can hone your skills.

REVIEW CONCEPTS

- SQL consists of statements for database definition (CREATE TABLE, ALTER TABLE, etc.), database manipulation (SELECT, INSERT, UPDATE, and DELETE), and database control (GRANT, REVOKE, etc.).
- The most recent SQL standard is known as SQL:1999. Because of the size and scope of this standard, no DBMS vendors claim conformance with the latest standard. Most DBMS vendors conform to the previous standard known as SQL-92.
- SELECT is a complex statement. Chapter 3 covered SELECT statements with the format:

```
SELECT <list of column and column expressions>
  FROM <list of tables and join operations>
  WHERE <list of row conditions connected by AND, OR, and NOT>
  GROUP BY <list of columns>
  HAVING <list of group conditions connected by AND, OR, and NOT>
  ORDER BY <list of sorting specifications>
```

- Use the standard comparison operators to select rows:

```
SELECT StdFirstName, StdLastName, StdCity, StdGPA
  FROM Student
  WHERE StdGPA >= 3.7
```

- Inexact matching is done with the LIKE operator and pattern-matching characters:

Oracle and SQL:1999

```
SELECT CourseNo, CrsDesc
  FROM Course
  WHERE CourseNo LIKE 'IS4%'
```

Access

```
SELECT CourseNo, CrsDesc
  FROM Course
  WHERE CourseNo LIKE 'IS4*'
```

- Use BETWEEN . . . AND to compare dates:

Oracle

```
SELECT FacFirstName, FacLastName, FacHireDate
  FROM Faculty
  WHERE FacHireDate BETWEEN '1-Jan-1994' AND '31-Dec-1995'
```

Access

```
SELECT FacFirstName, FacLastName, FacHireDate
  FROM Faculty
  WHERE FacHireDate BETWEEN #1/1/1994# AND #12/31/1995#
```

- Use Expressions in the SELECT and WHERE clauses:

Oracle

```
SELECT FacFirstName, FacLastName, FacCity, FacSalary*1.1 AS
         InflatedSalary, FacHireDate
  FROM Faculty
  WHERE to_number(to_char(FacHireDate, 'YYYY') ) > 1991
```

Access

```
SELECT FacFirstName, FacLastName, FacCity, FacSalary*1.1 AS
        InflatedSalary, FacHireDate
  FROM Faculty
  WHERE year(FacHireDate) > 1991
```

- Test for null values:

```
SELECT OfferNo, CourseNo
  FROM Offering
  WHERE FacSSN IS NULL AND OffTerm = 'SUMMER'
    AND OffYear = 2003
```

- Create complex logical expressions with AND and OR:

```
SELECT OfferNo, CourseNo, FacSSN
  FROM Offering
  WHERE (OffTerm = 'FALL' AND OffYear = 2002)
        OR (OffTerm = 'WINTER' AND OffYear = 2003)
```

- Sort results with the ORDER BY clause:

```
SELECT StdGPA, StdFirstName, StdLastName, StdCity, StdState
  FROM Student
  WHERE StdClass = 'JR'
  ORDER BY StdGPA
```

- Eliminate duplicates with the DISTINCT keyword:

```
SELECT DISTINCT FacCity, FacState
  FROM Faculty
```

- Qualify column names in join queries:

```
SELECT Course.CourseNo, CrsDesc
  FROM Offering, Course
  WHERE OffTerm = 'SPRING' AND OffYear = 2003
    AND Course.CourseNo = Offering.CourseNo
```

- Use the GROUP BY clause to summarize rows:

```
SELECT StdMajor, AVG(StdGPA) AS AvgGpa
  FROM Student
  GROUP BY StdMajor
```

- GROUP BY must precede HAVING:

```
SELECT StdMajor, AVG(StdGPA) AS AvgGpa
  FROM Student
  GROUP BY StdMajor
  HAVING AVG(StdGPA) > 3.1
```

- Use WHERE to test row conditions and HAVING to test group conditions:

```
SELECT StdMajor, AVG(StdGPA) AS AvgGpa
  FROM Student
  WHERE StdClass IN ('JR', 'SR')
  GROUP BY StdMajor
  HAVING AVG(StdGPA) > 3.1
```

- Difference between COUNT(*) and COUNT(DISTINCT column)—not supported by Access:

```
SELECT OffYear, COUNT(*) AS NumOfferings, COUNT(DISTINCT CourseNo)
        AS NumCourses
  FROM Offering
  GROUP BY OffYear
```

- Conceptual evaluation process lessons: use small sample tables, GROUP BY occurs after WHERE, only one grouping per SELECT statement.
- Query formulation questions: what tables?, how combined?, and row or group output?
- Join more than two tables with the cross product and join operator styles (not supported by Oracle 8i but supported by Oracle 9i):

```
SELECT OfferNo, Offering.CourseNo, CrsUnits, OffDays, OffLocation, OffTime
  FROM Faculty, Course, Offering
  WHERE Faculty.FacSSN = Offering.FacSSN
      AND Offering.CourseNo = Course.CourseNo
      AND OffYear = 2002 AND OffTerm = 'FALL'
      AND FacFirstName = 'LEONARD'
      AND FacLastName = 'VINCE'
```

```
SELECT OfferNo, Offering.CourseNo, CrsUnits, OffDays, OffLocation,
        OffTime
  FROM ( Faculty INNER JOIN Offering
        ON Faculty.FacSSN = Offering.FacSSN )
      INNER JOIN Course
        ON Offering.CourseNo = Course.CourseNo
  WHERE OffYear = 2002 AND OffTerm = 'FALL'
      AND FacFirstName = 'LEONARD'
      AND FacLastName = 'VINCE'
```

- Self-joins:

```
SELECT Subr.FacSSN, Subr.FacLastName, Subr.FacSalary, Supr.FacSSN,
        Supr.FacLastName, Supr.FacSalary
  FROM Faculty Subr, Faculty Supr
  WHERE Subr.FacSupervisor = Supr.FacSSN
      AND Subr.FacSalary > Supr.FacSalary
```

- Combine joins and grouping:

```
SELECT CourseNo, Enrollment.OfferNo, Count(*) AS NumStudents
  FROM Offering, Enrollment
  WHERE Offering.OfferNo = Enrollment.OfferNo
      AND OffYear = 2003 AND OffTerm = 'SPRING'
  GROUP BY Enrollment.OfferNo, CourseNo
```

- Traditional set operators and union compatibility:

```
SELECT FacSSN AS SSN, FacLastName AS LastName, FacCity AS City,
        FacState AS State
  FROM Faculty
      UNION
SELECT StdSSN AS SSN, StdLastName AS LastName, StdCity AS City,
        StdState AS State
  FROM Student
```

- Use the INSERT statement to add one or more rows:

  INSERT INTO Student
    (StdSSN, StdFirstName, StdLastName, StdCity, StdState, StdClass,
    StdMajor, StdGPA)
    VALUES ('999999999', 'JOE', 'STUDENT', 'SEATAC', 'WA', 'FR', 'IS', 0.0)

- Use the UPDATE statement to change columns in one or more rows:

  UPDATE Faculty
    SET FacSalary = FacSalary * 1.1
    WHERE FacDept = 'MS'

- Use the DELETE statement to remove one or more rows:

  DELETE FROM Student
    WHERE StdMajor = 'IS' AND StdClass = 'SR'

- Use a join operation inside a DELETE statement—Access only:

  DELETE Offering.*
    FROM Offering INNER JOIN Faculty
      ON Offering.FacSSN = Faculty.FacSSN
    WHERE FacFirstName = 'LEONARD' AND FacLastName = 'VINCE'

QUESTIONS

1. Why do some people pronounce SQL as "sequel"?

2. Why are the manipulation statements of SQL more widely used than the definition and control statements?

3. Is the SQL standard supported in whole or in part? Briefly explain.

4. How many levels of conformance does the SQL-92 standard have?

5. How many levels of conformance does the SQL:1999 standard have?

6. What is stand-alone SQL?

7. What is embedded SQL?

8. What is an expression in the context of database languages?

9. From the examples and the discussion in Chapter 3, what parts of SELECT are not supported by all DBMSs?

10. Recite the rule about GROUP BY and HAVING.

11. Recite the rule about columns in SELECT when a GROUP BY clause is used.

12. How does a row condition differ from a group condition?

13. Why should row conditions be placed in the WHERE clause rather than the HAVING clause?

14. Why are most DBMSs not case sensitive when matching on string conditions?

15. Explain how working with sample tables can provide insight about difficult problems.

16. When working with date columns, why is it necessary to refer to documentation of your DBMS?

17. How do exact and inexact matching differ in SQL?

18. How do you know when the output of a query relates to groups of rows as opposed to individual rows?

19. What tables belong in the FROM statement?

20. Explain the cross product style for join operations.

21. Explain the join operator style for join operations.

22. Discuss the pros and cons of the cross product versus the join operator styles. Do you need to know both the cross product and the join operator styles?

23. What is a self-join? When is a self-join useful?

24. Provide a SELECT statement example in which a table is needed even though the table does not provide conditions to test or columns to show in the result.

25. What is the requirement when using the traditional set operators in a SELECT statement?

26. When combining joins and grouping, what conceptually occurs first, joins or grouping?

27. How many times does grouping occur in a SELECT statement?

28. Why is the SELECT statement more widely used than the modification statements INSERT, UPDATE, and DELETE?

29. Provide an example of an INSERT statement that can insert multiple rows.

30. What is the relationship between the DELETE statement and the rules about deleting referenced rows?

31. What is the relationship between the UPDATE statement and the rules about updating the primary key of referenced rows?

32. How does COUNT(*) differ from COUNT(ColumnName)?

33. How does COUNT(DISTINCT ColumnName) differ from COUNT(ColumnName)?

PROBLEMS

ORDER

The problems use the tables of the Order Entry database, an extension of the order entry tables used in the problems of Chapter 2. Table 3.P1 lists the meaning of each table and Figure 3.P1 shows the Access Relationship window. After the relationship diagram, row listings and Oracle CREATE TABLE statements are shown for each table. Note that the primary key of the *OrdLine* table is a combination of *OrdNo* and *ProdNo*. The *Employee* table has a self-referencing (unary) relationship to itself through the foreign key, *SupEmpNo,* the employee number of the supervising employee. In the relationship diagram, the table *Employee_1* is a representation of the self-referencing relationship, not a real table. The relationship from *OrderTbl* to *OrdLine* cascades deletions and primary key updates of referenced rows. All other relationships restrict deletions and primary key updates of referenced rows if related rows exist.

TABLE 3.P1	Tables of the Order Entry Database

Table Name	Description
Customer	List of customers who have placed orders
OrderTbl	Contains the heading part of an order; Internet orders do not have an employee
Employee	List of employees who can take orders
OrdLine	Contains the detail part of an order
Product	List of products that may be ordered

Figure 3.P1	Relationship window for the order entry database.

Customer

CustNo	CustFirstName	CustLastName	CustStreet	CustCity	CustState	CustZip	CustBal
C0954327	Sheri	Gordon	336 Hill St.	Littleton	CO	80129–5543	$230.00
C1010398	Jim	Glussman	1432 E. Ravenna	Denver	CO	80111–0033	$200.00
C2388597	Beth	Taylor	2396 Rafter Rd	Seattle	WA	98103–1121	$500.00
C3340959	Betty	Wise	4334 153rd NW	Seattle	WA	98178–3311	$200.00
C3499503	Bob	Mann	1190 Lorraine Cir.	Monroe	WA	98013–1095	$0.00
C8543321	Ron	Thompson	789 122nd St.	Renton	WA	98666–1289	$85.00
C8574932	Wally	Jones	411 Webber Ave.	Seattle	WA	98105–1093	$1,500.00
C8654390	Candy	Kendall	456 Pine St.	Seattle	WA	98105–3345	$50.00
C9128574	Jerry	Wyatt	16212 123rd Ct.	Denver	CO	80222–0022	$100.00
C9403348	Mike	Boren	642 Crest Ave.	Englewood	CO	80113–5431	$0.00
C9432910	Larry	Styles	9825 S. Crest Lane	Bellevue	WA	98104–2211	$250.00
C9543029	Sharon	Johnson	1223 Meyer Way	Fife	WA	98222–1123	$856.00
C9549302	Todd	Hayes	1400 NW 88th	Lynnwood	WA	98036–2244	$0.00
C9857432	Homer	Wells	123 Main St.	Seattle	WA	98105–4322	$500.00
C9865874	Mary	Hill	206 McCaffrey	Littleton	CO	80129–5543	$150.00
C9943201	Harry	Sanders	1280 S. Hill Rd.	Fife	WA	98222–2258	$1,000.00

OrderTbl

OrdNo	OrdDate	CustNo	EmpNo	OrdName	OrdStreet	OrdCity	OrdState	OrdZip
O1116324	01/23/2004	C0954327	E8544399	Sheri Gordon	336 Hill St.	Littleton	CO	80129-5543
O1231231	01/23/2004	C9432910	E9954302	Larry Styles	9825 S. Crest Lane	Bellevue	WA	98104-2211
O1241518	02/10/2004	C9549302		Todd Hayes	1400 NW 88th	Lynnwood	WA	98036-2244
O1455122	01/09/2004	C8574932	E9345771	Wally Jones	411 Webber Ave.	Seattle	WA	98105-1093
O1579999	01/05/2004	C9543029	E8544399	Tom Johnson	1632 Ocean Dr.	Des Moines	WA	98222-1123
O1615141	01/23/2004	C8654390	E8544399	Candy Kendall	456 Pine St.	Seattle	WA	98105-3345
O1656777	02/11/2004	C8543321		Ron Thompson	789 122nd St.	Renton	WA	98666-1289
O2233457	01/12/2004	C2388597	E9884325	Beth Taylor	2396 Rafter Rd	Seattle	WA	98103-1121
O2334661	01/14/2004	C0954327	E1329594	Mrs. Ruth Gordon	233 S. 166th	Seattle	WA	98011
O3252629	01/23/2004	C9403348	E9954302	Mike Boren	642 Crest Ave.	Englewood	CO	80113-5431
O3331222	01/13/2004	C1010398		Jim Glussman	1432 E. Ravenna	Denver	CO	80111-0033
O3377543	01/15/2004	C9128574	E8843211	Jerry Wyatt	16212 123rd Ct.	Denver	CO	80222-0022
O4714645	01/11/2004	C2388597	E1329594	Beth Taylor	2396 Rafter Rd	Seattle	WA	98103-1121
O5511365	01/22/2004	C3340959	E9884325	Betty White	4334 153rd NW	Seattle	WA	98178-3311
O6565656	01/20/2004	C9865874	E8843211	Mr. Jack Sibley	166 E. 344th	Renton	WA	98006-5543
O7847172	01/23/2004	C9943201		Harry Sanders	1280 S. Hill Rd.	Fife	WA	98222-2258
O7959898	02/19/2004	C8543321	E8544399	Ron Thompson	789 122nd St.	Renton	WA	98666-1289
O7989497	01/16/2004	C3499503	E9345771	Bob Mann	1190 Lorraine Cir.	Monroe	WA	98013-1095
O8979495	01/23/2004	C9865874		Helen Sibley	206 McCaffrey	Renton	WA	98006-5543
O9919699	02/11/2004	C9857432	E9954302	Homer Wells	123 Main St.	Seattle	WA	98105-4322

Employee

EmpNo	EmpFirstName	EmpLastName	EmpPhone	SupEmpNo	EmpCommRate
E1329594	Landi	Santos	(303) 789–1234	E8843211	0.02
E8544399	Joe	Jenkins	(303) 221–9875	E8843211	0.02
E8843211	Amy	Tang	(303) 556–4321	E9884325	0.04
E9345771	Colin	White	(303) 221–4453	E9884325	0.04
E9884325	Thomas	Johnson	(303) 556–9987		0.05
E9954302	Mary	Hill	(303) 556–9871	E8843211	0.02

Product

ProdNo	ProdName	ProdMfg	ProdQOH	ProdPrice	ProdNextShipDate
P0036566	17 inch Color Monitor	ColorMeg, Inc.	12	$169.00	2/20/2004
P0036577	19 inch Color Monitor	ColorMeg, Inc.	10	$319.00	2/20/2004
P1114590	R3000 Color Laser Printer	Connex	5	$699.00	1/22/2004
P1412138	10 Foot Printer Cable	Ethlite	100	$12.00	
P1445671	8-Outlet Surge Protector	Intersafe	33	$14.99	
P1556678	CVP Ink Jet Color Printer	Connex	8	$99.00	1/22/2004
P3455443	Color Ink Jet Cartridge	Connex	24	$38.00	1/22/2004
P4200344	36-Bit Color Scanner	UV Components	16	$199.99	1/29/2004
P6677900	Black Ink Jet Cartridge	Connex	44	$25.69	
P9995676	Battery Back-up System	Cybercx	12	$89.00	2/1/2004

OrdLine

OrdNo	ProdNo	Qty
O1116324	P1445671	1
O1231231	P0036566	1
O1231231	P1445671	1
O1241518	P0036577	1
O1455122	P4200344	1
O1579999	P1556678	1
O1579999	P6677900	1
O1579999	P9995676	1
O1615141	P0036566	1
O1615141	P1445671	1
O1615141	P4200344	1
O1656777	P1445671	1
O1656777	P1556678	1
O2233457	P0036577	1
O2233457	P1445671	1
O2334661	P0036566	1
O2334661	P1412138	1
O2334661	P1556678	1
O3252629	P4200344	1
O3252629	P9995676	1
O3331222	P1412138	1
O3331222	P1556678	1

(continued)

OrdLine *(continued)*

OrdNo	ProdNo	Qty
O3331222	P3455443	1
O3377543	P1445671	1
O3377543	P9995676	1
O4714645	P0036566	1
O4714645	P9995676	1
O5511365	P1412138	1
O5511365	P1445671	1
O5511365	P1556678	1
O5511365	P3455443	1
O5511365	P6677900	1
O6565656	P0036566	10
O7847172	P1556678	1
O7847172	P6677900	1
O7959898	P1412138	5
O7959898	P1556678	5
O7959898	P3455443	5
O7959898	P6677900	5
O7989497	P1114590	2
O7989497	P1412138	2
O7989497	P1445671	3
O8979495	P1114590	1
O8979495	P1412138	1
O8979495	P1445671	1
O9919699	P0036577	1
O9919699	P1114590	1
O9919699	P4200344	1

```
CREATE TABLE Customer
(   CustNo              CHAR(8),
    CustFirstName       VARCHAR2(20) NOT NULL,
    CustLastName        VARCHAR2(30) NOT NULL,
    CustStreet          VARCHAR2(50),
    CustCity            VARCHAR2(30),
    CustState           CHAR(2),
    CustZip             CHAR(10),
    CustBal             DECIMAL(12, 2) DEFAULT 0,
    CONSTRAINT PKCustomer PRIMARY KEY (CustNo)   )

CREATE TABLE OrderTbl
(       OrdNo           CHAR(8),
        OrdDate         DATE NOT NULL,
        CustNo          CHAR(8) NOT NULL,
        EmpNo           CHAR(8),
        OrdName         VARCHAR2(50),
        OrdStreet       VARCHAR2(50),
        OrdCity         VARCHAR2(30),
```

```
        OrdState        CHAR(2),
        OrdZip          CHAR(10),
CONSTRAINT PKOrderTbl PRIMARY KEY (OrdNo),
CONSTRAINT FKCustNo FOREIGN KEY (CustNo) REFERENCES Customer,
CONSTRAINT FKEmpNo FOREIGN KEY (EmpNo) REFERENCES Employee )

CREATE TABLE OrdLine
(       OrdNo           CHAR(8),
        ProdNo          CHAR(8),
        Qty             INTEGER DEFAULT 1,
CONSTRAINT PKOrdLine PRIMARY KEY (OrdNo, ProdNo),
CONSTRAINT FKOrdNo FOREIGN KEY (OrdNo) REFERENCES OrderTbl
        ON DELETE CASCADE,
CONSTRAINT FKProdNo FOREIGN KEY (ProdNo) REFERENCES Product )

CREATE TABLE Employee
(       EmpNo           CHAR(8),
        EmpFirstName    VARCHAR2(20) NOT NULL,
        EmpLastName     VARCHAR2(30) NOT NULL,
        EmpPhone        CHAR(15),
        SupEmpNo        CHAR(8),
        EmpCommRate     DECIMAL(3,3) DEFAULT 0,
CONSTRAINT PKEmployee PRIMARY KEY (EmpNo),
CONSTRAINT FKSupEmpNo FOREIGN KEY (SupEmpNo) REFERENCES
        Employee )

CREATE TABLE Product
(       ProdNo              CHAR(8),
        ProdName            VARCHAR2(50) NOT NULL,
        ProdMfg             VARCHAR2(20) NOT NULL,
        ProdQOH             INTEGER DEFAULT 0,
        ProdPrice           DECIMAL(12,2) DEFAULT 0,
        ProdNextShipDate    DATE,
CONSTRAINT PKProduct PRIMARY KEY (ProdNo)   )
```

Part 1: SELECT

1. List the customer number, the name (first and last), and the balance of customers.

2. List the customer number, the name (first and last), and the balance of customers who reside in Colorado (CustState is CO).

3. List all columns of the *Product* table for products costing more than $50. Order the result by product manufacturer (*ProdMfg*) and product name.

4. List the order number, order date, and shipping name (*OrdName*) of orders sent to addresses in Denver or Englewood.

5. List the customer number, the name (first and last), the city, and the balance of customers who reside in Denver with a balance greater than $150 or who reside in Seattle with a balance greater than $300.

6. List the cities and states where orders have been placed. Remove duplicates from the result.

7. List all columns of the *OrderTbl* table for Internet orders placed in January 2004. An Internet order does not have an associated employee.

8. List all columns of the *OrderTbl* table for phone orders placed in February 2004. A phone order has an associated employee.

9. List all columns of the *Product* table that contain the words Ink Jet in the product name.

10. List the order number, order date, and customer number of orders placed after January 23, 2004, that are shipped to Washington recipients.

11. List the order number, order date, customer number, and customer name (first and last) of orders placed in January 2004 sent to Colorado recipients.

12. List the order number, order date, customer number, and customer name (first and last) of orders placed in January 2004 placed by Colorado customers (*CustState*) but sent to Washington recipients (*OrdState*).

13. List the customer number, name (first and last), and balance of Washington customers who have placed one or more orders in February 2004. Remove duplicate rows from the result.

14. List the order number, order date, customer number, customer name (first and last), employee number, and employee name (first and last) of January 2004 orders placed by Colorado customers.

15. List the employee number, name (first and last), and phone of employees who have taken orders in January 2004 from customers with balances greater than $300. Remove duplicate rows in the result.

16. List the product number, name, and price of products ordered by customer number C0954327 in January 2004. Remove duplicate products in the result.

17. List the customer number, name (first and last), order number, order date, employee number, employee name (first and last), product number, product name, and order cost (OrdLine.Qty * ProdPrice) for products ordered on January 23, 2004, in which the order cost exceeds $150.

18. List the average balance of customers by city. Include only customers residing in Washington state (WA).

19. List the average balance of customers by city and short zip code (the first five digits of the zip code). Include only customers residing in Washington state (WA). In Microsoft Access, the expression left(CustZip, 5) returns the first five digits of the zip code. In Oracle, the expression substr(CustZip, 1, 5) returns the first five digits.

20. List the average balance and number of customers by city. Only include customers residing in Washington state (WA). Eliminate cities in the result with less than two customers.

21. List the number of unique short zip codes and average customer balance by city. Only include customers residing in Washington state (WA). Eliminate cities in the result in which the average balance is less than $100. In Microsoft Access, the expression left(CustZip, 5) returns the first five digits of the zip code. In Oracle,

the expression substr(CustZip, 1, 5) returns the first five digits. (Note: this problem requires two SELECT statements in Access SQL or a nested query in the FROM clause—see Chapter 9).

22. List the order number and total amount of the order for orders on January 23, 2004. The total amount of an order is the sum of the quantity times the product price of each product on the order.

23. List the order number, order date, customer name (first and last), and total amount of the order for orders on January 23, 2004. The total amount of an order is the sum of the quantity times the product price of each product on the order.

24. List the customer number, customer name (first and last), the sum of the quantity of products ordered, and the total order amount (sum of the product price times the quantity) for orders placed in January 2004. Only include products in which the product name contains the string Ink Jet or Laser. Include only customers who have ordered more than two Ink Jet or Laser products in January 2004.

25. List the product number, product name, sum of the quantity of products ordered, and total order amount (sum of the product price times the quantity) for orders placed in January 2004. Only include products that have more than five products ordered in January 2004. Sort the result in descending order of the total amount.

26. List the order number, the order date, the customer number, the customer name (first and last), the customer state, and the shipping state (*OrdState*) in which the customer state differs from the shipping state.

27. List the employee number, the employee name (first and last), the commission rate, the supervising employee name (first and last), and the commission rate of the supervisor.

28. List the employee number, the employee name (first and last), and total amount of commissions on orders taken in January 2004. The amount of a commission is the sum of the dollar amount of products ordered times the commission rate of the employee.

29. List the union of the name, the street, the city, the state, and the zip of customers and order recipients. You need to use the concatenation function to combine the first and last names so that they can be compared to the order recipient name. In Access SQL, the & symbol is the concatenation function. In Oracle SQL, the || symbol is the concatenation function.

30. List the first and last name of customers who have the same name (first and last) as an employee.

31. List the employee number and the name (first and last) of second-level subordinates (subordinates of subordinates) of the employee named Thomas Johnson.

32. List the employee number and the name (first and last) of the first- and second-level subordinates of the employee named Thomas Johnson. To distinguish the level of subordinates, include a computed column with the subordinate level (1 or 2).

33. Using a mix of the join operator and the cross product styles, list the names (first and last) of customers who have placed orders taken by Amy Tang. Remove duplicate rows in the result. Note that Oracle 8i does not support the join operator style, but Oracle 9i does support the style.

34. Using the join operator style, list the product name and the price of all products ordered by Beth Taylor in January 2004. Remove duplicate rows from the result.

35. For Colorado customers, compute the number of orders placed in January 2004. The result should include the customer number, the last name, and the number of orders placed in January 2004.

36. For Colorado customers, compute the number of orders placed in January 2004 in which the orders contain products made by Connex. The result should include the customer number, the last name, and the number of orders placed in January 2004.

37. For each employee with a commission rate of less than 0.04, compute the number of orders taken in January 2004. The result should include the employee number, the employee last name, and the number of orders taken.

38. For each employee with a commission rate greater than 0.03, compute the total commission earned from orders taken in January 2004. The total commission earned is the total order amount times the commission rate. The result should include the employee number, the employee last name, and the total commission earned.

Part 2: INSERT, UPDATE, and DELETE Statements

1. Insert yourself as a new row in the *Customer* table.

2. Insert your roommate, best friend, or significant other as a new row in the *Employee* table.

3. Insert a new *OrderTbl* row with you as the customer, the person from problem 2 (Part 2) as the employee, and your choice of values for the other columns of the *OrderTbl* table.

4. Insert two rows in the *OrdLine* table corresponding to the *OrderTbl* row inserted in problem 3 (Part 2).

5. Increase the price by 10 percent of products containing the words Ink Jet.

6. Change the address (street, city, and zip) of the new row inserted in problem 1 (Part 2).

7. Identify an order that respects the rules about deleting referenced rows to delete the rows inserted in problems 1 to 4 (Part 2).

8. Delete the new row(s) of the table listed first in the order for problem 7 (Part 2).

9. Delete the new row(s) of the table listed second in the order for problem 7 (Part 2).

10. Delete the new row(s) of the remaining tables listed in the order for problem 7 (Part 2).

REFERENCES FOR FURTHER STUDY

Beyond the SQL coverage in this book, you will need specialized books on SQL-92 such as Bowman, Emerson, and Darnovsky (1996); Cannan and Otten (1992); Date and Darwen (1997); and Melton and Simon (1992). Groff and Weinberg (1999) provide a comprehensive review of the commercial dialects of SQL along with a CD-ROM with demonstration versions of Oracle, Microsoft SQL Server, Informix, Sybase, and DB2. Celko (1997) provides many interesting problems and SQL solutions. The *DBAZine* site (www.dbazine.com/) and the *DevX* help site (www.devx.com/gethelp/) have plenty of practical advice about query formulation and SQL. For product-specific SQL advice, the *Advisor.com* site (www.advisor.com/) features technical journals for Microsoft SQL Server and Microsoft Access. Oracle documentation can be found at the *Oracle Technet Site* (otn.oracle.com). You must register to use the Technet site although membership is free at this time.

Appendix 3.A **SQL:1999 Syntax Summary**

This appendix summarizes SQL:1999 syntax for the SELECT, INSERT, UPDATE, and DELETE statements presented in this chapter. The syntax is limited to the simplified statement structure presented in this chapter. More complex syntax is introduced in Part 3 of this textbook. The conventions used in the syntax notation are identical to those used at the end of Chapter 2.

SIMPLIFIED SELECT SYNTAX

```
<Select-Statement>: { <Simple-Select> | <Set-Select> }
                    [ ORDER BY <Sort-Specification>* ]

<Simple-Select>:
                SELECT [ DISTINCT ] <Column-Specification>*
                  FROM <Table-Specification>*
                  [ WHERE <Row-Condition> ]
                  [ GROUP BY ColumnName* ]
                  [ HAVING <Group-Condition> ]

<Column-Specification>: [ <Column-List> | <Column-Item> }

<Column-List>: { * | TableName.* }
                    –* is a literal here not a syntax symbol

<Column-Item>: <Column-Expression> [ AS ColumnName ]

<Column-Expression>:
                { <Scalar-Expression> | <Aggregate-Expression> }

<Scalar-Expression>:
                { <Scalar-Item> |
                  <Scalar-Item> <Arith-Operator> <Scalar-Item> }

<Scalar-Item>:
                { [ TableName.] ColumnName |
                  Constant |
                  FunctionName [ (Argument*) ] |
                  <Scalar-Expression> |
                  ( <Scalar-Expression> ) }

<Arith-Operator>: { + | – | * | / }
```

```
<Aggregate-Expression>:
                { SUM ( {<Scalar-Expression> | DISTINCT ColumnName } ) |
                  AVG ( {<Scalar-Expression> | DISTINCT ColumnName } ) |
                  MIN ( <Scalar-Expression> ) |
                  MAX ( <Scalar-Expression> ) |
                  COUNT ( [ DISTINCT ] ColumnName ) |
                  COUNT ( * ) }–* is a literal symbol here, not a special syntax symbol


<Table-Specification>: { <Simple-Table> |
                  <Join-Operation> }


<Simple-Table>: TableName [ [ AS ] AliasName ]


<Join-Operation>:
                { <Simple-Table> [INNER] JOIN <Simple-Table>
                  ON <Join-Condition> |
                  { <Simple-Table> | <Join-Operation> } [INNER] JOIN
                   { <Simple-Table> | <Join-Operation> }
                  ON <Join-Condition> |
                  ( <Join-Operation> ) }


<Join-Condition>: { <Simple-Join-Condition> |
                  <Compound-Join-Condition> }


<Simple-Join-Condition>:
                  <Scalar-Expression> <Comparison-Operator>
                  <Scalar-Expression>


<Compound-Join-Condition>:
                { NOT <Join-Condition> |
                  <Join-Condition> AND <Join-Condition> |
                  <Join-Condition> OR <Join-Condition> |
                  ( <Join-Condition> )


<Comparison-Operator>: { = | < | > | <= | >= | <> }


<Row-Condition>:
                { <Simple-Condition> | <Compound-Condition> }


<Simple-Condition>:
                { <Scalar-Expression> <Comparison-Operator>
                   <Scalar-Expression> |
                  <Scalar-Expression> [ NOT ] IN ( Constant* ) |
                  <Scalar-Expression> BETWEEN <Scalar-Expression> AND
                   <Scalar-Expression> |
                  <Scalar-Expression> IS [NOT] NULL |
                  ColumnName [ NOT ] LIKE StringPattern }
```

(Continued)

```
<Compound-Condition>:
            { NOT <Row-Condition> |
              <Row-Condition> AND <Row-Condition> |
              <Row-Condition> OR <Row-Condition> |
              ( <Row-Condition> ) }

<Group-Condition>:
            { <Simple-Group-Condition> | <Compound-Group-Condition> }

<Simple-Group-Condition>: –permits both scalar and aggregate expressions
            { <Column-Expression> <ComparisonOperator>
                < Column-Expression> |
              <Column-Expression> [ NOT ] IN ( Constant* ) |
              <Column-Expression> BETWEEN <Column-Expression> AND
              <Column-Expression> |
              <Column-Expression> IS [NOT] NULL |
              ColumnName [ NOT ] LIKE StringPattern }

<Compound-Group-Condition>:
            { NOT <Group-Condition> |
              <Group-Condition> AND <Group-Condition> |
              <Group-Condition> OR <Group-Condition> |
              ( <Group-Condition> ) }

<Sort-Specification>:
            { ColumnName | ColumnNumber } [ { ASC | DESC } ]

<Set-Select>:
            { <Simple-Select> | <Set-Select> } <Set-Operator>
            { <Simple-Select> | <Set-Select> }

<Set-Operator>: { UNION | INTERSECT | EXCEPT } [ ALL ]
```

INSERT SYNTAX

```
INSERT INTO TableName ( ColumnName* )
            VALUES ( Constant* )

INSERT INTO TableName [ ( ColumnName* ) ]
            <Simple-Select>
```

UPDATE SYNTAX

UPDATE TableName
             SET <Column-Assignment>*
             [WHERE <Row-Condition>]

<Column-Assignment>: ColumnName = <Scalar-Expression>

DELETE SYNTAX

DELETE FROM TableName
             [WHERE <Row-Condition>]

DELETE TableName.*   –* is a literal symbol here not a special syntax symbol
             FROM <Join-Operation>
             [WHERE <Row-Condition>]

Appendix 3.B   Syntax Differences among Major Database Products

Table 3B.1 summarizes syntax differences among Microsoft Access (1997, 2000, 2002 versions), Oracle 8i and 9i, Microsoft SQL Server, and IBM's DB2. The differences involve the parts of the SELECT statement presented in the chapter.

TABLE 3B.1   **SELECT Syntax Differences among Major Database Products**

Element Product	Oracle 8i, 9i	Access 97/2000/2002	MS SQL Server 2000	DB2
Pattern-matching characters	%, _	*, ? although the % and _ characters can be used in the 2002 version by setting the query mode	%, _	%, _
Case sensitivity in string matching	Yes	No	Yes	Yes
Date constants	Surround in single quotation marks	Surround in # symbols	Surround in single quotation marks	Surround in single quotation marks
Inequality symbol	<>	<>	!=	<>
Join operator style	No in 8i, Yes in 9i	Yes	Yes	Yes
Difference operations	MINUS keyword	Not supported	Not supported	EXCEPT keyword

DATABASE DEVELOPMENT

The chapters in Part 2 emphasize practical skills and design processes for the database development process. Chapter 4 introduces the context, objectives, phases, and tools of the database development process. Chapters 5 and 6 cover data modeling using the Entity Relationship Model. Chapter 5 emphasizes the Crow's Foot notation of the Entity Relationship Model and presents diagram rules to help prevent common diagram errors. Chapter 6 emphasizes the practice of data modeling on narrative problems and presents rules to convert entity relationship diagrams (ERDs) into relational tables. Chapter 6 presents design transformations and common design errors to sharpen data modeling skills. Chapter 7 covers the motivation, functional dependencies, normal forms, and practical considerations of data normalization. Chapter 8 contains broad coverage of physical database design including the objectives, inputs, file structure and query optimization background, and important design choices.

Introduction to Database Development

This chapter provides an overview of the database development process. After this chapter, the student should have acquired the following knowledge and skills:

- List the steps in the information systems life cycle.

- Describe the role of databases in an information system.

- List the goals of database development.

- Understand the relationships among phases in the database development process.

- List functions typically provided by CASE tools for database development.

OVERVIEW

Part 1 of this book provided a foundation for understanding relational databases. You learned about the features of DBMSs, the Relational Data Model, and query formulation with SQL. Part 2 explores the issues and skills involved in developing databases. This chapter broadly explains the context, goals, phases, and tools of database development to facilitate the learning of specific skills in later chapters of Part 2.

Before you can learn specific skills, you need to understand the broad context for database development. This chapter discusses a context for databases as part of an information system. You will learn about components of information systems, the life cycle of information systems, and the role of database development as part of information

123

systems development. This information systems context provides a background for database development. You will learn the phases of database development, the kind of skills used in database development, and software tools that can help you develop databases.

4.1 INFORMATION SYSTEMS

Databases exist as part of an information system. Before you can understand database development, you must understand the larger environment that surrounds a database. This section describes the components of an information system and several strategies to develop information systems.

4.1.1 Components of Information Systems

A <u>system</u> is a set of related components that work together to accomplish some objectives. Objectives are accomplished by interacting with the environment and performing functions. For example, the human circulatory system, consisting of blood, blood vessels, and the heart, makes blood flow to various parts of the body. The circulatory system interacts with other systems of the body to ensure that the right quantity and composition of blood arrives in a timely manner to various body parts.

An information system is similar to a physical system (such as the circulatory system) except that an information system manipulates data rather than a physical object like blood. An <u>information system</u> accepts data from its environment, processes data, and produces output data for decision making. For example, an information system for processing student loans (Figure 4.1) helps a service provider track loans for lending institutions. The environment of this system consists of lenders, students, and government agencies. Lenders send approved loan applications and students receive cash for school expenses. After graduation, students receive monthly statements and remit payments to retire their loans. If a student defaults, a government agency receives a delinquency notice.

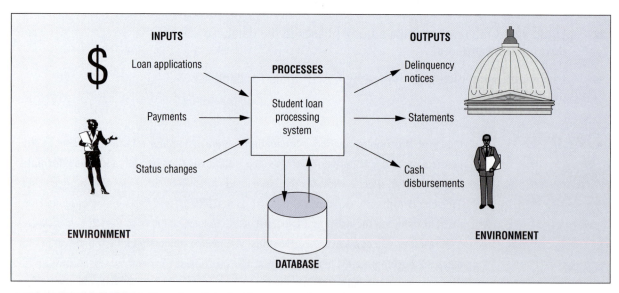

Figure 4.1   **Overview of student loan processing system.**

Databases are essential components of many information systems. The role of a database is to provide long-term memory for an information system. The long-term memory contains entities and relationships. For example, the database in Figure 4.1 contains data about students, loans, and payments so that the statements, cash disbursements, and delinquency notices can be generated. Information systems without permanent memory or with only a few variables in permanent memory are not considered in this book because most business information systems have databases with complex structures.

Databases are not the only components of information systems. Information systems also contain people, procedures, input data, output data, software, and hardware. Thus, developing an information system involves more than developing a database, as we will discuss next.

4.1.2 Information Systems Development Process

Figure 4.2 shows the phases of the traditional systems development life cycle. The particular phases of the life cycle are not standard. Different authors and organizations have proposed from 3 to 20 phases. The traditional life cycle is often known as the waterfall model or methodology because the result of each phase flows to the next phase. The traditional life cycle is mostly a reference framework. For most systems, the boundary

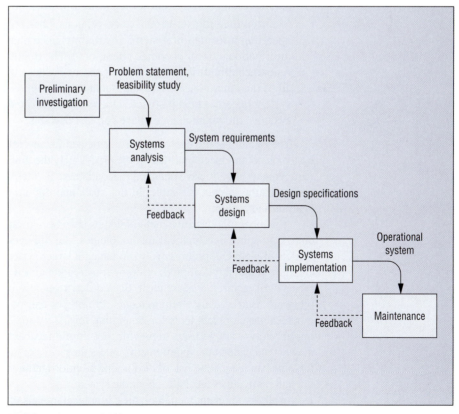

| **Figure 4.2** | **Traditional systems development life cycle.** |

between phases is blurred and there is considerable backtracking between phases. But the traditional life cycle is still useful because it describes the kind of activities and shows addition of detail until an operational system emerges. The following items describe the activities in each phase:

- **Preliminary investigation phase:** Produces a problem statement and feasibility study. The problem statement includes the objectives, constraints, and scope of the system. The feasibility study identifies the costs and benefits of the system. If the system is feasible, approval is given to begin systems analysis.
- **Systems analysis phase:** Produces requirements describing processes, data, and environment interactions. Diagramming techniques are used to document processes, data, and environment interactions. To produce the requirements, the current system is studied and users of the proposed system are interviewed.
- **Systems design phase:** Produces a plan to efficiently implement the requirements. Design specifications are created for processes, data, and environment interaction. The design specifications focus on choices to optimize resources given constraints.
- **Systems implementation phase:** Produces executable code, databases, and user documentation. To implement the system, the design specifications are coded and tested. Before making the new system operational, a transition plan from the old system to the new system is devised. To gain confidence and experience with the new system, an organization may run the old system in parallel to the new system for a period of time.
- **Maintenance phase:** Produces corrections, changes, and enhancements to an operating information system. The maintenance phase commences when an information system becomes operational. The maintenance phase is fundamentally different than other phases because it comprises activities from all of the other phases. The maintenance phase ends when developing a new system becomes cost justified. Due to the high fixed costs of developing new systems, the maintenance phase can last decades.

The traditional life cycle has been criticized for several reasons. First, an operating system is not produced until late in the process. By the time a system is operational, the requirements already have changed. Second, there is often a rush to begin implementation so that a product is visible. In this rush, appropriate time may not be devoted to analysis and design.

A number of alternative methodologies have been proposed to alleviate these difficulties. In spiral development methodologies, the life-cycle phases are performed for subsets of a system, progressively producing a larger system until the complete system emerges. Rapid application development methodologies delay producing design documents until requirements are clear. Scaled-down versions of a system known as proto-types are used to clarify requirements. Prototypes can be implemented rapidly using graphical development tools for generating forms, reports, and other code. Implementing a prototype allows users to provide meaningful feedback to developers. Often, users may not understand the requirements unless they can experience a prototype. Thus, prototyping can reduce the risk of developing an information system because it allows earlier and more direct feedback about the system.

In all development methodologies, graphical models of the data, processes, and environment interactions should be produced. The data model describes the kinds of data and relationships. The process model describes relationships among processes. A process can provide input data used by other processes and use the output data of other processes. The <u>environment interaction model</u> describes relationships between events and processes. An event such as the passage of time or an action from the environment can trigger a process to start or stop. The systems analysis phase produces an initial version of these models. The systems design phase adds more details so that the models can be efficiently implemented.

Even though models of data, processes, and environment interactions are necessary to develop an information system, this book emphasizes data models only. In many information systems development efforts, the data model is the most important. For business information systems, the process and environment interaction models are usually produced after the data model. Rather than present notation for the process and environment interaction models, this book emphasizes prototypes to depict connections among data, processes, and the environment. For more details about process and environment interaction models, please consult several references at the end of the chapter.

4.2 GOALS OF DATABASE DEVELOPMENT

Broadly, the goal of database development is to produce a database that provides an important resource for an organization. To fulfill this broad goal, the database should serve a large community of users, support organizational policies, contain high quality data, and allow efficient access. The remainder of this section describes the goals of database development that support these features.

4.2.1 Develop a Common Vocabulary

A database provides a common vocabulary for an organization. Before a common database is implemented, different parts of an organization may have different terminology. For example, there may be multiple formats for addresses, multiple ways to identify customers, and different ways to calculate interest rates. After a database is implemented, communication can improve among different parts of an organization. Thus, a database can unify an organization by establishing a common vocabulary.

Achieving a common vocabulary is not easy. Developing a database requires compromise to satisfy a large community of users. In some sense, a good database designer shares some characteristics with a good politician. A good politician often finds solutions with which everyone finds something to agree or disagree. In establishing a common vocabulary, a good database designer also finds similar imperfect solutions. Forging compromises can be difficult, but the results can improve productivity, customer satisfaction, and other measures of organizational performance.

4.2.2 Define the Meaning of Data

A database contains business rules to support organizational policies. Defining business rules is the essence of defining the semantics or meaning of the database. For example, in an order entry system, an important rule is that an order must precede a shipment. The database can contain an integrity constraint to support this rule. Defining business rules enables the database to actively support organizational policies. This active role contrasts with the more passive role that databases have in establishing a common vocabulary.

In establishing the meaning of data, a database designer must choose appropriate constraint levels. Selecting appropriate constraint levels may require compromise to balance the needs of different groups. Constraints that are too strict may force work-around solutions to handle exceptions. In contrast, constraints that are too loose may allow incorrect data in a database. For example, in a university database, a designer must decide if a course offering can be stored without knowing the instructor. Some user groups may want the instructor to be entered initially to ensure that course commitments can be met. Other user groups may want more flexibility because course catalogs are typically printed well in advance of the beginning of the academic period. Forcing the instructor to be entered at the time a course offering is stored may be too strict. If the database contains this constraint, users may be forced to circumvent it by using a default value such as TBA (to be announced). The appropriate constraint (forcing entry of the instructor or not) depends on the importance of the needs of the user groups to the goals of the organization.

4.2.3 Ensure Data Quality

The importance of data quality is analogous to the importance of product quality in manufacturing. Poor product quality can lead to loss of sales, lawsuits, and customer dissatisfaction. Because data are the product of an information system, data quality is equally important. Poor data quality can lead to poor decision making about communicating with customers, identifying repeat customers, tracking sales, and resolving customer problems. For example, communicating with customers can be difficult if addresses are outdated or customer names are inconsistently spelled on different orders.

Data quality has many dimensions or characteristics, as depicted in Table 4.1. The importance of data quality characteristics can depend on the part of the database in which they are applied. For example, in the product part of a retail grocery database, important characteristics of data quality may be the timeliness and correctness of prices. For other parts of the database, other characteristics may be more important.

A database design should help achieve adequate data quality. When evaluating alternatives, a database designer should consider data quality characteristics. For example, in a customer database, a database designer should consider the possibility that some customers may not have U.S. addresses. Therefore, the database design may be incomplete if it fails to support non-U.S. addresses.

Achieving adequate data quality may require a cost–benefit trade-off. For example, in a grocery store database, the benefits of timely price updates are reduced consumer complaints and less loss in fines from government agencies. Achieving data quality can

TABLE 4.1	Common Characteristics of Data Quality
Characteristic	*Meaning*
Completeness	Database represents all important parts of the information system
Lack of ambiguity	Each part of the database has only one meaning
Correctness	Database contains values perceived by the user
Timeliness	Business changes are posted to the database without excessive delays
Reliability	Failures or interference do not corrupt database
Consistency	Different parts of the database do not conflict

be costly both in preventative and monitoring activities. For example, to improve the timeliness and accuracy of price updates, automated data entry may be used (preventative activity) as well as sampling the accuracy of the prices charged to consumers (monitoring activity).

The cost–benefit trade-off for data quality should consider long-term as well as short-term costs and benefits. Often the benefits of data quality are long-term, especially data quality issues that cross individual databases. For example, consistency of customer identification across databases can be a crucial issue for strategic decision making. The issue may not be important for individual databases. Chapter 16 on data warehouses addresses issues of data quality related to strategic decision making.

4.2.4 Find an Efficient Implementation

Even if the other design goals are met, a slow-performing database will not be used. Thus, finding an efficient implementation is paramount. However, an efficient implementation should respect the other goals as much as possible. An efficient implementation that compromises the meaning of the database or database quality may be rejected by database users.

Finding an efficient implementation is an optimization problem with an objective and constraints. Informally, the objective is to maximize performance subject to constraints about resource usage, data quality, and data meaning. Finding an efficient implementation can be difficult because of the number of choices available, the interaction among choices, and the difficulty of describing inputs. In addition, finding an efficient implementation is a continuing effort. Performance should be monitored and design changes should be made if warranted.

4.3 DATABASE DEVELOPMENT PROCESS

This section describes the phases of the database development process and discusses relationships to the information systems development process. The other chapters in Part 2 elaborate on the framework provided here.

4.3.1 Phases of Database Development

The goal of the database development process is to produce an operational database for an information system. To produce an operational database, you need to define the three schemas (external, conceptual, and internal) and populate (supply with data) the database. To create these schemas, you can follow the process depicted in Figure 4.3. The first two phases are concerned with the information content of the database while the last two phases are concerned with efficient implementation. These phases are described in more detail in the remainder of this section.

Conceptual Data Modeling

The conceptual data modeling phase uses data requirements and produces entity relationship diagrams (ERDs) for the conceptual schema and for each external schema. Data requirements can have many formats such as interviews with users, documentation of existing systems, and proposed forms and reports. The conceptual schema should represent all the requirements and formats. In contrast, the external schemas (or

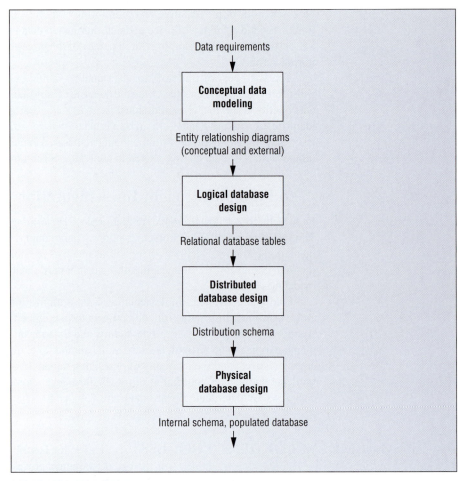

Data requirements

Conceptual data modeling

Entity relationship diagrams
(conceptual and external)

Logical database design

Relational database tables

Distributed database design

Distribution schema

Physical database design

Internal schema, populated database

Figure 4.3   Phases of database development.

views) represent the requirements of a particular usage of the database such as a form or report rather than all requirements. Thus, external schemas are generally much smaller than the conceptual schema.

The conceptual and external schemas follow the rules of the Entity Relationship Model, a graphical representation that depicts things of interest (entities) and relationships among entities. Figure 4.4 depicts an entity relationship diagram for part of a student loan system. The rectangles (*Student* and *Loan*) represent entity types and labeled lines (*Receives*) represent relationships. Attributes are listed inside the rectangle with the primary key attribute(s) underlined. Chapters 5 and 6 present more details about the Entity Relationship Model. Because the Entity Relationship Model is not fully supported by any DBMS, the conceptual schema is not biased toward any specific DBMS.

Logical Database Design

The logical database design phase transforms the conceptual data model into a format understandable by a commercial DBMS. The logical design phase is not concerned with efficient implementation. Rather, the logical design phase is concerned with refinements

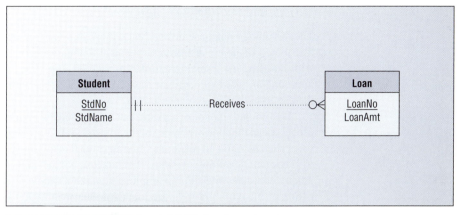

Figure 4.4   Partial ERD for the student loan system.

```
CREATE TABLE Student
(     StdNo           INTEGER        NOT NULL,
      StdName         CHAR(50),
      . . .
PRIMARY KEY (StdNo)   )
CREATE TABLE Loan
(     LoanNo          INTEGER        NOT NULL,
      LoanAmt         DECIMAL(10,2),
      StdNo           INTEGER        NOT NULL,
      . . .
PRIMARY KEY (LoanNo),
FOREIGN KEY (StdNo) REFERENCES Student    )
```

Figure 4.5   Conversion of Figure 4.4.

to the conceptual data model. The refinements preserve the information content of the conceptual data model while enabling implementation on a commercial DBMS. Because most business databases are implemented on relational DBMSs, the logical design phase usually produces a table design.

The logical database design phase consists of two refinement activities: conversion and normalization. The conversion activity transforms ERDs into table designs using conversion rules. As you have seen from Part 1 of this book, a table design includes tables, columns, primary keys, foreign keys, and other properties. For example, the ERD in Figure 4.4 is converted into two tables as depicted in Figure 4.5. The normalization activity removes redundancies in a table design using constraints or dependencies among columns. Chapter 6 presents conversion rules while Chapter 7 presents normalization techniques.

Distributed Database Design

The distributed database design phase marks a departure from the first two phases. The distributed database design and physical database design phases are both concerned with an efficient implementation. In contrast, the first two phases (conceptual data modeling and logical database design) are concerned with the information content of the database.

Distributed database design involves choices about the location of data and processes so that performance can be improved. Performance can be measured in many ways such as reduced response time, improved availability of data, and improved control. For data location decisions, the database can be split in many ways to distribute it among computer sites. For example, a loan table can be distributed according to the location of the bank granting the loan. Another technique to improve performance is to replicate or make copies of parts of the database. Replication improves availability of the database but makes updating more difficult because multiple copies must be kept consistent.

For process location decisions, some of the work is typically performed on a server and some of the work is performed by a client. For example, the server often retrieves data and sends them to the client. The client displays the results in an appealing manner. There are many other options about the location of data and processing that are explored in Chapter 17.

Physical Database Design

The physical database design phase, like the distributed database design phase, is concerned with an efficient implementation. Unlike distributed database design, physical database design is concerned with performance at one computer location only. If a database is distributed, physical design decisions are necessary for each location. An efficient implementation minimizes response time without using too many resources such as disk space and main memory. Because response time is difficult to directly measure, other measures such as the amount of disk input-output activity is often used as a substitute.

In the physical database design phase, two important choices are about indexes and data placement. An index is an auxiliary file that can improve performance. For each column of a table, the designer decides whether an index can improve performance. An index can improve performance on retrievals but reduce performance on updates. For example, an index on the primary key (*StdNo* and *LoanNo* in Figure 4.5) can usually improve performance. For data placement, the designer decides how data should be clustered or located close together on a disk. For example, performance might improve by placing student rows near the rows of associated loans. Chapter 8 describes details of physical database design including index selection and data placement.

Splitting Conceptual Design for Large Projects

The database development process shown in Figure 4.3 works well for moderate-size databases. For large databases, the conceptual modeling phase is usually modified. Designing large databases is a time-consuming and labor-intensive process often involving a team of designers. The development effort can involve requirements from many different groups of users. To manage complexity, the "divide and conquer" strategy is used in many areas of computing. Dividing a large problem into smaller problems allows the smaller problems to be solved independently. The solutions to the smaller problems are then combined into a solution for the entire problem.

View design and integration (Figure 4.6) is an approach to managing the complexity of large database development efforts. In view design, an ERD is constructed for each group of users. A view is typically small enough for a single person to design. Multiple designers can work on views covering different parts of the database. The view integration process merges the views into a complete, conceptual schema. Integration involves recognizing and resolving conflicts. To resolve conflicts, it is sometimes necessary to revise the conflicting views. Compromise is an important part of conflict resolution in the view integration process. Chapter 12 provides details about the view design and view integration processes.

Cross-Checking with Application Development

The database development process does not exist in isolation. Database development is conducted along with activities in the systems analysis, systems design, and systems implementation phases. The conceptual data modeling phase is performed as part of the systems analysis phase. The logical database design phase is performed during systems design. The distributed database design and physical database design phases are usually divided between systems design and systems implementation. Most of the preliminary decisions for the last two phases can be made in systems design. However, many physical design and distributed design decisions must be tested on a populated database. Thus, some activities in the last two phases occur in systems implementation.

To fulfill the goals of database development, the database development process must be tightly integrated with other parts of information systems development. To produce data, process, and interaction models that are consistent and complete, cross

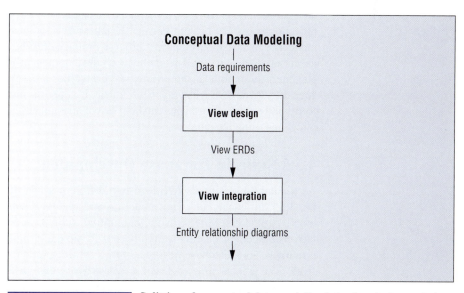

| **Figure 4.6** | Splitting of conceptual data modeling into view design and view integration. |

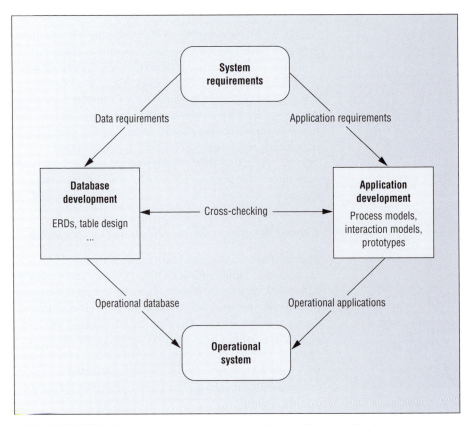

Figure 4.7 Interaction between database and application development.

checking can be performed, as depicted in Figure 4.7. The information systems development process can be split between database development and applications development. The database development process produces ERDs, table designs, and so on as described in this section. The applications development process produces process models, interaction models, and prototypes. Prototypes are especially important for cross-checking. A database has no value unless it supports intended applications such as forms and reports. Prototypes can help reveal mismatches between the database and applications using the database.

4.3.2 Skills in Database Development

As a database designer, you need two different kinds of skills as depicted in Figure 4.8. The conceptual data modeling and logical database design phases involve mostly <u>soft</u> skills. Soft skills are qualitative, subjective, and people-oriented. Qualitative skills emphasize the generation of feasible alternatives rather than the best alternatives. As a database designer, you want to generate a range of feasible alternatives. The choice among feasible alternatives can be subjective. As a database designer, you want to note the assumptions in which each feasible alternative is preferred. The alternative chosen is often subjective based on the designer's assessment of the most reasonable assumptions. Conceptual data modeling is especially people-

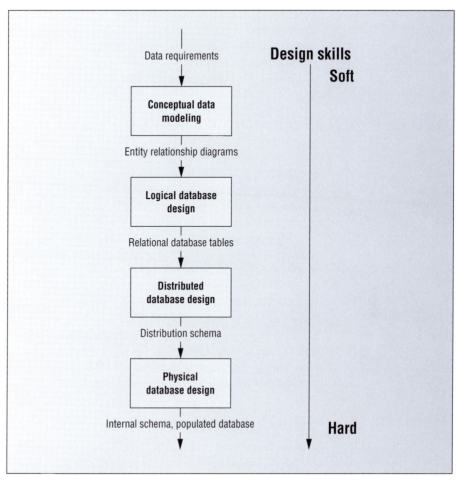

Data requirements

Design skills
Soft

Conceptual data modeling

Entity relationship diagrams

Logical database design

Relational database tables

Distributed database design

Distribution schema

Physical database design

Internal schema, populated database

Hard

Figure 4.8   Design skills used in database development.

oriented. In the role of data modeling, you need to obtain requirements from diverse groups of users. As mentioned earlier, compromise and effective listening are essential skills in data modeling.

Distributed database design and physical database design involve mostly <u>hard</u> skills. Hard skills are quantitative, objective, and data intensive. Background in quantitative disciplines such as statistics and operations management can be useful to understand mathematical models used in these phases. Many of the decisions in these phases can be modeled mathematically using an objective function and constraints. For example, the objective function for index selection is to minimize disk reads and writes with constraints about the amount of disk space and response time limitations. Many decisions cannot be based on objective criteria alone because of uncertainty about database usage. To resolve uncertainty, intensive data analysis can be useful. The database designer should collect and analyze data to understand patterns of database usage and database performance.

Because of the diverse skills and background knowledge required in different phases of database development, role specialization can occur. In large organizations, database design roles are divided between data modelers and database performance experts. Data modelers are mostly involved in the conceptual data modeling and logical database design phases. Database performance experts are mostly involved in the distributed and physical database design phases. Because the skills are different in these roles, the same person will not perform both roles in large organizations. In small organizations, the same person may fulfill both roles.

4.4 TOOLS OF DATABASE DEVELOPMENT

To improve productivity in developing information systems, computer-aided software engineering (CASE) tools have been created. CASE tools can help improve the productivity of information systems professionals working on large projects as well as end users working on small projects. A number of studies suggest that CASE tools facilitate improvements in the early phases of systems development leading to lower cost, higher quality, and faster implementations.

Most CASE tools support the database development process. Some CASE tools support database development as a part of information systems development. Other CASE tools target various phases of database development without supporting other aspects of information systems development.

CASE tools often are classified as front-end and back-end tools. Front-end CASE tools can help designers diagram, analyze, and document models used in the database development process. Back-end CASE tools create prototypes and generate code that can be used to cross check a database with other components of an information system. This section discusses the functions of CASE tools in more detail and demonstrates a commercial CASE tool, Visio Professional.

4.4.1 Diagramming

Diagramming is the most important and widely used function in CASE tools. Most CASE tools provide predefined shapes and connections among the shapes. The connection tools typically allow the shapes to be moved but stay connected as though "glued." This glue feature provides important flexibility because symbols on a diagram typically are rearranged many times.

For large drawings, CASE tools provide several features. Most CASE tools allow diagrams to span multiple pages. Multiple-page drawings can be printed so that the pages can be pasted together to make a wall display. Layout can be difficult for large drawings. Some CASE tools try to improve the visual appeal of a diagram by performing automatic layout. The automatic layout feature may minimize the number of crossing connections in a diagram. Although automated layout is not typically sufficient by itself, a designer can use it as a first step to improve the visual appearance of a diagram.

4.4.2 Documentation

Documentation is one of the oldest and most valuable functions of CASE tools. CASE tools can store various properties of a data model and link the properties to symbols on the diagram. Example properties stored in a CASE tool include alias names, integrity rules, data types, and owners. In addition to properties, CASE tools can store text describing assumptions, alternatives, and notes. Both the properties and text are stored in the data dictionary, the database of the CASE tool. The data dictionary is also known as the repository or encyclopedia.

To support system evolution, many CASE tools can document versions. A version is a group of changes and enhancements to a system that is released together. Because of the volume of changes, groups of changes rather than individual changes are typically released together. In the life of an information system, many versions can be made. To aid in understanding relationships between versions, many CASE tools support documentation for individual changes and entire versions.

4.4.3 Analysis

CASE tools can provide active assistance to database designers through analysis functions. In documentation and diagramming, CASE tools help make designers more proficient. In analysis functions, CASE tools can perform the work of a database designer. An analysis function is any form of reasoning applied to specifications produced in the database development process. For example, an important analysis function is to convert between an ERD and a table design. Converting from an ERD to a table design is known as forward engineering and converting in the reverse direction is known as reverse engineering.

Analysis functions can be provided in each phase of database development. In the conceptual data modeling phase, analysis functions can reveal conflicts in an ERD. In the logical database design phase, conversion and normalization are common analysis functions. Conversion produces a table design from an ERD. Normalization removes redundancy in a table design. In the distributed database design and physical database design phases, analysis functions can suggest decisions about data location and index selection. In addition, analysis functions for version control can cross database development phases. Analysis functions can convert between versions and show a list of differences between versions.

Because analysis functions are advanced features in CASE tools, availability of analysis functions varies widely. Some CASE tools support little or no analysis functions while others support extensive analysis functions. Because analysis functions can be useful in each phase of database development, no single CASE tool provides a complete range of analysis functions. CASE tools tend to specialize by the phases supported. CASE tools independent of a DBMS typically specialize in analysis functions in the conceptual data modeling phase. In contrast, CASE tools offered by a DBMS vendor often specialize in the distributed database design and physical database design phases.

4.4.4 Prototyping Tools

Prototyping tools provide a link between database development and application development. Prototyping tools can be used to create forms and reports that use a database. Because prototyping tools may generate code (SQL statements and programming language code), they are sometimes known as code generation tools. Prototyping tools are often provided as part of a DBMS. The prototyping tools may feature wizards to aid a developer in quickly creating applications that can be tested by users. Prototyping tools also can create an initial database design by retrieving existing designs from a library of designs. This kind of prototyping tool can be very useful to end users and novice database designers.

4.4.5 Commercial CASE Tools

As shown in Table 4.2, there are a number of CASE tools that provide extensive functionality for database development. Each of the products in Table 4.2 is a complex product that supports the full life cycle of information systems development.

TABLE 4.2	Prominent CASE Tools for Database Development	

Tool	Vendor	Innovative Features
PowerDesigner 9	Sybase	Forward and reverse engineering for relational databases and Java; model management support for comparing and merging models; application code generation; UML support; business process modeling; XML code generation; version control; data warehouse data modeling support
Oracle9i Designer	Oracle	Forward and reverse engineering for relational databases; reverse engineering of forms; application code generation; version control; dependency analysis; business process modeling; cross reference analysis
Visual Studio .NET Enterprise Architect	Microsoft	Forward and reverse engineering for relational databases and the Unified Modeling Language; code generation for XML Web Services; support for architectural guidance; generation of data models from natural language descriptions
AllFusion ERWin Data Modeler	Computer Associates	Forward and reverse engineering for relational databases; application code generation; data warehouse data modeling support
ER/Studio	Embarcadero Technologies	Forward and reverse engineering for relational databases; Java code generation; model management support for comparing and merging models; UML support; version control
Visible Analyst	Visible Systems Corporation	Forward and reverse engineering for relational databases; model management support for comparing and merging models; version control; methodology and rules checking support

Although the features of the products look similar, the quality, the depth, and the breadth of the features may vary across products. In addition, most of the products in Table 4.2 have several different versions that vary in price and features. All of the products are relatively neutral to a particular DBMS despite that companies with major DBMSs offer four of these products. There are a number of other products that specialize in one or more phases of database development, although the products are not listed in Table 4.2.

To provide a flavor for some features of commercial CASE tools, a brief depiction is given of Visio 2002 Professional Edition, an entry-level version of Visual Studio .NET Enterprise Architect. Visio Professional provides excellent drawing capabilities and a number of useful analysis tools. This section depicts Visio Professional because it is an easy-to-use and powerful tool for introductory database courses.

For database development, Visio Professional features several stencils (collections of shapes) and data dictionary support. As shown in Figure 4.9, Visio provides stencils for several data modeling notations (Relational, IDEF1X, Express-G, and Object Role Modeling notations) as well as the Unified Modeling Language (available in the software folder). Figure 4.10 depicts the Entity Relationship stencil (on the left) and the drawing window (on the right). If a symbol is moved, it stays connected to other symbols because of a feature known as "glue." For example, if the Product rectangle is moved, it stays connected to the OrdLine rectangle through the PurchasedIn line. Visio Professional can automatically lay out the entire diagram if requested.

Visio provides a data dictionary to accompany the Entity Relationship stencil. For entity types (rectangle symbols), Visio supports the name, data type, required (Req'd), primary key, and notes properties as shown in the Columns tab of Figure 4.11 as well as many other properties in the nonselected tabs. For relationships (connecting line

Figure 4.9   Data modeling stencils in Visio 2002 Professional.

Figure 4.10   Stencil and canvas windows in Visio Professional.

Figure 4.11   Database Properties window in Visio Professional for the *Product* entity type.

Figure 4.12   Database Properties window in Visio Professional for the *Places* relationship.

symbols), Visio supports properties about the definition, name, cardinality, and referential integrity as shown in Figure 4.12. For additional data dictionary support, custom properties and properties specific to a DBMS can be added.

Visio provides several analysis and prototyping tools beyond its stencil and data dictionary features. The analysis tools primarily support the schema conversion task in the logical database design phase. The Refresh Model Wizard detects and resolves differences between a Visio database diagram and an existing relational database. The Reverse Engineer Wizard performs the reverse task of converting a relational database definition into a Visio database diagram. Visio also supports various error checks to ensure consistent database diagrams. For prototyping, Visio can store shapes in relational databases. This feature can be particularly useful for providing a visual interface for hierarchical data such as organization charts and bill of material data. For more powerful prototyping, Visio supports the Visual Basic with Applications (VBA) language, an event-driven language integrated with Microsoft Office.

CLOSING THOUGHTS

This chapter described the role of databases in information systems and the nature of the database development process. Information systems are collections of related components that produce data for decision making. Databases provide the permanent memory for information systems. Development of an information system involves a repetitive process of analysis, design, and implementation. Database development occurs in all phases of systems development. Because a database is often a crucial part of an information system, database development can be the dominant part of information systems development. Development of the processing and environment interaction components is often performed after the database development. Cross-checking between the database and applications is the link that connects the database development process to the information systems development process.

This chapter described the goals, phases, and tools of database development. The goals emphasize both the information content of the database as well as efficient implementation. The phases of database development first establish the information content of the database and then find an efficient implementation. The conceptual data modeling and logical database design phases involve the information content of the database. The distributed database design and physical database design phases involve efficient implementation. Because developing databases can be a challenging process, computer-aided software engineering (CASE) tools have been created to improve productivity. CASE tools can be essential in helping the database designer to draw, document, and prototype the database. In addition, some CASE tools provide active assistance with analyzing a database design.

This chapter provides a context for the other chapters in Part 2. You might want to reread this chapter after completing other chapters in Part 2. The other chapters in Part 2 provide details about the phases of database development. Chapters 5 and 6 present details of the Entity Relationship Model, data modeling practice using the Entity Relationship Model, and conversion from the Entity Relationship Model to the Relational Model. Chapter 7 presents normalization techniques for relational tables. Chapter 8 presents physical database design techniques.

REVIEW CONCEPTS

- System: related components that work together to accomplish objectives.
- Information system: system that accepts, processes, and produces data.
- Waterfall model of information systems development: reference framework for activities in the information systems development process.
- Spiral development methodologies and rapid application development methodologies to alleviate the problems in the traditional waterfall development approach.
- Role of databases in information systems: provide permanent memory.
- Define a common vocabulary to unify an organization.
- Define business rules to support organizational processes.
- Ensure data quality to improve the quality of decision making.
- Evaluate investment in data quality using a cost–benefit approach.
- Find an efficient implementation to ensure adequate performance while not compromising other design goals.

- Conceptual data modeling to represent the information content independent of a target DBMS.
- View design and view integration to manage the complexity of large data modeling efforts.
- Logical database design to refine a conceptual data model to a target DBMS.
- Distributed database design to determine locations of data and processing to achieve an efficient and reliable implementation.
- Physical database design to achieve efficient implementations on each computer site.
- Develop prototype forms and reports to cross check among the database and applications using the database.
- Soft skills for conceptual data modeling: qualitative, subjective, and people-oriented.
- Hard skills for finding an efficient implementation: quantitative, objective, and data intensive.
- Computer-aided software engineering (CASE) tools to improve productivity in the database development process.
- Fundamental assistance of CASE tools: drawing and documenting.
- Active assistance of CASE tools: analysis and prototyping.

QUESTIONS

1. What is the relationship between a system and an information system?

2. Provide an example of a system that is not an information system.

3. For an information system of which you are aware, describe some of the components (input data, output data, people, software, hardware, and procedures).

4. Briefly describe some of the kinds of data in the database for the information system in question 3.

5. Describe the phases of the waterfall model.

6. Why is the waterfall model considered only a reference framework?

7. What are the shortcomings in the waterfall model?

8. What alternative methodologies have been proposed to alleviate the difficulties of the waterfall model?

9. What is the relationship of the database development process to the information systems development process?

10. What is a data model? Process model? Environment interaction model?

11. What is the purpose of prototyping in the information systems development process?

12. How is a database designer like a politician in establishing a common vocabulary?

13. Why should a database designer establish the meaning of data?

14. What factors should a database designer consider when choosing database constraints?

15. Why is data quality important?

16. Provide examples of data quality problems according to two characteristics mentioned in Section 4.2.3.

17. How does a database designer decide on the appropriate level of data quality?

18. Why is it important to find an efficient implementation?

19. What are the inputs and the outputs of the conceptual data modeling phase?

20. What are the inputs and the outputs of the logical database design phase?

21. What are the inputs and the outputs of the distributed database design phase?

22. What are the inputs and the outputs of the physical database design phase?

23. What does it mean to say that the conceptual data modeling phase and the logical database design phase are concerned with the information content of the database?

24. Why are there two phases (conceptual data modeling and logical database design) that involve the information content of the database?

25. What is the relationship of view design and view integration to conceptual data modeling?

26. What is a soft skill?

27. What is a hard skill?

28. What kind of background is appropriate for hard skills?

29. Why do large organizations sometimes have different people performing design phases dealing with information content and efficient implementation?

30. Why are CASE tools useful in the database development process?

31. What kinds of support can a CASE tool provide for drawing a database diagram?

32. What kinds of support can a CASE tool provide for documenting a database design?

33. What kinds of support can a CASE tool provide for analyzing a database design?

34. What kinds of support can a CASE tool provide for prototyping?

35. Should you expect to find one software vendor providing a full range of functions (drawing, documenting, analyzing, and prototyping) for the database development process? Why or why not?

PROBLEMS

Because of the introductory nature of this chapter, there are no problems in this chapter. Problems appear at the end of other chapters in Part 2.

REFERENCES FOR FURTHER STUDY

For a more detailed description of the database development process, you can consult specialized books on database design such as Batini, Ceri, and Navathe (1992) and Teorey (1999). For more details on the systems development process, you can consult books on systems analysis and design such as Whitten and Bentley (2001). For more details about data quality, consult Kimball (1996), Redman (1992), and Strong, Lee, and Wang (1997).

CHAPTER 5

Understanding Entity Relationship Diagrams

LEARNING OBJECTIVES

This chapter explains the notation of entity relationship diagrams as a prerequisite to applying entity relationship diagrams in the database development process. After this chapter, the student should have acquired the following knowledge and skills:

- Know the symbols and vocabulary of the Crow's Foot notation for entity relationship diagrams.

- Use the cardinality symbols to represent 1-1, 1-M, and M-N relationships.

- Compare the Crow's Foot notation to the representation of relational tables.

- Understand important relationship patterns.

- Use generalization hierarchies to represent similar entity types.

- Detect notational errors in an entity relationship diagram.

OVERVIEW

Chapter 4 provided a broad presentation about the database development process. You learned about the relationship between database development and information systems development, the phases of database development, and the kinds of skills you need to master. This chapter presents the notation of entity relationship diagrams to provide a foundation for using entity relationship diagrams in the database development process. To further develop your database design skills, Chapter 6 describes the process of using entity relationship diagrams to develop data models for business databases.

To become a good data modeler, you need to understand the notation in entity relationship diagrams and apply the notation on problems of increasing complexity. To help you master the notation, this chapter presents the symbols used in entity relationship diagrams and compares entity relationship diagrams to relational database diagrams that you have seen in earlier chapters. This chapter then probes deeper into relationships, the most distinguishing part of entity relationship diagrams. You will learn about identification dependency, relationship patterns, and an equivalence between two kinds of relationships. Finally, you will learn how to represent similarities among entities using generalization hierarchies. This chapter concludes with a summary of the Crow's Foot notation along with consistency and completeness rules to ensure valid use of the notation.

This chapter provides the basic skills of data modeling to enable you to understand the notation of entity relationship diagrams. To apply data modeling as part of the database development process, you should study Chapter 6 on developing data models for business databases. Chapter 6 emphasizes the problem-solving skills of generating alternative designs, mapping a problem statement to an entity relationship diagram, and justifying design decisions. With the background provided in both chapters, you will be prepared to perform data modeling on case studies and databases for moderate-size organizations.

5.1 INTRODUCTION TO ENTITY RELATIONSHIP DIAGRAMS

Gaining an initial understanding of entity relationship diagrams (ERDs) requires careful study. This section introduces the Crow's Foot notation for ERDs, a popular notation supported by many CASE tools. To get started, this section begins with the basic symbols of entity types, relationships, and attributes. This section then explains cardinalities and their appearance in the Crow's Foot notation. This section concludes by comparing the Crow's Foot notation to relational database diagrams. If you are covering data modeling before relational databases, you may want to skip this subsection.

5.1.1 Basic Symbols

Entity Type a collection of entities (persons, places, events, or things) of interest represented by a rectangle in an entity relationship diagram.

ERDs have three basic elements: entity types, relationships, and attributes. <u>Entity types</u> are collections of things of interest (entities) in an application. Entity types represent collections of physical things such as books, people, and places, as well as events such as payments. An entity is a member or instance of an entity type. Entities are uniquely identified to allow tracking across business processes. For example, customers have a unique identification to support order processing, shipment, and product warranty processes. In the Crow's Foot notation as well as most other notations, rectangles denote entity types. In Figure 5.1, the *Course* entity type represents the set of courses in the database.

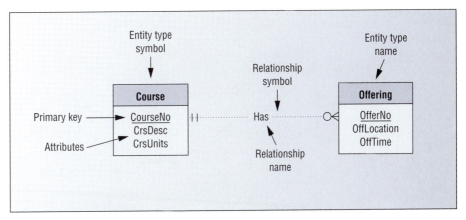

Figure 5.1   Entity relationship diagram illustrating basic symbols.

Attributes are properties of entity types or relationships. An entity type should have a primary key as well as other descriptive attributes. Attributes are shown inside an entity type rectangle. If there are many attributes, the attributes can be suppressed and listed on a separate page. Some ERD drawing tools show attributes in a zoomed view, separate from the rest of the diagram. Underlining indicates that the attribute(s) serves as the primary key of the entity type.

Relationships are named associations among entity types. In the Crow's Foot notation, relationship names appear on the line connecting the entity types involved in the relationship. In Figure 5.1, the *Has* relationship shows that the *Course* and *Offering* entity types are directly related. Relationships store associations in both directions. For example, the *Has* relationship shows the offerings for a given course and the associated course for a given offering. The *Has* relationship is binary because it involves two entity types. Section 5.2 presents examples of more complex relationships involving only one distinct entity type (unary relationships) and more than two entity types (M-way relationships).

In a loose sense, ERDs have a natural language correspondence. Entity types can correspond to nouns and relationships to verbs or prepositional phrases connecting nouns. In this sense, one can read an entity relationship diagram as a collection of sentences. For example, the ERD in Figure 5.1 can be read as "course has offerings." Note that there is an implied direction in relationships. In the other direction, one could write, "offering is given for a course." If practical, it is a good idea to use active rather than passive verbs for relationships. Therefore, *Has* is preferred as the relationship name. You should use the natural language correspondence as a guide rather than strict rule. For large ERDs, you will not always find a good natural language correspondence for all parts of the diagrams.

5.1.2 Relationship Cardinality

Cardinalities constrain the number of objects that participate in a relationship. To depict the meaning of cardinalities, an instance diagram is useful. Figure 5.2 shows a set of courses ({Course1, Course2, Course3}), a set of offerings ({Offering1, Offering2, Offering3, Offering4}), and connections between the two sets. In Figure 5.2, Course1 is related to Offering1, Offering2, and Offering3, Course2 is related to Offering4, and Course3 is

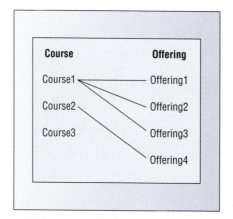

Figure 5.2   Instance diagram for the *Has* relationship.

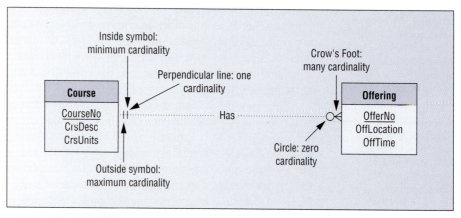

Figure 5.3   Entity relationship diagram with cardinalities noted.

not related to any *Offering* entities. Likewise, Offering1 is related to Course1, Offering2 is related to Course1, Offering3 is related to Course1, and Offering4 is related to Course2. From this instance diagram, we might conclude that each offering is related to exactly one course. In the other direction, each course is related to 0 or more offerings.

Crow's Foot Representation of Cardinalities

The Crow's Foot notation uses three symbols to represent cardinalities. The Crow's Foot symbol (two angled lines and one straight line) denotes many (zero or more) related entities. In Figure 5.3, the Crow's Foot symbol near the *Offering* entity type means that a course can be related to many offerings. The circle means a cardinality of zero, while a line perpendicular to the relationship line means a cardinality of one.

To depict minimum and maximum cardinalities, the cardinality symbols are placed adjacent to each entity type in a relationship. The minimum cardinality symbol appears toward the relationship name while the maximum cardinality symbol appears toward the

TABLE 5.1	Summary of Cardinality Classifications
Classification	*Cardinality Restrictions*
Mandatory	Minimum cardinality ≥ 1
Optional	Minimum cardinality $= 0$
Functional or single-valued	Maximum cardinality $= 1$
1-M	Maximum cardinality $= 1$ in one direction and maximum cardinality > 1 in the other direction
M-N	Maximum cardinality is > 1 in both directions
1-1	Maximum cardinality $= 1$ in both directions

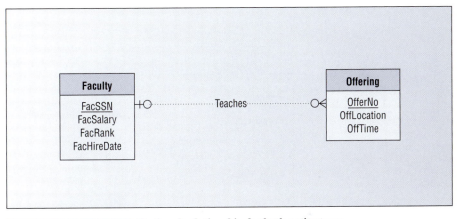

Figure 5.4   **Optional relationship for both entity types.**

entity type. In Figure 5.3, a course is related to a minimum of zero offerings (circle in the inside position) and a maximum of many offerings (Crow's Foot in the outside position). Similarly, an offering is related to exactly one (one and only one) course as shown by the single vertical lines in both inside and outside positions.

Classification of Cardinalities

Cardinalities are classified by common values for minimum and maximum cardinality. Table 5.1 shows two classifications for minimum cardinalities. A minimum cardinality of one or more indicates a <u>mandatory relationship.</u> For example, participation in the *Has* relationship is mandatory for each *Offering* entity due to the minimum cardinality of one. A mandatory relationship makes the entity type <u>existence dependent</u> on the relationship. The *Offering* entity type depends on the *Has* relationship because an *Offering* entity cannot be stored without a related *Course* entity. In contrast, a minimum cardinality of 0 indicates an <u>optional relationship.</u> For example, the *Has* relationship is optional to the *Course* entity type because a *Course* entity can be stored without being related to an *Offering* entity. Figure 5.4 shows that the *Teaches* relationship is optional for both entity types.

Existence Dependency an entity that cannot exist unless another related entity exists. A mandatory relationship produces an existence dependency.

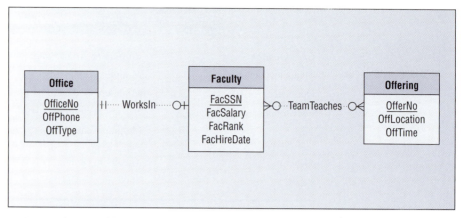

Figure 5.5   M-N and 1-1 relationship examples.

Figure 5.6   Instance diagram for the M-N *TeamTeaches* relationship.

Table 5.1 also shows several classifications for maximum cardinalities. A maximum cardinality of one means the relationship is *single-valued* or *functional*. For example, the *Has* and *Teaches* relationships are functional for *Offering* because an *Offering* entity can be related to a maximum of one *Course* and one *Faculty* entity. The word *function* comes from mathematics where a function gives one value. A relationship that has a maximum cardinality of one in one direction and more than one (many) in the other direction is called a 1-M (read one-to-many) relationship. Both the *Has* and *Teaches* relationships are 1-M.

Similarly, a relationship that has a maximum cardinality of more than one in both directions is known as an M-N (many-to-many) relationship. In Figure 5.5, the *TeamTeaches* relationship allows multiple professors to jointly teach the same offering, as shown in the instance diagram of Figure 5.6. M-N relationships are common in business databases. For example, M-N relationships usually represent the connection between parts and suppliers, authors and books, and skills and employees. A part can be supplied by many suppliers and a supplier can supply many parts.

Figure 5.7   **Relational database diagram for the *Course-Offering* example.**

Less common are 1-1 relationships in which the maximum cardinality equals one in both directions. For example, the *WorksIn* relationship in Figure 5.5 allows a faculty to be assigned to one office and an office to be occupied by at most one faculty.

5.1.3 Comparison to Relational Database Diagrams

To finish this section, let us compare the notation in Figure 5.3 with the relational database diagrams (from Microsoft Access) with which you are familiar. It is easy to become confused between the two notations. Some of the major differences are listed below.[1] To help you visualize these differences, Figure 5.7 shows a relational database diagram for the *Course-Offering* example.

1. Relational database diagrams do not use names for relationships. Instead foreign keys represent relationships. The ERD notation does not use foreign keys. For example, *Offering.CourseNo* is a column in Figure 5.7 but not an attribute in Figure 5.3.
2. Relational database diagrams show only maximum cardinalities.
3. Some ERD notations (including the Crow's Foot notation) allow both entity types and relationships to have attributes. Relational database diagrams only allow tables to have columns.
4. Relational database diagrams allow a relationship between two tables. Some ERD notations (although not the Crow's Foot notation) allow M-way relationships involving more than two entity types. The next section shows how to represent M-way relationships in the Crow's Foot notation.
5. In some ERD notations (although not the Crow's Foot notation), the position of the cardinalities is reversed.

5.2 UNDERSTANDING RELATIONSHIPS

This section explores the entity relationship notation in more depth by examining important aspects of relationships. The first subsection describes identification dependency, a specialized kind of existence dependency. The second subsection describes three important relationship

---

[1]Chapter 6 presents conversion rules that describe the differences more precisely.

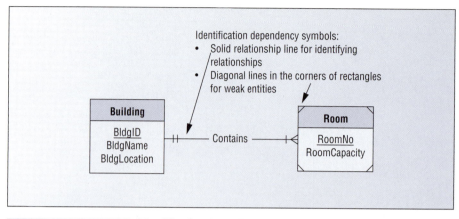

Figure 5.8 Identification dependency example.

patterns: (1) relationships with attributes, (2) self-referencing relationships, and (3) associative entity types representing multiway (M-way) relationships. The final subsection describes an important equivalence between M-N and 1-M relationships.

5.2.1 Identification Dependency (Weak Entities and Identifying Relationships)

In an ERD, some entity types may not have their own primary key. Entity types without their own primary key must borrow part (or all) of their primary key from other entity types. Entity types that borrow part or their entire primary key are known as <u>weak entities.</u> The relationship(s) that provides components of the primary key is known as an <u>identifying relationship</u>. Thus, an identification dependency involves a weak entity and one or more identifying relationships.

<u>Identification dependency</u> occurs because some entities are closely associated with other entities. For example, a room does not have a separate identity from its building because a room is physically contained in a building. You can reference a room only by providing its associated building identifier. In the ERD for buildings and rooms (Figure 5.8), the *Room* entity type is identification dependent on the *Building* entity type in the *Contains* relationship. A solid relationship line indicates an identifying relationship. For weak entities, the underlined attribute (if present) is part of the primary key, but not the entire primary key. Thus, the primary key of *Room* is a combination of *BldgID* and *RoomNo.* As another example, Figure 5.9 depicts an identification dependency involving the weak entity *State* and the identifying relationship *Holds.*

Identification dependency is a specialized kind of existence dependency. Recall that an existent-dependent entity type has a mandatory relationship (minimum cardinality of one). Weak entities are existent dependent on the identifying relationships. In addition to the existence dependency, a weak entity borrows at least part of its entire primary key. Because of the existence dependency and the primary key borrowing, the minimum and maximum cardinalities of a weak entity are always 1.

The next section shows several additional examples of identification dependency in the discussion of associative entity types and M-way relationships. The use of identification dependency is necessary for associative entity types.

Weak Entity an entity type that borrows all or part of its primary key from another entity type. Identifying relationships indicate the entity types that supply components of the borrowed primary key.

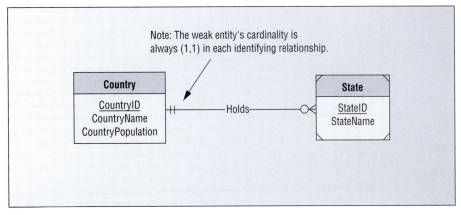

Figure 5.9   Another identification dependency example.

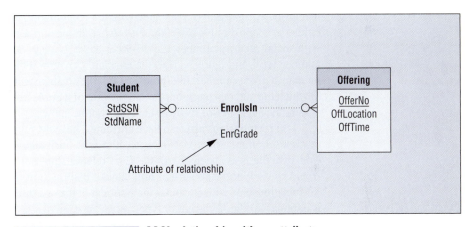

Figure 5.10   M-N relationship with an attribute.

5.2.2 Relationship Patterns

This section discusses three patterns for relationships that you may encounter in database development efforts: (1) M-N relationships with attributes; (2) self-referencing (unary) relationships; and (3) associative entity types representing M-way relationships. Although these relationship patterns do not dominate ERDs, they are important when they occur. You need to study these patterns carefully to apply them correctly in database development efforts.

M-N Relationships with Attributes

As briefly mentioned in Section 5.1, relationships can have attributes. This situation typically occurs with M-N relationships. In an M-N relationship, attributes are associated with the combination of entity types, not just one of the entity types. If an attribute is associated with only one entity type, then it should be part of that entity type, not the relationship. Figures 5.10 and 5.11 depict M-N relationships with attributes. In Figure 5.10,

Figure 5.11   **Additional M-N relationships with attributes.**

the attribute *EnrGrade* is associated with the combination of a student and offering, not either one alone. For example, the *EnrollsIn* relationship records the fact that the student with social security number 123-77-9993 has a grade of 3.5 in the offering with offer number 1256. In Figure 5.11(a), the attribute *Qty* represents the quantity of a part supplied by a given supplier. In Figure 5.11(b), the attribute *AuthOrder* represents the order in which the author's name appears in the title of a book. To reduce clutter on a large diagram, the attributes of relationships may not be shown.

1-M relationships also can have attributes, but 1-M relationships with attributes are much less common than M-N relationships with attributes. In Figure 5.12, the *Commission* attribute is associated with the *Lists* relationship, not with either the *Agent* or the *Home* entity type. A home will only have a commission if an agent lists it. Typically, 1-M relationships with attributes are optional in the one direction. The *Lists* relationship is optional for the *Home* entity type.

Self-Referencing (Unary) Relationships

Self-Referencing Relationship a relationship involving the same entity type. Self-referencing relationships represent associations among members of the same set.

A <u>self-referencing (unary) relationship</u> involves connections among members of the same set. Self-referencing relationships are sometimes called reflexive relationships because they are like a reflection in a mirror. Figure 5.13 displays two self-referencing relationships involving the *Faculty* and *Course* entity types. Both relationships involve two entity types that are the same (*Faculty* for *Supervises* and *Course* for *PreReqTo*). These relationships depict important concepts in a university database. The *Supervises* relationship depicts an organizational chart, while the *PreReqTo* relationship depicts course dependencies that can affect a student's course planning.

For self-referencing relationships, it is important to distinguish between 1-M and M-N relationships. An instance diagram can help you understand the difference. Figure 5.14(a) shows an instance diagram for the *Supervises* relationship. Notice that each faculty can have at most one superior. For example, Faculty2 and Faculty3 have Faculty1 as a superior. Therefore, *Supervises* is a 1-M relationship because each faculty can have at most one supervisor. In contrast, there is no such restriction in the instance diagram for the *PreReqTo* relationship [Figure 5.14(b)]. For example, both IS480 and IS460 are prerequisites to IS461. Therefore, *PreReqTo* is an M-N relationship because a course can be a prerequisite to many courses, and a course can have many prerequisites.

Figure 5.12   1-M relationship with an attribute.

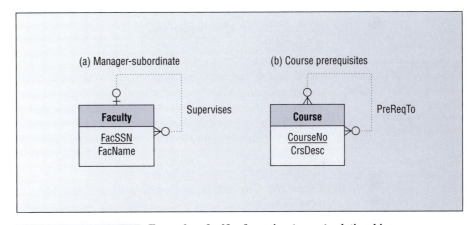

Figure 5.13   Examples of self-referencing (unary) relationships.

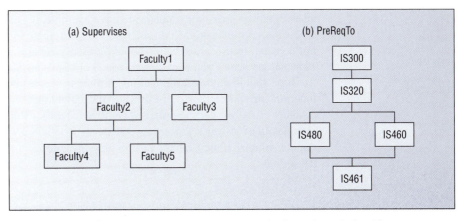

Figure 5.14   Instance diagrams for self-referencing relationships.

Self-referencing relationships occur in a variety of business situations. Any data that can be visualized like Figure 5.14 can be represented as a self-referencing relationship. Typical examples include hierarchical charts of accounts, genealogical charts, part designs, and transportation routes. In these examples, self-referencing relationships are an important part of the database.

There is one other noteworthy aspect of self-referencing relationships. Sometimes a self-referencing relationship is not needed. For example, if you only want to know whether an employee is a supervisor, a self-referencing relationship is not needed. Rather, an attribute can be used to indicate whether an employee is a supervisor.

Associative Entity Types Representing Multiway (M-Way) Relationships

Some ERD notations support relationships involving more than two entity types known as M-way (multiway) relationships where the *M* means more than two. For example, the Chen ERD notation (with diamonds for relationships) allows relationships to connect more than two entity types, as depicted in Figure 5.15.[2] The *Uses* relationship lists suppliers and parts used on projects. For example, a relationship instance involving Supplier1, Part1, and Project1 means that Supplier1 Supplies Part1 on Project1. An M-way relationship involving three entity types is called a ternary relationship.

Associative Entity Type a weak entity that replaces an M-way relationship. An associative entity type depends on two or more entity types for its primary key.

Although you cannot directly represent M-way relationships in the Crow's Foot notation, you should understand how to indirectly represent them. You use an associative entity type and a collection of binary relationships to represent an M-way relationship. In Figure 5.16, three 1-M relationships link the associative entity type, *Uses*, to the *Part*, the *Supplier*, and the *Project* entity types. The *Uses* entity type is associative because its role is to connect other entity types. Because associative entity types provide a connecting role, they are sometimes given names using active verbs. In addition, associative entity types are always weak as they must borrow the entire primary key. For example, the *Uses* entity type obtains its primary key through the three identifying relationships.

As another example, Figure 5.17 shows the associative entity type *Provides* that connects the *Employee, Skill,* and *Project* entity types. An example instance of the *Provides* entity type contains Employee1 providing Skill1 on Project1.

The issue of when to use an associative entity type representing an M-way relationship can be difficult to understand. If a database only needs to record pairs of facts, an associative entity type is not needed. For example, if a database only needs to record who supplies a part and what projects use a part, then an M-way relationship should not be used. In this case, there should be binary relationships between *Supplier* and *Part* and between *Project* and *Part*. You should use an M-way relationship when the database should record combinations of three (or more) entities rather than just combinations of two entities. For example, if a database needs to record which supplier provides parts on specific projects, an M-way relationship is needed. Because of the complexity of M-way relationships, Chapter 7 provides a way to reason about them using constraints, while Chapter 12 provides a way to reason about them using data entry forms.

[2]The Chen notation is named after Dr. Peter Chen, who published the paper defining the Entity Relationship Model in 1976.

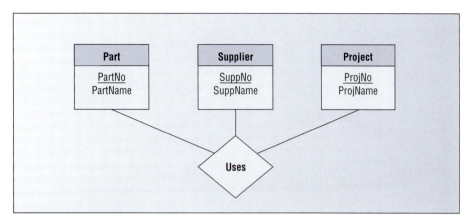

| **Figure 5.15** | M-way (ternary) relationship using the Chen notation. |

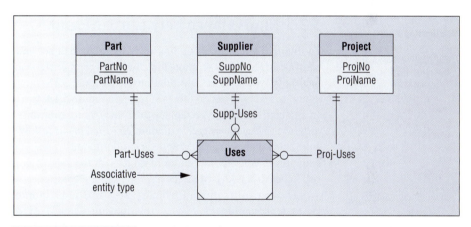

| **Figure 5.16** | Associative entity type to represent a ternary relationship. |

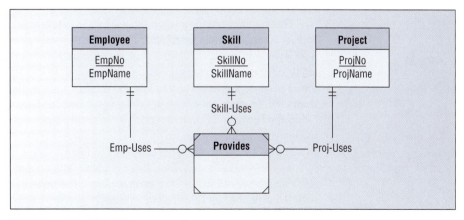

| **Figure 5.17** | Associative entity type connecting *Employee*, *Skill*, and *Project*. |

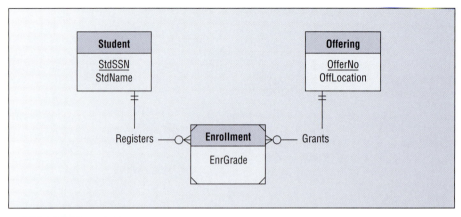

| **Figure 5.18** | *EnrollsIn* **M-N relationship (Figure 5.10) transformed into 1-M relationships.** |

5.2.3 Equivalence between 1-M and M-N Relationships

Relationship Equivalence
an M-N relationship can be replaced by an associative entity type and two identifying 1-M relationships.

To improve your understanding of M-N relationships, you should know an important equivalence for M-N relationships. An M-N relationship can be replaced by an associative entity type and two 1-M relationships. Figure 5.18 shows the *EnrollsIn* (Figure 5.10) relationship converted to this 1-M style. In Figure 5.18, two identifying relationships and an associative entity type replace the *EnrollsIn* relationship. The relationship name (*EnrollsIn*) has been changed to a noun (*Enrollment*) to follow the convention of nouns for entity type names. The 1-M style is similar to the representation in a relational database diagram. If you feel more comfortable with the 1-M style, then use it. In terms of the ERD, the M-N and 1-M styles have the same meaning.

The transformation of a binary M-N relationship into 1-M relationships is similar to representing an M-way relationship using 1-M relationships. Whenever an M-N relationship is represented as an associative relationship and two 1-M relationships, the new entity type is identification dependent on both 1-M relationships, as shown in Figure 5.18. Similarly, when representing M-way relationships, the associative entity type is identification dependent on all 1-M relationships as shown in Figures 5.16 and 5.17.

There is one situation when the 1-M style is preferred to the M-N style. When an M-N relationship must be related to other entity types in another relationship, use the 1-M style. For example, assume that in addition to enrollment in a course offering, attendance in each class session should be recorded. In this situation, the 1-M style is preferred because it is necessary to link an enrollment with attendance records. Figure 5.19 shows the *Attendance* entity type added to the ERD of Figure 5.18. Note that an M-N relationship between the *Student* and *Offering* entity types would not have allowed another relationship with *Attendance*.

Figure 5.19 provides other examples of identification dependencies. The solid line by *Attendance* means that *Attendance* is identification dependent on *Enrollment* in the *RecordedFor* relationship. The primary key of *Attendance* consists of *AttDate* along with the primary key of *Enrollment*. Similarly, *Enrollment* is identification dependent on both *Student* and *Offering*. The primary key of *Enrollment* is a combination of *StdSSN* and *OfferNo*.

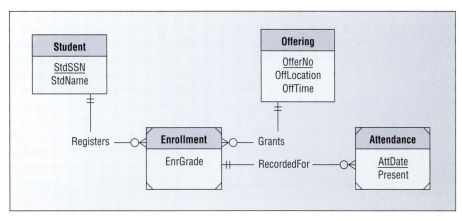

Figure 5.19   **Attendance entity type added to the ERD of Figure 5.18.**

5.3 CLASSIFICATION IN THE ENTITY RELATIONSHIP MODEL

People classify entities to better understand their environment. For example, animals are classified into mammals, reptiles, and other categories to understand the similarities and differences among different species. In business, classification is also pervasive. Classification can be applied to investments, employees, customers, loans, parts, and so on. For example, when applying for a home mortgage, an important distinction is between fixed- and adjustable-rate mortgages. Within each kind of mortgage, there are many variations distinguished by features such as the repayment period, the prepayment penalties, and the loan amount.

This section describes ERD notation to support classification. You will learn to use generalization hierarchies, specify cardinality constraints for generalization hierarchies, and use multiple level generalization hierarchies for complex classifications.

5.3.1 Generalization Hierarchies

Generalization Hierarchy a collection of entity types arranged in a hierarchical structure to show similarity in attributes. Each subtype or child entity type contains a subset of entities of its supertype or parent entity type.

Generalization hierarchies allow entity types to be related by the level of specialization. Figure 5.20 depicts a generalization hierarchy to classify employees as salaried versus hourly. Both salaried and hourly employees are specialized kinds of employees. The *Employee* entity type is known as the supertype (or parent). The entity types *SalaryEmp* and *HourlyEmp* are known as the subtypes (or children). Because each subtype entity *is a* supertype entity, the relationship between a subtype and supertype is known as ISA. For example, a salaried employee is an employee. Because the relationship name (ISA) is always the same, it is not shown on the diagram.

Inheritance a data modeling feature that supports sharing of attributes between a supertype and a subtype. Subtypes inherit attributes from their supertypes.

Inheritance supports sharing between a supertype and its subtypes. Because every subtype entity is also a supertype entity, the attributes of the supertype also apply to all subtypes. For example, every entity of *SalaryEmp* has an employee number, name, and hiring date because it is also an entity of *Employee*. Inheritance means that the attributes of a supertype are automatically part of its subtypes. That is, each subtype inherits the attributes of its supertype. For example, the attributes of the *SalaryEmp* entity type are its direct attribute (*EmpSalary*) and its inherited attributes from *Employee* (*EmpNo*, *EmpName, EmpHireDate,* etc.). Inherited attributes are not shown in an ERD. Whenever you have a subtype, assume that it inherits the attributes from its supertype.

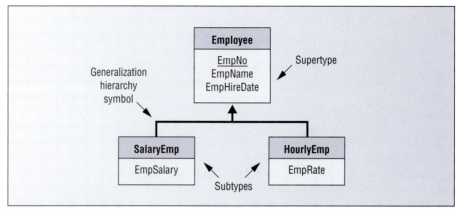

Figure 5.20   **Generalization hierarchy for employees.**

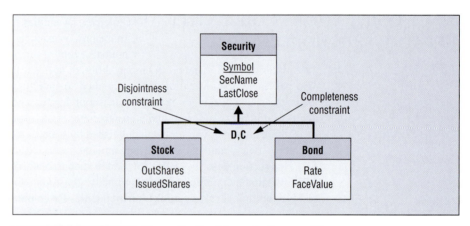

Figure 5.21   **Generalization hierarchy for securities.**

5.3.2 Disjointness and Completeness Constraints

Generalization hierarchies do not show cardinalities because they are always the same. Rather disjointness and completeness constraints can be shown. <u>Disjointness</u> means that subtypes in a generalization hierarchy do not have any entities in common. In Figure 5.21, the generalization hierarchy is disjoint because a security cannot be both a stock and a bond. In contrast, the generalization hierarchy in Figure 5.22 is not disjoint because teaching assistants can be considered both students and faculty. Thus, the set of students overlaps with the set of faculty. <u>Completeness</u> means that every entity of a supertype must be an entity in one of the subtypes in the generalization hierarchy. The completeness constraint in Figure 5.21 means that every security must be either a stock or a bond.

Some generalization hierarchies lack both disjointness and completeness constraints. In Figure 5.20, the lack of a disjointness constraint means that some employees can be both salaried and hourly. The lack of a completeness constraint indicates that some employees are not paid by salary or the hour (perhaps by commission).

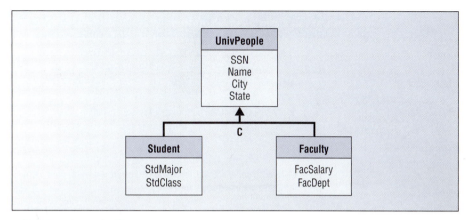

Figure 5.22   Generalization hierarchy for university people.

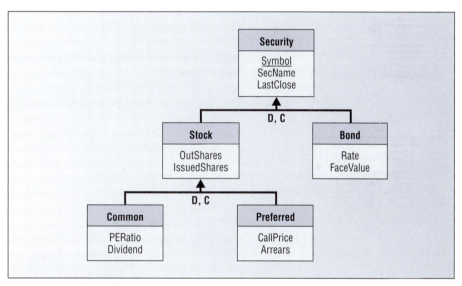

Figure 5.23   Multiple levels of generalization hierarchies.

5.3.3 Multiple Levels of Generalization

Generalization hierarchies can be extended to more than one level. This practice can be useful in disciplines such as investments where knowledge is highly structured. In Figure 5.23, there are two levels of subtypes beneath securities. Inheritance extends to all subtypes, direct and indirect. Thus, both the *Common* and *Preferred* entity types inherit the attributes of *Stock* (the immediate parent) and *Security* (the indirect parent). Note that disjointness and completeness constraints can be made for each group of subtypes.

5.4 NOTATION SUMMARY AND DIAGRAM RULES

You have seen a lot of ERD notation in the previous sections of this chapter. So that you do not become overwhelmed, this section provides a convenient summary as well as rules to help you avoid common diagramming errors.

TABLE 5.2	Summary of Crow's Foot Notation

Symbol	Meaning
Student (StdSSN, StdName, ...)	Entity type with attributes (primary key underlined).
Enrolls_In / EnrGrade	M-N relationship with attributes: attributes are shown if room permits; otherwise attributes are listed separately.
Contains	Identification dependency: identifying relationship(s) (solid relationship lines) and weak entity (diagonal lines in the corners of the rectangle). Associative entity types also are weak because they are (by definition) identification dependent.
D, C	Generalization hierarchy with disjointness and completeness constraints.
Contains	Existence dependent cardinality (minimum cardinality of 1): inner symbol is a line perpendicular to the relationship line.
Teaches	Optional cardinality (minimum cardinality of 0): inner symbol is a circle.
Has	Single-valued cardinality (maximum cardinality of 1): outer symbol is a perpendicular line.

5.4.1 Notation Summary

To help you recall the notation introduced in previous sections, Table 5.2 presents a summary while Figure 5.24 demonstrates the notation for the university database of Chapter 3. Figure 5.24 differs in some ways from the university database in Chapter 3 to depict most of the Crow's Foot notation. Figure 5.24 contains a generalization hierarchy to depict the similarities among students and faculty. You should note that the primary key of the *Student* and the *Faculty* entity types is *SSN,* an attribute inherited from the *UnivPerson* entity type. The *Enrollment* entity type (associative) and the identifying relationships (*Registers* and *Grants*) could appear as an M-N relationship as previously shown in Figure 5.10. In addition to these issues, Figure 5.24 omits some attributes for brevity.

5.4.2 Diagram Rules

To provide guidance about correct usage of the notation, Table 5.3 presents completeness and consistency rules. You should apply these rules when completing an ERD to ensure that there are no notation errors in your ERD. Thus, the diagram rules serve a purpose similar to syntax rules for a computer language. The absence of syntax errors does not mean that a computer program performs its tasks correctly. Likewise, the absence of

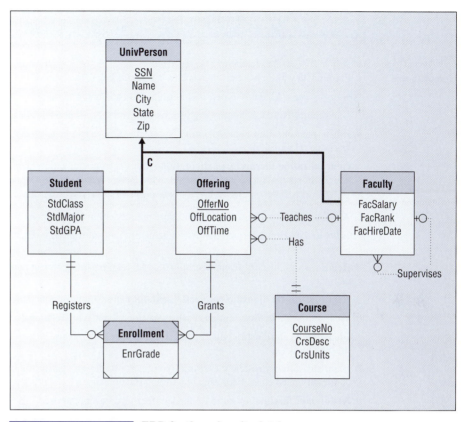

Figure 5.24   ERD for the university database.

notation errors does not mean that an ERD provides an adequate data representation. The diagram rules do *not* ensure that you have considered multiple alternatives, correctly represented user requirements, and properly documented your design. Chapter 6 discusses these issues to enhance your data modeling skills.

Most of the rules in Table 5.3 do not require much elaboration. The first three completeness rules and the first five consistency rules are simple to understand. Even though the rules are simple, you should still check your ERDs for compliance as it is easy to overlook a violation in a moderate-size ERD.

The consistency rules do not require unique relationship names because participating entity types provide a context for relationship names. However, it is good practice to use unique relationship names as much as possible to make relationships easy to distinguish. In addition, two or more relationships involving the same entity types should be unique because the entity types no longer provide a context to distinguish the relationships. Since it is uncommon to have more than one relationship between the same entity types, the consistency rules do not include this provision.

Completeness rules 4 (entity participation rule) and 5 (generalization hierarchy participation rule) require elaboration. Violating these rules is a warning, not necessarily an error. In most ERDs, all entity types not in a generalization hierarchy and all generalization hierarchies are connected to at least one other entity type. In rare situations, an ERD contains an unconnected entity type just to store a list of entities. Rule 5 applies to

TABLE 5.3	Completeness and Consistency Rules

Type of Check	Description
Completeness	1. **Primary key rule:** All entity types have a primary key (direct, borrowed, or inherited).
	2. **Naming rule:** All entity types, relationships, and attributes are named.
	3. **Cardinality rule:** Cardinality is given for both entity types in a relationship.
	4. **Entity participation rule:** All entity types except those in a generalization hierarchy participate in at least one relationship.
	5. **Generalization hierarchy participation rule:** Each generalization hierarchy participates in at least one relationship with an entity type not in the generalization hierarchy.
Consistency	1. **Entity name rule:** Entity type names are unique.
	2. **Attribute name rule:** Attribute names are unique within entity types and relationships.
	3. **Inherited attribute name rule:** Attribute names in a subtype do not match inherited (direct or indirect) attribute names.
	4. **Relationship/entity type connection rule:** All relationships connect two entity types (not necessarily distinct).
	5. **Relationship/relationship connection rule:** Relationships are not connected to other relationships.
	6. **Weak entity rule:** Weak entities have at least one identifying relationship.
	7. **Identifying relationship rule:** For each identifying relationship, at least one participating entity type must be weak.
	8. **Identification dependency cardinality rule:** For each weak entity, the minimum and maximum cardinality must equal 1 for each identifying relationship.
	9. **Redundant foreign key rule:** Redundant foreign keys are not used.

an entire generalization hierarchy, not to each entity type in a generalization hierarchy. In other words, at least one entity type in a generalization hierarchy should be connected to at least one entity type not in the generalization hierarchy. In many generalization hierarchies, multiple entity types participate in relationships. Generalization hierarchies permit subtypes to participate in relationships thus constraining relationship participation. For example in Figure 5.24, *Student* and *Faculty* participate in relationships.

Consistency rules 6 through 9 involve common errors in the ERDs of novice data modelers. Novice data modelers violate consistency rules 6 to 8 because of the complexity of identification dependency. Identification dependency involving a weak entity and identifying relationships provides more sources of errors than other parts of the Crow's Foot notation. In addition, each identifying relationship also requires a minimum and maximum cardinality of 1 that may be overlooked by novice data modelers. Novice data modelers violate consistency rule 9 (redundant foreign key rule) because of confusion between an ERD and the relational data model. The conversion process transforms 1-M relationships into foreign keys.

Example of Rule Violations and Resolutions

Because the identification dependency rules and the redundant foreign key rule are a frequent source of errors to novice designers, this section provides an example to depict rule violations and resolutions. Figure 5.25 demonstrates violations of the identification dependency rules (consistency rules 6 to 9) and the redundant foreign key rule (consistency rule 9) for the university database ERD. The following list explains the violations:

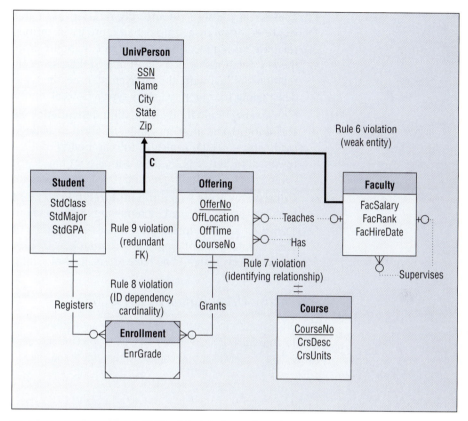

Figure 5.25   ERD with violations of consistency rules 6 to 9.

- **Consistency Rule 6 (weak entity rule) Violation:** *Faculty* cannot be a weak entity without at least one identifying relationship.
- **Consistency Rule 7 (identifying relationship rule) Violation:** The *Has* relationship is identifying but neither *Offering* nor *Course* is a weak entity.
- **Consistency Rule 8 (identification dependency cardinality rule) Violation:** The cardinality of the *Registers* relationship near *Student* should be (1, 1) not (0, Many).
- **Consistency Rule 9 (redundant foreign key rule) Violation:** The *CourseNo* attribute in the *Offering* entity type is redundant with the *Has* relationship. Because *CourseNo* is the primary key of *Course,* it should not be an attribute of *Offering* to link an *Offering* to a *Course.* The *Has* relationship provides the linkage to *Course.*

For most rules, resolving violations is easy. The major task is recognition of the violation. For the identification dependency rules, resolution can depend on the problem details. The following list suggests possible corrective actions for diagram errors:

- **Consistency Rule 6 (weak entity rule) Resolution:** The problem can be resolved either by adding one or more identifying relationships or by changing the weak entity into a regular entity. In Figure 5.25, the problem is resolved by making *Faculty* a regular entity. The more common resolution is to add one or more identifying relationships.

- **Consistency Rule 7 (identifying relationship rule) Resolution:** The problem can be resolved by adding one or more weak entities or making the relationship nonidentifying. In Figure 5.25, the problem is resolved by making the *Has* relationship nonidentifying. If there is more than one identifying relationship involving the same entity type, the typical resolution involves designating the common entity type as a weak entity.
- **Consistency Rule 8 (identification dependency cardinality rule) Resolution:** The problem can be resolved by changing the weak entity's cardinality to (1,1). Typically, the cardinality of the identifying relationship is reversed. In Figure 5.25, the cardinality of the *Registers* relationship should be reversed ((1,1) near *Student* and (0, Many) near *Enrollment*).
- **Consistency Rule 9 (redundant foreign key rule) Resolution:** Normally the problem can be resolved by removing the redundant foreign key. In Figure 5.25, *CourseNo* should be removed as an attribute of *Offering.* In some cases, the attribute may not represent a foreign key. If the attribute does not represent a foreign key, it should be renamed instead of removed.

Alternative Organization of Rules

The organization of rules in Table 5.3 may be difficult to remember. Table 5.4 provides an alternative grouping by rule purpose. If you find this organization more intuitive, you should use it. However you choose to remember the rules, the important point is to ap-

TABLE 5.4	Alternative Rule Organization
Category	*Rules*
Names	All entity types, relationships, and attributes are named. (Completeness rule 2)
	Entity type names are unique. (Consistency rule 1)
	Attribute names are unique within entity types and relationships. (Consistency rule 2)
	Attribute names in a subtype do not match inherited (direct or indirect) attribute names. (Consistency rule 3)
Content	All entity types have a primary key (direct, borrowed, or inherited). (Completeness rule 1)
	Cardinality is given for both entity types in a relationship. (Completeness rule 3)
Connection	All entity types except those in a generalization hierarchy participate in at least one relationship. (Completeness rule 4)
	Each generalization hierarchy participates in at least one relationship with an entity type not in the generalization hierarchy. (Completeness rule 5)
	All relationships connect two entity types. (Consistency rule 4)
	Relationships are not connected to other relationships. (Consistency rule 5)
	Redundant foreign keys are not used. (Consistency rule 9)
Identification Dependency	Weak entities have at least one identifying relationship. (Consistency rule 6)
	For each identifying relationship, at least one participating entity type must be weak. (Consistency rule 7)
	For each weak entity, the minimum and maximum cardinality must equal 1 for each identifying relationship. (Consistency rule 8)

ply them after you have completed an ERD. To help you apply diagram rules, most CASE tools perform checks specific to the notations supported by the tools. The next section describes diagram rule checking by the ER Assistant, the data modeling tool available with this textbook.

Support in the ER Assistant

To improve the productivity of novice data modelers, the ER Assistant supports the consistency and completeness rules listed in Table 5.3. The ER Assistant supports consistency rules 4 and 5 through its diagramming tools. Relationships must be connected to two entity types (not necessarily distinct) prohibiting violations of consistency rules 4 and 5. For the other completeness and consistency rules, the ER Assistant provides the Check Diagram button that generates a report of rule violations. Because the Check Diagram button may be used when an ERD is not complete, the ER Assistant does not require fixing rule violations found in an ERD. Before completing an ERD, you should address each violation noted by the ER Assistant.

For the redundant foreign key rule (consistency rule 9), the ER Assistant uses a simple implementation to determine if an ERD contains a redundant foreign key. The ER Assistant checks the child entity type (entity type on the many side of the relationship) for an attribute with the same name and data type as the primary key in the parent entity type (entity type on the one side of the relationship). If the ER Assistant finds an attribute with the same name and data type, a violation is listed in the Check Diagram report.

CLOSING THOUGHTS

This chapter has explained the notation of entity relationship diagrams as a prerequisite to applying entity relationship diagrams in the database development process. Using the Crow's Foot notation, this chapter described the symbols, important relationship patterns, and generalization hierarchies. The basic symbols are entity types, relationships, attributes, and cardinalities to depict the number of entities participating in a relationship. Four important relationship patterns were described: many-to-many (M-N) relationships with attributes, associative entity types representing M-way relationships, identifying relationships providing primary keys to weak entities, and self-referencing (unary) relationships. Generalization hierarchies allow classification of entity types to depict similarities among entity types.

To help you recall the notation and use the notation correctly, a convenient summary and diagram rules were presented. The diagram rules involve completeness and consistency requirements. The diagram rules ensure that an ERD does not contain obvious errors. To help you apply the rules, the ER Assistant provides a tool to check the rules on completed ERDs.

This chapter emphasized the notation of ERDs to provide a solid foundation for the more difficult study of applying the notation on complex problems. To master data modeling, you need to understand the ERD notation and obtain ample practice building ERDs. Chapter 6 emphasizes the practice of building ERDs for complex problems. Applying the notation involves consistent representation of user requirements, generation of alternative designs, and documentation of design decisions. In addition to these skills, Chapter 6 presents rules to convert an ERD into a table design and background on alternative ERD notations. With careful study, Chapters 5 and 6 provide a solid foundation to perform data modeling on business databases.

REVIEW CONCEPTS

- Basic concepts: entity types, relationships, and attributes.
- Minimum and maximum cardinalities to constrain relationship participation.
- Classification of cardinalities as optional, mandatory, and functional.
- Existence dependency for entities that cannot be stored without storage of related entities.
- Identification dependency involving weak entities and identifying relationships to support entity types that borrow at least part of the primary key.
- M-N relationships with attributes: attributes are associated with the combination of entity types, not just with one of the entity types.
- Equivalence between an M-N relationship and an associative entity type with identifying 1-M relationships.
- Associative entity types to represent M-way relationships among more than two entity types.
- Self-referencing (unary) relationships to represent associations among entities of the same entity type.
- Instance diagrams to help distinguish between 1-M and M-N self-referencing relationships.
- Generalization hierarchies to show similarities among entity types.
- Diagram rules to prevent obvious data modeling errors.
- Common sources of diagram errors: identification dependency and redundant foreign keys.
- Support for the diagram rules in the ER Assistant.

QUESTIONS

1. What is an entity type?

2. What is an attribute?

3. What is a relationship?

4. What is the natural language correspondence for entity types and relationships?

5. What is the difference between an ERD and an instance diagram?

6. What symbols are the ERD counterparts of foreign keys in the Relational Model?

7. What cardinalities indicate functional, optional, and mandatory relationships?

8. When is it important to convert an M-N relationship into 1-M relationships?

9. How can an instance diagram help to determine whether a self-referencing relationship is a 1-M or an M-N relationship?

10. When should an ERD contain weak entities?

11. What is the difference between an existence-dependent and a weak entity type?

12. Why is classification important in business?

13. What is inheritance in generalization hierarchies?

14. What is the purpose of disjointness and completeness constraints for a generalization hierarchy?

15. What symbols are used for cardinality in the Crow's Foot notation?

16. What are the two components of identification dependency?

17. How are M-way relationships represented in the Crow's Foot notation?

18. What is an associative entity type?

19. What is the equivalence between an M-N relationship and 1-M relationships?

20. What does it mean to say that part of a primary key is borrowed?

21. What is the purpose of the diagram rules?

22. What are the limitations of the diagram rules?

23. What consistency rules are commonly violated by novice data modelers?

24. Why do novice data modelers violate the identification dependency rules (consistency rules 6 through 8)?

25. Why do novice data modelers violate consistency rule 9 about redundant foreign keys?

26. Why should a CASE tool support diagram rules?

27. How does the ER Assistant support consistency rules 4 and 5?

28. How does the ER Assistant support all rules except consistency rules 4 and 5?

29. Why does the ER Assistant not require resolution of all diagram errors found in an ERD?

30. How does the ER Assistant implement consistency rule 9 about redundant foreign keys?

PROBLEMS

The problems emphasize correct usage of the Crow's Foot notation and application of the diagram rules. This emphasis is consistent with the pedagogy of the chapter. The more challenging problems in Chapter 6 emphasize user requirements, diagram transformations, design documentation, and schema conversion. To develop a good understanding of data modeling, you should complete the problems in both chapters.

ORDER

1. Draw an ERD containing the *Order* and the *Customer* entity types connected by a 1-M relationship from *Customer* to *Order*. Choose an appropriate relationship name using your common knowledge of interactions between customers and orders. Define minimum cardinalities so that an order is optional for a customer and a customer is mandatory for an order. For the *Customer* entity type, add attributes *CustNo* (primary key), *CustFirstName, CustLastName, CustStreet, CustCity, CustState, CustZip,* and *CustBal* (balance). For the *Order* entity type, add attributes for the *OrdNo* (primary key), *OrdDate, OrdName, OrdStreet, OrdCity, OrdState,* and *OrdZip.* If you are using the ER Assistant or another drawing tool that supports data type specification, choose appropriate data types for the attributes based on your common knowledge.

2. Extend the ERD from problem 1 with the *Employee* entity type and a 1-M relationship from *Employee* to *Order*. Choose an appropriate relationship name using your common knowledge of interactions between employees and orders. Define minimum cardinalities so that an employee is optional to an order and

an order is optional to an employee. For the *Employee* entity type, add attributes *EmpNo* (primary key), *EmpFirstName, EmpLastName, EmpPhone, EmpEmail, EmpCommRate* (commission rate), and *EmpDeptName.* If you are using the ER Assistant or another drawing tool that supports data type specification, choose appropriate data types for the attributes based on your common knowledge.

3. Extend the ERD from problem 2 with a self-referencing 1-M relationship involving the *Employee* entity type. Choose an appropriate relationship name using your common knowledge of organizational relationships among employees. Define minimum cardinalities so that the relationship is optional in both directions.

4. Extend the ERD from problem 3 with the *Product* entity type and an M-N relationship between *Product* and *Order.* Choose an appropriate relationship name using your common knowledge of connections between products and orders. Define minimum cardinalities so that an order is optional to a product, and a product is mandatory to an order. For the *Product* entity type, add attributes *ProdNo* (primary key), *ProdName, ProdQOH, ProdPrice,* and *ProdNextShipDate.* For the M-N relationship, add an attribute for the order quantity. If you are using the ER Assistant or another drawing tool that supports data type specification, choose appropriate data types for the attributes based on your common knowledge.

5. Revise the ERD from problem 4 by transforming the M-N relationship into an associative entity type and two identifying, 1-M relationships.

6. Check your ERDs from problems 4 and 5 for violations of the diagram rules. If you followed the problem directions, your diagrams should not have any errors. Perform the check without using the ER Assistant. Then use the Check Diagram feature of the ER Assistant.

7. Using your corrected ERD from problem 6, add violations of consistency rules 6 to 9. Use the Check Diagram feature of the ER Assistant to identify the errors.

8. Design an ERD for the *Task* entity type and an M-N self-referencing relationship. For the *Task* entity type, add attributes *TaskNo* (primary key), *TaskDesc, TaskEstDuration, TaskStatus, TaskStartTime,* and *TaskEndTime.* Choose an appropriate relationship name using your common knowledge of precedence connections among tasks. Define minimum cardinalities so that the relationship is optional in both directions.

9. Revise the ERD from problem 8 by transforming the M-N relationship into an associative entity type and two identifying, 1-M relationships.

10. Define a generalization hierarchy containing the *Student* entity type, the *UndStudent* entity type, and the *GradStudent* entity type. The *Student* entity type is the supertype and *UndStudent* and *GradStudent* are subtypes. The *Student* entity type has attributes *StdNo* (primary key), *StdName, StdGender, StdDOB* (date of birth), *StdEmail,* and *StdAdmitDate.* The *UndStudent* entity type has attributes *UndMajor, UndMinor,* and *UndClass.* The *GradStudent* entity type has attributes *GradAdvisor, GradThesisTitle,* and *GradAsstStatus* (assistantship status). The generalization hierarchy should be complete and disjoint.

11. Define a generalization hierarchy containing the *Employee* entity type, the *Faculty* entity type, and the *Administrator* entity type. The *Employee* entity type is the supertype and *Faculty* and *Administrator* are subtypes. The *Employee* entity type has attributes *EmpNo* (primary key), *EmpName, EmpGender, EmpDOB* (date of birth), *EmpPhone, EmpEmail,* and *EmpHireDate.* The *Faculty* entity type has attributes *FacRank, FacPayPeriods,* and *FacTenure.* The *Administrator* entity type has attributes *AdmTitle, AdmContractLength,* and *AdmAppointmentDate.* The generalization hierarchy should be complete and overlapping.

12. Combine the generalization hierarchies from problems 10 and 11. The root of the generalization hierarchy is the *UnivPerson* entity type. The primary key of *UnivPerson* is *UnvSSN.* The other attributes in the *UnivPerson* entity type should be the attributes common to *Employee* and *Student.* You should rename the attributes to be consistent with inclusion in the *UnivPerson* entity type. The generalization hierarchy should be complete and disjoint.

13. Draw an ERD containing the *Patient,* the *Physician,* and the *Visit* entity types connected by 1-M relationships from *Patient* to *Visit* and *Physician* to *Visit.* Choose appropriate names for the relationships. Define minimum cardinalities so that patients and physicians are mandatory for a visit, but visits are optional for patients and physicians. For the *Patient* entity type, add attributes *PatNo* (primary key), *PatFirstName, PatLastName, PatStreet, PatCity, PatState, PatZip,* and *PatHealthPlan.* For the *Physician* entity type, add attributes *PhyNo* (primary key), *PhyFirstName, PhyLastName, PhySpecialty, PhyPhone, PhyEmail, PhyHospital,* and *PhyCertification.* For the *Visit* entity type, add attributes for the *VisitNo* (primary key), *VisitDate, VisitPayMethod* (cash, check, or credit card), and *VisitCharge.* If you are using the ER Assistant or another drawing tool that supports data type specification, choose appropriate data types for the attributes based on your common knowledge.

14. Extend the ERD in problem 13 with the *Nurse,* the *Item,* and the *VisitDetail* entity types connected by 1-M relationships from *Visit* to *VisitDetail, Nurse* to *VisitDetail,* and *Item* to *VisitDetail. VisitDetail* is a weak entity with the 1-M relationship from *Visit* to *VisitDetail* an identifying relationship. Choose appropriate names for the relationships. Define minimum cardinalities so that a nurse is optional for a visit detail, an item is mandatory for a visit detail, and visit details are optional for nurses and items. For the *Item* entity type, add attributes *ItemNo* (primary key), *ItemDesc, ItemPrice,* and *ItemType.* For the *Nurse* entity type, add attributes *NurseNo* (primary key), *NurseFirstName, NurseLastName, NurseTitle, NursePhone, NurseSpecialty,* and *NursePayGrade.* For the *VisitDetail* entity type, add attributes for the *DetailNo* (part of the primary key) and *DetailCharge.* If you are using the ER Assistant or another drawing tool that supports data type specification, choose appropriate data types for the attributes based on your common knowledge.

15. Refine the ERD from problem 14 with a generalization hierarchy consisting of *Provider, Physician,* and *Nurse.* The root of the generalization hierarchy is the *Provider* entity type. The primary key of *Provider* is *ProvNo* replacing the attributes *PhyNo* and *NurseNo.* The other attributes in the *Provider* entity type should be the attributes common to *Nurse* and *Physician.* You should rename the attributes to be consistent with inclusion in the *Provider* entity type. The generalization hierarchy should be complete and disjoint.

16. Check your ERD from problem 15 for violations of the diagram rules. If you followed the problem directions, your diagram should not have any errors. Apply the consistency and completeness rules to ensure that your diagram does not have errors. If you are using the ER Assistant, you can use the Check Diagram feature after checking the rules yourself.

17. Using your corrected ERD from problem 16, add violations of consistency rules 3 and 6 to 9. If you are using the ER Assistant, you can use the Check Diagram feature after checking the rules yourself.

18. For each consistency error in Figure 5.P1, identify the consistency rule violated and suggest possible resolutions of the error. The ERD has generic names so that

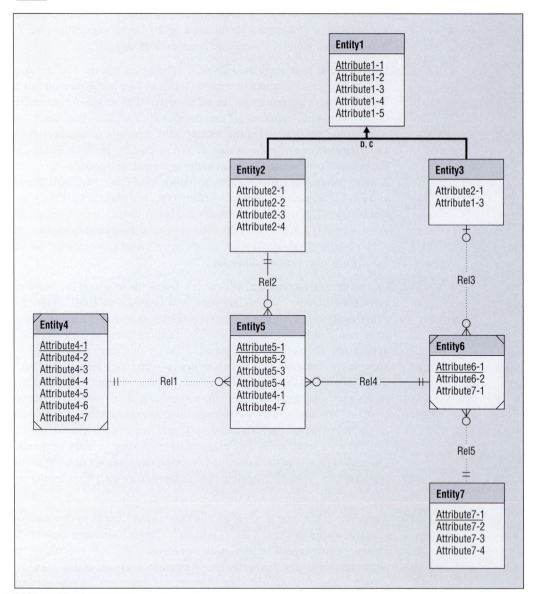

Figure 5.P1   **ERD for problem 18.**

you will concentrate on finding diagram errors rather than focusing on the meaning of the diagram. If you are using the ER Assistant, you can compare your solution to the result using the Check Diagram feature.

19. For each consistency error in Figure 5.P2, identify the consistency rule violated and suggest possible resolutions of the error. The ERD has generic names so that you will concentrate on finding diagram errors rather than focusing on the meaning of the diagram. If you are using the ER Assistant, you can compare your solution to the result using the Check Diagram feature.

20. For each consistency error in Figure 5.P3, identify the consistency rule violated and suggest possible resolutions of the error. The ERD has generic names so that you will concentrate on finding diagram errors rather than focusing on the meaning of the diagram. If you are using the ER Assistant, you can compare your solution to the result using the Check Diagram feature.

Figure 5.P2   **ERD for problem 19.**

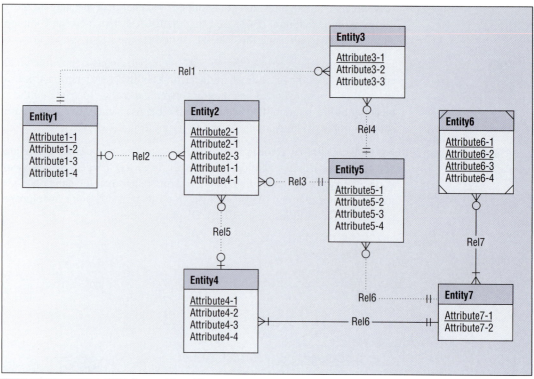

Figure 5.P3   ERD for problem 20.

REFERENCES FOR FURTHER STUDY

Four specialized books on database design are Batini, Ceri, and Navathe (1992); Nijssen and Halpin (1989); Teorey (1999); and Carlis and Maguire (2001). The *DBAZine* site (www.dbazine.com/) and the DevX help site (www.devx.com/gethelp/) also have plenty of practical advice about database development and data modeling.

CHAPTER 6

Developing Data Models for Business Databases

LEARNING OBJECTIVES

This chapter extends your knowledge of data modeling from the notation of entity relationship diagrams (ERDs) to the development of data models for business databases along with rules to convert entity relationship diagrams to relational tables. After this chapter, the student should have acquired the following knowledge and skills:

- Develop ERDs that are consistent with narrative problems.

- Use transformations to generate alternative ERDs.

- Document design decisions implicit in an ERD.

- Analyze an ERD for common design problems.

- Convert an ERD to a table design using conversion rules.

- Appreciate the diversity of notation for ERDs.

OVERVIEW

Chapter 5 explained the Crow's Foot notation for entity relationship diagrams. You learned about diagram symbols, relationship patterns, generalization hierarchies, and rules for consistency and completeness. Understanding the notation is a prerequisite for applying it to represent business databases. This chapter explains the development of data models for business databases using the Crow's Foot notation and rules to convert ERDs to table designs.

To become a good data modeler, you need to understand the notation in entity relationship diagrams and get plenty of practice building diagrams. This chapter provides practice with applying the notation. You will learn to analyze a narrative problem, refine a design through transformations, document important design decisions, and analyze a data model for common design errors. After finalizing an ERD, the diagram should be converted to relational tables so that it can be implemented with a commercial DBMS. This chapter presents rules to convert an entity relationship diagram to a table design. You will learn about the basic rules to convert common parts of a diagram along with specialized rules for less common parts of a diagram.

With this background, you are ready to build ERDs for moderate-size business situations. You should have confidence in your knowledge of the Crow's Foot notation, applying the notation to narrative problems, and converting diagrams to table designs. Because of the plethora of entity relationship notations, you may not have the opportunity to use the Crow's Foot notation exactly as shown in Chapters 5 and 6. To prepare you for understanding other notations, the chapter concludes with a presentation of diagram variations including the Class Diagram notation of the Unified Modeling Notation, one of the popular alternatives to the Crow's Foot notation.

6.1 DEVELOPING AN ERD FOR THE WATER UTILITY DATABASE

After studying the Crow's Foot notation, you are now ready to apply your knowledge. This section presents a small narrative problem and develops an ERD to represent the database needs described in the narrative. The discussion emphasizes strategies for developing an initial design, refining a design through transformations, documenting design decisions, and analyzing a diagram for common design errors.

6.1.1 Database Description

Let us begin with a brief description of a customer database for a municipal water utility. You can assume that this description is the result of an initial investigation with appropriate personnel at the water utility. The database should support recording of water usage and billing for water usage. To support these functions, the database should contain data about customers, rates, water usage, and bills. Other functions such as payment processing and customer service are omitted from this description for brevity. The following list describes the data requirements in more detail.

- Customer data include a unique customer number, a name, a billing address, a type (commercial or residential), an applicable rate, and a collection (one or more) of meters.
- Meter data include a unique meter number, an address, a size, and a model. A meter is associated with one customer at a time.
- An employee periodically reads each meter on a scheduled date. When a meter is read, a meter-reading document is created containing a unique meter reading number, an employee number, a meter number, a time stamp (includes date and time), and a consumption level. When a meter is first placed in service, there are no associated readings for it.

- A rate includes a unique rate code, a description, a fixed dollar amount, a consumption threshold, and a variable amount (dollars per cubic foot). Consumption up to the threshold is billed at the fixed amount. Consumption greater than the threshold is billed at the variable amount. Customers are assigned rates using a number of factors such as customer type, address, and adjustment factors. Many customers can be assigned the same rate. Rates are typically proposed months before approved and associated with customers.

- The water utility bills are based on customers' most recent meter readings and applicable rates. A bill consists of a heading part and a list of detail lines. The heading part contains a customer number, a preparation date, a payment due date, and a date range for the consumption period. Each detail line contains a meter number, a water consumption level, and an amount. The water consumption level is computed by subtracting the consumption levels in the two most recent meter readings. The amount is computed by multiplying the consumption level by the customer's rate.

6.1.2 Initial ERD

Let us begin by identifying potential entity types. Recall that nouns describing people, things, places, and events can represent entity types in an ERD. Prominent nouns in the narrative are customer, meter, bill, reading, and rate. For each of these nouns, the narrative describes associated attributes. Figure 6.1 shows a preliminary ERD with entity types for nouns and associated attributes. Note that collections of things are not attributes. For example, the fact that a customer has a collection of meters will be shown as a relationship, rather than as an attribute of the *Customer* entity type. In addition, references between these entity types will be shown as relationships rather than attributes. For example, the fact that a reading contains a meter number will be recorded as a relationship.

Identifying Primary Keys

Identification of primary keys is an important part of entity type identification. Ideally, primary keys should be stable and single purpose. Stable means that a primary key should never change after it has been assigned to an entity. Single purpose means that a

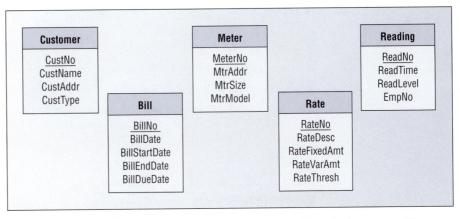

Figure 6.1   Preliminary entity types and attributes in the water utility database.

primary key attribute should have no purpose other than entity identification. Typically, good choices for primary keys are integer values automatically generated by a DBMS. For example, Access has the AutoNumber data type for primary keys and Oracle has the Sequence object for primary keys.

If the requirements indicate the primary key for an entity type, you should ensure that the proposed primary key is stable and single purpose. If the proposed primary key does not meet either criterion, you probably should reject it as a primary key. If the proposed primary key only meets one criterion, you should explore other attributes for the primary key. Sometimes, industry or organizational practices may dictate the choice of a primary key even if the choice is not ideal.

Besides primary keys, you should also identify other unique attributes (candidate keys). For example, an employee's e-mail address is often unique. The integrity of candidate keys may be important for searching and integration with external databases. Depending on the features of the CASE tool (if any) that you are using, you should note that an attribute is unique either in the attribute specification or in the documentation. Uniqueness constraints can be enforced after an ERD is converted to a table design.

Adding Relationships

After identifying entity types and attributes, let us continue by connecting entity types with relationships as shown in Figure 6.2. To reduce the size of the ERD, only the primary keys are shown in Figure 6.2. A good place to start is with parts of the narrative that indicate relationships among entity types. The following list explains the derivation of relationships from the narrative.

- For the *Assigned* relationship, the narrative states that a customer has a rate, and many customers can be assigned the same rate. These two statements indicate a 1-M relationship from *Rate* to *Customer*. For the minimum cardinalities, the narrative indicates that a rate is required for a customer, and that rates are proposed before being associated with customers.

- For the *Uses* relationship, the narrative states that a customer includes a collection of meters and a meter is associated with one customer at a time. These two statements indicate a 1-M relationship from *Customer* to *Meter*. For

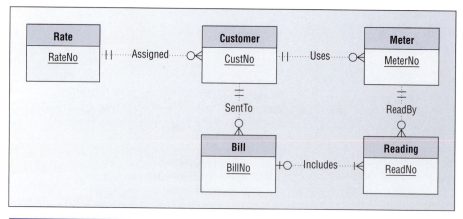

Figure 6.2   **Entity types connected by relationships.**

the minimum cardinalities, the narrative indicates that a customer must have at least one meter. The narrative does not indicate the minimum cardinality for a meter so either 0 or 1 can be chosen. The documentation should note this incompleteness in the specifications.

- For the *ReadBy* relationship, the narrative states that a meter reading contains a meter number, and meters are periodically read. These two statements indicate a 1-M relationship from *Meter* to *Reading*. For the minimum cardinalities, the narrative indicates that a meter is required for a reading, and a new meter does not have any associated readings.

- For the *SentTo* relationship, the narrative indicates that the heading part of a bill contains a customer number and bills are periodically sent to customers. These two statements indicate a 1-M relationship from *Customer* to *Bill*. For the minimum cardinalities, the narrative indicates that a customer is required for a bill, and a customer does not have an associated bill until the customer's meters are read.

The *Includes* relationship between the *Bill* and the *Reading* entity types is subtle. The *Includes* relationship is 1-M because a bill may involve a collection of readings (one on each detail line), and a reading relates to one bill. The consumption level and the amount on a detail line are calculated values. The *Includes* relationship connects a bill to its most recent meter readings, thus supporting the consumption and the amount calculations. These values can be stored if it is more efficient to store them rather than compute them when needed. If the values are stored, attributes can be added to the *Includes* relationship or the *Reading* entity type.

6.1.3 Refinements to the Initial ERD

Data modeling is usually an iterative or repetitive process. You construct a preliminary data model and then refine it many times. In refining a data model, you should generate feasible alternatives and evaluate them according to user requirements. You typically need to gather additional information from users to evaluate alternatives. This process of refinement and evaluation may continue many times for large databases. To depict the iterative nature of data modeling, this section describes some possible refinements to the initial ERD design.

Transforming Attributes into Entity Types

A common refinement is to transform an <u>attribute into an entity type.</u> When the database should contain more than just the identifier of an entity, this transformation is useful. This transformation involves the addition of an entity type and a 1-M relationship. In the water utility ERD, the *Reading* entity type contains the *EmpNo* attribute. If other data about an employee are needed, *EmpNo* can be expanded into an entity type and 1-M relationship as shown in Figure 6.3.

Splitting Compound Attributes

Another common refinement is to split <u>compound attributes into smaller attributes.</u> A compound attribute contains multiple kinds of data. For example, the *Customer* entity type has an address attribute containing data about a customer's street, city, state, and

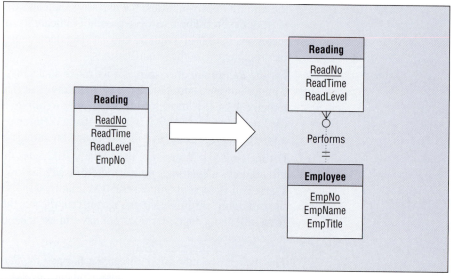

Figure 6.3   **Transformation of an attribute into an entity type.**

Figure 6.4   **Split of *CustAddr* attribute into component attributes.**

postal code. Splitting compound attributes can facilitate search of the embedded data. Splitting the address attribute as shown in Figure 6.4 supports searches by street, city, state, and postal code.

Expanding Entity Types

A third transformation is to make an <u>entity type into two entity types and a relationship.</u> This transformation can be useful to record a finer level of detail about an entity. For example, rates in the water utility database apply to all levels of consumption beyond a fixed level. It can be useful to have a more complex rate structure in which the variable amount depends on the consumption level. Figure 6.5 shows a transformation to the

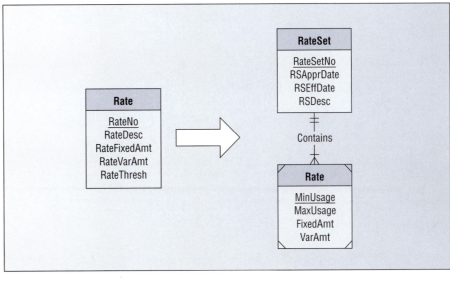

Figure 6.5   **Transformation of an entity type into two entity types and a relationship.**

Rate entity type to support a more complex rate structure. The *RateSet* entity type represents a set of rates approved by the utility's governing commission. The primary key of the *Rate* entity type borrows from the *RateSet* entity type. Identification dependency is not required when transforming an entity type into two entity types and a relationship. In this situation, identification dependency is useful, but in other situations, it may not be appropriate.

Transforming a Weak Entity into a Strong Entity

A fourth transformation is to make a <u>weak entity into a strong entity and change the associated identifying relationships into nonidentifying relationships.</u> This transformation can be useful to make it easier to reference an entity type after conversion to a table design. After conversion, a reference to a weak entity will involve a combined foreign key with more than one column. This transformation is most useful for associative entity types, especially associative entity types representing M-way relationships.

Figure 6.6 depicts the transformation of the weak entity *Rate* to a strong entity. The transformation involves changing the weak entity to a strong entity and changing each identifying relationship to a nonidentifying relationship. In addition, it may be necessary to add a new attribute to serve as the primary key. In Figure 6.6, the new attribute *RateNo* is the primary key as *MinUsage* does not uniquely identify rates.

Adding History

A fifth transformation is to add historical details to a data model. Historical details may be necessary for legal requirements as well as strategic reporting requirements. This transformation can be applied to attributes and relationships. When applied to attributes, the transformation is similar to the attribute to entity type transformation. For example, to maintain a history of employee titles, the *EmpTitle* attribute is replaced with an entity

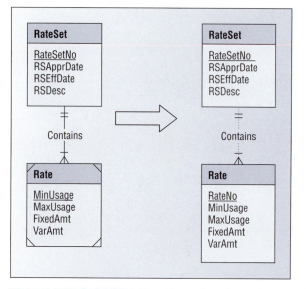

Figure 6.6   Transformation of a weak entity into a strong entity.

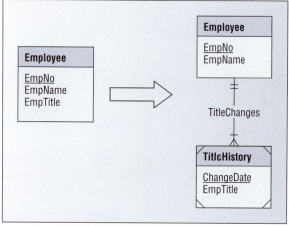

Figure 6.7   Adding history to the *EmpTitle* attribute.

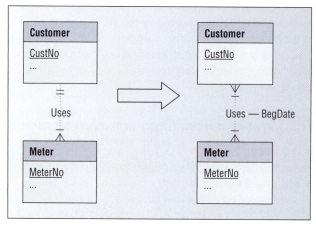

Figure 6.8   Adding history to a 1-M relationship.

type and a 1-M relationship. The new entity type typically contains a date attribute as part of its primary key and borrows from the original entity type for the remaining part of its primary key, as shown in Figure 6.7.

When applied to a relationship, this transformation typically involves changing a 1-M relationship into an M-N relationship with an attribute. Figure 6.8 depicts the transformation of the 1-M *Uses* relationship into an M-N relationship with a date attribute to record meter usage history. When applied to an M-N relationship, this transformation involves the conversion of the M-N relationship into an associative entity type along with the addition of a change date attribute that becomes part of the primary key of the associative entity type.

Figure 6.9   Generalization hierarchy transformation for water utility customers.

The transformations shown here support an unlimited history. For limited history, a number of attributes can be added. For example, to maintain a history of the current and the most recent employee titles, two attributes (*CurrEmpTitle* and *PrevEmpTitle*) can be used. To record the change dates for employee titles, one date attribute per title attribute can be added.

Adding Generalization Hierarchies

A sixth transformation is to make an <u>entity type into a generalization hierarchy.</u> This transformation should be used sparingly because the generalization hierarchy is a specialized modeling tool. If there are multiple attributes that do not apply to all entities and there is an accepted classification of entities, a generalization hierarchy may be useful. For example, water utility customers can be classified as commercial or residential. The attributes specific to commercial customers (*TaxPayerID* and *EnterpriseZone*) do not apply to residential customers and vice-versa. In Figure 6.9, the attributes specific to commercial and residential customers have been moved to the subtypes. An additional benefit of this transformation is the avoidance of null values. For example, entities in the *Commercial* and the *Residential* entity types will not have null values. Some entities in the original *Customer* entity type would have had null values. Residential customers would have had null values for *TaxPayerID* and *EnterpriseZone.*

This transformation also can be applied to a collection of entity types. In this situation, the transformation involves the addition of a supertype and a generalization hierarchy. In addition, the common attributes in the collection of entity types are moved to the supertype.

Summary of Transformations

When designing a database, you should carefully explore alternative designs. The transformations discussed in this section can help you consider alternative designs. The possible transformations are not limited to those discussed in this section. You can reverse most of these transformations. For example, you can eliminate a generalization hierarchy if the

TABLE 6.1	Summary of Transformations		
Transformation	*Details*		*When to Use*
Attribute to entity type	Replace attribute with an entity type and a 1-M relationship.		Add detail about an entity.
Split a compound attribute	Replace an attribute with a collection of attributes.		Standardize the data in an attribute.
Expand entity type	Add a new entity type and a 1-M relationship.		Add a finer level of detail about an entity.
Weak entity to strong entity	Remove identification dependency symbols and possibly add a primary key.		Remove combined foreign keys after conversion to tables.
Add history	For attribute history, replace an attribute with an entity type and a 1-M relationship. For relationship history, change relationship cardinality to M-N with an attribute.		Add detail for legal requirements or strategic reporting.
Add generalization hierarchy	Starting from a supertype: add subtypes, a generalization hierarchy, and redistribute attributes to subtypes. Starting from subtypes: add a supertype, a generalization hierarchy, and redistribute common attributes and relationships to the supertype.		Accepted classification of entities; specialized attributes and relationships for the subtypes.

subtypes do not have unique attributes. For additional transformations, you should check the references at the end of this chapter for specialized books on database design. To help you recall the transformations shown in this section, Table 6.1 presents a summary.

6.1.4 Documenting an ERD

Design Documentation include justification for design decisions involving multiple feasible choices and explanations of subtle design choices. Do not use documentation just to repeat the information already contained in an ERD. You also should provide a description for each attribute especially where an attribute's name does not indicate its purpose. As an ERD is developed, you should document incompleteness and inconsistency in the requirements.

Documentation plays an important role in resolving questions about a specification and in communicating the design to others. In the process of revising an ERD, you should carefully document inconsistency and incompleteness in a specification. A large specification typically contains many points of inconsistency and incompleteness. Recording each point allows systematic resolution through additional requirements-gathering activities.

As an example of inconsistency, the water utility requirements would be inconsistent if one part indicated that a meter is associated with one customer, but another part stated that a meter can be associated with multiple customers. In resolving an inconsistency, a user may indicate that the inconsistency is an exception. In this example, a user can indicate the circumstances in which a meter can be associated with multiple customers. The designer must decide on the resolution in the ERD such as permitting multiple customers for a meter, allowing a second responsible customer, or prohibiting more than one customer. The designer should carefully document the resolution of each inconsistency, including a justification for the chosen solution.

As an incompleteness example, the narrative does not specify the minimum cardinality for a meter in the *Uses* relationship of Figure 6.2. The designer should gather additional requirements to resolve the incomplete specification. Incomplete parts of a specification are common for relationships as complete specification involves two sets of cardinalities. It is easy to omit a cardinality in an initial specification.

Besides identifying problems in a specification, documentation should be used to communicate a design to others. Databases can have a long lifetime owing to the economics of information systems. An information system can undergo a long cycle of repair and enhancement before there is sufficient justification to redesign the system. Good documentation enhances an ERD by communicating the justification for impor-

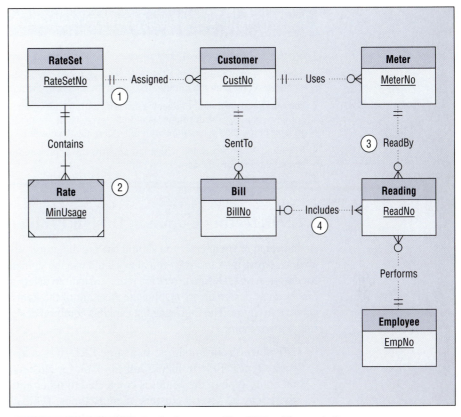

Figure 6.10 Revised water utility ERD with annotations.

tant design decisions. Your documentation should not repeat the constraints in an ERD. For example, you do not need to document that a customer can use many meters as the ERD contains this information.

You should document decisions in which there is more than one feasible choice. For example, you should carefully document alternative designs for rates (a single consumption level versus multiple consumption levels) as depicted in Figure 6.5. You should document your decision by recording who recommended the alternative and why. Although all transformations presented in the previous section can lead to feasible choices, you should focus on the transformations most relevant to the specification.

You also should document decisions that might be unclear to others even if there are no feasible alternatives. For example, the minimum cardinality of 0 from the *Reading* entity type to the *Bill* entity type might be unclear. You should document the need for this cardinality because of the time difference between the creation of a bill and its associated readings. A meter may be read days before an associated bill is created.

Design documentation should be incorporated into your ERD. If you are using an ERD tool that has a data dictionary, you should include design justifications in the data dictionary. The ER Assistant supports design justifications as well as comments associated with each item on a diagram. You can use the comments to describe the meaning of attributes. If you are not using a tool that supports documentation, you can list the justifications on a separate page and annotate your ERD as shown in Figure 6.10. The circled numbers in Figure 6.10 refer to explanations in Table 6.2. Note that some of the refinements shown previously were not used in the revised ERD.

TABLE 6.2	List of Design Justifications for the Revised ERD

1. A rate set is a collection of rates approved by the governing commission of the utility.

2. Rates are similar to lines on a tax table. An individual rate is identified by the rate set identifier along with the minimum consumption level of the rate.

3. The minimum cardinality indicates that a meter must always be associated with a customer. For new property, the developer is initially responsible for the meter. If a customer forecloses on a property, the financial institution holding the deed will be responsible.

4. A reading is not associated with a bill until the bill is prepared. A reading may be created several days before the associated bill.

6.1.5 Detecting Common Design Problems

As indicated in Chapter 5, you should use the diagram rules to ensure that there are no obvious errors in your ERD. You also should use the guidelines in this section to check for design errors. Design errors are more difficult to detect and resolve than diagram errors because design errors involve the meaning of the items on a diagram, not just a diagram's structure. The following list explains common design problems, while Table 6.3 summarizes them.

- **Misplaced relationships:** In a large ERD, it is easy to connect the wrong entity types. To help focus, you can look for clusters of entity types in which an entity type in the center is connected to other entity types. In a large ERD, there may be several clusters of entity types. Typically, entity type clusters involve important documents such as orders, purchases, and shipments. In the water utility database, the *Reading* entity type is the center of a cluster of entity types involving *Meter, Employee,* and *Bill.*

- **Incorrect cardinalities:** The typical error involves the usage of a 1-M relationship instead of an M-N relationship. This error can be caused by an omission in the requirements. For example, if the requirements just indicate that work assignments involve a collection of employees, you should not assume that an employee can be related to just one work assignment. You should gather additional requirements to determine if an employee can be associated with multiple work assignments. Other incorrect cardinality problems that you should consider are reversed cardinalities (1-M relationship should be in the opposite direction) and errors on a minimum cardinality.

- **Missing relationships:** If the requirements do not directly indicate a relationship, you should consider indirect implications to detect whether a relationship is required. For example, the requirements for the water utility database do not indicate directly the need for a relationship from *Bill* to *Reading.* However, careful consideration of the consumption calculation reveals the need for a relationship. The *Includes* relationship connects a bill to its most recent meter readings, thus supporting the consumption calculation.

- **Overuse of specialized data modeling tools:** Generalization hierarchies and M-way relationships are specialized data modeling tools. A typical novice mistake is to use them inappropriately. You should not use generalization hierarchies just because an entity can exist in multiple states. For example, the requirement that a project task can be not started, in process, or complete does not indicate the need for a generalization

TABLE 6.3	Summary of Design Errors	
Design Error	*Description*	*Resolution*
Misplaced relationship	Wrong entity types connected.	Use entity type clusters to reason about connections.
Incorrect cardinality	Typically using a 1-M relationship instead of an M-N relationship.	Incomplete requirements: inferences beyond the requirements.
Missing relationship	Entity types should be connected directly.	Examine implications of requirements.
Overuse of specialized data modeling tools	Generalization hierarchies and M-way relationships are not common. A typical novice mistake is to use them inappropriately.	For a generalization hierarchy, ensure that subtypes have specialized attributes and relationships. For an M-way relationship, ensure that the database records combinations of three or more entities.
Redundant relationship	Relationship derived from other relationships	Examine relationship cycles to see if a relationship can be derived from other relationships.

hierarchy. But if there is an established classification and there are specialized attributes and relationships for subtypes, a generalization hierarchy is an appropriate tool.

An associative entity type representing an M-way relationship should be used when the database is to record combinations of three (or more) objects rather than just combinations of two objects. In most cases, only combinations of two objects should be recorded. For example, if a database needs to record the skills provided by an employee and the skills required by a project, binary relationships should be used. If a database needs to record the skills provided by employees for specific projects, an M-way relationship is needed. Note that the former situation with binary relationships is more common than the latter situation with an M-way relationship.

- **Redundant relationships:** Cycles in an ERD may indicate redundant relationships. A cycle involves a collection of relationships arranged in a loop starting and ending with the same entity type. For example in Figure 6.10, there is a cycle of relationships connecting *Customer, Bill, Reading,* and *Meter.* In a cycle, a relationship is redundant if it can be derived from other relationships. For the *SentTo* relationship, the bills associated with a customer can be derived from the relationships *Uses, ReadBy,* and *Includes.* In the opposite direction, the customer associated with a bill can be derived from the *Includes, ReadBy,* and *Uses* relationships. Although a bill can be associated with a collection of readings, each associated reading must be associated with the same customer. Because the *SentTo* relationship can be derived, it is removed in the final ERD (see Figure 6.11).

  Another imaginable example of a redundant relationship (this relationship does not exist in the ERD) is the relationship between *Meter* and *Bill.* The meters associated with a bill can be derived using the *Includes* and the *ReadBy* relationships. Note that using clusters of entity types such as *Reading* in the center connected to *Meter, Employee,* and *Bill* avoids redundant relationships.

  You should take care when removing redundant relationships, as removing a necessary relationship is a more serious error than retaining a redundant relationship. When in doubt, you should retain the relationship.

Figure 6.11   **Final water utility ERD**

6.2 CONVERTING AN ERD TO RELATIONAL TABLES

Conversion from the ERD notation to relational tables is important because of industry practice. Computer-aided software engineering (CASE) tools support varying notations for ERDs. It is common practice to use a CASE tool as an aid in developing an ERD. Because most commercial DBMSs use the Relational Model, you must convert an ERD to relational tables to implement your database design.

This section describes the conversion process in two parts. First, the basic rules to convert entity types, relationships, and attributes are described. Second, specialized rules to convert optional 1-M relationships, generalization hierarchies, and 1-1 relationships are shown. All CREATE TABLE statements in this section conform to the SQL:1999 syntax.

6.2.1 Basic Conversion Rules

The rules that follow convert everything on an ERD except generalization hierarchies. You should apply these rules until everything in your ERD is converted. Use the first two rules before the other rules. As you apply these rules, you can use a check mark to indicate what parts of your ERD have been converted.

1. **Entity Type Rule:** Each entity type (except subtypes) becomes a table. The primary key of the entity type (if not weak) becomes the primary key of the table. The attributes of the entity type become columns in the table. This rule should be used first before the relationship rules.
2. **1-M Relationship Rule:** Each 1-M relationship becomes a foreign key in the table corresponding to the child entity type (the entity type near the Crow's Foot symbol). If the minimum cardinality is one, the foreign key cannot accept null values.

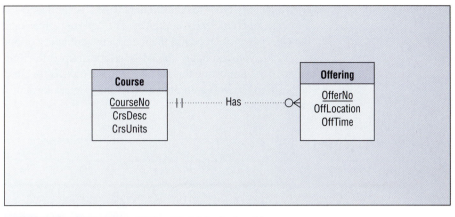

Figure 6.12   ERD with 1-M relationship.

```
CREATE TABLE Course
(    CourseNo   CHAR(6)      NOT NULL,
     CrsDesc    VARCHAR(30),
     CrsUnits   SMALLINT,
CONSTRAINT PKCourse PRIMARY KEY (CourseNo)   )

CREATE TABLE Offering
(    OfferNo         INTEGER         NOT NULL,
     OffLocation     CHAR(20),
     CourseNo        CHAR(6)         NOT NULL,
     OffTime         TIMESTAMP,
     . . .
CONSTRAINT PKOffering PRIMARY KEY (OfferNo),
CONSTRAINT FKCourseNo FOREIGN KEY (CourseNo) REFERENCES Course    )
```

Figure 6.13   Conversion of Figure 6.12 (SQL:1999 Syntax).

3. **M-N Relationship Rule:** Each M-N relationship becomes a separate table. The primary key of the table is a combined key consisting of the primary keys of the entity types participating in the M-N relationship.

4. **Identification Dependency Rule:** Each identifying relationship (denoted by a solid relationship line) adds a component to a primary key. The primary key of the table corresponding to the weak entity consists of (i) the underlined local key (if any) in the weak entity and (ii) the primary key(s) of the entity type(s) connected by the identifying relationship(s).

To understand these rules, you can apply them to some of the ERDs given previously in the chapter. Using Rules 1 and 2, you can convert Figure 6.12 into the CREATE TABLE statements shown in Figure 6.13. Rule 1 is applied to convert the *Course* and

Offering entity types to tables. Then, Rule 2 is applied to convert the *Has* relationship to a foreign key (*Offering.CourseNo*). The *Offering* table contains the foreign key because the *Offering* entity type has the maximum cardinality of one.

Next, you can apply the M-N relationship rule (Rule 3) to convert the ERD in Figure 6.14. Following this rule leads to the *Enrolls_In* table in Figure 6.15. The primary key of *Enrolls_In* is a combination of the primary keys of the *Student* and the *Offering* entity types.

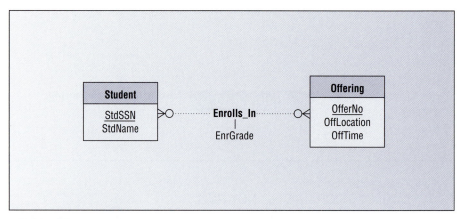

Figure 6.14   **M-N relationship with an attribute.**

```
CREATE TABLE Student
(     StdSSN                  CHAR(11)      NOT NULL,
      StdName                 VARCHAR(30),
      . . .
CONSTRAINT PKStudent PRIMARY KEY (StdSSN) )

CREATE TABLE Offering
(     OfferNo                 INTEGER       NOT NULL,
      OffLocation             VARCHAR(30),
      OffTime                 TIMESTAMP,
      . . .
CONSTRAINT PKOffering PRIMARY KEY (OfferNo) )

CREATE TABLE Enrolls_In
(     OfferNo                 INTEGER       NOT NULL,
      StdSSN                  CHAR(11)      NOT NULL,
      EnrGrade                DECIMAL(2,1),
CONSTRAINT PKEnrolls_In PRIMARY KEY (OfferNo, StdSSN),
CONSTRAINT FKOfferNo FOREIGN KEY (OfferNo) REFERENCES Offering,
CONSTRAINT FKStdSSN FOREIGN KEY (StdSSN) REFERENCES Student   )
```

Figure 6.15   **Conversion of Figure 6.14 (SQL:1999 Syntax).**

To gain practice with the identification dependency rule (Rule 4), you can use it to convert the ERD in Figure 6.16. The result of converting Figure 6.16 is identical to Figure 6.15 except that the *Enrolls_In* table is renamed *Enrollment.* The ERD in Figure 6.16 requires two applications of the identification dependency rule. Each application of the identification dependency rule adds a component to the primary key of the *Enrollment* table.

You can also apply the rules to convert self-referencing relationships. For example, you can apply the 1-M and M-N relationship rules to convert the self-referencing relationships in Figure 6.17. Using the 1-M relationship rule, the *Supervises* relationship converts to a foreign key in the *Faculty* table, as shown in Figure 6.18. Using the M-N relationship rule, the *Prereq_To* relationship converts to the *Prereq_To* table with a combined primary key of the course number of the prerequisite course and the course number of the dependent course.

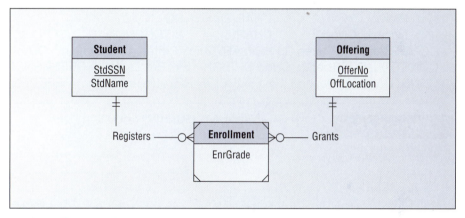

Figure 6.16 *Enrolls_in* **M-N relationship transformed into 1-M relationships.**

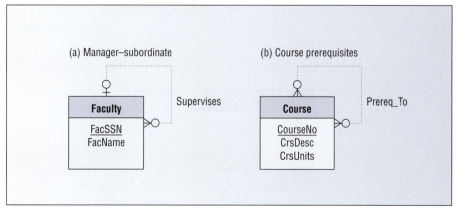

Figure 6.17 Examples of 1-M and M-N self-referencing relationships.

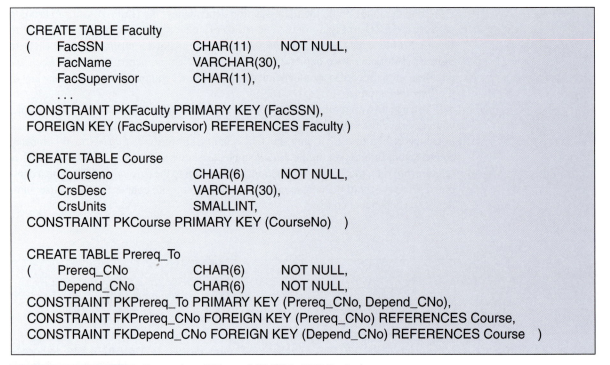

```
CREATE TABLE Faculty
(     FacSSN                CHAR(11)        NOT NULL,
      FacName               VARCHAR(30),
      FacSupervisor         CHAR(11),
      . . .
CONSTRAINT PKFaculty PRIMARY KEY (FacSSN),
FOREIGN KEY (FacSupervisor) REFERENCES Faculty )

CREATE TABLE Course
(     Courseno              CHAR(6)         NOT NULL,
      CrsDesc               VARCHAR(30),
      CrsUnits              SMALLINT,
CONSTRAINT PKCourse PRIMARY KEY (CourseNo)   )

CREATE TABLE Prereq_To
(     Prereq_CNo            CHAR(6)         NOT NULL,
      Depend_CNo            CHAR(6)         NOT NULL,
CONSTRAINT PKPrereq_To PRIMARY KEY (Prereq_CNo, Depend_CNo),
CONSTRAINT FKPrereq_CNo FOREIGN KEY (Prereq_CNo) REFERENCES Course,
CONSTRAINT FKDepend_CNo FOREIGN KEY (Depend_CNo) REFERENCES Course   )
```

Figure 6.18   Conversion of Figure 6.17 (SQL:1999 Syntax).

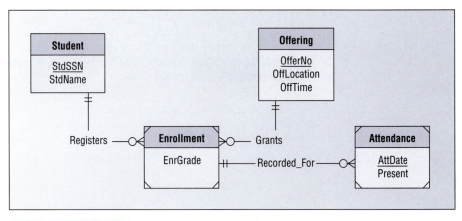

Figure 6.19   ERD with two weak entity types.

You also can apply conversion rules to more complex identification dependencies as depicted in Figure 6.19. The first part of the conversion is identical to the conversion of Figure 6.16. Application of the 1-M rule makes the combination of *StdSSN* and *OfferNo* foreign keys in the *Attendance* table (Figure 6.20). Note that the foreign keys in *Attendance* refer to *Enrollment,* not to *Student* and *Offering.* Finally, one application of the identification dependency rule makes the combination of *StdSSN, OfferNo,* and *Att-Date* the primary key of the *Attendance* table.

```
CREATE TABLE Attendance
(     OfferNo                    INTEGER       NOT NULL,
      StdSSN                     CHAR(11)      NOT NULL,
      AttDate                    DATE     NOT NULL,
      Present                    BOOLEAN,
CONSTRAINT PKAttendance PRIMARY KEY (OfferNo, StdSSN, AttDate),
CONSTRAINT FKOfferNoStdSSN FOREIGN KEY (OfferNo, StdSSN)
   REFERENCES Enrollment   )
```

Figure 6.20   Conversion of the *Attendance* entity type in Figure 6.19 (SQL:1999 Syntax).

Figure 6.21   Optional 1-M relationship.

The conversion in Figure 6.20 depicts a situation in which the transformation of a weak to a strong entity may apply (Section 6.1.3). In the conversion, the *Attendance* table contains a combined foreign key (*OfferNo, StdSSN*). Changing *Enrollment* into a strong entity will eliminate the combined foreign key in the *Attendance* table.

6.2.2 Converting Optional 1-M Relationships

When you use the 1-M relationship rule for optional relationships, the resulting foreign key contains null values. Recall that a relationship with a minimum cardinality of 0 is optional. For example, the *Teaches* relationship (Figure 6.21) is optional to *Offering* because an *Offering* entity can be stored without being related to a *Faculty* entity. Converting Figure 6.21 results in two tables (*Faculty* and *Offering*) as well as a foreign key (*FacSSN*) in the *Offering* table. The foreign key should allow null values because the minimum cardinality of the *Offering* entity type in the relationship is optional (0). However, null values can lead to complications in evaluating the results of queries.

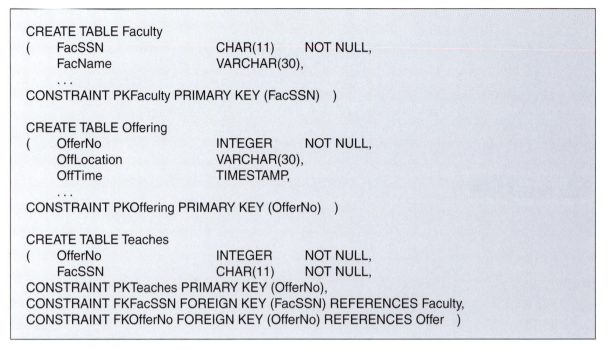

```
CREATE TABLE Faculty
(     FacSSN                    CHAR(11)        NOT NULL,
      FacName                   VARCHAR(30),
      . . .
CONSTRAINT PKFaculty PRIMARY KEY (FacSSN)   )

CREATE TABLE Offering
(     OfferNo                   INTEGER         NOT NULL,
      OffLocation               VARCHAR(30),
      OffTime                   TIMESTAMP,
      . . .
CONSTRAINT PKOffering PRIMARY KEY (OfferNo)   )

CREATE TABLE Teaches
(     OfferNo                   INTEGER         NOT NULL,
      FacSSN                    CHAR(11)        NOT NULL,
CONSTRAINT PKTeaches PRIMARY KEY (OfferNo),
CONSTRAINT FKFacSSN FOREIGN KEY (FacSSN) REFERENCES Faculty,
CONSTRAINT FKOfferNo FOREIGN KEY (OfferNo) REFERENCES Offer   )
```

Figure 6.22   **Conversion of Figure 6.21 (SQL:1999 Syntax).**

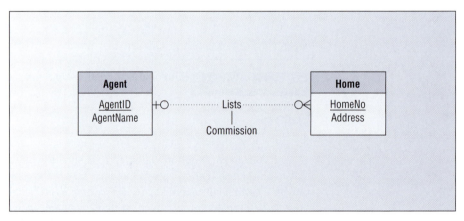

Figure 6.23   **Optional 1-M relationship with an attribute.**

To avoid null values when converting an optional 1-M relationship, you can apply Rule 5 to convert an optional 1-M relationship into a table instead of a foreign key. Figure 6.22 shows an application of Rule 5 to the ERD in Figure 6.21. The *Teaches* table contains the foreign keys *OfferNo* and *FacSSN* with null values not allowed for both columns. In addition, the *Offering* table no longer has a foreign key referring to the *Faculty* table. Figures 6.23 and 6.24 depict an example of converting an optional 1-M relationship with an attribute. Note that the *Lists* table contains the *Commission* column.

```
CREATE TABLE Agent
(    AgentId              CHAR(10)         NOT NULL,
     AgentName            VARCHAR(30),
     . . .
CONSTRAINT PKAgent PRIMARY KEY (AgentId)   )

CREATE TABLE Home
(    HomeNo               INTEGER          NOT NULL,
     HomeAddress          VARCHAR(50),

     . . .
CONSTRAINT PKHome PRIMARY KEY (HomeNo)   )

CREATE TABLE Lists
(    HomeNo               INTEGER          NOT NULL,
     AgentId              CHAR(10)         NOT NULL,
     Commission           DECIMAL(10,2),
CONSTRAINT PKLists PRIMARY KEY (HomeNo),
CONSTRAINT FKAgentId FOREIGN KEY (AgentId) REFERENCES Agent,
CONSTRAINT FKHomeNo FOREIGN KEY (HomeNo) REFERENCES Home    )
```

Figure 6.24   **Conversion of Figure 6.23 (SQL:1999 Syntax).**

5. **Optional 1-M Relationship Rule:** Each 1-M relationship with a minimum cardinality of 0 and a maximum cardinality of 1 becomes a new table. The primary key of the new table is the primary key of the entity type on the child (many) side of the relationship. The new table contains foreign keys for the primary keys of both entity types participating in the relationship. Both foreign keys in the new table do not permit null values. The new table also contains the attributes of the optional 1-M relationship.

Rule 5 is controversial. Using Rule 5 in place of Rule 2 (1-M Relationship Rule) avoids null values in foreign keys. However, the use of Rule 5 results in more tables. Query formulation can be more difficult with additional tables. In addition, query execution can be slower due to extra joins. The choice of using Rule 5 in place of Rule 2 depends on the importance of avoiding null values versus avoiding extra tables. In many databases, avoiding extra tables may be more important than avoiding null values.

6.2.3 Converting Generalization Hierarchies

The approach to convert generalization hierarchies mimics the entity relationship notation as much as possible. Rule 6 converts each entity type of a generalization hierarchy into a table. The only column appearing in a table that is different from the ERD is the inherited primary key. In Figure 6.25, *EmpNo* is a column in the *SalaryEmp* and *HourlyEmp* tables because it is the primary key of the parent entity type (*Employee*). In addition, the *SalaryEmp* and *HourlyEmp* tables have a foreign key constraint referring to the *Employee* table. The CASCADE delete option is set in both foreign key constraints (see Figure 6.26).

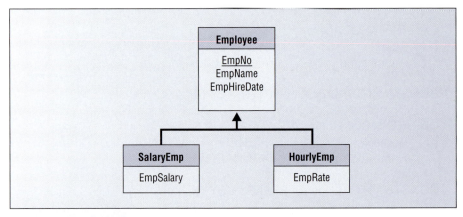

Figure 6.25 Generalization hierarchy for employees.

```
CREATE TABLE Employee
(    EmpNo                INTEGER      NOT NULL,
     EmpName              VARCHAR(30),
     EmpHireDate          DATE,
CONSTRAINT PKEmployee PRIMARY KEY (EmpNo)   )

CREATE TABLE SalaryEmp
(    EmpNo                INTEGER      NOT NULL,
     EmpSalary            DECIMAL(10,2),
CONSTRAINT PKSalaryEmp PRIMARY KEY (EmpNo),
CONSTRAINT FKSalaryEmp FOREIGN KEY (EmpNo) REFERENCES Employee
  ON DELETE CASCADE )

CREATE TABLE HourlyEmp
(    EmpNo                INTEGER      NOT NULL,
     EmpRate              DECIMAL(10,2),
CONSTRAINT PKHourlyEmp PRIMARY KEY (EmpNo),
CONSTRAINT FKHourlyEmp FOREIGN KEY (EmpNo) REFERENCES Employee
  ON DELETE CASCADE )
```

Figure 6.26 Conversion of the generalization hierarchy in Figure 6.25 (SQL:1999 Syntax).

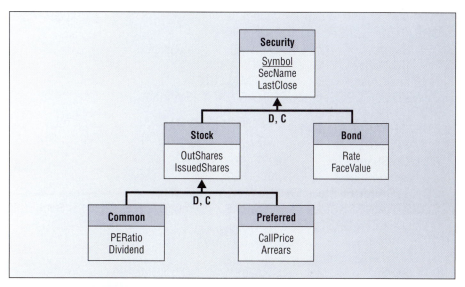

Figure 6.27   Multiple levels of generalization hierarchies.

6. **Generalization Hierarchy Rule:** Each entity type of a generalization hierarchy becomes a table. The columns of a table are the attributes of the corresponding entity type plus the primary key of the parent entity type. For each table representing a subtype, define a foreign key constraint that references the table corresponding to the parent entity type. Use the CASCADE option for deletions of referenced rows.

Rule 6 also applies to generalization hierarchies of more than one level. To convert the generalization hierarchy of Figure 6.27, five tables are produced (see Figure 6.28). In each table, the primary key of the parent (*Security*) is included. In addition, foreign key constraints are added in each table corresponding to a subtype.

Because the Relational Model does not directly support generalization hierarchies, there are several other ways to convert generalization hierarchies. The other approaches vary depending on the number of tables and the placement of inherited columns. Rule 6 may result in extra joins to gather all data about an entity, but there are no null values and only small amounts of duplicate data. For example, to collect all data about a common stock, you should join the *Common, Stock,* and *Security* tables. Other conversion approaches may require fewer joins, but result in more redundant data and null values. The references at the end of this chapter discuss the pros and cons of several approaches to convert generalization hierarchies.

You also should note that generalization hierarchies are directly supported in SQL:1999, the emerging standard for Object Relational databases presented in Chapter 18. Using SQL:1999 avoids loss of semantic information when converting generalization hierarchies.

```
CREATE TABLE Security
(      Symbol                CHAR(6)        NOT NULL,
       SecName               VARCHAR(30),
       LastClose             DECIMAL(10,2),
CONSTRAINT PKSecurity PRIMARY KEY (Symbol)   )


CREATE TABLE Stock
(      Symbol                CHAR(6)        NOT NULL,
       OutShares             INTEGER,
       IssuedShares          INTEGER,
CONSTRAINT PKStock PRIMARY KEY (Symbol),
CONSTRAINT FKStock FOREIGN KEY (Symbol) REFERENCES Security
   ON DELETE CASCADE   )


CREATE TABLE Bond
(      Symbol                CHAR(6)        NOT NULL,
       Rate                  DECIMAL(12,4),
       FaceValue             DECIMAL(10,2),
CONSTRAINT PKBond PRIMARY KEY (Symbol),
CONSTRAINT FKBond FOREIGN KEY (Symbol) REFERENCES Security
   ON DELETE CASCADE   )


CREATE TABLE Common
(      Symbol                CHAR(6)        NOT NULL,
       PERatio               DECIMAL(12,4),
       Dividend              DECIMAL(10,2),
CONSTRAINT PKCommon PRIMARY KEY (Symbol),
CONSTRAINT FKCommon FOREIGN KEY (Symbol) REFERENCES Stock
   ON DELETE CASCADE   )


CREATE TABLE Preferred
(      Symbol                CHAR(6)        NOT NULL,
       CallPrice             DECIMAL(12,2),
       Arrears               DECIMAL(10,2),
CONSTRAINT PKPreferred PRIMARY KEY (Symbol),
CONSTRAINT FKPreferred FOREIGN KEY (Symbol) REFERENCES Stock
   ON DELETE CASCADE   )
```

Figure 6.28 Conversion of the generalization hierarchy in Figure 6.27 (SQL:1999 Syntax).

6.2.4 Converting 1-1 Relationships

Outside of generalization hierarchies, 1-1 relationships are not common. They can occur when entities with separate identifiers are closely related. For example, Figure 6.29 shows the *Employee* and *Office* entity types connected by a 1-1 relationship. Separate entity types seem intuitive, but a 1-1 relationship connects the entity types. Rule 7 con-

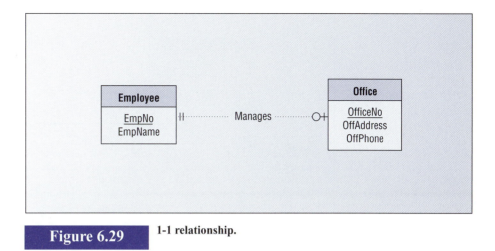

Figure 6.29   1-1 relationship.

```
CREATE TABLE Employee
(    EmpNo          INTEGER      NOT NULL,
     EmpName        VARCHAR(30),
CONSTRAINT PKEmployee PRIMARY KEY (EmpNo)   )

CREATE TABLE Office
(    OfficeNo       INTEGER      NOT NULL,
     OffAddress     VARCHAR(30),
     OffPhone       CHAR(10),
     EmpNo          INTEGER,
CONSTRAINT PKOffice PRIMARY KEY (OfficeNo),
CONSTRAINT FKEmpNo FOREIGN KEY (EmpNo) REFERENCES Employee,
CONSTRAINT EmpNoUnique UNIQUE (EmpNo)   )
```

Figure 6.30   Conversion of the 1-1 relationship in Figure 6.29 (SQL:1999 Syntax).

verts 1–1 relationships into two foreign keys unless many null values will result. In Figure 6.29, most employees will not manage offices. Thus, the conversion in Figure 6.30 eliminates the foreign key (*OfficeNo*) in the employee table.

7. **1-1 Relationship Rule:** The 1-1 relationship is converted into two foreign keys. If the relationship is optional with respect to one of the entity types, the corresponding foreign key may be dropped to eliminate null values.

6.2.5 Comprehensive Conversion Example

This section presents a larger example to integrate your knowledge of the conversion rules. Figure 6.31 shows an ERD similar to the final ERD for the water utility problem discussed in Section 6.1. For brevity, some attributes have been omitted. Figure 6.32 shows the relational tables derived through the conversion rules. Table 6.4 lists the conversion rules used along with brief explanations.

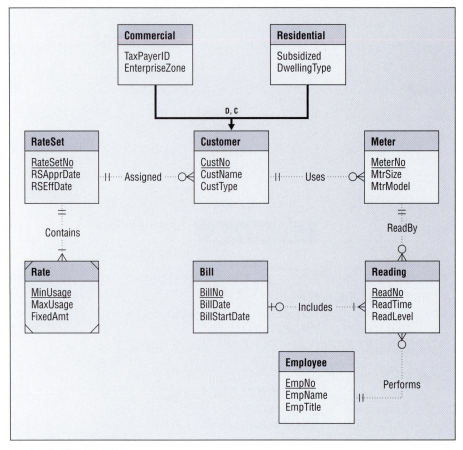

Figure 6.31   Water utility ERD with a generalization hierarchy.

```
CREATE TABLE Customer
(    CustNo              INTEGER        NOT NULL,
     CustName            VARCHAR(30),
     CustType            CHAR(6),
     RateSetNo           INTEGER        NOT NULL,
CONSTRAINT PKCustomer PRIMARY KEY (CustNo),
CONSTRAINT FKRateSetNo FOREIGN KEY (RateSetNo) REFERENCES RateSet   )

CREATE TABLE Commercial
(    CustNo              INTEGER        NOT NULL,
     TaxPayerID          CHAR(20)       NOT NULL,
     EnterpiseZone       BOOLEAN,
CONSTRAINT PKCommercial PRIMARY KEY (CustNo),
CONSTRAINT FKCommercial FOREIGN KEY (CustNo) REFERENCES Customer
  ON DELETE CASCADE   )
```

Figure 6.32   Conversion of the ERD in Figure 6.31 (SQL:1999 Syntax).

```
CREATE TABLE Residential
(    CustNo                INTEGER        NOT NULL,
     Subsidized            BOOLEAN,
     DwellingType          CHAR(6),
CONSTRAINT PKResidential PRIMARY KEY (CustNo),
CONSTRAINT FKResidential FOREIGN KEY (CustNo) REFERENCES Customer
   ON DELETE CASCADE   )


CREATE TABLE RateSet
(    RateSetNo             INTEGER        NOT NULL,
     RSApprDate            DATE,
     RSEffDate             DATE,
CONSTRAINT PKRateSet PRIMARY KEY (RateSetNo)   )


CREATE TABLE Rate
(    RateSetNo             INTEGER        NOT NULL,
     MinUsage              INTEGER,
     MaxUsage              INTEGER,
     FixedAmt              DECIMAL(10,2),
CONSTRAINT PKRate PRIMARY KEY (RateSetNo, MinUsage),
CONSTRAINT FKRateSetNo2 FOREIGN KEY(RateSetNo) REFERENCES RateSet   )


CREATE TABLE Meter
(    MeterNo               INTEGER        NOT NULL,
     MtrSize               INTEGER,
     MtrModel              CHAR(6),
     CustNo                INTEGER        NOT NULL,
CONSTRAINT PKMeter PRIMARY KEY (MeterNo),
CONSTRAINT FKCustNo FOREIGN KEY (CustNo) REFERENCES Customer   )


CREATE TABLE Reading
(    ReadNo                INTEGER        NOT NULL,
     ReadTime              TIMESTAMP,
     ReadLevel             INTEGER,
     MeterNo               INTEGER        NOT NULL,
     EmpNo                 INTEGER        NOT NULL,
     BillNo                INTEGER,
CONSTRAINT PKReading PRIMARY KEY (ReadNo),
CONSTRAINT FKEmpNo FOREIGN KEY (EmpNo) REFERENCES Employee,
CONSTRAINT FKMeterNo FOREIGN KEY (MeterNo) REFERENCES Meter,
CONSTRAINT FKBillNo FOREIGN KEY (BillNo) RERERENCES Bill   )


CREATE TABLE Bill
(    BillNo                INTEGER        NOT NULL,
     BillDate              DATE,
     BillStartDate         DATE,
CONSTRAINT PKBill PRIMARY KEY (BillNo)   )


CREATE TABLE Employee
(    EmpNo                 INTEGER        NOT NULL,
     EmpName               VARCHAR(50),
     EmpTitle              VARCHAR(20),
CONSTRAINT PKEmployee PRIMARY KEY (EmpNo)   )
```

Figure 6.32   Concluded.

TABLE 6.4	Conversion Rules Used for Figure 6.31

Rule	How Used
1	All entity types except subtypes converted to tables with primary keys.
2	1-M relationships converted to foreign keys: *Contains* relationship to *Rate.RateSetNo; Uses* relationship to *Meter.CustNo; ReadBy* relationship to *Reading.MeterNo; Includes* relationship to *Reading.BillNo; Performs* relationship to *Reading.EmpNo; Assigned* relationship to *Customer.RateSetNo.*
3	Not used because there are no M-N relationships.
4	Primary key of *Rate* table is a combination of *RateSetNo* and *MinUsage.*
5	Not used although it could have been used for the *Includes* relationship.
6	Subtypes (*Commercial* and *Residential*) converted to tables. Primary key of customer is added to the *Commercial* and *Residential* tables. Foreign key constraints with CASCADE delete options added to tables corresponding to the subtypes.

6.3 COMPARISON TO OTHER NOTATIONS

The ERD notation presented in this chapter is similar but not identical to what you may encounter later. There is no standard notation for ERDs. There are perhaps six reasonably popular ERD notations, each having its own small variations that appear in practice. The notation in this chapter comes from the Crow's Foot stencil in Visio Professional 5 with the addition of the generalization notation. The notations that you encounter in practice will depend on factors such as the data modeling tool (if any) used in your organization and the industry. One thing is certain: you should be prepared to adapt to the notation in use. This section describes ERD variations that you may encounter as well as the Class Diagram notation of the Unified Modeling Language (UML), an emerging standard for data modeling.

6.3.1 ERD Variations

Because there is no widely accepted ERD standard, different symbols can be used to represent the same concept. Relationship cardinalities are a source of wide variation. You should pay attention to the placement of the cardinality symbols. The notation in this chapter places the symbols close to the "far" entity type, while other notations place the cardinality symbols close to the "near" entity type. The notation in this chapter uses a visual representation of cardinalities with the minimum and maximum cardinalities given by three symbols. Other notations use a text representation with letters and integers instead of symbols. For example, Figure 6.33 shows a Chen ERD with the position of cardinalities reversed, cardinalities depicted with text, and relationships denoted by diamonds.

Other symbol variations are visual representations for certain kinds of entity types. In some notations, weak entities and M-N relationships have special representations. Weak entities are sometimes enclosed in double rectangles. Identifying relationships are sometimes enclosed in double diamonds. M-N relationships with attributes are sometimes shown as a rectangle with a diamond inside denoting the dual qualities (both relationship and entity type).

In addition to symbol variations, there are also rule variations, as shown in the following list. For each restriction there is a remedy. For example, if only binary relationships are supported, M-way relationships must be represented as an associative entity type with 1-M relationships.

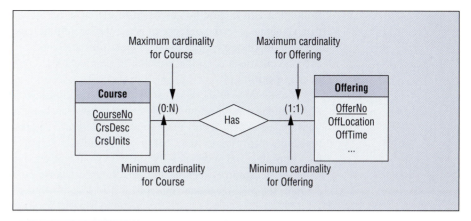

Figure 6.33   Chen notation for the course-offering ERD.

1. Some notations do not support M-way relationships.
2. Some notations do not support M-N relationships.
3. Some notations do not support relationships with attributes.
4. Some notations do not support self-referencing (unary) relationships.
5. Some notations permit relationships to be connected to other relationships.
6. Some notations show foreign keys as attributes.
7. Some notations allow attributes to have more than one value (multivalued attributes).

Relational database diagrams in Microsoft Access have most of these restrictions. Relational database diagrams do not support M-way relationships and M-N relationships. Despite these restrictions, relational database diagrams are no less expressive than notations without these restrictions. In certain situations, you may need additional symbols, but the same concept can be represented. For example, relational database diagrams may require more symbols to represent an M-N relationship, but an M-N relationship can still be represented.

6.3.2 Class Diagram Notation of the Unified Modeling Language

The Unified Modeling Language has become the standard notation for object-oriented modeling. Object-oriented modeling emphasizes objects rather than processes, as emphasized in traditional systems development approaches. In object-oriented modeling, one defines the objects first, followed by the features (attributes and operations) of the objects, and then the dynamic interaction among objects. The UML contains class diagrams, interface diagrams, and interaction diagrams to support object-oriented modeling. The class diagram notation provides an alternative to the ERD notations presented in this chapter.

Class diagrams contain classes (collections of objects), associations (binary relationships) among classes, and object features (attributes and operations). Figure 6.34 shows a simple class diagram containing the *Offering* and *Faculty* classes. The diagram was drawn with the UML template in Visio Professional. The association in Figure 6.34 represents a 1-M relationship. The UML supports role names and cardinalities (minimum and maximum) for each direction in an association. The 0..1 cardinality means that an offering object can be related to a minimum of zero faculty objects and a maximum of one faculty object. Operations are listed below the attributes. Each operation contains a parenthesized list of parameters along with the data type returned by the operation.

Associations in the UML are similar to relationships in the Crow's Foot notation. Associations can represent binary or unary relationships. To represent an M-way relationship, a class and a collection of associations are required. To represent an M-N relationship with attributes, the UML provides the association class to allow associations to have attributes and operations. Figure 6.35 shows an association class that represents an M-N relationship between the *Student* and the *Offering* classes. The association class contains the relationship attributes.

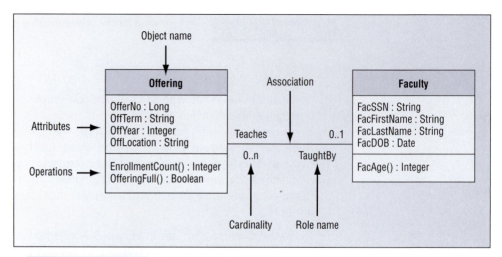

Figure 6.34 Simple class diagram.

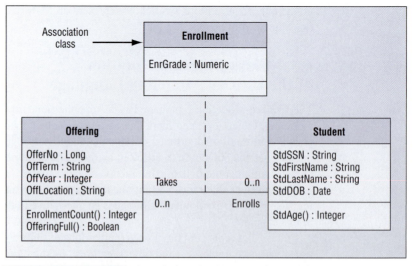

Figure 6.35 Association class representing an M-N relationship with attributes.

Unlike most ERD notations, support for generalization was built into the UML from its inception. In most ERD notations, generalization was added as an additional feature after a notation was well established. In Figure 6.36, the large empty arrow denotes a classification of the *Student* class into *Undergraduate* and *Graduate* classes. The UML supports generalization names and constraints. In Figure 6.36, the *Status* generalization is complete, meaning that every student must be an undergraduate or a graduate student.

The UML also provides a special symbol for composition relationships, similar to identification dependencies in ERD notations. In a composition relationship, the objects in a child class belong only to objects in the parent class. In Figure 6.37, each *OrdLine* object belongs to one *Order* object. Deletion of a parent object causes deletion of the related child objects. As a consequence, the child objects usually borrow part of their primary key from the parent object. However, the UML does not require this identification dependency.

UML class diagrams provide many other features not presented in this brief overview. The UML supports different kinds of classes to integrate programming language concerns with data modeling concerns. Other kinds of classes include value

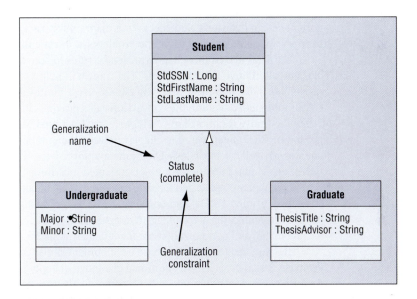

Figure 6.36 Class diagram with a generalization relationship.

Figure 6.37 Class diagram with a composition relationship.

classes, stereotype classes, parameterized classes, and abstract classes. For generalization, the UML supports additional constraints such as static and dynamic classification and different interpretations of generalization relationships (subtype and subclass). For data integrity, the UML supports the specification of constraints in a class diagram.

You should note that class diagrams are just one part of the UML. To some extent, class diagrams must be understood in the context of object-oriented modeling and the entire UML. You should expect to devote an entire academic term to understanding object-oriented modeling and the UML.

CLOSING THOUGHTS

This chapter has described the practice of data modeling, building on your understanding of the Crow's Foot notation presented in Chapter 5. To master data modeling, you need to understand the notation used in entity relationship diagrams (ERDs) and get plenty of practice building ERDs. To help you apply your knowledge of the ERD notation, a practice problem was presented. This chapter described how to derive an initial ERD for a narrative problem, refine the ERD through transformations, document important design decisions, and check your diagram for design errors. You are encouraged to apply this same process using the problems at the end of the chapter.

The remainder of this chapter presented rules to convert an ERD into relational tables and alternative ERD notations. The rules will help you convert modest-size ERDs into tables. For large problems, you should use a good CASE tool. Even if you use a CASE tool, understanding the conversion rules provides insight into the differences between the Entity Relationship Model and the Relational Model. To broaden your background of ERD notations, this chapter presented common variations that you may encounter as well as the Class Diagram notation of the Unified Modeling Language (UML), a standard notation for object-oriented modeling.

This chapter emphasized the data modeling skills of constructing ERDs for narrative problems, refining ERDs, and converting ERDs into relational tables. The next chapter presents normalization, a technique to remove redundancy from relational tables. Together, data modeling and normalization are fundamental skills for database development.

After you master these database development skills, you are ready to apply them to database design projects. An additional challenge of applying your skills is requirements definition. It is a lot of work to collect requirements from users with diverse interests and backgrounds. You may spend as much time gathering requirements as performing data modeling and normalization. With careful study and practice, you will find database development to be a challenging but highly rewarding activity.

REVIEW CONCEPTS

- Identifying entity types and attributes in a narrative.
- Criteria for primary keys: stable and single purpose.
- Identifying relationships in a narrative.
- Transformations to add detail to an ERD: attribute to entity type, expanding an entity type, adding history.
- Splitting an attribute to standardize information content.
- Changing a weak entity to a strong entity to remove combined foreign keys after conversion.
- Adding a generalization hierarchy to avoid null values.

- Documentation practices for important design decisions: justification for design decisions involving multiple feasible choices and explanations of subtle design choices.
- Poor documentation practices: just repeating the information already contained in an ERD.
- Common design errors: misplaced relationships, missing relationships, incorrect cardinalities, overuse of generalization hierarchies, and redundant relationships.
- Basic rules to convert entity types and relationships.
- Specialized conversion rules to convert optional 1-M relationships, generalization hierarchies, and 1-1 relationships.
- ERD variations: symbols and diagram rules.
- Class Diagram notation of the Unified Modeling Language as an alternative to the Entity Relationship Model.

QUESTIONS

1. What does it mean to say that constructing an ERD is an iterative process?
2. Why decompose a compound attribute into smaller attributes?
3. When is it appropriate to transform an attribute into an entity type?
4. Why transform an entity type into two entity types and a relationship?
5. Why transform a weak entity to a strong entity?
6. Why transform an entity type into a generalization hierarchy?
7. Why add history to an attribute or relationship?
8. What data model changes are involved in transforming an attribute to an entity type?
9. What data model changes are involved in splitting a compound attribute?
10. What data model changes are involved in expanding an entity type?
11. What data model changes are involved in transforming a weak entity to a strong entity?
12. What data model changes are involved in adding history to an attribute or a relationship?
13. What data model changes are involved in adding a generalization hierarchy?
14. What should you document about an ERD?
15. What should you omit in ERD documentation?
16. Why are design errors more difficult to detect and resolve than diagram errors?
17. What is a misplaced relationship and how is it resolved?
18. What is an incorrect cardinality and how is it resolved?
19. What is a missing relationship and how is it resolved?
20. What is overuse of a generalization hierarchy and how is it resolved?

21. What is a relationship cycle?

22. What is a redundant relationship and how is it resolved?

23. How is an M-N relationship converted to the Relational Model?

24. How is a 1-M relationship converted to the Relational Model?

25. What is the difference between the 1-M relationship rule and the optional 1-M relationship rule?

26. How is a weak entity type converted to the Relational Model?

27. How is a generalization hierarchy converted to the Relational Model?

28. How is a 1-1 relationship converted to the Relational Model?

29. List some symbol differences in ERD notation that you may experience in your career.

30. List some diagram rule differences in ERD notation that you may experience in your career.

31. What is the Unified Modeling Language (UML)?

32. What are the modeling elements in a UML class diagram?

33. What are the criteria for choosing a primary key?

34. What should you do if a proposed primary key does not meet the criteria?

PROBLEMS

The problems are divided between data modeling problems and conversion problems. Additional conversion problems are found in Chapter 7, where conversion is followed by normalization. In addition to the problems presented here, the case study in Chapter 13 provides practice on a larger problem.

Data Modeling Problems

1. Define an ERD for the following narrative. The database should track homes and owners. A home has a unique home identifier, a street address, a city, a state, a zip, a number of bedrooms, a number of bathrooms, and square feet. A home is either owner occupied or rented. An owner has a social security number, a name, an optional spouse name, a profession, and an optional spouse profession. An owner can possess one or more homes. Each home has only one owner.

2. Refine the ERD from problem 1 by adding an agent entity type. Agents represent owners in the sale of a home. An agent can list many homes, but only one agent can list a home. An agent has a unique agent identifier, a name, an office identifier, and a phone number. When an owner agrees to list a home with an agent, a commission (percentage of the sales price) and a selling price are determined.

3. In the ERD from problem 2, transform the attribute, office identifier, into an entity type. Data about an office include the phone number, the manager name, and the address.

4. In the ERD from problem 3, add a buyer entity type. A buyer entity type has a social security number, a name, a phone, preferences for the number of bedrooms and bathrooms, and a price range. An agent can work with many buyers, but a buyer works with only one agent.

5. Refine the ERD from problem 4 with a generalization hierarchy to depict similarities between buyers and owners.

6. Revise the ERD from problem 5 by adding an offer entity type. A buyer makes an offer on a home for a specified sales price. The offer starts on the submission date and time and expires on the specified date and time. A unique offer number identifies an offer. A buyer can submit multiple offers for the same home.

7. Construct an ERD to represent accounts in a database for personal financial software. The software supports checking accounts, credit cards, and two kinds of investments (mutual funds and stocks). No other kinds of accounts are supported, and every account must fall into one of these account types. For each kind of account, the software provides a separate data entry screen. The following list describes the fields on the data entry screens for each kind of account:
    *   For all accounts, the software requires the unique account identifier, the account name, date established, and the balance.
    *   For checking accounts, the software supports attributes for the bank name, the bank address, the checking account number, and the routing number.
    *   For credit cards, the software supports attributes for the credit card number, the expiration date, and the credit card limit.
    *   For stocks, the software supports attributes for the stock symbol, the stock type (common or preferred), the last dividend amount, the last dividend date, the exchange, the last closing price, and the number of shares (a whole number).
    *   For mutual funds, the software supports attributes for the mutual fund symbol, the share balance (a real number), the fund type (stock, bond, or mixed), the last closing price, the region (domestic, international, or global), and the tax-exempt status (yes or no).

8. Construct an ERD to represent categories in a database for personal financial software. A category has a unique category identifier, a name, a type (expense, asset, liability, or revenue), and a balance. Categories are organized hierarchically so that a category can have a parent category and one or more subcategories. For example, the category "household" can have subcategories for "cleaning" and "maintenance." A category can have any number of levels of subcategories. Make an instance diagram to depict the relationships among categories.

9. Design an ERD for parts and relationships among parts. A part has a unique identifier, a name, and a color. A part can have multiple subparts and multiple parts that use it. The quantity of each subpart should be recorded. Make an instance diagram to depict relationships among parts.

10. Design an ERD to represent a credit card statement. The statement has two parts: a heading containing the unique statement number, the account number of the credit card holder, and the statement date; and a detail section containing a list of zero or more transactions for which the balance is due. Each detail line contains a line number, a transaction date, a merchant name, and the amount of the transaction. The line number is unique within a statement.

11. Modify your ERD from problem 10. Everything is the same except that each detail line contains a unique transaction number in place of the line number. Transaction numbers are unique across statements.

12. Using the ERD in Figure 6.P1, transform the *ProvNo* attribute into an entity type (*Provider*) and a 1-M relationship (*Treats*). A provider has a unique provider number, a first name, a last name, a phone, a specialty, a hospital name in which the provider practices, an e-mail address, a certification, a pay grade, and a title. A provider is required for a visit. New providers do not have associated visits.

| Figure 6.P1 | ERD for Problem 12. |

13. In the result for problem 12, expand the *Visit* entity type to record details about a visit. A visit detail includes a detail number, a detail charge, an optional provider number, and an item number. The combination of the visit number and visit detail number is unique for a visit detail. An item includes a unique item number, an item description, an item price, and an item type. An item can be related to multiple visits. New items may not be related to any visit details. A provider can be related to multiple visit details. Some providers may not be associated with any visit details.

14. In the result for problem 13, add a generalization hierarchy to distinguish between nurse and physician providers. A nurse has a pay grade and a title. A physician has a residence hospital, e-mail address, and a certification. The other attributes of provider apply to both physicians and nurses. A visit involves a physician provider while a visit detail may involve a nurse provider.

15. In the result for problem 14, transform *VisitDetail* into a strong entity with *VisitDetailNo* as the primary key.

16. In the result for problem 15, add a history of item prices. Your solution should support the current price along with the two most recent prices. Include change dates for each item price.

17. In the result for problem 15, add a history of item prices. Your solution should support an unlimited number of prices and change dates.

18. Design an ERD with entity types for projects, specialties, and contractors. Add relationships and/or entity types as indicated in the following description. Each contractor has exactly one specialty, but many contractors can provide the same specialty. A contractor can provide the same specialty on multiple projects. A project can use many specialties, and a specialty can be used on many projects. Each combination of project and specialty should have at least two contractors.

19. For the following problem, define an ERD for the initial requirements and then revise the ERD for the new requirements. Your solution should have an initial ERD, a revised ERD, and a list of design decisions for each ERD. In performing the problem, you may want to follow the approach presented in Section 6.1.

    The database supports the placement office of a leading graduate school of business. The primary purpose of the database is to schedule interviews and facilitate searches by students and companies. Consider the following requirements in your initial ERD:

    - Student data include a unique student identifier, a name, a phone number, an e-mail address, a web address, a major, a minor, and a GPA.
    - The placement office maintains a standard list of positions based on the Labor Department's list of occupations. Position data include a unique position identifier and a position description.
    - Company data include a unique company identifier, a company name, and a list of positions and interviewers. Each company must map its positions into the position list maintained by the placement office. For each available position, the company lists the cities in which positions are available.
    - Interviewer data include a unique interviewer identifier, a name, a phone, an e-mail address, and a web address. Each interviewer works for one company.
    - An interview includes a unique interview identifier, a date, a time, a location (building and room), an interviewer, and a student.

    After reviewing your initial design, the placement office decides to revise the requirements. Make a separate ERD to show your refinements. Refine your original ERD to support the following new requirements:

    - Allow companies to use their own language to describe positions. The placement office will not maintain a list of standard positions.
    - Allow companies to reserve blocks of interview time. The interview blocks will not specify times for individual interviews. Rather a company will request a block of X hours during a specified week. Companies reserve interview blocks before the placement office schedules individual interviews. Thus, the placement office needs to store interviews as well as interview blocks.
    - Allow students to submit bids for interview blocks. Students receive a set amount of bid dollars that they can allocate among bids. The bid mechanism is a pseudo–market approach to allocating interviews, a scarce resource. A bid contains a unique bid identifier, a bid amount, and a company. A student can submit many bids and an interview block can receive many bids.

20. For the following problem, define an ERD for the initial requirements and then revise the ERD for the new requirements. Your solution should have an initial ERD, a revised ERD, and a list of design decisions for each ERD. In performing the problem, you may want to follow the approach presented in Section 6.1.

    Design a database for managing the task assignments on a work order. A work order records the set of tasks requested by a customer at a specified location.

    - A customer has a unique customer identifier, a name, and a billing address (street, city, state, zip).
    - A work order has a unique work order number, creation date, date required, a completion date, an optional supervising employee, a work address (street, city, state, zip), and a set of tasks.

- Each task has a unique task identifier, a task name, an hourly rate, and estimated hours. Tasks are standardized across work orders so that the same task can be performed on many work orders.
- Each task on a work order has a status (not started, in progress, or completed), actual hours, and a completion date. The completion date is not entered until the status changes to complete.

After reviewing your initial design, the company decides to revise the requirements. Make a separate ERD to show your refinements. Refine your original ERD to support the following new requirements:

- The company wants to maintain a list of materials. The data about materials include a unique material identifier, a name, and an estimated cost.
- Each work order also has a collection of material requirements. A material requirement includes a material, an estimated quantity of the material, and the actual quantity of the material used.
- The estimated number of hours for a task depends on the work order and task, not on the task alone. Each task of a work order includes an estimated number of hours.

21. For the following problem, define an ERD for the initial requirements and then revise the ERD for the new requirements. Your solution should have an initial ERD, a revised ERD, and a list of design decisions for each ERD. In performing the problem, you may want to follow the approach presented in Section 6.1.

Design a database to assist physical plant personnel in managing assignments of keys to employees. The primary purpose of the database is to ensure proper accounting for all keys.

- An employee has a unique employee number, a name, a position, and an optional office number.
- A building has a unique building number, a name, and a location within the campus.
- A room has a room number, a size (physical dimensions), a capacity, a number of entrances, and a description of equipment in the room. Because each room is located in exactly one building, the identification of a room depends on the identification of a building.
- Key types (also known as master keys) are designed to open one or more rooms. A room may have one or more key types that open it. A key type has a unique key type number, a date designed, and the employee authorizing the key type. A key type must be authorized before it is created.
- A copy of a key type is known as a key. Keys are assigned to employees. Each key is assigned to exactly one employee, but an employee can hold multiple keys. The key type number plus a copy number uniquely identify a key. The date the copy was made should be recorded in the database.

After reviewing your initial design, the physical plant supervisor decides to revise the requirements. Make a separate ERD to show your refinements. Refine your original ERD to support the following new requirements:

- The physical plant needs to know not only the current holder of a key but the past holders of a key. For past key holders, the date range that a key was held should be recorded.

- The physical plant needs to know the current status of each key: in use by an employee, in storage, or reported lost. If lost, the date reported lost should be stored.

22. Define an ERD that supports the generation of product explosion diagrams, assembly instructions, and parts lists. These documents are typically included in hardware products sold to the public. Your ERD should represent the final products as well as the parts comprising final products. The following points provide more details about the documents.

    - Your ERD should support the generation of product explosion diagrams as shown in Figure 6.P2 for a wheelbarrow with a hardwood handle. Your ERD should store the containment relationships along with the quantities required for each subpart. For line drawings and geometric position specifications, you can assume that image and position data types are available to store attribute values.

    - Your ERD should support the generation of assembly instructions. Each product can have a set of ordered steps for instruction. Table 6.P1 shows some of the assembly instructions for a wheelbarrow. The numbers in the instructions refer to the parts diagram.

    - Your ERD should support the generation of a parts list for each product. Table 6.P2 shows the parts list for the wheelbarrow.

Figure 6.P2   **Product explosion diagram.**

TABLE 6.P1	Sample Assembly Instructions for the Wheelbarrow

Step	Instructions
1	Assembly requires a few hand tools, screwdriver, box, or open wrench to fit the nuts.
2	Do NOT wrench-tighten nuts until entire wheelbarrow has been assembled.
3	Set the handles (1) on two boxes or two saw horses (one at either end).
4	Place a wedge (2) on top of each handle and align the bolt holes in the wedge with corresponding bolt holes in the handle.

TABLE 6.P2	Partial Parts List for the Wheelbarrow

Quantity	Part Description
1	Tray
2	Hardwood handle
2	Hardwood wedge
2	Leg

23. For the Expense Report ERD shown in Figure 6.P3, identify and resolve errors and note incompleteness in the specifications. Your solution should include a list of errors and a revised ERD. Note that the ERD may have both diagram and design errors. If you are using the ER Assistant, you can use the Check Diagram feature after checking the diagram rules yourself. Specifications for the ERD appear below:

- The Expense Reporting database tracks expense reports and expense report items along with users, expense categories, status codes, and limits on expense category spending.

- For each user, the database records the unique user number, the first name, the last name, the phone number, the e-mail address, the spending limit, the organizational relationships among users, and the expense categories (at least one) available to the user. A user can manage other users but have at most one manager. For each expense category available to a user, there is a limit amount.

- For each expense category, the database records the unique category number, the category description, the spending limit, and the users permitted to use the expense category. When an expense category is initially created, there may not be related users.

- For each status code, the database records the unique status number, the status description, and the expense reports using the status code.

- For each expense report, the database records the unique expense report number, the description, the submitted date, the status date, the status code (required), the user number (required), and the related expense items.

- For each expense item, the database records the unique item number, the description, the expense date, the amount, the expense category (required), and the expense report number (required).

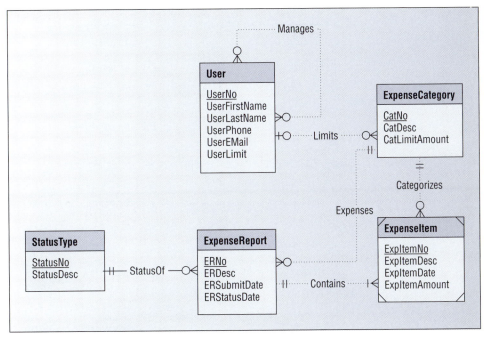

Figure 6.P3   **ERD for the expense reporting database.**

24. For the Intercollegiate Athletic ERD shown in Figure 6.P4, identify and resolve errors and note incompleteness in the specifications. Your solution should include a list of errors and a revised ERD. Note that the ERD may have both diagram and design errors. If you are using the ER Assistant, you can use the Check Diagram feature after checking the diagram rules yourself. Specifications for the ERD are as follows:

- The Intercollegiate Athletic database supports the scheduling and the operation of events along with tracking customers, facilities, locations within facilities, employees, and resources to support events. To schedule an event, a customer initiates an event request with the Intercollegiate Athletic Department. If an event request is approved, one or more event plans are made. Typically, event plans are made for the setup, the operation, and the cleanup of an event. An event plan consists of one or more event plan lines.

- For each event request, the database records the unique event number, the date held, the date requested, the date authorized, the status, an estimated cost, the estimated audience, the facility number (required), and the customer number (required).

- For each event plan, the database records the unique plan number, notes about the plan, the work date, the activity (setup, operation, or cleanup), the employee number (optional), and the event number (required).

- For each event plan line, the database records the line number (unique within a plan number), the plan number (required), the starting time, the ending time, the resource number (required), the location number (required), and the quantity of resources required.

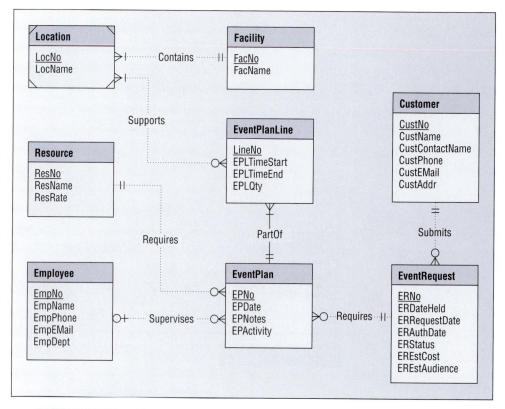

Figure 6.P4   **ERD for the intercollegiate athletic database.**

- For each customer, the database records the unique customer number, the name, the address, the contact name, the phone, the e-mail address, and the list of events requested by the customer. A customer is not stored in the database until submitting an event request.
- For each facility, the database records the unique facility number, the facility name, and the list of events in which the facility is requested.
- For each employee, the database records the unique employee number, the name, the department name, the e-mail address, the phone number, and the list of event plans supervised by the employee.
- For each location, the database records the related facility number, the location number (unique within a facility), the name, and the list of event plan lines in which the location is used.
- For each resource, the database records the unique resource number, the name, the rental rate, and the list of event plan lines in which the resource is needed.

25. Define an ERD that supports the generation of television viewing guides, movie listings, sports listings, public access listings, and cable conversion charts. These documents are typically included in television magazines bundled with Sunday newspapers. In addition, these documents are available online. The following points provide more details about the documents.

CHANNELS	6 PM	6:30	7 PM	7:30
	CABLE CHANNELS CONTINUED			
68 68	Life Makeover Project		Sixteen *Pepa's Fight* 'TVPG'	
58 7	Ed McMahon's Next Big Star		Candid Camera	
61 61	Home Projects With Rick & Dan			
52 76	◀Doctor Who ★ ★ ('96) 'TVPG'		The Addams Family ★ ★ ★	
25 25	Home Living - Lamps			
67 67	SoapTalk		Soapnet Special	
22 15 133	Bishop Jakes	Joyce Meyer	C. McClendon	Jack Hayford
57 6	◀U.S. Marshals ★ ★ ('98, Crime drama) *Tommy Lee Jones* 'TV14'			
64 82	A Face in the Crowd ★ ★ ★ ┐ ('57) *Andy Griffith, Patricia Neal*			
44 44	Beyond Tough		Junkyard Wars	
47 47	◀Arena Football (L)		Real TV	Real TV
51 51	◀The Peacemaker ★ ★ ┐ ('97, Action) *George Clooney* 'TV14' (CC)			
59 78	America's Best Waterparks		America's Best Beaches 3	
66 86	Beaver	Beaver	Batman	Batman
33 33	The Rage: Carrie 2 ★ ┐ ('99) *Emily Bergl, Jason London* (CC)			
45 45	◀Movie	Military Diaries	VH1 Special	
69 69	(:15) Wall Street ★ ★ ★ ┐ ('87, Drama) *Michael Douglas* 'R'			
10 62	◀Bull Durham ★ ★ ★ ('88)		Mutant X (R)	

Figure 6.P5   Sample television viewing guide.

- A television viewing guide lists the programs available during each time slot of a day as depicted in Figure 6.P5. For each program in a channel/time slot, a viewing guide may include some or all of these attributes: a program title, a television content rating, a description, a rerun status (yes or no), a duration, a closed caption status (yes or no), and a starting time if a program does not begin on a half-hour increment. For each movie, a guide also may include some or all of these attributes: an evaluative rating (number of stars from 1 to 4, with half-star increments), a list of major actors, an optional brief description, a motion picture content rating, and a release year. Public access programs are shown in a public access guide, not in a television viewing guide.
- A movie listing contains all movies shown in a television guide as depicted in Figure 6.P6. For each movie, a listing may include some or all of these attributes: a title, a release year, an evaluative rating, a content rating, a channel abbreviation, a list of days of the week/time combinations, a list of major actors, and a brief description. A movie listing is organized in ascending order by movie titles.

MOVIES

A

A.I.: ARTIFICIAL INTELLIGENCE *Science fiction* in the Future, a cutting-edge android in the form of a boy embarks on a jouney to discover its true nature. *Haley Joel Osment* (PG-13, 2:25) (AS, V) '01 *(Esp.)* iN1 June 2 3:30pm; 6 10:00am; 8 8:00am; 11 5:30pm; 13 10:00am; 25 10:00am; 29 9:00am (CC) ⌒ , iN2 June 1 7:30pm; 8 6:00am; 19 6:30am; 11 3:30pm; 12 7:30am; 13 11:00am (CC)⌒ , iN3 June 5 9:00am, 11:30am, 2:00pm, 4:30pm, 7:00pm, 9:30pm (CC)⌒ ,iN4 June 6 9:00am, 11:30am, 2:00pm, 4:30pm, 7:00pm, 9:30pm

A.K.A CASSIUS CLAY ★ ★ ' *Documentary* Heavyweight boxing champ Muhammad Ali speaks, visits comic Stepin Fetchit and appears in fight footage. (PG, 1:25) (AS, L, V) '70 *(Esp.)* TMC June 1 6:15am; 6 2:30pm; 19 6:20am, TMC-W June 1 9:15am; 6 5:30pm; 10 9:20am

ABANDON SHIFT ★ ★ ★ *Adventure* Short rations from a sunken liner force the officer of a packed lifeboat to sacrifice the weak. *Tyrone*

Power ⬭ (NR, 1:37) '57 **(Esp.)** TMAX June 4 6:05am; 21 4:40pm; 30 3:20pm

ABBOTT AND COSTELLO MEET THE KILLER, BORIS KARLOFF. ★ ★ ' *Comedy* A hotel detective and bellhop find dead bodies and a fake swami. *Bud Abbott* ⬭ (TVG, 1:30) '48 **AMC** June 28 5:30pm; 21 7:35am (CC)

ABBOTT AND COSTELLO MEET FRANKENSTEIN ★ ★ ★ ' *Comedy* The Wolf Man tries to warn a dimwitted porter that Dracula wants his brain for a monster's body. *Bud Abbott* ⬭ (TVG, 1:30) '48 **AMC** June 5 5:30pm (CC)

ABDUCTION OF INNOCENCE: A MOMENT OF TRUTH MOVIE ★ ★ *Drama* A lumber magnate's teen daughter stands trial for being an accomplice in her own kidnapping. *Katie Wright* (TVPG, 1:45) '96 **LMN** June 1 8:00pm; 2 9:30am (CC)

THE ABDUCTION OF KARI SWENSON ★ ★ *Docudrama* A U.S. Olympic biathlete is kidnapped in 1984 by father-and-son Montana mountain men. *Tracy Pollan* (TVPG, 1:45) (V) '87 **LMN** June 10 4:30pm; 11 6:00am

ABOUT ADAM ★ ★ ★ *Romance-comedy* A magnetic young man meets and romances an Irish waitress, then courts and beds the rest of the family. *Stuart Townsend* (R, 1:45) (AS, L) '00 **STARZIC** June 22 8:00pm; 23 1:10pm; 27 2:30pm, 10:15pm (CC)

ABOUT SARAH ★ ★ *Drama* A young woman decides whether to continue her medical career or care for her impaired mother. *Kellie*

discovery. Ed Harris (PG-13, 2:47) (AS, L, V) '89 **(Esp.)** ACTION June 2 12:05pm, 8:00pm, 3 6:45am; 13 12:20pm, 8:00pm; 22 8:10am, 5:35pm ⌒

THE ACCIDENT: A MOMENT OF THRUTH MOVIE ★ ★ *Docudrama* A teen, charged with manslaughter in a drunken driving crash that killed her best friend, uses alcohol to cope. *Bonnie Root* (TVPG, 1:45) '97 **LMN** June 8 2:45pm (CC)

THE ACCIDENTAL TOURIST ★ ★ ★ *Drama* A travel writer takes up with his dog trainer after his wife moves out. *William Hurt* (TVPG, 2:30) (AS, L) '88 **FOX-WXIX** June 23 12:00pm

THE ACCUSED ★ ★ ★ *Crime drama* A psychology professor goes to trial for killing a student who tried to seduce her. *Loretta Young* ⬭ (NR, 1:41) '48 **TCM** June 8 10:30am

AN ACT OF LOVE: THE PATRICIA NEAL STORY ★ ★ ★ *Docudrama* The actress recovers from a 1966 stroke with help from friends and her husband, writer Roald Dahl. *Glenda Jackson* (NR, 1:40) '81 **WE** June 26 11:10am

ACTIVE STEALTH *Action* When terrorists steal a stealth bomber, the Army calls upon a veteran fighter pilot and his squadron to retrieve it. *Daniel Baldwin* ✕ (R. 1:38) (AS, L, V) '99 **(Esp.)** AMAX June 2 2:45pm; 5 4:30pm; 7 8:00pm; 10 12:10pm; 15 6:20pm; 18 8:00pm; 24 12:50pm; 25 1:15pm; 30 1:15pm (CC) ⌒

THE ACTRESS ★ ★ ' *Drama* Supported by her mother, a New Englander finally tells her salty

| Figure 6.P6 | Sample movie listing. |

- A sports listing contains all sports programming in a television guide as depicted in Figure 6.P7. A sports listing is organized by sport and day within a sport. Each item in a sports listing may include some or all of these attributes: an event title, a time, a duration, a channel, an indicator for closed-captioning, an indicator if live, and an indicator if a rerun.

- A public access listing shows public access programming that does not appear elsewhere in a television guide as depicted in Figure 6.P8. A public access listing contains a list of community organizations (title, area, street address, city, state, zip code, and phone number). After the listing of community organizations, a public access listing contains programming for each day/time slot. Because public access shows do not occupy all time slots and are available on one channel only, there is a list of time slots for each day, not a grid as for a complete television guide. Each public access program has a title and an optional sponsoring community organization.

- A cable/conversion chart shows the mapping of channels across cable systems as depicted in Figure 6.P9. For each channel, a conversion chart shows a number on each cable system in the local geographic area.

Sports

8:00pm	**GOLF** Golf Murphy's Irish Open, First Round (R)
11:00pm	**GOLF** Golf Murphy's Irish Open, First Round (R)

FRIDAY, JUNE 28

10:00am	**GOLF** Golf Murphy's Irish Open, Second Round (L)
12:00pm	**ESPN** U.S. Senior Open, Second Round (L) (CC)
2:00pm	**ESPN** PGA FedEx St. Jude Classic, Second Round (L) (CC)
3:00pm	**GOLF** Golf ShopRite LPGA Classic, First Round (L)
4:00pm	**ESPN** Golf U.S. Senior Open, Second Round (L) (CC)
5:30pm	**GOLF** Scorecard Report
8:00pm	**GOLF** Golf ShopRite LPGA Classic, First Round (R)
10:00pm	**GOLF** Scoreboard Report
11:00pm	**GOLF** Golf Murphy's Irish Open, Second Round (R)

SATURDAY, JUNE 29

10:00am	**GOLF** Golf Murphy's Irish Open, Third Round (L)
3:00pm	**NBC-WLWT** Golf U.S. Senior Open, Third Round (L) (CC)
4:00pm	**ABC-WCPO** PGA FedEx St. Jude Classic, Third Round (L)
4:30pm	**GOLF** Golf ShopRite LPGA Classic, Second Round (L)
7:00pm	**GOLF** Scorecard Report
8:00pm	**GOLF** Haskins Award
8:30pm	**GOLF** Golf ShopRite LPGA Classic, Second Round (R)
10:00pm	**GOLF** Scorecard Report
11:00pm	**GOLF** Haskins Award
11:30PM	**GOLF** Golf Murphy's Irish Open, Third Round (R)

HORSE EVENTS

SUNDAY, JUNE 2

2:00pm	**ESPN** Equestrian Del Mar National (CC)

WEDNESDAY, JUNE 5

2:00pm	**ESPN2** Wire to Wire

FRIDAY, JUNE 7

5:00pm	**ESPN2** Horse Racing Acorn Stakes (L)

SATURDAY, JUNE 8

2:00pm	**ESPN2** Horse Racing Belmont Stakes Special (L) (CC)
5:00pm	**NBC-WLWT** Horse Racing Belmont Stakes (L) (CC)

WEDNESDAY, JUNE 12

2:00pm	**ESPN2** Wire to Wire

SATURDAY, JUNE 15

5:00pm	**CBS-WKRC** Horse Racing Stephen Foster Handicap (L)

WEDNESDAY, JUNE 19

2:00pm	**ESPN2** Wire to Wire

WEDNESDAY, JUNE 26

2:00pm	**ESPN2** Wire to Wire

SATURDAY, JUNE 29

3:00pm	**ESPN2** Budweiser Grand Prix of Devon
5:00pm	**CBS-WKRC** Horse Racing The Mothergoose (L) (CC)
11:00pm	**ESPN2** 2Day at the Races (L)

MARITAL ARTS

SATURDAY, JUNE 1

10:00pm	**iN2** World Championship Kickboxing Bad to the Bone (L)

MONDAY, JUNE 3

9:00pm	**iN2** World Championship Kickboxing Bad to the Bone (R)

SUNDAY, JUNE 16

9:00pm	**iN1** Ultimate Fighting Championship: Ultimate Royce Gracie

MONDAY, JUNE 17

1:00am	**iN2** Ultimate Fighting Championship: Ultimate Royce Gracie
11:30pm	**iN2** Ultimate Fighting Championship: Ultimate Royce Gracie

Figure 6.P7   **Sample sports listing.**

Public Access listings for Channel 24 in all Time Warner franchises in Greater Cincinnati:

Media Bridges Cincinnati, 1100 Race St., Cincinnati 45210. 651-4171.

Waycross Community Media (Forest Park-Greenhills-Springfield Twp.), 2086 Waycross Road, Forest Park 45240. 825-2429.

Intercommunity Cable Regulatory Commission, 2492 Commodity Circle, Cincinnati 45241. 772-4272.

Norwood Community Television, 2020 Sherman Ave., Norwood 45212. 396-5573.

SUNDAY
7 a.m.– Heart of Compassion
7:30 a.m.– Community Pentecostal
8 a.m.– ICRC Programming
8:30 a.m.– ICRC Programming
9 a.m.– St. John Church of Christ
10 a.m.– Beulah Missionary Baptist

MONDAY
6 a.m.– Sonshine Gospel Hour
7 a.m.– Latter Rain Ministry
8 a.m.– Dunamis of Faith
8:30 a.m.– In Jesus' Name
9 a.m.– Happy Gospel Time TV
10 a.m.– Greek Christian Hour
10:30 a.m.–Armor of God
11 a.m.– Delhi Christian Center
Noon – Humanist Perspective
12:30 p.m.– Waterway Hour
1:30 p.m.– Country Gospel Jubilee
2:30 p.m.– Know Your Government
4:30 p.m.– House of Yisrael
5:30 p.m.– Living Vine Presents
6:30 p.m.– Family Dialogue
7 p.m.– Goodwill Talks
8 p.m.– Pastor Nadie Johnson
9 p.m.– Delta Kings Barbershop Show
Midnight – Basement Flava 2
1 a.m.– Total Chaos Hour
2 a.m.– Commissioned by Christ
3 a.m.– From the Heart
3:30 a.m.– Words of Farrakhan
4:30 a.m.– Skyward Bound

11:30 p.m.– Fire Ball Minstry Church of God
12:30 a.m.– Second Peter Pentecostal Church
1:30 a.m.– Road to Glory Land
3:30 a.m.– Shadows of the Cross
WEDNESDAY
6 a.m.– Pure Gospal
8 a.m.– ICRC Programming
8:30 a.m.– Way of the Cross
9 a.m.– Church of Christ Hour
10 a.m.– A Challenge of Faith
10:30 a.m.– Miracles Still Happen
11 a.m.– Deerfield Digest
11:30 a.m.– Bob Schuler
Noon – Friendship Baptist Church
2 p.m.– Businese Talk
2:30 p.m.– ICRC Programming
3 p.m.– ICRC Programming
3:30 p.m.– Temple Fitness
4 p.m.– Church of God
5 p.m.– Around Cincinnati
5:30 p.m.– Countering the Silence
6 p.m.– Community Report
6:30 p.m.– ICRC Programming
7 p.m.– Inside Springdale
8 p.m.– ICRC Sports

Figure 6.P8   Sample public access listing.

CABLE CONVERSION CHART

Time Warner standard	Time Warner upgrade cable ready	Time Warner	Insight	Adelphia Amelia	Fairfield, Middletown	Time Warner Hamilton,	Adelphia Delhi
5	5	6	7	5	5	6
9	9	7	8	9	9	10
12	12	13	3	12	12	13
19	3	3	4	3	13	2
25	20	20–	25	25	20	15
48	13	8	13	6	6	8
64	11	11	11	11	11	11
2	–	–	–	–	2	–
7		–	–	–	7	–
14	14	14	14	14	14	14
16	16	16	–	16	16	16
22	–	–	–	–	8	–
43	–	–	–	–	3	–
45	–	–	–	–	10	–
54	21	21	2	–	–	4
A&E	39	39	52	28	27	46
AMC	46	46	31	29	26	40

Figure 6.P9   Sample conversion chart.

Conversion Problems

1. Convert the ERD shown in Figure 6.CP1 into tables. List the conversion rules used and the resulting changes to the tables.

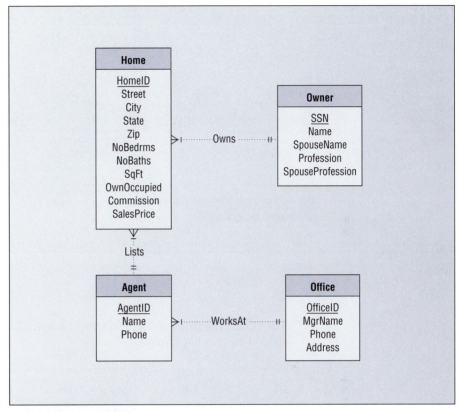

Figure 6.CP1   ERD for conversion problem 1.

2. Convert the ERD shown in Figure 6.CP2 into tables. List the conversion rules used and the resulting changes to the tables.

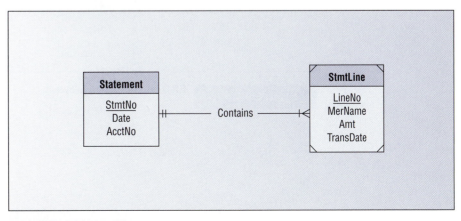

Figure 6.CP2   ERD for conversion problem 2.

3. Convert the ERD shown in Figure 6.CP3 into tables. List the conversion rules used and the resulting changes to the tables.

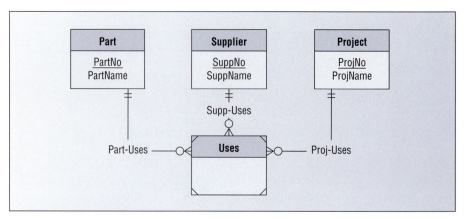

Figure 6.CP3   **ERD for conversion problem 3.**

4. Convert the ERD shown in Figure 6.CP4 into tables. List the conversion rules used and the resulting changes to the tables.

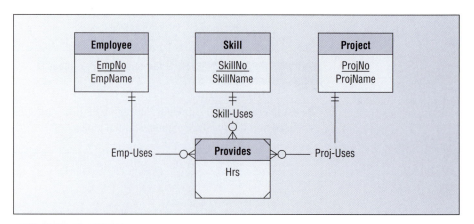

Figure 6.CP4   **ERD for conversion problem 4.**

5. Convert the ERD shown in Figure 6.CP5 into tables. List the conversion rules used and the resulting changes to the tables.

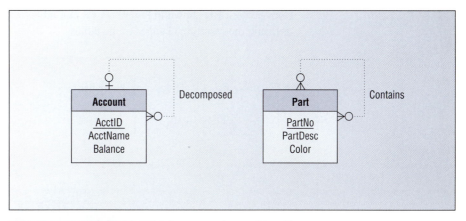

Figure 6.CP5 ERD for conversion problem 5.

6. Convert the ERD shown in Figure 6.CP6 into tables. List the conversion rules used and the resulting changes to the tables.

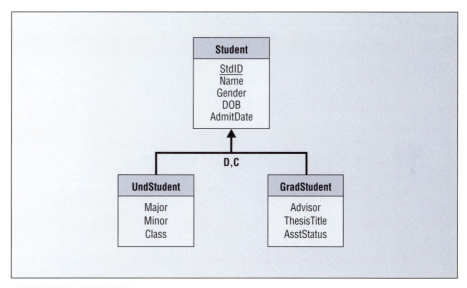

Figure 6.CP6 ERD for conversion problem 6.

7. Convert the ERD shown in Figure 6.CP7 into tables. List the conversion rules used and the resulting changes to the tables.

Figure 6.CP7 ERD for conversion problem 7.

8. Convert the ERD shown in Figure 6.CP8 into tables. List the conversion rules used and the resulting changes to the tables.

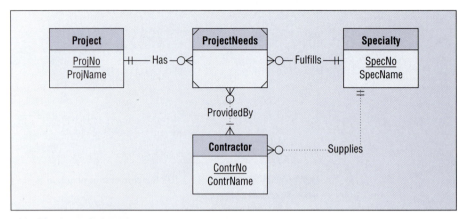

Figure 6.CP8   ERD for conversion problem 8.

9. Convert the ERD shown in Figure 6.CP9 into tables. List the conversion rules used and the resulting changes to the tables.

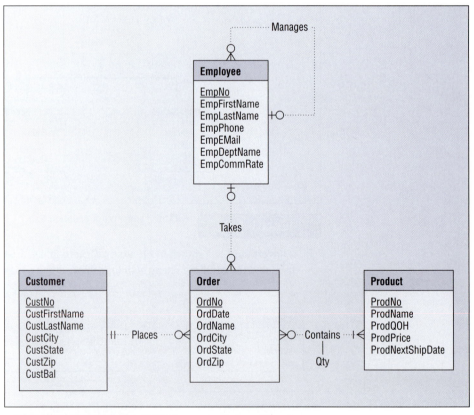

Figure 6.CP9   ERD for conversion problem 9.

10. Convert the ERD shown in Figure 6.CP10 into tables. List the conversion rules used and the resulting changes to the tables.

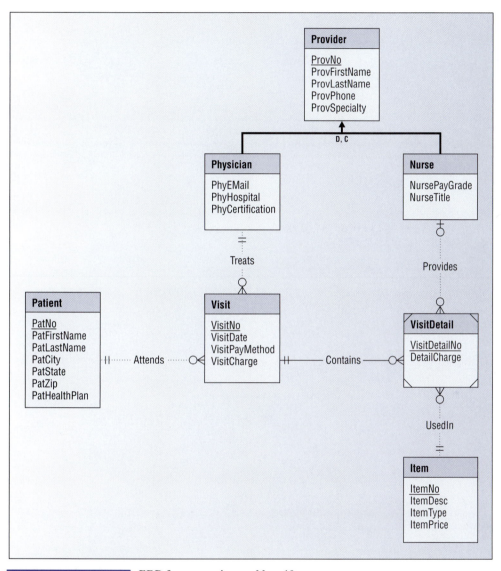

| **Figure 6.CP10** | ERD for conversion problem 10. |

REFERENCES FOR FURTHER STUDY

Chapter 3 of Batini, Ceri, and Navathe (1992) and Chapter 10 of Nijssen and Halpin (1989) provide more details on transformations to refine an ERD. For more details about conversion of generalization hierarchies, consult Chapter 11 of Batini, Ceri, and Navathe. If you would like more details about the UML, consult a specialized book on the topic such as the description by its developers (Booch, Jacobson, and Rumbaugh 1998); Fowler and Scott (1997); and Muller (1999). The *DBAZine* site (www.dbazine.com) and the DevX help site (www.devx.com/gethelp) have practical advice about database development and data modeling.

CHAPTER 7

Normalization of Relational Tables

This chapter describes normalization, a technique to eliminate unwanted redundancy in relational tables. After this chapter, the student should have acquired the following knowledge and skills:

■ Identify modification anomalies in tables with excessive redundancies.

■ Define functional dependencies among columns of a table.

■ Normalize tables by detecting violations of normal forms and applying normalization rules.

■ Analyze M-way relationships using the concept of independence.

■ Appreciate the usefulness and limitations of normalization.

OVERVIEW

Chapters 5 and 6 provided the tools for data modeling, a fundamental skill for database development. You learned about the notation used in entity relationship diagrams, important data modeling patterns, guidelines to avoid common modeling errors, and conversion of entity relationship diagrams (ERDs) into relational tables. You applied this knowledge to construct ERDs for small, narrative problems. This chapter extends your database design skills by presenting normalization techniques to remove redundancy in relational tables.

Redundancies can cause insert, update, and delete operations to produce unexpected side effects known as modification anomalies. This chapter prescribes normalization techniques to remove modification anomalies caused by redundancies. You will learn about functional dependencies, several normal forms, and a procedure to generate tables without redundancies. In addition, you will learn how to analyze M-way relationships for redundancies. This chapter concludes by briefly presenting additional normal forms and discussing the usefulness and limitations of normalization techniques in the database development process.

7.1 OVERVIEW OF RELATIONAL DATABASE DESIGN

After converting an ERD to relational tables, your work is not yet finished. You need to analyze the tables for redundancies that can make the tables difficult to use. This section describes why redundancies can make a table difficult to use and presents an important kind of constraint to analyze redundancies.

7.1.1 Avoidance of Modification Anomalies

Modification Anomaly an unexpected side effect that occurs when changing the data in a table with excessive redundancies.

A good database design ensures that users can change the contents of a database without unexpected side effects. For example, with a university database, a user should be able to insert a new course without having to simultaneously insert a new offering of the course and a new student enrolled in the course. Likewise, when a student is deleted from the database due to graduation, course data should not be inadvertently lost. These problems are examples of <u>modification anomalies</u>, unexpected side effects that occur when changing the contents of a table with excessive redundancies. A good database design avoids modification anomalies by eliminating excessive redundancies.

To understand more precisely the impact of modification anomalies, let us consider a poorly designed database. Imagine that a university database consists of the single table shown in Table 7.1. Such a poor design makes it easy to identify anomalies.[1] The following list describes some of the problems with this design.

- This table has insertion anomalies. An <u>insertion anomaly</u> occurs when extra data beyond the desired data must be added to the database. For example, to insert a course, it is necessary to know a student and an offering because the combination of *StdSSN* and *OfferNo* is the primary key. Remember that a row cannot exist with null values for part of its primary key.

TABLE 7.1	Sample Data for the Big University Database Table

StdSSN	StdCity	StdClass	OfferNo	OffTerm	OffYear	EnrGrade	CourseNo	CrsDesc
S1	SEATTLE	JUN	O1	FALL	2003	3.5	C1	DB
S1	SEATTLE	JUN	O2	FALL	2003	3.3	C2	VB
S2	BOTHELL	JUN	O3	WINTER	2003	3.1	C3	OO
S2	BOTHELL	JUN	O2	FALL	2003	3.4	C2	VB

---

[1]This single-table design is not as extreme as it may seem. Users without proper database training often design a database using a single table.

- This table has update anomalies. An <u>update anomaly</u> occurs when it is necessary to change multiple rows to modify only a single fact. For example, if we change the *StdClass* of student S1, two rows must be changed. If S1 was enrolled in 10 classes, 10 rows must be changed.

- This table has deletion anomalies. A <u>deletion anomaly</u> occurs whenever deleting a row inadvertently causes other data to be deleted. For example, if we delete the Enrollment of S2 in O3 (third row), we lose the information about offering O3 and course C3.

To deal with these anomalies, users may circumvent them (such as using a dummy primary key to insert a new course) or database programmers may write code to prevent inadvertent loss of data. A better solution is to modify the table design to remove the redundancies that cause the anomalies.

7.1.2 Functional Dependencies

Functional dependencies are important tools when analyzing a table for excessive redundancies. A functional dependency is a constraint about the database contents. Constraints can be characterized as value-based versus value-neutral (Figure 7.1). A <u>value-based</u> constraint involves a comparison of a column to a constant using a comparison operator such as $<$, $=$, or $>$. For example, age ≥ 21 is an important value-based constraint in a database used to restrict sales of alcohol to minors. A <u>value-neutral</u> constraint involves a comparison of columns. For example, a value-neutral constraint is that retirement age should be greater than current age in a database for retirement planning.

Primary key (PK) and foreign key (FK) constraints are important kinds of value-neutral constraints. A primary key can take any value as long as it does not match the primary key value in an existing row. A foreign key constraint requires that the value of a column in one table match the value of a primary key in another table.

A functional dependency is another important kind of value-neutral constraint. A <u>functional dependency</u> (FD) is a constraint about two or more columns of a table. X determines Y ($X \rightarrow Y$) if there exists at most one value of Y for every value of X. The word

Functional Dependency a constraint about two or more columns of a table. X determines Y ($X \rightarrow Y$) if there exists at most one value of Y for every value of X.

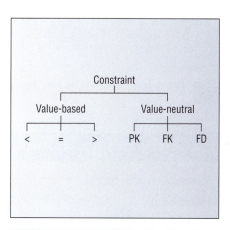

Figure 7.1 **Classification of database constraints.**

function comes from mathematics where a function gives one value. For example, social security number determines city (*StdSSN* → *StdCity*) in the university database table if there is at most one city value for every social security number. A column appearing on the left-hand side of an FD is called a <u>determinant</u> or, alternatively, an <u>LHS</u> for left-hand side. In this example, *StdSSN* is a determinant.

> **Determinant** the column(s) appearing on the left-hand side (LHS) of a functional dependency.

You also can think about functional dependencies as identifying *potential* primary keys for other tables. By stating that *X* → *Y*, if *X* and *Y* are placed together in a table without other columns, *X* is the primary key. Every determinant (LHS) is a potential primary key if it is placed in a table with the other columns that it determines. For example, if *StdSSN, StdCity,* and *StdClass* are placed in a table together and *StdSSN* → *StdCity* and *StdSSN* → *StdClass* then *StdSSN* is the primary key.

Functional Dependency Diagrams and Lists

A functional dependency diagram compactly displays the functional dependencies of a particular table. You should arrange FDs so that one can visually group columns sharing the same determinant. In Figure 7.2, it is easy to spot the dependencies where *StdSSN* is the determinant. By the position and height of lines, you also can see the dependencies where the combination of *StdSSN* and *OfferNo* is the determinant. A good visual arrangement can facilitate the normalization process described in the next section.

If you prefer, you can list FDs rather than arrange them in a diagram. With many FDs, you might find it difficult to make a diagram. If you list FDs, you can group them by LHS, as shown in Table 7.2.

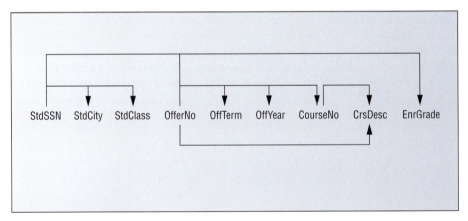

| **Figure 7.2** | Dependency diagram for the "big" university database table. |

| **TABLE 7.2** | **List of FDs for the University Database Table** |

StdSSN → StdCity, StdClass

OfferNo → OffTerm, OffYear, CourseNo, CrsDesc

CourseNo → CrsDesc

StdSSN, OfferNo → EnrGrade

Asserting Functional Dependencies

Functional dependencies are important business rules that are asserted during the database development process. The database designer interacts with users to understand the functional dependencies that exist for a table. For example, a user may state that each course offering has a unique offering number along with the year and term of the offering. From this statement, the designer can assert that the *OfferNo* column determines the *OffYear* and the *OffTerm* columns. Database designers must understand the meaning of functional dependencies so that functional dependencies can be identified during the database development process.

In recording functional dependencies, it is also important to distinguish when one column alone is the determinant versus a combination of columns. Part of this confusion is due to the meaning of columns in the left-hand versus right-hand side of a dependency. To record that student social security number determines city and class, you can write either *StdSSN → StdCity, StdClass* (more compact) or *StdSSN → StdCity* and *StdSSN → StdClass* (less compact). If you assume that the e-mail address is also unique for each student, then you can write *Email → StdCity, StdClass*. You should not write *StdSSN, Email → StdCity, StdClass* because these FDs imply that the combination of *StdSSN* and *Email* is the determinant. Thus, you should write FDs so that the LHS does not contain unneeded columns.[2]

Eliminating FDs Using Sample Data

Eliminating Potential FDs using sample data to eliminate potential FDs. If two rows have the same value for the LHS but different values for the RHS, an FD cannot exist. Some commercial normalization programs use this technique to help a user determine FDs.

A functional dependency cannot be proven to exist by examining the rows of a table. However, examining the contents of a table can prove that a functional dependency does not hold. For example, in the university database table we can conclude that *StdClass* does not determine *StdCity* because there are two rows with the same value for *StdClass* but a different value for *StdCity*. Thus, it is sometimes helpful to examine sample rows in a table to see what functional dependencies do *not* hold. There are several commercial database design tools that automate the process of eliminating dependencies through examination of sample rows. Ultimately, the database designer must make the final decision about what functional dependencies exist in a table.

7.2 NORMAL FORMS

Normalization is the process of removing redundancy in a table so that the table is easier to modify. A number of normal forms have been developed to remove redundancies. A normal form is a rule about allowable dependencies. Each normal form removes certain kinds of redundancies. As shown in Figure 7.3, first normal form (1NF) is the starting point. All tables without repeating groups are in 1NF. 2NF is stronger than 1NF. Only a subset of the 1NF tables is in 2NF. Each successive normal form refines the previous normal form to remove additional kinds of redundancies. Because BCNF (Boyce-Codd Normal Form) is a revised (and stronger) definition for 3NF, 3NF and BCNF are shown in the same part of Figure 7.3.

---

[2] This concept is more properly known as "full functional dependence." Full functional dependence means that the LHS is minimal.

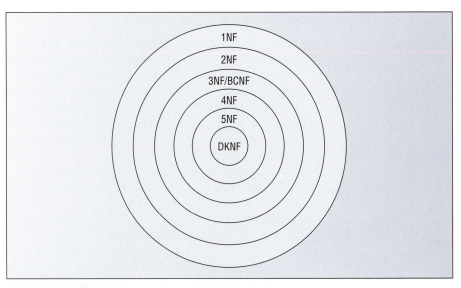

| Figure 7.3 | Relationship of normal forms. |

TABLE 7.3   **Unnormalized University Database Table**

StdSSN	StdCity	StdClass	OfferNo	OffTerm	OffYear	EnrGrade	CourseNo	CrsDesc
S1	SEATTLE	JUN	O1	FALL	2003	3.5	C1	DB
			O2	FALL	2003	3.3	C2	VB
S2	BOTHELL	JUN	O3	WINTER	2003	3.1	C3	OO
			O2	FALL	2003	3.4	C2	VB

2NF and 3NF/BCNF are rules about functional dependencies. If the functional dependencies for a table match the specified pattern, the table is in the specified normal form. 3NF/BCNF is the most important in practice because higher normal forms involve other kinds of dependencies that are less common and more difficult to understand. Therefore, most emphasis is given to 3NF/BCNF. Section 7.3 presents 4NF as a way to reason about M-way relationships. Section 7.4 presents 5NF and DKNF (domain key normal form) to show that higher normal forms have been proposed. DKNF is the ultimate normal form, but it remains an ideal rather than a practical normal form.

7.2.1 First Normal Form

1NF prohibits nesting or repeating groups in tables. A table not in 1NF is unnormalized or nonnormalized. In Table 7.3, the university table is unnormalized because the two rows contain repeating groups or nested tables. To convert an unnormalized table into 1NF, you replace each value of a repeating group with a row. In a new row, you copy the nonrepeating columns. You can see the conversion by comparing Table 7.3 with Table 7.1 (two rows with repeating groups versus four rows without repeating groups).

Because most commercial DBMSs require 1NF tables, you do not normally need to convert tables into 1NF.[3] However, you often need to perform the reverse process (1NF tables to unnormalized tables) for report generation. As discussed in Chapter 10, reports use nesting to show relationships. However, the underlying tables do not have nesting.

7.2.2 Second and Third Normal Forms

Combined Definition of 2NF and 3NF a table is in 3NF if every nonkey column is dependent on a candidate key, the whole candidate key, and nothing but candidate keys.[5]

The definitions of 2NF and 3NF distinguish between key and nonkey columns.[4] A column is a key column if it is part of a candidate key or a candidate key by itself. Recall that a *candidate key* is a minimal set of column(s) that has unique values in a table. Minimality means that none of the columns can be removed without removing the uniqueness property. Nonkey columns are any other columns. In Table 7.1, the combination of (*StdSSN, OfferNo*) is the only candidate key. Other columns such as *StdCity* and *StdClass* are nonkey columns.

The goal of 2NF and 3NF is to produce tables in which every key determines the other columns. An easy way to remember the definitions of both 2NF and 3NF is shown in the margin.

Second Normal Form

2NF Definition a table is in 2NF if every nonkey column is dependent on the whole key, not part of the key.

To understand this definition, let us break it down to the 2NF and 3NF parts. The 2NF definition uses the first part of the definition as shown in the margin.

To see if a table is in 2NF, you should look for FDs that violate the definition. An FD in which part of a key determines a nonkey column violates 2NF. If the key contains only one column, the table is in 2NF. Looking at the dependency diagram in Figure 7.2, you can easily detect violations of 2NF. For example, *StdCity* is a nonkey column but *StdSSN,* not the entire primary key (combination of *StdSSN* and *OfferNo*), determines it. The only FDs that satisfy the 2NF definition are *StdSSN, OfferNo → EnrGrade* and *CourseNo → CrsDesc.*

To place the table into 2NF, split the original table into smaller tables that satisfy the 2NF definition. In each smaller table, the entire primary key (not part of the primary key) should determine the nonkey columns. The splitting process involves the project operator of relational algebra. For the university database table, three projection operations split it so that the underlined primary key determines the nonkey columns in each table below.

UnivTable1 (<u>StdSSN</u>, StdCity, StdClass)
UnivTable2 (<u>OfferNo</u>, OffTerm, OffYear, CourseNo, CrsDesc)
UnivTable3 (<u>StdSSN</u>, <u>OfferNo</u>, EnrGrade)

The splitting process should preserve the original table in two ways. First, the original table should be recoverable by using natural join operations on the smaller tables. Second, the FDs in the original table should be derivable from the FDs in the smaller

---

[3]Although the SQL:1999 standard and Oracle 9i support nested tables, this feature does not appear important in most business applications. Thus, this chapter does not consider the complications of nested tables on normalization.
[4]In the literature, key columns are known as prime, and nonkey columns as nonprime.
[5]You can remember this definition by its analogy to the traditional justice oath: "Do you swear to tell the truth, the whole truth, and nothing but the truth, . . .".

tables. Technically, the splitting process is known as a nonloss, dependency-preserving decomposition. Some of the references at the end of this chapter explain the theory underlying the splitting process.

After splitting the original table into smaller tables, you should add referential integrity constraints to connect the tables. Whenever a table is split, the splitting attribute becomes a foreign key in the table in which it is not a primary key. For example, *StdSSN* is a foreign key in *UnivTable3* because the original university table was split on this column. Therefore, define a referential integrity constraint stating that *UnivTable3.StdSSN* refers to *UnivTable1.StdSSN*. The *UnivTable3* table is repeated below with its referential integrity constraints.

UnivTable3 (<u>StdSSN</u>, <u>OfferNo</u>, EnrGrade)
    FOREIGN KEY (StdSSN) REFERENCES UnivTable1
    FOREIGN KEY (OfferNo) REFERENCES UnivTable2

Third Normal Form

UnivTable2 still has modification anomalies. For example, you cannot add a new course unless the *OfferNo* column value is known. To eliminate the modification anomalies, the definition of 3NF should be applied.

> **3NF Definition** a table is in 3NF if it is in 2NF and every nonkey column is dependent only on the key.

An FD in which one nonkey column determines another nonkey column violates 3NF. In *UnivTable2* above, the FD (*CourseNo* → *CrsDesc*) violates 3NF because both columns, *CourseNo* and *CrsDesc,* are nonkey. To fix the violation, split *UnivTable2* into two tables, as shown below, and add a foreign key constraint.

UnivTable2-1 (<u>OfferNo</u>, OffTerm, OffYear, CourseNo)
    FOREIGN KEY (CourseNo) REFERENCES UnivTable2-2
UnivTable2-2 (<u>CourseNo</u>, CrsDesc)

> **Transitive Dependency** an FD derived by the law of transitivity. Transitive FDs should not be recorded as input to the normalization process.

An equivalent way to define 3NF is that 3NF prohibits <u>transitive dependencies</u>. A transitive dependency is a functional dependency derived by the law of transitivity. The law of transitivity says that if an object A is related to B, and B is related to C, then you can conclude that A is related to C. For example, the $<$ operator obeys the transitive law: $A < B$ and $B < C$ implies that $A < C$. Functional dependencies, like the $<$ operator, obey the law of transitivity: $A \rightarrow B$, $B \rightarrow C$, then $A \rightarrow C$. In Figure 7.2, *OfferNo* → *CrsDesc* is a transitive dependency derived from *OfferNo* → *CourseNo* and *CourseNo* → *CrsDesc*.

Because transitive dependencies are easy to overlook, the preferred definition of 3NF does not use transitive dependencies. In addition, you will learn in Section 7.2.4 that you should omit derived dependencies such as transitive dependencies in your analysis.

Combined Example of 2NF and 3NF

The big patient table as depicted in Table 7.4 provides another example for applying your knowledge of 2NF and 3NF. The big patient table contains facts about patients, health care providers, patient visits to a clinic, and diagnoses made by health care providers. The big patient table contains a combined primary key consisting of the combination of *VisitNo* and *ProvNo* (provider number). Like the big university database table depicted in Table 7.1, the big patient table reflects a poor table design with many redundancies. Table 7.5 lists the associated FDs. You should verify that the FDs do not violate the sample data in Table 7.4.

TABLE 7.4	Sample Data for the Big Patient Table

VisitNo	VisitDate	PatNo	PatAge	PatCity	PatZip	ProvNo	ProvSpecialty	Diagnosis
V10020	1/13/2004	P1	35	DENVER	80217	D1	INTERNIST	EAR INFECTION
V10020	1/13/2004	P1	35	DENVER	80217	D2	NURSE PRACTITIONER	INFLUENZA
V93030	1/20/2004	P3	17	ENGLEWOOD	80113	D2	NURSE PRACTITIONER	PREGNANCY
V82110	1/18/2004	P2	60	BOULDER	85932	D3	CARDIOLOGIST	MURMUR

TABLE 7.5	List of FDs for the Big Patient Table

PatNo → PatAge, PatCity, PatZip

PatZip → PatCity

ProvNo → ProvSpecialty

VisitNo → PatNo, VisitDate, PatAge, PatCity, PatZip

VisitNo, ProvNo → Diagnosis

As previously discussed, FDs that violate 2NF involve part of a key determining a nonkey. Many of the FDs in Table 7.5 violate the 2NF definition because the combination of *VisitNo* and *ProvNo* is the primary key. Thus, the FDs with only *VisitNo* or *ProvNo* in the LHS violate 2NF. To alleviate the 2NF violations, split the big patient table so that the violating FDs are associated with separate tables. In the revised list of tables, *PatientTable1* and *PatientTable2* contain the violating FDs. *PatientTable3* retains the remaining columns.

PatientTable1 (ProvNo, ProvSpecialty)
PatientTable2 (VisitNo, VisitDate, PatNo, PatAge, PatCity, PatZip)
PatientTable3 (VisitNo, ProvNo, Diagnosis)
        FOREIGN KEY (VisitNo) REFERENCES PatientTable2
        FOREIGN KEY (ProvNo) REFERENCES PatientTable1

PatientTable1 and *PatientTable3* are in 3NF because there are no nonkey columns that determine other nonkey columns. However, *PatientTable2* violates 3NF because the FDs *PatNo → PatZip, PatAge* and *PatZip → PatCity* involve nonkey columns that determine other nonkey columns. To alleviate the 3NF violations, split *PatientTable2* into three tables as shown in the revised table list. In the revised list of tables, *PatientTable2-1* and *PatientTable2-2* contain the violating FDs, while *PatientTable2-3* retains the remaining columns.

PatientTable2-1 (PatNo, PatAge, PatZip)
        FOREIGN KEY (PatZip) REFERENCES PatientTable2-2
PatientTable2-2 (PatZip, PatCity)
PatientTable2-3 (VisitNo, PatNo, VisitDate)
        FOREIGN KEY (PatNo) REFERENCES PatientTable2-1

Using 2NF and 3NF requires two normalization steps. The normalization process can be performed in one step using Boyce-Codd normal form, as presented in the next subsection.

7.2.3 Boyce-Codd Normal Form

The revised 3NF definition, known as <u>Boyce-Codd normal form (BCNF)</u>, is a better definition because it is simpler and covers a special case omitted by the original 3NF definition. The BCNF definition is simpler because it does not refer to 2NF.

Violations of BCNF involve FDs in which the determinant (LHS) is not a candidate key. In a poor table design such as the big university database table (sample data in Table 7.1 and FD list in Table 7.2), you can easily detect violations of BCNF. For example, *StdSSN* is a determinant but not a candidate key (it is part of a candidate key but not a candidate key itself). The only FD in Table 7.2 that does not violate BCNF is *StdSSN, OfferNo → EnrGrade*.

For another example, let us apply the BCNF definition to the FDs of the big patient table shown in Table 7.5. All of the FDs in Table 7.5 violate the BCNF definition except the last FD (*VisitNo, ProvNo → Diagnosis*). All of the other FDs have determinants that are not candidate keys (part of a candidate key in some cases but not an entire candidate key). To alleviate the BCNF violations, split the big patient table into smaller tables. Each determinant should be placed into a separate table along with the columns that it determines. The result is identical to the split for 3NF (see the result of the last 3NF example) with the *PatientTable1, PatientTable3, PatientTable2-1, PatientTable2-2,* and *PatientTable2-3* tables.

Relationship between 3NF and BCNF

Although BCNF and 3NF usually produce the same result, BCNF is a stronger definition than 3NF. Thus, every table in BCNF is by definition in 3NF. BCNF covers two special cases not covered by 3NF: (1) part of a key determines part of a key and (2) a nonkey column determines part of a key. These situations are only possible if there are multiple composite, candidate keys (candidate keys with multiple columns). Analyzing dependencies of tables with multiple composite candidate keys is difficult. Fortunately, tables with multiple, composite candidate keys are not common.

UnivTable4 (Figure 7.4) depicts a table in 3NF but not in BCNF according to the first exception (part of a key determines part of a key). *UnivTable4* (Figure 7.4) has two candidate keys: the combination of *StdSSN* and *OfferNo* (the primary key) and the combination of *Email* and *OfferNo*. In the FDs for *UnivTable4* (Figure 7.4), you should note that *StdSSN* and *Email* determine each other. Because of the FDs between *StdSSN* and *Email, UnivTable4* contains a redundancy as *Email* is repeated for each *StdSSN*. For example, the first two rows contain the same e-mail address because the *StdSSN* value is the same. The following points explain why *UnivTable4* is in 3NF but not in BCNF.

- **3NF:** *UnivTable4* is in 3NF because the only nonkey column (*EnrGrade*) depends on each candidate key (not just part of a candidate key). Since *EnrGrade* is the only nonkey column, it cannot depend on other nonkey columns.

- **BCNF:** The dependencies between *StdSSN* and *Email* violate BCNF. Both *StdSSN* and *Email* are determinants, but neither is an entire candidate key although they are both part of a key. To eliminate the redundancy, you can split *UnivTable4* into two tables, as shown in Figure 7.4.

UnivTable5 (Figure 7.5) depicts another example of a table with multiple, composite candidate keys. Like *UnivTable4, UnivTable5* is in 3NF but not in BCNF, because part of a key determines part of a key. *UnivTable5* has two candidate keys: the combination

UnivTable4-1 (<u>OfferNo</u>, <u>StdSSN</u>, EnrGrade)
      FOREIGN KEY (StdSSN) REFERENCES UnivTable4-2
UnivTable4-2 (<u>StdSSN</u>, Email)

Figure 7.4 Sample rows, dependency diagram, and normalized tables for *UnivTable4*.

UnivTable5-1 (<u>AdvisorNo</u>, <u>StdSSN</u>, Status)
      FOREIGN KEY (AdvisorNo) REFERENCES UnivTable5-2
UnivTable5-2 (<u>AdvisorNo</u>, Major)

Figure 7.5 Sample rows, dependency diagram, and normalized tables for *UnivTable5*.

of *StdSSN* and *AdvisorNo* (the primary key) and the combination of *StdSSN* and *Major*. *UnivTable5* has a redundancy as *Major* is repeated for each row with the same *AdvisorNo* value. The following points explain why *UnivTable5* is in 3NF but not in BCNF.

- **3NF:** *UnivTable5* is in 3NF because *Major* is a key column. *Status* is the only nonkey column. Since *Status* depends on the entire candidate keys (<*StdSSN, AdvisorNo*> and <*StdSSN, Major*>), *UnivTable5* is in 3NF.

- **BCNF:** The dependency diagram (Figure 7.5) shows that *AdvisorNo* is a determinant but not a candidate key by itself. Thus, *UnivTable5* is not in BCNF. To eliminate the redundancy, split *UnivTable5* into two tables as shown in Figure 7.5.

These examples demonstrate two points about normalization. First, tables with multiple, composite candidate keys are difficult to analyze. You need to study carefully the dependencies in each example (Figures 7.4 and 7.5) to understand the conclusions about the normal form violations. Second, most tables in 3NF (even ones with multiple composite, candidate keys) are also in BCNF. The examples in Figures 7.4 and 7.5 were purposely constructed to depict the difference between 3NF and BCNF. The importance of BCNF is that it is a simpler definition and can be applied in the procedure described in the next section.

7.2.4 Simple Synthesis Procedure

The <u>simple synthesis procedure</u> can be used to generate tables satisfying BCNF starting with a list of functional dependencies. The word *synthesis* means that the individual functional dependencies are combined to construct tables. This usage is similar to other disciplines such as music where synthesis involves combining individual sounds to construct larger units such as melodies, scores, and so on.

Figure 7.6 depicts the steps of the simple synthesis procedure. The first two steps ensure that the FDs are not redundant. The last three steps produce tables for collections of FDs. The tables produced in the last three steps may not be correct if the FDs are redundant.

Applying the Simple Synthesis Procedure

To understand this procedure, you can apply it to the FDs of the university database table (Table 7.2). In the first step, there are no extraneous columns in the determinants. To demonstrate an extraneous column, suppose there was the FD *StdSSN, StdCity → StdClass*. In this FD, if *StdCity* is removed from the left-hand side, then the FD *StdSSN → StdClass* still holds. The *StdCity* column is redundant in the FD and should be removed.

To apply the second step, you need to know how FDs can be derived from other FDs. Although there are a number of ways to derive FDs, the most prominent way is through the law of transitivity as stated in the discussion of 3NF (Section 7.2.2). For our purposes here, we will eliminate only transitively derived FDs in step 2. For details about the other ways to derive FDs, consult references listed at the end of the chapter.

In the second step, the FD *OfferNo → CrsDesc* is a transitive dependency because *OfferNo → CourseNo* and *CourseNo → CrsDesc* implies *OfferNo → CrsDesc*. Therefore, you should delete this dependency from the list of FDs.

In the third step, you should group the FDs by determinant. From Table 7.2, you can make the following FD groups:

- *StdSSN → StdCity, StdSSN → StdClass*
- *OfferNo → OffTerm, OfferNo → OffYear, OfferNo → CourseNo*

---

1. Eliminate extraneous columns from the LHS of FDs.

2. Remove derived FDs from the FD list.

3. Arrange the FDs into groups with each group having the same determinant.

4. For each FD group, make a table with the determinant as the primary key.

5. Merge tables in which one table contains all columns of the other table.

   5.1. Choose the primary key of one of the separate tables as the primary of the new, merged table.

   5.2. Define unique constraints for the other primary keys that were not designated as the primary key of the new table.

Figure 7.6   Steps of the simple synthesis procedure.

- *CourseNo → CrsDesc*
- *StdSSN, OfferNo → EnrGrade*

In the fourth step, you replace each FD group with a table having the common determinant as the primary key. Thus, you have four resulting BCNF tables as shown below. You should add table names for completeness.

Student(<u>StdSSN</u>, StdCity, StdClass)
Offering(<u>OfferNo</u>, OffTerm, OffYear, CourseNo)
Course(<u>CourseNo</u>, CrsDesc)
Enrollment(<u>StdSSN</u>, OfferNo, EnrGrade)

After defining the tables, you should add referential integrity constraints to connect the tables. To detect the need for a referential integrity constraint, you should look for a primary key in one table appearing in other tables. For example, *CourseNo* is the primary key of *Course,* but it also appears in *Offering.* Therefore, define a referential integrity constraint stating that *Offering.CourseNo* refers to *Course.CourseNo.* The tables are repeated below with the addition of referential integrity constraints.

Student(<u>StdSSN</u>, StdCity, StdClass)
Offering(<u>OfferNo</u>, OffTerm, OffYear, CourseNo)
   FOREIGN KEY (CourseNo) REFERENCES Course
Course(<u>CourseNo</u>, CrsDesc)
Enrollment(<u>StdSSN, OfferNo</u>, EnrGrade)
   FOREIGN KEY (StdSSN) REFERENCES Student
   FOREIGN KEY (OfferNo) REFERENCES Offering

The fifth step is not necessary because the FDs for this problem are simple. When there are multiple candidate keys for a table, the fifth step is necessary. For example, if *Email* is added as a column, then the FDs *Email → StdSSN* and *StdSSN → Email* should be added to the list. Note that the FDs *Email → StdCity, StdClass* should not be added to the list because they can be transitively derived from the other FDs. As a result of step 3, another group of FDs is added. In step 4, a new table (*Student2*) is added with *Email* as the primary key. Because the *Student* table contains the columns of the *Student2* table, the tables (*Student* and *Student2*) are merged in step 5. One of the candidate keys (*StdSSN* or *Email*) is chosen as the primary key. Since *Email* is chosen as the primary key, a unique constraint is defined for *StdSSN.*

   Email → StdSSN, StdSSN → Email
   Student2(<u>Email</u>, StdSSN, StdCity, StdClass)
    UNIQUE(<u>StdSSN</u>)

Multiple Candidate Keys a common misconception by novice database developers is that a table with multiple candidate keys violates BCNF. Multiple candidate keys do not violate BCNF or 3NF. Thus, you should not split a table just because it has multiple candidate keys.

As this additional example demonstrates, multiple candidate keys do not violate BCNF. The fifth step of the simple synthesis procedure creates tables with multiple candidate keys because it merges tables. Multiple candidate keys do not violate 3NF either. There is no reason to split a table just because it has multiple candidate keys. Splitting a table with multiple candidate keys can slow query performance due to extra joins.

You can use the simple synthesis procedure to analyze simple dependency structures. Most tables resulting from a conversion of an ERD should have simple dependency structures because the data modeling process has already done much of the normalization process. Most tables should be nearly normalized after the conversion process.

For complex dependency structures, you should use a commercial design tool to perform normalization. To make the synthesis procedure easy to use, some of the details have been omitted. In particular, step 2 can be rather involved because there are more ways to derive dependencies than transitivity. Even checking for transitivity can be difficult with many columns. The full details of step 2 can be found in references cited at the end of the chapter. Even if you understand the complex details, step 2 cannot be done by hand for complex dependency structures. For complex dependency structures, you need to use a CASE tool even if you are an experienced database designer.

Another Example Using the Simple Synthesis Procedure

To gain more experience with the simple synthesis procedure, you can follow along on another example. This example describes a database to track reviews of papers submitted to an academic conference. Prospective authors submit papers for review and possible acceptance in the published conference proceedings. Here are more details about authors, papers, reviews, and reviewers:

- Author information includes the unique author number, the name, the mailing address, and the unique but optional electronic address.
- Paper information includes the primary author, the unique paper number, the title, the abstract, and the review status (pending, accepted, rejected).
- Reviewer information includes the unique reviewer number, the name, the mailing address, and a unique but optional electronic address.
- A completed review includes the reviewer number, the date, the paper number, comments to the authors, comments to the program chairperson, and ratings (overall, originality, correctness, style, and relevance). The combination of reviewer number and paper number identifies a review.

Before beginning the procedure, you must identify the FDs in the problem. The following is a list of FDs for the problem:

$AuthNo \rightarrow AuthName, AuthEmail, AuthAddress$

$AuthEmail \rightarrow AuthNo$

$PaperNo \rightarrow Primary\text{-}AuthNo, Title, Abstract, Status$

$RevNo \rightarrow RevName, RevEmail, RevAddress$

$RevEmail \rightarrow RevNo$

$RevNo, PaperNo \rightarrow Auth\text{-}Comm, Prog\text{-}Comm, Date, Rating1, Rating2,$
$\qquad\qquad\qquad\qquad Rating3, Rating4, Rating5$

Because the LHS is minimal in each FD, the first step is finished. The second step is not necessary because there are no transitive dependencies. Note that the FDs *AuthEmail* → *AuthName, AuthAddress,* and *RevEmail* → *RevName, RevAddress* can be transitively derived. If any of these FDs were part of the original list, they should be removed. For each of the six FD groups, you can list a table. In the last step, you combine the FD groups with *AuthNo* and *AuthEmail* and *RevNo* and *RevEmail* as determinants. In addition, you should add unique constraints for *AuthEmail* and *RevEmail* because these columns were not selected as the primary key of the new tables.

Author(<u>AuthNo</u>, AuthName, AuthEmail, AuthAddress)
    UNIQUE (AuthEmail)

Paper(PaperNo, Primary-Auth, Title, Abstract, Status)
   FOREIGN KEY (Primary-Auth) REFERENCES Author
Reviewer(RevNo, RevName, RevEmail, RevAddress)
   UNIQUE (RevEmail)
Review(PaperNo, RevNo, Auth-Comm, Prog-Comm, Date, Rating1, Rating2,
     Rating3, Rating4, Rating5)
   FOREIGN KEY (PaperNo) REFERENCES Paper
   FOREIGN KEY (RevNo) REFERENCES Reviewer

7.3 REFINING M-WAY RELATIONSHIPS

Beyond BCNF, a remaining concern is the analysis of M-way relationships. Recall that M-way relationships are represented by associative entity types in the Crow's Foot ERD notation. In the conversion process, an associative entity type converts into a table with a combined primary key consisting of three or more components. The concept of independence, underlying 4NF, is an important tool used to analyze M-way relationships. Using the concept of independence, you may find that an M-way relationship should be split into two or more binary relationships to avoid redundancy. In Chapter 12, you will use forms to analyze the need for M-way relationships. The following sections describe the concept of relationship independence and 4NF.

7.3.1 Relationship Independence

Before you study how independence can influence a database design, let us discuss the meaning of independence in statistics. Two variables are statistically independent if knowing something about one variable tells you nothing about another variable. More precisely, two variables are independent if the probability of both variables (the joint probability) can be derived from the probability of each variable alone. For example, one variable may be the age of a rock, and another variable may be the age of the person holding the rock. Because the age of a rock and the age of a person holding the rock are unrelated, these variables are considered independent. However, the age of a person and a person's marital status are related. Knowing a person's age tells us something about the probability of being single, married, or divorced. If two variables are independent, it is redundant to store data about how they are related. You can use probabilities about individual variables to derive joint probabilities.

Relationship Independence
a relationship that can be derived from two independent relationships.

The concept of relationship independence is similar to statistical independence. If two relationships are independent (that is, not related), it is redundant to store data about a third relationship. You can derive the third relationship by combining the two essential relationships through a join operation. If you store the derived relationship, modification anomalies can result. Thus, the essential idea of relationship independence is not to store relationships that can be derived by joining other (independent) relationships.

Relationship Independence Example

To clarify relationship independence, consider the associative entity type *Enroll* (Figure 7.7) representing a three-way relationship among students, offerings, and textbooks. The *Enroll* entity type converts to the *Enroll* table (Table 7.6) that consists only of a combined primary key: *StdSSN, OfferNo,* and *TextNo.*

Figure 7.7 M-way relationship example.

TABLE 7.6 **Sample Rows of the *Enroll* Table**

StdSSN	OfferNo	TextNo
S1	O1	T1
S1	O2	T2
S1	O1	T2
S1	O2	T1

The design question is whether the *Enroll* table has redundancies. If there is redundancy, modification anomalies may result. The *Enroll* table is in BCNF, so there are no anomalies due to functional dependencies. However, the concept of independence leads to the discovery of redundancies. The *Enroll* table can be divided into three combinations of columns representing three binary relationships: *StdSSN–OfferNo* representing the relationship between students and offerings, *OfferNo–TextNo* representing the relationship between offerings and textbooks, and *StdSSN–TextNo* representing the relationship between students and textbooks. If any of the binary relationships can be derived from the other two, there is a redundancy.

- The relationship between students and offerings (*StdSSN–OfferNo*) cannot be derived from the other two relationships. For example, suppose that textbook T1 is used in two offerings, O1 and O2, and by two students, S1 and S2. Knowing these two facts, you do not know the relationship between students and offerings. For example, S1 could be enrolled in O1 or perhaps O2.
- Likewise, the relationship between offerings and textbooks (*OfferNo–TextNo*) cannot be derived. A professor's choice for a collection of textbooks cannot be derived by knowing who enrolls in an offering and what textbooks a student uses.
- However, the relationship between students and textbooks (*StdSSN–TextNo*) can be derived by the other two relationships. For example, if student S1 is enrolled in offering O1 and offering O1 uses textbook T1, then you can conclude that student S1 uses textbook T1 in offering O1. Because the *Student–Offering* and the *Offering–Textbook* relationships are independent, you know the textbooks used by a student without storing the relationship instances.

Because of this independence, the *Enroll* table and the related associative entity type *Enroll* have redundancy. To remove the redundancy, replace the *Enroll* entity type with two binary relationships (Figure 7.8). Each binary relationship converts to a table as shown in Tables 7.7 and 7.8. The *Enroll* and *Orders* tables have no redundancies. For example, to delete a student's enrollment in an offering (say S1 in O1), only one row must be deleted from Table 7.7. In contrast, two rows must be deleted from Table 7.6.

If the assumptions change slightly, an argument can be made for an associative entity type representing a three-way relationship. Suppose that the bookstore wants to record textbook purchases by offering and by student to estimate textbook demand. Then the relationship between students and textbooks is no longer independent of the other two relationships. Even though a student is enrolled in an offering and the offering uses a textbook, the student may not purchase the textbook (perhaps borrow it) for the offering. In this situation, there is no independence and a three-way relationship is needed. In addition to the M-N relationships in Figure 7.8, there should be a new associative entity type and three 1-M relationships, as shown in Figure 7.9. You need the

Figure 7.8   Decomposed relationships example.

TABLE 7.7	Sample Rows of the Binary *Enroll* Table

StdSSN	OfferNo
S1	O1
S1	O2

TABLE 7.8	Sample Rows of the Binary *Orders* Table

OfferNo	TextNo
O1	T1
O1	T2
O2	T1
O2	T2

Figure 7.9   **M-way and binary relationships example.**

A	B	C
A1	B1	C1
A1	B2	C2
A1	B2	C1
A1	B1	C2

Figure 7.10   **Table representation of an MVD.**

Enroll relationship to record student selections of offerings and the *Orders* relationship to record professor selections of textbooks. The *Purchase* entity type records purchases of textbooks by students in a course offering. However, a purchase cannot be known from the other relationships.

7.3.2 Multivalued Dependencies and Fourth Normal Form (4NF)

MVD Definition The multivalued dependency (MVD) $A \rightarrow \rightarrow B \mid C$ (read A multidetermines B or C) means that

1. A given A value is associated with a collection of B and C values, and

2. B and C are independent given the relationships between A and B and A and C.

In relational database terminology, a relationship that can be derived from other relationships is known as a multivalued dependency (MVD). An MVD involves three columns as described in the marginal definition. Like in the discussion of relationship independence, the three columns comprise a combined primary key of an associative table. The nonessential or derived relationship involves the columns B and C. The definition states that the nonessential relationship (involving the columns B and C) can be derived from the relationships A-B and A-C. The word *multivalued* means that A can be associated with a collection of B and C values, not just single values as in a functional dependency.

MVDs can lead to redundancies because of independence among columns. You can see the redundancy by using a table to depict an MVD as shown in Figure 7.10. If the two rows above the line exist and the MVD $A \rightarrow \rightarrow B \mid C$ is true, then the two rows below the line will exist. The two rows below the line will exist because the relationship between B and C can be derived from the relationships A-B and A-C. In Figure 7.10,

OfferNo	StdSSN	TextNo
O1	S1	T1
O1	S2	T2
O1	S2	T1
O1	S1	T2

Figure 7.11   **Representation of the MVD in the *Enroll* table.**

value A1 is associated with two *B* values (B1 and B2) and two *C* values (C1 and C2). Because of independence, value A1 will be associated with every combination of its related *B* and *C* values. The two rows below the line are redundant because they can be derived.

To apply this concept to the *Enroll* table, consider the possible MVD *OfferNo* → → *StdSSN | TextNo*. In the first two rows of Figure 7.11, offering O1 is associated with students S1 and S2 and textbooks T1 and T2. If the MVD is true, then the two rows below the line will exist. The last two rows do not need to be stored if you know the first two rows and the MVD exists.

MVDs are generalizations of functional dependencies (FDs). Every FD is an MVD but not every MVD is an FD. An MVD in which a value of *A* is associated with only one value of *B* and one value of *C* is also an FD. In this section, we are interested only in MVDs that are <u>not</u> also FDs. An MVD that is not an FD is known as a <u>nontrivial MVD</u>.

Fourth Normal Form (4NF)

4NF Definition a table is in 4NF if it does not contain any nontrivial MVDs (MVDs that are not also FDs).

<u>Fourth normal form (4NF)</u> prohibits redundancies caused by multivalued dependencies. As an example, the table *Enroll(StdSSN, OfferNo, TextNo)* (Table 7.6) is not in 4NF if the MVD *OfferNo* → → *StdSSN | TextNo* exists. To eliminate the MVD, split the M-way table *Enroll* into the binary tables *Enroll* (Table 7.7) and *Orders* (Table 7.8).

The ideas of MVDs and 4NF are somewhat difficult to understand. The ideas are somewhat easier to understand if you think of an MVD as a relationship that can be derived by other relationships because of independence. Chapter 12 presents another way to reason about M-way relationships using patterns in data entry forms.

7.4 HIGHER-LEVEL NORMAL FORMS

The normalization story does not end with 4NF. Other normal forms have been proposed, but their practicality has not been demonstrated. This section briefly describes two higher normal forms to complete your normalization background.

7.4.1 Fifth Normal Form (5NF)

5NF applies to M-way relationships like 4NF. Unlike 4NF, 5NF involves situations when a three-way relationship should be replaced with three binary relationships, not two binary relationships as for 4NF. Because situations in which 5NF applies (as opposed to 4NF) are rare, 5NF is generally not considered a practical normal form. Understanding the details of 5NF requires a lot of intellectual investment, but the return on your study time is rarely applicable.

Figure 7.12   Associative entity type.

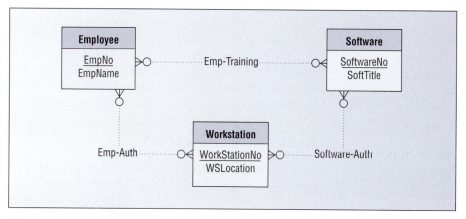

Figure 7.13   Replacement of associative entity type with three binary relationships.

The example in Figure 7.12 demonstrates a situation in which 5NF could apply. The *Authorization* entity type represents authorized combinations of employees, workstations, and software. This associative entity type has redundancy because it can be divided into three binary relationships as shown in Figure 7.13. If you know employees authorized to use workstations, software licensed for workstations, and employees trained to use software, then you know the valid combinations of employees, workstations, and software. Thus, it is necessary to record the three binary combinations (employee–workstation, software–workstation, and employee–software), not the three-way combination of employee, workstation, and software.

Whether the situation depicted in Figure 7.13 is realistic is debatable. For example, if software is licensed for servers rather than workstations, the *Software-Auth* relationship may not be necessary. Even though it is possible to depict situations in which 5NF applies, these situations may not exist in real organizations.

7.4.2 Domain Key Normal Form (DKNF)

After reading about so many normal forms, you may be asking questions such as "Where does it stop?" and "Is there an ultimate normal form?" Fortunately, the answer to the last question is yes. In a 1981 paper, Dr. Ronald Fagin proposed domain key normal form (DKNF) as the ultimate normal form. In DKNF, domain refers to a data type: a set of values with allowable operations. A set of values is defined by the kind of values (e.g., whole numbers versus floating-point numbers) and the integrity rules about the values (e.g., values greater than 21). Key refers to the uniqueness property of candidate keys. A table is in DKNF if every constraint on a table can be derived from keys and domains. A table in DKNF cannot have modification anomalies.

Unfortunately, DKNF remains an ideal rather than a practical normal form. There is no known algorithm for converting a table into DKNF. In addition, it is not even known what tables can be converted to DKNF. As an ideal, you should try to define tables in which most constraints result from keys and domains. These kinds of constraints are easy to test and understand.

7.5 PRACTICAL CONCERNS ABOUT NORMALIZATION

After reading this far, you should be well acquainted with the tools of relational database design. Before you are ready to use these tools, some practical advice is useful. This section discusses the role of normalization in the database development process and the importance of thinking carefully about the objective of eliminating modification anomalies.

7.5.1 Role of Normalization in the Database Development Process

There are two opposite ways to use normalization in the database development process: (1) as a refinement tool or (2) as an initial design tool. In the refinement approach, you perform conceptual data modeling using the Entity Relationship Model. If the design is large, you can design ERDs for individual views and then integrate them as described in Chapter 12. After you achieve a conceptual database design, the logical design step follows. In logical design, you transform the ERD into tables using the conversion rules. Then, you apply normalization techniques to analyze each table: identify FDs, use the simple synthesis procedure to remove redundancies, and analyze a table for independence if the table represents an M-way relationship.

In the initial design approach, you use normalization techniques in conceptual data modeling. Instead of drawing an ERD, you identify functional dependencies and apply a normalization procedure like the simple synthesis procedure. After defining the tables, you identify the referential integrity constraints and construct a relational model diagram such as that available in Microsoft Access. If needed, an ERD can be generated from the relational database diagram.

This book clearly favors using normalization as a refinement tool, not as an initial design tool. Through development of an ERD, you intuitively group related fields. Much normalization is accomplished in an informal manner without the tedious process of recording functional dependencies. As a refinement tool, there is usually less normalization to perform. The purpose is to ensure that you have not overlooked any redundancies. Normalization provides a rigorous way to reason about the quality of the design.

Another reason for favoring the refinement approach is that M-N relationships can be overlooked when using normalization as the initial design approach. If an M-N relationship has no attributes, there will not be any functional dependencies that show the need for a table. For example, in a design about textbooks and course offerings, if the relationship between them has no attributes, there are no functional dependencies that relate textbooks and course offerings.[6] In drawing an ERD, however, the need for an M-N relationship becomes clear.

7.5.2 Analyzing the Normalization Objective

As a design criterion, avoidance of modification anomalies is biased toward database changes. As you have seen, removing anomalies usually results in a database with many tables. A design with many tables makes a database easier to change but more difficult to query. If a database is used predominantly for queries, avoiding modification anomalies may not be an appropriate design goal. Chapter 16 describes databases for decision support in which the primary use is query rather than modification. In this situation, a design that is not fully normalized may be appropriate. Denormalization is the process of combining tables so that they are easier to query. In addition, physical design goals may conflict with logical design goals. Chapter 8 describes physical database design goals and the use of denormalization as a technique to improve query performance.

Another time to consider denormalization is when an FD is not important. The classic example contains the FDs $Zip \rightarrow City, State$ in a customer table where $City$ means the post office city. In some databases, these dependencies may not be important to maintain. If there is not a need to manipulate zip codes independent of customers, the FDs can be safely ignored. However, there are databases in which it is important to maintain a table of zip codes independent of customer information. For example, if a retailer does business in many states and countries, a zip code table is useful to record sales tax rates.[7] If you ignore an FD in the normalization process, you should note that it exists but will not lead to any significant anomalies. Proceed with caution: *most* FDs will lead to anomalies if ignored.

CLOSING THOUGHTS

This chapter described how redundancies could make a table difficult to change causing modification anomalies. Avoiding modification anomalies is the goal of normalization techniques. As a prerequisite to normalizing a table, you should list the functional dependencies (FDs). This chapter described three normal forms (2NF, 3NF, and BCNF) based on functional dependencies. The simple synthesis procedure was presented to analyze functional dependencies and produce tables in BCNF. Providing a complete list of FDs is the most important part of the normalization process. Even if you do not understand the normal forms, you can purchase a CASE tool to perform normalization. CASE tools are not capable of providing a complete list of FDs, however.

---

[6]An FD can be written with a null right-hand side to represent M-N relationships. The FD for the offering–textbook relationship can be expressed as *TextId, OfferNo* $\rightarrow \varnothing$. However, this kind of FD is awkward to state. It is much easier to define an M-N relationship.

[7]A former database student made this comment about the database of a large computer retailer.

This chapter also described an approach to analyze M-way relationships (represented by associative entity types) using the concept of independence. If two relationships are independent, a third relationship can be derived from them. There is no need to store the third relationship. The independence concept is equivalent to a multivalued dependency. 4NF prohibits redundancy caused by multivalued dependencies.

This chapter and the data modeling chapters, Chapters 5 and 6, emphasized data modeling and normalization, fundamental skills for database development. After data modeling and normalization are complete, you are ready to implement the design usually with a relational DBMS. Chapter 8 describes physical database design concepts and practices to facilitate your implementation work on relational DBMSs

REVIEW CONCEPTS

- Redundancies in a table cause modification anomalies.
- Modification anomalies: unexpected side effects when inserting, updating, or deleting.
- Functional dependencies: a value neutral constraint similar to a primary key.
- 2NF: nonkey columns dependent on the entire key, not a subset of the key.
- 3NF: nonkey columns dependent only on the key, not on other nonkey columns.
- BCNF: every determinant is a candidate key.
- Simple synthesis procedure: analyze FDs and produce tables in BCNF.
- Use the simple synthesis procedure to analyze simple dependency structures.
- Use commercial design software to analyze complex dependency structures.
- Use relationship independence as a criterion to split M-way relationships into smaller relationships.
- MVD: association with collections of values and independence among columns.
- MVDs cause redundancy because rows can be derived using independence.
- 4NF: no redundancies due to MVDs.
- Use normalization techniques as a refinement tool rather than as an initial design tool.
- Denormalize a table if FDs do not cause modification anomalies.

QUESTIONS

1. What is an insertion anomaly?
2. What is an update anomaly?
3. What is a deletion anomaly?
4. What is the cause of modification anomalies?
5. What is a functional dependency?
6. How is a functional dependency like a candidate key?
7. Can a software design tool identify functional dependencies? Briefly explain your answer.
8. What is the meaning of an FD with multiple columns on the right-hand side?
9. Why should you be careful when writing FDs with multiple columns on the left-hand side?

10. What is a normal form?

11. What does 1NF prohibit?

12. What is a key column?

13. What is a nonkey column?

14. What kinds of FDs are not allowed in 2NF?

15. What kinds of FDs are not allowed in 3NF?

16. What is the combined definition of 2NF and 3NF?

17. What kinds of FDs are not allowed in BCNF?

18. What is the relationship between BCNF and 3NF? Is BCNF a stricter normal form than 3NF? Briefly explain your answer.

19. Why is the BCNF definition preferred to the 3NF definition?

20. What are the special cases covered by BCNF but not covered by 3NF?

21. Are the special cases covered by BCNF but not 3NF significant?

22. What is the goal of the simple synthesis procedure?

23. What is a limitation of the simple synthesis procedure?

24. What is a transitive dependency?

25. Are transitive dependencies permitted in 3NF tables? Explain why or why not.

26. Why eliminate transitive dependencies in the simple synthesis procedure?

27. When is it necessary to perform the fifth step of the simple synthesis procedure?

28. How is relationship independence similar to statistical independence?

29. What kind of redundancy is caused by relationship independence?

30. How many columns does an MVD involve?

31. What is a multivalued dependency (MVD)?

32. What is the relationship between MVDs and FDs?

33. What is a nontrivial MVD?

34. What is the goal of 4NF?

35. What are the advantages of using normalization as a refinement tool rather than as an initial design tool?

36. Why is 5NF not considered a practical normal form?

37. Why is DKNF not considered a practical normal form?

38. When is denormalization useful? Provide an example to depict when it may be beneficial for a table to violate 3NF.

39. What are the two ways to use normalization in the database development process?

40. Why does this book recommend using normalization as a refinement tool, not as an initial design tool?

PROBLEMS

ORDER

Besides the problems presented here, the case study in Chapter 13 provides additional practice. To supplement the examples in this chapter, Chapter 13 provides a complete database design case including conceptual data modeling, schema conversion, and normalization.

1. For the big university database table, list FDs with the column *StdCity* as the determinant that are *not* true due to the sample data. With each FD that does not hold, show the sample data that violate it. Remember that it takes two rows to demonstrate a violation of an FD. The sample data are repeated in Table 7.P1 for your reference.

2. Following on problem 1, list FDs with the column *StdCity* as the determinant that the sample data do not violate. For each FD, add one or more sample rows and then identify the sample data that violate the FD. Remember that it takes two rows to demonstrate a violation of an FD.

3. For the big patient table, list FDs with the column *PatZip* as the determinant that are *not* true due to the sample data. Exclude the FD *PatZip → PatCity* because it is a valid FD. With each FD that does not hold, show the sample data that violate it. Remember that it takes two rows to demonstrate a violation of an FD. The sample data are repeated in Table 7.P2 for your reference.

4. Following on problem 3, list FDs with the column *PatZip* as the determinant that sample data do not violate. Exclude the FD *PatZip → PatCity* because it is a valid FD. For each FD, add one or more sample rows and then identify the sample data that violate the FD. Remember that it takes two rows to demonstrate a violation of an FD.

5. Apply the simple synthesis procedure to the FDs of the big patient table. The FDs are repeated in Table 7.P3 for your reference. Show the result of each step in the procedure. Include the primary keys and the foreign keys in the final list of tables.

TABLE 7.P1   Sample Data for the "Big" University Database Table

StdSSN	StdCity	StdClass	OfferNo	OffTerm	OffYear	EnrGrade	CourseNo	CrsDesc
S1	SEATTLE	JUN	O1	FALL	2003	3.5	C1	DB
S1	SEATTLE	JUN	O2	FALL	2003	3.3	C2	VB
S2	BOTHELL	JUN	O3	WINTER	2003	3.1	C3	OO
S2	BOTHELL	JUN	O2	FALL	2003	3.4	C2	VB

TABLE 7.P2   Sample Data for the Big Patient Table

VisitNo	VisitDate	PatNo	PatAge	PatCity	PatZip	ProvNo	ProvSpecialty	Diagnosis
V10020	1/13/2004	P1	35	DENVER	80217	D1	INTERNIST	EAR INFECTION
V10020	1/13/2004	P1	35	DENVER	80217	D2	NURSE PRACTITIONER	INFLUENZA
V93030	1/20/2004	P3	17	ENGELWOOD	80113	D2	NURSE PRACTITIONER	PREGNANCY
V82110	1/18/2004	P2	60	BOULDER	85932	D3	CARDIOLOGIST	MURMUR

TABLE 7.P3	List of FDs for the Big Patient Table

PatNo → PatAge, PatCity, PatZip

PatZip → PatCity

ProvNo → ProvSpecialty

VisitNo → PatNo, VisitDate, PatAge, PatCity, PatZip

VisitNo, ProvNo → Diagnosis

6. The FD diagram in Figure 7.P1 depicts FDs among columns in an order entry database. Figure 7.P1 shows FDs with determinants *CustNo, OrderNo, ItemNo,* the combination of *OrderNo* and *ItemNo,* the combination of *ItemNo* and *PlantNo,* and the combination of *OrderNo* and *LineNo.* In the bottom FDs, the combination of *LineNo* and *OrderNo* determines *ItemNo* and the combination of *OrderNo* and *ItemNo* determines *LineNo.* To test your understanding of dependency diagrams, convert the dependency diagram into a list of dependencies organized by the LHSs.

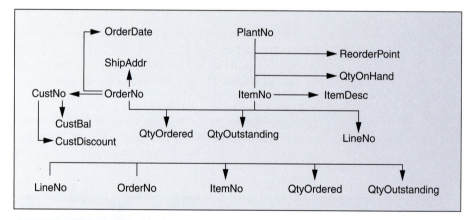

Figure 7.P1	Dependency diagram for the big order entry table.

7. Using the FD diagram (Figure 7.P1) and the FD list (solution to problem 6) as guidelines, make a table with sample data. There are two candidate keys for the underlying table: the combination of *OrderNo, ItemNo,* and *PlantNo* and the combination of *OrderNo, LineNo,* and *PlantNo.* Using the sample data, identify insertion, update, and deletion anomalies in the table.

8. Derive 2NF tables starting with the FD list from problem 6 and the table from problem 7.

9. Derive 3NF tables starting with the FD list from problem 6 and the 2NF tables from problem 8.

10. Following on problems 6 and 7, apply the simple synthesis procedure to produce BCNF tables.

11. Modify your table design in problem 10 if the shipping address (*ShipAddr*) column determines customer number (*CustNo*). Do you think that this additional FD is reasonable? Briefly explain your answer.

12. Go back to the original FD diagram in which *ShipAddr* does not determine *CustNo.* How does your table design change if you want to keep track of a master list of shipping addresses for each customer? Assume that you do not want to lose a shipping address when an order is deleted.

13. Convert the ERD in Figure 7.P2 into tables and perform further normalization as needed. After converting to tables, write down FDs for each table. If a table is not in BCNF, explain why and split it into two or more tables that are in BCNF.

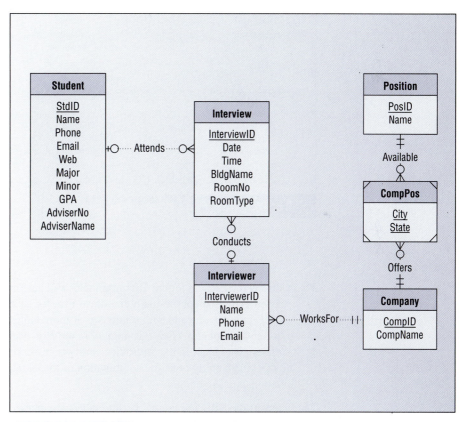

Figure 7.P2   ERD for problem 13.

14. Convert the ERD in Figure 7.P3 into tables and perform further normalization as needed. After the conversion, write down FDs for each table. If a table is not in BCNF, explain why and split it into two or more tables that are in BCNF. Note that in the *Owner* and *Buyer* entity types, the primary key (*SSN*) is included although it is inherited from the *Person* entity type.

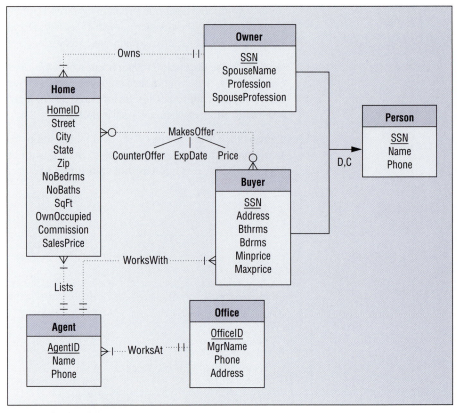

Figure 7.P3   **ERD for problem 14.**

15. Convert the ERD in Figure 7.P4 into tables and perform further normalization as needed. After the conversion, write down FDs for each table. If a table is not in BCNF, explain why and split it into two or more tables that are in BCNF. In the *User* entity type, *UserEmail* is unique. In the *ExpenseCategory* entity type, *CatDesc* is unique. In the *StatusType* entity type, *StatusDesc* is unique. For the *ExpenseItem* entity type, the combination of the *Categorizes* and *Contains* relationships are unique.

16. Convert the ERD in Figure 7.P5 into tables and perform further normalization as needed. After the conversion, write down FDs for each table. If a table is not in BCNF, explain why and split it into two or more tables that are in BCNF. In the employee entity type, each department has one manager. All employees in a department are supervised by the same manager. For the other entity types, *FacName* is unique in *Facility, ResName* is unique in *Resource,* and *CustName* and *CustEmail* are unique in *Customer.*

17. Extend the solution to the problem described in Section 7.2.4 about a database to track submitted conference papers. In the description, underlined parts are new. Write down the new FDs. Using the simple synthesis procedure, design a

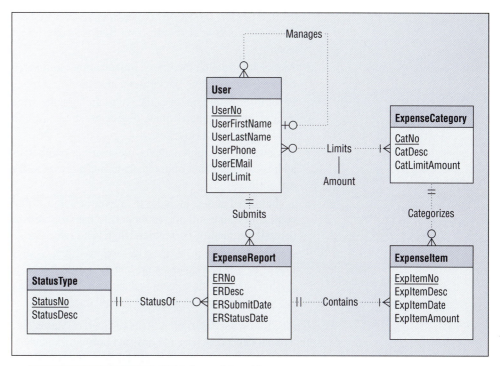

Figure 7.P4   ERD for problem 15.

Figure 7.P5   ERD for problem 16.

collection of tables in BCNF. Note dependencies that are not important to the problem and relax your design from BCNF as appropriate. Justify your reasoning.

- Author information includes a unique author number, a name, a mailing address, and a unique but optional electronic address.
- Paper information includes the <u>list of authors</u>, the primary author, the paper number, the title, the abstract, the review status (pending, accepted, rejected), and a <u>list of subject categories</u>.
- Reviewer information includes the reviewer number, the name, the mailing address, a unique but optional electronic address, and a <u>list of expertise categories</u>.
- A completed review includes the reviewer number, the date, the paper number, comments to the authors, comments to the program chairperson, and ratings (overall, originality, correctness, style, and relevance).
- <u>Accepted papers are assigned to sessions. Each session has a unique session identifier, a list of papers, a presentation order for each paper, a session title, a session chairperson, a room, a date, a start time, and a duration. Note that each accepted paper can be assigned to only one session.</u>

18. For the following description of an airline reservation database, identify functional dependencies and construct normalized tables. Using the simple synthesis procedure, design a collection of tables in BCNF. Note dependencies that are not important to the problem and relax your design from BCNF as appropriate. Justify your reasoning.

The Fly by Night Operation is a newly formed airline aimed at the burgeoning market of clandestine travelers (fugitives, spies, con artists, scoundrels, deadbeats, cheating spouses, politicians, etc.). The Fly by Night Operation needs a database to track flights, customers, fares, airplane performance, and personnel assignment. Since the Fly by Night Operation is touted as a "fast way out of town," individual seats are not assigned, and flights of other carriers are not tracked. More specific notes about different parts of the database are listed below:

- Information about a flight includes its unique flight number, its origin, its (supposed) destination, and (roughly) estimated departure and arrival times. To reduce costs, the Fly by Night Operation only has nonstop flights with a single origin and destination.
- Flights are scheduled for one or more dates with an airplane and a crew assigned to each scheduled flight, and the remaining capacity (seats remaining) noted. In a crew assignment, the employee number and the role (e.g., captain, flight attendant) are noted.
- Airplanes have a unique serial number, a model, a capacity, and a next scheduled maintenance date.
- The maintenance record of an airplane includes a unique maintenance number, a date, a description, the serial number of the plane, and the employee responsible for the repairs.
- Employees have a unique employee number, a name, a phone, and a job title.
- Customers have a unique customer number, a phone number, and a name (typically an alias).

- Records are maintained for reservations of scheduled flights including a unique reservation number, a flight number, a flight date, a customer number, a reservation date, a fare, and the payment method (usually cash but occasionally someone else's check or credit card). If the payment is by credit card, a credit card number and an expiration date are part of the reservation record.

19. For the following description of an accounting database, identify functional dependencies and construct normalized tables. Using the simple synthesis procedure, design a collection of tables in BCNF. Note dependencies that are not important to the problem and relax your design from BCNF as appropriate. Justify your reasoning.

    - The primary function of the database is to record entries into a register. A user can have multiple accounts and there is a register for each account.
    - Information about users includes a unique user number, a name, a street address, a city, a state, a zip, and an e-mail address (optional).
    - Accounts have attributes including a unique number, a unique name, a start date, a last check number, a type (checking, investment, etc.), a user number, and a current balance (computed). For checking accounts, the bank number (unique), the bank name, and the bank address are also recorded.
    - An entry contains a unique number, a type, an optional check number, a payee, a date, an amount, a description, an account number, and a list of entry lines. The *type* can have various values including ATM, next check number, deposit, and debit card.
    - In the list of entry lines, the user allocates the total amount of the entry to categories. An entry line includes a category name, a description of the entry line, and an amount.
    - Categories have other attributes not shown in an entry line: a unique category number (name is also unique), a description, a type (asset, expense, revenue, or liability), and a tax-related status (yes or no).
    - Categories are organized in hierarchies. For example, there is a category Auto with subcategories Auto:fuel and Auto:repair. Categories can have multiple levels of subcategories.

20. For the ERDs in Figure 7.P6, describe assumptions under which the ERDs correctly depict the relationships among operators, machines, and tasks. In each case, choose appropriate names for the relationships and describe the meaning of the relationships. In part (b) you should also choose the name for the new entity type.

21. For the following description of a database to support physical plant operations, identify functional dependencies and construct normalized tables. Using the simple synthesis procedure, design a collection of tables in BCNF. Note dependencies that are not important to the problem and relax your design from BCNF as appropriate. Justify your reasoning.

    Design a database to assist physical plant personnel in managing key cards for access to buildings and rooms. The primary purpose of the database is to ensure proper accounting for all key cards.

    - A building has a unique building number, a unique name, and a location within the campus.

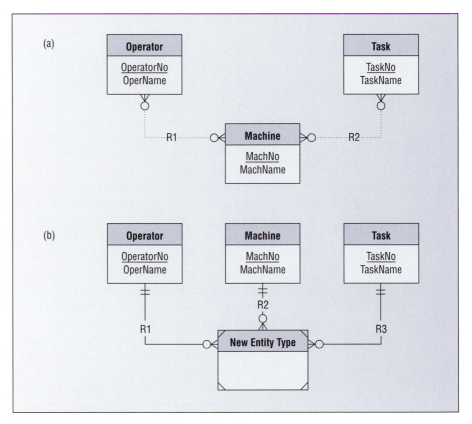

Figure 7.P6 ERDs for problem 20.

- A room has a unique room number, a size (physical dimensions), a capacity, a number of entrances, and a description of equipment in the room. Each room is located in exactly one building. The room number includes a building identification followed by an integer number. For example, room number KC100 identifies room 100 in the King Center (KC) building.
- An employee has a unique employee number, a name, a position, a unique e-mail address, a phone, and an optional room number in which the employee works.
- Magnetically encoded key cards are designed to open one or more rooms. A key card has a unique card number, a date encoded, a list of room numbers that the key card opens, and the number of the employee authorizing the key card. A room may have one or more key cards that open it. A key type must be authorized before it is created.

22. For the ERDs in Figure 7.P7, describe assumptions under which the ERDs correctly depict the relationships among work assignments, tasks, and materials. A work assignment contains the scheduled work for a construction job at a specific location. Scheduled work includes the tasks and materials needed for the construction job. In each case, choose appropriate names for the relationships and describe the meaning of the relationships. In part (b) you should also choose the name for the new entity type.

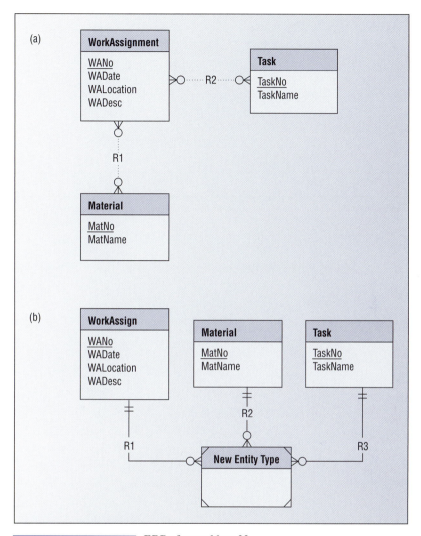

Figure 7.P7   **ERDs for problem 22.**

REFERENCES FOR FURTHER STUDY

The subject of normalization can be much more detailed than described in this chapter. For a more detailed description of normalization, consult computer science books such as Date (1995), Elmasri and Navathe (1994), and Teorey (1999). The simple synthesis procedure was adapted from Hawryszkiewycz (1984). For a classic tutorial on normalization, consult Kent (1983). Fagin (1981) describes domain key normal form, the ultimate normal form. The *DBAZine* site (www.dbazine.com) and the DevX help site (www.devx.com/gethelp) have practical advice about database development and normalization.

Physical Database Design

LEARNING OBJECTIVES

This chapter describes physical database design, the final phase of the database development process. Physical database design transforms a table design from the logical design phase into an efficient implementation that supports all applications using the database. After this chapter, the student should have acquired the following knowledge and skills:

- Describe the inputs, outputs, and objectives of physical database design.

- List characteristics of sequential, Btree, hash, and bitmap index file structures.

- Appreciate the difficulties of performing physical database design and the need for periodic review of physical database design choices.

- Understand the trade-offs in index selection and denormalization decisions.

- Understand the need for good tools to help make physical database design decisions.

OVERVIEW

Chapters 5 to 7 covered the conceptual and the logical design phases of database development. You learned about entity relationship diagrams, data modeling practice, schema conversion, and normalization. This chapter extends your database design skills by showing you how to achieve an efficient implementation of your table design.

To become proficient in physical database design, you need to understand the process and environment. This chapter describes the process of physical database design including the inputs, the outputs, and the objectives along with two critical parts of the environment, file structures and query optimization. Most of the choices in physical database design relate to characteristics of file structures and query optimization decisions.

After understanding the process and environment, you are ready to perform physical database design. In performing physical database design, you should provide good inputs and make choices to balance the needs of retrieval and update applications. This chapter describes table profiles and application profiles as important but sometimes difficult-to-define inputs. Index selection is the most important choice of physical database design. This chapter describes trade-offs in index selection and provides index selection rules that you can apply to moderate-size databases. In addition to index selection, this chapter presents denormalization, record formatting, and parallel processing as techniques to improve database performance.

8.1 OVERVIEW OF PHYSICAL DATABASE DESIGN

Decisions in the physical database design phase involve the storage level of a database. Collectively, the storage-level decisions are known as the internal schema. This section describes the storage level as well as the objectives, the inputs, and the outputs used in physical database design.

8.1.1 Storage Level of Databases

Physical Record collection of bytes that are transferred between volatile storage in main memory and stable storage on a disk. The number of physical record accesses is an important measure of database performance.

The storage level is closest to the hardware and operating system. At the storage level, a database consists of physical records (also known as blocks or pages) organized into files. A <u>physical record</u> is a collection of bytes that are transferred between volatile storage in main memory and stable storage on a disk. Main memory is considered volatile storage because the contents of main memory may be lost if a failure occurs. A <u>file</u> is a collection of physical records organized for efficient access. Figure 8.1 depicts relation-

Figure 8.1   **Relationships between logical records (LR) and physical records (PR).**

ships between logical records (rows of a table) and physical records stored in a file. Typically, a physical record contains multiple logical records. The size of a physical record is a power of two such as 1024 (2^{10}) or 4096 (2^{12}) bytes. A large logical record may be split over multiple physical records. Another possibility is that logical records from more than one table are stored in the same physical record.

The DBMS and the operating system work together to satisfy requests for logical records made by applications. Figure 8.2 depicts the process of transferring physical and logical records between a disk, DBMS buffers, and application buffers. Normally, the DBMS and the application have separate memory areas known as buffers. When an application makes a request for a logical record, the DBMS locates the physical record containing it. In the case of a read operation, the operating system transfers the physical record from disk to the memory area of the DBMS. The DBMS then transfers the logical record to the application's buffer. In the case of a write operation, the transfer process is reversed.

A logical record request may not result in a physical record transfer because of buffering. The DBMS tries to anticipate the needs of applications so that corresponding physical records already reside in the DBMS buffers. A significant difficulty about predicting database performance is knowing when a logical record request leads to a physical record transfer. For example, if multiple applications are accessing the same logical records, the corresponding physical records may reside in the DBMS buffers. Consequently, the uncertainty about the contents of DBMS buffers can make physical database design difficult.

8.1.2 Objectives and Constraints

The goal of physical database design is to minimize response time to access and change a database. Because response time is difficult to estimate directly, minimizing computing resources is used as a substitute measure. The resources that are consumed by database processing are physical record transfers, central processing unit (CPU)

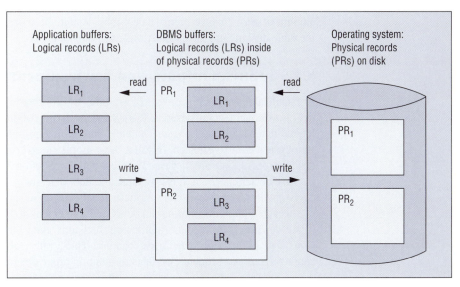

| Figure 8.2 | **Transferring physical records.** |

operations, main memory, and disk space. The latter two resources (main memory and disk space) are considered as constraints rather than resources to minimize. Minimizing main memory and disk space can lead to high response times.

The number of physical record accesses limits the performance of most database applications. A physical record access may involve mechanical movement of a disk including rotation and magnetic head movement. Mechanical movement is generally much slower than electronic switching of main memory. The speed of a disk access is measured in milliseconds (thousandths of a second) whereas a memory access is measured in nanoseconds (billionths of a second). Thus, a physical record access may be many times slower than a main memory access. Reducing the number of physical record accesses will usually improve response time.

CPU usage also can be a factor in some database applications. For example, sorting requires a large number of comparisons and assignments. These operations, performed by the CPU, are many times faster than a physical record access, however. To accommodate both physical record accesses and CPU usage, a weight can be used to combine them into one measure. The weight is usually close to 0 to reflect that many CPU operations can be performed in the time to perform one physical record transfer.

The objective of physical database design is to minimize the combined measure for all applications using the database. Generally, improving performance on retrieval applications comes at the expense of update applications and vice versa. Therefore, an important theme of physical database design is to balance the needs of retrieval and update applications.

The measures of performance are too detailed to estimate by hand except for simple situations. Complex optimization software calculates estimates using detailed cost formulas. The optimization software is usually part of the SQL compiler. Understanding the nature of the performance measure helps one to interpret choices made by the optimization software.

For most choices in physical database design, the amounts of main memory and disk space are usually fixed. In other words, main memory and disk space are constraints of the physical database design process. As with constraints in other optimization problems, you should consider the effects of changing the given amounts of main memory and disk space. Increasing the amounts of these resources can improve performance. The amount of performance improvement may depend on many factors such as the DBMS, the table design, and the applications using the database.

> **Combined Measure of Database Performance** *PRA* + *W* * *CPU-OP* where *PRA* is the number of physical record accesses, *CPU-OP* is the number of CPU operations such as comparisons and assignments, and *W* is a weight, a real number between 0 and 1.

8.1.3 Inputs, Outputs, and Environment

Physical database design consists of a number of different inputs and outputs as depicted in Figure 8.3 and summarized in Table 8.1. The starting point is the table design from the logical database design phase. The table and application profiles are used specifically for physical database design. Because these inputs are so critical to the physical database design process, they are discussed in more detail in Section 8.2. The most important outputs are decisions about file structures and data placement. Section 8.5 discusses these decisions in more detail. For simplicity, decisions about other outputs are made separately even though the outputs can be related. For example, file structures are usually selected separately from denormalization decisions even though denormalization decisions can affect file structure decisions. Thus, physical database design is better characterized as a sequence of decision-making processes rather than one large process.

Knowledge about file structures and query optimization is in the environment of physical database design rather than being an input. The knowledge can be embedded in database design tools. If database design tools are not available, a designer informally

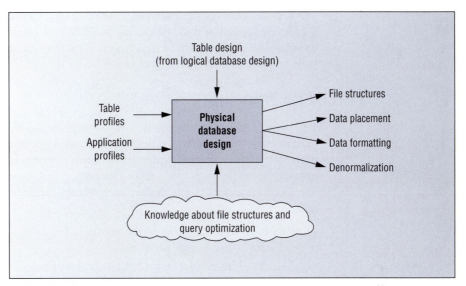

| **Figure 8.3** | Inputs, outputs, and environment of physical database design. |

| **TABLE 8.1** | **Summary of Inputs, Outputs, and Environment of Physical Database Design** |

Item	*Description*
Inputs	
Table profiles	Statistics for each table such as the number of rows and unique column values
Application profiles	Statistics for each form, report, and query such as the tables accessed/updated and the frequency of access/update
Outputs	
File structures	Method of organizing physical records for each table
Data placement	Criteria for arranging physical records in close proximity
Data formatting	Usage of compression and derived data
Denormalization	Combining separate tables into a single table
Environment knowledge	
File structures	Characteristics such as kind of access supported and cost formulas
Query optimization	Access decisions made by the optimization component for each query

uses knowledge about the environment to make physical database decisions. Acquiring the knowledge can be difficult because much of it is specific to each DBMS. Because knowledge of the environment is so crucial in the physical database design process, Sections 8.3 and 8.4 discuss it in more detail.

8.1.4 Difficulties

Before proceeding to more details about physical database design, it is important to understand why physical database design is difficult. The difficulty is due to the number of decisions, relationships among decisions, detailed inputs, complex environment, and uncertainty in predicting physical record accesses. These factors are briefly discussed below. In the remainder of this chapter, keep these difficulties in mind.

- The number of possible choices available to the designer can be large. For databases with many fields, the number of possible choices can be too large to evaluate even on large computers.
- The decisions cannot be made in isolation of each other. For example, file structure decisions for one table can influence the decisions for other tables.
- The quality of decisions is limited to the precision of the table and application profiles. However, these inputs can be large and difficult to collect. In addition, the inputs change over time so that periodic collection is necessary.
- The environment knowledge is specific to each DBMS. Much of the knowledge is either a trade secret or too complex to fully know.
- The number of physical record accesses is difficult to predict because of uncertainty about the contents of DBMS buffers. The uncertainty arises because the mix of applications accessing the database is constantly changing.

8.2 Inputs of Physical Database Design

Physical database design requires inputs specified in sufficient detail. Inputs specified without enough detail can lead to poor decisions in physical database design and query optimization. This section describes the level of detail recommended for both table profiles and application profiles.

8.2.1 Table Profiles

A table profile summarizes a table as a whole, the columns within a table, and the relationships between tables as shown in Table 8.2. Because table profiles are tedious to construct manually, most DBMSs provide statistics programs to construct them automatically. The designer may need to periodically run the statistics program so that the

TABLE 8.2	Typical Components of a Table Profile

Component	Statistics
Table	Number of rows and physical records
Column	Number of unique values, distribution of values
Relationship	Distribution of the number of related rows

profiles do not become obsolete. For large databases, table profiles may be estimated on samples of the database. Using the entire database can be too time consuming and disruptive.

For column and relationship summaries, the distribution conveys the number of rows and related rows for column values. The distribution of values can be specified in a number of ways. A simple way is to assume that the column values are uniformly distributed. Uniform distribution means that each value has an equal number of rows. If the uniform value assumption is made, only the minimum and maximum values must be specified.

A more detailed way to specify a distribution is to use a histogram. A <u>histogram</u> is a two-dimensional graph where the *x*-axis represents column ranges and the *y*-axis represents the number of rows containing the range of values. For example, the first bar in Figure 8.4 means that 1,500 rows have a salary greater than or equal to 0 and less than or equal to 20,000. The number of ranges to encode a distribution depends on the column and the method of choosing ranges. References at the end of the chapter describe methods to choose ranges.

Table profiles are used to calculate estimates of the combined measure of performance presented in Section 8.1.2. For example, the number of physical records is used to calculate the physical record accesses to retrieve all rows of a table. The distribution of column values is needed to estimate the fraction of rows that satisfy a condition in a query. For example, to estimate the fraction of rows that satisfy the condition Salary > 45000, you would sum the number of rows in the first three bars of Figure 8.4 and use linear interpolation in the fourth bar.

It is sometimes useful to store more detailed data about columns. If columns are related, errors can be made when estimating the fraction of rows that satisfy conditions connected by Boolean operators. For example, if the salary and age columns are related, the fraction of rows satisfying the Boolean expression Salary > 45000 AND Age < 25 cannot be accurately estimated by knowing the distribution of salary and age alone. Data about the statistical relationship between salary and age are also necessary. Because summaries about column relationships are costly to collect and store, many DBMSs assume that columns are independent.

| **Figure 8.4** | **Example histogram for salary column.** |

8.2.2 Application Profiles

Application profiles summarize the queries, forms, and reports that access a database as shown in Table 8.3. For forms, the frequency of using the main form and the subform for each kind of operation (insert, update, delete, and retrieval) should be specified. For queries and reports, the distribution of parameter values encodes the number of times the query/report is executed with various parameter values. Unfortunately, DBMSs are not as helpful to collect application profiles as table profiles. The database designer may need to write specialized software or find third-party software to collect application profiles.

Table 8.4 depicts profiles for several applications of the university database. The frequency data are specified as an average per unit time period such as per day. Sometimes it is useful to summarize frequencies in more detail. Specifying peak frequencies and variance in frequencies can help avoid problems with demand spikes. In addition, specifying response time limits indicates the importance of applications. Response time limits can allow designs to be tilted toward critical applications.

TABLE 8.3	**Typical Components of an Application Profile**
Application Type	*Statistics*
Query	Frequency, distribution of parameter values
Form	Frequency of insert, update, delete, and retrieval operations to the main form and the subform
Report	Frequency, distribution of parameter values

TABLE 8.4	**Example Application Profiles**		
Application Name	*Tables*	*Operation*	*Frequency*
Enrollment Query	*Course, Offering, Enrollment*	Retrieval	100 per day during the registration period; 50 per day during the drop/add period
Registration Main Form	*Registration*	Insert	1,000 per day during the registration period
Registration Subform	*Enrollment*	Insert	5,000 per day during the registration period; 1,000 per day during the drop/add period
Registration Main Form	*Registration*	Delete	100 per day during the registration period; 10 per day during the drop/add period
Registration Subform	*Enrollment*	Delete	1,000 per day during the registration period; 500 per day during the drop/add period
Registration Main Form	*Registration, Student*	Retrieval	6,000 per day during the registration period; 1,500 per day during the drop/add period
Registration Subform	*Enrollment, Course, Offering, Faculty*	Retrieval	6,000 per day during the registration period; 1,500 per day during the drop/add period
Faculty Workload Report	*Faculty, Course, Offering, Enrollment*	Retrieval	50 per day during the last week of the academic period; 10 per day otherwise; typical parameters: current year and academic period

8.3 FILE STRUCTURES

As mentioned in Section 8.1, selecting among alternative file structures is one of the most important choices in physical database design. In order to choose intelligently, you must understand characteristics of available file structures. This section describes the characteristics of common file structures available in most DBMSs.

8.3.1 Sequential Files

The simplest kind of file structure stores logical records in insertion order. New logical records are appended to the last physical record in the file, as shown in Figure 8.5. Unless logical records are inserted in a particular order and no deletions are made, the file becomes unordered. Unordered files are sometimes known as heap files because of the lack of order.

> **Sequential File** a simple file organization in which records are stored in insertion order or by key value. Sequential files are simple to maintain and provide good performance for processing large numbers of records.

The primary advantage of unordered sequential files is fast insertion. However, when logical records are deleted, insertion becomes more complicated. For example, if the second logical record in PR_1 is deleted, space is available in PR_1. A list of free space must be maintained to tell if a new record can be inserted into the empty space instead of into the last physical record. Alternately, new logical records can always be inserted in the last physical record. However, periodic reorganization to reclaim lost space due to deletions is necessary.

Because ordered retrieval is sometimes needed, ordered sequential files can be preferable to unordered sequential files. Logical records are arranged in key order where the key can be any column, although it is often the primary key. Ordered sequential files are faster when retrieving in key order, either the entire file or a subset of records. The primary disadvantage to ordered sequential files is slow insertion speed. Figure 8.6 demonstrates that records must sometimes be rearranged during the insertion process. The rearrangement process can involve movement of logical records between blocks and maintenance of an ordered list of physical records.

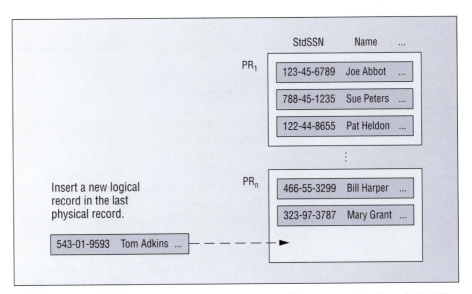

Figure 8.5   **Inserting a new logical record into an unordered sequential file.**

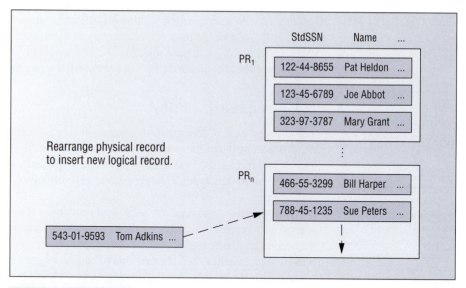

Figure 8.6 Inserting a new logical record into an ordered sequential file.

TABLE 8.5	Hash Function Calculations for *StdSSN* Values

StdSSN	StdSSN Mod 97	PR Number
122448655	26	176
123456789	39	189
323973787	92	242
466553299	80	230
788451235	24	174
543019593	13	163

8.3.2 Hash Files

Hash File a specialized file structure that supports search by key. Hash files transform a key value into an address to provide fast access.

Hash files, in contrast to sequential files, support fast access of records by primary key value. The basic idea behind hash files is a function that converts a key value into a physical record address. The mod function (remainder division) is a simple hash function. Table 8.5 applies the mod function to the *StdSSN* column values in Figure 8.6. For simplicity, assume that the file capacity is 100 physical records. The divisor for the mod function is 97, a large prime number close to the file capacity. The physical record number is the result of the hash function result plus the starting physical record number, assumed to be 150. Figure 8.7 shows selected physical records of the hash file.

Hash functions may assign more than one key to the same physical record address. A collision occurs when two keys hash to the same physical record address. As long as the physical record has free space, a collision is no problem. However, if the original or home physical record is full, a collision-handling procedure locates a physical record with free space. Figure 8.8 demonstrates the linear probe procedure for collision handling. In

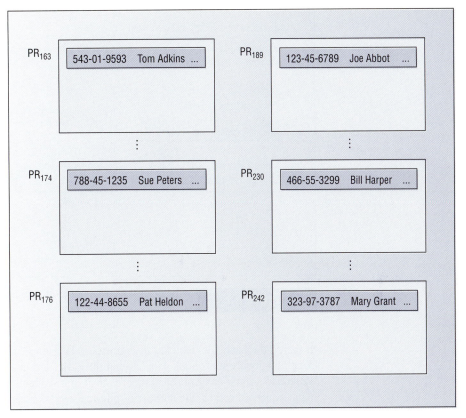

Figure 8.7   Hash file after insertions.

the linear probe procedure, a logical record is placed in the next available physical record if its home address is occupied. To retrieve a record by its key, the home address is initially searched. If the record is not found in its home address, a linear probe is initiated.

The existence of collisions highlights a potential problem with hash files. If collisions do not occur often, insertions and retrievals are very fast. If collisions occur often, insertions and retrievals can be slow. The likelihood of a collision depends on how full the file is. Generally, if the file is less than 70 percent full, collisions do not occur often. However, maintaining a hash file that is only 70 percent full can be a problem if the table grows. If the hash file becomes too full, a reorganization is necessary. A reorganization can be time consuming and disruptive because a larger hash file is allocated and all logical records are inserted into the new file.

To eliminate reorganizations, dynamic hash files have been proposed. In a dynamic hash file, periodic reorganization is never necessary and search performance does not degrade after many insert operations. However, the average number of physical record accesses to retrieve a record may be slightly higher as compared to a static hash file that is not too full. The basic idea in dynamic hashing is that the size of the hash file grows as records are inserted. For details of the various approaches, consult the references at the end of this chapter.

Another problem with hash files is sequential search. Good hash functions tend to spread logical records uniformly among physical records. Because of gaps between physical records, sequential search may examine empty physical records. For example,

| **Figure 8.8** | **Linear probe collision handling during an insert operation.** |

to search the hash file depicted in Figure 8.7, 100 physical records must be examined even though only six contain data. Even if the hash file is reasonably full, logical records are spread among more physical records than in a sequential file. Thus, when performing a sequential search, the number of physical record accesses may be higher in a hash file than in a sequential file.

8.3.3 Multiway Tree (Btrees) Files

Sequential files and hash files provide good performance on some operations but poor performance on other operations. Sequential files perform well on sequential search but poorly on key search. Hash files perform well on key search but poorly on sequential search. The multiway tree or <u>Btree</u> as it is popularly known, is a compromise and widely used file structure. The Btree provides good performance on both sequential search and key search. This section describes characteristics of the Btree, shows examples of Btree operations, and discusses the cost of operations.

Btree File a popular file structure supported by most DBMSs because it provides good performance both on key search as well as sequential search. A Btree file is a balanced, multiway tree.

Btree Characteristics: What's in a Name?

A Btree is a special kind of tree, as depicted in Figure 8.9. A tree is a structure in which each node has at most one parent except for the root or top node. The Btree structure possesses a number of characteristics, discussed in the following list, that make it a useful file structure. Some of the characteristics are possible meanings for the letter *B* in the name.[1]

- **Balanced:** all leaf nodes (nodes without children) reside on the same level of the tree. In Figure 8.9, all leaf nodes are two levels beneath the root. A balanced tree ensures that all leaf nodes can be retrieved with the same access cost.

---

[1] Another possible meaning for the letter *B* is Bayer, for the inventor of the Btree, Professor Rudolph Bayer. In a private conversation, Professor Bayer denied naming the Btree after himself or for his employer at the time, Boeing. When pressed, Professor Bayer only said that the *B* represents the *B*.

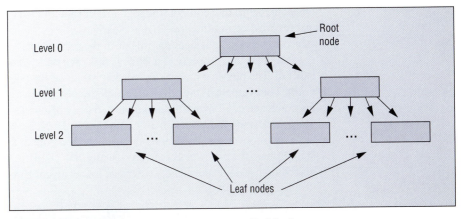

Figure 8.9   Structure of a Btree of height 3.

Figure 8.10   Btree node containing keys and pointers.

- **Bushy:** the number of branches from a node is large, perhaps 10 to 100 branches. Multiway, meaning more than two, is a synonym for bushy. The width (number of arrows from a node) and height (number of nodes between root and leaf nodes) are inversely related: increase width, decrease height. The ideal Btree is wide (bushy) but short (few levels).

- **Block-Oriented:** each node in a Btree is a block or physical record. To search a Btree, you start in the root node and follow a path to a leaf node containing data of interest. The height of a Btree is important because it determines the number of physical record accesses for searching.

- **Dynamic:** the shape of a Btree changes as logical records are inserted and deleted. Periodic reorganization is never necessary for a Btree. The next subsection describes node splitting and concatenation, the ways that a Btree changes as records are inserted and deleted.

- **Ubiquitous:** the Btree is a widely implemented and used file structure.

Before studying the dynamic nature, let us look more carefully at the contents of a node as depicted in Figure 8.10. Each node consists of pairs with a key value and a pointer (physical record address), sorted by key value. The pointer identifies the physical record that contains the logical record with the key value. Other data in a logical record, besides the key, do not usually reside in the nodes. The other data may be stored in separate physical records or in the leaf nodes.

An important property of a Btree is that each node, except the root, must be at least half full. The physical record size, the key size, and the pointer size determine node capacity. For example, if the physical record size is 1,024 bytes, the key size is 4 bytes, and the pointer size is 4 bytes, the maximum capacity of a node is 128 <key, pointer> pairs. Thus, each node must contain at least 64 pairs. Because the designer usually does not have control over the physical record size and the pointer size, the key size determines the number of branches. Btrees are usually not good for large key sizes due to less branching per node and, hence, taller and less efficient Btrees.

Node Splitting and Concatenation

Insertions are handled by placing the new key in a nonfull node or by splitting nodes, as depicted in Figure 8.11. In the partial Btree in Figure 8.11(a), each node contains a maximum of four keys. Inserting the key value 55 in Figure 8.11(b) requires rearrangement in the right-most leaf node. Inserting the key value 58 in Figure 8.11(c) requires more work because the right-most leaf node is full. To accommodate the new value, the node is split into two nodes and a key value is moved to the root node. In Figure 8.11(d), a split occurs at two levels because both nodes are full. When a split occurs at the root, the tree grows another level.

Deletions are handled by removing the deleted key from a node and repairing the structure if needed, as demonstrated in Figure 8.12. If the node is still at least half full, no additional action is necessary [Figure 8.12(b)]. However, if the node is less than half full, the structure must be changed. If a neighboring node contains more than half capacity, a key can be borrowed, as shown in Figure 8.12(c). If a key cannot be borrowed, nodes must be concatenated, as shown in Figure 8.12(d).

Cost of Operations

The height of a Btree is small even for a large table when the branching factor is large. An upper bound or limit on the height (h) of a Btree is

$$h \leq ceil(\log_d (n + 1)/ 2)$$

where

$ceil$ is the ceiling function ($ceil(x)$ is the smallest integer $\geq x$)

d is the minimum number of keys in a node

n is the number of keys to store in the index

Example: $h \leq 4$ for $n = 1,000,000$ and $d = 42$

The height dominates the number of physical record accesses in Btree operations. The cost in terms of physical record accesses to find a key is less than or equal to the height. If the row data are not stored in the tree, another physical record access is necessary to retrieve the row data after finding the key. The cost to insert a key includes the cost to locate the nearest key plus the cost to change nodes. In the best case [Figure 8.11(b)], the additional cost is one physical record access to change the index record and one physical record access to write the row data. The worst case occurs when a new level is added to the tree, as depicted in Figure 8.11(d). Even in the worst case, the height of the tree still dominates. Another $2h$ write operations are necessary to split the tree at each level.

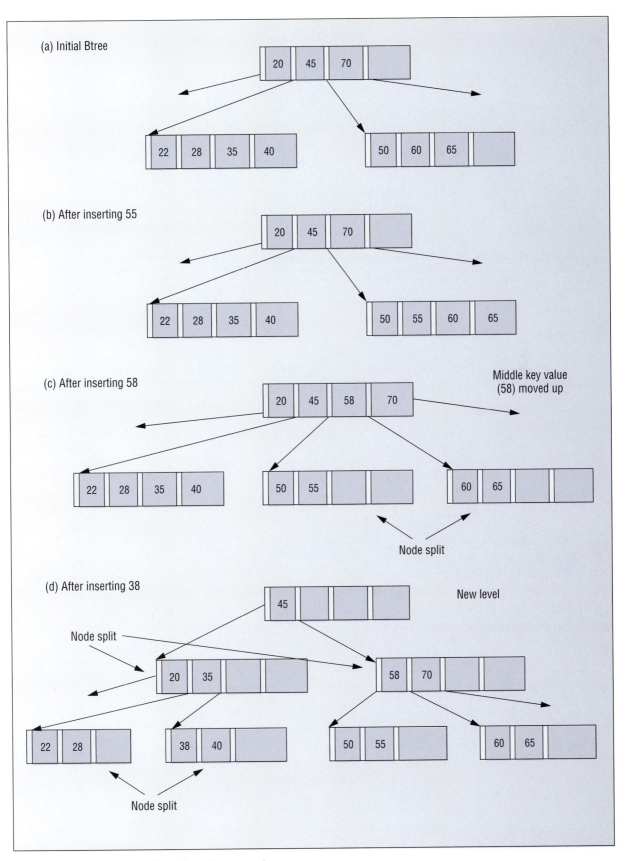

(a) Initial Btree

(b) After inserting 55

(c) After inserting 58

Middle key value
(58) moved up

Node split

(d) After inserting 38

New level

Node split

Node split

Figure 8.11   Btree insertion examples.

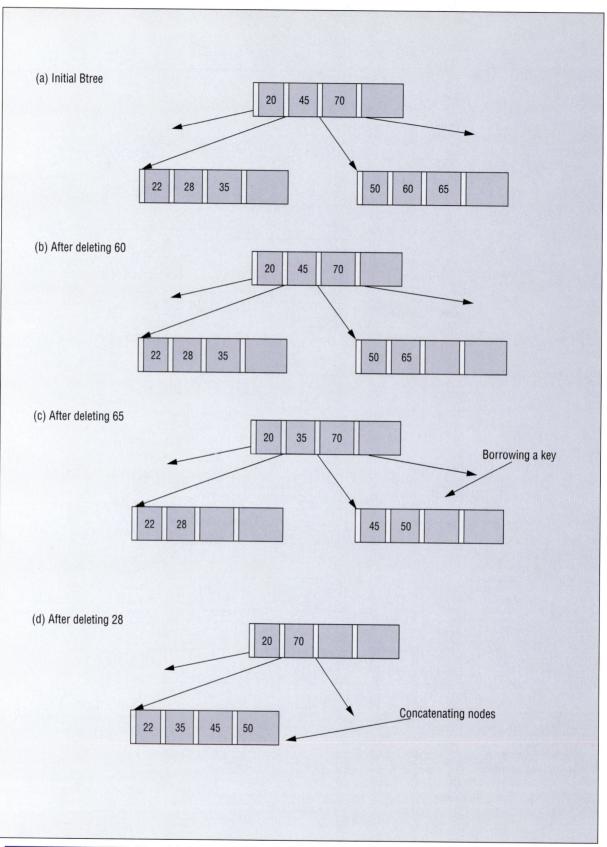

(a) Initial Btree

(b) After deleting 60

(c) After deleting 65

Borrowing a key

(d) After deleting 28

Concatenating nodes

Figure 8.12   Btree deletion examples.

B+Tree

B+tree File the most popular variation of the Btree. In a B+tree, all keys are redundantly stored in the leaf nodes. The B+tree provides improved performance on sequential and range searches.

Sequential searches can be a problem with Btrees. To perform a range search, the search procedure must travel up and down the tree. For example, to retrieve keys in the range 28 to 60 in Figure 8.12(a), the search process starts in the root, descends to the left leaf node, returns to the root, and then descends to the right leaf node. This procedure has problems with retention of physical records in memory. Operating systems may replace physical records if there have not been recent accesses. Because some time may elapse before a parent node is accessed again, the operating system may replace it with another physical record if main memory becomes full. Thus, another physical record access may be necessary when the parent node is accessed again.

To ensure that physical records are not replaced, the B+tree variation is usually implemented. Figure 8.13 shows the two parts of a B+tree. The triangle (index set) represents a normal Btree index. The lower part (sequence set) contains the leaf nodes. All keys reside in the leaf nodes even if a key appears in the index set. The leaf nodes are connected together so that sequential searches do not need to move up the tree. Once the initial key is found, the search process accesses only nodes in the sequence set.

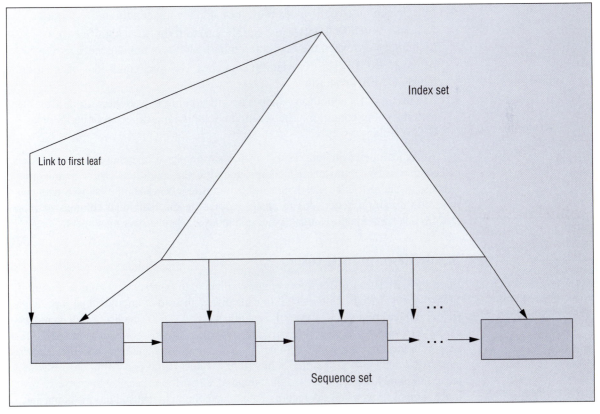

Figure 8.13   **B+tree structure.**

Index Matching

A Btree can be used to store all data in the nodes (primary file structure) or just pointers to the data records (secondary file structure or index). A Btree is especially versatile as an index because it can be used for a variety of queries. Determining whether an index can be used in a query is known as index matching. When a condition in a WHERE clause references an indexed column, the DBMS must determine if the index can be used. The complexity of a condition determines whether an index can be used. For single-column indexes, an index matches a condition if the column appears alone without functions or operators and the comparison operator matches one of the following items:

$= , >, <, > = , < =$ (but not $< >$)

BETWEEN

IS NULL

IN $<$list of constant values$>$

LIKE 'Pattern' in which pattern does not contain a meta character (%, _) as the first part of the pattern

For composite indexes involving more than one column, the matching rules are more complex and restrictive. Composite indexes are ordered by the most significant (first column in the index) to the least significant (last column in the index) column. A composite index matches conditions according to the following rules:

- The first column of the index must have a matching condition.
- Columns match from left (most significant) to right (least significant). Matching stops when the next column in the index is not matched.
- At most, one BETWEEN condition matches. No other conditions match after the BETWEEN condition.
- At most, one IN condition matches an index column. Matching stops after the next matching condition. The second matching condition cannot be IN or BETWEEN.

To depict index matching, Table 8.6 shows examples of matching between indexes and conditions. When matching a composite index, the conditions can be in any order. Because of the restrictive matching rules, composite indexes should be used with caution. It is usually a better idea to create indexes on the individual columns as most DBMSs can combine the results of multiple indexes when answering a query.

8.3.4 Bitmap Indexes

Bitmap Index a secondary file structure consisting of a column value and a bitmap. A bitmap contains one bit position for each row of a referenced table. A bitmap column index references the rows containing the column value. A bitmap join index references the rows of a child table that join with rows of the parent table containing the column. Bitmap indexes work well for stable columns with few values typical of tables in a data warehouse.

Btree and hash files work best for columns with unique values. For nonunique columns, Btree index nodes can store a list of row identifiers instead of an individual row identifier for unique columns. However, if a column has few values, the list of row identifiers can be very long. As an alternative structure for columns with few values, many DBMSs support bitmap indexes. Figure 8.14 depicts a bitmap column index for a sample *Faculty* table. A bitmap contains a string of bits (0 or 1 values) with one bit for each row of a table. In Figure 8.14, the length of the bitmap is 12 positions because there are 12 rows in the sample *Faculty* table. A record of a bitmap column index contains a column and a bitmap. A 0 value in a bitmap indicates that the associated row does not have the column value. A 1 value indicates that the associated row has the column value. The DBMS provides an efficient way to convert a position in a bitmap to a row identifier.

TABLE 8.6	Index Matching Examples

Condition	Index	Matching Notes
C1 = 10	C1	Matches index on C1
C2 BETWEEN 10 AND 20	C2	Matches index on C2
C3 IN (10, 20)	C3	Matches index on C3
C1 < > 10	C1	Does not match index on C1
C4 LIKE 'A%'	C4	Matches index on C4
C4 LIKE '%A'	C4	Does not match index on C4
C1 = 10 AND C2 = 5 AND C3 = 20 AND C4 = 25	(C1,C2,C3,C4)	Matches all columns of the index
C2 = 5 AND C3 = 20 AND C1 = 10	(C1,C2,C3,C4)	Matches the first three columns of the index
C2 = 5 AND C4 = 22 AND C1 = 10 AND C6 = 35	(C1,C2,C3,C4)	Matches the first two columns of the index
C2 = 5 AND C3 = 20 AND C4 = 25	(C1,C2,C3,C4)	Does not match any columns of the index: missing condition on C1
C1 IN (6, 8, 10) AND C2 = 5 AND C3 IN (20, 30, 40)	(C1,C2,C3,C4)	Matches the first two columns of the index: at most one matching IN condition
C2 = 5 AND C1 BETWEEN 6 AND 10	(C1,C2,C3,C4)	Matches the first column of the index: matching stops after the BETWEEN condition

Faculty Table

RowId	FacSSN	. . .	FacRank
1	098-55-1234		Asst
2	123-45-6789		Asst
3	456-89-1243		Assc
4	111-09-0245		Prof
5	931-99-2034		Asst
6	998-00-1245		Prof
7	287-44-3341		Assc
8	230-21-9432		Asst
9	321-44-5588		Prof
10	443-22-3356		Assc
11	559-87-3211		Prof
12	220-44-5688		Asst

Bitmap Column Index on *FacRank*

FacRank	Bitmap
Asst	110010010001
Assc	001000100100
Prof	000101001010

Figure 8.14   Sample faculty table and bitmap column index on *FacRank*.

A variation of the bitmap column index is the bitmap join index. In a bitmap join index, the bitmap identifies the rows of a related table, not the table containing the indexed column. Thus, a bitmap join index represents a precomputed join from a column in a parent table to the rows of a child table that join with rows of the parent table. A join bitmap index can be defined for a join column such as *FacSSN* or a nonjoin column such as *FacRank*. Figure 8.15 depicts a bitmap join index for the *FacRank* column in the *Faculty* table to the rows in the sample *Offering* table. The length of the bitmap is 24 bits because there are 24 rows in the sample *Offering* table. A 1 value in a bitmap indicates that a parent row containing the column value joins with the child table in the specified bit position. For example, a 1 in the first bit position of the Asst row of the join index means that a *Faculty* row with the Asst value joins with the first row of the *Offering* table.

Offering Table

RowId	OfferNo	. . .	FacSSN
1	1111		098-55-1234
2	1234		123-45-6789
3	1345		456-89-1243
4	1599		111-09-0245
5	1807		931-99-2034
6	1944		998-00-1245
7	2100		287-44-3341
8	2200		230-21-9432
9	2301		321-44-5588
10	2487		443-22-3356
11	2500		559-87-3211
12	2600		220-44-5688
13	2703		098-55-1234
14	2801		123-45-6789
15	2944		456-89-1243
16	3100		111-09-0245
17	3200		931-99-2034
18	3258		998-00-1245
19	3302		287-44-3341
20	3901		230-21-9432
21	4001		321-44-5588
22	4205		443-22-3356
23	4301		559-87-3211
24	4455		220-44-5688

Bitmap Join Index on *FacRank*

FacRank	Bitmap
Asst	110010010001110010010001
Assc	001000100100001000100100
Prof	000101001010000101001010

| **Figure 8.15** | Sample offering table and bitmap join index on *FacRank*. |

Table 8.7	**Summary of File Structures**				
	Unordered	*Ordered*	*Hash*	*B+tree*	*Bitmap*
Sequential search	Y	Y	Extra PRs	Y	N
Key search	Linear	Linear	Constant time	Logarithmic	Y
Range search	N	Y	N	Y	Y
Usage	Primary only	Primary only	Primary or secondary	Primary or secondary	Secondary only

Bitmap indexes work well for stable columns with few values. The *FacRank* column would be attractive for a bitmap column index because it contains few values and faculty members do not change rank often. The size of the bitmap is not an important issue because compression techniques can reduce the size significantly. Due to the requirement for stable columns, bitmap indexes are most common for data warehouse tables especially as join indexes. A data warehouse is a decision support database that is mostly used for retrievals and periodic insertion of new data. Chapter 16 discusses the use of bitmap indexes for data warehouse tables.

8.3.5 Summary of File Structures

To help you recall the file structures, Table 8.7 summarizes the major characteristics of each structure. In the first row, hash files can be used for sequential access, but there may be extra physical records because keys are evenly spread among physical records. In the second row, unordered and ordered sequential files must examine on average half the physical records (linear). Hash files examine a constant number (usually close to 1) of physical records, assuming that the file is not too full. Btrees have logarithmic search costs because of the relationship between the height, the log function, and search cost formulas. File structures can store all the data of a table (primary file structure) or store only key data along with pointers to the data records (secondary file structure). A secondary file structure or index provides an alternative path to the data. A bitmap index supports range searches by performing union operations on the bitmaps for each column value in the range.

8.4 QUERY OPTIMIZATION

In most relational DBMSs, you do not have the choice of how queries are implemented on the physical database. The query optimization component assumes this responsibility. Your productivity increases because you do not need to make these tedious decisions. However, you can sometimes improve the optimization process if you understand it. To provide you with an understanding of the optimization process, this section describes the tasks performed and discusses tips to improve optimization results.

8.4.1 Translation Tasks

When you submit an SQL statement for execution, the query optimization component translates your query in four phases as shown in Figure 8.16. The first and fourth phases are common to any computer language translation process. The second phase has some unique aspects. The third phase is unique to translation of database languages.

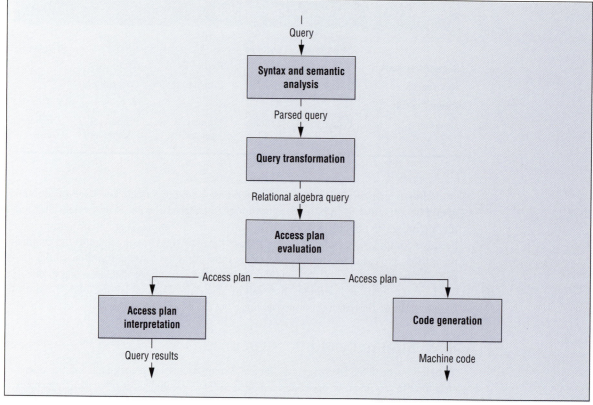

Figure 8.16   Tasks in database language translation.

Syntax and Semantic Analysis

The first phase analyzes a query for syntax and simple semantic errors. Syntax errors involve misuse of keywords such as if the FROM keyword was misspelled in Example 8.1. Semantic errors involve misuse of columns and tables. The data language compiler can detect only simple semantic errors involving incompatible data types. For example, a WHERE condition that compares the *CourseNo* column with the *FacSalary* column results in a semantic error because these columns have incompatible data types. To find semantic errors, the DBMS uses table, column, and relationship definitions as stored in the data dictionary.

**Example 8.1
(Oracle)**

Joining Three Tables

```
SELECT FacName, CourseNo, Enrollment.OfferNo, EnrGrade
  FROM Enrollment, Offering, Faculty
  WHERE CourseNo LIKE 'IS%' AND OffYear = 2002
    AND OffTerm = 'FALL'
    AND Enrollment.OfferNo = Offering.OfferNo
    AND Faculty.FacSSN = Offering.FacSSN
```

Query Transformation

The second phase transforms a query into a simplified and standardized format. As with optimizing programming language compilers, database language translators can eliminate redundant parts of a logical expression. For example, the logical expression (OffYear = 2003 AND OffTerm = 'WINTER') OR (OffYear = 2003 AND OffTerm = 'SPRING') can be simplified to OffYear = 2003 AND (OffTerm = 'WINTER' OR OffTerm = 'SPRING'). Join simplification is unique to database languages. For example, if Example 8.1 contained a join with the *Student* table, this table could be eliminated if no columns or conditions involving the *Student* table are used in the query.

The standardized format is usually based on relational algebra. The relational algebra operations are rearranged so that the query can be executed faster. Typical rearrangement operations are described below. Because the query optimization component performs this rearrangement, you do not have to be careful about writing your query in an efficient way.

- Restriction operations are combined so that they can be tested together.
- Projection and restriction operations are moved before join operations to eliminate unneeded columns and rows before expensive join operations.
- Cross product operations are transformed into join operations if a join condition exists in the WHERE clause.

Access Plan Evaluation

Access Plan a tree that encodes decisions about file structures to access individual tables, the order of joining tables, and the algorithm to join tables.

The third phase determines how to implement the rearranged relational algebra expression as an access plan. An access plan indicates how to implement a query as operations on files, as depicted in Figure 8.17. In an access plan, the leaf nodes are individual tables in the query, and the arrows point upward to indicate the flow of data. The nodes above the leaf nodes indicate decisions about accessing individual tables. In Figure 8.17,

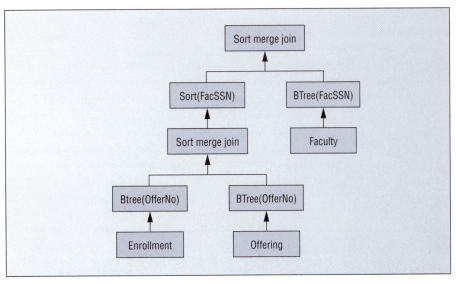

Figure 8.17 Example access plan for Example 8.1.

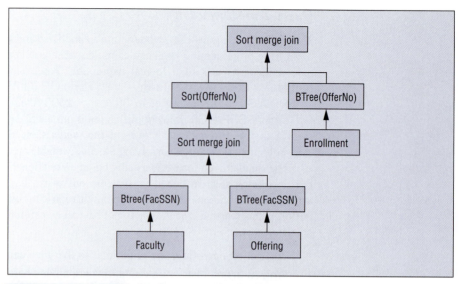

Figure 8.18   **Another access plan for Example 8.1.**

Btree indexes are used to access individual tables. The first join combines the *Enrollment* and the *Offering* tables. The Btree file structures provide the sorting needed for the merge join algorithm. The second join combines the result of the first join with the *Faculty* table. The intermediate result must be sorted on *FacSSN* before the merge join algorithm can be used.

The query optimization component evaluates a large number of access plans. Access plans vary by join orders, file structures, and join algorithms. For example, Figure 8.18 shows a variation of the access plan in Figure 8.17 in which the join order is changed. For file structures, some optimization components can consider set operations to combine the results of multiple indexes on the same table. The query optimization component can evaluate many more access plans than you can mentally comprehend. Typically, the query optimization component evaluates thousands of access plans. Evaluating access plans can involve a significant amount of time when the query contains more than four tables.

Most optimization components use a small set of join algorithms. Table 8.8 summarizes common join algorithms employed by optimization components. For each join operation in a query, the optimization component considers each supported join algorithm. For the nested loops and the hybrid algorithms, the optimization component also must choose the outer table and the inner table. All algorithms except the star join involve two tables at a time. The star join can combine any number of tables matching the star pattern (a child table surrounded by parent tables in 1-M relationships). The nested loops algorithm can be used with any join operation, not just an equi-join operation.

The query optimization component uses cost formulas to evaluate access plans. Each operation in an access plan has a corresponding cost formula that estimates the physical record accesses and CPU operations. The cost formulas use table profiles to estimate the number of rows in a result. For example, the number of rows resulting from a WHERE condition can be estimated using distribution data such as a histogram. The query optimization component chooses the access plan with the lowest cost.

TABLE 8.8	Summary of Common Join Algorithms	
Algorithm	*Requirements*	*When to Use*
Nested loops	Choose outer table and inner table; can be used for all joins	Appropriate when there are few rows in the outer table or when all pages of the inner table fit into memory. An index on a foreign key join column allows efficient usage of the nested loops algorithm when there are restrictive conditions on the parent table
Sort merge	Both tables must be sorted (or use an index) on the join columns; only used for equi-joins	Appropriate if sort cost is small or if a clustered join index exists
Hybrid join	Combination of sort merge and nested loops; outer table must be sorted (or use a join column index); inner table must have an index on the join column; only used for equi-joins	Performs better than sort merge when there is a nonclustering index (see the next section) on the join column of the inner table
Hash join	Internal hash file built for both tables; only used for equi-joins	Hash join performs better than sort merge when the tables are not sorted or indexes do not exist
Star join	Join multiple tables in which there is one child table related to multiple parent tables in 1-M relationships; bitmap join index required on each parent table; only used for equi-joins	Best join algorithm for tables matching the star pattern with bitmap join indexes especially when there are highly selective conditions on the parent tables; widely used to optimize data warehouse queries (see Chapter 16)

Access Plan Execution

The last phase executes the selected access plan. The query optimization component either generates machine code or interprets the access plan. Execution of machine code results in faster response than interpreting an access plan. However, most DBMSs interpret access plans because of the variety of hardware supported. The performance difference between interpretation and machine code execution is usually not significant for most users.

8.4.2 Optimization Tips

Even though the query optimization component performs its role automatically, the database designer also has a role to play. In some situations, you can influence the quality of solutions produced and improve the speed of the optimization process. Perhaps the largest impact is to choose a DBMS with a good optimization component. Here is a list of choices available to the database designer to improve the optimization process:

- The query optimization component needs detailed and current statistics to evaluate access plans. Statistics that are not detailed enough or outdated can lead to the choice of poor access plans.
- The optimization process can be time consuming, especially for queries containing more than four tables. To reduce optimization time, some DBMSs save access plans to avoid the time-consuming phases of the translation process. Query binding is the process of associating a query with an access plan. Most DBMSs rebind automatically if a query changes or the database changes (file structures, table profiles, data types, etc.).

- Some DBMSs allow reviewing of access plans. For queries with poor performance, reviewing access plans can be useful to see if an index might improve performance or to change the order in which tables are joined.
- Some DBMSs allow hints that influence the choice of access plans. For example, Oracle allows hints to choose the optimization goal, the file structure for a particular table, the join algorithm, and the join order. Hints should be used with great caution because a hint overrides the judgment of the optimizer.
- You should avoid Type II nested queries (Chapter 9), especially when the nested query performs grouping with aggregate calculation. Many DBMSs perform poorly as query optimization components often do not consider efficient ways to implement Type II queries. Query execution speed can improve by replacing a Type II nested query with a separate query.
- For queries involving 1-M relationships in which there is a condition on the join column, make the condition on the parent table rather than the child table. The condition on the parent table can significantly reduce the effort in joining the tables.
- For queries involving the HAVING clause, eliminate conditions that do not involve aggregate functions. Conditions involving simple comparisons of columns in the GROUP BY clause belong in the WHERE clause, not the HAVING clause. Moving these conditions to the WHERE clause will eliminate rows sooner, thus providing faster execution.

The first point about detailed statistics needs further elaboration. Optimizers using the uniform value assumption often choose sequential file access rather than Btree access. For example, consider a query to list employees with salaries greater than $100,000. If the salary range is $10,000 to $2,000,000, about 95 percent of the employee table should satisfy this condition using the uniform value assumption. For most companies, however, few employees would have a salary greater than $100,000. Using the estimate from the uniform value assumption, the optimizer will choose a sequential file instead of a Btree to access the employee table. Using a histogram instead of the uniform value assumption should provide a more accurate estimate.

Hints may be necessary if an optimization component does not maintain detailed statistics on frequently used columns. A hint can be used to force an optimization component to use an index instead of using sequential file access. A hint also can be useful for conditions involving parameter values. If a database designer knows that the typical parameter values result in the selection of few rows, a hint can be used to force an optimization component to use an index.

In addition to detailed statistics about individual columns, an optimization component sometimes needs detailed statistics on combinations of columns. If a combination of columns appears in the WHERE clause of a query, statistics on the column combination are important if the columns are not independent. Most optimization components assume that combinations of columns are statistically independent to simplify the computation of the estimation of the fraction of rows. Unfortunately, few DBMSs maintain statistics on combinations of columns. If a DBMS does not maintain statistics on column combinations, a database designer may want to use hints to override the judgment of the DBMS when a joint condition in a WHERE clause generates few rows. Using a hint could force the optimization component to combine indexes when accessing a table rather than using a sequential table scan.

8.5 INDEX SELECTION

Index selection is the most important decision available to the physical database designer. However, it also can be one of the most difficult decisions. As a designer, you need to understand why index selection is difficult and the limitations of performing index selection without an automated tool. This section helps you gain this knowledge by defining the index selection problem, discussing trade-offs in selecting indexes, and presenting index selection rules for moderate-size databases.

8.5.1 Problem Definition

Index a secondary file structure that provides an alternative path to the data. In a clustering index, the order of the data records is close to the index order. In a nonclustering index, the order of the data records is unrelated to the index order.

Index selection involves two kinds of indexes, clustering and nonclustering. In a <u>clustering index</u>, the order of the rows is close to the index order. Close means that physical records containing rows will not have to be accessed more than one time if the index is accessed sequentially. Figure 8.19 shows the sequence set of a B+tree index pointing to associated rows inside physical records. Note that for a given node in the sequence set, most associated rows are clustered inside the same physical record. Ordering the row data by the index field is a simple way to make a clustered index.

In contrast, a <u>nonclustering index</u> does not have this closeness property. In a nonclustered index, the order of the rows is not related to the index order. Figure 8.20 shows that the same physical record may be repeatedly accessed when using the sequence set. The pointers from the sequence set nodes to the rows cross many times, indicating that the index order is different from the row order.

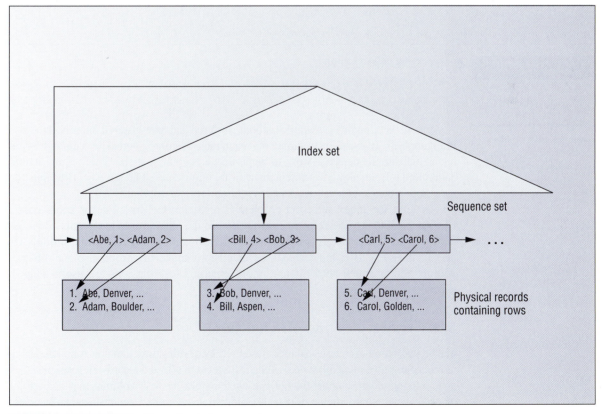

Figure 8.19   Clustering index example.

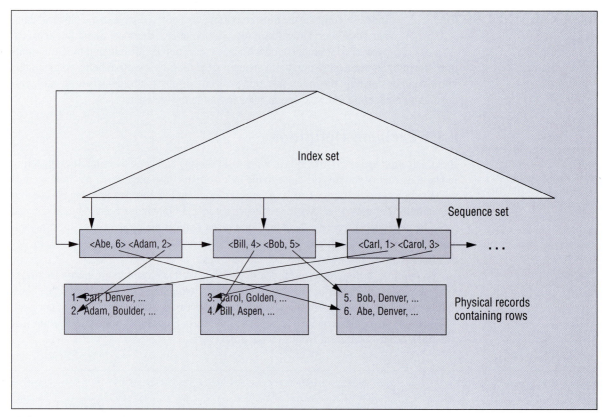

Figure 8.20 **Nonclustering index example.**

Index Selection Problem
for each table, select at most
one clustering index and zero
or more nonclustering
indexes.

Index selection involves choices about clustered and nonclustered indexes, as shown in Figure 8.21. It is usually assumed that each table is stored in one file. The SQL statements indicate the database work to be performed by applications. The weights should combine the frequency of a statement with its importance. The table profiles must be specified in the same level of detail as required for query optimization.

Usually, the index selection problem is restricted to Btree indexes and separate files for each table. The references at the end of the chapter provide details about using other kinds of indexes (such as hash indexes) and placing data from multiple tables in the same file. However, these extensions make the problem more difficult without adding much performance improvement. The extensions are useful only in specialized situations.

8.5.2 Trade-offs and Difficulties

The best selection of indexes balances faster retrieval with slower updates. A nonclustering index can improve retrievals by providing fast access to selected records. In Example 8.2, a nonclustering index on either the *OffYear, OffTerm,* or *CourseNo* columns may be useful if relatively few rows satisfy the associated condition in the query. Usually, less than 5 percent of the rows must satisfy a condition for a nonclustering index to be useful. It is unlikely that any of the conditions in Example 8.2 will yield such a small fraction of the rows.

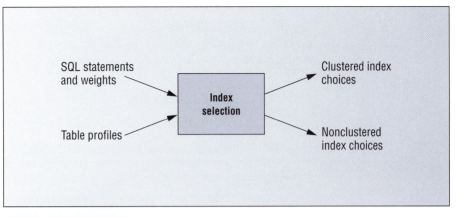

Figure 8.21   Inputs and outputs of index selection.

A nonclustering index also can be useful in a join if a small number of rows result in one table. For example, if only a few *Offering* rows meet all three conditions in Example 8.2, a nonclustering index on the *Faculty.FacSSN* column may be useful when joining the *Faculty* and *Offering* tables.

Example 8.2 (Oracle)

Join of the Faculty and Offering Tables

```
SELECT FacName, CourseNo, OfferNo
  FROM Offering, Faculty
  WHERE CourseNo LIKE 'IS%' AND OffYear = 2002
    AND OffTerm = 'FALL'
    AND Faculty.FacSSN = Offering.FacSSN
```

A clustering index can improve retrievals under more situations than a nonclustering index. A clustering index is useful in the same situations as a nonclustering index except that the number of resulting rows can be larger. For example, a clustering index on either the *CourseNo, OffYear,* or *OffTerm* columns may be useful if perhaps 20 percent of the rows satisfy the associated condition in the query.

A clustering index also can be useful on joins because it avoids the need to sort. For example, using clustering indexes on the *Offering.FacSSN* and *Faculty.FacSSN* columns, the *Offering* and *Faculty* tables can be joined by merging the rows from each table. Merging rows is often a fast way to join tables if the tables do not need to be sorted (clustered indexes exist).

The cost to maintain indexes as a result of INSERT, UPDATE, and DELETE statements balances retrieval improvements. INSERT and DELETE statements affect all indexes of a table. Thus, many indexes on a table are not preferred if the table has frequent insert and delete operations. UPDATE statements affect only the columns listed in the SET clause. If UPDATE statements on a column are frequent, the benefit of an index is usually lost.

Clustering index choices are more sensitive to maintenance than nonclustering index choices. Clustering indexes are more expensive to maintain than nonclustering indexes because the data file must be changed similar to an ordered sequential file. For nonclustering indexes, the data file can be maintained as an unordered sequential file.

Difficulties of Index Selection

Index selection is difficult to perform well for a variety of reasons:

- Application weights are difficult to specify. Judgments that combine frequency and importance can make the result subjective.
- Distribution of parameter values is sometimes needed. Many SQL statements in reports and forms use parameter values. If parameter values vary from being highly selective to not very selective, selecting indexes is difficult.
- The behavior of the query optimization component must be known. Even if an index appears useful for a query, the query optimization component must use it. There may be subtle reasons why the query optimization component does not use an index, especially a nonclustering index.
- The number of choices is large. Even if indexes on combinations of columns are ignored, the theoretical number of choices is exponential in the number of columns (2^{NC} where NC is the number of columns). Although many of these choices can be easily eliminated, the number of practical choices is still quite large.
- Index choices can be interrelated. The interrelationships can be subtle, especially when choosing indexes to improve join performance.

An index selection tool can help with the last three problems. A good tool should use the query optimization component to derive cost estimates for each query under a given choice of indexes. However, a good tool cannot help alleviate the difficulty of specifying application weights and parameter value distributions.

8.5.3 Selection Rules

Despite the difficulties previously discussed, you usually can avoid poor index choices by following some simple rules. You also can use the rules as a starting point for a more careful selection process.

Rule 1: A primary key is a good candidate for a clustering index.

Rule 2: To support joins, consider indexes on foreign keys. A nonclustering index on a foreign key is a good idea when there are important queries with highly selective conditions on the related primary key table. A clustering index is a good choice when most joins use a parent table with a clustering index on its primary key, and the queries do not have highly selective conditions on the parent table.

Rule 3: A column with many values may be a good choice for a nonclustering index if it is used in equality conditions. The term *many values* means that the column is almost unique.

Rule 4: A column used in highly selective range conditions is a good candidate for a nonclustering index.

Rule 5: A frequently updated column is not a good index candidate.

Rule 6: Volatile tables (lots of insertions and deletions) should not have many indexes.

Rule 7: Stable columns with few values are good candidates for bitmap indexes if the columns appear in WHERE conditions.

Rule 8: Avoid indexes on combinations of columns. Most optimization components can use multiple indexes on the same table. An index on a combination of columns is not as flexible as multiple indexes on the individual columns.

Applying the Selection Rules

Let us apply these rules to the *Student, Enrollment,* and *Offering* tables of the university database. Table 8.9 lists SQL statements and frequencies for these tables. The names beginning with $ represent parameters supplied by a user. The frequencies assume a student population of 30,000, in which students enroll in an average of four offerings per

TABLE 8.9	SQL Statements and Frequencies for Several University Database Tables

SQL Statement	Frequency	Comments
1. INSERT INTO Student . . .	7,500/year	Beginning of year
2. INSERT INTO Enrollment . . .	120,000/term	During registration
3. INSERT INTO Offering . . .	1,000/year	Just before scheduling deadline
4. DELETE Student WHERE StdSSN = $X	8,000/year	After separation
5. DELETE Offering WHERE OfferNo = $X	1,000/year	End of year
6. DELETE Enrollment WHERE OfferNo = $X AND StdSSN = $Y	64,000/year	End of year
7. SELECT * FROM Student WHERE StdGPA > $X	1,200/year	$X is usually very large or small
8. SELECT * FROM Student WHERE StdSSN = $X	30,000/term	

9. SELECT * FROM Offering
    WHERE OffTerm = $X AND OffYear = $Y
    AND CourseNo LIKE '$Z%'
	60,000/term	Few rows in result

10. SELECT * FROM Offering, Enrollment
    WHERE StdSSN = $X AND OffTerm = $Y
    AND OffYear = $Z
    AND Offering.OfferNo = Enrollment.OfferNo
	30,000/term	Few rows in result

11. UPDATE Student SET StdGPA = $X WHERE StdSSN = $Y	30,000/term	Updated at end of reporting form
12. UPDATE Enrollment SET EnrGrade = $X WHERE StdSSN = $Y AND OfferNo = $Z	120,000/term	Part of grade reporting form
13. UPDATE OfferNo SET FacSSN = $X WHERE OfferNo = $Y	500/year	

14. SELECT FacSSN, FacFirstName, FacLastName
    FROM Faculty
    WHERE FacRank = $X AND FacDept = $Y
	1,000/term	Most occurring during registration

TABLE 8.10	Table Profiles

Table	Number of Rows	Column (Number of Unique Values)
Student	30,000	StdSSN (PK), StdLastName (29,000), StdAddress (20,000), StdCity (500), StdZip (1,000), StdState (50), StdMajor (100), StdGPA (400)
Enrollment	300,000	StdSSN (30,000), OfferNo (2,000), EnrGrade (400)
Offering	10,000	OfferNo (PK), CourseNo (900), OffTime (20), OffLocation (500), FacSSN (1,500), OffTerm (4), OffYear (10), OffDays (10)
Course	1,000	CourseNo (PK), CrsDesc (1,000), CrsUnits (6)
Faculty	2,000	FacSSN (PK), FacLastName (1,900), FacAddress (1,950), FacCity (50), FacZip (200), FacState (3), FacHireDate (300), FacSalary (1,500), FacRank (10), FacDept (100)

TABLE 8.11	Index Selections for the University Database Tables

Column	Index Kind	Rule
Student.StdSSN	Clustering	1
Student.StdGPA	Nonclustering	4
Offering.OfferNo	Clustering	1
Enrollment.OfferNo	Clustering	2
Faculty.FacRank	Bitmap	7
Faculty.Dept	Bitmap	7
Offering.OffTerm	Bitmap	7
Offering.OffYear	Bitmap	7

term. After a student graduates or leaves the university, the *Student* and *Enrollment* rows are archived. Table 8.10 lists summaries of the table profiles. More detail about column and relationship distributions can be encoded in histograms.

Table 8.11 lists index choices according to the index selection rules. Only a few indexes are recommended because of the frequency of maintenance statements and the absence of highly selective conditions on columns other than the primary key. In queries 9 and 10, although the individual conditions on *OffTerm* and *OffYear* are not highly selective, the joint condition may be reasonably selective to recommend bitmap indexes, especially in query 9 with the additional condition on *CourseNo*. There is an index on *StdGPA* because parameter values should be very high or low, providing high selectivity. A more detailed study of the *StdGPA* index may be necessary because it has a considerable amount of update activity. Even though not suggested by the SQL statements, the *StdLastName* and *FacLastName* columns also may be good index choices because they are almost unique (a few duplicates) and reasonably stable. If there are additional SQL statements that use these columns in conditions, nonclustered indexes should be considered.

Although SQL:1999 does not support statements for indexes, most DBMSs do support index statements. In Example 8.3, the word following the INDEX keyword is the name of the index. The CREATE INDEX statement also can be used to create an index on a combination of columns by listing multiple columns in the parentheses. The Oracle CREATE INDEX statement cannot be used to create a clustered index. To create a clustered index, Oracle provides the ORGANIZATION INDEX clause as part of the CREATE TABLE statement.

Example 8.3 (Oracle)	CREATE INDEX Statements

CREATE UNIQUE INDEX StdSSNIndex ON Student (StdSSN)
CREATE INDEX StdGPAIndex ON Student (StdGPA)
CREATE UNIQUE INDEX OfferNoIndex ON Offering (OfferNo)
CREATE INDEX EnrollOfferNoIndex ON Enrollment (OfferNo)
CREATE BITMAP INDEX OffYearIndex ON Offering (OffYear)
CREATE BITMAP INDEX OffTermIndex ON Offering (OffTerm)
CREATE BITMAP INDEX FacRankIndex ON Faculty (FacRank)
CREATE BITMAP INDEX FacDeptIndex ON Faculty (FacDept)

8.6 ADDITIONAL CHOICES IN PHYSICAL DATABASE DESIGN

Although index selection is the most important decision of physical database design, there are other decisions that can significantly improve performance. This section discusses two decisions, denormalization and record formatting, that can improve performance in selected situations. Next, this section presents parallel processing to improve database performance, an increasingly popular alternative. Finally, several ways to improve performance related to specific kinds of processing are briefly discussed.

8.6.1 Denormalization

Normalized Designs
- Have better update performance.
- Require less coding to enforce integrity constraints.
- Support more indexes to improve query performance.

Denormalization combines tables so that they are easier to query. After combining tables, the new table may violate a normal form such as BCNF. Although some of the denormalization techniques do not lead to violations in a normal form, they still make a design easier to query and more difficult to update. Denormalization should always be done with extreme care because a normalized design has important advantages. Chapter 7 described one situation for denormalization: ignoring a functional dependency if it does not lead to significant modification anomalies. This section describes additional situations under which denormalization may be justified.

Repeating Groups

A repeating group is a collection of associated values such as sales history, lines of an order, or payment history. The rules of normalization force repeating groups to be stored in a child table separate from the associated parent table. For example, the lines of an order are stored in an order line table, separate from a related order table. If a repeating group is always accessed with its associated parent table, denormalization may be a reasonable alternative.

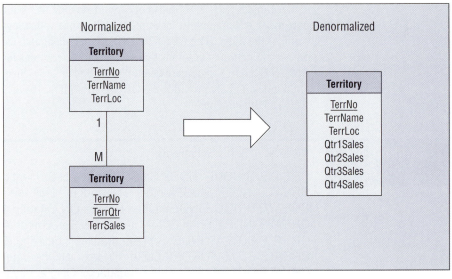

Figure 8.22 Denormalizing a repeating group.

Figure 8.22 shows a denormalization example of quarterly sales data. Although the denormalized design does not violate BCNF, it is less flexible for updating than the normalized design. The normalized design supports an unlimited number of quarterly sales as compared to only four quarters of sales results for the denormalized design. However, the denormalized design does not require a join to combine territory and sales data.

Generalization Hierarchies

Following the conversion rule for generalization hierarchies in Chapter 6 can result in many tables. If queries often need to combine these separate tables, it may be reasonable to store the separate tables as one table. Figure 8.23 demonstrates denormalization of the *Emp, HourlyEmp,* and *SalaryEmp* tables. They have 1-1 relationships because they represent a generalization hierarchy. Although the denormalized design does not violate BCNF, the combined table may waste much space because of null values. However, the denormalized design avoids the outer join operator to combine the tables.

Codes and Meanings

Normalization rules require that foreign keys be stored alone to represent 1-M relationships. If a foreign key represents a code, the user often requests an associated name or description in addition to the foreign key value. For example, the user may want to see the state name in addition to the state code. Storing the name or description column along with the code violates BCNF, but it eliminates some join operations. If the name or description column is not changed often, denormalization may be a reasonable choice. Figure 8.24 demonstrates denormalization for the *Dept* and *Emp* tables. In the denormalized design, the *DeptName* column has been added to the *Emp* table.

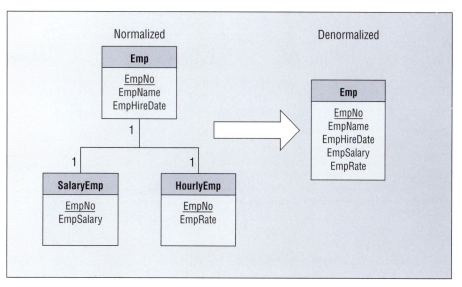

Figure 8.23   Denormalizing a generalization hierarchy.

Figure 8.24   Denormalizing to combine code and meaning columns.

8.6.2 Record Formatting

Record formatting decisions involve compression and derived data. With an increasing emphasis on storing complex data types such as audio, video, and images, compression is becoming an important issue. In some situations, there are multiple compression alternatives available. Compression is a trade-off between input–output and processing effort. Compression reduces the number of physical records transferred but may require considerable processing effort to compress and decompress the data.

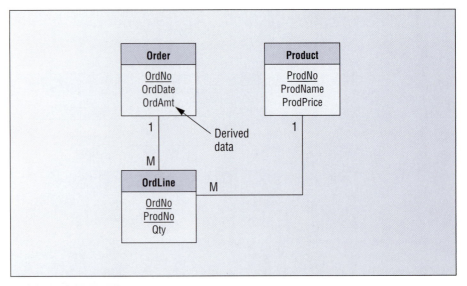

Figure 8.25   Storing derived data to improve query performance.

Decisions about derived data involve trade-offs between query and update operations. For query purposes, storing derived data reduces the need to retrieve data needed to calculate the derived data. However, updates to the underlying data require additional updates to the derived data. Storing derived data to reduce join operations may be reasonable. Figure 8.25 demonstrates derived data in the *Order* table. If the total amount of an order is frequently requested, storing the derived column *OrdAmt* may be reasonable. Calculating order amount requires a summary or aggregate calculation of related *Ord-Line* and *Product* rows to obtain the *Qty* and *ProdPrice* columns. Storing the *OrdAmt* column avoids two join operations.

8.6.3 Parallel Processing

Retrieval and modification performance can be improved significantly through parallel processing. Retrievals involving many records can be improved by reading physical records in parallel. For example, a report to summarize daily sales activity may read thousands of records from several tables. Parallel reading of physical records can reduce significantly the execution time of the report. In addition, performance can be improved significantly for batch applications with many write operations and read/write of large logical records such as images.

As a response to the potential performance improvements, many DBMSs provide parallel processing capabilities. These capabilities require hardware and software support for Redundant Arrays of Independent Disks (RAID).[2] The RAID controller (Figure 8.26) enables an array of disks to appear as one large disk to the DBMS. For very high performance, a RAID controller can control as many as 90 disks. Because of the

RAID a collection of disks (a disk array) that operates as a single disk. RAID storage supports parallel read and write operations with high reliability.

[2]RAID originally was an acronym for Redundant Arrays of Inexpensive Disks. Because prices of disk drives have fallen dramatically since the invention of the RAID idea (1988), *inexpensive* has been replaced by *independent.*

Figure 8.26   **Components of a RAID storage system.**

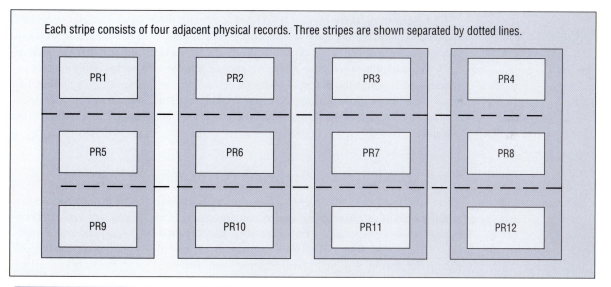

Figure 8.27   **Striping in RAID storage systems.**

controller, RAID storage requires no changes in applications and queries. However, the query optimization component may be changed to account for the effect of parallel processing on access plan evaluation.

Striping is an important concept for RAID storage. Striping involves the allocation of physical records to different disks. A stripe is the set of physical records that can be read or written in parallel. Normally, a stripe contains a set of adjacent physical records. Figure 8.27 depicts an array of four disks that allows the reading or writing of four physical records in parallel.

To utilize RAID storage, a number of architectures have emerged. The architectures, known as RAID-X, support parallel processing with varying amounts of performance and reliability. Reliability is an important issue because the mean time between failures (a measure of disk drive reliability) decreases as the number of disk drives increases. To combat reliability concerns, RAID architectures incorporate redundancy using mirrored disks, error-correcting codes, and spare disks. For most purposes, two RAID architectures dominate although many variations of these basic architectures exist.

- **RAID-1:** involves a full mirror or redundant array of disks to improve reliability. Each physical record is written to both disk arrays in parallel. Read operations from separate queries can access a disk array in parallel to improve performance across queries. RAID-1 involves the most storage overhead as compared to other RAID architectures.

- **RAID-5:** uses both data and error-correcting pages (known as parity pages) to improve reliability. Read operations can be performed in parallel on stripes. Write operations involve a data page and an error-correcting page on another disk. To reduce disk contention, the error-correcting pages are randomly located across disks. RAID-5 uses storage space more efficiently than RAID-1 but can involve slower write times because of the error-correcting pages. Thus, RAID-1 is often preferred for highly volatile parts of a database.

To increase capacity beyond RAID and to remove the reliance on storage devices attached to a server, Storage Area Networks (SANs) have been developed. A SAN is a specialized high-speed network that connects storage devices and servers. The goal of SAN technology is to integrate different types of storage subsystems into a single system and to eliminate the potential bottleneck of a single server controlling storage devices. Many large organizations are using SANs to integrate storage systems for operational databases, data warehouses, archival storage of documents, and traditional file systems.

8.6.4 Other Ways to Improve Performance

There are a number of other ways to improve database performance that are related to a specific kind of processing. For transaction processing (Chapter 15), you can add computing capacity (faster and more processors, memory, and hard disk) and make trade-offs in transaction design. For data warehouses (Chapter 16), you can add computing capacity and design new tables with derived data. For distributed database processing (Chapter 17), you can allocate processing and data to various computing locations. Data can be allocated by partitioning a table vertically (column subset) and horizontally (row subset) to locate data close to its usage. These design choices are discussed in the respective chapters in Part 4.

In addition to tuning performance for specific processing requirements, you also can improve performance by utilizing options specific to a DBMS. Fragmentation is an important concern in database storage as it is with any disk storage. Most DBMSs provide guidelines and tools to monitor and control fragmentation. In addition, most DBMSs have options for file structures that can improve performance. You must carefully study the specific DBMS to understand these options. It may take several years of experience and specialized education to understand options of a particular DBMS. However, the payoff of increased salary and demand for your knowledge can be worth the study.

CLOSING THOUGHTS

This chapter has described the nature of the physical database design process and details about the inputs, environment, and design decisions. Physical database design involves details closest to the operating system such as movement of physical records. The objective of physical database design is to minimize certain computing resources (physical record accesses and processing effort) without compromising the meaning of the database. Physical database design is a difficult process because the inputs can be difficult to specify, the environment is complex, and the number of choices can be overwhelming.

To improve your proficiency in performing physical database design, this chapter described details about the inputs and the environment of physical database design. This chapter described table profiles and application profiles as inputs that must be specified in sufficient detail to achieve an efficient design. The environment consists of file structures and the query optimization component of the DBMS. For file structures, this chapter described characteristics of sequential, hash, Btree file, and bitmap structures used by many DBMSs. For query optimization, this chapter described the tasks of query optimization and tips to produce better optimization results.

After establishing the background for the physical database design process, the inputs, and the environment, this chapter described decisions about index selection, denormalization, and record formatting. For index selection, this chapter described trade-offs between retrieval and update applications and presented rules for selecting indexes. For denormalization and data formatting, this chapter presented a number of situations when they are useful.

This chapter concludes the database development process. After completing these steps, you should have an efficient table design that represents the needs of an organization. To complete your understanding of the database development process, Chapter 13 provides a detailed case study in which to apply the ideas in Parts 2 and 3 of this book.

REVIEW CONCEPTS

- Relationship between physical records and logical records.
- Objective of physical database design.
- Difficulties of physical database design.
- Level of detail in table and application profiles.
- Histograms to specify column distributions.
- Characteristics of sequential, hash, and Btree file structures.
- Possible meanings of the letter *B* in the name *Btree:* balanced, bushy, block-oriented.
- Bitmap indexes for stable columns with few values.
- Tasks of data language translation.
- The usage of cost formulas and table profiles to evaluate access plans.
- The importance of table profiles with sufficient detail for access plan evaluation.
- The difference between clustered and nonclustered indexes.
- Trade-offs in selecting indexes.
- Index selection rules to avoid poor index choices.
- Denormalization to improve join performance.
- Record formatting to reduce physical record accesses and improve query performance.

- RAID storage to provide parallel processing for retrievals and updates.
- RAID architectures to provide parallel processing with high reliability.
- Storage Area Networks (SANs) to integrate storage subsystems and to eliminate reliance upon server-attached storage devices.

QUESTIONS

1. What is the difference between a physical record access and a logical record access?

2. Why is it difficult to know when a logical record access results in a physical record access?

3. What is the objective of physical database design?

4. What computing resources are constraints rather than being part of the objective of physical database design?

5. What are the contents of table profiles?

6. What are the contents of application profiles?

7. Describe two ways to specify distributions of columns used in table and application profiles.

8. What is a file structure?

9. What is the difference between a primary and a secondary file structure?

10. Describe the uses of sequential files for sequential search, range search, and key search.

11. What is the purpose of a hash function?

12. Describe the uses of hash files for sequential search, range search, and key search.

13. What is the difference between a static hash file and a dynamic hash file?

14. Define the terms *balanced, bushy,* and *block-oriented* as they relate to Btree files.

15. Briefly explain the use of node splits and concatenations in the maintenance of Btree files.

16. What does it mean to say that Btrees have logarithmic search cost?

17. What is the difference between a Btree and a B+tree?

18. What is a bitmap?

19. How does a DBMS use a bitmap?

20. What are the components of a bitmap index record?

21. What is the difference between a bitmap column index and a bitmap join index?

22. When should bitmap indexes be used?

23. What is the difference between a primary and secondary file structure?

24. What does it mean to say that an index matches a column?

25. Why should composite indexes be used sparingly?

26. What happens in the query transformation phase of database language translation?

27. What is an access plan?

28. How are access plans evaluated in query optimization?

29. Why does the uniform value assumption sometimes lead to poor access plans?

30. What does it mean to bind a query?

31. What join algorithm can be used for all join operations?

32. For what join algorithms must the optimization component choose the outer and inner tables?

33. What join algorithm can combine more than two tables at a time?

34. When is the sort merge algorithm a good choice for combining tables?

35. When is the hash join algorithm a good choice for combining tables?

36. What is an optimizer hint? Why should hints be used cautiously?

37. Identify a situation in which an optimizer hint may be appropriate.

38. What is the difference between a clustered and a nonclustered index?

39. When is a nonclustered index useful?

40. When is a clustered index useful?

41. What is the relationship of index selection to query optimization?

42. What are the trade-offs in index selection?

43. Why is index selection difficult?

44. When should you use the index selection rules?

45. Why should you be careful about denormalization?

46. Identify two situations when denormalization may be useful.

47. What is RAID storage?

48. For what kinds of applications can RAID storage improve performance?

49. What is striping in relation to RAID storage?

50. What techniques are used in RAID storage to improve reliability?

51. What are the advantages and disadvantages of RAID-1 versus RAID-5?

52. What is a Storage Area Network (SAN)?

53. What is the relationship of a SAN to RAID storage?

54. What are the trade-offs in storing derived data?

55. What processing environments also involve physical database design decisions?

56. What are some DBMS-specific concerns for performance improvement?

PROBLEMS

Besides the problems presented here, the case study in Chapter 13 provides additional practice. To supplement the examples in this chapter, Chapter 13 provides a complete database design case including physical database design.

1. Use the following data to perform the indicated calculations. Show formulas that you used to perform the calculations.

> Row size = 100 bytes
> Number of rows = 100,000
> Primary key size = 6 bytes
> Physical record size = 4,096 bytes
> Pointer size = 4 bytes
> Floor(X) is the largest integer less than or equal to X.
> Ceil(X) is the smallest integer greater than or equal to X.

1.1. Calculate the number of rows that can fit in a physical record. Assume that only complete rows can be stored (use the Floor function).

1.2. Calculate the number of physical records necessary for a sequential file. Assume that physical records are filled to capacity except for perhaps the last physical record (use the Ceil function).

1.3. If an unordered sequential file is used, calculate the number of physical record accesses on the average to retrieve a row with a specified key value.

1.4. If an ordered sequential file is used, calculate the number of physical record accesses on the average to retrieve a row with a specified key value. Assume that the key exists in the file.

1.5. Calculate the average number of physical record accesses to find a key that does not exist in an unordered sequential file and an ordered sequential file.

1.6. Calculate the number of physical records for a static hash file. Assume that each physical record of the hash file is 70 percent full.

1.7. Calculate the maximum branching factor on a node in a Btree. Assume that each record in a Btree consists of <key value, pointer> pairs.

1.8. Using your calculation from problem 1.7, calculate the maximum height of a Btree index.

1.9. Calculate the maximum number of physical record accesses to find a node in the Btree with a specific key value.

2. Answer query optimization questions for the following SQL statement:

```
SELECT * FROM Customer
WHERE CustCity = 'DENVER' AND CustBalance >5000
    AND CustState = 'CO'
```

ORDER

2.1. Show four access plans for this query assuming that nonclustered indexes exist on the columns *CustCity, CustBalance,* and *CustState.* There is also a clustered index on the primary key column, *CustNo.*

2.2. Using the uniform value assumption, estimate the fraction of rows that satisfy the condition on *CustBalance.* The smallest balance is 0 and the largest balance is $10,000.

2.3. Using the following histogram, estimate the fraction of rows that satisfy the condition on *CustBalance.*

Histogram for *CustBalance*

Range	Rows
0–100	1,000
101–250	950
251–500	1,050
501–1,000	1,030
1,001–2,000	975
2,001–4,500	1,035
4,501 –	1,200

3. Answer query optimization questions for the following SQL statement:

```
SELECT OrdNo, OrdDate, Vehicle.ModelNo
  FROM Customer, Order, Vehicle
  WHERE CustBalance > 5000
      AND Customer.CustNo = Vehicle.CustNo
      AND Vehicle.SerialNo = Order.SerialNo
```

3.1. List the possible orders to join the *Customer, Order,* and *Vehicle* tables.

3.2. For one of these join orders, make an access plan. Assume that Btree indexes exist for only the primary keys, *Customer.CustNo, Order.OrdNo,* and *Vehicle.SerialNo.*

4. For the following tables and SQL statements, select indexes that balance retrieval and update requirements. For each table, justify your choice using the rules discussed in Section 8.5.3.

Customer(CustNo, CustName, CustCity, CustState, CustZip, CustBal)
Order(OrdNo, OrdDate, CustNo)
     FOREIGN KEY CustNo REFERENCES Customer
OrdLine(OrdNo, ProdNo, OrdQty)
     FOREIGN KEY OrdNo REFERENCES Order
     FOREIGN KEY ProdNo REFERENCES Product
Product(ProdNo, ProdName, ProdColor, ProdPrice)

4.1. For the *Customer* table, what columns are good choices for the clustered index? Nonclustered indexes?

4.2. For the *Product* table, what columns are good choices for the clustered index? Nonclustered indexes?

4.3. For the *Order* table, what columns are good choices for the clustered index? Nonclustered indexes?

4.4. For the *OrdLine* table, what columns are good choices for the clustered index? Nonclustered indexes?

SQL Statement	Frequency
1. INSERT INTO Customer . . .	100/day
2. INSERT INTO Product . . .	100/month
3. INSERT INTO Order . . .	3,000/day
4. INSERT INTO OrdLine . . .	9,000/day
5. DELETE Product WHERE ProdNo = $X	100/year
6. DELETE Customer WHERE CustNo = $X	1,000/year
7. SELECT * FROM Order, Customer WHERE OrdNo = $X AND Order.CustNo = Customer.CustNo	300/day
8. SELECT * FROM OrdLine, Product WHERE OrdNo = $X AND OrdLine.ProdNo = Product.ProdNo	300/day

9. SELECT * FROM Customer, Order, OrdLine, Product
    WHERE CustName = $X AND OrdDate = $Y
       AND Customer.CustNo = Order.CustNo
       AND Order.OrdNo = OrdLine.OrdNo
       AND Product.ProdNo = OrdLine.ProdNo
	500/day

10. UPDATE OrdLine SET OrdQty = $X WHERE OrdNo = $Y	300/day
11. UPDATE Product SET ProdPrice = $X WHERE ProdNo = $Y	300/month

5. Indexes on combinations of columns are not as useful as indexes on individual columns. Consider a combination index on two columns, *CustState* and *CustCity*, where *CustState* is the primary ordering and *CustCity* is the secondary ordering. For what kinds of conditions can the index be used? For what kinds of conditions is the index not useful?

6. For query 9 in problem 4, list the possible join orders considered by the query optimization component.

7. For the following tables of a financial planning database, identify possible uses of denormalization and derived data to improve performance. In addition, identify denormalization and derived data already appearing in the tables.

   The tables track financial assets held and trades made by customers. A trade involves a purchase or sale of a specified quantity of an asset by a customer. Assets include stocks and bonds. The *Holding* table contains the *net* quantity of each asset held by a customer. For example, if a customer has purchased 10,000 shares of IBM and sold 4,000, the *Holding* table shows a net quantity of 6,000. A frequent query is to list the most recent valuation for each asset held by a customer. The most recent valuation is the net quantity of the asset times the most recent price.

   Customer(<u>CustNo,</u> CustName, CustAddress, CustCity, CustState, CustZip, CustPhone)
   Asset(<u>AssetNo,</u> SecName, LastClose)
   Stock(<u>AssetNo,</u> OutShares, IssShares)
   Bond(<u>AssetNo,</u> BondRating, FacValue)
   PriceHistory(<u>AssetNo, PHistDate,</u> PHistPrice)
       FOREIGN KEY AssetNo REFERENCES Asset
   Holding(<u>CustNo, AssetNo,</u> NetQty)
       FOREIGN KEY CustNo REFERENCES Customer
       FOREIGN KEY AssetNo REFERENCES Asset

Trade(<u>TradeNo,</u> CustNo, AssetNo, TrdQty, TrdPrice, TrdDate, TrdType, TrdStatus)
    FOREIGN KEY CustNo REFERENCES Customer
    FOREIGN KEY AssetNo REFERENCES Asset

8. Rewrite the following SQL statement to improve its performance on most DBMSs. Use the tips in Section 8.4.2 to rewrite the statement. The Access SQL statement uses the financial trading database shown in problem 7. The purpose of the statement is to list the customer number and the name of customers and the sum of the amount of their completed October 2003 buy trades. The amount of a trade is the quantity (number of shares) times the price per share. A customer should be in the result if the sum of the amount of his/her completed October 2003 buy trades exceeds by 25 percent the sum of the amount of his/her completed September 2003 buy trades.

```
SELECT Customer.CustNo, CustName,
        SUM(TrdQty * TrdPrice) AS SumTradeAmt
  FROM Customer, Trade
  WHERE Customer.CustNo = Trade.CustNo AND TrdType = 'BUY'
    AND TrdDate BETWEEN #10/1/2003# AND #10/31/2003#
  GROUP BY Customer.CustNo, CustName
  HAVING SUM(TrdQty * TrdPrice) >
    (  SELECT 1.25 * SUM(TrdQty * TrdPrice) FROM Trade
        WHERE TrdDate BETWEEN #9/1/2003# AND #9/30/2003#
          AND TrdType = 'BUY'
          AND Trade.CustNo = Customer.CustNo   )
```

9. Rewrite the following SELECT statement to improve its performance on most DBMSs. Use the tips in Section 8.4.2 to rewrite the statement. The Access SQL statement uses the financial trading database shown in problem 7.

```
SELECT Customer.CustNo, CustName,
        TrdQty * TrdPrice, TrdDate, SecName
  FROM Customer, Trade, Asset
  WHERE Customer.CustNo = Trade.CustNo
    AND Trade.AssetNo = Asset.AssetNo
    AND TrdType = 'BUY'
    AND TrdDate BETWEEN #10/1/2003# AND #10/31/2003#
    AND Trade.CustNo = 'C10001'
```

10. For the following conditions and indexes, indicate if the index matches the condition.
    - Index on TrdDate: TrdDate BETWEEN #10/1/2003# AND #10/31/2003#.
    - Index on CustPhone: CustPhone LIKE '(303)%'.
    - Index on TrdType: TrdType < > 'BUY'.
    - Bitmap column index on BondRating: BondRating IN ('AAA', 'AA', 'A').
    - Index on <CustState, CustCity, CustZip>:.
      - CustState = 'CO' AND CustCity = 'Denver'.
      - CustState IN ('CO', 'CA') AND CustCity LIKE '%er'.
      - CustState IN ('CO', 'CA') AND CustZip LIKE '8%'.
      - CustState = 'CO' AND CustCity IN ('Denver', 'Boulder') AND CustZip LIKE '8%'.

11. For the sample *Customer* and *Trade* tables below, construct bitmap indexes as indicated.

- Bitmap column index on *Customer.CustState.*
- Join bitmap index on *Customer.CustNo* to the *Trade* table.
- Bitmap join index on *Customer.CustState* to the *Trade* table.

Customer Table

RowID	CustNo	. . .	CustState
1	113344		CO
2	123789		CA
3	145789		UT
4	111245		NM
5	931034		CO
6	998245		CA
7	287341		UT
8	230432		CO
9	321588		CA
10	443356		CA
11	559211		UT
12	220688		NM

Trade Table

RowID	TradeNo	. . .	CustNo
1	1111		113344
2	1234		123789
3	1345		123789
4	1599		145789
5	1807		145789
6	1944		931034
7	2100		111245
8	2200		287341
9	2301		287341
10	2487		230432
11	2500		443356
12	2600		559211
13	2703		220688
14	2801		220688
15	2944		220688
16	3100		230432
17	3200		230432
18	3258		321588
19	3302		321588
20	3901		559211
21	4001		998245
22	4205		998245
23	4301		931034
24	4455		443356

12. For the following tables and SQL statements, select indexes (clustering and nonclustering) that balance retrieval and update requirements. For each table, justify your choice using the rules discussed in Section 8.5.3.

> **Customer**(CustNo, CustName, CustAddress, CustCity, CustState, CustZip, CustPhone)
> **Asset**(AssetNo, AssetName, AssetType)
> **PriceHistory**(AssetNo, PHistDate, PHistPrice)
> > FOREIGN KEY AssetNo REFERENCES Asset
> **Holding**(CustNo, AssetNo, NetQty)
> > FOREIGN KEY CustNo REFERENCES Customer
> > FOREIGN KEY AssetNo REFERENCES Asset
> **Trade**(TradeNo, CustNo, AssetNo, TrdQty, TrdPrice, TrdDate, TrdType, TrdStatus)
> > FOREIGN KEY CustNo REFERENCES Customer
> > FOREIGN KEY AssetNo REFERENCES Asset

SQL Statement	Frequency
1. INSERT INTO Customer . . .	100/day
2. INSERT INTO Asset . . .	100/quarter
3. INSERT INTO Trade . . .	10,000/day
4. INSERT INTO Holding . . .	200/day
5. INSERT INTO PriceHistory . . .	5,000/day
5. DELETE Asset WHERE AssetNo = $X	300/year
6. DELETE Customer WHERE CustNo = $X	3,000/year
7. SELECT * FROM Holding, Customer, Asset, PriceHistory 　　WHERE CustNo = $X AND Holding.CustNo = Customer.CustNo 　　　AND Holding.AssetNo = Asset.AssetNo 　　　AND Asset.AssetNo = PriceHistory.AssetNo 　　　AND PHistDate = $Y	15,000/month
8. SELECT * FROM Trade 　　WHERE TradeNo = $X	1,000/day
9. SELECT * FROM Customer, Trade, Asset 　　WHERE Customer.CustNo = $X AND TrdDate BETWEEN $Y AND $Z 　　　AND Customer.CustNo = Trade.CustNo 　　　AND Trade.AssetNo = Asset.AssetNo	10,000/month
10. UPDATE Trade SET TrdStatus = $X 　　WHERE TradeNo = $Y	1,000/day
11. UPDATE Holding SET NetQty = $X 　　WHERE CustNo = $Y AND AssetNo = $Z	10,000/day
12. SELECT * FROM Customer WHERE CustZip = $X 　　AND CustPhone LIKE '$Y%'	500/day
13. SELECT * FROM Trade WHERE TrdStatus = $X AND TrdDate = $Y	10/day
14. SELECT * FROM Asset WHERE AssetName LIKE '$X%'	500/day

13. For the workload of problem 12, are there any SELECT statements that a DBA might want to use optimizer hints? Please explain the kind of hint that could be used and your reasoning for using it.

REFERENCES FOR FURTHER STUDY

The subject of physical database design can be much more detailed and mathematical than described in this chapter. For a more detailed description of file structures and physical database design, consult computer science books such as Elmasri and Navathe (2002) and Teorey and Fry (1982). For detailed tutorials about query optimization, consult Chaudhuri (1998), Jarke and Koch (1984), and Mannino, Chu, and Sager (1988). Finkelstein, Schkolnick, and Tiberio (1988) describe DBDSGN, an index selection tool for SQL/DS, an IBM relational DBMS. Chaudhuri and Narasayya (1997, 2001) describe tools for index selection and statistics management for Microsoft SQL Server. For practical descriptions of physical database design, consult Gibson, Hughes, and Remington (1989), Rodgers (1989), Schumacher (1994), and Viehman (1994). Books on physical database design for specific DBMSs include Ensor and Stevenson (1997) and Gillette, Muench, and Tabaka (1996). The Benchmark Factory (www.csrad.com) provides tools for performance evaluation of major DBMSs. The *DBAZine* site (www.dbazine.com) provides practical advice about physical database design.

APPLICATION DEVELOPMENT WITH RELATIONAL DATABASES

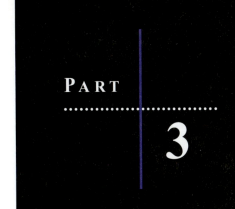

Part 3 provides a foundation for building database applications by helping students acquire skills in advanced query formulation, specification of data requirements for data entry forms and reports, coding triggers and stored procedures, and using views in the design of complex databases. Chapter 9 presents additional examples of intermediate and advanced SQL along with corresponding query formulation skills. Chapter 10 describes the motivation, definition, and usage of relational views along with specification of view definitions for data entry forms and reports. Chapter 11 presents concepts and coding practices of database programming languages, stored procedures, and triggers for customization of database applications. Chapter 12 describes view design and view integration, data modeling concepts for large database development efforts. Chapter 13 provides a comprehensive case study that enables students to gain insights about the difficulties of applying database design and application development skills to a realistic business situation.

Advanced Query Formulation with SQL

LEARNING OBJECTIVES

This chapter extends your query formulation skills by explaining advanced table matching problems involving the outer join, difference, and division operators. Other parts of the SELECT statement are demonstrated to explain these advanced matching problems. In addition, the subtle effects of null values are explained to provide a deeper understanding of query formulation. After this chapter, you should have acquired the following knowledge and skills:

■ Recognize Type I nested queries for joins and understand the conceptual evaluation process.

■ Recognize Type II nested queries and understand the conceptual evaluation process.

■ Recognize problems involving the outer join, difference, and division operators.

■ Formulate problems involving the outer join, difference, and division operators.

■ Understand the effect of null values on conditions, aggregate calculations, and grouping.

OVERVIEW

As the first chapter in Part 3 of the textbook, this chapter builds on material covered in Chapters 2 and 3. Chapter 3 provided a foundation for query formulation using SQL. Most importantly, you learned an important subset of SELECT and how to apply it to problems involving joins and grouping. This chapter extends your knowledge of query formulation to advanced matching problems. To solve these advanced matching problems, additional parts of the SELECT statement are introduced.

This chapter continues with the learning approaches of Chapter 3: provide many examples to imitate and conceptual models to help you reason through difficult problems. You first will learn how to formulate problems involving the outer join operator using new keywords in the FROM clause. You next will learn about nested queries and how they can be used in advanced matching problems. Then you will learn how to formulate problems involving the division operator using the GROUP BY clause and the COUNT function. Finally, you will learn the effect of null values on simple conditions, compound conditions with Boolean operators, aggregate calculations, and grouping. As in Chapter 3, all examples execute in both Microsoft Access 2002 and Oracle 9i except where noted. Because the outer join notation in Oracle changed between versions 8i and 9i, both notations are shown.

9.1 OUTER JOIN PROBLEMS

One of the powerful but sometimes confusing aspects of SQL is the number of ways to express a join. In Chapter 3, you formulated joins using the cross product style and the join operator style. In the cross product style, you list the tables in the FROM clause and the join conditions in the WHERE clause. In the join operator style, you write join operations directly in the FROM clause using the INNER JOIN and ON keywords.

The major advantage of the join operator style is that problems involving the outer join operator can be formulated. Outer join problems cannot be formulated with the cross product style except with proprietary SQL extensions. This section demonstrates the join operator style for outer join problems and combinations of inner and outer joins. In addition, the proprietary outer join extension of Oracle is shown. For your reference, the relationship diagram of the university database is repeated from Chapter 3 (see Figure 9.1).

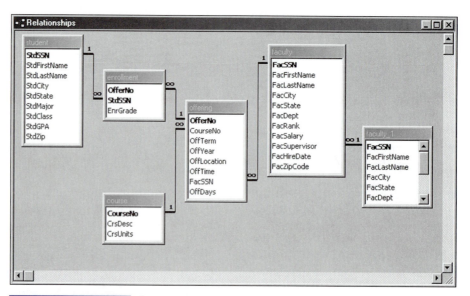

| **Figure 9.1** | Relationship window for the university database. |

9.1.1 SQL Support for Outer Join Problems

A join between two tables generates a table with the rows that match on the join column(s). The outer join operator generates the join result (the matching rows) plus the nonmatching rows. A <u>one-sided outer join</u> generates a new table with the matching rows plus the nonmatching rows from <u>one</u> of the tables. For example, it can be useful to see all offerings listed in the output even if an offering does not have an assigned faculty.

One-Sided Outer Join an operator that generates the join result (the matching rows) plus the nonmatching rows from one of the input tables. SQL supports the one-sided outer join operator through the LEFT JOIN and RIGHT JOIN keywords.

SQL uses the LEFT JOIN and RIGHT JOIN keywords to produce a one-sided outer join.[1] The LEFT JOIN keyword means to generate a table containing the matching rows and the nonmatching rows of the left table. The RIGHT JOIN keyword means to generate a table containing the matching rows and the nonmatching rows of the right table. Thus, the result of a one-sided outer join depends on the direction (RIGHT or LEFT) and the position of the table names. Examples 9.1 and 9.2 demonstrate one-sided outer joins using both the LEFT and RIGHT keywords. The result rows with blank values for certain columns are nonmatched rows.

Example 9.1 (Access)	One-Sided Outer Join Using LEFT JOIN

For IS course offerings, retrieve the offer number, the course number, the faculty number, and the faculty name. Include an offering in the result even if the faculty is not yet assigned. The Oracle 9i counterpart of this example uses % instead of * as the wild card character.

```
SELECT OfferNo, CourseNo, Offering.FacSSN, Faculty.FacSSN,
        FacFirstName, FacLastName
FROM Offering LEFT JOIN Faculty
        ON Offering.FacSSN = Faculty.FacSSN
WHERE CourseNo LIKE 'IS*'
```

OfferNo	CourseNo	Offering.FacSSN	Faculty.FacSSN	FacFirstName	FacLastName
1111	IS320				
2222	IS460				
1234	IS320	098-76-5432	098-76-5432	LEONARD	VINCE
3333	IS320	098-76-5432	098-76-5432	LEONARD	VINCE
4321	IS320	098-76-5432	098-76-5432	LEONARD	VINCE
4444	IS320	543-21-0987	543-21-0987	VICTORIA	EMMANUEL
8888	IS320	654-32-1098	654-32-1098	LEONARD	FIBON
9876	IS460	654-32-1098	654-32-1098	LEONARD	FIBON
5679	IS480	876-54-3210	876-54-3210	CRISTOPHER	COLAN
5678	IS480	987-65-4321	987-65-4321	JULIA	MILLS

Example 9.2 (Access)	One-Sided Outer Join Using RIGHT JOIN

For IS course offerings, retrieve the offer number, the course number, the faculty number, and the faculty name. Include an offering in the result even if the faculty is not yet assigned. The result is identical to Example 9.1. The Oracle 9i counterpart of this example uses % instead of * as the wild card character.

```
SELECT OfferNo, CourseNo, Offering.FacSSN, Faculty.FacSSN,
        FacFirstName, FacLastName
```

---

[1]The full SQL keywords are LEFT OUTER JOIN and RIGHT OUTER JOIN. The SQL:1999 standard and most DBMSs allow omission of the OUTER keyword.

```
FROM Faculty RIGHT JOIN Offering
       ON Offering.FacSSN = Faculty.FacSSN
WHERE CourseNo LIKE 'IS*'
```

Until the current release (9i), Oracle used a proprietary extension for one-sided outer joins. To express a one-sided outer join in Oracle 8i SQL, use the notation (+) as part of a join condition in the WHERE clause. You place the (+) notation just after the join column of the null table, that is, the table with null values in the result. This placement reverses the usage of the SQL:1999 LEFT and RIGHT keywords by the table to preserve. The Oracle 8i formulations of Examples 9.1 and 9.2 demonstrate the (+) notation.

Example 9.1 (Oracle 8i)

One-Sided Outer Join Using LEFT JOIN

The (+) notation is placed after the *Faculty.FacSSN* column in the join condition because *Faculty* is the null table in the result.

```
SELECT OfferNo, CourseNo, Offering.FacSSN, Faculty.FacSSN,
       FacFirstName, FacLastName
 FROM Faculty, Offering
 WHERE Offering.FacSSN = Faculty.FacSSN (+)
    AND CourseNo LIKE 'IS%'
```

Example 9.2 (Oracle 8i)

One-Sided Outer Join Using RIGHT JOIN

The (+) notation is placed after the *Faculty.FacSSN* column in the join condition because *Faculty* is the null table in the result.

```
SELECT OfferNo, CourseNo, Offering.FacSSN, Faculty.FacSSN,
       FacFirstName, FacLastName
 FROM Faculty, Offering
 WHERE Faculty.FacSSN (+) = Offering.FacSSN
    AND CourseNo LIKE 'IS%'
```

It should be noted that the proprietary extension of Oracle is inferior to the SQL:1999 notation. The proprietary extension does not allow specification of the order of performing outer joins. This limitation can be problematic on difficult problems involving more than one outer join. Thus, you should use the SQL:1999 outer join syntax although Oracle 9i still supports the proprietary extension using the (+) symbol.

Another use of the one-sided outer join operator is to generate a table with only non-matching rows. The IS NULL comparison operator can remove rows that match, as demonstrated in Example 9.3.

Example 9.3

One-Sided Outer Join with Only Nonmatching Rows

Retrieve the social security number, the name, the department, and the salary of faculty who are *not* students.

```
SELECT FacSSN, FacFirstName, FacLastName, FacSalary
  FROM Faculty LEFT JOIN Student
        ON Faculty.FacSSN = Student.StdSSN
  WHERE Student.StdSSN IS NULL
```

FacSSN	FacFirstName	FacLastName	FacSalary
098-76-5432	LEONARD	VINCE	$35,000.00
543-21-0987	VICTORIA	EMMANUEL	$120,000.00
654-32-1098	LEONARD	FIBON	$70,000.00
765-43-2109	NICKI	MACON	$65,000.00
987-65-4321	JULIA	MILLS	$75,000.00

Example 9.3 (Oracle 8i)

One-Sided Outer Join with Only Nonmatching Rows

Retrieve the social security number, the name, the department, and the salary of faculty who are *not* students.

```
SELECT FacSSN, FacFirstName, FacLastName, FacSalary
  FROM Faculty, Student
  WHERE Faculty.FacSSN = Student.StdSSN (+)
        AND Student.StdSSN IS NULL
```

Full Outer Join an operator that generates the join result (the matching rows) plus the non-matching rows from both input tables. SQL supports the full outer join operator through the FULL JOIN keyword.

A <u>full outer join</u> generates a table with the matching rows plus the nonmatching rows from both tables. Typically, a full outer join is used to combine two similar but not union compatible tables. For example, the *Student* and *Faculty* tables are similar because they contain information about university people. However, they are not union compatible. They have common columns such as last name, city, and social security number but also unique columns such as GPA and salary. Occasionally, you will need to write a query that combines both tables. For example, find all university people within a certain city. A full outer join is used in such problems.

SQL:1999 provides the FULL JOIN keyword as demonstrated in Example 9.4. Note the null values in both halves (*Student* and *Faculty*) of the result.

Example 9.4 (SQL:1999 and Oracle 9i)

Full Outer Join

Combine the *Faculty* and *Student* tables using a full outer join. List the social security number, the name (first and last), the salary (faculty only), and the GPA (students only) in the result. This SQL statement does not execute in Microsoft Access.

```
SELECT FacSSN, FacFirstName, FacLastName, FacSalary,
        StdSSN, StdFirstName, StdLastName, StdGPA
  FROM Faculty FULL JOIN Student
        ON Student.StdSSN = Faculty.FacSSN
```

FacSSN	FacFirstName	FacLastName	FacSalary	StdSSN	StdFirstName	StdLastName	StdGPA
				123456789	HOMER	WELLS	3
				124567890	BOB	NORBERT	2.7
				234567890	CANDY	KENDALL	3.5
				345678901	WALLY	KENDALL	2.8
				456789012	JOE	ESTRADA	3.2
				567890123	MARIAH	DODGE	3.6
				678901234	TESS	DODGE	3.3
				789012345	ROBERTO	MORALES	2.5
				890123456	LUKE	BRAZZI	2.2
				901234567	WILLIAM	PILGRIM	3.8
098765432	LEONARD	VINCE	35000				
543210987	VICTORIA	EMMANUEL	120000				
654321098	LEONARD	FIBON	70000				
765432109	NICKI	MACON	65000				
876543210	CRISTOPHER	COLAN	40000	876543210	CRISTOPHER	COLAN	4
987654321	JULIA	MILLS	75000				

Some DBMSs (such as Microsoft Access 2002 and Oracle 8i) do not directly support the full outer join operator. In these systems, a full outer join can be formulated by taking the union of two one-sided outer joins using the steps shown below. The SELECT statement implementing these steps is shown in Example 9.5.

1. Construct a right join of *Faculty* and *Student* (nonmatched rows of *Student*).
2. Construct a left join of *Faculty* and *Student* (nonmatched rows of *Faculty*).
3. Construct a union of these two temporary tables. Remember when using the UNION operator, the two table arguments must be "union compatible": each corresponding column from both tables must have compatible data types. Otherwise, the UNION operator will not work as expected.

Example 9.5 (Access)

Full Outer Join Using a Union of Two One-Sided Outer Joins
Combine the *Faculty* and *Student* tables using a full outer join. List the social security number, the name (first and last), the salary (faculty only), and the GPA (students only) in the result. The result is identical to Example 9.4.

```
SELECT FacSSN, FacFirstName, FacLastName, FacSalary,
       StdSSN, StdFirstName, StdLastName, StdGPA
FROM Faculty RIGHT JOIN Student
     ON Student.StdSSN = Faculty.FacSSN
         UNION
SELECT FacSSN, FacFirstName, FacLastName, FacSalary,
       StdSSN, StdFirstName, StdLastName, StdGPA
FROM Faculty LEFT JOIN Student
     ON Student.StdSSN = Faculty.FacSSN
```

Example 9.5 (Oracle 8i)

Full Outer Join Using a Union of Two One-sided Outer Joins
Combine the *Faculty* and *Student* tables using a full outer join. List the social security number, the name (first and last), the salary (faculty only), and the GPA (students only) in the result. The result is identical to Example 9.4.

```
SELECT FacSSN, FacFirstName, FacLastName, FacSalary,
       StdSSN, StdFirstName, StdLastName, StdGPA
```

```
FROM Faculty, Student
WHERE Student.StdSSN = Faculty.FacSSN (+)
        UNION
SELECT FacSSN, FacFirstName, FacLastName, FacSalary,
        StdSSN, StdFirstName, StdLastName, StdGPA
 FROM Faculty, Student
 WHERE Student.StdSSN (+) = Faculty.FacSSN
```

9.1.2 Mixing Inner and Outer Joins

Inner and outer joins can be mixed as demonstrated in Examples 9.6 and 9.7. For readability, it is generally preferred to use the join operator style rather than to mix the join operator and cross product styles.

Example 9.6 (Access)	Mixing a One-Sided Outer Join and an Inner Join

Combine columns from the *Faculty, Offering,* and *Course* tables for IS courses offered in 2003. Include a row in the result even if there is not an assigned instructor. The Oracle 9i counterpart of this example uses % instead of * as the wild card character.

```
SELECT OfferNo, Offering.CourseNo, OffTerm, CrsDesc,
        Faculty.FacSSN, FacFirstName, FacLastName
 FROM (   Faculty RIGHT JOIN Offering
        ON Offering.FacSSN = Faculty.FacSSN   )
      INNER JOIN Course
        ON Course.CourseNo = Offering.CourseNo
 WHERE Course.CourseNo LIKE 'IS*' AND OffYear = 2003
```

OfferNo	CourseNo	OffTerm	CrsDesc	FacSSN	FacFirstName	FacLastName
1111	IS320	SUMMER	FUNDAMENTALS OF BUSINESS PROGRAMMING			
3333	IS320	SPRING	FUNDAMENTALS OF BUSINESS PROGRAMMING	098-76-5432	LEONARD	VINCE
4444	IS320	WINTER	FUNDAMENTALS OF BUSINESS PROGRAMMING	543-21-0987	VICTORIA	EMMANUEL
5678	IS480	WINTER	FUNDAMENTALS OF DATABASE MANAGEMENT	987-65-4321	JULIA	MILLS
5679	IS480	SPRING	FUNDAMENTALS OF DATABASE MANAGEMENT	876-54-3210	CRISTOPHER	COLAN
8888	IS320	SUMMER	FUNDAMENTALS OF BUSINESS PROGRAMMING	654-32-1098	LEONARD	FIBON
9876	IS460	SPRING	SYSTEMS ANALYSIS	654-32-1098	LEONARD	FIBON

Example 9.6 (Oracle 8i)	Mixing a One-Sided Outer Join and an Inner Join

Combine columns from the *Faculty, Offering,* and *Course* tables for IS courses offered in 2003. Include a row in the result even if there is not an assigned instructor.

```
SELECT OfferNo, Offering.CourseNo, OffTerm, CrsDesc,
        Faculty.FacSSN, FacFirstName, FacLastName
 FROM Faculty, Offering, Course
 WHERE Offering.FacSSN = Faculty.FacSSN (+)
      AND Course.CourseNo = Offering.CourseNo
      AND Course.CourseNo LIKE 'IS%' AND OffYear = 2003
```

**Example 9.7
(Access)**

Mixing a One-Sided Outer Join and Two Inner Joins

List the rows of the *Offering* table where there is at least one student enrolled, in addition to the requirements of Example 9.6. Remove duplicate rows when there is more than one student enrolled in an offering. The Oracle 9i counterpart of this example uses % instead of * as the wild card character.

```
SELECT DISTINCT Offering.OfferNo, Offering.CourseNo,
        OffTerm, CrsDesc, Faculty.FacSSN, FacFirstName,
        FacLastName
  FROM (  (   Faculty RIGHT JOIN Offering
        ON Offering.FacSSN = Faculty.FacSSN )
        INNER JOIN Course
        ON Course.CourseNo = Offering.CourseNo )
        INNER JOIN Enrollment
        ON Offering.OfferNo = Enrollment.OfferNo
  WHERE Offering.CourseNo LIKE 'IS*' AND OffYear = 2003
```

OfferNo	CourseNo	OffTerm	CrsDesc	FacSSN	FacFirstName	FacLastName
5678	IS480	WINTER	FUNDAMENTALS OF DATABASE MANAGEMENT	987-65-4321	JULIA	MILLS
5679	IS480	SPRING	FUNDAMENTALS OF DATABASE MANAGEMENT	876-54-3210	CRISTOPHER	COLAN
9876	IS460	SPRING	SYSTEMS ANALYSIS	654-32-1098	LEONARD	FIBON

**Example 9.7
(Oracle 8i)**

Mixing a One-Sided Outer Join and Two Inner Joins

List the rows of the *Offering* table where there is at least one student enrolled, in addition to the requirements of Example 9.6. Remove duplicate rows when there is more than one student enrolled in an offering.

```
SELECT DISTINCT Offering.OfferNo, Offering.CourseNo,
        OffTerm, CrsDesc, Faculty.FacSSN, FacFirstName,
        FacLastName
  FROM Faculty, Offering, Course, Enrollment
  WHERE Offering.FacSSN = Faculty.FacSSN (+)
        AND Course.CourseNo = Offering.CourseNo
        AND Offering.OfferNo = Enrollment.OfferNo
        AND Course.CourseNo LIKE 'IS%' AND OffYear = 2003
```

9.2 UNDERSTANDING NESTED QUERIES

A nested query or subquery is a query (SELECT statement) inside a query. A nested query typically appears as part of a condition in the WHERE or HAVING clauses. Nested queries also can be used in the FROM clause. Nested queries can be used like a procedure (Type I nested query) in which the nested query is executed one time or like a loop (Type II nested query) in which the nested query is executed repeatedly. This section demonstrates examples of both kinds of nested queries and explains problems in which they can be applied.

Type I Nested Query a nested query in which the inner query does not reference any tables used in the outer query. Type I nested queries can be used for some join problems and some difference problems.

9.2.1 Type I Nested Queries

Type I nested queries are like procedures in a programming language. The nested query evaluates one time and produces a table. The nested (or inner) query does not reference the outer query. Using the IN comparison operator, a Type I nested query can be used to express a join. In Example 9.8, the nested query on the *Enrollment* table generates a list of qualifying social security number values. A row is selected in the outer query on *Student* if the social security number is an element of the nested query result.

Example 9.8

Using a Type I Nested Query to Perform a Join
List the social security number, the name, and the major of students who have a high grade ($\geq$ 3.5) in a course offering.

```
SELECT StdSSN, StdFirstName, StdLastName, StdMajor
  FROM Student
  WHERE Student.StdSSN IN
    (   SELECT StdSSN FROM Enrollment
        WHERE EnrGrade >= 3.5   )
```

StdSSN	StdFirstName	StdLastName	StdMajor
123-45-6789	HOMER	WELLS	IS
124-56-7890	BOB	NORBERT	FIN
234-56-7890	CANDY	KENDALL	ACCT
567-89-0123	MARIAH	DODGE	IS
789-01-2345	ROBERTO	MORALES	FIN
890-12-3456	LUKE	BRAZZI	IS
901-23-4567	WILLIAM	PILGRIM	IS

Type I nested queries should be used only when the result does not contain any columns from the nested query. In Example 9.8, no columns from *Enrollment* are used in the result. In Example 9.9, the join between *Student* and *Enrollment* cannot be performed with a Type I nested query because *EnrGrade* appears in the result.

Example 9.9

Combining a Type I Nested Query and the Join Operator Style
Retrieve the name, the city, and the grade of students who have a high grade ($\geq$ 3.5) in a course offered in fall 2002.

```
SELECT StdFirstName, StdLastName, StdCity, EnrGrade
  FROM Student INNER JOIN Enrollment
        ON Student.StdSSN = Enrollment.StdSSN
  WHERE EnrGrade >= 3.5 AND Enrollment.OfferNo IN
    (   SELECT OfferNo FROM Offering
        WHERE OffTerm = 'FALL' AND OffYear = 2002   )
```

StdFirstName	StdLastName	StdCity	EnrGrade
CANDY	KENDALL	TACOMA	3.5
MARIAH	DODGE	SEATTLE	3.8
HOMER	WELLS	SEATTLE	3.5
ROBERTO	MORALES	SEATTLE	3.5

It is possible to have multiple levels of nested queries if desired. In a nested query, you can have another nested query using the IN comparison operator in the WHERE clause. In Example 9.10, the nested query on the *Offering* table has a nested query on the *Faculty* table. No *Faculty* columns are needed in the main query or in the nested query on *Offering*.

Example 9.10

Using a Type I Nested Query Inside Another Type I Nested Query

Retrieve the name, the city, and the grade of students who have a high grade (≥ 3.5) in a course offered in fall 2002 taught by Leonard Vince.

```
SELECT StdFirstName, StdLastName, StdCity, EnrGrade
  FROM Student, Enrollment
  WHERE Student.StdSSN = Enrollment.StdSSN
     AND EnrGrade >= 3.5 AND Enrollment.OfferNo IN
     (   SELECT OfferNo FROM Offering
            WHERE OffTerm = 'FALL' AND OffYear = 2002
               AND FacSSN IN
                  (   SELECT FacSSN FROM Faculty
                        WHERE FacFirstName = 'LEONARD'
                           AND FacLastName = 'VINCE'   )   )
```

StdFirstName	StdLastName	StdCity	EnrGrade
CANDY	KENDALL	TACOMA	3.5
MARIAH	DODGE	SEATTLE	3.8
HOMER	WELLS	SEATTLE	3.5
ROBERTO	MORALES	SEATTLE	3.5

The Type I style gives a visual feel to a query. You can visualize a Type I subquery as navigating between tables. Visit the table in the subquery to collect join values that can be used to select rows from the table in the outer query. The use of Type I nested queries is largely a matter of preference. Even if you do not prefer this join style, you should be prepared to interpret queries written by others with Type I nested queries.

The DELETE statement provides another use of a Type I nested query. A Type I nested query is useful when the deleted rows are related to other rows, as demonstrated in Example 9.11. Using a Type I nested query is the standard way to reference related tables in DELETE statements. Chapter 3 demonstrated the join operator style inside a DELETE statement, a proprietary extension of Microsoft Access. For your reference, Example 9.12 shows a DELETE statement using the join operator style that removes the same rows as Example 9.11.

Example 9.11

DELETE Statement Using a Type I Nested Query

Delete offerings taught by Leonard Vince. Three *Offering* rows are deleted. In addition, this statement deletes related rows in the *Enrollment* table because the ON DELETE clause is set to CASCADE.

```
DELETE FROM Offering
  WHERE Offering.FacSSN IN
     (   SELECT FacSSN FROM Faculty
            WHERE FacFirstName = 'LEONARD'
               AND FacLastName = 'VINCE'   )
```

**Example 9.12
(Access)**

DELETE Statement Using INNER JOIN Operation

Delete offerings taught by Leonard Vince. Three *Offering* rows are deleted. In addition, this statement deletes related rows in the *Enrollment* table because the ON DELETE clause is set to CASCADE.

```
DELETE Offering.*
  FROM Offering INNER JOIN Faculty
        ON Offering.FacSSN = Faculty.FacSSN
  WHERE FacFirstName = 'LEONARD'
        AND FacLastName = 'VINCE'
```

Type II Nested Query a nested query in which the inner query references a table used in the outer query. Type II nested queries are very useful for difference problems but should be avoided for join problems.
···

9.2.2 Type II Nested Queries

Type II nested queries have two distinguishing features. First, Type II nested queries reference one or more columns from an outer query. Type II nested queries are sometimes known as <u>correlated</u> subqueries because they reference columns used in outer queries. In contrast, Type I nested queries are not correlated with outer queries. In Example 9.13, note that *Student.StdSSN* in the inner query refers to the *Student* table used in the outer query. Whenever you see such a reference, the inner query is Type II.

Example 9.13

Using a Type II Nested Query to Perform a Join

List the social security number, the name (first and last), and the major of students who have a high grade (≥ 3.5) in a course offering. The result is identical to Example 9.8.

```
SELECT StdSSN, StdFirstName, StdLastName, StdMajor
  FROM Student
  WHERE EXISTS
    (   SELECT StdSSN FROM Enrollment
         WHERE Student.StdSSN = Enrollment.StdSSN
            AND EnrGrade >= 3.5 )
```

The second distinguishing feature of Type II nested queries involves execution. A Type II nested query executes one time for <u>each</u> row in the outer query. In this sense, a Type II nested query is similar to a nested loop that executes one time for each execution of the outer loop. In each execution of the inner loop, variables used in the outer loop are used in the inner loop. In other words, the inner query uses one or more values from the outer query in each execution.

In Example 9.13, each execution of the inner query uses the *Student.StdSSN* value from the current row of the outer query. To help you understand Example 9.13, Table 9.3 traces the execution of the nested query using Tables 9.1 and 9.2. The nested query executes three times, one time for each row in Table 9.1. For example, the first nested query execution uses the *StdSSN* value "123-45-6789" and retrieves the two matching rows in Table 9.2. The EXISTS comparison operator is true if the inner query evaluates to a nonempty table (one or more rows in the result). Thus, the result contains the first *Student* row because the EXISTS condition is true.

TABLE 9.1	Sample *Student* Table

StdSSN	StdFirstName	StdLastName	StdMajor
123-45-6789	HOMER	WELLS	IS
124-56-7890	BOB	NORBERT	FIN
234-56-7890	CANDY	KENDALL	ACCT

TABLE 9.2	Sample *Enrollment* Table

OfferNo	StdSSN	EnrGrade
1234	123-45-6789	3.6
4321	123-45-6789	3.5
4321	124-56-7890	3.2

TABLE 9.3	Execution Trace of Nested Query in Example 9.13

StdSSN	Result of subquery execution	EXISTS
123-45-6789	2 rows retrieved	true
124-56-7890	0 rows retrieved	false
234-56-7890	0 rows retrieved	false

Type II nested queries can be combined with other join styles similar to Type I nested queries, as demonstrated in Example 9.14. Note that Type II nested queries should not be used for a join when a column from the inner query is needed in the result.

Example 9.14

Combining a Type II Nested Query and the Join Operator Style
Retrieve the name, the city, and the grade of students who have a high grade ($\geq$ 3.5) in a course offered in fall 2002. The result is identical to Example 9.9.

```
SELECT StdFirstName, StdLastName, StdCity, EnrGrade
  FROM Student INNER JOIN Enrollment
        ON Student.StdSSN = Enrollment.StdSSN
  WHERE EnrGrade >= 3.5 AND EXISTS
     (   SELECT * FROM Offering
           WHERE Enrollment.OfferNo = Offering.OfferNo
             AND OffTerm = 'FALL' AND OffYear = 2002   )
```

Because conceptually Type II nested queries are repeatedly executed, they are not typically used for join problems. Many SQL compilers will not recognize that some Type II nested queries are actually join operations. Thus, one of the other join styles is generally preferred for efficiency reasons. Type II nested queries are more typically used for difference problems, as demonstrated in the next subsection.

9.2.3 Solving Difference Problems with Type II Nested Queries

Type II nested queries are useful for problems involving the difference operator, as demonstrated in Example 9.15. The placement of the word "not" in the problem statement indicates that the result contains rows only in the *Faculty* table, not in the *Student* table. This requirement involves a difference operation. The Type II nested query provides a way to remove faculty members who are also students.

Example 9.15	Using a Type II Nested Query for a Difference Problem

Retrieve the social security number, the name (first and last), the department, and the salary of faculty who are not students.

```
SELECT FacSSN, FacFirstName, FacLastName, FacDept,
       FacSalary
 FROM Faculty
 WHERE NOT EXISTS
    (   SELECT * FROM Student
         WHERE Student.StdSSN = Faculty.FacSSN )
```

FacSSN	FacFirstName	FacLastName	FacDept	FacSalary
098-76-5432	LEONARD	VINCE	MS	$35,000.00
543-21-0987	VICTORIA	EMMANUEL	MS	$120,000.00
654-32-1098	LEONARD	FIBON	MS	$70,000.00
765-43-2109	NICKI	MACON	FIN	$65,000.00
987-65-4321	JULIA	MILLS	FIN	$75,000.00

To help you understand Example 9.15, Table 9.6 traces the execution of the nested query using Tables 9.4 and 9.5. The NOT EXISTS operator is true if the nested query returns 0 rows. Thus, a faculty row in the outer query is selected only if there are no matching student rows in the nested query. For example, the first two rows in Table 9.4 are selected because there are no matching rows in Table 9.5. The third row is not selected because the nested query returns one row (the third row of Table 9.5).

TABLE 9.4	Sample *Faculty* Table

FacSSN	FacFirstName	FacLastName	FacRank
098-76-5432	LEONARD	VINCE	ASST
543-21-0987	VICTORIA	EMMANUEL	PROF
876-54-3210	CRISTOPHER	COLAN	ASST

TABLE 9.5	Sample *Student* Table

StdSSN	StdFirstName	StdLastName	StdMajor
123-45-6789	HOMER	WELLS	IS
124-56-7890	BOB	NORBERT	FIN
876-54-3210	CRISTOPHER	COLAN	IS

TABLE 9.6	Execution Trace of Nested Query in Example 9.15	

FacSSN	Result of subquery execution	NOT EXISTS
098-76-5432	0 rows retrieved	true
543-21-0987	0 rows retrieved	true
876-54-3210	1 row retrieved	false

Example 9.16 shows another formulation that clarifies the meaning of the NOT EXISTS operator. Here, a faculty row is selected if the number of rows in the nested query is 0. Using the sample tables (Tables 9.4 and 9.5), the nested query result is 0 for the first two faculty rows.

Example 9.16

Using a Type II Nested Query with the COUNT Function

Retrieve the social security number, the name, the department, and the salary of faculty who are <u>not</u> students. The result is the same as Example 9.15.

```
SELECT FacSSN, FacFirstName, FacLastName, FacDept,
       FacSalary
 FROM Faculty
 WHERE 0 =
   (  SELECT COUNT(*) FROM Student
      WHERE Student.StdSSN = Faculty.FacSSN   )
```

Other SQL Solutions for Difference Problems

Some difference problems can be solved using a Type I nested query in place of a Type II nested query, as demonstrated in Example 9.17. As long as the comparison among tables involves a single column (*FacSSN* in this problem), a Type I nested query can be used. On some DBMSs, the formulation with the Type I nested query will execute much faster than the formulation with the Type II nested query.

Example 9.17

Using a Type I Nested Query for a Difference Problem

Retrieve the social security number, the name (first and last), the department, and the salary of faculty who are <u>not</u> students. The result is identical to Example 9.15.

```
SELECT FacSSN, FacFirstName, FacLastName, FacDept,
       FacSalary
 FROM Faculty
 WHERE FacSSN NOT IN
   (  SELECT StdSSN FROM Student   )
```

Although SQL:1999 does have a difference operator (the EXCEPT keyword), it is sometimes not convenient because only the common columns can be shown in the result. Example 9.18 does not provide the same result as Example 9.15 because the columns unique to the *Faculty* table (*FacDept* and *FacSalary*) are not in the result. Another query that uses the first result must be formulated to retrieve the unique *Faculty* columns.

Example 9.18 (Oracle)	**Difference Query**

Show faculty who are <u>not</u> students (pure faculty). Only show the common columns in the result. Note that Microsoft Access does not support the EXCEPT keyword. Oracle uses the MINUS keyword instead of EXCEPT. The result is identical to Example 9.15 except for *FacCity* and *FacState* instead of *FacDept* and *FacSalary*.

```
SELECT FacSSN AS SSN, FacFirstName AS FirstName,
        FacLastName AS LastName, FacCity AS City,
        FacState AS State
 FROM Faculty
        MINUS
SELECT StdSSN AS SSN, StdFirstName AS FirstName,
        StdLastName AS LastName, StdCity AS City,
        StdState AS State
 FROM Student
```

Difference Problems Cannot Be Solved with Inequality Joins

It is important to note that difference problems such as Example 9.15 cannot be solved with a join alone. Example 9.15 requires that every row of the *Student* table be searched to select a faculty row. In contrast, a join selects a faculty row when the first matching student row is found. To contrast difference and join problems, examine Example 9.19. Although it looks correct, it is not. Every faculty row will be in the result because there is at least one student row that does not match every faculty row.

Example 9.19	**Inequality Join**

Erroneous formulation for the problem "Retrieve the social security number, name (first and last), and rank of faculty who are <u>not</u> students." The result contains all faculty rows.

```
SELECT DISTINCT FacSSN, FacFirstName, FacLastName,
                FacRank
 FROM Faculty, Student
 WHERE Student.StdSSN <> Faculty.FacSSN
```

To understand Example 9.19, you can use the conceptual process discussed in Section 3.3. The result tables show the cross product (Table 9.7) of Tables 9.4 and 9.5 followed by the rows that satisfy the WHERE condition (Table 9.8). Notice that only one row of the cross product is deleted. The final result (Table 9.9) contains all rows of Table 9.4.

TABLE 9.7	Cross Product of the Sample *Student* and *Faculty* Tables						
FacSSN	FacFirstName	FacLastName	FacRank	StdSSN	StdFirstName	StdLastName	StdMajor
098-76-5432	LEONARD	VINCE	ASST	123-45-6789	HOMER	WELLS	IS
098-76-5432	LEONARD	VINCE	ASST	124-56-7890	BOB	NORBERT	FIN
098-76-5432	LEONARD	VINCE	ASST	876-54-3210	CRISTOPHER	COLAN	IS
543-21-0987	VICTORIA	EMMANUEL	PROF	123-45-6789	HOMER	WELLS	IS
543-21-0987	VICTORIA	EMMANUEL	PROF	124-56-7890	BOB	NORBERT	FIN
543-21-0987	VICTORIA	EMMANUEL	PROF	876-54-3210	CRISTOPHER	COLAN	IS
876-54-3210	CRISTOPHER	COLAN	ASST	123-45-6789	HOMER	WELLS	IS
876-54-3210	CRISTOPHER	COLAN	ASST	124-56-7890	BOB	NORBERT	FIN
876-54-3210	CRISTOPHER	COLAN	ASST	876-54-3210	CRISTOPHER	COLAN	IS

TABLE 9.8	Restriction of Table 9.7 to Eliminate Matching Rows						
FacSSN	FacFirstName	FacLastName	FacRank	StdSSN	StdFirstName	StdLastName	StdMajor
098-76-5432	LEONARD	VINCE	ASST	123-45-6789	HOMER	WELLS	IS
098-76-5432	LEONARD	VINCE	ASST	124-56-7890	BOB	NORBERT	FIN
098-76-5432	LEONARD	VINCE	ASST	876-54-3210	CRISTOPHER	COLAN	IS
543-21-0987	VICTORIA	EMMANUEL	PROF	123-45-6789	HOMER	WELLS	IS
543-21-0987	VICTORIA	EMMANUEL	PROF	124-56-7890	BOB	NORBERT	FIN
543-21-0987	VICTORIA	EMMANUEL	PROF	876-54-3210	CRISTOPHER	COLAN	IS
876-54-3210	CRISTOPHER	COLAN	ASST	123-45-6789	HOMER	WELLS	IS
876-54-3210	CRISTOPHER	COLAN	ASST	124-56-7890	BOB	NORBERT	FIN

TABLE 9.9	Projection of Table 9.8 to Eliminate *Student* Columns		
FacSSN	FacFirstName	FacLastName	FacRank
098-76-5432	LEONARD	VINCE	ASST
543-21-0987	VICTORIA	EMMANUEL	PROF
876-54-3210	CRISTOPHER	COLAN	ASST

More Difficult Difference Problems

More difficult difference problems combine a difference operation with join operations. For example, consider the query to list students who took all of their IS offerings in winter 2003 from the same instructor. The query results should include students who took only one offering as well as students who took more than one offering.

- Construct a list of students who have taken IS courses in winter 2003 (a join operation).
- Construct another list of students who have taken IS courses in winter 2003 from more than one instructor (a join operation).
- Use a difference operation (first student list minus the second student list) to produce the result.

Conceptualizing a problem in this manner forces you to recognize that it involves a difference operation. If you recognize the difference operation, you can make a formulation in SQL involving a nested query (Type II with NOT EXISTS or Type I with NOT

IN) or the EXCEPT keyword. Example 9.20 shows a NOT EXISTS solution in which the outer query retrieves a student row if the student does not have an offering from a <u>different</u> instructor in the inner query.

Example 9.20 (Access)	**More Difficult Difference Problem Using a Type II Nested Query**

List the social security number and the name of students who took all of their IS offerings in winter 2003 from the same instructor. Include students who took only one offering as well as students who took more than one offering. Note that in the nested query, the columns *Enrollment.StdSSN* and *Offering.FacSSN* refer to the outer query.

```
SELECT DISTINCT Enrollment.StdSSN, StdFirstName,
                StdLastName
 FROM Student, Enrollment, Offering
 WHERE Student.StdSSN = Enrollment.StdSSN
     AND Enrollment.OfferNo = Offering.OfferNo
     AND CourseNo LIKE 'IS*' AND OffTerm = 'WINTER'
     AND OffYear = 2003 AND NOT EXISTS
     (  SELECT * FROM Enrollment E1, Offering O1
         WHERE E1.OfferNo = O1.OfferNo
             AND Enrollment.StdSSN = E1.StdSSN
             AND O1.CourseNo LIKE 'IS*'
             AND O1.OffYear = 2003
             AND O1.OffTerm = 'WINTER'
             AND Offering.FacSSN <> O1.FacSSN   )
```

StdSSN	StdFirstName	StdLastName
123-45-6789	HOMER	WELLS
234-56-7890	CANDY	KENDALL
345-67-8901	WALLY	KENDALL
456-78-9012	JOE	ESTRADA
567-89-0123	MARIAH	DODGE

Example 9.20 (Oracle)	**More Difficult Difference Problem Using a Type II Nested Query**

List the social security number and name of the students who took all of their IS offerings in winter 2003 from the same instructor. Include students who took only one offering as well as students who took more than one offering.

```
SELECT DISTINCT Enrollment.StdSSN, StdFirstName,
                StdLastName
 FROM Student, Enrollment, Offering
 WHERE Student.StdSSN = Enrollment.StdSSN
     AND Enrollment.OfferNo = Offering.OfferNo
     AND CourseNo LIKE 'IS%' AND OffTerm = 'WINTER'
     AND OffYear = 2003 AND NOT EXISTS
     (  SELECT * FROM Enrollment E1, Offering O1
         WHERE E1.OfferNo = O1.OfferNo
             AND Enrollment.StdSSN = E1.StdSSN
             AND O1.CourseNo LIKE 'IS%'
             AND O1.OffYear = 2003
```

```
        AND O1.OFFTERM = 'WINTER'
        AND OFFERING.FacSSN <> O1.FacSSN   )
```

Example 9.21 shows another example using the NOT EXISTS operator to solve a difference problem. Conceptually this problem involves a difference operation between two sets: the set of all faculty members and the set of faculty members teaching in the specified term. The difference operation can be implemented by selecting a faculty in the outer query list if the faculty does not teach an offering during the specified term in the inner query result.

| **Example 9.21** | Another Difference Problem Using a Type II Nested Query |

List the name (first and last) and the department of faculty who are <u>not</u> teaching in winter term 2003.

```
SELECT FacFirstName, FacLastName, FacDept
  FROM Faculty
  WHERE NOT EXISTS
     (   SELECT * FROM Offering
          WHERE Offering.FacSSN = Faculty.FacSSN
             AND OffTerm = 'WINTER' AND OffYear = 2003   )
```

FacFirstName	FacLastName	FacDept
CRISTOPHER	COLAN	MS
LEONARD	FIBON	MS
LEONARD	VINCE	MS

9.2.4 Nested Queries in the FROM Clause

So far, you have seen nested queries in the WHERE clause with certain comparison operators (IN and EXISTS) as well as with traditional comparison operators when the nested query produces a single value such as the count of the number of rows. Similar to the usage in the WHERE clause, nested queries also can appear in the HAVING clause as demonstrated in the next section. Nested queries in the WHERE and the HAVING clauses have been part of the SQL design since its initial design.

In contrast, nested queries in the FROM clause are a recent extension in SQL:1999. SQL:1999 follows a philosophy of consistency in language design. Consistency means that wherever an object is permitted, an object expression should be permitted. In the FROM clause, this philosophy means that wherever a table is permitted, a table expression (a nested query) should be allowed. Nested queries in the FROM clause are not as widely used as nested queries in the WHERE and HAVING clauses. The remainder of this section demonstrates some specialized uses of nested queries in the FROM clause.

One usage of nested queries in the FROM clause is to compute an aggregate function within an aggregate function (nested aggregates). SQL does not permit an aggregate function inside another aggregate function. A nested query in the FROM clause overcomes the prohibition against nested aggregates as demonstrated in Example 9.22. Without a nested query in the FROM clause, two queries would be necessary to produce the output. In Access, the nested query would be a stored query. In Oracle, the nested query would be a view (see Chapter 10 for an explanation of views).

Example 9.22

Using a Nested Query in the FROM Clause

List the course number, the course description, the number of offerings, and the average enrollment across offerings.

```
SELECT T.CourseNo, T.CrsDesc, COUNT(*) AS NumOfferings,
        Avg(T.EnrollCount) AS AvgEnroll
  FROM
  (   SELECT Course.CourseNo, CrsDesc,
              Offering.OfferNo, COUNT(*) AS EnrollCount
      FROM Offering, Enrollment, Course
      WHERE Offering.OfferNo = Enrollment.OfferNo
          AND Course.CourseNo = Offering.CourseNo
      GROUP BY Course.CourseNo, CrsDesc, Offering.OfferNo   ) T
  GROUP BY T.CourseNo, T.CrsDesc
```

CourseNo	CrsDesc	NumOfferings	AvgEnroll
FIN300	FUNDAMENTALS OF FINANCE	1	2
FIN450	PRINCIPLES OF INVESTMENTS	1	2
FIN480	CORPORATE FINANCE	1	3
IS320	FUNDAMENTALS OF BUSINESS PROGRAMMING	2	6
IS460	SYSTEMS ANALYSIS	1	7
IS480	FUNDAMENTALS OF DATABASE MANAGEMENT	2	5.5

Another usage of a nested query in the FROM clause is to compute aggregates from multiple groupings. Without a nested query in the FROM clause, a query can contain aggregates from one grouping. For example, multiple groupings are needed to summarize the number of students per offering and the number of resources per offering. This query would be useful if the design of the university database was extended with a *Resource* table and an associative table (*ResourceUsage*) connected to the *Offering* and the *Resource* tables via 1-M relationships. The query would require two nested queries in the FROM clause, one to retrieve the enrollment count for offerings and the other to retrieve the resource count for offerings.

In Access, a nested query in the FROM clause can compensate for the inability to use the DISTINCT keyword inside aggregate functions. For example, the DISTINCT keyword is necessary to compute the number of distinct courses taught by faculty as shown in Example 9.23. To produce the same results in Access, a nested query in the FROM clause is necessary as shown in Example 9.24. The nested query in the FROM clause uses the DISTINCT keyword to eliminate duplicate course numbers. Section 9.3.3 contains additional examples using nested queries in the FROM clause to compensate for the DISTINCT keyword inside the COUNT function.

Example 9.23 (Oracle)

Using the DISTINCT Keyword inside the COUNT Function

List the social security number, the last name, and the number of unique courses taught.

```
SELECT Faculty.FacSSN, FacLastName,
        COUNT(DISTINCT CourseNo) AS NumPreparations
  FROM Faculty, Offering
  WHERE Faculty.FacSSN = Offering.FacSSN
  GROUP BY Faculty.FacSSN, FacLastName
```

FacSSN	FacLastName	NumPreparations
098-76-5432	VINCE	1
543-21-0987	EMMANUEL	1
654-32-1098	FIBON	2
765-43-2109	MACON	2
876-54-3210	COLAN	1
987-65-4321	MILLS	2

Example 9.24

Using a Nested Query in the FROM Clause Instead of the DISTINCT Keyword inside the COUNT Function

List the social security number, the last name, and the number of unique courses taught. The result is identical to Example 9.23. Although this SELECT statement executes in Access and Oracle, you should use the statement in Example 9.23 in Oracle because it will execute faster.

```
SELECT T.FacSSN, T.FacLastName,
        COUNT(*) AS NumPreparations
FROM
  (   SELECT DISTINCT Faculty.FacSSN, FacLastName, CourseNo
      FROM Offering, Faculty
      WHERE Offering.FacSSN = Faculty.FacSSN   ) T
GROUP BY T.FacSSN, T.FacLastName
```

9.3 FORMULATING DIVISION PROBLEMS

Division problems can be some of the most difficult problems. Because of the difficulty, the division operator of Chapter 2 is briefly reviewed. After this review, this section discusses some easier division problems before moving to more advanced problems.

9.3.1 Review of the Divide Operator

Divide an operator of relational algebra that combines rows from two tables. The divide operator produces a table in which values of a column from one input table are associated with all the values from a column of the second table.

To review the divide operator, consider a simplified university database consisting of three tables: *Student1* (Table 9.10), *Club* (Table 9.11), and *StdClub* (Table 9.12) showing student membership in clubs. The divide operator is typically applied to linking tables showing M-N relationships. The *StdClub* table links the *Student1* and *Club* tables: a student may belong to many clubs and a club may have many students.

The divide operator builds a table consisting of the values of one column (*StdNo*) that match all of the values in a specified column (*ClubNo*) of a second table (*Club*). A typical division problem is to list the students who belong to all clubs. The resulting table contains only student S1 because S1 is associated with all four clubs.

Division is more conceptually difficult than join because division matches on all of the values whereas join matches on a single value. If this problem involved a join, it would be stated as "list students who belong to any club." The key difference is the word "any" versus "all." Most division problems can be written with adjectives "every" or "all" between a verb phrase representing a table and a noun representing another table. In this example, the phrase "students who belong to all of the clubs" fits this pattern. Another example is "students who have taken every course."

TABLE 9.10		*Student1* Table Listing

StdNo	SName	SCity
S1	JOE	SEATTLE
S2	SALLY	SEATTLE
S3	SUE	PORTLAND

TABLE 9.11		*Club* Table Listing

ClubNo	CName	CPurpose	CBudget	CActual
C1	DELTA	SOCIAL	$1,000.00	$1,200.00
C2	BITS	ACADEMIC	$500.00	$350.00
C3	HELPS	SERVICE	$300.00	$330.00
C4	SIGMA	SOCIAL		$150.00

TABLE 9.12		*StdClub* Table Listing

StdNo	ClubNo
S1	C1
S1	C2
S1	C3
S1	C4
S2	C1
S2	C4
S3	C3

9.3.2 Simple Division Problems

There are a number of ways to perform division in SQL. Some books describe an approach using Type II nested queries. Because this approach can be difficult to understand if you have not had a course in logic, a different approach is used here. The approach here uses the COUNT function with a nested query in the HAVING clause.

The basic idea is to compare the number of students associated with a club in the *StdClub* table with the number of clubs in the *Club* table. To perform this operation, group the *StdClub* table on *StdNo* and compare the number of rows in each *StdNo* group with the number of rows in the *Club* table. You can make this comparison using a nested query in the HAVING clause as shown in Example 9.25.

Example 9.25

Simplest Division Problem

List the student number of students who belong to all of the clubs.

SELECT StdNo
 FROM StdClub

```
GROUP BY StdNo
HAVING COUNT(*) = (   SELECT COUNT(*) FROM Club   )
```

StdNo
S1

Note that the COUNT(*) on the left-hand side tallies the number of rows in the *StdNo* group. The right-hand side contains a nested query with only a COUNT(*) in the result. The nested query is Type I because there is no connection to the outer query. Therefore, the nested query only executes one time and returns a single row with a single value (the number of rows in the *Club* table).

Now let us examine some variations of the first problem. The most typical variation is to retrieve students who belong to a subset of the clubs rather than all of the clubs. For example, retrieve students who belong to all of the social clubs. To accomplish this change, you should modify Example 9.25 by including a WHERE condition in both the outer and the nested query. Instead of counting all *Student1* rows in a *StdNo* group, count only the rows where the club's purpose is social. Compare this count to the number of social clubs in the *Club* table. Example 9.26 shows these modifications.

Example 9.26

Division Problem to Find a Subset Match

List the student number of students who belong to all of the social clubs.

```
SELECT StdNo
 FROM StdClub, Club
 WHERE StdClub.ClubNo = Club.ClubNo
    AND CPurpose = 'SOCIAL'
 GROUP BY StdNo
 HAVING COUNT(*) =
    (   SELECT COUNT(*) FROM Club
        WHERE CPURPOSE = 'SOCIAL'   )
```

StdNo
S1
S2

Other variations are shown in Examples 9.27 and 9.28. In Example 9.27, a join between *StdClub* and *Student* is necessary to obtain the student name. Example 9.28 reverses the previous problems by looking for clubs rather than students.

Example 9.27

Division Problem with Joins

List the student number and the name of students who belong to all of the social clubs.

```
SELECT Student1.StdNo, SName
 FROM StdClub, Club, Student1
 WHERE StdClub.ClubNo = Club.ClubNo
    AND Student1.StdNo = StdClub.StdNo
```

```
        AND CPurpose = 'SOCIAL'
    GROUP BY Student1.StdNo, SName
    HAVING COUNT(*) =
       (   SELECT COUNT(*) FROM Club
            WHERE CPurpose = 'SOCIAL'   )
```

StdNo	SName
S1	JOE
S2	SALLY

Example 9.28

Another Division Problem

List the club numbers of clubs that have all of the Seattle students as members.

```
SELECT ClubNo
  FROM StdClub, Student1
  WHERE Student1.StdNo = StdClub.StdNo
     AND SCity = 'SEATTLE'
  GROUP BY ClubNo
  HAVING COUNT(*) =
      (   SELECT COUNT(*) FROM Student1
           WHERE SCity = 'SEATTLE'   )
```

ClubNo
C1
C4

9.3.3 Advanced Division Problems

Example 9.29 (using the original university database tables) depicts another complication of division problems in SQL. Before tackling this additional complication, let us examine a simpler problem. Example 9.29 can be formulated with the same technique as shown in Section 9.3.2. First, join the *Faculty* and *Offering* tables, select rows matching the WHERE conditions, and group the result by faculty name (first and last). Then, compare the count of the rows in each faculty *name* group with the number of fall 2002 IS offerings from the *Offering* table.

**Example 9.29
(Access)**

Division Problem with a Join

List the social security number and the name (first and last) of faculty who teach all of the fall 2002 IS offerings.

```
SELECT Faculty.FacSSN, FacFirstName, FacLastName
  FROM Faculty, Offering
  WHERE Faculty.FacSSN = Offering.FacSSN
     AND OffTerm = 'FALL' AND CourseNo LIKE 'IS*'
     AND OffYear = 2002
  GROUP BY Faculty.FacSSN, FacFirstName, FacLastName
  HAVING COUNT(*) =
```

```
(   SELECT COUNT(*) FROM Offering
     WHERE OffTerm = 'FALL' AND OffYear = 2002
       AND CourseNo LIKE 'IS*'   )
```

FacSSN	FacFirstName	FacLastName
098-76-5432	LEONARD	VINCE

Example 9.29 (Oracle)

Division Problem with a Join

List the social security number and the name (first and last) of faculty who teach all of the fall 2002 IS courses.

```
SELECT Faculty.FacSSN, FacFirstName, FacLastName
 FROM Faculty, Offering
 WHERE Faculty.FacSSN = Offering.FacSSN
    AND OffTerm = 'FALL' AND CourseNo LIKE 'IS%'
    AND OffYear = 2002
 GROUP BY Faculty.FacSSN, FacFirstName, FacLastName
 HAVING COUNT(*) =
    (   SELECT COUNT(*) FROM Offering
         WHERE OffTerm = 'FALL' AND OffYear = 2002
           AND CourseNo LIKE 'IS%'   )
```

Example 9.29 is not particularly useful because it is unlikely that an instructor has taught every offering. Rather, it is more useful that an instructor has taught one offering of every course as demonstrated in Example 9.30. Rather than counting the rows in each group, count the unique *CourseNo* values. This change is necessary because *CourseNo* is not unique in the *Offering* table. There can be multiple rows with the same *CourseNo,* corresponding to a situation where there are multiple offerings for the same course. The solution only executes in Oracle because Access does not support the DISTINCT keyword in aggregate functions. Example 9.31 shows an Access solution using two nested queries in FROM clauses. The second nested query occurs inside the nested query in the HAVING clause. Appendix 9.A shows an alternative to nested queries in the FROM clause using multiple SELECT statements.

Example 9.30 (Oracle)

Division Problem with DISTINCT inside COUNT

List the social security number and the name (first and last) of faculty who teach at least one section of all of the fall 2002 IS courses.

```
SELECT Faculty.FacSSN, FacFirstName, FacLastName
 FROM Faculty, Offering
 WHERE Faculty.FacSSN = Offering.FacSSN
    AND OffTerm = 'FALL' AND CourseNo LIKE 'IS%'
    AND OffYear = 2002
 GROUP BY Faculty.FacSSN, FacFirstName, FacLastName
 HAVING COUNT(DISTINCT CourseNo) =
    (   SELECT COUNT(DISTINCT CourseNo) FROM Offering
         WHERE OffTerm = 'FALL' AND OffYear = 2002
           AND CourseNo LIKE 'IS%'   )
```

FacSSN	FacFirstName	FacLastName
098-76-5432	LEONARD	VINCE

Example 9.31 (Access)

Division Problem Using Nested Queries in the FROM Clauses Instead of the DISTINCT Keyword inside the COUNT Function

List the social security number and the name (first and last) of faculty who teach at least one section of all of the fall 2002 IS courses. The result is the same as Example 9.30.

```
SELECT FacSSN, FacFirstName, FacLastName
 FROM
   (SELECT DISTINCT Faculty.FacSSN, FacFirstName,
           FacLastName, CourseNo
    FROM Faculty, Offering
    WHERE Faculty.FacSSN = Offering.FacSSN
        AND OffTerm = 'FALL' AND OffYear = 2002
        AND CourseNo LIKE 'IS*' )
 GROUP BY FacSSN, FacFirstName, FacLastName
 HAVING COUNT(*) =
   (   SELECT COUNT(*) FROM
       (   SELECT DISTINCT CourseNo
           FROM Offering
           WHERE OffTerm = 'FALL' AND OffYear = 2002
               AND CourseNo LIKE 'IS*'   )   )
```

Example 9.32 is another variation of the technique used in Example 9.30. The DISTINCT keyword is necessary so that students taking more than one offering from the same instructor are not counted twice. Note that the DISTINCT keyword is not necessary for the nested query because only rows of the *Student* table are counted. Example 9.33 shows an Access solution using a nested query in the FROM clause.

Example 9.32 (Oracle)

Another Division Problem with DISTINCT inside COUNT

List the faculty who have taught all of the seniors in their fall 2002 IS offerings.

```
SELECT Faculty.FacSSN, FacFirstName, FacLastName
 FROM Faculty, Offering, Enrollment, Student
 WHERE Faculty.FacSSN = Offering.FacSSN
     AND OffTerm = 'FALL' AND CourseNo LIKE 'IS%'
     AND OffYear = 2002 AND StdClass = 'SR'
     AND Offering.OfferNo = Enrollment.OfferNo
     AND Student.StdSSN = Enrollment.StdSSN
  GROUP BY Faculty.FacSSN, FacFirstName, FacLastName
  HAVING COUNT(DISTINCT Student.StdSSN) =
    (   SELECT COUNT(*) FROM Student
        WHERE StdClass = 'SR'   )
```

FacSSN	FacFirstName	FacLastName
098-76-5432	LEONARD	VINCE

Example 9.33
(Access)

Another Division Problem Using Nested Queries in the FROM Clauses Instead of the DISTINCT Keyword inside the COUNT Function

List the faculty who have taught all seniors in their fall 2002 IS offerings. The result is identical to Example 9.32.

```
SELECT FacSSN, FacFirstName, FacLastName
 FROM
    (  SELECT DISTINCT Faculty.FacSSN, FacFirstName,
                FacLastName, Student.StdSSN
       FROM Faculty, Offering, Enrollment, Student
       WHERE Faculty.FacSSN = Offering.FacSSN
          AND OffTerm = 'FALL' AND CourseNo LIKE 'IS*'
          AND OffYear = 2002 AND StdClass = 'SR'
          AND Offering.OfferNo = Enrollment.OfferNo
          AND Student.StdSSN = Enrollment.StdSSN )
 GROUP BY FacSSN, FacFirstName, FacLastName
 HAVING COUNT(*) =
    (  SELECT COUNT(*) FROM Student
       WHERE StdClass = 'SR'   )
```

9.4 NULL VALUE CONSIDERATIONS

The last section of this chapter does not involve difficult matching problems or new parts of SQL. Rather, this section presents interpretation of query results when tables contain null values. These effects have largely been ignored until this section to simplify the presentation. Because most databases use null values, you need to understand the effects to attain a deeper understanding of query formulation.

Null values affect simple conditions involving comparison operators, compound conditions involving Boolean operators, aggregate calculations, and grouping. As you will see, some of the null value effects are rather subtle. Because of these subtle effects, a good table design minimizes, although it usually does not eliminate, the use of null values. The null effects described in this section are specified in the SQL-92 and SQL:1999 standards. Because specific DBMSs may provide different results, you may need to experiment with your DBMS.

9.4.1 Effect on Simple Conditions

Simple conditions involve a comparison operator, a column or column expression and a constant, column, or column expression. A simple condition results in a null value if either column (or column expression) in a comparison is null. A row qualifies in the result if the simple condition evaluates to true for the row. Rows evaluating to false and null are discarded. Example 9.34 depicts a simple condition evaluating to null for one of the rows.

Example 9.34

Simple Condition Using a Column with Null Values

List the clubs (Table 9.11) with a budget greater than $200. The club with a null budget (C4) is omitted because the condition evaluates as a null value.

```
SELECT *
 FROM Club
 WHERE CBudget > 200
```

ClubNo	CName	CPurpose	CBudget	CActual
C1	DELTA	SOCIAL	$1,000.00	$1,200.00
C2	BITS	ACADEMIC	$500.00	$350.00
C3	HELPS	SERVICE	$300.00	$330.00

A more subtle result can occur when a simple condition involves two columns and at least one column contains null values. If neither column contains null values, every row will be in the result of either the simple condition or the opposite (negation) of the simple condition. For example, if $<$ is the operator of a simple condition, the opposite condition contains $\geq$ as its operator assuming the columns remain in the same positions. If at least one column contains null values, some rows will not appear in the result of either the simple condition or its negation. More precisely, rows containing null values will be excluded in both results, as demonstrated in Examples 9.35 and 9.36.

Example 9.35

Simple Condition Involving Two Columns

List the clubs with the budget greater than the actual spending. The club with a null budget (C4) is omitted because the condition evaluates as a null value.

```
SELECT *
  FROM Club
  WHERE CBudget > CActual
```

ClubNo	CName	CPurpose	CBudget	CActual
C2	BITS	ACADEMIC	$500.00	$350.00

Example 9.36

Opposite Condition of Example 9.30

List the clubs with the budget less than or equal to the actual spending. The club with a null budget (C4) is omitted because the condition evaluates as a null value.

```
SELECT *
  FROM Club
  WHERE CBudget <= CActual
```

ClubNo	CName	CPurpose	CBudget	CActual
C1	DELTA	SOCIAL	$1,000.00	$1,200.00
C3	HELPS	SERVICE	$300.00	$330.00

9.4.2 Effect on Compound Conditions

Compound conditions involve one or more simple conditions connected by the Boolean operators AND, OR, and NOT. Like simple conditions, compound conditions evaluate to true, false, or null. A row is selected if the entire compound condition in the WHERE clause evaluates to true.

To evaluate the result of a compound condition, the SQL:1999 standard uses truth tables with three values. A truth table shows how combinations of values (true, false, and null) combine with the Boolean operators. Truth tables with three values define a three-valued logic. Tables 9.13 through 9.15 depict truth tables for the AND, OR, and

TABLE 9.13	AND Truth Table		
AND	*True*	*False*	*Null*
True	True	False	Null
False	False	False	False
Null	Null	False	Null

TABLE 9.14	OR Truth Table		
OR	*True*	*False*	*Null*
True	True	True	True
False	True	False	Null
Null	True	Null	Null

TABLE 9.15	NOT Truth Table		
NOT	*True*	*False*	*Null*
	False	True	Null

NOT operators. The internal cells in these tables are the result values. For example, the first internal cell (True) in Table 9.13 results from the AND operator applied to two conditions with true values. You can test your understanding of the truth tables using Examples 9.37 and 9.38.

Example 9.37   Evaluation of a Compound OR Condition with a Null Value
List the clubs with the budget less than or equal to the actual spending or the actual spending less than $200. The club with a null budget (C4) is included because the second condition results in a true value.

```
SELECT *
 FROM Club
 WHERE CBudget <= CActual OR CActual < 200
```

ClubNo	CName	CPurpose	CBudget	CActual
C1	DELTA	SOCIAL	$1,000.00	$1,200.00
C3	HELPS	SERVICE	$300.00	$330.00
C4	SIGMA	SOCIAL		$150.00

Example 9.38   Evaluation of a Compound AND Condition with a Null Value
List the clubs (Table 9.11) with the budget less than or equal to the actual spending and the actual spending less than $500. The club with a null budget (C4) is not included because the first condition results in a null value.

```
SELECT *
   FROM Club
   WHERE CBudget <= CActual AND CActual < 500
```

ClubNo	CName	CPurpose	CBudget	CActual
C3	HELPS	SERVICE	$300.00	$330.00

9.4.3 Effect on Aggregate Calculations and Grouping

Null values are ignored in aggregate calculations. Although this statement sounds simple, the results can be subtle. For the COUNT function, COUNT(*) returns a different value than COUNT(column) if the column contains null values. COUNT(*) always returns the number of rows. COUNT(column) returns the number of non-null values in the column. Example 9.39 demonstrates the difference between COUNT(*) and COUNT(column).

Example 9.39

COUNT Function with Null Values

List the number of rows in the *Club* table and the number of values in the *CBudget* column.

```
SELECT COUNT(*) AS NumRows,
         COUNT(CBudget) AS NumBudgets
   FROM Club
```

NumRows	NumBudgets
4	3

An even more subtle effect can occur if the SUM or AVG functions are applied to a column with null values. Without regard to null values, the following equation is true: SUM(Column1) + SUM(Column2) = SUM(Column1 + Column2). With null values in at least one of the columns, the equation may not be true because a calculation involving a null value yields a null value. If Column1 has a null value in one row, the plus operation in SUM(Column1 + Column2) produces a null value for that row. However, the value of Column2 in the same row is counted in SUM(Column2). Example 9.40 demonstrates this subtle effect using the minus operator instead of the plus operator.

Example 9.40

SUM Function with Null Values

Using the *Club* table, list the sum of the budget values, the sum of the actual values, the difference of the two sums, and the sum of the differences (budget – actual). The last two columns differ because of a null value in the *CBudget* column. Parentheses enclose negative values in the result.

```
SELECT SUM(CBudget) AS SumBudget,
         SUM(CActual) AS SumActual,
         SUM(CBudget)-SUM(CActual) AS SumDifference,
         SUM(CBudget-CActual) AS SumOfDifferences
   FROM Club
```

SumBudget	SumActual	SumDifference	SumOfDifferences
$1,800.00	$2,030.00	($230.00)	($80.00)

Null values also can affect grouping operations performed in the GROUP BY clause. The SQL standard stipulates that all rows with null values are grouped together. The grouping column shows null values in the result. In the university database, this kind of grouping operation is useful to find course offerings without assigned professors, as demonstrated in Example 9.41.

Example 9.41

Grouping on a Column with Null Values

For each faculty social security number in the *Offering* table, list the number of offerings. In Microsoft Access and Oracle, an Offering row with a null *FacSSN* value displays as a blank. In Access, the null row displays before the non-null rows as shown below. In Oracle, the null row displays after the non-null rows.

```
SELECT FacSSN, COUNT(*) AS NumRows
  FROM Offering
  GROUP BY FacSSN
```

FacSSN	NumRows
	2
098-76-5432	3
543-21-0987	1
654-32-1098	2
765-43-2109	2
876-54-3210	1
987-65-4321	2

CLOSING THOUGHTS

Chapter 9 has discussed advanced query formulation skills with an emphasis on complex matching between tables and a wider subset of SQL. Complex matching problems include the outer join with its variations (one-sided and full) as well as problems requiring the difference and division operators of relational algebra. In addition to new kinds of problems and new parts of the SELECT statement, this chapter explained the subtle effects of null values to provide a deeper understanding of query formulation.

Two new parts of the SELECT statement were covered. The keywords LEFT, RIGHT, and FULL as part of the join operator style support outer join operations. Nested queries are a query inside another query. To understand the effect of a nested query, look for tables used in both an outer and an inner query. If there are no common tables, the nested query executes one time (Type I nested query). Otherwise, the nested query executes one time for each row of the outer query (Type II nested query). Type I nested queries are typically used to formulate joins as part of the SELECT and DELETE statements. Type I nested queries with the NOT IN operator and Type II nested queries with the NOT EXISTS operator are useful for problems involving the difference operator. Type I nested queries in the HAVING clause are useful for problems involving the divide operator.

Although advanced query skills are not as widely applied as the fundamental skills covered in Chapter 3, they are important when required. You may find that you gain a competitive edge by mastering advanced skills.

Chapters 3 and 9 have covered important query formulation skills and a large part of the SELECT statement of SQL. Despite this significant coverage, there is still much left to learn. There are even more complex matching problems and other parts of the SELECT statement that were not described. You are encouraged to extend your skills by consulting the references cited at the end of the chapter. In addition, you have not learned how to apply your query formulation skills to building applications. Chapter 10 applies your skills to building applications with views, while Chapter 11 applies your skills to stored procedures and triggers.

REVIEW CONCEPTS

- Formulating one-sided outer joins.

Access and Oracle 9i:

```
SELECT OfferNo, CourseNo, Offering.FacSSN, Faculty.FacSSN,
        FacFirstName, FacLastName
  FROM Offering LEFT JOIN Faculty
        ON Offering.FacSSN = Faculty.FacSSN
  WHERE CourseNo = 'IS480'
```

Oracle 8i:

```
SELECT OfferNo, CourseNo, Offering.FacSSN, Faculty.FacSSN,
        FacFirstName, FacLastName
  FROM Offering, Faculty
  WHERE Offering.FacSSN = Faculty.FacSSN (+)
        AND CourseNo = 'IS480'
```

- Formulating full outer joins using the FULL JOIN keyword (SQL:1999 and Oracle 9i).

```
SELECT FacSSN, FacFirstName, FacLastName, FacSalary,
        StdSSN, StdFirstName, StdLastName, StdGPA
  FROM Faculty FULL JOIN Student
        ON Student.StdSSN = Faculty.FacSSN
```

- Formulating full outer joins by combining two one-sided outer joins.

Access:

```
SELECT FacSSN, FacFirstName, FacLastName, FacSalary,
        StdSSN, StdFirstName, StdLastName, StdGPA
  FROM Faculty RIGHT JOIN Student
        ON Student.StdSSN = Faculty.FacSSN UNION
SELECT FacSSN, FacFirstName, FacLastName, FacSalary,
        StdSSN, StdFirstName, StdLastName, StdGPA
  FROM Faculty LEFT JOIN Student
        ON Student.StdSSN = Faculty.FacSSN
```

Oracle 8i:

```
SELECT FacSSN, FacFirstName, FacLastName, FacSalary,
        StdSSN, StdFirstName, StdLastName, StdGPA
  FROM Faculty, Student
  WHERE Student.StdSSN = Faculty.FacSSN (+)
        UNION
```

```
SELECT FacSSN, FacFirstName, FacLastName, FacSalary,
        StdSSN, StdFirstName, StdLastName, StdGPA
 FROM Faculty, Student
 WHERE Student.StdSSN (+) = Faculty.FacSSN
```

- Mixing inner and outer joins.

Access and Oracle 9i:

```
SELECT OfferNo, Offering.CourseNo, OffTerm, CrsDesc,
        Faculty.FacSSN, FacFirstName, FacLastName
 FROM (   Faculty RIGHT JOIN Offering
        ON Offering.FacSSN = Faculty.FacSSN )
        INNER JOIN Course
        ON Course.CourseNo = Offering.CourseNo
 WHERE OffYear = 2003
```

Oracle 8i:

```
SELECT OfferNo, Offering.CourseNo, OffTerm, CrsDesc,
        Faculty.FacSSN, FacFirstName, FacLastName
 FROM Faculty, Offering, Course
 WHERE Offering.FacSSN = Faculty.FacSSN (+)
        AND Course.CourseNo = Offering.CourseNo
        AND OffYear = 2003
```

- Understanding that conditions in the WHERE or HAVING clause can use SELECT statements in addition to scalar (individual) values.
- Identifying Type I nested queries by the IN keyword and the lack of a reference to a table used in an outer query.
- Identifying Type II (correlated) nested queries by a reference to a table used in an outer query.
- Using a Type I nested query to formulate a join.

```
SELECT DISTINCT StdSSN, StdFirstName, StdLastName,
                StdMajor
 FROM Student
 WHERE Student.StdSSN IN
    (   SELECT StdSSN FROM Enrollment
        WHERE EnrGrade >= 3.5   )
```

- Using a Type I nested query inside a DELETE statement to test conditions on a related table.

```
DELETE FROM Offering
 WHERE Offering.FacSSN IN
    (   SELECT FacSSN FROM Faculty
        WHERE FacFirstName = 'LEONARD'
        AND FacLastName = 'VINCE' )
```

- Not using a Type I nested query for a join when a column from the nested query is needed in the final query result.
- Using a Type II nested query for a difference problem.

```
SELECT FacSSN, FacFirstName, FacLastName, FacDept,
        FacSalary
 FROM Faculty
```

```
WHERE NOT EXISTS
  (  SELECT * FROM Student
     WHERE Student.StdSSN = Faculty.FacSSN )
```

- Using a nested query in the FROM clause to compute nested aggregates or aggregates for more than one grouping.

```
SELECT T.CourseNo, T.CrsDesc, COUNT(*) AS NumOfferings,
       Avg(T.EnrollCount) AS AvgEnroll
FROM
  (  SELECT Course.CourseNo, CrsDesc,
            Offering.OfferNo, COUNT(*) AS EnrollCount
     FROM Offering, Enrollment, Course
     WHERE Offering.OfferNo = Enrollment.OfferNo
       AND Course.CourseNo = Offering.CourseNo
     GROUP BY Course.CourseNo, CrsDesc, Offering.OfferNo   ) T
GROUP BY T.CourseNo, T.CrsDesc
```

- Noting that division problems often have the word <u>every</u> or <u>all</u> to connect different parts of a problem statement.
- Using the count method to formulate division problems.

```
SELECT StdNo
FROM StdClub
GROUP BY StdNo
HAVING COUNT(*) = (  SELECT COUNT(*) FROM Club  )
```

- Evaluating a simple condition containing a null value in a column expression.
- Using three-valued logic and truth tables to evaluate compound conditions with null values.
- Understanding the result of aggregate calculations with null values.
- Understanding the result of grouping on a column with null values.

QUESTIONS

1. Explain a situation when a one-sided outer join is useful.

2. Explain a situation when a full outer join is useful.

3. How do you interpret the meaning of the LEFT and RIGHT JOIN keywords in the FROM clause?

4. How do you interpret the meaning of the (+) Oracle 8i notation in the WHERE clause?

5. What is meant by the "null table" when using the (+) Oracle 8i notation?

6. What is a nested query?

7. What is the distinguishing feature about Type I nested queries?

8. What is the distinguishing feature about Type II nested queries?

9. How many times is a Type I nested query executed as part of an outer query?

10. How is a Type I nested query like a procedure in a program?

11. How many times is a Type II nested query executed as part of an outer query?

12. How is a Type II nested query like a nested loop in a program?

13. What is the meaning of the IN comparison operator?

14. What is the meaning of the EXISTS comparison operator?

15. What is the meaning of the NOT EXISTS comparison operator?

16. When can you not use a Type I nested query to perform a join?

17. Why is a Type I nested query a good join method when you need a join in a DELETE statement?

18. Why does SQL:1999 permit nested queries in the FROM clause?

19. Identify two situations in which nested queries in the FROM clause are necessary.

20. How do you detect that a problem involves a division operation?

21. Explain the "count" method for formulating division problems.

22. Why is it sometimes necessary to use the DISTINCT keyword inside the COUNT function for division problems?

23. What is the result of a simple condition when a column expression in the condition evaluates to null?

24. What is a truth table?

25. How many values do truth tables have in the SQL:1999 standard?

26. How do you use truth tables to evaluate compound conditions?

27. How do null values affect aggregate calculations?

28. Explain why the following equation may not be true if Column1 or Column2 contains null values: SUM(Column1) − SUM(Column2) = SUM(Column1 − Column2)

29. How are null values handled in a grouping column?

30. In Access, how do you compensate for the lack of the DISTINCT keyword inside the COUNT function?

PROBLEMS

ORDER

The problems use the tables of the Order Entry database introduced in the Problems section of Chapter 3. When formulating the problems, remember that the *EmpNo* foreign key in the *OrderTbl* table allows null values. An order does not have an associated employee if taken over the Internet.

1. Using a Type I nested query, list the customer number, the name (first and last), and the city of each customer who has a balance greater than $150 and placed an order in February 2004.

2. Using a Type II nested query, list the customer number, the name (first and last), and the city of each customer who has a balance greater than $150 and placed an order in February 2004.

3. Using two Type I nested queries, list the product number, the name, and the price of products with a price greater than $150 that were ordered on January 23, 2004.

4. Using two Type I nested queries and another join style, list the product number, the name, and the price of products with a price greater than $150 that were ordered in January 2004 by customers with balances greater than $400.

5. List the order number, the order date, the employee number, and the employee name (first and last) of orders placed on January 23, 2004. List the order even if there is not an associated employee.

6. List the order number, the order date, the employee number, the employee name (first and last), the customer number, and the customer name (first and last) of orders placed on January 23, 2004. List the order even if there is not an associated employee.

7. List all the people in the database. The resulting table should have all columns of the *Customer* and *Employee* tables. Match the *Customer* and *Employee* tables on first and last names. If a customer does not match any employees, the columns pertaining to the *Employee* table will be blank. Similarly for an employee who does not match any customers, the columns pertaining to the *Customer* table will be blank.

8. For each Ink Jet product ordered in January 2004, list the order number, the order date, the customer number, the customer name (first and last), the employee number (if present), the employee name (first and last), the quantity ordered, the product number, and the product name. Include products containing Ink Jet in the product name. Include both Internet (no employee) and phone orders (taken by an employee).

9. Using a Type II nested query, list the customer number and the customer name of Colorado customers who have not placed orders in February 2004.

10. Repeat problem 9 using a Type I nested query instead of a Type II nested query.

11. Repeat problem 9 using the MINUS keyword. Note that Access does not support the MINUS keyword.

12. List the order number and the order date of orders containing only one Ink Jet product. An Ink Jet product contains the words Ink Jet in the product description.

13. List the customer number and the name (first and last) of customers who have ordered products only manufactured by Connex. Include only customers who have ordered at least one product manufactured by Connex. Remove duplicate rows from the result.

14. List the order number and the order date of orders containing every Ink Jet product.

15. List the product number and the name of products contained on every order placed on January 7, 2004, through January 9, 2004.

16. List the customer number and name (first and last) of customers who have ordered every product manufactured by ColorMeg, Inc., in January 2004.

17. Using a Type I nested query, delete orders placed by customer Betty Wise in January 2004. The CASCADE DELETE action will delete related rows in the *OrdLine* table.

18. Using a Type I nested query, delete orders placed by Colorado customers that were taken by Landi Santos in January 2004. The CASCADE DELETE action will delete related rows in the *OrdLine* table.

19. List the order number and the order date of orders in which any part of the shipping address (street, city, state, and zip) differs from the customer's address.

20. List the employee number and the employee name (first and last) of employees who have taken orders in January 2004 from every Seattle customer.

21. For Colorado customers, compute the average amount of their orders. The average amount of a customer's orders is the sum of the amount (quantity ordered times the product price) on each order divided by the number of orders. The result should include the customer number, the customer last name, and the average order amount.

22. For Colorado customers, compute the average amount of their orders and the number of orders placed. The result should include the customer number, the customer last name, the average order amount, and the number of orders placed. In Access, this problem is especially difficult to formulate.

23. For Colorado customers, compute the number of unique products ordered. If a product is purchased on multiple orders, it should be counted only one time. The result should include the customer number, the customer last name, and the number of unique products ordered.

24. For each employee with a commission less than 0.04, compute the number of orders taken and the average number of products per order. The result should include the employee number, the employee last name, the number of orders taken, and the average number of products per order. In Access, this problem is especially difficult to formulate as a single SELECT statement.

25. For each Connex product, compute the number of unique customers who ordered the product in January 2004. The result should include the product number, the product name, and the number of unique customers.

Null Value Problems

The following problems are based on the *Product* table of the Order Entry database. The table is repeated below for your convenience. The *ProdNextShipDate* column contains the next expected shipment date for the product. If the value is null, a new shipment has not been arranged. A shipment may not be scheduled for a variety of reasons, such as the large quantity on hand or unavailability of the product from the manufacturer.

Product

ProdNo	ProdName	ProdMfg	ProdQOH	ProdPrice	ProdNextShipDate
P0036566	17 inch Color Monitor	ColorMeg, Inc.	12	$169.00	2/20/2004
P0036577	19 inch Color Monitor	ColorMeg, Inc.	10	$319.00	2/20/2004
P1114590	R3000 Color Laser Printer	Connex	5	$699.00	1/22/2004
P1412138	10 Foot Printer Cable	Ethlite	100	$12.00	
P1445671	8-Outlet Surge Protector	Intersafe	33	$14.99	
P1556678	CVP Ink Jet Color Printer	Connex	8	$99.00	1/22/2004
P3455443	Color Ink Jet Cartridge	Connex	24	$38.00	1/22/2004
P4200344	36-Bit Color Scanner	UV Components	16	$199.99	1/29/2004
P6677900	Black Ink Jet Cartridge	Connex	44	$25.69	
P9995676	Battery Back-up System	Cybercx	12	$89.00	2/1/2004

1. Identify the result rows in the following SELECT statement. Both Access and Oracle versions of the statement are shown.

   Access:

   ```
   SELECT *
    FROM Product
    WHERE ProdNextShipDate = #1/22/2004#
   ```

   Oracle:

   ```
   SELECT *
    FROM Product
    WHERE ProdNextShipDate = '22-Jan-2004';
   ```

2. Identify the result rows in the following SELECT statement:

   Access:

   ```
   SELECT *
    FROM Product
    WHERE ProdNextShipDate = #1/22/2004#
        AND ProdPrice < 100
   ```

   Oracle:

   ```
   SELECT *
    FROM Product
    WHERE ProdNextShipDate = '22-Jan-2004'
        AND ProdPrice < 100;
   ```

3. Identify the result rows in the following SELECT statement:

   Access:

   ```
   SELECT *
    FROM Product
    WHERE ProdNextShipDate = #1/22/2004#
        OR ProdPrice < 100
   ```

   Oracle:

   ```
   SELECT *
    FROM Product
    WHERE ProdNextShipDate = '22-Jan-2004'
        OR ProdPrice < 100;
   ```

4. Calculate the result of the following SELECT statement:

   ```
   SELECT COUNT(*) AS NumRows,
           COUNT(ProdNextShipDate) AS NumShipDates
    FROM Product
   ```

5. Calculate the result of the following SELECT statement:

   ```
   SELECT ProdNextShipDate, COUNT(*) AS NumRows
    FROM Product
    GROUP BY ProdNextShipDate
   ```

6. Calculate the result of the following SELECT statement:

```
SELECT ProdMfg, ProdNextShipDate, COUNT(*) AS NumRows
  FROM Product
  GROUP BY ProdMfg, ProdNextShipDate
```

7. Calculate the result of the following SELECT statement:

```
SELECT ProdNextShipDate, ProdMfg, COUNT(*) AS NumRows
  FROM Product
  GROUP BY ProdNextShipDate, ProdMfg
```

REFERENCES FOR FURTHER STUDY

Most textbooks for the business student do not cover query formulation and SQL in as much detail as here. Specialized books on SQL-92 such as Bowman, Emerson, and Darnovsky (1996); Cannan and Otten (1992); Date and Darwen (1997); and Melton and Simon (1992) cover a larger subset of SQL but lack the pedagogy found here. For new features in SQL:1999, you should read Melton and Simon (2001). Celko (1997) provides many interesting problems and SQL solutions. Groff and Weinberg (1999) cover the various notations for outer joins available in commercial DBMSs. The *DBAZine* site (www.dbazine.com) and the DevX help site (www.devx.com/gethelp) have plenty of practical advice about query formulation and SQL. For product-specific SQL advice, the Advisor.com site (www.advisor.com) features technical journals for Microsoft SQL Server and Microsoft Access. Oracle documentation can be found at the Oracle Technet Site (otn.oracle.com).

Usage of Multiple Statements in Microsoft Access

In Microsoft Access, you can use multiple SELECT statements instead of nested queries in the FROM clause. Using multiple statements can provide simpler formulation in some cases than using nested queries in the FROM clause. For example, instead of using DISTINCT inside COUNT as in Example 9.30, you can use a stored query with the DISTINCT keyword following the SELECT keyword. In Example 9A.1, the first stored query (**Temp9A-1**) finds the unique combinations of faculty name and course number. Note the use of the DISTINCT keyword to eliminate duplicates. The second stored query (**Temp9A-2**) finds the unique course numbers in the *Offering* table. The final query combines the two stored queries. Note that you can use stored queries similar to the way tables are used. Simply use the stored query name in the FROM clause.

Example 9A.1

Using Stored Queries Instead Nested Queries in the FROM Clause
List the name of faculty who teach in at least one section of all fall 2002 IS courses. The result is identical to that in Example 9.30.

Temp9A-1:

```
SELECT DISTINCT Faculty.FacSSN, FacFirstName, FacLastName, CourseNo
  FROM Faculty, Offering
  WHERE Faculty.FacSSN = Offering.FacSSN
    AND OffTerm = 'FALL' AND OffYear = 2002
    AND CourseNo LIKE 'IS*'
```

Temp9A-2:

```
SELECT DISTINCT CourseNo
  FROM Offering
  WHERE OffTerm = 'FALL' AND OffYear = 2002
    AND CourseNo LIKE 'IS*'
```

```
SELECT FacSSN, FacFirstName, FacLastName
  FROM [Temp9A-1]
  GROUP BY FacSSN, FacFirstName, FacLastName
  HAVING COUNT(*) = (   SELECT COUNT(*) FROM [Temp9A-2]   )
```

Appendix 9.B   SQL:1999 Syntax Summary

This appendix summarizes the SQL:1999 syntax for nested SELECT statements (subqueries) and outer join operations presented in Chapter 9. For the syntax of other variations of the nested SELECT and outer join operations not presented in Chapter 9, consult an SQL:1999 reference book. Nested SELECT statements can be used in the FROM clause and the WHERE clause of the SELECT, UPDATE, and DELETE statements. The conventions used in the syntax notation are identical to those used at the end of Chapter 2.

EXPANDED SYNTAX FOR NESTED QUERIES IN THE FROM CLAUSE

```
<Table-Specification>:
                    {  <Simple-Table>   |  -- defined in Chapter 3
                       <Join-Operation>   |  -- defined in Chapter 3
                       <Simple-Select>  [ [ AS ] AliasName ]  }
                    -- <Simple-Select> is defined in Chapter 3
```

EXPANDED SYNTAX FOR ROW CONDITIONS

```
<Row-Condition>:
{   <Simple-Condition>   |  -- defined in Chapter 3
                    <Compound-Condition>   | -- defined in Chapter 3
                    <Exists-Condition> |
                    <Element-Condition>   }

<Exists-Condition>: [ NOT ] EXISTS <Simple-Select>

<Simple-Select>:   --   defined in Chapter 3

<Element-Condition>:
 <Scalar-Expression> <Element-Operator> (  <Simple-Select>   )

<Element-Operator>:
{   =  |  <  |  >  |  >=  |  <=  |  <>  |  [ NOT ] IN  }

<Scalar-Expression>: -- defined in Chapter 3
```

EXPANDED SYNTAX FOR GROUP CONDITIONS

```
<Simple-Group-Condition>: -- Last choice is new
{   <Column-Expression> ComparisonOperator < Column-Expression> |
    <Column-Expression> [ NOT ] IN (   Constant*   )   |
    <Column-Expression> BETWEEN <Column-Expression>
      AND <Column-Expression>   |
    <Column-Expression> IS [ NOT ] NULL   |
    ColumnName [ NOT ] LIKE StringPattern   |
    <Exists-Condition>   |
    <Column-Expression> <Element-Operator> <Simple-Select>   }

<Column-Expression>: -- defined in Chapter 3
```

EXPANDED SYNTAX FOR OUTER JOIN OPERATIONS

```
<Join-Operation>:
                    {   <Simple-Table> <Join-Operator> <Simple-Table>
                        ON <Join-Condition>   |
                    {   <Simple-Table>   |   <Join-Operation>   }   <Join-Operator>
                        {   <Simple-Table>   |   <Join-Operation> }
                        ON <Join-Condition> |
                        (   <Join-Operation>   )   }

<Join-Operator>:
{   [   INNER   ]   JOIN                |
    LEFT   [   OUTER   ] JOIN           |
    RIGHT   [   OUTER   ]   JOIN   |
    FULL   [   OUTER   ]   JOIN   }
```

Application Development with Views

LEARNING OBJECTIVES

This chapter describes concepts underlying views and demonstrates how to use views when developing forms, reports, and other database applications. After this chapter, the student should have acquired the following knowledge and skills:

- Write CREATE VIEW statements.

- Write queries that use views.

- Apply rules to determine if single-table and multiple-table views are updatable.

- Identify the relationship and join column used in a hierarchical form.

- Write queries that provide data for hierarchical forms.

- Formulate queries that provide input for hierarchical reports.

OVERVIEW

Chapters 2, 3, and 9 provided the foundation for understanding relational databases and formulating queries in SQL. Most importantly, you gained practice with a large number of examples, acquired conceptual skills for query formulation, and learned different parts of SQL. This chapter shows you how to apply your query formulation skills to building applications with views.

This chapter emphasizes views as the foundation for building database applications. Before discussing the link between views and database applications, essential background is provided. You will learn the motivation for views, the CREATE VIEW statement, and usage of views in SELECT and data manipulation (INSERT, UPDATE, and DELETE) statements. Most view examples in Sections 10.2 and 10.3 are supported in Microsoft Access as stored queries and in Oracle as views. After this background, you will learn about using views to build database applications based on hierarchical forms and reports.

10.1 BACKGROUND

View a table derived from base or physical tables using a query.

A <u>view</u> is a virtual or derived table. Virtual means that a view behaves like a base table but no physical table exists. A view can be used in a query like a base table. However, the rows of a view do not exist until they are derived from base tables. This section describes why views are important and how to define them in SQL.

10.1.1 Motivation

Views provide the external level of the Three Schema Architecture described in Chapter 1. The Three Schema Architecture promotes <u>data independence</u> to reduce the impact of database definition changes on applications that use a database. If an application accesses the database through a view, most changes to the conceptual schema will not affect the application. For example, if a table name used in a view changes, the view definition must be changed, but applications using the view do not have to be changed.

<u>Simplification</u> of tasks is another important benefit of views. Many queries can be easier to formulate if a view is used rather than base tables. Without a view, a SELECT statement may involve two, three, or more tables and require grouping if summary data are needed. With a view, the SELECT statement can just reference a view without joins or grouping. Training users to write single table queries is much easier than training them to write multiple table queries with grouping.

Views provide simplification similar to macros in programming languages and spreadsheets. A macro is a named collection of commands. Using a macro removes the burden of specifying the commands just as using a view removes the burden of writing the underlying query.

Views also provide a flexible level of <u>security.</u> Restricting access by views is more flexible than restrictions for fields and tables because a view is any derived part of a database. Data not in the view are hidden from the user. For example, you can restrict a user to selected departments, products, or geographic regions in a view. Security using tables and fields cannot specify conditions and computations, which can be done in a view. A view even can include aggregate calculations to restrict users to row summaries rather than individual rows.

The only drawback to views can be performance. For most views, using the views instead of base tables directly will not involve a significant performance penalty. For some complex views, using the views can involve a significant performance penalty as opposed to using the base tables directly. The performance penalty can vary by DBMS. Before using complex views, you are encouraged to compare performance to using the base tables directly.

10.1.2 View Definition

Defining a view is no more difficult than writing a query. SQL provides the CREATE VIEW statement in which the view name and the underlying SELECT statement must be specified, as shown in Examples 10.1 and 10.2. In Microsoft Access, the SELECT statement part of the examples can be saved as a stored query to achieve the same effect as a view. In Oracle, the CREATE VIEW statement executes directly.

Example 10.1

Define a Single-Table View

Define a view named IS_View consisting of students majoring in IS.

```
CREATE VIEW IS_View AS
  SELECT * FROM Student
    WHERE StdMajor = 'IS'
```

StdSSN	StdFirstName	StdLastName	StdCity	StdState	StdZip	StdMajor	StdClass	StdGPA
123-45-6789	HOMER	WELLS	SEATTLE	WA	98121-1111	IS	FR	3.00
345-67-8901	WALLY	KENDALL	SEATTLE	WA	98123-1141	IS	SR	2.80
567-89-0123	MARIAH	DODGE	SEATTLE	WA	98114-0021	IS	JR	3.60
876-54-3210	CRISTOPHER	COLAN	SEATTLE	WA	98114-1332	IS	SR	4.00
890-12-3456	LUKE	BRAZZI	SEATTLE	WA	98116-0021	IS	SR	2.20
901-23-4567	WILLIAM	PILGRIM	BOTHEL	WA	98113-1885	IS	SO	3.80

Example 10.2

Define a Multiple Table View

Define a view named MS_View consisting of offerings taught by faculty in the Management Science department.

```
CREATE VIEW MS_View AS
    SELECT OfferNo, Offering.CourseNo, CrsUnits, OffTerm,
           OffYear, Offering.FacSSN, FacFirstName,
           FacLastName, OffTime, OffDays
    FROM Faculty, Course, Offering
    WHERE FacDept = 'MS'
        AND Faculty.FacSSN = Offering.FacSSN
        AND Offering.CourseNo = Course.CourseNo
```

OfferNo	CourseNo	CrsUnits	OffTerm	OffYear	FacSSN	FacFirstName	FacLastName	OffTime	OffDays
1234	IS320	4	FALL	2002	098-76-5432	LEONARD	VINCE	10:30 AM	MW
3333	IS320	4	SPRING	2003	098-76-5432	LEONARD	VINCE	8:30 AM	MW
4321	IS320	4	FALL	2002	098-76-5432	LEONARD	VINCE	3:30 PM	TTH
4444	IS320	4	WINTER	2003	543-21-0987	VICTORIA	EMMANUEL	3:30 PM	TTH
8888	IS320	4	SUMMER	2003	654-32-1098	LEONARD	FIBON	1:30 PM	MW
9876	IS460	4	SPRING	2003	654-32-1098	LEONARD	FIBON	1:30 PM	TTH
5679	IS480	4	SPRING	2003	876-54-3210	CRISTOPHER	COLAN	3:30 PM	TTH

In the CREATE VIEW statement, a list of column names enclosed in parentheses can follow the view name. A list of column names is required when you want to rename one or more columns from the names used in the SELECT clause. The column list is omitted in MS_View because there are no renamed columns. The column list is required in Example 10.3 to rename the aggregate calculation (COUNT(*)) column. If one column is renamed, the entire list of column names must be given.

Example 10.3

Define a View with Renamed Columns

Define a view named Enrollment_View consisting of offering data and the number of students enrolled.

```
CREATE VIEW Enrollment_View
(OfferNo, CourseNo, Term, Year, Instructor, NumStudents)
 AS
 SELECT Offering.OfferNo, CourseNo, OffTerm, OffYear,
        FacLastName, COUNT(*)
  FROM Offering, Faculty, Enrollment
  WHERE Offering.FacSSN = Faculty.FacSSN
    AND Offering.OfferNo = Enrollment.OfferNo
  GROUP BY Offering.OfferNo, CourseNo, OffTerm, OffYear,
           FacLastName
```

OfferNo	CourseNo	Term	Year	Instructor	NumStudents
1234	IS320	FALL	2002	VINCE	6
4321	IS320	FALL	2002	VINCE	6
5555	FIN300	WINTER	2003	MACON	2
5678	IS480	WINTER	2003	MILLS	5
5679	IS480	SPRING	2003	COLAN	6
6666	FIN450	WINTER	2003	MILLS	2
7777	FIN480	SPRING	2003	MACON	3
9876	IS460	SPRING	2003	FIBON	7

In some DBMSs such as Microsoft Access, a view is merely a stored query.[1] You create a stored query simply by writing it and then supplying a name when saving it.

10.2 USING VIEWS FOR RETRIEVAL

This section shows examples of queries that use views and explains how queries with views are processed. After showing examples in Section 10.2.1, two methods to process queries with views are described in Section 10.2.2.

10.2.1 Using Views in SELECT Statements

Once a view is defined, it can be used in SELECT statements. Simply use the view name in the FROM clause and the view columns in other parts of the statement. You can add other conditions and select a subset of the columns as demonstrated in Examples 10.4 and 10.5.

Example 10.4

Query Using a Multiple-Table View

List the spring 2003 courses in MS_View.

```
SELECT OfferNo, CourseNo, FacFirstName, FacLastName,
       OffTime, OffDays
```

---

[1]Microsoft Access 2002 supports the CREATE VIEW statement through the Microsoft OLE DB provider for the native Access Jet engine. Views cannot be created in the SQL Window of Access 2002.

FROM MS_View
WHERE OffTerm = 'SPRING' AND OffYear = 2003

OfferNo	CourseNo	FacFirstName	FacLastName	OffTime	OffDays
3333	IS320	LEONARD	VINCE	8:30 AM	MW
9876	IS460	LEONARD	FIBON	1:30 PM	TTH
5679	IS480	CRISTOPHER	COLAN	3:30 PM	TTH

Example 10.5 (Access)

Query Using a Grouping View

List the spring 2003 offerings of IS courses in the Enrollment_View. In Oracle, the % should be used in place of the * for wild card matching.

SELECT OfferNo, CourseNo, Instructor, NumStudents
 FROM Enrollment_View
 WHERE Term = 'SPRING' AND Year = 2003
   AND CourseNo LIKE 'IS*'

OfferNo	CourseNo	Instructor	NumStudents
5679	IS480	COLAN	6
9876	IS460	FIBON	7

Both queries are much easier to write than the original queries. A novice user can probably write both queries with just a little training. In contrast, it may take many hours of training for a novice user to write queries with multiple tables and grouping.

According to SQL:1999, a view can be used in any query. In practice, most DBMSs have some limitations on view usage in queries. For example, some DBMSs do not support the queries shown in Examples 10.6 and 10.7.[2]

Example 10.6

Grouping Query Using a View Derived from a Grouping Query

List the average number of students by instructor name using Enrollment_View.

SELECT Instructor, AVG(NumStudents) AS AvgStdCount
 FROM Enrollment_View
 GROUP BY Instructor

Instructor	AvgStdCount
COLAN	6
FIBON	7
MACON	2.5
MILLS	3.5
VINCE	6

Example 10.7

Joining a Base Table with a View Derived from a Grouping Query

List the offering number, instructor, number of students, and course units using the *Enrollment_View* view and the *Course* table.

[2]Microsoft Access 97, 2000, and 2002 and Oracle 8i and 9i both support Examples 10.6 and 10.7.

Query_d: Query that defines a view   Query_v: Query that references a view

Figure 10.1   **Process flow of view materialization.**

SELECT OfferNo, Instructor, NumStudents, CrsUnits
 FROM Enrollment_View, Course
 WHERE Enrollment_View.CourseNo = Course.CourseNo
  AND NumStudents < 5

OfferNo	Instructor	NumStudents	CrsUnits
5555	MACON	2	4
6666	MILLS	2	4
7777	MACON	3	4

10.2.2 PROCESSING QUERIES WITH VIEW REFERENCES

View Materialization a method to process a query on a view by executing the query directly on the stored view. The stored view can be materialized on demand (when the view query is submitted) or periodically rebuilding the view from the base tables. For databases with a mixture of retrieval and update activity, materialization usually is not an efficient way to process a query on a view.

To process queries that reference a view, the DBMS can use either a materialization or modification strategy. Materialization requires the storage of views. The simplest way to store a view is to build the view from the base tables on demand (when the view query is submitted). Processing a query with a view reference requires that a DBMS execute two queries, as depicted in Figure 10.1. A user submits a query using a view (Query_v). The query defining the view (Query_d) is executed and a temporary view table is created. Figure 10.1 depicts this action by the arrow into the view. Then, the query using the view is executed using the temporary view table.

Materialization is usually not the preferred strategy because it requires the DBMS to execute two queries. However, on certain queries such as Examples 10.6 and 10.7, materialization may be necessary. In addition, materialization is preferred in data warehouses in which retrievals dominate. In a data warehouse environment, views are periodically refreshed from base tables rather than materialized on demand. Chapter 16 discusses materialized views used in data warehouses.

Query$_V$: query that references a view

Query$_B$: modification of Query$_V$ such that references to the view are replaced by references to base tables.

| **Figure 10.2** | **Process flow of view modification.** |

View Modification a method to process a query on a view involving the execution of only one query. A query using a view is translated into a query using base tables by replacing references to the view with its definition. In most cases, modification provides an efficient way to process a query on a view.

Modification usually provides better performance than materialization because the DBMS only executes one query. Figure 10.2 shows that a query using a view is modified or rewritten as a query using base tables only; then the modified query is executed using the base tables. The modification process happens automatically without any user knowledge or action. In most DBMSs, the modified query cannot be seen even if you want to review it.

As a modification example, consider the transformation shown from Example 10.8 to Example 10.9. When you submit a query using a view, the reference to the view is replaced with the definition of the view. The view name in the FROM clause is replaced by base tables. In addition, the conditions in the WHERE clause are combined using the Boolean AND with the conditions in the query defining the view. The underlined parts in Example 10.9 indicate substitutions made in the modification process.

| **Example 10.8** | Query Using MS_View |

```
SELECT OfferNo, CourseNo, FacFirstName, FacLastName,
       OffTime, OffDays
FROM MS_View
WHERE OffTerm = 'SPRING' AND OffYear = 2003
```

OfferNo	CourseNo	FacFirstName	FacLastName	OffTime	OffDays
3333	IS320	LEONARD	VINCE	8:30 AM	MW
9876	IS460	LEONARD	FIBON	1:30 PM	TTH
5679	IS480	CRISTOPHER	COLAN	3:30 PM	TTH

Example 10.9	Modification of Example 10.8

Example 10.8 is modified by replacing references to MS_View with base table references.

```
SELECT OfferNo, Course.CourseNo, FacFirstName,
       FacLastName, OffTime, OffDays
 FROM Faculty, Course, Offering
 WHERE FacDept = 'MS'
     AND Faculty.FacSSN = Offering.FacSSN
     AND Offering.CourseNo = Course.CourseNo
     AND OffTerm = 'SPRING' AND OffYear = 2003
```

If the DBMS is intelligent, it can sometimes simplify modified queries. For example, the *Course* table is not needed because there are no conditions and columns from the *Course* table in Example 10.9. In addition, the join between the *Offering* and the *Course* tables is not necessary because every *Offering* row is related to a *Course* row (null is not allowed). As a result the modified query can be simplified by removing the *Course* table. Such simplification will result in a faster execution time, as the most important factor in execution time is the number of tables.

Example 10.10	Further Simplification of Example 10.9

Simplify by removing the *Course* table because it is not needed in Example 10.9.

```
SELECT OfferNo, CourseNo, FacFirstName, FacLastName,
       OffTime, OffDays
 FROM Faculty, Offering
 WHERE FacDept = 'MS'
     AND Faculty.FacSSN = Offering.FacSSN
     AND OffTerm = 'SPRING' AND OffYear = 2003
```

10.3 UPDATING USING VIEWS

Depending on its definition, a view can be read-only or updatable. A <u>read-only view</u> can be used in SELECT statements as demonstrated in Section 10.2. All views are at least read-only. A read-only view cannot be used in queries involving INSERT, UPDATE, and DELETE statements. A view that can be used in modification statements as well as SELECT statements is known as an <u>updatable view.</u> This section describes rules for defining both single-table and multiple-table updatable views.

Updatable View a view that can be used in SELECT statements as well as UPDATE, INSERT, and DELETE statements. Views that can be used only with SELECT statements are known as read-only views.

10.3.1 Single-Table Updatable Views

An updatable view allows you to insert, update, or delete rows in the underlying base tables by performing the corresponding operation on the view. Whenever a modification is made to a view row, a corresponding operation is performed on the base table. Intuitively, this means that the rows of an updatable view correspond in a one-to-one manner with rows from the underlying base tables. If a view contains the primary key of the base table, then each view row matches a base table row. A single-table view is updatable if it satisfies the following three rules that include the primary key requirement.

Rules for Single-Table Updatable Views

1. The view includes the primary key of the base table.
2. All required fields (NOT NULL) of the base table are in the view.
3. The view's query does not include GROUP BY or DISTINCT.

Following these rules, *Fac_View1* (Example 10.11) is updatable while *Fac_View2* (Example 10.12) and *Fac_View3* (Example 10.13) are read-only. *Fac_View1* is updatable assuming the missing *Faculty* columns are not required. *Fac_View2* violates Rules 1 and 2 while *Fac_View3* violates all three rules making them read-only.

Example 10.11

Single-Table Updatable View
Create a row and column subset view with the primary key.

```
CREATE VIEW Fac_View1 AS
  SELECT FacSSN, FacFirstName, FacLastName, FacRank,
         FacSalary, FacDept, FacCity, FacState, FacZipCode
  FROM Faculty
  WHERE FacDept = 'MS'
```

FacSSN	FacFirstName	FacLastName	FacRank	FacSalary	FacDept	FacCity	FacState	FacZipCode
098-76-5432	LEONARD	VINCE	ASST	35000.00	MS	SEATTLE	WA	98111-9921
543-21-0987	VICTORIA	EMMANUEL	PROF	120000.00	MS	BOTHELL	WA	98011-2242
654-32-1098	LEONARD	FIBON	ASSC	70000.00	MS	SEATTLE	WA	98121-0094
876-54-3210	CRISTOPHER	COLAN	ASST	40000.00	MS	SEATTLE	WA	98114-1332

Example 10.12

Single-Table Read-Only View
Create a row and column subset without the primary key.

```
CREATE VIEW Fac_View2 AS
  SELECT FacDept, FacRank, FacSalary
  FROM Faculty
  WHERE FacSalary > 50000
```

FacDept	FacRank	FacSalary
MS	PROF	120000.00
MS	ASSC	70000.00
FIN	PROF	65000.00
FIN	ASSC	75000.00

Example 10.13

Single-Table Read-Only View
Create a grouping view with faculty department and average salary.

```
CREATE VIEW Fac_View3 (FacDept, AvgSalary) AS
  SELECT FacDept, AVG(FacSalary)
  FROM Faculty
  WHERE FacRank = 'PROF'
  GROUP BY FacDept
```

FacDept	AvgSalary
FIN	65000
MS	120000

Because *Fac_View1* is updatable, it can be used in INSERT, UPDATE, and DELETE statements to change the *Faculty* table. In Chapters 3 and 9, you used these statements to change rows in base tables. Examples 10.14 through 10.16 demonstrate that these statements can be used to change view rows and rows of the underlying base tables. Note that modifications to views are subject to the integrity rules of the underlying base table. The insertion in Example 10.14 is rejected if another *Faculty* row has 999-99-8888 as the social security number. When deleting rows in a view or changing the primary key column, the rules on referenced rows apply (Section 2.4). For example, the deletion in Example 10.16 is rejected if the Faculty with *FacSSN* 098-76-5432 has related rows in the *Offering* table and the delete rule for the *Faculty-Offering* relationship is set to RESTRICT.

Example 10.14

Insert Operation on Updatable View
Insert a new faculty row into the MS department.

```
INSERT INTO Fac_View1
  (FacSSN, FacFirstName, FacLastName, FacRank, FacSalary,
   FacDept, FacCity, FacState, FacZipCode)
  VALUES (   '999-99-8888', 'JOE', 'SMITH', 'PROF', 80000,
             'MS', 'SEATTLE', 'WA', '98011-011' )
```

Example 10.15

Update Operation on Updatable View
Give assistant professors in Fac_View1 a 10 percent raise.

```
UPDATE Fac_View1
  SET FacSalary = FacSalary * 1.1
  WHERE FacRank = 'ASST'
```

Example 10.16

Delete Operation on Updatable View
Delete a specific faculty member from Fac_View1.

```
DELETE FROM Fac_View1
  WHERE FacSSN = '999-99-8888'
```

View Updates with Side Effects

Some modifications to updatable views can be problematic, as demonstrated in Example 10.17 and Tables 10.1 and 10.2. The update statement in Example 10.17 changes the department of the last row (Victoria Emmanuel) in the view and the corresponding row in the base table. Upon regenerating the view, however, the changed row disappears (Table 10.2). The update has the side effect of causing the row to disappear from the view. This kind of side effect can occur whenever a column in the WHERE clause of the

TABLE 10.1		**Fac_View1 before Update**						

FacSSN	FacFirstName	FacLastName	FacRank	FacSalary	FacDept	FacCity	FacState	FacZipCode
098-76-5432	LEONARD	VINCE	ASST	35000.00	MS	SEATTLE	WA	98111-9921
543-21-0987	VICTORIA	EMMANUEL	PROF	120000.00	MS	BOTHELL	WA	98011-2242
654-32-1098	LEONARD	FIBON	ASSC	70000.00	MS	SEATTLE	WA	98121-0094
876-54-3210	CRISTOPHER	COLAN	ASST	40000.00	MS	SEATTLE	WA	98114-1332

TABLE 10.2		**Fac_View1 after Example 10.17 Update**						

FacSSN	FacFirstName	FacLastName	FacRank	FacSalary	FacDept	FacCity	FacState	FacZipCode
098-76-5432	LEONARD	VINCE	ASST	35000.00	MS	SEATTLE	WA	98111-9921
654-32-1098	LEONARD	FIBON	ASSC	70000.00	MS	SEATTLE	WA	98121-0094
876-54-3210	CRISTOPHER	COLAN	ASST	40000.00	MS	SEATTLE	WA	98114-1332

view definition is changed by an UPDATE statement. Example 10.17 updates the *FacDept* column, the column used in the WHERE clause of the definition of the *Fac_View1* view.

Example 10.17

Update Operation on Updatable View with a Side Effect
Change the department of highly paid faculty members to the finance department.

```
UPDATE Fac_View1
  SET FacDept = 'FIN'
  WHERE FacSalary > 100000
```

WITH CHECK OPTION a clause in the CREATE VIEW statement that prevents side effects when updating a view. The WITH CHECK OPTION clause prevents UPDATE and INSERT statements that violate a view's WHERE clause.

Because this side effect can be confusing to a user, the WITH CHECK OPTION clause can be used to prevent updates with side effects. If the WITH CHECK OPTION is specified in the CREATE VIEW statement (Example 10.18), INSERT or UPDATE statements that violate the WHERE clause are rejected. The update in Example 10.17 would be rejected if *Fac_View1* contained a CHECK OPTION clause because changing *FacDept* to FIN violates the WHERE condition.

Example 10.18

Single Table Updatable View Using the WITH CHECK OPTION
Create a row and column subset view with the primary key.

```
CREATE VIEW Fac_View1_Revised AS
  SELECT FacSSN, FacFirstName, FacLastName, FacRank,
           FacSalary, FacDept, FacCity, FacState, FacZipCode
  FROM Faculty
  WHERE FacDept = 'MS'
WITH CHECK OPTION
```

10.3.2 Multiple-Table Updatable Views

It may be surprising but some multiple-table views are also updatable. A multiple-table view may correspond in a one-to-one manner with rows from more than one table if the view contains the primary key of each table. Because multiple-table views are more complex than single-table views, there is not wide agreement on updatability rules for multiple-table views.

Some DBMSs may not support updatability for any multiple-table views. Other systems support updatability for a large number of multiple-table views. In this section, the updatability rules in Microsoft Access are described as they support a wide range of multiple-table views. In addition, the rules for updatable views in Access are linked to the presentation of hierarchical forms in Section 10.4.

To complement the presentation of the Access updatability rules, Appendix 10.B describes the rules for updatable join views in Oracle 9i. The rules for updatable join views in Oracle 9i are similar to Microsoft Access although Oracle is more restrictive on the allowable manipulation operations and the number of updatable tables.

In Access, multiple-table queries that support updates are known as 1-M updatable queries. A 1-M updatable query involves two or more tables with one table playing the role of the parent or 1 table and another table playing the role of the child or M table. For example, in a query involving the *Course* and the *Offering* tables, *Course* plays the role of the parent table and *Offering* the child table. To make a 1-M query updatable, follow these rules:

Rules for 1-M Updatable Queries

1. The query includes the primary key of the child table.
2. The query contains all required columns (NOT NULL) of the child table.
3. The query does not include GROUP BY or DISTINCT.
4. The join field of the parent table should be unique (either a primary key or a unique specification).
5. The query contains the foreign key column(s) of the child table.
6. The query includes the primary key and required columns of the parent table if the view supports insert operations on the parent table. Update operations are supported on the parent table even if the query does not contain the primary key of the parent table.

Using these rules, Course_Offering_View1 (Example 10.19) and Faculty_Offering_View1 (Example 10.21) are updatable. Course_Offering_View2 (Example 10.20) is not updatable because *Offering.CourseNo* (the foreign key in the child table) is missing. In the SELECT statements, the join operator style (INNER JOIN keywords) is used because Microsoft Access requires it for 1-M updatable queries.

Example 10.19 **(Access)**	1-M Updatable Query Create a 1-M updatable query (saved as Course_Offering_View1) with a join between the *Course* and the *Offering* tables.

Course_Offering_View1:
```
SELECT Course.CourseNo, CrsDesc, CrsUnits,
       Offering.OfferNo, OffTerm, OffYear,
       Offering.CourseNo, OffLocation, OffTime, FacSSN,
       OffDays
```

FROM Course INNER JOIN Offering
      ON Course.CourseNo = Offering.CourseNo

**Example 10.20
(Access)**

Multiple-Table Read-Only Query
This query (saved as Course_Offering_View2) is read-only because it does not contain *Offering.CourseNo.*

    Course_Offering_View2:
SELECT CrsDesc, CrsUnits, Offering.OfferNo,
      Course.CourseNo, OffTerm, OffYear, OffLocation,
      OffTime, FacSSN, OffDays
FROM Course INNER JOIN Offering
      ON Course.CourseNo = Offering.CourseNo

**Example 10.21
(Access)**

1-M Updatable Query
Create a 1-M updatable query (saved as Faculty_Offering_View1) with a join between the *Faculty* and the *Offering* tables.

    Faculty_Offering_View1:
SELECT Offering.OfferNo, Offering.FacSSN, CourseNo,
      OffTerm, OffYear, OffLocation, OffTime, OffDays,
      FacFirstName, FacLastName, FacDept
FROM Faculty INNER JOIN Offering
      ON Faculty.FacSSN = Offering.FacSSN

Inserting Rows in 1-M Updatable Queries

Inserting a new row in a 1-M updatable query is more involved than inserting a row in a single-table view. This complication results because there is a choice about the tables that support insert operations. Rows from the parent and/or the child tables can be inserted as a result of a view update. To insert a row into the child table, supply only the values needed to insert a row into the child table as demonstrated in Example 10.22. Note that the value for *Offering.CourseNo* and *Offering.FacSSN* must match existing rows in the *Course* and the *Faculty* tables, respectively.

**Example 10.22
(Access)**

Inserting a Row into the Child Table as a Result of a View Update
Insert a new row into *Offering* as a result of using Course_Offering_View1.

INSERT INTO Course_Offering_View1
(Offering.OfferNo, Offering.CourseNo, OffTerm, OffYear,
  OffLocation, OffTime, FacSSN, OffDays   )
VALUES (7799, 'IS480', 'SPRING', 2003, 'BLM201',
      #1:30PM#, '098-76-5432', 'MW'   )

To insert a row into both tables (parent and child tables), the view must include the primary key and the required columns of the parent table. If the view includes these columns, supplying values for all columns inserts a row into both tables as demonstrated in Example 10.23. Supplying values for just the parent table inserts a row only into the parent table as demonstrated in Example 10.24. In both examples, the value for *Course.CourseNo* must <u>not</u> match an existing row in *Course*.

Example 10.23 (Access)	Inserting a Row into Both Tables as a Result of a View Update

Insert a new row into *Course* and *Offering* as a result of using Course_Offering_View1.

```
INSERT INTO Course_Offering_View1
   (   Course.CourseNo, CrsUnits, CrsDesc, Offering.OfferNo,
       OffTerm, OffYear, OffLocation, OffTime, FacSSN,
       OffDays )
   VALUES (   'IS423', 4, 'OBJECT ORIENTED COMPUTING', 8877,
               'SPRING', 2003, 'BLM201', #3:30PM#,
               '123-45-6789', 'MW'   )
```

Example 10.24	Inserting a Row into the Parent Table as a Result of a View Update

Insert a new row into the *Course* table as a result of using the Course_Offering_View1.

```
INSERT INTO Course_Offering_View1
   (   Course.CourseNo, CrsUnits, CrsDesc)
   VALUES (   'IS481', 4, 'ADVANCED DATABASE'   )
```

1-M Updatable Queries with More Than Two Tables

Queries involving more than two tables also can be updatable. The same rules apply to 1-M updatable queries with more than two tables. However, you should apply the rules to each join in the query. For example, if a query has three tables (two joins), then apply the rules to both joins. In Faculty_Offering_Course_View1 (Example 10.25), *Offering* is the child table in both joins. Thus, the foreign keys (*Offering.CourseNo* and *Offering. FacSSN*) must be in the query result. In the Faculty_Offering_Course_Enrollment_ View1 (Example 10.26), *Enrollment* is the child table in one join and *Offering* is the child table in the other two joins. The primary key of the *Offering* table is not needed in the result unless *Offering* rows should be inserted using the view. In Example 10.26, only the *Enrollment* table is updatable.

Example 10.25 (Access)	1-M Updatable Query with Three Tables

```
        Faculty_Offering_Course_View1:
SELECT CrsDesc, CrsUnits, Offering.OfferNo,
        Offering.CourseNo, OffTerm, OffYear, OffLocation,
        OffTime, Offering.FacSSN, OffDays, FacFirstName,
        FacLastName
FROM (   Course INNER JOIN Offering
        ON   Course.CourseNo = Offering.CourseNo   )
        INNER JOIN Faculty
        ON Offering.FacSSN = Faculty.FacSSN
```

Example 10.26 (Access)

1-M Updatable Query with Four Tables

Faculty_Offering_Course_Enrollment_View1:
```
SELECT CrsDesc, CrsUnits, Offering.CourseNo,
        Offering.FacSSN, FacFirstName, FacLastName,
        OffTerm, OffYear, OffLocation, OffTime, OffDays,
        Enrollment.OfferNo, Enrollment.StdSSN,
        Enrollment.EnrGrade
FROM (    (   Course INNER JOIN Offering
            ON Course.CourseNo = Offering.CourseNo   )
        INNER JOIN Faculty
            ON Offering.FacSSN = Faculty.FacSSN    )
        INNER JOIN Enrollment
            ON Enrollment.OfferNo = Offering.OfferNo
```

The specific rules about which insert, update, and delete operations are supported on 1-M updatable queries are more complex than what is described here. The purpose here is to demonstrate that multiple-table views can be updatable and the rules can be complex. The Microsoft Access documentation provides a complete description of the rules.

The choices about updatable tables in a 1-M updatable query can be confusing especially when the query includes more than two tables. Typically, only the child table should be updatable, so the considerations in Examples 10.23 and 10.24 do not apply. The choices are usually dictated by the needs of data entry forms, which are discussed in the next section.

10.4 USING VIEWS IN HIERARCHICAL FORMS

One of the most important benefits of views is that they are the building blocks for applications. Data entry forms, a cornerstone of most database applications, support retrieval and modification of tables. Data entry forms are formatted so that they are visually appealing and easy to use. In contrast, the plain formatting of query results may not appeal to most users. This section describes the hierarchical form, a powerful kind of data entry form, and the relationships between views and hierarchical forms.

10.4.1 What Is a Hierarchical Form?

A form is a document used in a business process. A form is designed to support a business task such as processing an order, registering for a class, or making an airline reservation. Hierarchical forms support business tasks with a fixed and a variable part. The fixed part of a hierarchical form is known as the main form, while the variable (repeating) part is known as the subform. For example, a hierarchical form for course offerings (Figure 10.3) shows course data in the main form and offering data in the subform. A hierarchical form for class registration (Figure 10.4) shows registration and student data in the main form and enrollment in course offerings in the subform. The billing calculation fields below the subform are part of the main form. In each form, the subform can display multiple records while the main form shows only one record.

Hierarchical Form a formatted window for data entry and display using a fixed (main form) and a variable (subform) part. One record is shown in the main form and multiple, related records are shown in the subform.

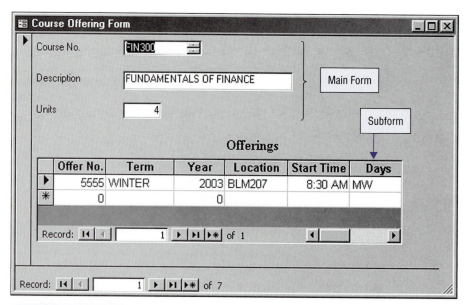

Figure 10.3   Example Course Offering Form.

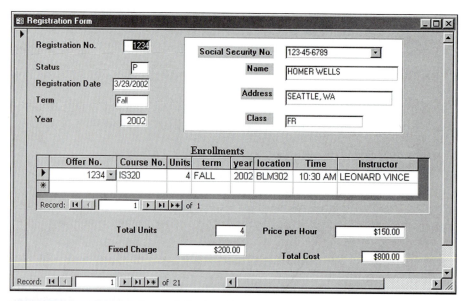

Figure 10.4   Example Registration Form.

Hierarchical forms can be part of a system of related forms. For example, a student information system may have forms for student admissions, grade recording, course approval, course scheduling, and faculty assignments to courses. These forms may be related through updates to the database or by directly sending data between forms. For example, updates to a database made by processing a registration form are used at the end of a term by a grade recording form. This chapter emphasizes the data

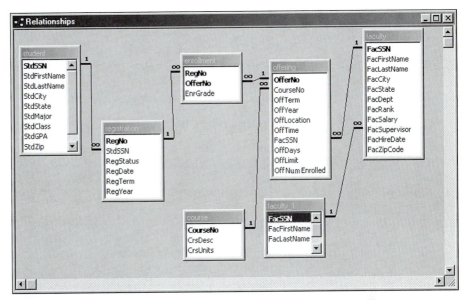

Figure 10.5 Relationships in the revised university database.

requirements of individual forms, an important skill of application development. This skill complements other application development skills such as user interface design and workflow design.

10.4.2 Relationship between Hierarchical Forms and Tables

Hierarchical forms support operations on 1-M relationships. A hierarchy or tree is a structure with 1-M relationships. Each 1-M relationship has a parent (the 1 table) and child (the M table). A hierarchical form allows the user to insert, update, delete, and retrieve records in both tables of a 1-M relationship. A hierarchical form is designed to manipulate (display, insert, update, and delete) the parent table in the main form and the child table in the subform. In essence, a hierarchical form is a nice interface for operations on a 1-M relationship.

As examples, consider the hierarchical forms shown in Figures 10.3 and 10.4. In the Course Offering Form (Figure 10.3), the relationship between the *Course* and the *Offering* tables enables the form to display a *Course* row in the main form and related *Offering* rows in the subform. The Registration Form (Figure 10.4) operates on the *Registration* and the *Enrollment* tables as well as the 1-M relationship between these tables. The *Registration* table is a new table in the university database. Figure 10.5 shows a revised relationship diagram.

To better support a business process, it is often useful to display other information in the main form and the subform. Other information (outside of the parent and the child tables) is usually for display purposes. Although it is possible to design a form to allow fields from other tables to be changed, the requirements of a particular business process may not warrant it. For example, the Registration Form (Figure 10.4) contains fields from the *Student* table so that the user can be authenticated. Likewise, fields from the *Offering,* the *Faculty,* and the *Course* tables are shown in the subform so that the user can make an informed enrollment choice. If a business process permits fields from other tables to be changed, this task is usually done using another form.

10.4.3 Query Formulation Skills for Hierarchical Forms

To implement a hierarchical form, you should make decisions for each step listed below. These steps help to clarify the relationship between a form and its related database tables. In addition, these steps can be used directly to implement the form in some DBMSs such as Microsoft Access.

1. Identify the 1-M relationship manipulated by the form.
2. Identify the join or linking columns for the 1-M relationship.
3. Identify the other tables in the main form and the subform.
4. Determine the updatability of the tables in the hierarchical form.
5. Write queries for the main form and the subform.

Step 1: Identify the 1-M Relationship

The most important decision is matching the form to a 1-M relationship in the database. If you are starting from a picture of a form (such as Figure 10.3 or 10.4), look for a relationship that has columns from the parent table in the main form and columns from the child table in the subform. Usually, the parent table contains the primary key of the main form. In Figure 10.3, the Course No. field is the primary key of the main form so the *Course* table is the parent table. In Figure 10.4, the Registration No. field is the primary key of the main form, so the *Registration* table is the parent table. If you are performing the form design and layout yourself, decide on the 1-M relationship before you sketch the form layout.

Step 2: Identify the Linking Columns

If you can identify the 1-M relationship, identifying the linking columns is usually easy. The linking columns are simply the join columns from both tables (parent and child) in the relationship. In the Course Offering Form, the linking columns are *Course.CourseNo* and *Offering.CourseNo.* In the Registration Form, the linking columns are *Registration.RegNo* and *Enrollment.RegNo.* It is important to remember that the linking columns connect the main form to the subform. With this connection, the subform only shows rows that match the value in the linking column of the main form. Without this connection, the subform displays all rows, not just the rows related to the record displayed in the main form.

Step 3: Determine Other Tables

In addition to the 1-M relationship, other tables can be shown in the main form and the subform to provide a context to a user. If you see columns from other tables, you should note those tables so that you can use them in step 5 when writing queries for the form. For example, the Registration Form includes columns from the *Student* table in the main form. The subform includes columns from the *Offering,* the *Faculty,* and the *Course* tables. Computed columns, such as Total Units, are not a concern until the form is implemented.

Step 4: Determine Updatable Tables

The fourth step requires that you understand the tables that can be changed when using the form. Typically, there is only one table in the main form and one table in the subform that should be changed as the user enters data. In the Registration Form, the *Registration* table is changed when the user manipulates the main form and the *Enrollment* table is changed when the user manipulates the subform. Usually the tables identified in step 3 are read-only. The *Student,* the *Offering,* the *Faculty,* and the *Course* tables are read-only in the subform.

Sometimes the main form does not support updates to any tables. In the Course Offering Form, the *Course* table is not changed when using the main form. The reason for making the main form read-only is to support the course approval process. Most universities require a separate approval process for new courses using a separate form. The Course Offering Form is designed only for adding offerings to existing courses. If a university does not have this constraint, the main form can be used to change the *Course* table. As part of designing a hierarchical form, you should clearly understand the requirements of the underlying business process. These requirements should then be transformed into decisions about which tables are affected by user actions in the form such as updating a field or inserting a new record.

Step 5: Write Form Queries

The last step integrates decisions made in the other steps. You should write a query for the main form and a query for the subform. These queries must support updates to the tables you identified in step 4. You should follow the rules for formulating updatable views (both single-table and multiple-table) given in Section 10.3. Some DBMSs may require that you use a CREATE VIEW statement for these queries while other DBMSs may allow you to type the SELECT statements directly.

Examples 10.27 to 10.30 show queries for the main forms and subforms of Figures 10.3 and 10.4. In Example 10.29, the *Address* form field (Figure 10.4) is derived from the *StdCity* and *StdState* columns. In Example 10.30, the primary key of the *Offering* table is not needed because the query does not support insert operations on the *Offering* table. The query only supports insert operations on the *Enrollment* table. Note that all examples conform to the Access 97/2000/2002 rules for 1-M updatable queries.

Example 10.27 (Access)	Query for the Main Form of the Course Offering Form
	SELECT CourseNo, CrsDesc, CrsUnits FROM Course

Example 10.28 (Access)	Query for the Subform of the Course Offering Form
	SELECT * FROM Offering

Example 10.29 (Access)	Query for the Main Form of the Registration Form

```
SELECT RegNo, RegTerm, RegYear, RegDate,
          Registration.StdSSN, RegStatus, StdFirstName,
          StdLastName, StdClass, StdCity, StdState
    FROM Registration INNER JOIN Student
        ON Registration.StdSSN = Student.StdSSN
```

Example 10.30 (Access)	Query for the Subform of the Registration Form

```
SELECT RegNo, Enrollment.OfferNo, Offer.CourseNo, OffTime, OffLocation,
          OffTerm, OffYear, Offering.FacSSN, FacFirstName, FacLastName,
          CrsDesc, CrsUnits
    FROM (   (   Enrollment INNER JOIN Offering
              ON Enrollment.OfferNo = Offering.OfferNo   )
          INNER JOIN Faculty
              ON Faculty.FacSSN = Offering.FacSSN )
          INNER JOIN Course
              ON Course.CourseNo = Offering.CourseNo
```

In the subform query for the Registration Form (Example 10.30), there is one other issue. The subform query will display an *Offering* row only if there is an associated *Faculty* row. If you want the subform to display *Offering* rows regardless of whether there is an associated *Faculty* row, a one-sided outer join should be used, as shown in Example 10.31. You can tell if an outer join is needed by looking at example copies of the form. If you can find offerings listed without an assigned faculty, then you need a one-sided outer join in the query.

Example 10.31 (Access)	Revised Subform Query with a One-Sided Outer Join

```
SELECT RegNo, Enrollment.OfferNo, Offering.CourseNo,
          OffTime, OffLocation, OffTerm, OffYear,
          Offering.FacSSN, FacFirstName, FacLastName,
          CrsDesc, CrsUnits
    FROM (   (   Enrollment INNER JOIN Offering
              ON Enrollment.OfferNo = Offering.OfferNo)
          INNER JOIN Course
              ON Offering.CourseNo = Course.CourseNo   )
          LEFT JOIN Faculty
              ON Faculty.FacSSN = Offering.FacSSN
```

As another example, Table 10.3 summarizes responses to the five query formulation steps for the Faculty Assignment Form shown in Figure 10.6. The goal of this form is to support administrators in assigning *Faculty* to course offerings. The 1-M relationship for the form is the relationship from the *Faculty* table to the *Offering* table. This form cannot be used to insert new *Faculty* rows or change data about *Faculty*. In addition, this form cannot be used to insert new *Offering* rows. The only update operation supported by this form is to change the *Faculty* assigned to teach an existing *Offering.* Examples 10.32 and 10.33 show the main form and the subform queries.

TABLE 10.3	Summary of Query Formulation Steps for the Faculty Assignment Form

Step	Response
1	*Faculty* (parent table), *Offering* (child table)
2	*Faculty.FacSSN, Offering.FacSSN*
3	Only data from the *Faculty* and *Offering* tables
4	Update *Offering.FacSSN*

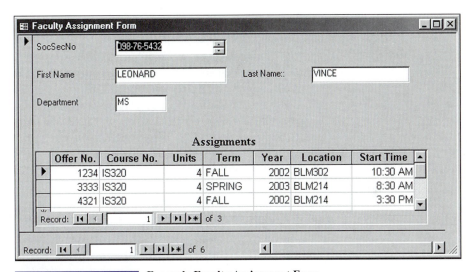

Figure 10.6   Example Faculty Assignment Form.

**Example 10.32
(Access)**

Main Form Query for the Faculty Assignment Form

```
SELECT FacSSN, FacFirstName, FacLastName, FacDept
  FROM Faculty
```

**Example 10.33
(Access)**

Subform Query for the Faculty Assignment Form

```
SELECT OfferNo, Offering.CourseNo, FacSSN, OffTime,
        OffDays, OffLocation, CrsUnits
  FROM Offering INNER JOIN Course
        ON Offering.CourseNo = Course.CourseNo
```

10.5 USING VIEWS IN REPORTS

Besides being the building blocks of data entry forms, views are also the building blocks of reports. A <u>report</u> is a stylized presentation of data appropriate to a selected audience. A report is similar to a form in that both use views and present the data much differently than it appears in the base tables. A report differs from a form in that a report does not change the base tables while a form can make changes to the base tables. This section describes the hierarchical report, a powerful kind of report, and the relationship between views and hierarchical reports.

10.5.1 What Is a Hierarchical Report?

Hierarchical Report a formatted display of a query using indentation to show grouping and sorting.

<u>Hierarchical reports</u> (also known as control break reports) use nesting or indentation to provide a visually appealing format. The Faculty Schedule Report (Figure 10.7) shows data arranged by department, faculty name, and quarter. Each indented field is known as a <u>group</u>. The nesting of the groups indicates the sorting order of the report. The innermost line in a report is known as the <u>detail line.</u> In the Faculty Schedule Report, detail lines show the course number, offering number, and other details of the assigned course. The detail lines also can be sorted. In the Faculty Schedule Report, the detail lines are sorted by course number.

The major advantage of hierarchical reports is that users can grasp more readily the meaning of data that are sorted and arranged in an indented manner. The standard output of a query (a datasheet) is not easy to inspect. For example, compare the Faculty Schedule Report with the datasheet (Figure 10.8) showing the same information. It can be distracting to see the department, faculty name, and term repeated.

To improve appearance, hierarchical reports can show summary data in the detail lines, computed columns, and calculations after groups. The detail lines in Figure 10.9 show the enrollment (number of students enrolled) in each course offering taught by a

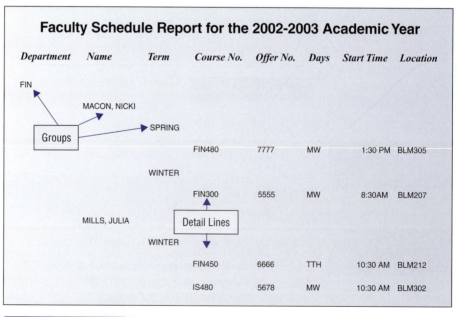

Figure 10.7   Faculty Schedule Report.

professor. In SQL, the number of students is computed with the COUNT function. The columns Percent Full ((Enrollment/Limit) * 100%) and Low Enrollment (a true/false value) are computed. A check box is a visually appealing way to display true/false columns. Many reports show summary calculations after each group. In the Faculty Work Load Report, summary calculations show the total units and students as well as average percentage full of course offerings.

10.5.2 Query Formulation Skills for Hierarchical Reports

Formulating queries for reports is similar to formulating queries for forms. In formulating a query for a report, you should (1) match fields in the report to database columns, (2) determine the needed tables, and (3) identify the join conditions. Most report queries will involve joins and possibly one-sided outer joins. More difficult queries involving difference and division are not common. These steps can be followed to formulate the query, shown in Example 10.34, for the Faculty Schedule Report (Figure 10.7).

FacDept	FacLastName	FacFirstName	OffTerm	CourseNo	OfferNo	OffLocation	OffTime	OffDays
FIN	MACON	NICKI	SPRING	FIN480	7777	BLM305	1:30 PM	MW
FIN	MACON	NICKI	WINTER	FIN300	5555	BLM207	8:30 AM	MW
FIN	MILLS	JULIA	WINTER	FIN450	6666	BLM212	10:30 AM	TTH
FIN	MILLS	JULIA	WINTER	IS480	5678	BLM302	10:30 AM	MW
MS	COLAN	CRISTOPHER	SPRING	IS480	5679	BLM412	3:30 PM	TTH
MS	EMMANUEL	VICTORIA	WINTER	IS320	4444	BLM302	3:30 PM	TTH
MS	FIBON	LEONARD	SPRING	IS460	9876	BLM307	1:30 PM	TTH
MS	VINCE	LEONARD	FALL	IS320	4321	BLM214	3:30 PM	TTH
MS	VINCE	LEONARD	FALL	IS320	1234	BLM302	10:30 AM	MW
MS	VINCE	LEONARD	SPRING	IS320	3333	BLM214	8:30 AM	MW

Figure 10.8   Datasheet showing the contents of the Faculty Schedule Report.

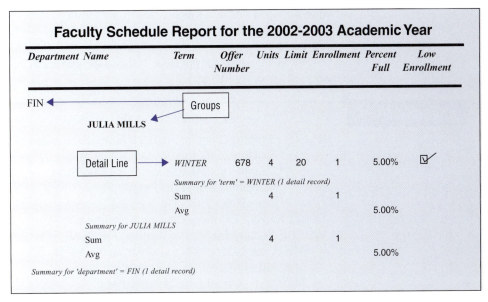

Figure 10.9   Faculty Work Load Report.

Example 10.34   Query for the Faculty Scheduling Report

```
SELECT Faculty.FacSSN, Faculty.FacFirstName, FacLastName,
        Faculty.FacDept, Offering.OfferNo,
        Offering.CourseNo, Offering.OffTerm,
        Offering.OffYear, Offering.OffLocation,
        Offering.OffTime, Offering.OffDays
 FROM Faculty, Offering
 WHERE Faculty.FacSSN = Offering.FacSSN
   AND (  (   Offering.OffTerm = 'FALL'
   AND Offering.OffYear = 2002 )
    OR (   Offering.OffTerm = 'WINTER'
   AND Offering.OffYear = 2003 )
    OR (   Offering.OffTerm = 'SPRING'
   AND Offering.OffYear = 2003   )   )
```

In some ways, formulating queries for hierarchical reports is easier than for hierarchical forms. Queries for reports do not need to be updatable (they usually are not updatable). In addition, there is only one query for a report as opposed to two or more queries for a hierarchical form.

The major query formulation issue for hierarchical reports is the <u>level</u> of the output. Sometimes there is a choice between whether the query's output contains individual rows or groups of rows. A rule of thumb is that the query should produce data for detail lines on the report. The query for the Faculty Work Load Report (Example 10.35) groups the data and counts the number of students enrolled. The query directly produces data for detail lines on the report. If the query produced one row per student enrolled in a course (a finer level of detail), then the report must calculate the number of students enrolled. With most reporting tools, it is easier to perform aggregate calculations in the query when the detail line of the report shows only summary data.

The other calculations (*PercentFull* and *LowEnrollment*) in Example 10.35 can be performed in the query or report with about the same effort. Note that the field *OffLimit* is a new field in the *Offering* table. It shows the maximum number of students that can enroll in a course offering.

Example 10.35   Query for the Faculty Work Load Report with Summary Data in Detail Lines

```
SELECT Offering.OfferNo, FacFirstName, FacLastName,
        FacDept, OffTerm, CrsUnits, OffLimit,
        Count(Enrollment.RegNo) AS NumStds,
        NumStds/Offlimit AS PercentFull,
        (NumStds/Offlimit) < 0.25 AS LowEnrollment
 FROM Faculty, Offering, Course, Enrollment
 WHERE Faculty.FacSSN = Offering.FacSSN
   AND Course.CourseNo = Offering.CourseNo
   AND Offering.OfferNo = Enrollment.OfferNo
   AND (   (   Offering.OffTerm = 'FALL'
   AND Offering.OffYear = 2002   )
    OR (   Offering.OffTerm = 'WINTER'
   AND Offering.OffYear = 2003 )
```

```
OR (   Offering.OffTerm = 'SPRING'
AND Offering.OffYear = 2003   )   )
GROUP BY Offering.OfferNo, FacFirstName, FacLastName,
       FacDept, OffTerm, CrsUnits, OffLimit
```

CLOSING THOUGHTS

This chapter has described views, which are virtual tables derived from base tables with queries. The important concepts about views are the motivation for views and how views can be used to retrieve and change a database. The major benefit of views is data independence. Changes to the definition of base tables usually do not impact applications that use views. Views also can simplify queries written by users as well as provide a flexible security tool. To effectively use views, you need to understand the difference between read-only and updatable views. A read-only view can be used in a query just like a base table. All views are at least read-only, but only some views are updatable. With an updatable view, changes to rows in the view are propagated to the underlying base tables. Both single-table and multiple-table views can be updatable. The most important determinant of updatability is that the view contains primary keys of the underlying base tables.

Views have become the building blocks of database applications because form and report tools use views. Data entry forms support retrieval and changes to a database. Hierarchical forms manipulate 1-M relationships in the database. To define a hierarchical form, you need to identify the 1-M relationship and define updatable views for the fixed (main form) and variable (subform) part of the form. Hierarchical reports provide a visually appealing presentation of data. To define a hierarchical report, you need to identify grouping levels and formulate a query to produce data for the detail lines of the report.

This chapter continues Part 3 by emphasizing application development with relational databases. In Chapter 9, you extended the query formulation skills and understanding of relational databases begun in the Part 1 chapters. This chapter stressed the application of query formulation skills in building applications based on views. To cement your understanding of application development with views, you need to use a relational DBMS especially to build forms and reports. It is only by applying the concepts to an actual DBMS that you will really learn the concepts.

REVIEW CONCEPTS

- Benefits of views: data independence, simplified query formulation, security.
- View definition in SQL:

  ```
  CREATE VIEW IS_Students AS
    SELECT * FROM Student WHERE StdMajor = 'IS'
  ```

- Using a view in a query:

  ```
  SELECT StdFirstName, StdLastName, StdCity, StdGPA
    FROM IS_Students
    WHERE StdGPA >= 3.7
  ```

- Using an updatable view in INSERT, UPDATE, and DELETE statements:

  ```
  UPDATE IS_Students
    SET StdGPA = 3.5
    WHERE StdClass = 'SR'
  ```

- View modification: DBMS service that modifies view references to base table references.
- View materialization: DBMS service that executes the query defining the view followed by execution of the view query.
- Typical usage of view processing by view modification for databases that have a mix of update and retrieval usage.
- Rules for defining single-table updatable views: primary key and required columns.
- Rules for defining multiple-table updatable views: primary key and required columns of each updatable table along with foreign keys of the child tables.
- Components of a hierarchical form: main form and subform.
- Relationship of hierarchical forms and 1-M relationships.
- Query formulation steps for hierarchical forms: identify the 1-M relationship, identify the linking columns, identify other tables on the form, determine updatability of tables, write the form queries.
- Writing updatable queries for the main form and the subform.
- Hierarchical reports: grouping fields and detail lines.
- Writing queries for hierarchical reports: provide data for detail lines.

QUESTIONS

1. How do views provide data independence?

2. How can views simplify queries written by users?

3. How is a view like a macro in a spreadsheet?

4. What is view materialization?

5. What is view modification?

6. Why do most DBMSs use modification rather than materialization to process view queries?

7. What is an updatable view?

8. Why are some views read-only?

9. What are the rules for single-table updatable views?

10. What are the rules for multiple-table updatable views?

11. What is the purpose of the WITH CHECK clause?

12. What is a hierarchical form?

13. Briefly describe how a hierarchical form can be used in a business process that you know about. For example, if you know something about order processing, describe how a hierarchical form can support this process.

14. What is the difference between a main form and a subform?

15. What is the purpose of linking columns in hierarchical forms?

16. Why should you write updatable queries for a main form and a subform?

17. Why are tables used in a hierarchical form even when the tables cannot be changed as a result of using the form?

18. What is the first step of the query formulation process for hierarchical forms?

19. What is the second step of the query formulation process for hierarchical forms?

20. What is the third step of the query formulation process for hierarchical forms?

21. What is the fourth step of the query formulation process for hierarchical forms?

22. What is the fifth step of the query formulation process for hierarchical forms?

23. Provide an example of a hierarchical form in which the main form is not updatable. Explain the business reason that determines the read-only status of the hierarchical form.

24. What is a hierarchical report?

25. What is a grouping column in a hierarchical report?

26. How do you identify grouping columns in a report?

27. What is a detail line in a hierarchical report?

28. What is the relationship of grouping columns in a report to sorting columns?

29. Why is it often easier to write a query for a hierarchical report than for a hierarchical form?

30. What does it mean that a query should produce data for the detail line of a hierarchical report?

PROBLEMS

The problems use the extended order entry database depicted in Figure 10.P1 and Table 10.P1. Oracle CREATE TABLE statements for the new tables and the revised *Product* table follow Table 10.P1. This database extends the order entry database used in the problems of Chapters 3 and 9 with three tables: (1) *Supplier,* containing the list of suppliers for products carried in inventory; (2) *Purchase,* recording the general details of purchases to replenish

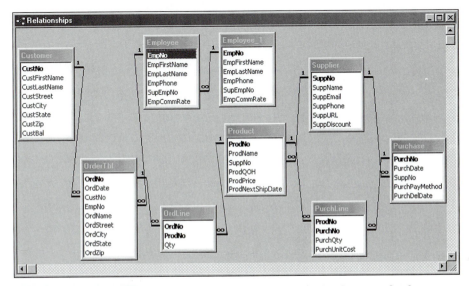

Figure 10.P1   Relationship diagram for the revised order entry database.

TABLE 10.P1	Explanations of Selected Columns in the Revised Order Entry Database

Column Name	Description
PurchDate	Date of making the purchase
PurchPayMethod	Payment method for the purchase (Credit, P.O., or Cash)
PurchDelDate	Expected delivery date of the purchase
SuppDiscount	Discount provided by the supplier
PurchQty	Quantity of product purchased
PurchUnitCost	Unit cost of the product purchased

inventory; and (3) *PurchLine,* containing the products requested on a purchase. In addition, the extended order entry database contains a new 1-M relationship (*Supplier* to *Product*) that replaces the *Product.ProdMfg* field in the original database.

In addition to the revisions noted in the previous paragraph, you should be aware of several assumptions made in the design of the extended order entry database:

- The design makes the simplifying assumption that there is only one supplier for each product. This assumption is appropriate for a single retail store that orders directly from manufacturers.

- The 1-M relationship from *Supplier* to *Purchase* supports the purchasing process. In this process, a user designates the supplier before selecting items to order from the supplier. Without this relationship, the business process and associated data entry forms would be more difficult to implement.

```
CREATE TABLE Product
(     ProdNo                CHAR(8) NOT NULL,
      ProdName              VARCHAR2(50) NOT NULL,
      SuppNo                CHAR(8) NOT NULL,
      ProdQOH               INTEGER DEFAULT 0,
      ProdPrice             DECIMAL(12,2) DEFAULT 0,
      ProdNextShipDate      DATE,
CONSTRAINT PKProduct   PRIMARY KEY (ProdNo),
CONSTRAINT SuppNoFK1 FOREIGN KEY (SuppNo) REFERENCES Supplier
   ON DELETE CASCADE   )
```

```
CREATE TABLE Supplier
(     SuppNo                CHAR(8) NOT NULL,
      SuppName              VARCHAR2(30) NOT NULL,
      SuppEmail             VARCHAR2(50),
      SuppPhone             CHAR(13),
      SuppURL               VARCHAR2(100),
      SuppDiscount          DECIMAL(3,3),
CONSTRAINT PKSupplier PRIMARY KEY (SuppNo)   )
```

```
CREATE TABLE Purchase
(       PurchNo             CHAR(8) NOT NULL,
        PurchDate           DATE NOT NULL,
        SuppNo              CHAR(8) NOT NULL,
        PurchPayMethod      CHAR(6) DEFAULT 'PO',
        PurchDelDate        DATE,
CONSTRAINT PKPurchase PRIMARY KEY (PurchNo),
CONSTRAINT SuppNoFK2 FOREIGN KEY (SuppNo) REFERENCES Supplier   )
```

```
CREATE TABLE PurchLine
(       ProdNo              CHAR(8) NOT NULL,
        PurchNo             CHAR(8) NOT NULL,
        PurchQty            INTEGER DEFAULT 1 NOT NULL,
        PurchUnitCost       DECIMAL(12,2),
CONSTRAINT PKPurchLine PRIMARY KEY (PurchNo, ProdNo),
CONSTRAINT FKPurchNo FOREIGN KEY (PurchNo) REFERENCES Purchase
        ON DELETE CASCADE,
CONSTRAINT FKProdNo2 FOREIGN KEY (ProdNo) REFERENCES Product   )
```

1. Define a view containing products from supplier number S3399214. Include all *Product* columns in the view.

2. Define a view containing the details of orders placed in January 2004. Include all *OrderTbl* columns, *OrdLine.Qty,* and the product name in the view.

3. Define a view containing the product number, name, price, and quantity on hand along with the number of orders in which the product appears.

4. Using the view defined in problem 1, write a query to list the products with a price larger than $300. Include all view columns in the result.

5. Using the view defined in problem 2, write a query to list the rows containing the words Ink Jet in the product name. Include all view columns in the result.

6. Using the view defined in problem 3, write a query to list the products in which more than five orders have been placed. Include the product name and the number of orders in the result.

7. For the query in problem 4, modify the query so that it uses base tables only.

8. For the query in problem 5, modify the query so that it uses base tables only.

9. For the query in problem 6, modify the query so that it uses base tables only.

10. Is the view in problem 1 updatable? Explain why or why not.

11. Is the view in problem 2 updatable? Explain why or why not. What database tables can be changed by modifying rows in the view?

12. Is the view in problem 3 updatable? Explain why or why not.

13. For the view in problem 1, write an INSERT statement that references the view. The effect of the INSERT statement should add a new row to the *Product* table.

14. For the view in problem 1, write an UPDATE statement that references the view. The effect of the UPDATE statement should modify the *ProdQOH* column of the row added in problem 13.

15. For the view in problem 1, write a DELETE statement that references the view. The effect of the DELETE statement should remove the row added in problem 13.

16. Modify the view definition of problem 1 to prevent side effects. Use a different name for the view than the name used in problem 1. This problem cannot be done in Access using the SQL window.

17. Write an UPDATE statement for the view in problem 1 to modify the *SuppNo* of the row with *ProdNo* of P6677900 to S4420948. The UPDATE statement should be rejected by the revised view definition in problem 16 but accepted by the original view definition in problem 1. This problem cannot be done in Access using the SQL window.

18. Define a 1-M updatable query involving the *Customer* and the *OrderTbl* tables. The query should support updates to the *OrderTbl* table. The query should include all columns of the *OrderTbl* table and the name (first and last), street, city, state, and zip of the *Customer* table. Note that this problem is specific to Microsoft Access.

19. Define a 1-M updatable query involving the *Customer* table, the *OrderTbl* table, and the *Employee* table. The query should support updates to the *OrderTbl* table. Include all rows in the *OrderTbl* table even if there is a null employee number. The query should include all columns of the *OrderTbl* table, the name (first and last), street, city, state, and zip of the *Customer* table, and the name (first and last) and phone of the *Employee* table. Note that this problem is specific to Microsoft Access.

20. Define a 1-M updatable query involving the *OrdLine* and the *Product* tables. The query should support updates to the *OrdLine* table. The query should include all columns of the *OrdLine* table and the name, the quantity on hand, and the price of the *Product* table. Note that this problem is specific to Microsoft Access.

21. Define a 1-M updatable query involving the *Purchase* and the *Supplier* tables. The query should support updates and inserts to the *Product* and the *Supplier* tables. Include the necessary columns so that both tables are updatable. Note that this problem is specific to Microsoft Access.

22. For the sample Simple Order Form shown in Figure 10.P2, answer the five query formulation questions discussed in Section 10.4.3. The form supports manipulation of the heading and the details of orders.

23. For the sample Order Form shown in Figure 10.P3, answer the five query formulation questions discussed in Section 10.4.3. Like the Simple Order Form depicted in Figure 10.P2, the Order Form supports manipulation of the heading and the details of orders. In addition, the Order Form displays data from other tables to provide a context for the user when completing an order. The Order Form supports both phone (an employee taking the order) and Web (without an employee taking the order) orders. The subform query should compute the Amount field as Oty * ProdPrice. Do not compute the Total Amount field in either the main form query or the subform query. It is computed in the form.

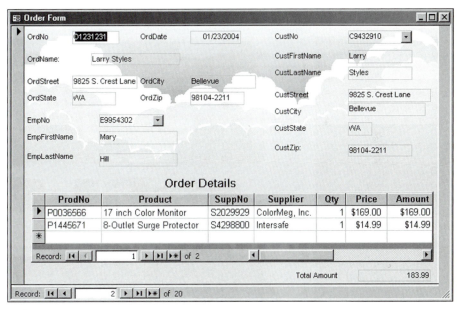

Figure 10.P2   Simple Order Form.

Figure 10.P3   Order Form.

24. Modify your answer to problem 23 assuming that the Order Form supports only phone orders, not Web orders.

25. For the sample Simple Purchasing Form shown in Figure 10.P4, answer the five query formulation questions discussed in Section 10.4.3. The form supports manipulation of the heading and the details of purchases.

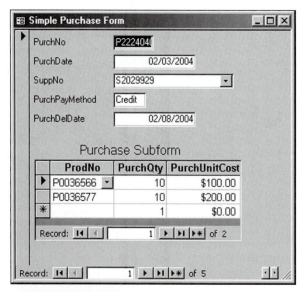

Figure 10.P4   Simple Purchase Form.

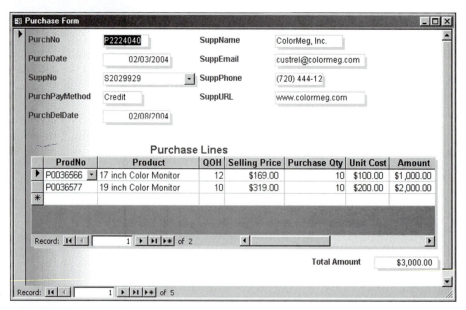

Figure 10.P5   Purchase Form.

26. For the sample Purchase Form shown in Figure 10.P5, use the five query formulation steps presented in Section 10.4.3. Like the Simple Purchase Form depicted in Figure 10.P4, the Purchase Form supports manipulation of the heading and the details of purchases. In addition, the Purchase Form displays data from other tables to provide a context for the user when completing a purchase. The subform query should compute the Amount field as **PurchQty *** **PurchUnitCost**. Do not compute the Total Amount field in either the main form query or the subform query. It is computed in the form.

Figure 10.P6   Supplier Main Form.

27. For the sample Supplier Form shown in Figure 10.P6, use the five query formulation steps presented in Section 10.4.3. The main form supports the manipulation of supplier data whereas the subform supports the manipulation of only the product number and the product name of the products provided by the supplier in the main form.

28. For the Order Detail Report, write a SELECT statement to produce the data for the detail lines. The grouping column in the report is *OrdNo*. The report should list the orders for customer number O2233457 in January 2004.

Order Detail Report

Order Number	Order Date	Product No	Qty	Price	Amount
O2233457	1/12/2004	P1441567	1	$14.99	$14.99
		P0036577	2	$319.00	$638.00
Total Order Amount					$652.99
O4714645	1/11/2004	P9995676	2	$89.00	$178.00
		P0036566	1	$369.00	$369.00
Total Order Amount					$447.00

29. For the sample Order Summary Report, write a SELECT statement to produce the data for the detail lines. The Zip Code report field is the first five characters of the *CustZip* column. The grouping field in the report is the first five characters of the *CustZip* column. The Order Amount Sum report field is the sum of the quantity times the product price. Limit the report to year 2004 orders. You should also include the month number in the SELECT statement so that the report can be sorted by the month number instead of the Month report field. Use the following expressions to derive columns used in the report:

   • In Microsoft Access, the expression left(CustZip, 5) derives the Zip Code report field. In Oracle, the expression substr(CustZip, 1, 5) derives the Zip Code report field.

- In Microsoft Access, the expression format(OrdDate, "mmmm yyyy") derives the Month report field. In Oracle, the expression to_char(OrdDate, 'MONTH YYYY') derives the Month report field.
- In Microsoft Access, the expression month(OrdDate) derives the month. In Oracle, the expression to_number(to_char(OrdDate, 'MM')) derives the month.

Order Summary Report

Zip Code	Month	Order Line Count	Order Amount Sum
80111	January 2004	10	$1,149
	February 2004	21	$2,050
Summary of 80111		31	$3,199
80113	January 2004	15	$1,541
	February 2004	11	$1,450
Summary of 80113		26	$2,991

30. Revise the Order Summary Report to list the number of orders and the average order amount instead of the Order Line Count and Order Amount Sum. The revised report appears below. You will need to use a SELECT statement in the FROM clause or write two statements to produce the data for the detail lines.

Order Summary Report

Zip Code	Month	Order Count	Average Order Amount
80111	January 2004	4	$287.25
	February 2004	10	$205.00
Summary of 80111		15	$213.27
80113	January 2004	5	$308.20
	February 2004	4	$362.50
Summary of 80113		9	$243.44

REFERENCES FOR FURTHER STUDY

The *DBAZine* site (www.dbazine.com) and the DevX help site (www.devx.com/gethelp) have plenty of practical advice about query formulation and application development. For product-specific SQL advice, the Advisor.com site (www.advisor.com) features technical journals for Microsoft SQL Server and Microsoft Access. Oracle documentation can be found at the Oracle Technet Site (otn.oracle.com). In Chapter 17, Date (1995) provides additional details of view updatability issues especially related to multiple table views. Melton and Simon (2001) describe updatable query specifications in SQL:1999.

Appendix 10.A SQL:1999 Syntax Summary

This appendix summarizes the SQL:1999 syntax for the CREATE VIEW statement presented in Chapter 10 and a simple companion statement (DROP VIEW). The conventions used in the syntax notation are identical to those used at the end of Chapter 2.

CREATE VIEW STATEMENT

```
CREATE VIEW ViewName   [   (   ColumnName*   )   ]
                AS <Select-Statement>
                [ WITH CHECK OPTION ]

<Select-Statement>: --defined in Chapter 3 and extended in Chapter 9
```

DROP VIEW STATEMENT.

```
DROP VIEW ViewName   [   {   CASCADE | RESTRICT   }   ]

                --CASCADE deletes the view and any views that use its definition.
                --RESTRICT means that the view is not deleted if any views use its definition.
```

Appendix 10.B Rules for Updatable Join Views in Oracle 9i

In Oracle 9i, a join view contains one or more tables or views in its defining FROM clause. Fundamental to updatable join views is the concept of a <u>key preserving table.</u> A join view preserves a table if every candidate key of the table can be a candidate key of the join result table. This statement means that the rows of an updatable join view can be mapped in a 1-1 manner with each key preserved table. In a join involving a 1-M relationship, the child table could be key preserved because each child row is associated with at most one parent row.

Using the definition of key preserving table, a join view is updatable if it satisfies the following conditions:

- It does not contain the DISTINCT keyword, the GROUP BY clause, aggregation functions, or set operations (UNION, MINUS, and INTERSECT).
- It contains at least one key preserving table.
- The CREATE VIEW statement does not contain the WITH CHECK OPTION.

An updatable join view supports insert, update, and delete operations on one underlying table per manipulation statement. The updatable table is the key preserving table. An UPDATE statement can modify (in the SET clause) only columns of one key preserving table. An INSERT statement can add values for columns of one key preserved table. An INSERT statement cannot contain columns from nonkey preserving tables. Rows can be deleted as long as the join view contains only one key preserving table. Join views with more than one key preserving table do not support DELETE statements.

CHAPTER 11

Stored Procedures and Triggers

LEARNING OBJECTIVES

This chapter explains the motivation for stored procedures and triggers as well as the practice of writing them using PL/SQL, the database programming language of Oracle. After this chapter, the student should have acquired the following knowledge and skills:

- Explain the reasons for writing stored procedures and triggers.

- Understand the design issues of language style, binding, database connection, and result processing for database programming languages.

- Write PL/SQL procedures.

- Understand the classification of triggers.

- Understand trigger execution procedures.

- Write PL/SQL triggers.

OVERVIEW

Chapter 10 provided details about application development with views. You learned about defining user views, updating base tables with views, and using views in forms and reports. This chapter augments your database application development skills with stored procedures and triggers. Stored procedures provide reuse of common code, while triggers provide rule processing for common tasks. Together, stored procedures and triggers support customization of database applications and improved productivity in developing database applications.

To become skilled in database application development as well as in database administration, you need to understand stored procedures and triggers. Since both stored procedures and triggers are coded in a database programming language, this chapter first provides background about the motivation and design issues for database programming languages as well as specific details about PL/SQL, the proprietary database programming language of Oracle.

After the background about database programming languages and PL/SQL, this chapter then presents stored procedures and triggers. For stored procedures, you will learn about the motivation and coding practices for simple and more advanced procedures. For triggers, you will learn about the classification of triggers, trigger execution procedures, and coding practices for triggers.

The presentation of PL/SQL details in Sections 11.1 to 11.3 assumes that you have had a previous course in computer programming using a business programming language such as Visual Basic, COBOL, or Java. If you would like a broader treatment of the material without the computer programming details, you should read Sections 11.1.1, 11.1.2, 11.3.1, and the introductory material in Section 11.2 before the beginning of Section 11.2.1. In addition, the trigger examples in Section 11.3.2 mostly involve SQL statements so that you can understand the triggers without detailed knowledge of PL/SQL statements.

For continuity, all examples about stored procedures and triggers use the revised university database of Chapter 10. Figure 11.1 shows the Access relationship window of the revised university database for convenient reference.

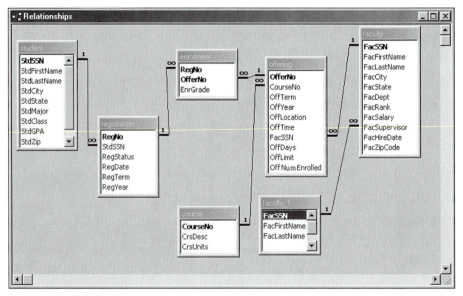

Figure 11.1   **Relationship window for the revised university database.**

11.1 DATABASE PROGRAMMING LANGUAGES AND PL/SQL

After learning about the power of nonprocedural access and application development tools, you might think that procedural languages are not necessary for database application development. However, these tools despite their power are not complete solutions for commercial database application development. This section presents the motivation for database programming languages, design issues for database programming languages, and details about PL/SQL, the database programming language of Oracle.

11.1.1 Motivation for Database Programming Languages

Database Programming Language a procedural language with an interface to one or more DBMSs. The interface allows a program to combine procedural statements with nonprocedural database access.

A <u>database programming language</u> is a procedural language with an interface to one or more DBMSs. The interface allows a program to combine procedural statements with database access, usually nonprocedural database access. This subsection discusses three primary motivations (customization, batch processing, and complex operations) for using a database programming language and two secondary motivations (efficiency and portability).

Customization

Most database application development tools support customization. Customization is necessary because no tool provides a complete solution for the development of complex database applications. Customization allows an organization to use the built-in power of a tool along with customized code to change the tool's default actions and to add new actions beyond those supported by the tool.

To support customized code, most database application development tools use event-driven coding. In this coding style, an event triggers the execution of a procedure. An event model includes events for user actions such as clicking a button, as well as internal events such as before a database record is updated. An event procedure may access the values of controls on forms and reports as well as retrieve and update database records. Event procedures are coded using a database programming language, often a proprietary language provided by a DBMS vendor. For commercial application development, event coding is common.

Batch Processing

Despite the growth of online database processing, batch processing continues to be an important way to process database work. For example, check processing typically is a batch process in which a clearinghouse bank processes large groups or batches of checks during nonpeak hours. Batch processing usually involves a delay from the occurrence of an event to its capture in a database. In the check processing case, checks are presented for payment to a merchant but not processed by a clearinghouse bank until later. Some batch processing such as billing statement preparation does not involve a time delay. Even with the continued growth of commercial Web commerce, batch processing will remain an important method of processing database work.

Application development for batch processing involves writing computer programs in a database programming language. Since few development tools support batch processing, coding can be detailed and labor intensive. The programmer typically must write code to read input data, perform database manipulation, and create output records to show the processing result.

Complex Operations

Nonprocedural database access by definition does not support all possible database retrievals. The design of a nonprocedural language involves a trade-off between amount of code and computational completeness. To allow general purpose computation, a procedural language is necessary. To reduce coding, nonprocedural languages support compact specification of important and common operations. The SELECT statement of SQL supports the operations of relational algebra along with ordering and grouping. To perform database retrievals beyond the operations of relational algebra, coding in a database programming language is necessary.

The transitive closure is an important operation not supported by most SQL implementations. This operation is important for queries involving self-referencing relationships. For example, to retrieve all employees managed directly or indirectly using a self-referencing relationship, the transitive closure operator is needed. This operation involves self-join operations, but the number of self-join operations depends on the depth (number of layers of subordinates) in an organization chart. Although SQL:1999 supports the WITH RECURSIVE clause for transitive closure operations, most DBMSs have not implemented this part of SQL:1999. With most DBMSs, transitive closure operations must be coded using a database programming language. To code a transitive closure operation, a self-join query must be repetitively executed inside a loop until the query returns an empty result.

Other Motivations

Efficiency and portability are two additional reasons for using a database programming language. When distrust in optimizing database compilers was high (until the mid-1990s), efficiency was a primary motivation for using a database programming language. To avoid the optimizing compilers, some DBMS vendors supported record-at-a-time access with the programmer determining the access plan for complex queries. As confidence has grown in optimizing database compilers, the efficiency need has become less important. However, with complex Web applications and immature Web development tools, efficiency has become an important issue in some applications. As Web development tools mature, efficiency should become a less important issue.

Portability can be important in some environments. Most application development tools and database programming languages are proprietary. If an organization wants to remain vendor neutral, an application can be built using a nonproprietary programming language (such as Java) along with a standard database interface. If just DBMS neutrality is desired (not neutrality from an application development tool), some application development tools allow connection with a variety of DBMSs through database interfaces such as the Open Database Connectivity (ODBC) and the Java Database Connectivity (JDBC). Portability is a particular concern for Web database access in which an application must be compatible with many types of servers and browsers.

11.1.2 Design Issues

Before undertaking the study of any database programming language, you should understand design issues about integrating a procedural language with a nonprocedural language. Understanding the issues will help you differentiate among the many languages in the marketplace and understand the features of a specific language. Each DBMS usually provides several alternatives for database programming languages. This section discusses the design issues of language style, binding, database connection, and result processing with an emphasis on the design choices specified in SQL:1999. Many DBMS vendors are adapting to the specifications in SQL:1999.

Language Style

Statement-Level Interface
a language style for integrating a programming language with a nonprocedural language such as SQL. A statement-level interface involves changes to the syntax of a host programming language to accommodate embedded SQL statements.

SQL:1999 provides two language styles for integrating a procedural language with SQL. A statement-level interface involves changes to the syntax of a host programming language to accommodate embedded SQL statements. The host language contains additional statements to establish database connections, execute SQL statements, use the results of an SQL statement, associate programming variables with database columns, handle exceptions in SQL statements, and manipulate database descriptors. Statement-level interfaces are available for standard and proprietary languages. For standard languages such as C, Java, and COBOL, some DBMSs provide a precompiler to process the statements before invoking the programming language compiler. Most DBMSs also provide proprietary languages such as the Oracle language PL/SQL with a statement-level interface to support embedded SQL.

Call-Level Interface (CLI)
a language style for integrating a programming language with a non-procedural language such as SQL. A CLI includes a set of procedures and a set of type definitions for manipulating the results of SQL statements in computer programs.

The second language style provided by SQL:1999 is known as a call-level interface (CLI). The SQL:1999 CLI contains a set of procedures and a set of type definitions for SQL data types. The procedures provide similar functionality to the additional statements in a statement-level interface. The SQL:1999 CLI is more difficult to learn and use than a statement-level interface. However, the SQL:1999 CLI is portable across host languages, whereas the statement-level interface is not portable and not supported for all programming languages.

The most widely used call-level interfaces are the Open Database Connectivity (ODBC) supported by Microsoft and the Java Database Connectivity (JDBC) supported by Oracle. Because both Microsoft and Oracle have cooperated with the SQL standards efforts, the most recent versions of these proprietary CLIs are compatible to the SQL:1999 CLI. Because of the established user bases, these interfaces probably will continue to be more widely used than the SQL:1999 CLI.

Binding

Binding for a database programming language involves the association of an SQL statement with its access plan. Recall from Chapter 8 that the SQL compiler determines the best access plan for an SQL statement after a detailed search of possible access plans. Static binding involves the determination of the access plan at compile time. Because the optimization process can consume considerable computing resources, it is desirable to determine the access plan at compile time and to reuse the access plan for repetitively executed statements. However, in some applications, the data to retrieve cannot be predetermined. In these situations, dynamic binding is necessary in which the access plan for a statement is determined when the statement is executed during run-time of the application. Even in these dynamic situations, it is useful to reuse the access plan for a statement if the statement is repetitively executed by the application.

SQL:1999 specifies both static and dynamic binding to support a range of database applications. A statement-level interface can support both static and dynamic binding. Embedded SQL statements have static binding. Dynamic SQL statements can be supported by the SQL:1999 EXECUTE statement that contains an SQL statement as an input parameter. If a dynamic statement is repetitively executed by an application, the

SQL:1999 PREPARE statement supports reuse of the access plan. The SQL:1999 CLI supports only dynamic binding. If a dynamic statement is repetitively executed by an application, the SQL:1999 CLI provides the Prepare() procedure to reuse the access plan.

Database Connection

A database connection identifies the database used by an application. A database connection can be implicit or explicit. For procedures and triggers stored in a database, the connection is implicit. The SQL statements in triggers and procedures implicitly access the database that contains the triggers and procedures.

In programs external to a database, the connection is explicit. SQL:1999 specifies the CONNECT statement and other related statements for statement-level interfaces and the Connect() procedure and related procedures in the CLI. A database is identified by a Web address or a database identifier that contains a Web address. Using a database identifier relieves the database programmer from knowing the specific Web address for a database as well as providing the server administrator more flexibility to relocate a database to a different location on a server.

Result Processing

To process the results of SQL statements, database programming languages must resolve differences in data types and processing orientation. The data types in a programming language may not correspond exactly to the standard SQL data types. To resolve this problem, the database interface provides statements or procedures to map between the programming language data types and the SQL data types.

The result of a SELECT statement can be one row or a collection of rows. For SELECT statements that return at most one row (for example, retrieval by primary key), the SQL:1999 specification allows the result values to be stored in program variables. In the statement-level interface, SQL:1999 provides the USING clause to store result values in program variables. The SQL:1999 CLI provides for implicit storage of result values using predefined descriptor records that can be accessed in a program.

Cursor a construct in a database programming language that allows storage and iteration of a set of records returned by a SELECT statement. A cursor is similar to a dynamic array in which the array size is determined by the size of the query result.

For SELECT statements that return more than one row, a <u>cursor</u> must be used. A cursor allows storage and iteration of a set of records returned by a SELECT statement. A cursor is similar to a dynamic array in which the array size is determined by the size of the query result. For statement-level interfaces, SQL:1999 provides statements to declare cursors, open and close cursors, position cursors, and retrieve values from cursors. The SQL:1999 CLI provides procedures with similar functionality to the statement-level interface. Section 11.2.3 presents details about cursors for PL/SQL.

11.1.3 PL/SQL Statements

Programming Language/Structured Query Language (PL/SQL) is a proprietary database programming language for the Oracle DBMS. Since its introduction in 1992, Oracle has steadily added features to PL/SQL so that it has the features of a modern programming language as well as a statement-level interface for SQL. Because PL/SQL is a widely used language among Oracle developers and Oracle is a widely used enterprise DBMS, this chapter uses PL/SQL to depict stored procedures and triggers.

To prepare you to read and code stored procedures and triggers, this section presents examples of PL/SQL statements. After reading this section, you should understand the structure of PL/SQL statements and be able to write PL/SQL statements using the example statements as guidelines. This section shows enough PL/SQL statement examples to allow you to read and write stored procedures and triggers of modest complexity after you complete the chapter. However, this section depicts neither all PL/SQL statements nor all statement variations.

This section is not a tutorial about computer programming. To follow the remainder of this chapter, you should have taken a previous course in computer programming or have equivalent experience. You will find that PL/SQL statements are similar to statements in other modern programming languages such as C, Java, and Visual Basic.

Basics of PL/SQL

PL/SQL statements contain reserved words and symbols, user identifiers, and constant values. Reserved words in PL/SQL are not case sensitive. Reserved symbols include the semicolon (;) for terminating statements as well as operators such as $+$ and $-$. User identifiers provide names for variables, constants, and other PL/SQL constructs. User identifiers like reserved words are not case sensitive. The following list defines restrictions on user identifiers:

- Must have a maximum of 30 characters.
- Must begin with a letter.
- Allowable characters are letters (upper- or lowercase), numbers, the dollar sign, the pound symbol (#), and the underscore.
- Must not be identical to any reserved word or symbol.
- Must not be identical to other identifiers, table names, or column names.

A PL/SQL statement may contain constant values for numbers, character strings, and Booleans. The following list provides background about PL/SQL constants:

- Numeric constants can be whole numbers (100), numbers with a decimal point (1.67), negative numbers (-150.15), and numbers in scientific notation (3.14E7).
- String constants are surrounded in single quotation marks, such as 'this is a string'. Do not use single quotation marks to surround numeric or Boolean constants. String constants are case sensitive so that 'This is a string' is a different value than 'this is a string'. To use a single quotation mark in a string constant, use two single quotation marks as 'today''s date'.
- Boolean constants are the TRUE and FALSE reserved words.
- The reserved word *NULL* can be used as a number, string, or Boolean constant. For strings, two single quotation marks '' without anything inside denote the NULL value.
- PL/SQL does not provide date constants. You should use the **To_Date** function to convert a string constant to a date value.

Variable Declaration and Assignment Statements

A variable declaration contains a variable name (a user identifier), a data type, and an optional default value. Table 11.1 lists common PL/SQL data types. Besides using the predefined types, a variable's type can be a user-defined type created with a TYPE statement. A default value can be indicated with the DEFAULT keyword or the assignment (:=) symbol. The DECLARE keyword should precede the first variable declaration as shown in Example 11.1.

TABLE 11.1	**Summary of Common PL/SQL Data Types**	

Category	Data Types	Comments
String	CHAR(L), VARCHAR2(L)	CHAR for fixed length strings; VARCHAR2 for variable length strings; L for the maximum length
Numeric	INTEGER, SMALLINT, POSITIVE, NUMBER(W,D), DECIMAL(W,D), FLOAT, REAL	W for the width; D for the number of digits to the right of the decimal point
Logical	BOOLEAN	TRUE, FALSE values
Date	DATE	Stores both date and time information including the century, the year, the month, the day, the hour, the minute, and the second. A date occupies 7 bytes.

Example 11.1

PL/SQL Variable Declarations
Lines beginning with double hyphens are comments.

```
DECLARE
  aFixedLengthString        CHAR(6) DEFAULT 'ABCDEF';
  aVariableLengthString     VARCHAR2(30);
  anIntegerVariable         INTEGER := 0;
  aFixedPrecisionVariable   DECIMAL(10,2);
  -- Uses the SysDate function for the default value
  aDateVariable             DATE DEFAULT SysDate;
```

For variables associated with columns of a database table, PL/SQL provides anchored declarations. Anchored declarations relieve the programmer from knowing the data types of database columns. An anchored declaration includes a fully qualified column name followed by the keyword %TYPE. Example 11.2 demonstrates anchored variable declarations using columns from the revised university database of Chapter 10. The last anchored declaration involves a variable using the type associated with a previously defined variable.

Example 11.2

PL/SQL Anchored Variable Declarations

```
DECLARE
  anOffTerm Offering.OffTerm%TYPE;
  anOffYear Offering.OffYear%TYPE;
  aCrsUnits Course.CrsUnits%TYPE;
  aSalary1 DECIMAL(10,2);
  aSalary2 aSalary1%TYPE;
```

Oracle also provides structured data types for combining primitive data types. Oracle supports variable-length arrays (VARRAY), tables (TABLE), and records (RECORD) for combining data types. For information about the structured data types, you should consult the online Oracle documentation such as the *PL/SQL User's Guide.*

Assignment statements involve a variable, the assignment symbol (:=), and an expression on the right. Expressions can include combinations of constants, variables, functions, and operators. When evaluated, an expression produces a value. Example 11.3 demonstrates assignment statements with various expression elements.

Example 11.3	PL/SQL Assignment Examples.

It is assumed that variables used in the examples have been previously declared. Lines beginning with double hyphens are comments.

```
aFixedLengthString := 'XYZABC';
-- I I is the string concatenation function
aVariableLengthString := aFixedLengthString I I 'ABCDEF';
anIntegerVariable := anAge + 1;
aFixedPrecisionVariable := aSalary * 0.10;
-- To_Date is the date conversion function
aDateVariable := To_Date( '30-Jun-2003' );
```

Conditional Statements

PL/SQL provides the IF and CASE statements for conditional decision making. In an IF statement, a logical expression or condition evaluating to TRUE, FALSE, or NULL, follows the IF keyword. Conditions include comparison expressions using the comparison operators (Table 11.2) connected using the logical operators AND, OR, and NOT. Parentheses can be used to clarify the order of evaluation in complex conditions. When mixing the AND and OR operators, you should use parentheses to clarify the order of evaluation. Conditions are evaluated using the three-valued logic described in Chapter 9 (Section 9.4).

As in other languages, the PL/SQL IF statement has multiple variations. Example 11.4 depicts the first variation known as the IF-THEN statement. Any number of statements can be used between the THEN and END IF keywords. Example 11.5 depicts the second variation known as the IF-THEN-ELSE statement. This statement allows a set of alternative statements if the condition is false. The third variation (IF-THEN-ELSIF) depicted in Example 11.6 allows a condition for each ELSIF clause along with a final ELSE clause if all conditions are false.

TABLE 11.2	**List of PL/SQL Comparison Operators**

Operator	Meaning
=	Equal to
<>	Not equal to
>	Greater than
<	Less than
>=	Greater than or equal to
<=	Less than or equal to

IF-THEN Statement:
    IF condition THEN
        sequence of statements
    END IF;

IF-THEN-ELSE Statement:
    IF condition THEN
        sequence of statements 1
    ELSE
        sequence of statements 2
    END IF;

IF-THEN-ELSIF Statement:
    IF condition1 THEN
        sequence of statements 1
    ELSIF condition2 THEN
        sequence of statements 2
    ELSIF conditionN THEN
        sequence of statements N
    ELSE
        sequence of statements N+1
    END IF;

Example 11.4

IF-THEN Statement Examples

It is assumed that variables used in the examples have been previously declared.

```
IF aCrsUnits > 3 THEN
    CourseFee := BaseFee + aCrsUnits * VarFee;
END IF;

IF anOffLimit > NumEnrolled OR CourseOverRide = TRUE THEN
    NumEnrolled := NumEnrolled + 1;
    EnrDate := SysDate;
END IF;
```

Example 11.5

IF-THEN-ELSE Statement Examples

It is assumed that variables used in the examples have been previously declared.

```
IF aCrsUnits > 3 THEN
    CourseFee := BaseFee + ((aCrsUnits – 3) * VarFee);
ELSE
    CourseFee := BaseFee;
END IF;

IF anOffLimit > NumEnrolled OR CourseOverRide = TRUE THEN
    NumEnrolled := NumEnrolled + 1;
    EnrDate := SysDate;
ELSE
    Enrolled := FALSE;
END IF;
```

Example 11.6   IF-THEN-ELSIF Statement Examples
It is assumed that variables used in the examples have been previously declared.

```
IF anOffTerm = 'Fall' AND Enrolled := TRUE THEN
    FallEnrolled := FallEnrolled + 1;
ELSIF anOffTerm = 'Spring' AND Enrolled := TRUE THEN
    SpringEnrolled := SpringEnrolled + 1;
ELSE
    SummerEnrolled := SummerEnrolled + 1;
END IF;


IF aStdClass = 'FR' THEN
    NumFR := NumFR + 1;
    NumStudents := NumStudents + 1;
ELSIF aStdClass = 'SO' THEN
    NumSO := NumSO + 1;
    NumStudents := NumStudents + 1;
ELSIF aStdClass = 'JR' THEN
    NumJR := NumJR + 1;
    NumStudents := NumStudents + 1;
ELSIF aStdClass = 'SR' THEN
    NumSR := NumSR + 1;
    NumStudents := NumStudents + 1;
END IF;
```

The CASE statement uses a selector instead of condition. A selector is an expression whose value determines a decision. Example 11.7 shows a CASE statement corresponding to the second part of Example 11.6. Note that the CASE statement is not part of PL/SQL for Oracle 8i. It is part of PL/SQL for Oracle 9i. All Oracle 8i versions give a syntax error for Example 11.7.

Example 11.7   CASE Statement Example Corresponding to the Second Part of Example 11.6
It is assumed that variables used in the example have been previously declared.

```
CASE aStdClass
 WHEN 'FR' THEN
    NumFR := NumFR + 1;
    NumStudents := NumStudents + 1;
 WHEN 'SO' THEN
    NumSO := NumSO + 1;
    NumStudents := NumStudents + 1;
 WHEN 'JR' THEN
    NumJR := NumJR + 1;
    NumStudents := NumStudents + 1;
 WHEN 'SR' THEN
    NumSR := NumSR + 1;
    NumStudents := NumStudents + 1;
END CASE;
```

CASE Statement:

```
CASE selector
    WHEN expression1 THEN sequence of statements 1
    WHEN expression2 THEN sequence of statements 2
    WHEN expressionN THEN sequence of statements N
    [   ELSE sequence of statements N+1   ]
END CASE;
```

Iteration Statements

PL/SQL contains three iteration statements along with a statement to terminate a loop. The FOR LOOP statement iterates over a range of integer values, as shown in Example 11.8. The WHILE LOOP statement iterates until a stopping condition is false, as shown in Example 11.9. The LOOP statement iterates until an EXIT statement causes termination, as shown in Example 11.10. Note that the EXIT statement can also be used in the FOR LOOP and the WHILE LOOP statements to cause early termination of a loop.

Example 11.8

FOR LOOP Statement Example

It is assumed that variables used in the example have been previously declared.

```
FOR Idx IN 1 . . NumStudents LOOP
    TotalUnits := TotalUnits + (Idx * aCrsUnits);
END LOOP;
```

Example 11.9

WHILE LOOP Statement Corresponding to Example 11.8

```
Idx := 1;
WHILE Idx < = NumStudents LOOP
    TotalUnits := TotalUnits + (Idx * aCrsUnits);
    Idx := Idx + 1;
END LOOP;
```

Example 11.10

LOOP Statement Corresponding to Example 11.8

```
Idx := 1;
LOOP
    TotalUnits := TotalUnits + (Idx * aCrsUnits);
    Idx := Idx + 1;
    EXIT WHEN Idx > NumStudents;
END LOOP;
```

FOR LOOP Statement:

```
FOR variable IN BeginExpr .. EndExpr LOOP
    sequence of statements
END LOOP;
```

WHILE LOOP Statement:

```
WHILE condition LOOP
    sequence of statements
END LOOP;
```

LOOP Statement:

```
LOOP
    sequence of statements containing an EXIT statement
END LOOP;
```

11.1.4 Executing PL/SQL Statements in Anonymous Blocks

PL/SQL is a block structured language. You will learn about named blocks in Section 11.2. This section introduces anonymous blocks so that you can execute statement examples in SQL *Plus, the most widely used tool for execution of PL/SQL statements. Anonymous blocks also are useful for testing procedures and triggers. Before presenting anonymous blocks, a brief introduction to SQL *Plus is provided.

To use SQL *Plus, you need an Oracle login name and password. Authentication to SQL *Plus is different than authentication to your operating system. After connecting to SQL *Plus, you will see the SQL> prompt. At the prompt, you can enter SQL statements, PL/SQL blocks, and SQL *Plus commands. Table 11.3 lists common SQL *Plus commands. To terminate an individual statement or SQL *Plus command, you use a semicolon at the end of the statement or command. To terminate a collection of statements or commands, you should use a slash (/) on a line by itself.

A PL/SQL block contains an optional declaration section (DECLARE keyword), an executable section (BEGIN keyword), and an optional exception section (EXCEPTION keyword). This section depicts anonymous blocks containing declaration and executable sections. Section 11.2 depicts the exception section.

TABLE 11.3	List of Common SQL *Plus Commands

Command	Example and Meaning
CONNECT	CONNECT UserName@DatabaseId/Password opens a connection to DatabaseId for UserName with Password
DESCRIBE	DESCRIBE TableName lists the columns of TableName
EXECUTE	EXECUTE Statement executes the PL/SQL statement
HELP	HELP ColumnName describes ColumnName
SET	SET SERVEROUTPUT ON causes the results of PL/SQL statements to be displayed
SHOW	SHOW ERRORS causes compilation errors to be displayed
SPOOL	SPOOL FileName causes the output to be written to FileName; SPOOL OFF stops spooling to a file
/	Use on a line by itself to terminate a collection of statements or SQL *Plus commands

Block Structure:
```
[  DECLARE
      sequence of declarations    ]
BEGIN
      sequence of statements
[  EXCEPTION
      sequence of statements to respond to exceptions    ]
END;
```

To demonstrate anonymous blocks, Example 11.11 computes the sum and product of integers 1 to 10. The *Dbms_Output.Put_Line* procedure displays the results. The *Dbms_Output* package contains procedures and functions to read and write lines in a buffer. Example 11.12 modifies Example 11.11 to compute the sum of the odd numbers and the product of the even numbers.

Example 11.11

Anonymous Block to Compute the Sum and the Product
The first line (SET command) and the last line (/) are not part of the anonymous block.

```
-- SQL *Plus command
SET SERVEROUTPUT ON;
-- Anonymous block
DECLARE
  TmpSum      INTEGER;
  TmpProd     INTEGER;
  Idx         INTEGER;
BEGIN
-- Initialize temporary variables
  TmpSum := 0;
  TmpProd := 1;
  -- Use a loop to compute the sum and product
  FOR Idx IN 1 .. 10 LOOP
      TmpSum := TmpSum + Idx;
      TmpProd := TmpProd * Idx;
  END LOOP;
  -- Display the results
  Dbms_Output.Put_Line('Sum is' | | To_Char(TmpSum) );
  Dbms_Output.Put_Line('Product is' | | To_Char(TmpProd) );
END;
/
```

Example 11.12

Anonymous Block to Compute the Sum of the Even Numbers and the Product of the Even Numbers.
The SET command is not necessary if it was used for Example 11.11 in the same session of SQL *Plus.

```
SET SERVEROUTPUT ON;
DECLARE
  TmpSum      INTEGER;
  TmpProd     INTEGER;
  Idx         INTEGER;
```

```
BEGIN
-- Initialize temporary variables
  TmpSum := 0;
  TmpProd := 1;
  -- Use a loop to compute the sum and product
  -- Mod(X,Y) returns the integer remainder of X/Y.
  FOR Idx IN 1 .. 10 LOOP
      IF Mod(Idx,2) = 0 THEN -- even number
        TmpSum := TmpSum + Idx;
      ELSE
        TmpProd := TmpProd * Idx;
      END IF;
  END LOOP;
  -- Display the results
  Dbms_Output.Put_Line('Sum is' | | To_Char(TmpSum) );
  Dbms_Output.Put_Line('Product is' | | To_Char(TmpProd) );
END;
/
```

11.2 STORED PROCEDURES

With background about database programming languages and PL/SQL, you are now ready to learn about stored procedures. Programming languages have supported procedures since the early days of business computing. Procedures support the management of complexity by allowing computing tasks to be divided into manageable chunks. A database procedure is like a programming language procedure except that it is managed by the DBMS, not the programming environment. The following list explains the reasons for a DBMS to manage procedures:

- A DBMS can compile the programming language code along with the SQL statements in a stored procedure. In addition, a DBMS can detect when the SQL statements in a procedure need to be recompiled due to changes in database definitions.

- Stored procedures allow flexibility for client–server development. The stored procedures are saved on a server and not replicated on each client. In the early days of client–server computing, the ability to store procedures on a server was a major motivation for stored procedures. With the development of distributed objects on the Web, this motivation is not as important now because there are other technologies for managing stored procedures.

- Stored procedures allow for the development of more complex operators and functions than supported by SQL. Chapter 18 describes the importance of specialized procedures and functions in object-oriented databases.

- Database administrators can manage stored procedures with the same tools for managing other parts of a database application. Most importantly, stored procedures are managed by the security system of the DBMS.

This section covers PL/SQL procedures, functions, and packages. Some additional parts of PL/SQL (cursors and exceptions) are shown to demonstrate the utility of stored procedures. Testing scripts assume that the university tables are populated according to the data on the textbook's website.

11.2.1 PL/SQL Procedures

In PL/SQL, a procedure is a named block with an optional set of parameters. Each parameter contains a parameter name, a usage (IN, OUT, IN OUT), and a data type. An input parameter (IN) should not be changed inside a procedure. An output parameter (OUT) is given a value inside a procedure. An input–output parameter (IN OUT) should have a value provided outside a procedure but can be changed inside a procedure. The data type specification should not include any constraints such as length. For example, for a string parameter you should use the data type VARCHAR2. You do not provide a length in the specification of the data type for a parameter.

PROCEDURE STRUCTURE:
```
CREATE [OR REPLACE] PROCEDURE ProcedureName
    [  (Parameter1, . . ., ParameterN)   ]
IS
    [   sequence of declarations   ]
BEGIN
    sequence of statements
[   EXCEPTION
    sequence of statements to respond to exceptions   ]
END;
```

As a simple example, the procedure *pr_InsertRegistration* in Example 11.13 inserts a row into the *Registration* table of the university database. The input parameters provide the values to insert. The *Dbms_Output.Put_Line* procedure call displays a message that the insert was successful.

Example 11.13

Procedure to Insert a Row into the *Registration* Table Along with Code to Test the Procedure

```
CREATE OR REPLACE PROCEDURE pr_InsertRegistration
 (aRegNo IN Registration.RegNo%TYPE,
  aStdSSN IN Registration.StdSSN%TYPE,
  aRegStatus IN Registration.RegStatus%TYPE,
  aRegDate IN Registration.RegDate%TYPE,
  aRegTerm IN Registration.RegTerm%TYPE,
  aRegYear IN Registration.RegYear%TYPE) IS
-- Create a new registration
BEGIN

INSERT INTO Registration
        (RegNo, StdSSN, RegStatus, RegDate, RegTerm, RegYear)
VALUES (aRegNo, aStdSSN, aRegStatus, aRegDate, aRegTerm, aRegYear);

dbms_output.put_line('Added a row to the Registration table');

END;
/

-- Testing code
SET SERVEROUTPUT ON;
```

```
-- Number of rows before the procedure execution
SELECT COUNT(*) FROM Registration;

BEGIN
pr_InsertRegistration
   (1275, '901-23-4567','F',To_Date('27-Feb-2003'),'Spring',2003);
END;
/
-- Number of rows after the procedure execution
SELECT COUNT(*) FROM Registration;
-- Delete the inserted row using the ROLLBACK statement
ROLLBACK;
```

To enable *pr_InsertRegistration* to be used by other procedures, a better design would replace the output display with an output parameter indicating the success or failure of the insertion. Example 11.14 modifies Example 11.13 to use an output parameter. The OTHERS exception catches a variety of errors such as a violation of a primary key constraint or a foreign key constraint. You should use the OTHERS exception when you do not need specialized code for each kind of exception. To catch a specific error, you should use a predefined exception (Table 11.4) or create a user-defined exception. A later section contains an example of a user-defined exception. After the procedure, the script includes test cases for a successful insert as well as a primary key constraint violation.

| **Example 11.14** | Procedure to Insert a Row into the *Registration* Table Along with Code to Test the Procedure |

```
CREATE OR REPLACE PROCEDURE pr_InsertRegistration
 (aRegNo IN Registration.RegNo%TYPE,
  aStdSSN IN Registration.StdSSN%TYPE,
  aRegStatus IN Registration.RegStatus%TYPE,
  aRegDate IN Registration.RegDate%TYPE,
  aRegTerm IN Registration.RegTerm%TYPE,
  aRegYear IN Registration.RegYear%TYPE,
  aResult OUT BOOLEAN ) IS
-- Create a new registration
-- aResult is TRUE if successful, false otherwise.
BEGIN
aResult := TRUE;
INSERT INTO Registration
        (RegNo, StdSSN, RegStatus, RegDate, RegTerm, RegYear)
VALUES (aRegNo, aStdSSN, aRegStatus, aRegDate, aRegTerm, aRegYear);

EXCEPTION
WHEN OTHERS THEN aResult := FALSE;
END;
/
```

```
-- Testing code
SET SERVEROUTPUT ON;
-- Number of rows before the procedure execution
SELECT COUNT(*) FROM Registration;
DECLARE
  -- Output parameter must be declared in the calling block
  Result BOOLEAN;
BEGIN
-- This test should succeed.
-- Procedure assigns value to the output parameter (Result).
pr_InsertRegistration
(1275,'901-23-4567','F', To_Date('27-Feb-2003'),'Spring',2003,Result);
IF Result THEN
    dbms_output.put_line('Added a row to the Registration table');
ELSE
    dbms_output.put_line('Row not added to the Registration table');
END IF;

-- This test should fail because of the duplicate primary key.
pr_InsertRegistration
(1275,'901-23-4567','F',To_Date('27-Feb-2003'),'Spring',2003,Result);
IF Result THEN
    dbms_output.put_line('Added a row to the Registration table');
ELSE
    dbms_output.put_line('Row not added to the Registration table');
END IF;
END;
/

-- Number of rows after the procedure executions
SELECT COUNT(*) FROM Registration;
-- Delete inserted row
ROLLBACK;
```

Table 11.4	**List of Common Predefined PL/SQL Exceptions**
Exception	*When Raised*
Cursor_Already_Open	Attempt to open a cursor that has been previously opened
Dup_Val_On_Index	Attempt to store a duplicate value in a unique index
Invalid_Cursor	Attempt to perform an invalid operation on a cursor such as closing a cursor that was not previously opened
No_Data_Found	SELECT INTO statement returns no rows
Rowtype_Mismatch	Attempt to assign values with incompatible data types between a cursor and a variable
Timeout_On_Resource	Timeout occurs such as when waiting for an exclusive lock
Too_Many_Rows	SELECT INTO statement returns more than one row

11.2.2 PL/SQL Functions

Functions should return values instead of manipulating output variables and having side effects such as inserting a row. You should always use a procedure if you want to have more than one result and/or have a side effect. Functions should be usable in expressions, meaning that a function call can be replaced by the value it returns. A PL/SQL function is similar to a procedure in that both contain a parameter list. However, a function should use only input parameters. After the parameter list, the return data type is defined. In the function body, the sequence of statements should include a RETURN statement to generate the function's output value.

Function Structure:

```
CREATE [OR REPLACE] FUNCTION FunctionName
    [  (Parameter1, . . ., ParameterN)   ]
RETURN DataType
IS
    [  sequence of declarations   ]
BEGIN
    sequence of statements including a RETURN statement
[  EXCEPTION
    sequence of statements to respond to exceptions   ]
END;
```

As a simple example, the function *fn_RetrieveStdName* in Example 11.15 retrieves the name of a student given the social security number. The predefined exception *No_Data_Found* is true if the SELECT statement does not return at least one row. The SELECT statement uses the INTO clause to associate the variables with the database columns. The INTO clause can be used only when the SELECT statement returns at most one row. If an INTO clause is used when a SELECT statement returns more than one row, an exception is generated. The *Raise_Application_Error* procedure displays an error message and an error number. This predefined procedure is useful to handle unexpected errors.

Example 11.15   Function to Retrieve the Student Name Given the Student SSN

```
CREATE OR REPLACE FUNCTION fn_RetrieveStdName
(aStdSSN IN Student.StdSSN%type) RETURN VARCHAR2 IS
-- Retrieves the student name (concatenate first and last name)
-- given a student SSN. If the student does not exist,
-- return null.
aFirstName Student.StdFirstName%TYPE;
aLastName Student.StdLastName%TYPE;

BEGIN

SELECT StdFirstName, StdLastName
  INTO aFirstName, aLastName
  FROM Student
  WHERE StdSSN = aStdSSN;

RETURN(aLastName | | ', ' | | aFirstName);
```

```
EXCEPTION
-- No_Data_Found is raised if the SELECT statement returns no data.
  WHEN No_Data_Found THEN
    RETURN(NULL);

  WHEN OTHERS THEN
    raise_application_error(-20001, 'Database error');

END;
/
-- Testing code
SET SERVEROUTPUT ON;
DECLARE
aStdName VARCHAR2(50);
BEGIN
-- This call should display a student name.
aStdName := fn_RetrieveStdName('901-23-4567');
IF aStdName IS NULL THEN
    dbms_output.put_line('Student not found');
ELSE
    dbms_output.put_line('Name is ' || aStdName);
END IF;

-- This call should not display a student name.
aStdName := fn_RetrieveStdName('905-23-4567');
IF aStdName IS NULL THEN
    dbms_output.put_line('Student not found');
ELSE
    dbms_output.put_line('Name is ' || aStdName);
END IF;
END;
/
```

Example 11.16 shows a function with a more complex query than the function in Example 11.15. The testing code contains two cases to test for an existing student and a nonexisting student along with a SELECT statement that uses the function in the result. An important benefit of functions is that they can be used in expressions in SELECT statements.

Example 11.16   Function to Compute the Weighted GPA Given the Student SSN and Year

```
CREATE OR REPLACE FUNCTION fn_ComputeWeightedGPA
(aStdSSN IN Student.StdSSN%TYPE, aYear IN Offering.OffYear%TYPE)
  RETURN NUMBER IS
-- Computes the weighted GPA given a student SSN and year.
-- Weighted GPA is the sum of units times the grade
-- divided by the total units.
-- If the student does not exist, return null.
```

```
WeightedGPA NUMBER;

BEGIN
SELECT SUM(EnrGrade*CrsUnits)/ SUM(CrsUnits)
  INTO WeightedGPA
  FROM Student, Registration, Enrollment, Offering, Course
  WHERE Student.StdSSN = aStdSSN
      AND Offering.OffYear = aYear
      AND Student.StdSSN = Registration.StdSSN
      AND Registration.RegNo = Enrollment.RegNo
      AND Enrollment.OfferNo = Offering.OfferNo
      AND Offering.CourseNo = Course.CourseNo;

RETURN(WeightedGPA);

EXCEPTION
  WHEN No_Data_Found THEN
    RETURN(NULL);

  WHEN OTHERS THEN
    raise_application_error(-20001, 'Database error');

END;
/
-- Testing code
SET SERVEROUTPUT ON;
DECLARE
aGPA DECIMAL(3,2);
BEGIN
-- This call should display a weighted GPA.
aGPA := fn_ComputeWeightedGPA('901-23-4567', 2003);
IF aGPA IS NULL THEN
    dbms_output.put_line('Student or enrollments not found');
ELSE
    dbms_output.put_line('Weighted GPA is ' || to_char(aGPA));
END IF;

-- This call should not display a weighted GPA.
aGPA := fn_ComputeWeightedGPA('905-23-4567', 2003);
IF aGPA IS NULL THEN
    dbms_output.put_line('Student or enrollments not found');
ELSE
    dbms_output.put_line('Weighted GPA is ' || to_char(aGPA));
END IF;
END;
/
-- Use the function in a query
SELECT StdSSN, StdFirstName, StdLastName,
        fn_ComputeWeightedGPA(StdSSN, 2003) AS WeightedGPA
FROM Student;
```

11.2.3 Using Cursors

The previous procedures and functions are rather simple as they involve retrieval of a single row. More complex procedures and functions involve iteration through multiple rows using a cursor. PL/SQL provides cursor declaration (explicit or implicit), a specialized FOR statement for cursor iteration, cursor attributes to indicate the status of cursor operations, and statements to perform actions on explicit cursors. PL/SQL supports static cursors in which the SQL statement is known at compile-time as well as dynamic cursors in which the SQL statement is not determined until run-time.

Example 11.17 depicts an implicit cursor to return the class rank of a student in an offering. Implicit cursors are not declared in the DECLARE section. Instead, implicit cursors are declared, opened, and iterated inside a FOR statement. In Example 11.17, the FOR statement iterates through each row of the SELECT statement using the implicit cursor *EnrollRec*. The SELECT statement sorts the result in descending order by enrollment grade. The function exits the FOR statement when the *StdSSN* value matches the parameter value. The class rank is incremented only when the grade changes so that two students with the same grade have the same rank.

Implicit PL/SQL Cursor a cursor that is neither explicitly declared nor explicitly opened. Instead a special version of the FOR statement declares, opens, iterates, and closes a locally named SELECT statement. An implicit cursor cannot be referenced outside of the FOR statement in which it is declared.

....

Example 11.17   Using an implicit cursor to determine the class rank of a given student and offering

```
CREATE OR REPLACE FUNCTION fn_DetermineRank
(aStdSSN IN Student.StdSSN%TYPE, anOfferNo IN Offering.OfferNo%TYPE)
    RETURN INTEGER IS
-- Determines the class rank for a given student SSN and OfferNo.
-- Uses an implicit cursor.
-- If the student or offering does not exist, return 0.
TmpRank INTEGER := 0;
PrevEnrGrade Enrollment.EnrGrade%TYPE := 9.9;
FOUND BOOLEAN := FALSE;

BEGIN
-- Loop through implicit cursor
FOR EnrollRec IN
  (   SELECT Student.StdSSN, EnrGrade
      FROM Student, Registration, Enrollment
      WHERE Enrollment.OfferNo = anOfferNo
        AND Student.StdSSN = Registration.StdSSN
        AND Registration.RegNo = Enrollment.RegNo
      ORDER BY EnrGrade DESC   ) LOOP

      IF EnrollRec.EnrGrade < PrevEnrGrade THEN
      -- Increment the class rank when the grade changes
        TmpRank := TmpRank + 1;
        PrevEnrGrade := EnrollRec.EnrGrade;
      END IF;
      IF   EnrollRec.StdSSN = aStdSSN THEN
          Found := TRUE;
          EXIT;
      END IF;
  END LOOP;
```

```
IF Found THEN
    RETURN(TmpRank);
ELSE
    RETURN(0);
END IF;

EXCEPTION
WHEN OTHERS THEN
        raise_application_error(-20001, 'Database error');

END;
/
-- Testing code
SET SERVEROUTPUT ON;
-- Execute query to see test data
SELECT Student.StdSSN, EnrGrade
  FROM Student, Registration, Enrollment
  WHERE Enrollment.OfferNo = 5679
      AND Student.StdSSN = Registration.StdSSN
      AND Registration.RegNo = Enrollment.RegNo
  ORDER BY EnrGrade DESC;

-- Test script
DECLARE
aRank INTEGER;
BEGIN
-- This call should return a rank of 6.
aRank := fn_DetermineRank('789-01-2345', 5679);
IF aRank > 0 THEN
    dbms_output.put_line('Rank is ' | | to_char(aRank));
ELSE
    dbms_output.put_line('Student is not enrolled.');
END IF;

-- This call should return a rank of 0.
aRank := fn_DetermineRank('789-01-2005', 5679);
IF aRank > 0 THEN
    dbms_output.put_line('Rank is ' | | to_char(aRank));
ELSE
    dbms_output.put_line('Student is not enrolled.');
END IF;
END;
/
```

Explicit PL/SQL Cursor a cursor that is declared with the CURSOR statement in the DECLARE section. Explicit cursors are usually manipulated by the OPEN, CLOSE, and FETCH statements. Explicit cursors can be referenced anyplace inside the BEGIN section.

Example 11.18 depicts a procedure with an explicit cursor to return the class rank and the grade of a student in an offering. The explicit cursor *EnrollCursor* in the CURSOR statement contains offer number as a parameter. Explicit cursors must use parameters for nonconstant search values in the associated SELECT statement. The

OPEN, FETCH, and CLOSE statements replace the FOR statement of Example 11.17. After the FETCH statement, the condition *EnrollCursor%NotFound* tests for the empty cursor.

Example 11.18   Using an Explicit Cursor to Determine the Class Rank and Grade of a Given Student and Offering

```
CREATE OR REPLACE PROCEDURE pr_DetermineRank
(aStdSSN IN Student.StdSSN%TYPE, anOfferNo IN Offering.OfferNo%TYPE,
 OutRank OUT INTEGER, OutGrade OUT Enrollment.EnrGrade%TYPE  ) IS
-- Determines the class rank and grade for a given student SSN
-- and OfferNo using an explicit cursor.
-- If the student or offering does not exist, return 0.
TmpRank INTEGER := 0;
PrevEnrGrade Enrollment.EnrGrade%TYPE := 9.9;
Found BOOLEAN := FALSE;
TmpGrade Enrollment.EnrGrade%TYPE;
TmpStdSSN Student.StdSSN%TYPE;
-- Explicit cursor
CURSOR EnrollCursor (tmpOfferNo Offering.OfferNo%TYPE) IS
  SELECT Student.StdSSN, EnrGrade
    FROM Student, Registration, Enrollment
    WHERE Enrollment.OfferNo = anOfferNo
       AND Student.StdSSN = Registration.StdSSN
       AND Registration.RegNo = Enrollment.RegNo
    ORDER BY EnrGrade DESC;

BEGIN
-- Open and loop through explicit cursor
OPEN EnrollCursor(anOfferNo);
LOOP
      FETCH EnrollCursor INTO TmpStdSSN, TmpGrade;
      EXIT WHEN EnrollCursor%NotFound;
      IF TmpGrade < PrevEnrGrade THEN
      -- Increment the class rank when the grade changes
        TmpRank := TmpRank + 1;
        PrevEnrGrade := TmpGrade;
      END IF;
      IF TmpStdSSN = aStdSSN THEN
        Found := TRUE;
        EXIT;
      END IF;
END LOOP;

CLOSE EnrollCursor;
IF Found THEN
  OutRank := TmpRank;
  OutGrade := PrevEnrGrade;
ELSE
```

```
        OutRank := 0;
        OutGrade := 0;
END IF;

EXCEPTION
WHEN OTHERS THEN
    raise_application_error(-20001, 'Database error');
END;
/
-- Testing code
SET SERVEROUTPUT ON;
-- Execute query to see test data
SELECT Student.StdSSN, EnrGrade
  FROM Student, Registration, Enrollment
  WHERE Student.StdSSN = Registration.StdSSN
      AND Registration.RegNo = Enrollment.RegNo
      AND Enrollment.OfferNo = 5679
  ORDER BY EnrGrade DESC;

-- Test script
DECLARE
aRank INTEGER;
aGrade Enrollment.EnrGrade%TYPE;
BEGIN
-- This call should produce a rank of 6.
pr_DetermineRank('789-01-2345', 5679, aRank, aGrade);
IF aRank > 0 THEN
    dbms_output.put_line('Rank is ' || to_char(aRank) || '.');
    dbms_output.put_line('Grade is ' || to_char(aGrade) || '.');
ELSE
    dbms_output.put_line('Student is not enrolled.');
END IF;

-- This call should produce a rank of 0.
pr_DetermineRank('789-01-2005', 5679, aRank, aGrade);
IF aRank > 0 THEN
    dbms_output.put_line('Rank is ' || to_char(aRank) || '.');
    dbms_output.put_line('Grade is ' || to_char(aGrade) || '.');
ELSE
    dbms_output.put_line('Student is not enrolled.');
END IF;
END;
/
```

PL/SQL supports a number of cursor attributes as listed in Table 11.5. When used with an explicit cursor, the cursor name precedes the cursor attribute. When used with an implicit cursor, the SQL keyword precedes the cursor attribute. For example, *SQL%RowCount* denotes the number of rows in an implicit cursor. The implicit cursor name is not used.

Table 11.5	List of Common Cursor Attributes

Cursor Attribute	Value
%IsOpen	True if cursor is open.
%Found	True if cursor is not empty following a FETCH statement.
%NotFound	True if cursor is empty following a FETCH statement.
%RowCount	Number of rows fetched. After each FETCH, the RowCount is incremented.

11.2.4 PL/SQL Packages

Packages support a larger unit of modularity than procedures or functions. A package may contain procedures, functions, exceptions, variables, constants, types, and cursors. By grouping related objects together, a package provides easier reuse than individual procedures and functions. Oracle provides many predefined packages such as the *DBMS_Output* package containing groups of related objects. In addition, a package separates a public interface from a private implementation to support reduced software maintenance efforts. Changes to a private implementation do not affect the usage of a package through its interface. Chapter 18 on object databases provides more details about the benefits of larger units of modularity.

A package interface contains the definitions of procedures and functions along with other objects that can be specified in the DECLARE section of a PL/SQL block. All objects in a package interface are public. Example 11.19 demonstrates the interface for a package combining some of the procedures and functions presented in previous sections.

Package Interface Structure
```
CREATE [OR REPLACE] PACKAGE PackageName IS
[   Constant, variable, and type declarations   ]
[   Cursor declarations   ]
[   Exception declarations   ]
[   Procedure definitions   ]
[   Function definitions   ]
END PackageName;
```

Example 11.19	Package Interface Containing Related Procedures and Functions for the University Database

```
CREATE OR REPLACE PACKAGE pck_University IS
PROCEDURE pr_DetermineRank
 (aStdSSN IN Student.StdSSN%TYPE, anOfferNo IN Offering.OfferNo%TYPE,
    OutRank OUT INTEGER, OutGrade OUT Enrollment.EnrGrade%TYPE );
FUNCTION fn_ComputeWeightedGPA
(aStdSSN IN Student.StdSSN%TYPE, aYear IN Offering.OffYear%TYPE)
    RETURN NUMBER;
END pck_University;
/
```

A package implementation or body contains the private details of a package. For each object in the package interface, the package body must define an implementation. In addition, private objects can be defined in a package body. Private objects can be used only inside the package body. External users of a package cannot access private objects. Example 11.20 demonstrates the body for the package interface in Example 11.19. Note that each procedure or function terminates with an END statement containing the procedure or function name. Otherwise the procedure and function implementations are identical to creating a procedure or function outside of a package.

Package Body Structure:

```
CREATE [OR REPLACE] PACKAGE BODY PackageName IS
[   Variable and type declarations   ]
[   Cursor declarations   ]
[   Exception declarations   ]
[   Procedure implementations   ]
[   Function implementations   ]
[   BEGIN sequence of statements   ]
[   EXCEPTION exception handling statements   ]
END PackageName;
```

| *Example 11.20* | Package Body Containing Implementations of Procedures and Functions |

```
CREATE OR REPLACE PACKAGE BODY pck_University IS
PROCEDURE pr_DetermineRank
  (aStdSSN IN Student.StdSSN%TYPE, anOfferNo IN Offering.OfferNo%TYPE,
     OutRank OUT INTEGER, OutGrade OUT Enrollment.EnrGrade%TYPE ) IS
-- Determines the class rank and grade for a given student SSN
-- and OfferNo using an explicit cursor.
-- If the student or offering does not exist, return 0.
TmpRank INTEGER := 0;
PrevEnrGrade Enrollment.EnrGrade%TYPE := 9.9;
Found BOOLEAN := FALSE;
TmpGrade Enrollment.EnrGrade%TYPE;
TmpStdSSN Student.StdSSN%TYPE;
-- Explicit cursor
CURSOR EnrollCursor (tmpOfferNo Offering.OfferNo%TYPE) IS
    SELECT Student.StdSSN, EnrGrade
    FROM Student, Registration, Enrollment
    WHERE Enrollment.OfferNo = anOfferNo
      AND Student.StdSSN = Registration.StdSSN
      AND Registration.RegNo = Enrollment.RegNo
    ORDER BY EnrGrade DESC;

BEGIN
-- Open and loop through explicit cursor
OPEN EnrollCursor(anOfferNo);
LOOP
    FETCH EnrollCursor INTO TmpStdSSN, TmpGrade;
    EXIT WHEN EnrollCursor%NotFound;
```

```
            IF TmpGrade < PrevEnrGrade THEN
            -- Increment the class rank when the grade changes
               TmpRank := TmpRank + 1;
               PrevEnrGrade := TmpGrade;
            END IF;
            IF TmpStdSSN = aStdSSN THEN
               Found := TRUE;
               EXIT;
            END IF;
   END LOOP;

   CLOSE EnrollCursor;
   IF Found THEN
      OutRank := TmpRank;
      OutGrade := PrevEnrGrade;
   ELSE
      OutRank := 0;
      OutGrade := 0;
   END IF;

   EXCEPTION
   WHEN OTHERS THEN
      raise_application_error(-20001, 'Database error');
   END pr_DetermineRank;

   FUNCTION fn_ComputeWeightedGPA
   (aStdSSN IN Student.StdSSN%TYPE, aYear IN Offering.OffYear%TYPE)
      RETURN NUMBER IS
   -- Computes the weighted GPA given a student SSN and year.
   -- Weighted GPA is the sum of units times the grade
   -- divided by the total units.
   -- If the student does not exist, return null.
   WeightedGPA NUMBER;

   BEGIN

   SELECT SUM(EnrGrade*CrsUnits)/ SUM(CrsUnits)
      INTO WeightedGPA
      FROM Student, Registration, Enrollment, Offering, Course
      WHERE Student.StdSSN = aStdSSN
         AND Offering.OffYear = aYear
         AND Student.StdSSN = Registration.StdSSN
         AND Registration.RegNo = Enrollment.RegNo
         AND Enrollment.OfferNo = Offering.OfferNo
         AND Offering.CourseNo = Course.CourseNo;

   RETURN(WeightedGPA);

   EXCEPTION
    WHEN no_data_found THEN
```

```
    RETURN(NULL);

  WHEN OTHERS THEN
    raise_application_error(-20001, 'Database error');

END fn_ComputeWeightedGPA;
END pck_University;
/
```

To use the objects in a package, you need to use the package name before the object name. In Example 11.21, you should note that the package name (*pck_University*) precedes the procedure and function names.

Example 11.21   Script to Use the Procedures and Functions of the University Package

```
SET SERVEROUTPUT ON;
DECLARE
aRank INTEGER;
aGrade Enrollment.EnrGrade%TYPE;
aGPA NUMBER;
BEGIN
-- This call should produce a rank of 6.
pck_University.pr_DetermineRank('789-01-2345', 5679, aRank, aGrade);
IF aRank > 0 THEN
    dbms_output.put_line('Rank is ' || to_char(aRank) || '.');
    dbms_output.put_line('Grade is ' || to_char(aGrade) || '.');
ELSE
    dbms_output.put_line('Student is not enrolled.');
END IF;
-- This call should display a weighted GPA.
aGPA := pck_University.fn_ComputeWeightedGPA('901-23-4567', 2003);
IF aGPA IS NULL THEN
    dbms_output.put_line('Student or enrollments not found');
ELSE
    dbms_output.put_line('Weighted GPA is ' || to_char(aGPA) );
END IF;
END;
/
```

11.3 TRIGGERS

Trigger a rule that is stored and executed by a DBMS. Because a trigger involves an event, a condition, and a sequence of actions, it also is known as an event-condition-action rule.

Triggers are rules managed by a DBMS. Because a trigger involves an event, a condition, and a sequence of actions, it also is known as an event-condition-action rule. Writing the action part or trigger body is similar to writing a procedure or a function except that a trigger has no parameters. Triggers are executed by the rule system of the DBMS not by explicit calls as for procedures and functions. Triggers are part of SQL:1999 although not part of SQL-92. However most DBMS vendors implemented triggers long before the release of SQL:1999.

This section covers Oracle triggers with background about SQL:1999 triggers. The first part of this section discusses the reasons that triggers are important parts of database application development and provides a classification of triggers. The second part demonstrates trigger coding in PL/SQL. The final part presents the trigger execution procedures of Oracle and SQL:1999.

11.3.1 Motivation and Classification of Triggers

Triggers are widely implemented in DBMSs because they have a variety of uses in business applications. The following list explains typical uses of triggers.

- **Complex integrity constraints:** Integrity constraints that cannot be declaratively specified by check constraints in CREATE TABLE statements and assertions (see Chapter 14). Most DBMSs impose limitations on check constraints and do not support assertions.
- **Transition constraints:** Integrity constraints that compare the values before and after an update occurs. For example, you can write a trigger to enforce the transition constraint that salary increases do not exceed 10 percent.
- **Update propagation:** Update derived columns in related tables such as to maintain perpetual inventory balance or the seats remaining on a scheduled flight.
- **Exception reporting:** Create a record of unusual conditions as an alternative to rejecting a transaction. A trigger also can send a notification in an e-mail message. For example, instead of rejecting a salary increase of 10 percent, a trigger can create an exception record and notify a manager to review the salary increase.
- **Audit trail:** Create a historical record of a transaction such as a history of automated teller usage.

SQL:1999 classifies triggers by granularity, timing, and applicable event. For granularity, a trigger can involve each row affected by an SQL statement or an entire SQL statement. Row triggers are more common than statement triggers. For timing, a trigger can fire before or after an event. Typically, triggers for constraint checking fire before an event, while triggers updating related tables and performing other actions fire after an event. For applicable event, a trigger can apply to INSERT, UPDATE, and DELETE statements. Update triggers can specify a list of applicable columns.

Because the SQL:1999 trigger specification was defined in response to vendor implementations, most trigger implementations vary from the SQL:1999 specification. Oracle supports most parts of the specification while adding proprietary extensions. An important extension is the INSTEAD trigger that fires in place of an event, not before or after an event. Oracle also supports data definition events and other database events. SQL Server 2000 provides statement triggers with access to row data in place of row triggers. Thus, most DBMSs support the spirit of the SQL:1999 trigger specification in trigger granularity, timing, and applicable events but do not adhere strictly to the SQL:1999 trigger syntax.

11.3.2 Oracle Triggers

An Oracle trigger contains a trigger name, a timing specification, an optional referencing clause, an optional granularity, an optional condition, and a PL/SQL block for the body. The timing specification involves the keywords BEFORE, AFTER, or INSTEAD OF along with a triggering event using the keywords INSERT, UPDATE, or DELETE.

With the UPDATE event, you can specify an optional list of columns. To specify multiple events, you can use the OR keyword. Oracle also supports data definition and other database events, but these events are beyond the scope of this chapter. The referencing clause allows alias names for the old and new data that can be referenced in a trigger. The granularity is specified by the FOR EACH ROW keywords. If you omit these keywords, the trigger is a statement trigger. Because Oracle has numerous restrictions on the condition in the WHEN clause, the WHEN clause is used infrequently. The body of a trigger looks like other PL/SQL blocks except that triggers have more restrictions on the statements in a block.

Oracle Trigger Structure:

```
CREATE [OR REPLACE] TRIGGER TriggerName
TriggerTiming TriggerEvent
[   Referencing clause   ]
[   FOR EACH ROW   ]
[   WHEN (   Condition   )   ]
[   DECLARE sequence of declarative statements   ]
BEGIN sequence of statements
[   EXCEPTION exception handling statements   ]
END;
```

Introductory Triggers and Testing Code

To start on some simple Oracle triggers, Examples 11.22 through 11.24 contain triggers that fire respectively on every INSERT, UPDATE, and DELETE statement on the *Course* table. Example 11.25 demonstrates a trigger with a combined event that fires for every action on the *Course* table. The triggers in Examples 11.22 through 11.25 have no purpose except to depict a wide range of trigger syntax as explained in the following list.

- A common naming scheme for triggers identifies the table name, the triggering actions (*I* for INSERT, *U* for UPDATE, and *D* for DELETE), and the timing (*B* for BEFORE and *A* for AFTER). For example, the last part of the trigger name (DIUA) in Example 11.25 denotes the DELETE, INSERT, and UPDATE events along with the AFTER timing.
- In Example 11.25, the OR keyword in the trigger event specification supports compound events involving more than one event.
- There is no referencing clause as the default names for the old (*:OLD*) and the new (*:NEW*) row are used in the trigger bodies.

Example 11.22   Trigger That Fires for INSERT Statement on the *Course* Table Along with Testing Code to Fire the Trigger

```
CREATE OR REPLACE TRIGGER tr_Course_IA
AFTER INSERT
ON Course
FOR EACH ROW
BEGIN
        -- No references to OLD row because only NEW exists for INSERT
        dbms_output.put_line('Inserted Row');
        dbms_output.put_line('CourseNo: ' | | :NEW.CourseNo);
        dbms_output.put_line('Course Description: ' | | :NEW.CrsDesc);
```

```
            dbms_output.put_line('Course Units: ' | | To_Char(:NEW.CrsUnits));
END;
/
-- Testing statements
SET SERVEROUTPUT ON;
INSERT INTO Course (CourseNo, CrsDesc, CrsUnits)
VALUES ('IS485','Advanced Database Management',4);
ROLLBACK;
```

| **Example 11.23** | Trigger That Fires for Every UPDATE Statement on the *Course* Table Along with Testing Code to Fire the Trigger |

```
CREATE OR REPLACE TRIGGER tr_Course_UA
AFTER UPDATE
ON Course
FOR EACH ROW
BEGIN
      dbms_output.put_line('New Row Values');
      dbms_output.put_line('CourseNo: ' | | :NEW.CourseNo);
      dbms_output.put_line('Course Description: ' | | :NEW.CrsDesc);
      dbms_output.put_line('Course Units: ' | | To_Char(:NEW.CrsUnits));

      dbms_output.put_line('Old Row Values');
      dbms_output.put_line('CourseNo: ' | | :OLD.CourseNo);
      dbms_output.put_line('Course Description: ' | | :OLD.CrsDesc);
      dbms_output.put_line('Course Units: ' | | To_Char(:OLD.CrsUnits));
END;
/
-- Testing statements
SET SERVEROUTPUT ON;
-- Add row so it can be updated
INSERT INTO Course (CourseNo, CrsDesc, CrsUnits)
 VALUES ('IS485','Advanced Database Management',4);

UPDATE Course
 SET CrsUnits = 3
 WHERE CourseNo = 'IS485';

ROLLBACK;
```

| **Example 11.24** | Trigger That Fires for Every DELETE Statement on the *Course* Table Along with Testing Code to Fire the Trigger |

```
CREATE OR REPLACE TRIGGER tr_Course_DA
AFTER DELETE
ON Course
FOR EACH ROW
BEGIN
      -- No references to NEW row because only OLD exists for DELETE
      dbms_output.put_line('Deleted Row');
      dbms_output.put_line('CourseNo: ' | | :OLD.CourseNo);
```

```
        dbms_output.put_line('Course Description: ' || :OLD.CrsDesc);
        dbms_output.put_line('Course Units: ' || To_Char(:OLD.CrsUnits) ) ;
END;
/
-- Testing statements
SET SERVEROUTPUT ON;
-- Insert row so that it can be deleted
INSERT INTO Course (CourseNo, CrsDesc, CrsUnits)
 VALUES ('IS485','Advanced Database Management',4);

DELETE FROM Course
 WHERE CourseNo = 'IS485';

ROLLBACK;
```

| **Example 11.25** | Trigger with a Combined Event That Fires for Every Action on the *Course* Table Along with Testing Code to Fire the Trigger |

```
CREATE OR REPLACE TRIGGER tr_Course_DIUA
AFTER INSERT OR UPDATE OR DELETE
ON Course
FOR EACH ROW
BEGIN
        dbms_output.put_line('Inserted Table');
        dbms_output.put_line('CourseNo: ' || :NEW.CourseNo);
        dbms_output.put_line('Course Description: ' || :NEW.CrsDesc);
        dbms_output.put_line('Course Units: ' || To_Char(:NEW.CrsUnits) );

        dbms_output.put_line('Deleted Table');
        dbms_output.put_line('CourseNo: ' || :OLD.CourseNo);
        dbms_output.put_line('Course Description: ' || :OLD.CrsDesc);
        dbms_output.put_line('Course Units: ' || To_Char(:OLD.CrsUnits) );
END;
/
-- Testing statements
SET SERVEROUTPUT ON;
INSERT INTO Course (CourseNo, CrsDesc, CrsUnits)
 VALUES ('IS485','Advanced Database Management',4);

UPDATE Course
 SET CrsUnits = 3
 WHERE CourseNo = 'IS485';

DELETE FROM Course
 WHERE CourseNo = 'IS485';

ROLLBACK;
```

Triggers, unlike procedures, cannot be tested directly. Instead, you use SQL statements that cause the triggers to fire. When the trigger in Example 11.25 fires for an INSERT statement, the old values are null. Likewise, when the trigger fires for a DELETE statement, the new values are null. When the trigger fires for an UPDATE statement, the old and new values are not null unless the table had null values before the update.

BEFORE ROW Trigger for Constraint Checking

BEFORE ROW triggers typically are used for complex integrity constraints because they should not contain SQL manipulation statements. For example, enrolling in an offering involves a complex integrity constraint to ensure that a seat exists in the related offering. Example 11.26 demonstrates a BEFORE trigger to ensure that a seat remains when a student enrolls in an offering. The trigger ensures that the number of students enrolled in the offering is less than the limit. The testing code inserts students and modifies the number of students enrolled so that the next insertion raises an error. The trigger uses a user-defined exception to handle the error.

Example 11.26   Trigger to Ensure That a Seat Remains in an Offering

```
CREATE OR REPLACE TRIGGER tr_Enrollment_IB
-- This trigger ensures that the number of enrolled
-- students is less than the offering limit.
BEFORE INSERT
ON Enrollment
FOR EACH ROW
DECLARE
    anOffLimit Offering.OffLimit%TYPE;
    anOffNumEnrolled Offering.OffNumEnrolled%TYPE;
    -- user defined exception declaration
    NoSeats EXCEPTION;
    ExMessage VARCHAR(200);
BEGIN
    SELECT OffLimit, OffNumEnrolled
      INTO anOffLimit, anOffNumEnrolled
      FROM Offering
      WHERE Offering.OfferNo = :NEW.OfferNo;

    IF anOffLimit <= anOffNumEnrolled THEN
      RAISE NoSeats;
    END IF;
EXCEPTION
  WHEN NoSeats THEN
    -- error number between -20000 and -20999
    ExMessage := 'No seats remaining in offering' ||
                to_char(:NEW.OfferNo) || '.';
    ExMessage := ExMessage || 'Number enrolled: ' ||
                to_char(anOffNumEnrolled) || '.';
    ExMessage := ExMessage || 'Offering limit: ' ||
                to_char(anOffLimit);
    Raise_Application_Error(-20001, ExMessage);
END;
/
```

```
-- Testing statements
SET SERVEROUTPUT ON;
-- See offering limit and number enrolled
SELECT OffLimit, OffNumEnrolled
  FROM Offering
  WHERE Offering.OfferNo = 5679;
-- Insert the last student
INSERT INTO Enrollment (RegNo, OfferNo, EnrGrade)
  VALUES (1234,5679,0);

-- update the number of enrolled students
UPDATE Offering
  SET OffNumEnrolled = OffNumEnrolled + 1
  WHERE OfferNo = 5679;

-- See offering limit and number enrolled
SELECT OffLimit, OffNumEnrolled
  FROM Offering
  WHERE Offering.OfferNo = 5679;
-- Insert a student beyond the limit
INSERT INTO Enrollment (RegNo, OfferNo, EnrGrade)
  VALUES (1236,5679,0);

ROLLBACK;
```

AFTER ROW Trigger for Update Propagation

The testing code for the BEFORE ROW trigger in Example 11.26 includes an UPDATE statement to increment the number of students enrolled. An AFTER trigger can automate this task as shown in Example 11.27. The triggers in Examples 11.26 and 11.27 work in tandem. The BEFORE ROW trigger ensures that a seat remains in the offering. The AFTER ROW trigger then updates the related *Offering* row.

Example 11.27   Trigger to Update the Number of Enrolled Students in an Offering

```
CREATE OR REPLACE TRIGGER tr_Enrollment_IA
-- This trigger updates the number of enrolled
-- students in the related offering row.
AFTER INSERT
ON Enrollment
FOR EACH ROW
BEGIN
    UPDATE Offering
      SET OffNumEnrolled = OffNumEnrolled + 1
      WHERE OfferNo = :NEW.OfferNo;
EXCEPTION
  WHEN OTHERS THEN
    Raise_Application_Error(-20001, 'Database error');
END;
/
```

```
-- Testing statements
SET SERVEROUTPUT ON;
-- See the offering limit and number enrolled
SELECT OffLimit, OffNumEnrolled
  FROM Offering
  WHERE Offering.OfferNo = 5679;
-- Insert the last student
INSERT INTO Enrollment (RegNo, OfferNo, EnrGrade)
  VALUES (1234,5679,0);

-- See the offering limit and number enrolled
SELECT OffLimit, OffNumEnrolled
  FROM Offering
  WHERE Offering.OfferNo = 5679;

ROLLBACK;
```

Combining Trigger Events to Reduce the Number of Triggers

The triggers in Examples 11.26 and 11.27 involve insertions to the *Enrollment* table. Additional triggers are needed for updates to the *Enrollment.OfferNo* column and deletions of *Enrollment* rows.

As an alternative to separate triggers for events on the same table, one large BEFORE trigger and one large AFTER trigger can be written. Each trigger contains multiple events as shown in Examples 11.28 and 11.29. The action part of the trigger in Example 11.29 uses the keywords INSERTING, UPDATING, and DELETING to determine the triggering event. The script in Example 11.30 is rather complex because it tests two complex triggers.

Example 11.28	Trigger to Ensure That a Seat Remains in an Offering When Inserting or Updating an *Enrollment* Row

```
-- Drop the previous trigger to avoid interactions
DROP TRIGGER tr_Enrollment_IB;
CREATE OR REPLACE TRIGGER tr_Enrollment_IUB
-- This trigger ensures that the number of enrolled
-- students is less than the offering limit.
BEFORE INSERT OR UPDATE OF OfferNo
ON Enrollment
FOR EACH ROW
DECLARE
      anOffLimit Offering.OffLimit%TYPE;
      anOffNumEnrolled Offering.OffNumEnrolled%TYPE;
      NoSeats EXCEPTION;
      ExMessage VARCHAR(200);
BEGIN
```

```
            SELECT OffLimit, OffNumEnrolled
               INTO anOffLimit, anOffNumEnrolled
               FROM Offering
               WHERE Offering.OfferNo = :NEW.OfferNo;

            IF anOffLimit <= anOffNumEnrolled THEN
               RAISE NoSeats;
            END IF;
      EXCEPTION
        WHEN NoSeats THEN
          -- error number between -20000 and -20999
             ExMessage := 'No seats remaining in offering ' ||
                             to_char(:NEW.OfferNo) || '.';
             ExMessage := ExMessage || 'Number enrolled: ' ||
                             to_char(anOffNumEnrolled) || '.';
             ExMessage := ExMessage || 'Offering limit: ' ||
                             to_char(anOffLimit);
             raise_application_error(-20001, ExMessage);
      END;
```

Example 11.29 Trigger to Update the Number of Enrolled Students in an Offering When Inserting,
Updating, or Deleting an *Enrollment* Row

```
-- Drop the previous trigger to avoid interactions
DROP TRIGGER tr_Enrollment_IA;
CREATE OR REPLACE TRIGGER tr_Enrollment_DIUA
-- This trigger updates the number of enrolled
-- students in the related offering row.
AFTER INSERT OR DELETE OR UPDATE of OfferNo
ON Enrollment
FOR EACH ROW
BEGIN
  -- Increment the number of enrolled students for insert, update
  IF INSERTING OR UPDATING THEN
     UPDATE Offering
        SET OffNumEnrolled = OffNumEnrolled + 1
        WHERE OfferNo = :NEW.OfferNo;
  END IF;
-- Decrease the number of enrolled students for delete, update
IF UPDATING OR DELETING THEN
     UPDATE Offering
        SET OffNumEnrolled = OffNumEnrolled - 1
        WHERE OfferNo = :OLD.OfferNo;
END IF;

EXCEPTION
 WHEN OTHERS THEN
    raise_application_error(-20001, 'Database error');
END;
```

Example 11.30

Script to Test the Triggers in Examples 11.28 and 11.29

```
-- Test case 1
-- See the offering limit and number enrolled
SELECT OffLimit, OffNumEnrolled
  FROM Offering
  WHERE Offering.OfferNo = 5679;
-- Insert the last student
INSERT INTO Enrollment (RegNo, OfferNo, EnrGrade)
  VALUES (1234,5679,0);
-- See the offering limit and the number enrolled
SELECT OffLimit, OffNumEnrolled
  FROM Offering
  WHERE Offering.OfferNo = 5679;

-- Test case 2
-- Insert a student beyond the limit: exception raised
INSERT INTO Enrollment (RegNo, OfferNo, EnrGrade)
  VALUES (1236,5679,0);
-- Transfer a student to offer 5679: exception raised
UPDATE Enrollment
  SET OfferNo = 5679
  WHERE RegNo = 1234 AND OfferNo = 1234;

-- Test case 3
-- See the offering limit and the number enrolled before update
SELECT OffLimit, OffNumEnrolled
  FROM Offering
  WHERE Offering.OfferNo = 4444;
-- Update a student to a non full offering
UPDATE Enrollment
  SET OfferNo = 4444
  WHERE RegNo = 1234 AND OfferNo = 1234;
-- See the offering limit and the number enrolled after update
SELECT OffLimit, OffNumEnrolled
  FROM Offering
  WHERE Offering.OfferNo = 4444;

-- Test case 4
-- See the offering limit and the number enrolled before delete
SELECT OffLimit, OffNumEnrolled
  FROM Offering
  WHERE Offering.OfferNo = 1234;
-- Delete an enrollment
DELETE Enrollment
  WHERE OfferNo = 1234;
-- See the offering limit and the number enrolled
SELECT OffLimit, OffNumEnrolled
  FROM Offering
  WHERE Offering.OfferNo = 1234;
```

```
-- Erase all changes
ROLLBACK;
```

There is no clear preference for many smaller triggers or fewer larger triggers. Although smaller triggers are easier to understand than larger triggers, the number of triggers is a complicating factor to understand interactions among triggers. The next subsection explains trigger execution procedures to clarify issues of trigger interactions.

Additional BEFORE ROW Trigger Examples

This subsection finishes with two additional BEFORE triggers. Example 11.31 depicts a trigger for a transition constraint. The trigger contains a WHEN clause to restrict the trigger execution. Example 11.32 depicts a trigger to enforce uppercase usage for the faculty name columns. Although BEFORE triggers should not perform updates with SQL statements, they can change the new values as the trigger in Example 11.32 demonstrates.

| **Example 11.31** | Trigger to Ensure That a Salary Increase Does Not Exceed 10 Percent |

Note that the NEW and OLD keywords should not be preceded by a colon (:) when used in a WHEN condition.

```
CREATE OR REPLACE TRIGGER tr_FacultySalary_UB
-- This trigger ensures that a salary increase does not exceed
-- 10%.
BEFORE UPDATE OF FacSalary
ON Faculty
FOR EACH ROW
WHEN (NEW.FacSalary > 1.1 * OLD.FacSalary)
DECLARE
     SalaryIncreaseTooHigh EXCEPTION;
     ExMessage VARCHAR(200);
BEGIN
     RAISE SalaryIncreaseTooHigh;
EXCEPTION
  WHEN SalaryIncreaseTooHigh THEN
    -- error number between -20000 and -20999
      ExMessage := 'Salary increase exceeds 10% . ';
      ExMessage := ExMessage || 'Current salary: ' ||
                    to_char(:OLD.FacSalary) || '.';
      ExMessage := ExMessage || 'New salary: ' ||
                    to_char(:NEW.FacSalary) || '.';
      Raise_Application_Error(-20001, ExMessage);
END;
/
SET SERVEROUTPUT ON;
-- Test case 1: salary increase of 5%
UPDATE Faculty
 SET FacSalary = FacSalary * 1.05
 WHERE FacSSN = '543-21-0987';
```

```
SELECT FacSalary FROM Faculty WHERE FacSSN = '543-21-0987';
-- Test case 2: salary increase of 20%  should generate an exception.
UPDATE Faculty
  SET FacSalary = FacSalary * 1.20
  WHERE FacSSN = '543-21-0987';
ROLLBACK;
```

Example 11.32	Trigger to Change the Case of the Faculty First Name and Last Name

```
CREATE OR REPLACE TRIGGER tr_FacultyName_IUB
-- This trigger changes the case of FacFirstName and FacLastName.
BEFORE INSERT OR UPDATE OF FacFirstName, FacLastName
ON Faculty
FOR EACH ROW
BEGIN
    :NEW.FacFirstName := Upper(:NEW.FacFirstName);
    :NEW.FacLastName := Upper(:NEW.FacLastName);
END;
/
-- Testing statements
UPDATE Faculty
  SET FacFirstName = 'Joe', FacLastName = 'Smith'
  WHERE FacSSN = '543-21-0987';
-- Display the changed faculty name.
SELECT FacFirstName, FacLastName
  FROM Faculty
  WHERE FacSSN = '543-21-0987';
ROLLBACK;
```

11.3.3 Understanding Trigger Execution

As the previous subsection demonstrated, individual triggers usually are easy to understand. Collectively, however, triggers can be difficult to understand especially in conjunction with integrity constraint enforcement and database actions. To understand the collective behavior of triggers, integrity constraints, and database manipulation actions, you need to understand the execution procedure used by a DBMS. Although SQL:1999 specifies a <u>trigger execution procedure</u>, most DBMSs do not adhere strictly to it. Therefore, this subsection emphasizes the Oracle trigger execution procedure with comments about the differences between the Oracle and the SQL:1999 execution procedures.

Trigger Execution Procedure specifies the order of execution among the various kinds of triggers, integrity constraints, and database manipulation statements. Trigger execution procedures can be complex because the actions of a trigger may fire other triggers.

Simplified Trigger Execution Procedure

The trigger execution procedure that follows applies to the data manipulation statements (INSERT, UPDATE, and DELETE). Before this procedure begins, Oracle determines the applicable triggers for a statement. A trigger is applicable to a statement if the trigger contains an event that matches the statement type. To match an UPDATE statement with a column list, at least one column in the triggering event must be in the list of columns updated by the statement. After determining the applicable triggers, Oracle executes triggers in the order of BEFORE STATEMENT, BEFORE ROW, AFTER ROW, and AFTER STATEMENT. An applicable trigger does not execute if its WHEN condition is not true.

Simplified Oracle Trigger Execution Procedure

1. Execute the applicable BEFORE STATEMENT triggers.
2. For each row affected by the SQL manipulation statement:
   2.1. Execute the applicable BEFORE ROW triggers.
   2.2. Perform the data manipulation operation on the row.
   2.3. Perform integrity constraint checking.
   2.4. Execute the applicable AFTER ROW triggers.
3. Perform deferred integrity constraint checking.
4. Execute the applicable AFTER statement triggers.

Overlapping Triggers two or more triggers with the same timing, granularity, and applicable table. The triggers overlap if an SQL statement may cause both triggers to fire. You should not depend on a particular firing order for overlapping triggers.

The trigger execution procedure of Oracle differs from the SQL:1999 execution procedure about <u>overlapping triggers</u>. Two triggers with the same timing, granularity, and applicable table overlap if an SQL statement may cause both triggers to fire. For example a BEFORE ROW trigger with the UPDATE ON Customer event overlaps with a BEFORE ROW trigger with the UPDATE OF CustBal ON Customer event. Both triggers fire when updating the *CustBal* column. For overlapping triggers, Oracle specifies that the execution order is arbitrary. For SQL:1999, the execution order depends on the time in which the trigger is defined. Overlapping triggers are executed in the order in which the triggers were created.

Most constraint checking occurs after executing the applicable BEFORE ROW triggers but before executing the applicable AFTER ROW triggers. Deferred constraint checking is performed at the end of a transaction. Chapter 15 on transaction management presents SQL statements for deferred constraint checking. In most applications, few constraints are declared with deferred checking.

Trigger Execution Procedure with Recursive Execution

Data manipulation statements in a trigger complicate the simplified execution procedure. Data manipulation statements in a trigger may cause other triggers to fire. Consider the AFTER ROW trigger in Example 11.29 that fires when an *Enrollment* row is added. The trigger updates the *NumEnrolled* column enrolled in the related *Offering* row. Suppose there is another trigger on the *NumEnrolled* column of the *Offering* table that fires when the *NumEnrolled* column becomes large (say within two of the limit). This second trigger should fire as a result of the first trigger firing when an offering becomes almost full.

When a data manipulation statement is encountered in a trigger, the trigger execution procedure is recursively executed. Recursive execution means that a procedure calls itself. In the previous example, the trigger execution procedure is recursively executed when a data manipulation statement is encountered in the trigger in Example 11.29. In the Oracle execution procedure, steps 2.1 and 2.4 may involve recursive execution of the procedure. In the SQL:1999 execution procedure, only step 2.4 may involve recursive execution because SQL:1999 prohibits data manipulation statements in BEFORE triggers.

Actions on referenced rows also complicate the simplified execution procedure. When deleting or updating a referenced row, the foreign key constraint can specify actions (CASCADE, SET NULL, and SET DEFAULT) on related rows. For example, a foreign key constraint containing ON DELETE CASCADE for *Offering.CourseNo* means that deletion of a *Course* row causes deletion of the related *Offering* rows. Actions on referenced rows can cause other triggers to fire leading to recursive execution of the trigger execution procedure in step 2.3 for both Oracle and SQL:1999. Actions on referenced rows are performed as part of constraint checking in step 2.3.

With these complications that cause recursive execution, the full trigger execution procedure is presented below. Most DBMSs such as Oracle limit the recursion depth in steps 2.1, 2.3, and 2.4.

Oracle Trigger Execution Procedure with Recursive Execution

1. Execute the applicable BEFORE STATEMENT triggers.
2. For each row affected by the SQL manipulation statement:
    2.1. Execute the applicable BEFORE ROW triggers. Recursively execute the procedure for data manipulation statements in a trigger.
    2.2. Perform the data manipulation operation on the row.
    2.3. Perform integrity constraint checking. Recursively execute the procedure for actions on referenced rows.
    2.4. Execute the applicable AFTER ROW triggers. Recursively execute the procedure for data manipulation statements in a trigger.
3. Perform deferred integrity constraint checking.
4. Execute the applicable AFTER statement triggers.

The full execution procedure shows considerable complexity when executing a trigger. To control complexity among a collection of triggers, you should follow these guidelines:

- Do not use data manipulation statements in BEFORE triggers.
- Limit data manipulation statements in AFTER triggers.
- For triggers that fire on UPDATE statements, always list the columns in which the trigger applies.
- Ensure that overlapping triggers do not depend on a specific order to fire. In most DBMSs, the firing order is arbitrary. Even if the order is not arbitrary (as in SQL:1999), it is risky to depend on a specific firing order.
- Be cautious about triggers on tables affected by actions on referenced rows. These triggers will fire as a result of actions on the parent tables.

Mutating Table Errors

Oracle has a restriction on trigger execution that can impede the development of specialized triggers. In trigger actions, Oracle prohibits SQL statements on the table in which the trigger is defined or on related tables affected by DELETE CASCADE actions. The underlying trigger table and the related tables are known as mutating tables. For example, on a trigger for the *Registration* table, Oracle prohibits SQL statements on the *Registration* table as well as on the *Enrollment* table if the *Enrollment* table contains a foreign key constraint on *Registration.RegNo* with the ON DELETE CASCADE action. If a trigger executes an SQL statement on a mutating table, a run-time error occurs.

For most triggers, you can avoid mutating table errors by using row triggers with new and old values. In specialized situations, you must redesign a trigger to avoid a mutating table error. One situation involves a trigger to enforce an integrity constraint involving other rows of the same table. For example, a trigger to ensure that no more than five rows contain the same value for a column would have a mutating table error. Another example would be a trigger that ensures that a row cannot be deleted if it is the last row associated with a parent table. A second situation involves a trigger for a parent table that inserts rows into a child table if the child table has a foreign key constraint with ON DELETE CASCADE.

To write a trigger in these situations, you will need a more complex solution. For complete details, you should consult some websites that show solutions to avoid mutating table errors. The Oracle documentation mentions the following two approaches:

1. Write a package and a collection of triggers that use procedures in the package. The package maintains a private array that contains the old and new values of the mutating table. Typically, you will need a BEFORE

STATEMENT trigger to initialize the private array, an AFTER ROW trigger to insert into the private array, and an AFTER STATEMENT trigger to enforce the integrity constraint using the private array.

2. Create a view and use an INSTEAD OF trigger for the view. View triggers do not have any mutating table restrictions.

CLOSING THOUGHTS

This chapter has augmented your knowledge of database application development with details about database programming languages, stored procedures, and triggers. Database programming languages are procedural languages with an interface to one or more DBMSs. Database programming languages support customization, batch processing, and complex operations beyond the SQL SELECT statement as well as improved efficiency and portability in some cases. The major design issues in a database programming language are language style, binding, database connections, and result processing. This chapter presented background about PL/SQL, a widely used database programming language available as part of Oracle.

After learning about database programming languages and PL/SQL, the chapter presented stored procedures. Stored procedures provide modularity like programming language procedures. Stored procedures managed by a DBMS provide additional benefits including reuse of access plans, flexibility for client–server development, and usage of the same tools for managing other parts of a database application. You learned about PL/SQL procedure coding through examples demonstrating procedures, functions, exception processing, and embedded SQL containing single row results and multiple row results with cursors. You also learned about PL/SQL packages that group related procedures, functions, and other PL/SQL objects.

The final part of the chapter covered triggers for rule processing. A trigger involves an event, a condition, and a sequence of actions. You learned the varied uses for triggers as well as a classification of triggers by granularity, timing, and applicable event. After this background material, you learned about coding Oracle triggers using PL/SQL statements in a trigger body. To provide understanding about the complexity of large collections of triggers, you learned about trigger execution procedures specifying the order of execution among various kinds of triggers, integrity constraints, and SQL statements.

The material in this chapter is important for both application developers and database administrators. Stored procedures and triggers can be a significant part of large applications, perhaps as much as 25 percent of the code. Application developers use database programming languages to code stored procedures and triggers, while database administrators provide oversight in the development process. In addition, database administrators may write stored procedures and triggers to support the process of database monitoring. Thus, database programming languages, stored procedures, and triggers are important tools for careers in both application development and database administration.

REVIEW CONCEPTS

- Primary motivation for database programming languages: customization, batch processing, and complex operations.
- Secondary motivation for database programming languages: efficiency and portability.
- Statement-level interface to support embedded SQL in a programming language.
- Call-level interface to provide procedures to invoke SQL statements in a programming language.

- Popularity of proprietary call-level interfaces (ODBC and JDBC) instead of the SQL:1999 call-level interface.
- Support for static and dynamic binding of SQL statements in statement-level interfaces.
- Support for dynamic binding with reuse of access plans in call-level interfaces.
- Implicit versus explicit database connections.
- Usage of cursors to integrate set-at-a-time processing of SQL with record-at-a-time processing of programming languages.
- PL/SQL data types and variable declaration.
- Anchored variable declaration in PL/SQL.
- Conditional statements in PL/SQL: IF-THEN, IF-THEN-ELSE, IF-THEN-ELSIF, and CASE.
- Looping statements in PL/SQL: FOR LOOP, WHILE LOOP, and LOOP with an EXIT statement.
- Anonymous blocks to execute PL/SQL statements and test stored procedures and triggers.
- Motivations for stored procedures: compilation of access plans, flexibility in client–server development, implementation of complex operators, and convenient management using DBMS tools such as security control.
- Specification of parameters in PL/SQL procedures and functions.
- Exception processing in PL/SQL procedures and functions.
- Using static cursors in PL/SQL procedures and functions.
- Implicit versus explicit cursors in PL/SQL.
- PL/SQL packages to group related procedures, functions, and other objects.
- Public versus private specification of packages.
- Motivation for triggers: complex integrity constraints, transition constraints, update propagation, exception reporting, and audit trails.
- Trigger granularity: statement versus row-level triggers.
- Trigger timing: before or after an event.
- Trigger events: INSERT, UPDATE, or DELETE as well as compound events with combinations of these events.
- SQL:1999 trigger specification versus proprietary trigger syntax.
- Oracle BEFORE ROW triggers for complex integrity constraints, transition constraints, data entry standardization.
- Oracle AFTER ROW triggers for update propagation.
- The order of trigger execution in a trigger execution procedure: BEFORE STATEMENT, BEFORE ROW, AFTER ROW, AFTER STATEMENT.
- The order of integrity constraint enforcement in a trigger execution procedure.
- Arbitrary execution order for overlapping triggers.
- Recursive execution of a trigger execution procedure for data manipulation statements in a trigger body and actions on referenced rows.

QUESTIONS

1. What is a database programming language?
2. Why is customization an important motivation for database programming languages?
3. How do database programming languages support customization?

4. Why is batch processing an important motivation for database programming languages?

5. Why is support for complex operations an important motivation for database programming languages?

6. Why is efficiency a secondary motivation for database programming languages, not a primary motivation?

7. Why is portability a secondary motivation for database programming languages, not a primary motivation?

8. What is a statement-level interface?

9. What is a call-level interface?

10. What is binding for a database programming language?

11. What is the difference between dynamic and static binding?

12. What is the relationship between language style and binding?

13. What SQL:1999 statements and procedures support explicit database connections?

14. What differences must be resolved to process the results of an SQL statement in a computer program?

15. What is a cursor?

16. What statements and procedures does SQL:1999 provide for cursor processing?

17. Why study PL/SQL?

18. Explain case sensitivity in PL/SQL. Why are most elements case insensitive?

19. What is an anchored variable declaration?

20. What is a logical expression?

21. What conditional statements are provided by PL/SQL?

22. What iteration statements are provided by PL/SQL?

23. Why use an anonymous block?

24. Why should a DBMS manage stored procedures rather than a programming environment?

25. What are the usages of a parameter in a stored procedure?

26. What is the restriction on the data type in a parameter specification?

27. Why use predefined exceptions and user-defined exceptions?

28. Why use the OTHERS exception?

29. How does a function differ from a procedure?

30. What are the two kinds of cursor declaration in PL/SQL?

31. What is the difference between a static and a dynamic cursor in PL/SQL?

32. What is a cursor attribute?

33. How are cursor attributes referenced?

34. What is the purpose of a PL/SQL package?

35. Why separate the interface from the implementation in a PL/SQL package?

36. What does a package interface contain?

37. What does a package implementation contain?

38. What is an alternative name for a trigger?

39. What are typical uses for triggers?

40. How does SQL:1999 classify triggers?

41. Why do most trigger implementations differ from the SQL:1999 specification?

42. How are compound events specified in a trigger?

43. How are triggers tested?

44. Is it preferable to write many smaller triggers or fewer larger triggers?

45. What is a trigger execution procedure?

46. What is the order of execution for various kinds of triggers?

47. What is an overlapping trigger? What is the execution order of overlapping triggers?

48. What situations lead to recursive execution of the trigger execution procedure?

49. List at least two ways to reduce the complexity of a collection of triggers.

50. What is a mutating table error in an Oracle trigger?

51. How are mutating table errors avoided?

52. What are typical uses of BEFORE ROW triggers?

53. What are typical uses of AFTER ROW triggers?

PROBLEMS

Each problem uses the revised order entry database shown in Chapter 10. For your reference, Figure 11.P1 shows a relationship window for the revised order entry database. More details about the revised database can be found in Chapter 10 problems.

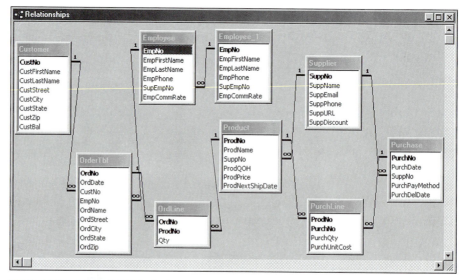

Figure 11.P1   Relationship diagram for the revised order entry database.

The problems provide practice with PL/SQL coding and development of procedures, functions, packages, and triggers. In addition, some problems involve anonymous blocks and scripts to test the procedures, functions, packages, and triggers.

1. Write a PL/SQL anonymous block to calculate the number of days in a non–leap year. Your code should loop through the months of the year (1 to 12) using a FOR LOOP. You should use an IF-THEN-ELSIF statement to determine the number of days to add for the month. You can group months together that have the same number of days. Display the number of days after the loop terminates.

2. Revise problem 1 to calculate the number of days in a leap year. If working in Oracle 9i, use a CASE statement instead of an IF-THEN-ELSIF statement. Note that you cannot use a CASE statement in Oracle 8i.

3. Write a PL/SQL anonymous block to calculate the future value of $1,000 at 8 percent interest, compounded annually for 10 years. The future value at the end of year i is the amount at the beginning of the year plus the beginning amount times the yearly interest rate. Use a WHILE LOOP to calculate the future value. Display the future amount after the loop terminates.

4. Write a PL/SQL anonymous block to display the price of product number P0036577. Use an anchored variable declaration and a SELECT INTO statement to determine the price. If the price is less than $100, display a message that the product is a good buy. If the price is between $100 and $300, display a message that the product is competitively priced. If the price is greater than $300, display a message that the product is feature laden.

5. Write a PL/SQL procedure to insert a new row into the *Product* table using input parameters for the product number, product name, product price, next ship date, quantity on hand, and supplier number. For a successful insert, display an appropriate message. If an error occurs in the INSERT statement, raise an exception with an appropriate error message.

6. Revise problem 5 to generate an output value instead of displaying a message about a successful insert. In addition, the revised procedure should catch a duplicate primary key error. If the user tries to insert a row with an existing product number, your procedure should raise an exception with an appropriate error message.

7. Write testing scripts for the procedures in problems 5 and 6. For the procedure in problem 6, your script should test for a primary key violation and a foreign key violation.

8. Write a PL/SQL function to determine if the most recent order for a given customer number was sent to the customer's billing address. The function should return TRUE if each order address column (street, city, state, and zip) is equal to the corresponding customer address column. If any address column is not equal, return false. The most recent order has the largest order date. Return NULL if the customer does not exist or there are no orders for the customer.

9. Create a testing script for the PL/SQL function in problem 8.

10. Create a procedure to compute the commission amount for a given order number. The commission amount is the commission rate of the employee taking the order times the amount of the order. The amount of an order is the sum of the product of the quantity of a product ordered times the product price. If the order does not

have a related employee (a Web order), the commission is zero. The procedure should have an output variable for the commission amount. The output variable should be null if an order does not exist.

11. Create a testing script for the PL/SQL procedure in problem 10.

12. Create a function to check the quantity on hand of a product. The input parameters are a product number and a quantity ordered. Return FALSE if the quantity on hand is less than the quantity ordered. Return TRUE if the quantity on hand is greater than or equal to the quantity ordered. Return NULL if the product does not exist.

13. Create a procedure to insert an order line. Use the function from problem 12 to check for adequate stock. If there is not sufficient stock, the output parameter should be FALSE. Raise an exception if there is an insertion error such as a duplicate primary key.

14. Create testing scripts for the function in problem 12 and the procedure in problem 13.

15. Write a function to compute the median of the customer balance column. The median is the middle value in a list of numbers. If the list size is even, the median is the average of the two middle values. For example, if there are 18 customer balances, the median is the average of the ninth and tenth balances. You should use an implicit cursor in your function. You may want to use the Oracle SQL functions *Trunc* and *Mod* in writing your function. Write a test script for your function. Note that this function does not have any parameters. Do not use parentheses in the function declaration or in the function invocation when a function does not have parameters.

16. Revise the function in problem 15 with an explicit cursor using the CURSOR, the OPEN, the FETCH, and the CLOSE statements. Write a test script for your revised function.

17. Create a package containing the function in problem 15, the procedure in problem 13, the procedure in problem 10, the function in problem 8, and the procedure in problem 6. The function in problem 12 should be private to the package. Write a testing script to execute each public object in the package. You do not need to completely test each public object. One execution per public object is fine because you previously tested the procedures and functions outside the package.

18. Write an AFTER ROW trigger to fire for every action on the *Customer* table. In the trigger, display the new and old customer values every time that the trigger fires. Write a script to test the trigger.

19. Write a trigger for a transition constraint on the *Employee* table. The trigger should prevent updates that increase or decrease the commission rate by more than 10 percent. Write a script to test your trigger.

20. Write a trigger to remove the prefix http:// in the column *Supplier.SuppURL* on insert and update operations. Your trigger should work regardless of the case of the prefix http://. You need to use Oracle SQL functions for string manipulation. You should study Oracle SQL functions such as *SubStr, Lower,* and *LTrim.* Write a script to test your trigger.

21. Write a trigger to ensure that there is adequate stock when inserting a new *OrdLine* row or updating the quantity of an *OrdLine* row. On insert operations, the *ProdQOH* of the related row should be greater than or equal to the quantity in the new row. On update operations, the *ProdQOH* should be greater than or equal to the difference in the quantity (new quantity minus old quantity).

22. Write a trigger to propagate updates to the *Product* table after an operation on the *OrdLine* table. For insertions, the trigger should decrease the quantity on hand by the order quantity. For updates, the trigger should decrease the quantity on hand by the difference between the new order quantity minus the old order quantity. For deletions, the trigger should increase the quantity on hand by the old order quantity.

23. Write a script to test the triggers from problems 21 and 22.

24. Write a trigger to propagate updates to the *Product* table after insert operations on the *PurchLine* table. The quantity on hand should increase by the purchase quantity. Write a script to test the trigger.

25. Write a trigger to propagate updates to the *Product* table after update operations on the *PurchLine* table. The quantity on hand should increase by the difference between the new purchase quantity and the old purchase quantity. Write a script to test the trigger.

26. Write a trigger to propagate updates to the *Product* table after delete operations on the *PurchLine* table. The quantity on hand should decrease by the old purchase quantity. Write a script to test the trigger.

27. Write a trigger to propagate updates to the *Product* table updates to the *ProdNo* column of the *PurchLine* table. The quantity on hand of the old product should decrease while the quantity on hand of the new product should increase. Write a script to test the trigger.

28. Suppose that you have an UPDATE statement that changes both the *ProdNo* column and the *PurchQty* column of the *PurchLine* table. What triggers (that you wrote in previous problems) fire for such an UPDATE statement? If more than one trigger fires, why do the triggers overlap and what is the firing order? Modify the overlapping triggers and prepare a test script so that you can determine the firing order. Does the Oracle trigger execution procedure guarantee the firing order?

29. For the UPDATE statement in problem 28, do the triggers that you created in previous problems work correctly? Write a script to test your triggers for such an UPDATE statement. If the triggers do not work correctly, rewrite them so that they work correctly for an UPDATE statement on both columns as well as UPDATE statements on the individual columns. Write a script to test the revised triggers. *Hint:* you need to specify the column in the UPDATING keyword in the trigger body. For example, you can specify UPDATING('PurchQty') to check if the *PurchQty* is being updated.

30. Can you devise another solution to the problem of UPDATE statements that change both *ProdNo* and *PurchQty*? Is it reasonable to support such UPDATE statements in online applications?

REFERENCES FOR FURTHER STUDY

The Oracle Technology Network (otn.oracle.com) contains a wealth of material about PL/SQL, stored procedures, and triggers. There is no charge for access to most materials although you must register to gain access to the materials. The *PL/SQL User's Guide* provides details about PL/SQL and stored procedures. The *Oracle SQL Reference* provides details about triggers as well as descriptions of predefined functions such as *Mod* and *SubStr*. More details and examples can be found in the *Oracle Concepts* and the *Oracle Application Developers Guide*. Melton and Simon (2001) describe triggers in SQL:1999.

SQL:1999 Syntax Summary

This appendix summarizes the SQL:1999 syntax for the trigger statement. The conventions used in the syntax notation are identical to those used at the end of Chapter 2.

TRIGGER STATEMENT

```
CREATE TRIGGER TriggerName
            <TriggerTiming> <TriggerEvent> ON TableName
            [  REFERENCING <AliasClause> [  <AliasClause>  ]  ]
            [  <GranularityClause>  [  WHEN  (  <Row-Condition>  )  ]  ]
            <ActionBlock>

<TriggerTiming>:  {  BEFORE  |  AFTER  }

<TriggerEvent>:  {  INSERT  |  DELETE  |
            UPDATE  [  OF ColumnName*  ]  }

<AliasClause>:  {  <RowAlias>  |  <TableAlias>  }

<RowAlias>:
            {  OLD  [ROW]  [AS]  AliasName  |
            NEW  [ROW]  [AS]  AliasName  }

<TableAlias>:
            {  OLD TABLE  [AS]  AliasName  |
            NEW TABLE  [AS]  AliasName  }

<GranularityClause>: FOR EACH  {  ROW  |  STATEMENT  }

<Row-Condition>: -- defined in Chapter 3

<ActionBlock>:
            -- can be a procedure call or an SQL:1999 block
```

View Design
and Integration

Learning Objectives |

• |

This chapter describes the practice of designing user views and combining user views into a complete conceptual design. After this chapter, the student should have acquired the following knowledge and skills:

■ Understand the motivation for view design and integration.

■ Analyze a form and construct an ERD to represent it.

■ Determine an integration strategy for a database development effort.

■ Perform both incremental and parallel integration approaches.

■ Recognize and resolve synonyms and homonyms in the view integration process.

Overview

Chapters 5, 6, and 7 provided tools for data modeling and normalization, fundamental skills for database design. You applied this knowledge to construct entity relationship diagrams (ERDs) for modest-size problems, convert ERDs into relational tables, and normalize the tables. This chapter extends your database design skills by showing you how to analyze views and integrate user views into a complete, conceptual schema. This approach is an applications-oriented approach appropriate for designing complex databases.

To become a good database designer, you need to extend your skills to larger problems. To motivate you about the importance of extending your skills, this chapter describes the nature of large database development projects. This chapter then presents a methodology for view design with an emphasis on constructing an ERD to represent a data entry form. Forms can provide important sources of requirements for database design. You will learn to analyze individual forms, construct an ERD, and check the ERD for consistency against the form. Because of the emphasis on views and forms, this chapter logically follows Chapter 10 on application development with views. While studying this chapter, you may want to review important concepts from Chapter 10, such as updatable views.

After the presentation of view design, this chapter describes the process of view integration, combining ERDs derived from individual views. You will learn about the incremental and parallel integration approaches, determination of an integration strategy by analyzing relationships among forms, and application of the integration process using both the incremental and parallel approaches.

12.1 MOTIVATION FOR VIEW DESIGN AND INTEGRATION

The complexity of a database reflects the complexity of the underlying organization and the functions that a database supports. Many factors can contribute to the complexity of an organization. Size is certainly an important determinant of complexity. Size can be measured in many ways such as by sales volume, the number of employees, the number of products, and the number of countries in which an organization operates. Size alone is not the only determinant, however. Other factors that contribute to organizational complexity are the regulatory environment, the competitive environment, and the organizational structure. For example, the areas of payroll and personnel can be tremendously complex because of the number of employee types, details of compensation packages, union agreements, and government regulations.

Large organizations have many databases with individual databases supporting groups of functions such as payroll, personnel, accounting, material requirements, and so on. These individual databases can be very complex, as measured by the size of the ERDs. An ERD for a large database can have hundreds of entity types and relationships. When converted to a relational database, the database can have hundreds to perhaps thousands of tables. A large ERD is difficult to visually inspect because it can fill an entire wall. Other measures of complexity involve the use of the database through forms, reports, computer programs, and validation rules. A large database can have hundreds to thousands of forms, reports, computer programs, and validation rules.

Designing large databases is a time-consuming and labor-intensive process. The design effort often involves collecting requirements from many different groups of users. Requirements can be notoriously difficult to capture. Users often need to experience a database to clarify their requirements. Because of the volume of requirements and the difficulty of capturing requirements, a large database design effort can involve a team of designers. Coordination among designers is an important part of the database design effort.

To manage complexity, the "divide and conquer" strategy is used in many areas of computing. Dividing a large problem allows smaller problems to be independently solved. The solutions to the smaller problems are then combined into a solution for the entire problem.

View design and integration (Figure 12.1) supports management of the complexity of a database design effort. In view design, an ERD is constructed for each group of users. The requirements can come in many formats such as interviews, documentation of an existing system, and proposed forms and reports. A view is typically small enough

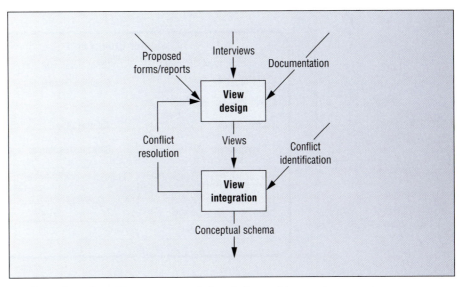

Figure 12.1 Overview of view design and integration.

for a single person to design. Multiple designers can work on views covering different parts of a database. The view integration process merges the views into a complete, conceptual schema. Integration involves recognizing and resolving conflicts. To resolve conflicts, it is sometimes necessary to revise the conflicting views. Compromise is an important part of conflict resolution in the integration process.

The remaining sections of this chapter provide details about the view design and integration activities. A special emphasis is given to data entry forms as a source of requirements.

12.2 VIEW DESIGN WITH FORMS

Forms can provide an important source of requirements for database design. Because of familiarity, users can effectively communicate many requirements through the forms they use. To aid you in using forms as database requirements, this section describes a procedure to design views using data entry forms. The procedure enables you to analyze the data requirements of a form. After the form analysis procedure, application of the procedure to forms with M-way relationships is discussed.

12.2.1 Form Analysis

In using forms for database design, you reverse the traditional database development process. In the traditional process, a database design precedes application development. With a form-driven approach to database design, forms are defined before or concurrently with the database design. Forms often may exist in paper format or as part of an existing system. The form definition does not need to be as complete as required after the database design is complete. For example, the entire set of events defining user interaction with the form need not be defined. Instead, form definition can involve a sketch on a word processor (Figure 12.2) or drawing tool. In addition, you may need several sample instances of a form.

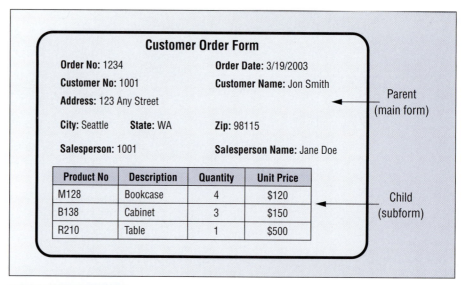

Figure 12.2   Sample Customer Order Form.

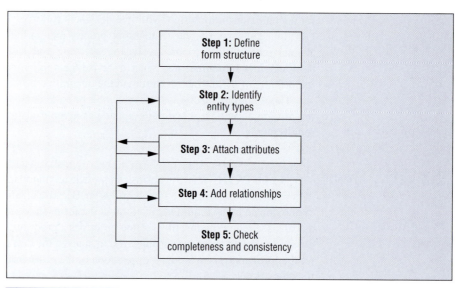

Figure 12.3   Steps in the form analysis process.

The use of forms in view design does not preclude requirements in other formats such as interviews and documentation of an existing system. You should use all kinds of requirements in the view design process. As an important source of requirements, forms should be analyzed carefully.

In form analysis (Figure 12.3), you create an entity relationship diagram to represent a form. The resulting ERD is a view of the database. The ERD should be general enough to support the form and other anticipated processing. The backtracking in Figure 12.3 shows that the form analysis process can return to previous steps. It is not nec-

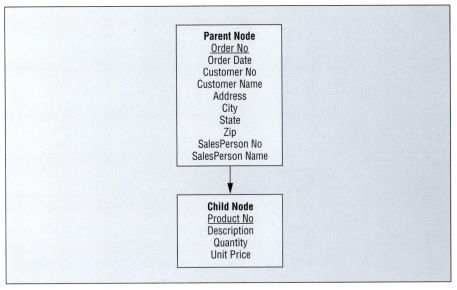

Figure 12.4   **Hierarchical structure for the Customer Order Form.**

essary to perform the steps sequentially. In particular, if any problems are found in the last step, other steps must be repeated to correct the problems. The remainder of this section explains the form analysis steps in more detail and applies the form analysis process to example forms.

Step 1: Define Form Structure

In the first step, you construct a hierarchy that depicts the form structure. Most forms consist of a simple hierarchy where the main form is the parent and the subform is the child. For example, Figure 12.4 depicts the structure of the customer order form in Figure 12.2. A rectangle (parent or child) in the hierarchy diagram is called a node. Complex forms can have more nodes (parallel subforms) and more levels (subforms inside subforms) in the hierarchy. For example, an automotive service order form may have a subform (child) showing part charges and another subform (child) showing labor charges. Complex forms such as a service order form are not as common because they can be difficult for users to understand.

As part of making the form structure, you should identify keys within each node in the hierarchy. In Figure 12.4, node keys are underlined. In the parent node, the node key value is unique among all form instances. In the child node, the node key value is unique within the parent node. For example, a product number is unique on an order. However, two orders may use the same product number.

Step 2: Identify Entity Types

In the second step, you may split each node in the hierarchical structure into one or more entity types. Typically, each node in the hierarchical structure represents more than one entity type. You should look for form fields that can be primary keys of an entity type in the database. You should make an entity type if the form field is a potential primary key

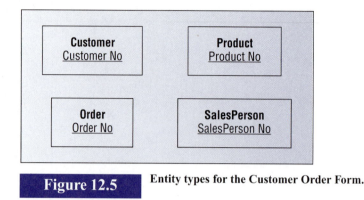

Figure 12.5   Entity types for the Customer Order Form.

and there are other associated fields in the form. Equivalently, you group form fields into entity types using functional dependencies (FDs). All form fields determined by the same field(s) should be placed together in the same entity type.

As an example of step 2, there are three entity types in the parent node of Figure 12.4 as shown in Figure 12.5: *Customer* identified by *Customer No, Order* identified by *Order No,* and *SalesPerson* identified by *SalesPerson No.* The parent node key (*Order No*) usually designates an entity type. *Customer No* and *SalesPerson No* are good choices because there are other associated fields (*Customer Name* and *SalesPerson Name*). In the child node, there is one entity type: *Product* designated by *Product No* because *Product No* can be a primary key with other associated fields.

Step 3: Attach Attributes

In the third step, you attach attributes to the entity types identified in the previous step. It is usually easy to associate form fields with the entity types. You should group together fields that are associated with the primary keys found in step 2. Sometimes the proximity of fields can provide clues to their grouping: form fields close together often belong in the same entity type. In this example, group the fields as shown in Figure 12.6. *Order* with *Order No* and *Order Date, Customer* with *Customer No, Customer Name, Address, City, State,* and *Zip, SalesPerson* with *SalesPerson No* and *SalesPerson Name,* and *Product* with *Product No, Description,* and *Unit Price.*

If you are observant, you might notice that *Quantity* does not seem to belong to *Product* because the combination of *Order No* and *Product No* determines *Quantity.* You can create a new entity type (*OrderLine*) with *Quantity* as an attribute. If you miss this entity type, *Quantity* can be made an attribute of a relationship in the next step. In addition, the *Unit Price* attribute can be considered an attribute of the *OrderLine* entity type if the historical price rather than the current price of a product is tracked.

Step 4: Add Relationships

In the fourth step, you connect entity types with relationships and specify cardinalities. Table 12.1 summarizes rules about connecting entity types. You should begin with the entity type containing the primary key of the form. Let us call this the form entity type. Make the form entity type the center of the ERD. Typically, several relationships connect the form entity type to other entity types derived from the parent and the child nodes. In Figure 12.5, *Order* is the form entity type.

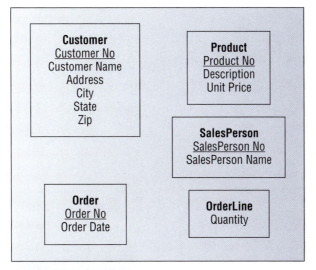

Figure 12.6   **Attributes added to the entity types of Figure 12.5.**

TABLE 12.1	**Rules to Connect Entity Types**

1. Place the form entity type in the center of the ERD.
2. Add relationships between the form entity type and other entity types derived from the parent node. The relationships are usually 1-M.
3. Add a relationship to connect the form entity type to an entity type in the child node.
4. Add relationships to connect entity types derived from the child node if not already connected.

After identifying the form entity type, you should add 1-M relationships with other entity types derived from fields in the main form. This leaves us with *Order* connected to *Customer* and *SalesPerson* through 1-M relationships as shown in Figure 12.7. You should verify that the same customer can make many orders and the same salesperson can take many orders by examining additional form instances and talking to knowledgeable users.

Next connect the entity types derived from fields in the subform. *Product* and *OrderLine* can be connected by a 1-M relationship. An order line contains one product, but the same product may appear in order lines of different forms.

To finish the relationships, you need to connect an entity type derived from main form fields with an entity type derived from subform fields. Typically, the relationship will connect the form entity type (*Order*) with an entity type derived from the child node. This relationship can be 1-M or M-N. In Figure 12.7, you can assume that an order can be associated with many products. If you examine other order form instances, you could see the same product associated with different orders. Therefore, a product can be associated with many orders. Here, it is important to note that *Quantity* is not associated with either *Product* or *Order* but with the combination. The combination can be considered a relationship or entity type. In Figure 12.7, *OrderLine* is an entity type. Figure 12.8 shows an alternative representation as an M-N relationship.

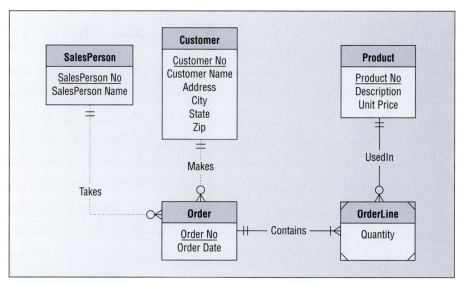

Figure 12.7   Entity relationship diagram for the Customer Order Form.

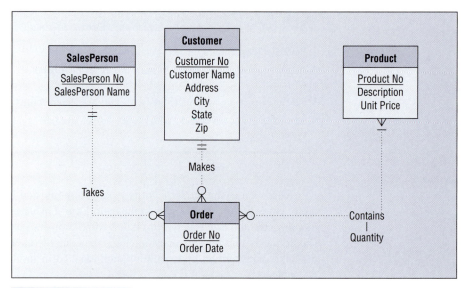

Figure 12.8   Alternative ERD for the Customer Order Form.

Step 5: Check Completeness and Consistency

In the fifth step, you check the ERD for consistency and completeness with the form structure. The ERD should adhere to the diagram rules defined in Chapter 5 (Section 5.4.2). For example, the ERD should contain minimum and maximum cardinalities for all relationships, a primary key for all entity types, and a name for all relationships.

For consistency, the form structure provides several constraints on the relationship cardinalities as summarized in Table 12.2. The first rule is necessary because only one value is displayed on the form. For example, there is only one value displayed for the

TABLE 12.2	Consistency Rules for Relationship Cardinalities

1. In at least one direction, the maximum cardinality should be one for relationships connecting entity types derived from the same node (parent or child).

2. In at least one direction, the maximum cardinality should be greater than one for relationships connecting entity types derived from nodes on different levels of the form hierarchy.

Invoice Form

Customer No.: 1273
Name: Contemporary Designs
Address: 123 Any Street
City: Seattle **State:** WA

Invoice No.: 06389
Date: 3/28/2003
Order No.: 61384
Zip: 98105

Product No	Description	Qty Ord	Qty Ship	Qty Back	Unit Price	Total Price
B381	Cabinet	2	2		150.00	300.00
R210	Table	1	1		500.00	500.00
M128	Bookcase	4	2	2	200.00	400.00
				Total Amount		$1200.00
				Discount		60.00
				Amount Due		$1140.00

Figure 12.9 Sample Invoice Form.

customer number, name, and so on. As an example of the first rule, the maximum cardinality is one in the relationship from *Order* to *Customer* and from *Order* to *SalesPerson*. The second rule ensures that there is a 1-M relationship from the parent to the child node. A given record in the parent node can be related to many records in the child node. As an example of the second rule, the relationship from *Order* to *OrderLine* has a maximum cardinality of M. In the alternative ERD (Figure 12.8), the maximum cardinality is M from *Order* to *Product*.

After following the steps of form analysis, you also can explore transformations as discussed in Chapter 6 (Section 6.1). The attribute to entity type transformation is often useful. If the form only displays a primary key, you may not initially create an entity type. For example, if only the salesperson number is displayed, you may not create a separate salesperson entity type. You can ask the user whether other data about a salesperson should be maintained. If yes, transform the salesperson number into an entity type.

Another Form Analysis Example

The Invoice Form (Figure 12.9) provides another example for form analysis. A customer receives an invoice form along with the products ordered. In the main form, an invoice contains fields to identify the customer and the order. In the subform, an invoice identifies the

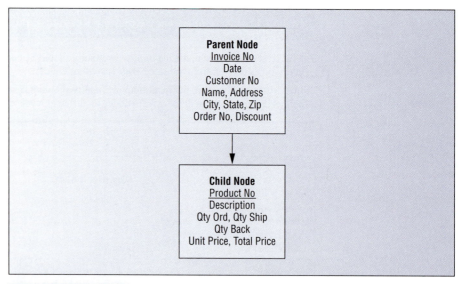

Figure 12.10   Hierarchical structure for the Invoice Form.

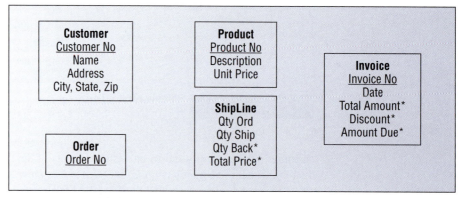

Figure 12.11   Entity types for the Invoice Form.

products and the quantities shipped, ordered, and backordered. The quantity backordered equals the quantity ordered less the quantity shipped. Corresponding to this form, Figure 12.10 shows the hierarchical structure.

Figure 12.11 shows the result of steps 2 and 3 for the Customer Invoice form. The asterisks denote computed fields. *Invoice, Customer,* and *Order* are derived from the parent node. *Product* and *ShipLine* are derived from the child node. If you miss *ShipLine,* you can add it later as a relationship.

Figure 12.12 displays the ERD for the Invoice Form. The *SentTo* and *ShipFor* relationships connect entity types from the parent node. The *ShipsIn* relationship connects an entity type in the parent node (*Invoice*) with an entity type in the child node (*ShipLine*). Figure 12.13 shows an alternative ERD with the *ShipLine* entity type replaced by an M-N relationship.

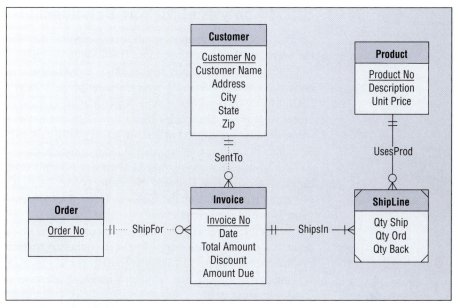

Figure 12.12   ERD for the Invoice Form.

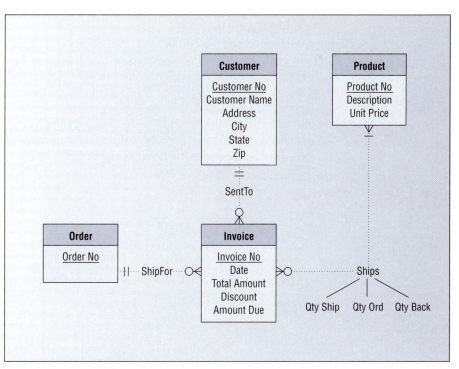

Figure 12.13   Alternative ERD for the Invoice Form.

12.2.2 Analysis of M-Way Relationships Using Forms

Chapter 7 described the concept of relationship independence as a way to reason about the need for M-way relationships. This section describes a more application-oriented way to reason about M-way relationships. You can use data entry forms to help determine if an associative entity type representing an M-way relationship is needed in an ERD. M-way relationships can be difficult to understand because they involve three or more entity types. Data entry forms provide a context to understand M-way relationships. Without the context of a form, it can be difficult to determine that an M-way relationship is necessary as opposed to binary relationships.

An M-way relationship may be needed if a form shows a data entry pattern involving three entity types. Typically, one entity type resides on the main form and the other two entity types reside on the subform. Figure 12.14 shows a form with a project in the main form and part–supplier combinations (two entity types) in the subform. This form can be used to purchase parts for a particular project (localized purchasing). Because purchasing decisions are made by projects, both Part No and Supplier No can be updated in the subform. Figure 12.15 shows an ERD for this form. An associative entity type involving purchase, part, and supplier is necessary because a purchase can involve many combinations of parts and suppliers.

As an alternative to localized purchasing for each project, some organizations may prefer centralized purchasing. Figure 12.16 shows a form to support centralized purchasing with the supplier in the main form and related parts (one entity type) in the subform. The ERD in Figure 12.17 shows a binary relationship between *Purchase* and *Part*. To allocate parts to projects, there is another form with the project in the main form and the parts used by the project in the subform. The ERD for the other form would need a binary relationship between project and part.

Even if there are two or more entity types in a subform, binary relationships may suffice if only one entity type is updatable. In Figure 12.14, both Supplier No and Part No are updatable in the subform. Thus, an M-way relationship is necessary. As a counter example, Figure 12.18 shows a form for course registration. The subform shows primary keys of the *Offering, Faculty,* and *Course* entity types, but only *Offering* is updatable in the subform. Faculty No and Course No are read only. The selection of a faculty member and the course corresponding to the offering are made in other forms. Thus, the ERD only contains binary relationships as Figure 12.19 shows.

Project Purchasing Form			
Purchase No.: P1234 **Project No.:** PR1		**Purchase Date:** 3/19/2003 **Project Manager:** Jon Smith	
Part No.	Supplier No.	Quantity	Unit Price
M128	S100	4	$120
M128	S101	3	$150
R210	S102	1	$500

Figure 12.14   **Sample Project Purchasing Form.**

Figure 12.15   **Entity relationship diagram for the Project Purchase Form.**

Purchasing Form

Purchase No.: P1234   **Purchase Date:** 3/19/2003
Supplier No.: S101   **Supplier Name:** Anytime Supply

Part No.	Quantity	Unit Price
M128	4	$120
M129	3	$150
R210	1	$500

Figure 12.16   **Sample Purchasing Form.**

Figure 12.17   **Entity relationship diagram for the Purchasing Form.**

Registration No: 1273 Quarter: Fall Student No: 123489					Date: 5/15/2003 Year: 2003 Student Name: Sue Thomas	
Offer No	Course No	Days	Time	Location	Faculty No	Faculty Name
1234	IS480	MW	10:30	BLM211	1111	Sally Hope
3331	IS460	MW	8:30	BLM411	2121	George Jetstone
2222	IS470	MW	1:30	BLM305	1111	Sally Hope

Figure 12.18 Registration form.

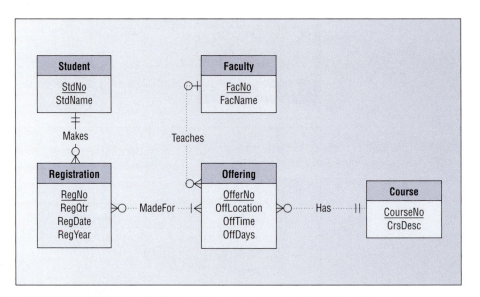

Figure 12.19 Entity relationship diagram for the registration form.

12.3 VIEW INTEGRATION

With a large database project, even skilled database designers need a way to manage the complexity of the design process. Together, view design and integration can help you manage a large database design project by providing a way to break a large effort into smaller parts. In the last section, you studied how to design an ERD that represents the data requirements of a form. This section describes the process to combine individual views into a complete database design. Two approaches for view integration are presented along with an example of each approach.

12.3.1 Incremental and Parallel Integration Approaches

The incremental and parallel approaches are opposite ways to perform view integration. In the <u>incremental approach</u> (Figure 12.20), a view and partially integrated ERD are merged in each integration step. Initially, the designer chooses a view and constructs an ERD for it. For subsequent views, the designer performs integration while analyzing the

Figure 12.20   Incremental integration process.

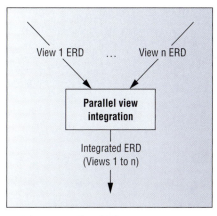

Figure 12.21   Parallel integration process.

next view. The view design and integration processes are performed jointly for each view after the first one. This approach is incremental as a partially integrated ERD is produced after each step. This approach is also binary as the current view is analyzed along with the partially integrated ERD.

In the <u>parallel approach</u> (Figure 12.21), ERDs are produced for each view and then the view ERDs are merged. The integration occurs in one large step after all views are analyzed. This approach is parallel because different designers can perform view designs at the same time. Integration can be more complex in the parallel approach because integration is postponed until the end when all views are integrated to produce the final ERD.

Both approaches have advantages and disadvantages. The incremental approach has more integration steps, but each integration step is smaller. The parallel approach postpones integration until the end when a large integration effort may be necessary. The incremental approach is well suited to closely related views. For example, the order and the invoice forms are closely related because an order precedes an invoice. The parallel approach works well on large projects with views that are not closely related. Independent teams can work on different parts of a design in parallel. On a large project with many database designers, the parallel approach supports more independent work.

Determining an Integration Strategy

Integration Strategy a mix of incremental and parallel approaches to integrate a set of views. The views are divided into subsets. For each subset of views, incremental integration is used. Parallel integration is usually applied to the ERDs resulting from integrating the view subsets.

The incremental and parallel approaches are typically combined in a large database design project. An <u>integration strategy</u> (Figure 12.22) specifies a mix of incremental and parallel approaches to integrate a set of views. To choose an integration strategy, you divide the views into subsets (say *n* subsets). For each subset of views, the incremental approach is followed. You should choose subsets of views so that the views in a subset are closely related. Views in different subsets should not be closely related. Incremental integration across subsets of views can proceed in parallel. After an integrated ERD is produced for each subset of views, a parallel integration produces the final, integrated ERD. If the ERDs from each subset of views do not overlap much, the final integration should not be difficult. If there is significant overlap among the subset of views, incremental integration can be used to combine the ERDs from the view subsets.

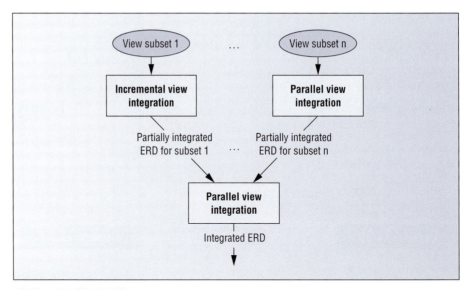

Figure 12.22   Outline of a general integration strategy.

As an example, consider a database to support a consulting firm. The database should support marketing to potential customers, billing on existing projects, and conducting work on projects. The database design effort can be divided into three parts (marketing, billing, and working). A separate design team may work incrementally on each part. If the marketing part has requirements for customer contacts and promotions, two incremental ERDs should be produced. After working independently, the teams can perform a parallel integration to combine their work.

Precedence Relationships among Forms

To help determine an integration strategy, you should identify precedence relationships among forms. Form A precedes form B if form A must be complete before form B is used. Form A typically provides some data used in form B. For example, the invoice form (Figure 12.9) uses the quantity of each product ordered (from the order form) to determine the quantity to ship. A good rule of thumb is to place forms with precedence relationships in the same view subset. Thus, the invoice and order forms should be in the same subset of views.

To further depict the use of precedence relationships, let us extend the order and invoice example. Figure 12.23 shows precedence relationships among forms for a custom manufacturing company. The product design form contains data about the components of a product. The product manufacturing form contains data about the sequence of physical operations necessary to manufacture a product. The customer and product forms contain data only about customers and products, respectively. The precedence relationships indicate that instances of the customer and product forms must be complete before an order is taken. Likewise, the product and product design forms must be complete before a manufacturing form is completed.

Using these precedence relationships, the forms can be divided into two groups: (i) an ordering process consisting of the customer, product, order, and invoice forms and (ii) a manufacturing process consisting of the product, product design, and product manufacturing forms.

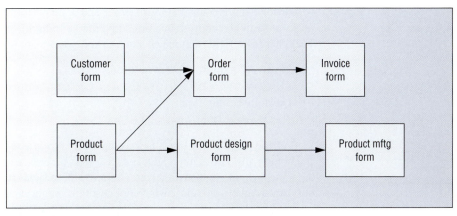

Figure 12.23   **Precedence relationships among forms.**

Resolving Synonyms and Homonyms

Resolution of Synonyms and Homonyms A synonym is a group of words that are spelled differently but have the same meaning. A homonym is a group of words that have the same sound and often the same spelling but have different meanings. The use of naming standards and a corporate data dictionary can aid in the identification and resolution of synonyms and homonyms.

In any integration approach, resolution of synonyms and homonyms is a very important issue. A <u>synonym</u> is a group of words that are spelled differently but have the same meaning. For example, OrdNo, Order Number, and ONO are likely synonyms. Synonyms occur when different parts of an organization use different vocabulary to describe the same things. This situation is especially likely if a common database did not exist before.

A <u>homonym</u> is a group of words that have the same sound and often the same spelling but have different meanings. In database design, homonyms arise because of context of usage. For example, two forms may show an address field. In one form, the address may represent the street address while in the other form, it represents the street, city, state, and zip. Even when both address fields represent the street address, they may not be the same. One form might contain the billing address while the other form contains the shipping address.

Resolving synonyms and homonyms is a major part of standardizing a vocabulary that is a large part of database development. The use of naming standards and a corporate data dictionary can aid in the identification and resolution of synonyms and homonyms. You can create and maintain a corporate data dictionary with a CASE tool. Some CASE tools help with the enforcement of naming standards. Even with these tools, recognizing synonyms and homonyms can be difficult. The most important point is to be alert for their existence. Resolving them is easier: rename synonyms the same (or establish an official list of synonyms) and rename homonyms differently.

12.3.2 View Integration Examples

This section depicts the incremental and parallel approaches to view integration using the customer order and invoice forms. The final result is identical with both approaches, but the path to this result is different.

Incremental Integration Example

To demonstrate the incremental integration approach, let us integrate the customer invoice form (Figure 12.9) with the ERD from Figure 12.7. The hierarchical structure of the invoice form is shown in Figure 12.10. You can start by adding an entity for invoice with invoice number and date. As steps 2 and 3 are performed (Figure 12.11), it is useful to see how the entity types should be merged into the existing ERD (Figure 12.7). The other form fields that match existing entity types are listed below.

- *Order No* matches the *Order* entity type.
- *Customer No, Customer Name, Address, City, State,* and *Zip* match the *Customer* entity type.
- *Product No, Description,* and *Unit Price* match the *Product* entity type.

As you match form fields to existing entity types, you should check for synonyms and homonyms. For example, it is not clear that *Address, City, State,* and *Zip* fields have the same meaning in the two forms. Certainly these fields have the same general meaning. However, it is not clear whether a customer might have a different address for ordering purposes than for shipping purposes. You may need to conduct additional interviews and examine additional form instances to resolve this issue. If you determine that the two sets of fields are homonyms (an order may be billed to one address and shipped to another), there are a number of data modeling alternatives as listed below.

- Revise the *Customer* entity type with two sets of address fields: billing address fields and shipping address fields. This solution restricts the customer to having only a single shipping address. If more than one shipping address is possible, this solution is not feasible.
- Add shipping address fields to the *Invoice* entity type. This solution supports multiple shipping addresses per customer. However, if an invoice is deleted, the shipping address is lost.
- Create a new entity type (*ShipAddress*) with the shipping address fields. This solution supports multiple shipping addresses per customer. It may require overhead to gather the shipping addresses. If shipping addresses are maintained separate from invoices, this solution is the best.

The integrated ERD in Figure 12.24 uses the second alternative. In a real problem, more information should be gathered from the users before making the decision.

In the incremental integration process, the usual process of connecting entity types (step 4 of Figure 12.3) should be followed. For example, there is an M cardinality relating an entity type derived from the parent node with an entity type derived from the child node. The maximum cardinality in *ShipsIn* from *Invoice* to *ShipLine* satisfies this constraint. Note that *ShipLine* could be represented as an M-N relationship instead of as an entity type with two 1-M relationships.

As another point of interest from Figure 12.24, there is no relationship from *Invoice* to *Customer.* At first thought, a relationship may seem necessary because customer data appear on the main form of an invoice. If the invoice customer can be different from the order customer, a relationship between *Invoice* and *Customer* is needed. If the customer on an order is the same as the customer on the related invoice, a relationship is not needed. The customer for an invoice can be found by navigating from *Invoice* to *Order* and *Order* to *Customer.* In Figure 12.24, the assumption is that the order customer and the invoice customer are identical.

Parallel Integration Example

To demonstrate the parallel integration process, let us integrate the customer invoice form (Figure 12.9) with the order form (Figure 12.2). The major difference between the parallel and incremental approaches is that integration occurs later in the parallel ap-

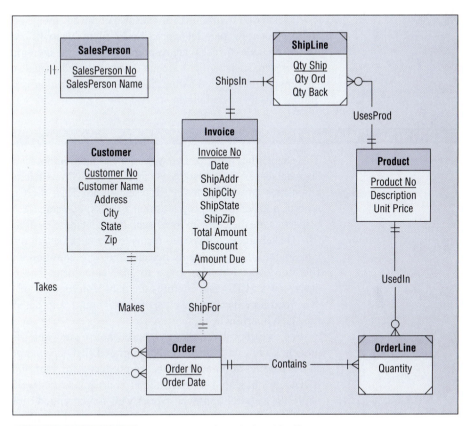

Figure 12.24   **Integrated entity relationship diagram.**

proach. Thus, the first step is to construct an ERD for each form using the steps of form analysis described previously. In the ERD for the invoice form (Figure 12.12), *Invoice* is directly connected to both *Customer* and *Order.* The direct connection follows the practice of making the form entity type (*Invoice*) the center of the diagram.

The integration process merges the order form ERD (Figure 12.7) with the invoice form ERD (Figure 12.12) to produce the ERD shown in Figure 12.24. The final ERD should be the same whether you use the incremental or the parallel approach.

Again, a major integration issue is the resolution of homonyms for the address fields. In the two ERDs (Figures 12.7 and 12.12), the *Customer* entity type contains the address fields. Working independently on the two forms, it is easy to overlook the two uses of the address fields: billing and shipping. Unless you note that the address fields in the invoice form are for shipping purposes, you may not notice that the fields are homonyms.

Another integration issue is the connections among *Invoice, Order,* and *Customer.* In Figure 12.7, *Customer* is directly connected to *Order,* but in Figure 12.12, *Order* and *Customer* are not directly connected by a relationship. The integration process must resolve this difference. The relationship between *Order* and *Customer* is needed because orders precede invoices. A relationship between *Invoice* and *Customer* is not needed if the customer shown on an invoice is the same customer shown on the associated order. Assuming that the customer on an order is identical to the customer on the associated invoices, *Invoice* is not directly connected to *Customer* in Figure 12.24.

These two integration examples depict the advantage of the incremental integration approach over the parallel approach. Conflicts due to different uses of fields and timing (orders precede invoices) are resolved sooner in the incremental approach. In the parallel approach, such conflicts are not detected until the final step. This discussion conveys the sentiment discussed earlier: incremental integration is most appropriate when integrating closely related views.

CLOSING THOUGHTS

This chapter has described view design and integration, an important skill for designing large databases. Large databases can involve ERDs with hundreds of entity types and relationships. In addition to the large size of the ERDs, there are often hundreds of forms, reports, and computer programs that will use the database. View design and integration helps manage the complexity of such large database design efforts.

This chapter emphasized forms in the view design process. Forms are an important source of requirements because they are common and easily communicated. A five-step procedure was given to analyze a form. The result of the form analysis process is an ERD that captures the data requirements of the form. This chapter also described how the form analysis process could help detect the need for M-way relationships in an ERD.

This chapter described two approaches to view integration. In the incremental approach, a view and the partially integrated ERD are merged in each integration step. In the parallel approach, ERDs are produced for each view, and then the individual ERDs are merged. The incremental approach works well for closely related views, while the parallel approach works well for unrelated views. This chapter discussed how to determine an integration strategy to combine the incremental and parallel approaches. In any integration approach, resolving synonyms and homonyms is critical. This chapter demonstrated that forms provide a context to resolve synonyms and homonyms.

This chapter concludes your study of the first two phases (conceptual data modeling and logical database design) of database development and provides a link between application development and database development. After completing these steps, you should have a high-quality relational database design: a design that represents the needs of the organization and is free of unwanted redundancies. Chapter 13 provides a detailed case study to apply the ideas in Parts 2 and 3 of this book.

REVIEW CONCEPTS

- Characteristics of large database design efforts.
- Importance of forms as sources of database requirements.
- Five steps of form analysis.
- Form structure: nodes and node keys.
- Rules for adding relationships in form analysis.
- Rules to check cardinalities for consistency in form analysis.
- Using form analysis to detect the need for M-way relationships.
- Using the incremental and parallel integration approaches.
- Determining an integration strategy by combining incremental and parallel approaches.
- Detection of synonyms and homonyms during view integration.

QUESTIONS

1. What factors influence the size of a conceptual schema?

2. How does the view design and integration process help to manage the complexity of large database design efforts?

3. What is the goal of form analysis?

4. What are node keys in a form structure?

5. How do nodes in a form structure correspond to main forms and subforms?

6. What is the form entity type?

7. Why does the ERD for a form often have a different structure than the form?

8. Why is it recommended to place the "form" entity type in the center of the ERD?

9. Explain the first consistency rule in Table 12.2.

10. Explain the second consistency rule in Table 12.2.

11. How many integration steps are necessary to perform incremental integration with 10 views?

12. How many view design steps are necessary to perform parallel integration with 10 views?

13. In the incremental integration approach, why are view design and integration performed together?

14. When is the incremental integration approach appropriate?

15. When is the parallel integration approach appropriate?

16. What is an integration strategy?

17. When does a form depend on another form?

18. What criteria can you use to decide how to group views in an integration strategy?

19. What is a synonym in view integration?

20. What is a homonym in view integration?

21. Why do synonyms and homonyms occur when designing a database?

22. How can using forms in database design help you to detect synonyms and homonyms?

PROBLEMS

Besides the problems presented here, the case studies in this book's website provide additional practice. To supplement the examples in this chapter, Chapter 13 provides a complete database design case including view design and integration.

1. Perform form analysis for the Simple Order Form (problem 22 of Chapter 10). Your solution should include a hierarchical structure for the form, an ERD that represents the form, and design justifications. Ignore the database design in Chapter 10 when performing the analysis. In your analysis, you can assume that an order must contain at least one product.

2. Perform form analysis for the Order Form (problem 23 of Chapter 10). Your solution should include a hierarchical structure for the form, an ERD that represents the form, and design justifications. Ignore the database design in Chapter 10 when performing the analysis. Here are a number of additional points to supplement the sample form shown in problem 23 of Chapter 10:

    - In all additional form instances, customer data appear on the main form.
    - In some additional form instances, the employee data do not appear on the main form.
    - In some additional form instances, the price for the same product varies. For example, the price for product P0036566 is $169.00 on some instances and $150.00 on other instances.
    - The supplier number cannot be updated on the subform. In addition, the supplier number and name are identical for all instances of the subform with the same product number.

3. Perform form analysis for the Simple Purchasing Form (problem 25 of Chapter 10). Your solution should include a hierarchical structure for the form, an ERD that represents the form, and design justifications. Ignore the database design in Chapter 10 when performing the analysis. Here are a number of additional points to supplement the sample form shown in problem 25 of Chapter 10:

    - The purchase unit price can vary across form instances containing the same product number.
    - A purchase must contain at least one product.

4. Perform form analysis for the Purchasing Form (problem 26 of Chapter 10). Your solution should include a hierarchical structure for the form, an ERD that represents the form, and design justifications. Ignore the database design in Chapter 10 when performing the analysis. Here are a number of additional points to supplement the sample form shown in problem 26 of Chapter 10:

    - In all additional form instances, supplier data appear on the main form.
    - The selling price can vary across form instances containing the same product number.
    - The unit cost and QOH are identical across subform instances for a given product.

5. Perform form analysis for the Supplier Form (problem 27 of Chapter 10). Your solution should include a hierarchical structure for the form, an ERD that represents the form, and design justifications. Ignore the database design in Chapter 10 when performing the analysis. In analyzing the form, you can assume that a given product only appears on one Supplier Form instance.

6. Perform parallel integration using the ERDs that you created in problems 2, 4, and 5. Ignore the database design in Chapter 10 when performing the analysis. In performing the integration, you should assume that every product on a purchase form must come from the same supplier. In addition, you should assume that a Supplier Form instance must be completed before products can be ordered or purchased.

7. Perform form analysis on the Project Staffing Form that follows. Projects have a manager, a start date, an end date, a category, a budget (hours and dollars), and a list of staff assigned. For each staff assigned, the available hours and the assigned hours are shown.

Project Staffing Form

Project ID: PR1234
Category: Auditing
Budget Hours: 170
Begin Date: 6/1/2003

Project Name: A/P testing
Manager: Scott Jones
Budget Dollars: $10,000
End Date: 6/30/2003

Staff ID	Staff Name	Avail Hours	Assigned Hours
S128	Rob Scott	10	10
S129	Sharon Store	20	5
S130	Sue Kendall	20	15

8. Perform incremental integration using the ERD from problem 7 and the Program Form that follows. A project is divided into a number of programs. Each program is assigned to one employee. An employee can be assigned to a program only if the employee has been assigned to the project.

Program Form

Staff ID: S128
Project ID: PR1234

Name: Rob Scott
Project Manager: Scott Jones

Program ID	Hours	Status	Due Date
PR1234-1	10	completed	6/25/2003
PR1234-2	10	pending	6/27/2003
PR1234-3	20	pending	6/15/2003

9. Perform incremental integration using the ERD from problem 8 and the Timesheet Form that follows. The Timesheet Form allows an employee to record hours worked on various programs during a time period.

Timesheet Form

Timesheet ID: TS100
Total Hours: 18
Staff ID: S128
Begin Date: 5/1/2003

Time Period No: 5

Name: Rob Scott
End Date: 5/31/2003

Program ID	Hours	Pay Type	Date
PR1234-1	4	regular	5/2/2003
PR1234-1	6	overtime	5/2/2003
PR1234-2	8	regular	5/3/2003

10. Define an integration strategy for the Project Staffing, Program, and Timesheet forms. Briefly justify your integration strategy.

REFERENCES FOR FURTHER STUDY

View design and integration is covered in more detail in specialized books on database design. The best reference on view design and integration is Batini, Ceri, and Navathe (1992). Other database design books such as Nijssen and Halpin (1989) and Teorey (1999) also cover view design and integration. More details about the methodology for form analysis and view integration can be found in Choobineh, Mannino, Konsynski, and Nunamaker (1988) and Choobineh, Mannino, and Tseng (1992). Batra (1997) provides a recent update to this work on form analysis.

CHAPTER 13

Database Development for Student Loan, Limited

This chapter applies the knowledge and skills presented in the chapters of Parts 2 and 3 to a moderate-size case. After this chapter, the student should have acquired the following knowledge and skills:

■ Perform conceptual data modeling for a comparable case.

■ Refine an ERD using conversion and normalization for a comparable case.

■ Estimate a workload on a table design of moderate size.

■ Perform index selection for a comparable case.

■ Specify the data requirements for applications in a comparable case.

OVERVIEW The chapters of Parts 2 and 3 have provided knowledge and techniques about using the database development process. You learned about using the Entity Relationship Model (Chapters 5 and 6), refining a conceptual schema through conversion and normalization (Chapters 6 and 7), using the view modeling and view integration processes for large conceptual data modeling efforts (Chapter 12), and finding an efficient implementation (Chapter 8). In addition, you learned about the broad context of database development

(Chapter 4). This chapter applies the specific design techniques of other chapters to a moderate-size case. By carefully following the case and its solution, you should reinforce your design skills, gain insights about the database development process, and obtain a model for database development of comparable cases.

This chapter presents a case derived from discussions with information systems professionals of a large commercial processor of student loans. Servicing student loans is a rather complex business owing to the many different kinds of loans, changing government regulations, and numerous billing conditions. To adapt the case for this chapter, many details have been omitted. The database for the actual information system is more than 150 tables. The case presented here preserves the essential concepts of student loan processing but is understandable in one chapter. You should find the case challenging and informative. You might even learn how to have your student loans forgiven!

13.1 CASE DESCRIPTION

This section describes the purpose and environment of student loan processing as well as the work flow of a proposed system for Student Loan, Limited. In addition to the details in this section, Appendix 13.A contains a glossary of fields contained in the forms and reports.

13.1.1 Overview

The Guaranteed Student Loan (GSL) program was created to help students pay for their college education. GSL loans are classified according to subsidy status: (1) <u>subsidized,</u> in which the federal government pays interest accruing during school years and (2) <u>unsubsidized,</u> in which the federal government does not pay interest accruing during school years. On unsubsidized loans, the interest accruing during school years is added to the principal when repayment begins. Repayment of loans begins about six months after separation from school. A given student can receive multiple GSL loans with each loan possibly having a different interest rate and subsidy status.

To support the GSL program, different organizations may play the role of lender, guarantor, and service provider. Students apply for loans from <u>lenders,</u> including banks, savings and loans, and credit unions. The U.S. Department of Education makes loans possible by guaranteeing repayment if certain conditions are met. Lenders ensure that applicants are eligible for the GSL program. The <u>service provider</u> tracks student status, calculates repayment schedules, and collects payments. The <u>guarantor</u> ensures that loans are serviced properly by monitoring the work of the service provider. If a loan enters claim (nonpayment) status and the loan has not been serviced according to Department of Education guidelines, the guarantor can become liable. To reduce their risk, lenders usually do not service or guarantee their loans. Instead, lenders typically contract with a service provider and guarantor.

Student Loan, Limited is a leading service provider for GSL and other types of student loans. Student Loan, Limited currently uses a legacy system with older file technology. They want to switch to a client–server architecture using a relational DBMS. The new architecture should allow them to respond to new regulations easier as well as to pursue new business such as the direct lending program.

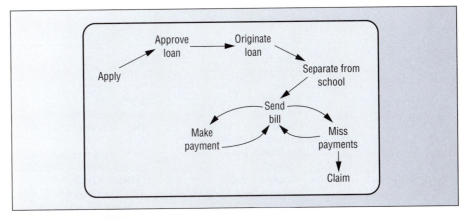

Figure 13.1   **Loan processing work flow.**

13.1.2 Flow of Work

Processing of student loans follows the pattern shown in Figure 13.1. Students apply for a loan from a lender. In the approval process, the lender usually identifies a guarantor. If the loan is approved, the student signs a promissory note that describes the interest rate and the repayment terms. After the promissory note is signed, the lender sends a loan origination form to Student Loan, Limited. Student Loan, Limited then disburses funds as specified in the loan origination form. Typically, funds are disbursed in each period of an academic year.

Upon separating from school (graduation or leaving school), the repayment process begins. Shortly after a student separates from school, Student Loan, Limited sends a disclosure letter. A disclosure letter provides an estimate of the monthly payment required to repay an outstanding loan by the end of the payment period. The student receives one disclosure letter per note except if the notes have been consolidated into a single note. Notes are consolidated if the interest rate, subsidy status, and repayment period are similar.

About six months after separation, Student Loan, Limited sends the first bill. For convenience, Student Loan, Limited sends one consolidated statement even if the student has multiple outstanding loans. With most students, Student Loan, Limited processes periodic bills and payments until all loans are repaid. If a student becomes delinquent, collection activities begin. If collection is successful, the student returns to the billing-payment cycle. Otherwise, the loan enters claim (default) and may be given to a collection agency.

Loan Origination Form

The Loan Origination Form, an electronic document sent from a lender, triggers involvement of Student Loan, Limited. Figures 13.2 and 13.3 depict sample forms with student, loan, and disbursement data. An origination form includes only one loan identified by a unique loan number. Each time a loan is approved, the lender sends a new loan origination form. The disbursement method can be electronic funds transfer (EFT) or check. If the disbursement method is EFT (Figure 13.2), the routing number, the account number,

<table>
<tr><td colspan="3" align="center">**Loan Origination Form**</td></tr>
<tr><td>**Loan No.** L101</td><td>**Date**</td><td>6 Sept. 2004</td></tr>
<tr><td>**Student No.**</td><td colspan="2">S100</td></tr>
<tr><td>**Name**</td><td colspan="2">Sam Student</td></tr>
<tr><td>**Address**</td><td colspan="2">15400 Any Street</td></tr>
<tr><td>**City, State, Zip**</td><td colspan="2">Anytown, USA 00999</td></tr>
<tr><td>**Phone** (341) 555-2222</td><td colspan="2">**Date of Birth** 11/11/1985</td></tr>
<tr><td>**Expected Graduation**</td><td colspan="2">May 2002</td></tr>
<tr><td>**Institution ID:** U100</td><td colspan="2">**Institution Name:** University of Colorado</td></tr>
<tr><td>**Address**</td><td colspan="2">1250 14th Street, Suite 700</td></tr>
<tr><td>**City, State, Zip**</td><td colspan="2">Denver CO 80217</td></tr>
<tr><td>**Disbursement Method**</td><td colspan="2">*EFT* **X** *Check*</td></tr>
<tr><td>**Routing No.** R10001</td><td colspan="2">**Account No.** A111000</td></tr>
<tr><td>**Disbursement Bank**</td><td colspan="2">Any Student Bank USA</td></tr>
<tr><td>**Lender No.** LE100</td><td colspan="2">**Lender Name** Any Bank USA</td></tr>
<tr><td>**Guarantor No.** G100</td><td colspan="2">**Guarantor Name** Any Guarantor USA</td></tr>
<tr><td>**Note Value:** $10000</td><td>**Subsidized:** Yes</td><td>**Rate:** 8.5%</td></tr>
</table>

Disbursement Plan

Date	Amount	Origination Fee	Guarantee Fee
30 Sept 2004	$3,200	$100	$100
30 Dec 2004	$3,200	$100	$100
30 Mar 2005	$3,000	$100	$100

Figure 13.2   Sample Loan Origination Form.

and the financial institution must be given. The disbursement plan shows the date of disbursement, the amount, and any fees. Note that the total amount of the loan is the sum of the amounts disbursed plus the fees. Fees typically amount to 6 percent of the loan.

Disclosure Letter

After a student graduates but before repayment begins, Student Loan, Limited is required to send disclosure letters for each outstanding loan. Typically, disclosure letters are sent about 60 days after a student separates from school. In some cases, more than one disclosure letter per loan may be sent at different times. A disclosure letter includes fields for the amount of the loan, amount of the monthly payment, number of payments, interest rate, total finance charge, and due date of the first and last payments. In the sample disclosure letter (Figure 13.4), the fields in the form letter are underlined. Student Loan, Limited is required to retain copies of disclosure letters in case the guarantor needs to review the loan processing of a student.

Statement of Account

About six months after a student separates, Student Loan, Limited sends the first bill. For most students, additional bills follow monthly. In Student Loan, Limited vocabulary, a bill is known as a Statement of Account. Figures 13.5 and 13.6 depict sample

Loan Origination Form

Loan No. L100	**Date** 7 Sept. 2003
Student No.	S100
Name	Sam Student
Address	15400 Any Street
City, State, Zip	Anytown, USA 00999
Phone (341) 555-2222	**Date of Birth** 11/11/1985
Expected Graduation	May 2002
Institution Id: U100	**Institution Name:** University of Colorado
Address	1250 14th Street, Suite 700
City, State, Zip	Denver CO 80217
Disbursement Method	*EFT Check* **X**
Routing No. —	**Account No.** —
Disbursement Bank	—
Lender No. LE100	**Lender Name** Any Bank USA
Guarantor No. G100	**Guarantor Name** Any Guarantor USA
Note Value: $10000	**Subsidized:** No **Rate:** 8.0%

Disbursement Plan

Date	Amount	Origination Fee	Guarantee Fee
29 Sept 2003	$3,200	$100	$100
30 Dec 2003	$3,200	$100	$100
28 Mar 2004	$3,000	$100	$100

Figure 13.3   Sample Loan Origination Form.

Disclosure Letter

1 July 2005
Subject: Loan L101

Dear Mr. Student,

According to our records, your guaranteed student loan enters repayment status in September 2005. The total amount that you borrowed was $10,000. Your payment schedule includes 120 payments with an interest rate of 8.5%. Your estimated finance charge is $4,877.96. Your first payment will be due on October 31, 2005. Your monthly payment will be $246.37. Your last payment is due September 30, 2015.

Sincerely,

Anne Administrator, Student Loan, Limited

Figure 13.4   Sample Disclosure Letter.

Statement of Account

Statement No.	B100	**Date**	1 Oct. 2005
Student No.	S100	**Name**	Sam Student
Street	123 Any Street	**Zip**	00011
City	Any City	**State**	Any State
Amount Due	$246.37	**Due Date**	31 Oct 2005
Payment Method	*Check* **X** *EFT*	**Amount Enclosed**	

Loan Summary

Loan No.	Balance	Rate
L100	$10,000	8.5%
L101	$10,000	8.2%

For Office Use Only

Date Paid:

Figure 13.5   Sample Statement of Account for check payment.

Statement of Account

Statement No.	B101	**Date**	1 Nov. 2005
Student No.	S100	**Name**	Sam Student
Street	123 Any Street	**Zip**	00011
City	Any City	**State**	Any State
Amount Due	$246.37	**Due Date**	30 Nov. 2005
Payment Method	*Check* *EFT* **X**	**Amount Enclosed**	

Note: $246.37 will be deducted from your account on 30 Nov 2005

Loan Summary

Loan No.	Balance	Rate
L100	$9,946.84	8.5%
L101	$9,944.34	8.2%

For Office Use Only

Date Paid:

Figure 13.6   Sample Statement of Account for EFT payment.

statements. The top half of a statement contains the unique statement number, amount due, due date, amount paid, and payment method (EFT or check). If the payment method is by check (Figure 13.5), the student returns the statement to Student Loan, Limited with the check enclosed. In this case, the amount paid is completed either by the student when the bill is returned or by data entry personnel of Student Loan, Limited when the statement is processed. If the payment method is EFT (Figure 13.6), the

Loan Activity Report

Student No.	S100	**Date**	1 Feb. 2006	
Street	123 Any Street	**Name**	Sam Student	
City	Any City	**Zip**	00011	
		State	Any State	

Payment Summary for 2005

Loan No.	Beg. Balance	Principal	Interest	Ending Balance
L100	$10,000	160.60	211.37	$9,839.40
L101	$10,000	168.12	203.85	$9,831.88

For Office Use Only

Date Paid:

Figure 13.7 Sample Loan Activity Report.

amount paid is shown on the statement along with the date that the transfer will be made. The date paid is completed by Student Loan, Limited when a payment is received. The lower half of a statement lists the status of each loan. For each loan, the loan number, outstanding balance, and interest rate are shown.

After a payment is received, Student Loan, Limited applies the principal amount of the payment to outstanding loan balances. The payment is apportioned among each outstanding loan according to an associated payment schedule. If a student pays more than the specified amount, the extra amount may be applied in a number of ways such as the loan with highest interest rate is reduced first or all outstanding loans are reduced equally. The method of applying extra amounts is determined by Department of Education policy. As with most government policies, it is subject to change. Applications of a payment to loan balances can be seen by comparing two consecutive statements. Figures 13.5 and 13.6 show that $53.16 of the October 2005 payment was applied to loan L100.

Loan Activity Report

After the end of each year, Student Loan, Limited sends each student a report summarizing all loan activity. For each loan, the report (Figure 13.7) shows the loan balance at the beginning of the year, the total amount applied to reduce the principal, the total interest paid, and the loan balance at the end of the year. Student Loan, Limited is required to retain copies of loan activity reports in case the guarantor needs to review the loan processing of a student.

New Technology

To reduce paper, Student Loan, Limited is interested in imaging the documents (disclosure letters and loan activity reports) required by guarantors. After imaging the documents, they would like to store recent documents in the student loan database and nonrecent documents in archival storage.

13.2 CONCEPTUAL DATA MODELING

The conceptual data modeling phases use the incremental integration approach because the case is not too large and the forms are related. Incremental integration begins with the loan origination form because it triggers involvement of Student Loan, Limited with a loan.

13.2.1 ERD for the Loan Origination Form

The Loan Origination Form contains two nodes, as shown in Figure 13.8. The child node contains the repeating disbursement fields. The *Loan* entity type is the center of the ERD, as shown in Figure 13.9. The surrounding entity types (*Guarantor, Lender, Institution,* and *Student*) and associated relationships are derived from the parent node. The minimum cardinality is 0 from *Loan* to *Guarantor* because some loans do not have a guarantor (lender performs role). The *DisburseLine* entity type and associated relationship are derived from the child node. Table 13.1 shows assumptions corresponding to the annotations in Figure 13.9.

13.2.2 Incremental Integration after Adding the Disclosure Letter

The disclosure letter contains only a single node (Figure 13.10) because it has no repeating groups. Figure 13.11 shows the integrated ERD, with corresponding assumptions shown in Table 13.2. The ERD in Figure 13.11 assumes that images can be stored in the database. Therefore, the particular fields of a disclosure letter are not stored. The unique *LetterNo* field has been added as a convenient identifier of a disclosure letter. If images cannot be stored in the database, some of the fields in the disclosure letter may need to be stored because they are difficult to compute.

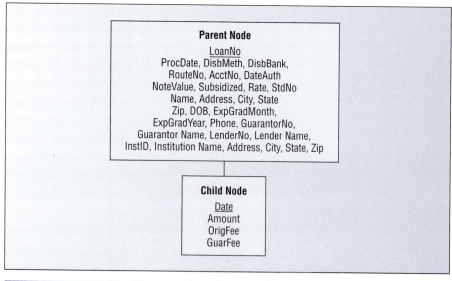

Figure 13.8   **Structure of the Loan Origination Form.**

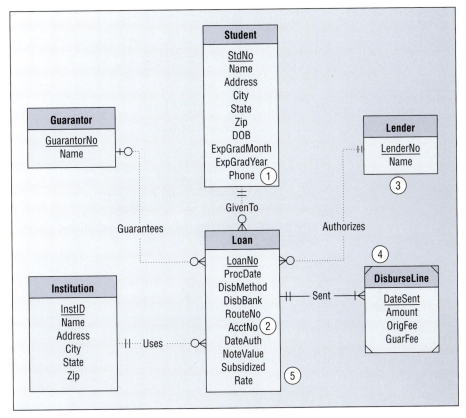

| **Figure 13.9** | ERD for the Loan Origination Form. |

| **TABLE 13.1** | **Assumptions for the ERD in Figure 13.9** |

Annotation Number	*Explanation*
1	The expected graduation fields can be combined into one field or kept as two fields.
2	Routing number (*RouteNo*), account number (*AcctNo*), and disbursement bank (*DisbBank*) are required if the disbursement method is EFT. Otherwise, they are not used.
3	There would probably be other data about lenders and guarantors that is stored. Because the form only shows the identifying number and name, the ERD does not include extra fields.
4	*DisburseLine* is identification dependent on *Loan*. Because *DisburseLine.DateSent* is a local key, there cannot be two disbursements of the same loan on the same date. The primary key of *DisburseLine* is a concatenation of *LoanNo* and *DateSent*.
5	The sum of the amount, the origination fee, and the guarantee fee in the disbursement plan should equal the note value.

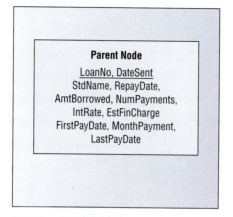

Figure 13.10   Structure of the disclosure letter.

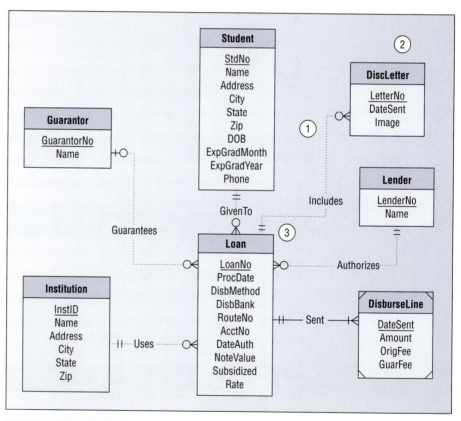

Figure 13.11   ERD after adding the disclosure letter.

TABLE 13.2	Assumptions for the ERD in Figure 13.11

Annotation Number	*Explanation*
1	The relationship between *DiscLetter* and *Loan* allows multiple letters per loan. As stated in the case, multiple disclosure letters may be sent for the same loan.
2	The *Image* field contains a scanned image of the letter. The guarantor may require a copy of the letter if the loan is audited. As an alternative to storing the image, an indicator of the physical location could be stored if imaging technology is not used.
3	The minimum cardinality of 0 is needed because a payment plan is not created until a student has separated from school.

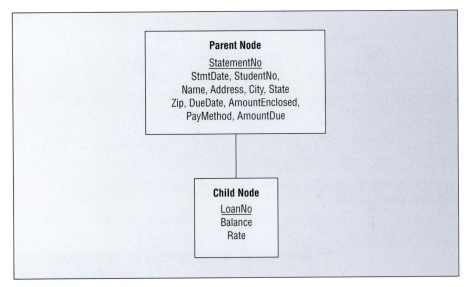

Figure 13.12	Structure of the statement of account.

13.2.3 Incremental Integration after Adding the Statement of Account

The statement of account contains both parent and child nodes (Figure 13.12) because it has a repeating group. Figure 13.13 shows the integrated ERD with corresponding assumptions shown in Table 13.3. The *Applied* relationship in Figure 13.13 represents the parent–child relationship in the form hierarchy. The minimum cardinality is 0 from *Loan* to *Statement* because a loan does not have any amounts applied until after it enters payment status.

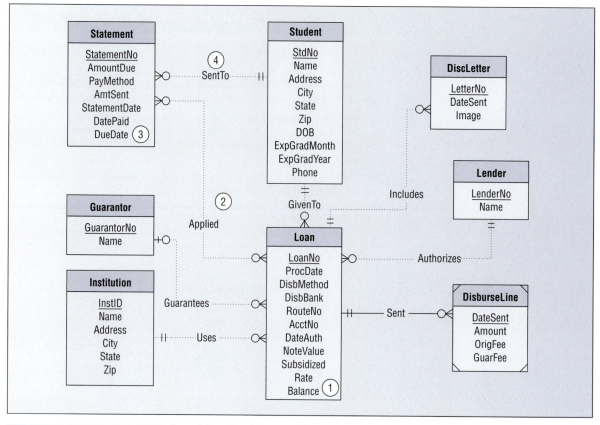

Figure 13.13 ERD after adding the statement of account.

TABLE 13.3	Assumptions for the ERD in Figure 13.13

Annotation Number	*Explanation*
1	*Balance* is added as a field to reflect the loan summary on a statement. The balance reflects the last payment made on a loan.
2	The *Applied* relationship is created at the same time as the statement. However, the principal and interest fields are not updated until after a payment is received. The attributes (*Principal, Interest, CumPrincipal*, and *CumInterest*) of the applied relationship are not shown in the diagram to reduce clutter. *CumPrinicipal* and *CumInterest* are derived columns that facilitate the Loan Activity Report.
3	If the payment method is EFT, other attributes such as routing number and account number might be needed in *Statement*. Since these attributes are not shown in a statement, they are omitted from the *Statement* entity type.
4	The *SentTo* relationship is redundant. It can be derived from the *Applied* and *GivenTo* relationships. If time to derive the *SentTo* relationship is not onerous, it can be dropped.

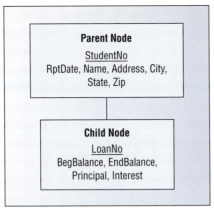

Figure 13.14　Structure of the loan activity report.

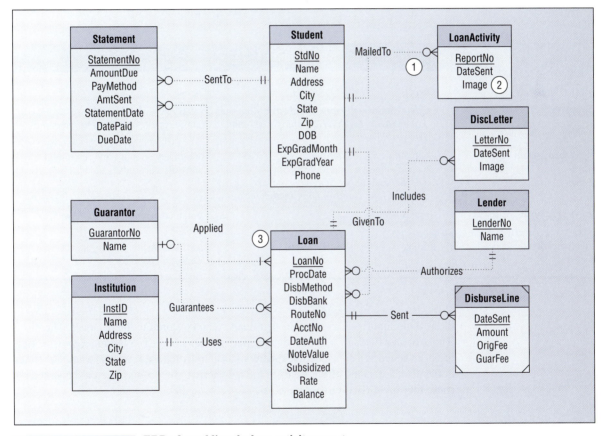

Figure 13.15　ERD after adding the loan activity report.

13.2.4 Incremental Integration after Adding the Loan Activity Report

The loan activity report contains both parent and child nodes (Figure 13.14) because it has a repeating group. Figure 13.15 shows the integrated ERD with corresponding assumptions shown in Table 13.4. Like the ERD for the disclosure letter (Figure 13.11),

TABLE 13.4	**Assumptions for the ERD in Figure 13.15**

Annotation Number	Explanation
1	The *LoanActivity* entity type is not directly related to the *Loan* entity type because it is assumed that an activity report summarizes all loans of a student.
2	The *Image* field contains a scanned image of the report. The guarantor may require a copy of the report if the loan is audited. As an alternative to storing the image, an indicator of the physical location could be stored if imaging technology is not used.
3	To make the calculations easier, fields for annual principal and interest could be added to the *Loan* entity type. These fields would be updated after every payment is received. These fields should be considered during physical database design.

TABLE 13.5	**Rules Used to Convert the ERD of Figure 13.15**

Conversion Rule	Objects	Comments
Entity type rule	*Student, Statement, Loan, DiscLetter, LoanActivity, Lender, Guarantor, Institution, DisburseLine* tables	Primary keys in each table are identical to entity types except for *DisburseLine*
1-M relationship rule	*Loan.StdNo, Loan.GuarantorNo, Loan.LenderNo, LoanActivity.StdNo, DiscLetter.LoanNo, Statement.StdNo, DisburseLine.LoanNo, Loan.InstID*	Foreign key columns and referential integrity constraints added
M-N relationship rule	*Applies* table	Combined primary key: *StatementNo, LoanNo*
Identification dependency rule	Primary key (*LoanNo, DateSent*)	*LoanNo* added to primary key of *DisburseLine* table

the ERD in Figure 13.15 assumes that images can be stored in the database. Therefore, the particular fields of a loan activity report are not stored. The unique *ReportNo* field has been added as a convenient identifier of an activity report. If images cannot be stored in the database, some of the fields in the loan activity report may need to be stored because they are difficult to compute.

13.3 REFINING THE CONCEPTUAL SCHEMA

After building a conceptual ERD, you refine it by applying conversion rules to produce an initial table design and using normalization rules to remove excessive redundancies from your initial table design. This section describes refinements of the conceptual ERD that produce a good table design for Student Loan, Limited.

13.3.1 Schema Conversion

The conversion can be performed using the first four rules (Chapter 6) as depicted in Table 13.5. The optional 1-M relationship rule (Rule 5) could be applied to the *Guarantees* relationship. However, the number of loans without guarantors appears small

TABLE 13.6	List of Tables after Conversion

Student(<u>StdNo</u>, Name, Address, Phone, City, State, Zip, ExpGradMonth, ExpGradYear, DOB)

Lender(<u>LenderNo</u>, Name)

Guarantor(<u>GuarantorNo</u>, Name)

Institution(<u>InstID</u>, Name, Address, City, State, Zip)

Loan(<u>LoanNo</u>, ProcDate, DisbMethod, DisbBank, RouteNo, AcctNo, DateAuth, NoteValue, Subsidized, Rate, Balance, *StdNo, InstID, GuarantorNo, LendNo*)

DiscLetter(<u>LetterNo</u>, DateSent, Image, *LoanNo*)

LoanActivity(<u>ReportNo</u>, DateSent, Image, *StdNo*)

DisburseLine(<u>*LoanNo*</u>, <u>DateSent</u>, Amount, OrigFee, GuarFee)

Statement(<u>StatementNo</u>, AmtDue, PayMethod, AmtSent, StatementDate, DatePaid, DueDate, *StdNo*)

Applied(<u>*LoanNo*</u>, <u>*StatementNo*</u>, Principal, Interest, CumPrincipal, CumInterest)

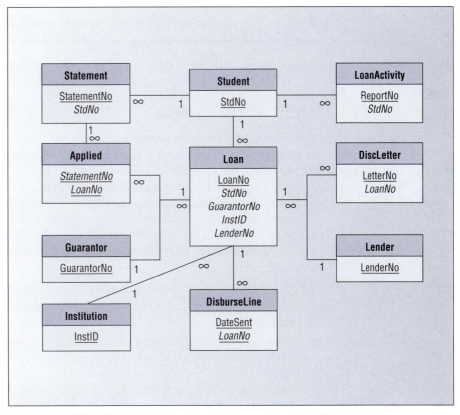

Figure 13.16	Relational model diagram for the initial table design.

so the 1-M relationship rule is used instead. The generalization hierarchy rule (Rule 6) is not needed because the ERD (Figure 13.9) does not have any generalization hierarchies. The conversion result is shown in Table 13.6 (primary keys underlined and foreign keys italicized) and Figure 13.16 (graphical depiction of tables, primary keys, and foreign keys).

TABLE 13.7	List of FDs

Table	FDs
Student	StdNo → Name, Address, City, State, Zip, ExpGradMonth, ExpGradYear, DOB, Phone; Zip → State
Lender	LenderNo → Name
Guarantor	GuarantorNo → Name
Institution	InstID → Name, Address, City, State, Zip; Zip → City, State
Loan	LoanNo → ProcDate, DisbMethod, DisbBank, RouteNo, AcctNo, DateAuth, NoteValue, Subsidized, Rate, Balance, StdNo, InstID, GuarantorNo, LenderNo; RouteNo → DisbBank
Discletter	LetterNo → DateSent, Image, LoanNo; LoanNo, DateSent → LetterNo, Image
LoanReport	ReportNo → DateSent, Image, StdNo; StdNo, DateSent → ReportNo, Image
DisburseLine	LoanNo, DateSent → Amount, OrigFee, GuarFee
Statement	StatementNo → AmtDue, PayMethod, AmtSent, StatementDate, DatePaid, DueDate, StdNo
Applied	LoanNo, StatementNo → Principal, Interest, CumPrincipal, CumInterest

13.3.2 Normalization

The tables resulting from the conversion process may still have redundancy. To eliminate redundancy, you should list the FDs for each table and apply the normalization rules or the simple synthesis procedure. Table 13.7 lists the FDs for each table.

Because most FDs involve a primary key on the left-hand side, there is not much normalization work. However, the *Loan, Student,* and *Institution* tables violate BCNF as these tables have determinants that are not candidate keys. The *DiscLetter* and *LoanReport* tables do not violate BCNF because all determinants are candidate keys. For the tables violating BCNF, here are explanations and options about splitting the tables:

- *Student* is not in BCNF because of the FD with *Zip.* If Student Loan, Limited wants to update zip codes independently of students, a separate table should be added.
- *Loan* is not in BCNF because of the FD involving *RouteNo.* If Student Loan, Limited wants to update banks independently of loans, a separate table should be created.
- *Institution* is not in BCNF because of the FDs with *Zip.* If Student Loan, Limited wants to update zip codes independently of institutions, a separate table should be added. Only one zip table is needed for both *Student* and *Institution.*

In the revised table design (Figure 13.17), the *ZipCode* table and the *Bank* table are added to remove redundancies. Appendix 13.B shows CREATE TABLE statements with the revised list of tables. Delete and update actions are also included in Appendix 13.B.

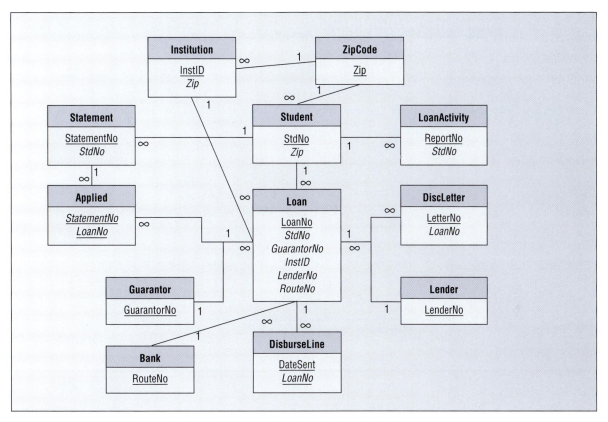

Figure 13.17   **Relational model diagram for the revised table design.**

For most foreign keys, deletions are restricted because the corresponding parent and child tables are not closely related. For example, deletions are restricted for the foreign key *Loan.InstID* because the *Institution* and *Loan* tables are not closely related. In contrast, deletions cascade for the foreign key *DisburseLine.LoanNo* because disbursement lines are identification dependent on the related loan. Deletions also cascade for the foreign key *Applied.StatementNo* because applied rows represent statement lines that have no meaning without the statement. The update action of most foreign keys was set to cascade to allow easy changing of primary key values.

13.4 PHYSICAL DATABASE DESIGN AND APPLICATION DEVELOPMENT

After producing a good table design, you are ready to implement the database. This section describes physical database design decisions including index selection, derived data, and denormalization for the Student Loan, Limited database. Before describing these decisions, table and application profiles are defined. After physical database design decisions are presented, application development of some forms and reports is depicted as a cross check on database development.

TABLE 13.8	Application Characteristics

Application	Tables	Conditions
Verify data (for loan origination)	Student, Lender, Institution, Guarantor	StdNo = $X; LenderNo = $Y; InstID = $Z; GuarantorNo = $W
Create loan (for loan origination)	Loan, DisburseLine	1 row inserted in Loan; multiple rows inserted in DisburseLine
Create student (for loan origination)	Student	1 row inserted
Create disclosure letter	Student, Loan, DiscLetter	Insert row in DiscLetter; retrieve rows from Student and Loan (LoanNo = $X)
Display disclosure letter	DiscLetter	LoanNo = $X
Create loan activity report	Student, Loan, LoanActivity, Applied, Statement	Insert row in LoanActivity; retrieve rows from Student (StdNo = $X) and Statement (DatePaid in past year)
Display loan activity report	LoanActivity	StdNo = $X
Create statement of account	Statement	1 row inserted in Statement; multiple rows inserted in Applied
Display statement of account	Statement, Student, Applied, Loan	StdNo = $X AND DateSent = $Y; sometimes using StatementNo = $Z
Apply payment	Applied, Statement, Loan	Applied rows updated; LoanNo = $X AND StatementNo = $Y; Balance updated in the Loan table

13.4.1 Application and Table Profiles

To clarify anticipated usage of the database, the documents described in Section 13.1 are split into database access applications as summarized in Table 13.8. Three separate applications are associated with the Loan Origination Form. Verifying data involves retrievals to ensure that the student, lender, institution, and guarantor exist. If a student does not exist, a new row is added. Creating a loan involves inserting a row in the *Loan* table and multiple rows in the *DisburseLine* table. For the other documents, there is an application to create the document and retrieve the document. For statements of account, there is also an application to update the *Applied* and *Loan* tables when payments are received.

To make physical database design decisions, the relative importance of applications must be specified. The frequencies in Table 13.9 assume 100,000 new loans per year and 100,000 students in repayment per year. The loan origination applications and the statement of account applications dominate the workload. The coarse frequencies (per year) are sufficient to indicate the relative importance of applications. A finer specification (e.g., by month or day) may be needed to schedule work such as to arrange for batch processing instead of online processing. For example, applications involving loan origination forms may be processed in batch instead of online.

After defining the application profiles, table profiles can be defined. The volume of modification activity (inserts, updates, deletes) can help in the estimation of table profiles. In addition, you should use statistics from existing systems and interviews with key application personnel to help make the estimates. Table 13.10 provides an overview of the profiles. More detail about column distributions and relationship distributions can be added after the system is partially populated.

TABLE 13.9	Application Frequencies

Application	Frequency	Comments
Verify data	100,000/year	Most activity at beginning of term
Create loan	100,000/year	Most activity at beginning of term
Create student	20,000/year	Most students are repeat
Create disclosure letter	50,000/year	Spread evenly throughout year
Display disclosure letter	5,000/year	Spread evenly throughout year
Create loan activity report	30,000/year	End-of-year processing
Display loan activity report	5,000/year	Spread evenly throughout year
Create statement of account	100,000/year	Once per month
Display statement of account	10,000/year	Spread evenly throughout year
Apply payment	100,000/year	Spread evenly throughout month

TABLE 13.10	Table Profiles

Table	Number of Rows	Column (Number of Unique Values)
Student	100,000	StdNo (PK), Name (99,000), Address (90,000), City (1,000), Zip (1,000), DOB (365), ExpGradMonth (12), ExpGradYear (10)
Loan	300,000	LoanNo (PK), ProcDate (350), DisbMethod (3), DisbBank (3,000), RouteNo (3,000), AcctNo (90,000), DateAuth (350), NoteValue (1,000), Subsidized (2), Rate (1,000), Balance (10,000), StdNo (100,000), InstID (2,000), GuarantorNo (100), LenderNo (2,000)
Institution	2,000	InstID (PK), Name (2,000), Address (2,000), City (500), State (50), Zip (500)
DiscLetter	1,000,000	LetterNo (PK), DateSent (350), Image (1,000,000), LoanNo (300,000)
Statement	2,000,000	StatementNo (PK), AmtDue (100,000), PayMethod (3), AmtSent (200,000), StatementDate (350), DatePaid (350), DueDate (350), StdNo (100,000)
Guarantor	100	GuarantorNo (PK), Name (100)
Bank	3,000	RouteNo (PK), DisbBank (3,000)
DisburseLine	900,000	LoanNo (300,000), DateSent (350), Amount (5,000), OrigFee (5,000), GuarFee (5,000)
Applied	6,000,000	LoanNo (300,000), StatementNo (2,000,000), Principal (100,000), Interest (1,000,000)
ZipCode	1,000	Zip (PK), State (50)
Lender	2,000	LenderNo (PK), Name (2,000)

13.4.2 Index Selection

You can select indexes using the application profiles and the rules described in Chapter 8. To clarify the selection process, let us consider retrieval needs before manipulation needs. Recall that Rules 1 through 4 (Chapter 8) involve the selection of indexes for retrieval needs. The following list discusses useful index choices for retrieval purposes:

- Indexes on the primary keys of the *Student, Lender, Guarantor, Institution, DiscLetter, LoanActivity, Statement,* and *Bank* tables support the verify loan, display disclosure letter, display activity report, and display statement of account applications.
- A nonclustering index on student name may be a good choice to support the retrieval of statements of account and the loan activity reports.
- To support joins, nonclustering indexes on foreign keys *Loan.StdNo, Statement.StdNo, Applied.LoanNo,* and *Applied.StatementNo* may be useful. For example, an index on *Loan.StdNo* facilitates joining the *Student* and the *Loan* tables when given a specific *StdNo* value.

Because the *Applied* and *Loan* tables have lots of modifications, you should proceed with caution about indexes on the component fields. Some mitigating factors may offset the impact of the modification activity, however. The updates in the apply payment application do not affect the foreign key fields in these tables. Batch processing can reduce the impact of the insertions on the *Loan* and the *Applied* tables. The create loan and create statement of account applications may be performed in batch because loan origination forms are received in batch and statements of account can be produced in batch. If the indexes are too much of a burden for batch processing, it may be possible to destroy the indexes before batch processing and re-create them after finishing.

Table 13.11 shows index choices based on the previous discussion. The choices assume that foreign key indexes on the *Applied* and the *Loan* tables do not impede the insertion activity. Further investigation is probably necessary to determine the impact of indexes on insertions in the *Loan* and the *Applied* tables.

13.4.3 Derived Data and Denormalization Decisions

There are some derived data in the revised table design. The *NoteValue* column in the *Loan* table can be derived from columns in related rows of the *DisburseLine* table. The *CumPrincipal* and *CumInterest* columns are derived in the *Applied* table. The *DiscLetter* and the *LoanActivity* tables have lots of derived data in the *Image* columns. In all of these cases, the derived data seem justified because of the difficulty of computing it.

Denormalization may be useful for some foreign keys. If users frequently request the name along with the foreign key, denormalization may be useful for the foreign keys in the *Loan* table. For example, storing both *LenderNo* and *Lender.Name* in the *Loan* table violates BCNF, but it may reduce joins between the *Loan* and the *Lender* tables. The usage of the database should be monitored carefully to determine whether the *Loan* table should be denormalized by adding name columns in addition to the *LenderNo, GuarantorNo, InstID,* and *RouteNo* columns. If performance can be significantly improved, denormalization is a good idea because the *Lender, Guarantor, Institution,* and *Bank* tables are relatively static.

TABLE 13.11	Index Selections for the Revised Table Design		
Column		*Index Kind*	*Rule*
	Student.StdNo	Clustering	1
	Student.Name	Nonclustering	3
	Statement.StatementNo	Clustering	1
	DiscLetter.LetterNo	Clustering	1
	Loan.LoanNo	Clustering	1
	Institution.InstID	Clustering	1
	Guarantor.GuarantorNo	Clustering	1
	Lender.LenderNo	Clustering	1
	LoanActivity.ReportNo	Clustering	1
	ZipCode.Zip	Clustering	1
	Bank.RouteNo	Clustering	1
	Statement.StdNo	Nonclustering	2
	Loan.StdNo	Nonclustering	2
	Applied.StatementNo	Clustering	2
	Applied.LoanNo	Nonclustering	2

13.4.4 Other Implementation Decisions

There are a number of implementation decisions that involve the database development process. Because these decisions can have a large impact on the success of the loan servicing system, they are highlighted in this section.

- Smooth conversion from the old system to the new system is an important issue. One impediment to smooth conversion is processing volumes. Sometimes processing volumes in a new system can be much larger than in the old system. One way to alleviate potential performance problems is to execute the old and the new systems in parallel with more work shifted to the new system over time.

- An important part of the conversion process involves the old data. Converting the old data to the new format is not usually difficult except for data quality concerns. Sometimes, the poor quality of old data causes many rejections in the conversion process. The conversion process needs to be sensitive to rejecting poor-quality data because rejections can require extensive manual corrections.

- The size of the image data (loan activity reports and disclosure letters) can impact the performance of the database. Archival of the image data can improve performance for images that are infrequently retrieved.

13.4.5 Application Development

To complete the development of the database, you should implement the forms and reports used in the database design requirements. Implementing the forms and reports provides a cross check on the conceptual and logical design phases. Your table design should support queries for each form and report. Often, limitations in a table design appear as a result of implementing forms and reports. After implementing the forms and reports, you should use them under typical workloads to ensure adequate performance. It is likely that you will need to adjust your physical design to achieve acceptable performance.

This section demonstrates implementation of the data requirements for some of the forms and reports in Section 13.1 along with a trigger for maintenance of derived data. The implementations of the data requirements for the other forms and reports are left as end-of-chapter problems.

Data Requirements for the Loan Origination Form

The following list provides answers to the five data requirement steps including the main form and subform queries. For reference, Figures 13.2 and 13.3 show instances of the Loan Origination Form.

- **Identify the 1-M relationship manipulated by the form:** The 1-M relationship connects the *Loan* table to the *DisburseLine* table.
- **Identify the join or linking columns for the 1-M relationship:** *Loan.LoanNo* and *DisburseLine.LoanNo* are the linking columns.
- **Identify the other tables in the main form and the subform:** In addition to the *Loan* table, the main form contains the *Student* table, the *Instituition* table, the *Bank* table, the *Lender* table, and the *Guarantor* table. The subform does not contain additional tables beyond the *DisburseLine* table.
- **Determine the updatability of the tables in the hierarchical form:** The *Loan* table in the main form and the *DisburseLine* table in the subform are updatable. The other tables are read-only. Separate forms should be provided to update the other tables that appear in the main form.
- **Write the main form query:** The one-sided outer join with the *Bank* table preserves the *Loan* table. The one-sided outer join allows the bank data optionally to appear on the form. The bank data appear on the form when the disbursement method is electronic. The SELECT statement retrieves some additional columns that do not appear on the form such as *Bank.RouteNo*. These additional columns do not affect the updatability of the query.

```
SELECT Loan.*, Student.*, Institution.*, Bank.*, Institution.*,
       Lender.*
  FROM ( ( ( ( Student INNER JOIN Loan ON Student.StdNo = Loan.StdNo  )
    INNER JOIN Institution ON Institution.InstId = Loan.InstId   )
    INNER JOIN Lender ON Lender.LenderNo = Loan.LenderNo )
    INNER JOIN Guarantor ON Guarantor.GuarantorNo = Loan.GuarantorNo   )
    LEFT JOIN Bank ON Bank.RouteNo = Loan.RouteNo
```

- **Write the subform query:**
```
SELECT DisburseLine.*
  FROM DisburseLine
```

Data Requirements for the Loan Activity Report

The report query is difficult to formulate because each line of the Loan Activity Report shows the beginning and the ending loan balances. Two rows in the *Applied* and the *Statement* tables must be used to calculate the beginning and the ending loan balances.

The ending loan balance is calculated as the note value of the loan minus the cumulative principal payment reflected on the last *Applied* row in the report year. The beginning loan balance is calculated as the note value of the loan minus the cumulative principal payment reflected on the last *Applied* row in the year prior to the report year. To determine the last *Applied* row for a given year, the *Applied* table is joined to the *Statement* row having the largest *DatePaid* in the year. The nested queries in the WHERE clause retrieve the *Statement* rows with the maximum *DatePaid* for the report year and the year prior to the report. The identifier *$ReportYear* is the parameter for the report year. The **Year** function is a Microsoft Access function that retrieves the year part of a date.

```
SELECT Student.StdNo, Name, Address, Phone, City, State, Zip,
          Loan.LoanNo, NoteValue, ACurr.CumPrincipal, ACurr.CumInterest,
          APrev.CumPrincipal
  FROM Student, Loan, Applied ACurr, Applied APrev,
          Statement SCurr, Statement SPrev
  WHERE Student.StdNo = Loan.StdNo
     AND Loan.LoanNo = SCurr.LoanNo
     AND SCurr.StatementNo = ACurr.StatementNo
     AND ACurr.LoanNo = Loan.LoanNo
     AND SCurr.DatePaid =
     (   SELECT MAX(DatePaid) FROM Statement
         WHERE Year(DatePaid) = $ReportYear   )
     AND Loan.LoanNo = SPrev.LoanNo
     AND SPrev.StatementNo = APrev.StatementNo
     AND APrev.LoanNo = Loan.LoanNo
     AND SPrev.DatePaid =
     (   SELECT MAX(DatePaid) FROM Statement
         WHERE Year(DatePaid) = $ReportYear - 1   )
```

This report query demonstrates the need for the computed columns *CumPrincipal* and *CumInterest*. The report query would be very difficult to formulate without these derived columns.

Derived Data Maintenance

AFTER ROW triggers can be defined to maintain the derived columns in the *Loan* and the *Applied* tables. The code below shows an Oracle trigger to maintain the *Loan.Balance* column after creating an *Applied* row. The triggers to maintain the *Applied.CumPrincipal* and *Applied.CumInterest* columns would involve mutating table considerations in Oracle. Because solutions to triggers with mutating tables were not shown in Chapter 11, the solution to maintain these columns will not be shown here either. The solution involves either an INSTEAD OF trigger with a view or an Oracle package with a collection of triggers.

```
CREATE OR REPLACE TRIGGER tr_Applied_IA
-- This trigger updates the Balance column
-- of the related Loan row.
AFTER INSERT
ON Applied
```

```
FOR EACH ROW
BEGIN
     UPDATE Loan
      SET Balance = Balance - :NEW.Principal
      WHERE LoanNo = :NEW.LoanNo;
EXCEPTION
   WHEN OTHERS THEN
       RAISE_Application_Error(-20001, 'Database error');
END;
```

CLOSING THOUGHTS

This chapter presented a moderate-size case study as a capstone of the database development process. The Student Loan, Limited case described a significant subset of commercial student loan processing including accepting loans from lenders, notifying students of repayment, billing and processing payments, and reporting loan status. The case solution integrated techniques presented in the chapters of Parts 2 and 3. The solution depicted models and documentation produced in the conceptual modeling, logical database design, and physical database design phases as well as data requirements for forms, reports, and triggers.

After careful reading of this chapter, you are ready to tackle database development for a real organization. You are encouraged to work cases available through the textbook's website to solidify your understanding of the database development process. This case, although presenting you with a larger, more integrated problem than the other database development chapters, is still not comparable to performing database development for a real organization. For a real organization, requirements are often open-ended, unclear, and continuous. Deciding on the database boundary and modifying the database design in response to requirement changes are crucial to long-term success. Monitoring the operation of the database allows you to improve performance as dictated by database usage. These challenges make database development a stimulating intellectual activity.

REVIEW CONCEPTS

- Guaranteed Student Loan (GSL) program providing subsidized and unsubsidized loans.
- Roles of students, lenders, service providers, guarantors, and government regulators in the GSL program.
- Workflow for processing student loans involving loan applications, loan approval, loan origination, separation from school, and loan repayment.
- Important documents for loan processing: the loan origination form, the disclosure letter, the statement of account, and the loan activity report.
- Conceptual data modeling: incremental integration strategy for the loan origination form, the disclosure letter, the statement of account, and the loan activity report.
- Converting the ERD using the basic conversion rules.
- Removing normal form violations in the *Loan, Student,* and *Institution* tables.
- Specification of table and application profiles for physical database design.
- Applying the index selection rules for clustering indexes on primary keys and nonclustering indexes on foreign keys.
- Using denormalization for the *Loan* table.

- Specifying data requirements for the loan origination form and the loan activity report to cross check the result of the conceptual data modeling and logical design phases.
- Writing triggers to maintain derived data in the *Loan* and *Applied* tables.

QUESTIONS

1. Why is the student application process not considered in the conceptual design phase?

2. Why is the incremental integration approach used to analyze the requirements?

3. Why is the Loan Origination Form analyzed first?

4. How is the note value field on the Loan Origination Form related to other data on the form?

5. Explain how the 1-M relationship in the Loan Origination Form is represented in the ERD of Figure 13.9.

6. What is the primary key of the *DisburseLine* entity type in Figure 13.9?

7. What data are contained in the image field of the *DiscLetter* entity type in Figure 13.11?

8. Explain how the 1-M relationship in the statement of account is represented in the ERD of Figure 13.13.

9. Why is the optional 1-M relationship rule (Rule 5 of Chapter 9) not used to convert the ERD of Figure 13.15?

10. Explain how the *Authorizes* relationship in Figure 13.15 is converted in Figure 13.16.

11. Explain how the identification dependency in Figure 13.15 is converted in Figure 13.16.

12. Explain how the *Applied* relationship in Figure 13.15 is converted in Figure 13.16.

13. Explain why the *DiscLetter* table is in BCNF.

14. Discuss a possible justification for violating BCNF with the *Student* table depicted in Table 13.7.

15. Why decompose the documents into multiple database applications as depicted in Table 13.8?

16. Explain the difference between batch and online processing of loan origination forms. Why is batch processing feasible for loan origination forms?

17. How can batch processing reduce the impact of maintaining indexes?

18. Explain why a clustered index is recommended for the *Applied.StatementNo* column.

19. Explain why a nonclustered index is recommended for the *Applied.LoanNo* column.

20. Why is it reasonable to store the *NoteValue* column in the *Loan* table rather than compute it when needed?

PROBLEMS

The following problems involve extensions to the Student Loan, Limited case. For additional cases of similar complexity, visit this book's website.

1. Use the optional 1-M relationship rule to convert the *Guarantees* relationship in Figure 13.15. Modify the relational model diagram in Figure 13.16 with the conversion change.

2. Simplify the ERD for the loan origination form (Figure 13.9) by combining the *Loan* entity type with entity types associated with a loan (*Lender* and *Guarantor*). What transformation (see Chapter 6) is used to combine the entity types? What transformation can be used to split bank attributes (*RouteNo* and *DisbBank*) into a separate entity type?

3. Modify the ERD in Figure 13.15 to reflect a change in the relationship between an activity report and associated loans of a student. The assumption in the case is that an activity report summarizes all of a student's loans. The new assumption is that an activity report may summarize only a subset of a student's loans.

4. Explain how denormalization can be used to combine the *LoanActivity* and the *Student* tables. Do the same for the *DiscLetter* and the *Loan* tables.

5. Student Loan, Limited has decided to enter the direct lending business. A direct lending loan is similar to a guaranteed student loan except there is neither a lender nor a guarantor for a direct lending loan. Due to the lack of a lender and guarantor, there are no origination and guarantee fees. However, there is a service fee of about 3 percent per note value. In addition, a student may choose income-contingent repayment after separating from school. If a student chooses income contingent repayment, the terms of the loan and payment amount are revised.

   a. Modify the ERD in Figure 13.15 to reflect these new requirements.
   b. Convert the ERD changes to a table design. Show your conversion result as a modification to the relational database diagram in Figure 13.16.

6. Student Loan, Limited cannot justify the expense of imaging software and hardware. Therefore, the database design must be modified. The *Image* columns in the *DiscLetter* and the *LoanActivity* tables cannot be stored. Instead, the data stored inside the image fields must be stored or computed on demand.

   a. Make recommendations for storing or computing the underlined fields in a disclosure letter. Modify the table design as necessary. Consider update and retrieval trade-offs in your recommendation.
   b. Make recommendations for storing or computing the fields in a loan activity report. Modify the table design as necessary. Consider update and retrieval trade-offs in your recommendation.

7. Write a SELECT statement to indicate the data requirements for the disclosure letter depicted in Figure 13.4.

8. Use the five steps presented in Chapter 10 to specify the data requirements for the Statement of Account form depicted in Figure 13.5.

Appendix 13.A Glossary of Form and Report Fields

Appendix 13.A provides a brief description of the fields found on the documents presented in Section 13.1. The field names are the captions from the associated document.

LOAN ORIGINATION FORM

- **Loan No.:** unique alphanumeric value that identifies a Loan Origination Form.
- **Date:** date that the Loan Origination Form was completed.
- **Student No.:** unique alphanumeric value that identifies a student.
- **Name:** name of student applying.
- **Address:** street address of student applying.
- **City, State, Zip:** concatenation of the student's city, state, and zip code.
- **Phone:** phone number including area code of the student applying.
- **Date of Birth:** birth date of student applying.
- **Expected Graduation:** month and year of expected graduation.
- **Institution ID:** federal identification number of the university or school.
- **Institution Name:** name of the university or school.
- **Address:** street address of the university or school.
- **City, State, Zip:** concatenation of the institution's city, state, and zip code.
- **Disbursement Method:** the method used to distribute funds to the student applicant; the values can be EFT (electronic funds transfer) or check.
- **Routing No.:** unique alphanumeric value that identifies a bank to disburse the funds; only used if disbursement method is EFT.
- **Account No.:** unique alphanumeric value that identifies an account of the student applicant; Account No. is only guaranteed to be unique within the student's bank (identified by routing number).
- **Disbursement Bank:** name of the bank from which the funds are disbursed; used only if the disbursement method is EFT.
- **Lender No.:** unique alphanumeric value that identifies the financial institution lending funds to the student applicant.
- **Lender Name:** name of the financial institution lending to the student applicant.
- **Guarantor No.:** unique alphanumeric value that identifies the financial institution ensuring the loan is properly serviced.
- **Guarantor Name:** name of the guaranteeing financial institution.
- **Note Value:** amount (in dollars) borrowed by the student applicant; note value is equal to the sum of the disbursement amounts and the fees (origination and guarantee).
- **Subsidized:** yes/no value indicating whether the government pays the interest while the student is in school.

- **Rate:** interest rate on the loan.
- **Date:** disbursement date; this is the *Date* field under Disbursement Plan.
- **Amount:** disbursement amount in dollars.
- **Origination Fee:** fee (in dollars) charged by the lending institution.
- **Guarantee Fee:** fee (in dollars) charged by the guarantor.

DISCLOSURE LETTER

- **Date:** date (1 July 2005) that the letter was sent to the student applicant.
- **Loan No:** loan number of the associated loan.
- **Last Name:** title and last name (Mr. Student) of student applicant.
- **Repayment Starting:** month and year (September 2005) when loans enter repayment status.
- **Amount Borrowed:** sum of amounts ($10,000) borrowed in all loans covered by payment plan.
- **Number of Payments:** estimated number of scheduled payments (120) to retire the amount borrowed.
- **Interest Rate:** weighted average percentage rate (8.5 percent) of loans covered by the payment plan.
- **Finance Charge:** estimated finance charge ($4,877.96) if amount borrowed is repaid according to the payment plan.
- **Payment Amount:** amount of payment ($246.37) required for each month (except perhaps for the last month). If a student does not pay this amount each month, the student will be in arrears unless other arrangements are made.
- **First Payment Date:** date (October 31, 2005) when the first payment is due if the payment plan is followed.
- **Last Payment Date:** date (September 30, 2015) when the last payment is due if the payment plan is followed.

STATEMENT OF ACCOUNT

- **Statement No:** unique alphanumeric value (B100) that identifies the statement of account form.
- **Date:** date that the statement was sent.
- **Student No.:** unique alphanumeric value that identifies a student.
- **Name:** name of student applying.
- **Address:** street address of student applicant (part of the mailing address).
- **City:** city of the student applicant (part of the mailing address).
- **State:** two-letter state abbreviation of the student applicant (part of the mailing address).
- **Zip:** five- or nine-digit zip code of the student applicant (part of the mailing address).
- **Amount Due:** amount (in dollars) that the student should remit.
- **Due Date:** date when repayment should be received by Student Loan, Limited. A late penalty may be assessed if the amount is received at a later date.

- **Payment Method:** check or EFT.
- **Amount Enclosed:** amount (in dollars) sent with the payment. If payment method is EFT, the applicant does not complete this field.
- **Loan No.:** unique alphanumeric value that identifies a loan of the applicant.
- **Balance:** outstanding loan balance (in dollars) before repayment.
- **Rate:** percentage interest rate applying to the loan.
- **Date Paid:** date when the payment is received; this field should be completed by staff at Student Loan, Limited.

LOAN ACTIVITY REPORT

- **Date:** date that the report was prepared.
- **Student No.:** unique alphanumeric value that identifies a student.
- **Name:** name of student applying.
- **Street:** street address of student applicant (part of the mailing address).
- **City:** city of the student applicant (part of the mailing address).
- **State:** two-letter state abbreviation of the student applicant (part of the mailing address).
- **Zip:** five- or nine-digit zip code of the student applicant (part of the mailing address).
- **Loan No.:** unique alphanumeric value that identifies a loan of the applicant.
- **Beg. Balance:** outstanding loan balance (in dollars) at beginning of year.
- **Principal:** total amount of payments applied to principal.
- **Interest:** total amount of payments applied to interest.
- **Ending Balance:** outstanding loan balance (in dollars) at the end of year after applying payments.

Appendix 13.B CREATE TABLE Statements

Appendix 13.B contains CREATE TABLE statements for the tables resulting from the conversion and normalization process described in Section 13.3. The CREATE TABLE statements conform to SQL:1999 syntax.

```
CREATE TABLE Student
                (  StdNo            CHAR(10)          NOT NULL,
                   Name             CHAR(30)          NOT NULL,
                   Address          VARCHAR(50)       NOT NULL,
                   Phone            CHAR(9),
                   City             CHAR(30)          NOT NULL,
                   Zip              CHAR(9)           NOT NULL,
                   ExpGradMonth     SMALLINT,
                   ExpGradYear      INTEGER,
                   DOB              DATE              NOT NULL,
CONSTRAINT FKZip1 FOREIGN KEY (Zip) REFERENCES ZipCode
                   ON DELETE RESTRICT
                   ON UPDATE CASCADE,
CONSTRAINT PKStudent PRIMARY KEY (StdNo)   )
```

```
CREATE TABLE Lender
                (  LenderNo         INTEGER           NOT NULL,
                   Name             CHAR(30)          NOT NULL,
CONSTRAINT PKLender PRIMARY KEY (LenderNo)   )
```

```
CREATE TABLE Guarantor
                (  GuarantorNo      CHAR(10)          NOT NULL,
                   Name             CHAR(30)          NOT NULL,
CONSTRAINT PKGuarantor PRIMARY KEY (GuarantorNo)   )
```

```
CREATE TABLE Institution
                (  InstID           CHAR(10)          NOT NULL,
                   Name             CHAR(30)          NOT NULL,
                   Address          VARCHAR(50)       NOT NULL,
                   City             CHAR(30)          NOT NULL,
                   Zip              CHAR(9)           NOT NULL,
CONSTRAINT FKZip2 FOREIGN KEY (Zip) REFERENCES ZipCode
                   ON DELETE RESTRICT
                   ON UPDATE CASCADE,
CONSTRAINT PKInstitution PRIMARY KEY (InstID)   )
```

```
CREATE TABLE ZipCode
                ( Zip            CHAR(9)        NOT NULL,
                  State          CHAR(2)        NOT NULL,
CONSTRAINT PKZipCode PRIMARY KEY (Zip)   )
```

```
CREATE TABLE Loan
                ( LoanNo         CHAR(10)       NOT NULL,
                  ProcDate       DATE           NOT NULL,
                  DisbMethod     CHAR(6)        NOT NULL,
                  RouteNo        CHAR(10),
                  AcctNo         CHAR(10),
                  DateAuth       INTEGER        NOT NULL,
                  NoteValue      DECIMAL(10,2)  NOT NULL,
                  Subsidized     BOOLEAN        NOT NULL,
                  Rate           FLOAT          NOT NULL,
                  Balance        DECIMAL(10,2),
                  StdNo          CHAR(10)       NOT NULL,
                  InstID         CHAR(10)       NOT NULL,
                  GuarantorNo    CHAR(10),
                  LenderNo       CHAR(10)       NOT NULL,
CONSTRAINT FKStdNo1 FOREIGN KEY (StdNo) REFERENCES Student
                ON DELETE RESTRICT
                ON UPDATE CASCADE,
CONSTRAINT FKInstID FOREIGN KEY (InstID) REFERENCES Institution
                ON DELETE RESTRICT
                ON UPDATE CASCADE,
CONSTRAINT FKGuarantorNo FOREIGN KEY (GuarantorNo)  REFERENCES Guarantor
                ON DELETE RESTRICT
                ON UPDATE CASCADE,
CONSTRAINT FKLenderNo FOREIGN KEY (LenderNo) REFERENCES Lender
                ON DELETE RESTRICT
                ON UPDATE CASCADE,
CONSTRAINT FKRouteNo FOREIGN KEY (RouteNo) REFERENCES Bank
                ON DELETE RESTRICT
                ON UPDATE CASCADE,
CONSTRAINT PKLoan PRIMARY KEY (LoanNo)   )
```

```
CREATE TABLE Bank
                ( RouteNo        CHAR(10)       NOT NULL,
                  Name           CHAR(30)       NOT NULL,
CONSTRAINT PKBank PRIMARY KEY (RouteNo)   )
```

```
CREATE TABLE DisburseLine
              (   LoanNo        CHAR(10)           NOT NULL,
                  DateSent      DATE               NOT NULL,
                  Amount        DECIMAL(10,2)      NOT NULL,
                  OrigFee       DECIMAL(10,2)      NOT NULL,
                  GuarFee       DECIMAL(10,2)      NOT NULL,
CONSTRAINT FKLoanNo1 FOREIGN KEY (LoanNo) REFERENCES Loan
              ON DELETE CASCADE
              ON UPDATE CASCADE,
CONSTRAINT PKDisburseLine PRIMARY KEY (LoanNo, DateSent)   )
```

```
CREATE TABLE DiscLetter
              (   LetterNo      INTEGER        NOT NULL,
                  DateSent      DATE           NOT NULL,
                  Image         BLOB           NOT NULL,
                  LoanNo        CHAR(10)       NOT NULL,
CONSTRAINT FKLoanNo2 FOREIGN KEY (LoanNo) REFERENCES Loan
              ON DELETE RESTRICT
              ON UPDATE CASCADE,
CONSTRAINT PKDiscLetter PRIMARY KEY (LetterNo)   )
```

```
CREATE TABLE LoanActivity
              (   ReportNo      INTEGER        NOT NULL,
                  DateSent      DATE           NOT NULL,
                  Image         BLOB           NOT NULL,
                  StdNo         CHAR(10)       NOT NULL,
CONSTRAINT FKStdNo2 FOREIGN KEY (StdNo) REFERENCES Student
              ON DELETE RESTRICT
              ON UPDATE CASCADE,
CONSTRAINT PKLoanActivity PRIMARY KEY (ReportNo)   )
```

```
CREATE TABLE Statement
              (   StatementNo        CHAR(10)           NOT NULL,
                  StatementDate      DATE               NOT NULL,
                  PayMethod          CHAR(6)            NOT NULL,
                  StdNo              CHAR(10)           NOT NULL,
                  AmtDue             DECIMAL(10,2)      NOT NULL,
                  DueDate            DATE               NOT NULL,
                  AmtSent            DECIMAL(10,2),
                  DatePaid           DATE,
CONSTRAINT FKStdNo3 FOREIGN KEY (StdNo) REFERENCES Student
              ON DELETE RESTRICT
              ON UPDATE CASCADE,
CONSTRAINT PKStatement PRIMARY KEY (StatementNo)   )
```

```
CREATE TABLE Applied
                    (  LoanNo              CHAR(10)              NOT NULL,
                       StatementNo         CHAR(10)              NOT NULL,
                       Principal           DECIMAL(10,2)         NOT NULL,
                       Interest            DECIMAL(10,2)         NOT NULL,
                       CumPrincipal        DECIMAL(10,2)         NOT NULL,
                       CumInterest         DECIMAL(10,2)         NOT NULL,
CONSTRAINT FKLoanNo3 FOREIGN KEY (LoanNo) REFERENCES Loan
                       ON DELETE RESTRICT
                       ON UPDATE CASCADE,
CONSTRAINT FKStatementNo FOREIGN KEY (StatementNo) REFERENCES Statement
                       ON DELETE CASCADE
                       ON UPDATE CASCADE,
CONSTRAINT PKApplied PRIMARY KEY (LoanNo, StatementNo)   )
```

MANAGING DATABASE ENVIRONMENTS

The chapters in Part 4 emphasize the role of database specialists and the details of managing databases in various operating environments. Chapter 14 provides a context for the other chapters through coverage of the responsibilities, tools, and processes used by database administrators and data administrators. The other chapters in Part 4 provide a foundation for managing databases in important environments: Chapter 15 on transaction processing, Chapter 16 on data warehouses, Chapter 17 on distributed processing and data, and Chapter 18 on object database management. These chapters emphasize concepts, architectures, and design choices important to database specialists. In addition, Chapters 15, 16, and 18 provide details about SQL statements used in transaction processing, data warehouse development, and object database development.

CHAPTER 14

Data and Database Administration

LEARNING OBJECTIVES

This chapter provides an overview of the responsibilities and tools of database specialists known as data administrators and database administrators. After this chapter, the student should have acquired the following knowledge and skills:

■ Compare and contrast the responsibilities of database administrators and data administrators.

■ Control databases using SQL statements for security and integrity.

■ Manage the usage of stored procedures and triggers.

■ Understand the roles of data dictionary tables and the information resource dictionary.

■ Describe the data planning process.

■ Understand the process to select and evaluate DBMSs.

■ Perceive the processing environments in which database technology exists.

OVERVIEW

Part 3 of this book provided a foundation for database application development. You learned about advanced query formulation, application development with views, stored procedures, and triggers, and database development using requirements represented as views. Utilizing the knowledge and skills in Parts 1 through 3, you should be able to develop databases and implement applications that use the databases. Part 4 explores issues and skills involved in managing databases in different processing environments. This chapter describes the responsibilities and tools of data specialists (data administrators and database administrators) and provides an introduction to the different processing environments for databases.

Before learning the details of the processing environments, you need to understand the organizational context in which databases exist and learn tools and processes for managing databases. This chapter first discusses an organizational context for databases. You will learn about database support for management decision making, the goals of information resource management, and the responsibilities of data and database administrators. After explaining the organizational context, this chapter presents new tools and processes to manage databases. You will learn SQL statements for security and integrity, management of triggers and stored procedures, and data dictionary manipulation as well as processes for data planning and DBMS selection. This chapter concludes with an introduction to the different processing environments that will be presented in more detail in the other chapters of Part 4.

14.1 ORGANIZATIONAL CONTEXT FOR MANAGING DATABASES

This section reviews management decision-making levels and discusses database support for decision making at all levels. After this background, this section describes the function of information resource management and the responsibilities of data specialists to manage information resources.

14.1.1 Database Support for Management Decision Making

Databases support business operations and management decision making at various levels. Most large organizations have developed many <u>operational databases</u> to help conduct business efficiently. Operational databases directly support major functions such as order processing, manufacturing, accounts payable, and product distribution. The reasons for investing in an operational database are typically faster processing, larger volumes of business, and reduced personnel costs.

Operational Database a database to support the daily functions of an organization.

As organizations achieve improved operations, they begin to realize the decision-making potential of their databases. Operational databases provide the raw materials for management decision making as depicted in Figure 14.1. Lower-level management can obtain exception and problem reports directly from operational databases. However, much value must be added to leverage the operational databases for middle and upper management. The operational databases must be cleaned, integrated, and summarized to provide value for tactical and strategic decision making. Integration is necessary because operational databases often are developed in isolation without regard for the information needs of tactical and strategic decision making.

Table 14.1 provides examples of management decisions and data requirements. Lower-level management deals with short-term problems related to individual transactions. Periodic summaries of operational databases and exception reports assist operational management. Middle management relies on summarized data that are integrated

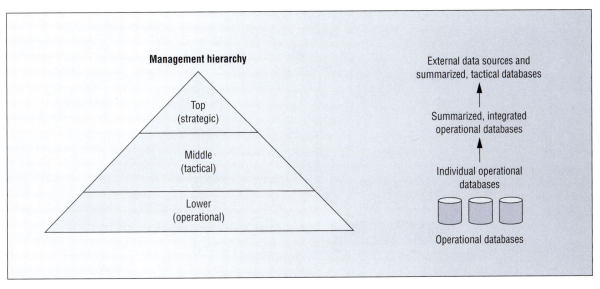

Figure 14.1   Database support for management levels.

TABLE 14.1	Examples of Management Decision Making

Level	Example Decisions	Data Requirements
Top	Identify new markets and products; plan growth; reallocate resources across divisions	Economic and technology forecasts; news summaries; industry reports; medium-term performance reports
Middle	Choose suppliers; forecast sales, inventory, and cash; revise staffing levels; prepare budgets	Historical trends; supplier performance; critical path analysis; short-term and medium-term plans
Lower	Schedule employees; correct order delays; find production bottlenecks; monitor resource usage	Problem reports; exception reports; employee schedules; daily production results; inventory levels

across operational databases. Middle management may want to integrate data across different departments, manufacturing plants, and retail stores. Top management relies on the results of middle management analysis and external data sources. Top management needs to integrate data so that customers, products, suppliers, and other important entities can be tracked across the entire organization. In addition, external data must be summarized and then integrated with internal data.

14.1.2 Information Resource Management to Knowledge Management

Information Life Cycle the stages of information transformation in an organization. Each entity has its own information life cycle that should be managed and integrated with the life cycles of other entities.

As a response to the challenges of leveraging operational databases and information technology for management decision making, the philosophy of information resource management has arisen. Information resource management involves processing, distributing, and integrating information throughout an organization. A key element of information resource management is the control of information life cycles (Figure 14.2).

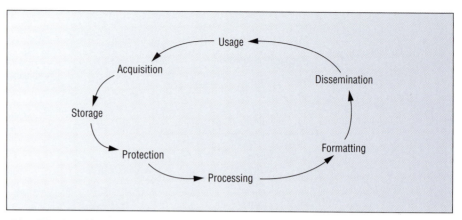

Figure 14.2	**Typical stages of an information life cycle.**

Each level of management decision making and business operations has its own information life cycle. For effective decision making, the life cycles must be integrated to provide timely and consistent information. For example, information life cycles for operations provide input to life cycles for management decision making.

Data quality is a particular concern for information resource management because of the impact of data quality on management decision making. As discussed in Chapter 4, data quality involves a number of dimensions such as correctness, timeliness, consistency, completeness, and reliability. Often the level of data quality that suffices for business operations may be insufficient for decision making at upper levels of management. This conflict is especially true for the consistency dimension. For example, inconsistency of customer identification across operational databases can impair decision making at the upper management level. Information resource management emphasizes a long-term perspective on data quality to ensure support for management decision making.

In recent years, there has been a movement to extend information resource management into <u>knowledge management.</u> Traditionally, information resource management has emphasized technology to support predefined recipes for decision making rather than the ability to react to a constantly changing business environment. To succeed in today's business environment, organizations must emphasize fast response and adaptation rather than planning. To meet this challenge, Dr. Yogesh Malhotra, a well-known management consultant, argues that organizations should develop systems that facilitate knowledge creation rather than information management. For knowledge creation, he advocates a greater emphasis on human information processing and organization dynamics to balance the technology emphasis, as shown in Figure 14.3.

This vision for knowledge management provides a context for the use of information technology to solve business problems. The best information technology will fail if not aligned with the human and organization elements. Information technology should amplify individual intellectual capacity, compensate for limitations in human processing, and support positive organization dynamics.

Knowledge Management
applying information technology with human information processing capabilities and organization processes to support rapid adaptation to change.

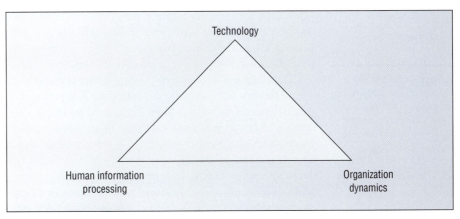

| **Figure 14.3** | **Three pillars of knowledge management.** |

TABLE 14.2	**Responsibilities of Data Administrators and Database Administrators**

Position	*Responsibilities*
Data administrator	Develops an enterprise data model
	Establishes interdatabase standards and policies about naming, data sharing, and data ownership
	Negotiates contractual terms with information technology vendors
	Develops long-range plans for information technology
Database administrator	Develops detailed knowledge of individual DBMSs
	Consults on application development
	Performs data modeling and logical database design
	Enforces data administration standards
	Monitors database performance
	Performs technical evaluation of DBMSs
	Creates security, integrity, and rule-processing statements
	Devises standards and policies related to individual databases and DBMSs

14.1.3 Responsibilities of Data Administrators and Database Administrators

As part of controlling information resources, new management responsibilities have arisen. The <u>data administrator (DA)</u> is a middle- or upper-management position with broad responsibilities for information resource management. The *database administrator* (DBA) is a support role with responsibilities related to individual databases and DBMSs. Table 14.2 compares the responsibilities of data administrators and database administrators. The data administrator views the information resource in a broader context than the database administrator. The data administrator considers all kinds of data whether stored in relational databases, files, Web pages, or external sources. The database administrator typically considers only data stored in databases.

Enterprise Data Model a conceptual data model of an organization. An enterprise data model can be used for data planning and decision support.

Development of an <u>enterprise data model</u> is one of the most important responsibilities of the data administrator. An enterprise data model provides an integrated model of all databases of an organization. Because of its scope, an enterprise data model is less detailed than the individual databases that it encompasses. The enterprise data model concentrates on the major subjects in operational databases rather the full details. An enterprise data model can be developed for data planning (what databases to develop) or decision support (how to integrate and summarize existing databases). Section 14.3 describes the details of data planning while Chapter 16 describes the details of developing an enterprise data model for decision support. The data administrator is usually heavily involved in both efforts.

Large organizations may offer much specialization in data administration and database administration. For data administration, specialization can occur by task and environment. On the task side, data administrators can specialize in planning versus policy establishment. On the environment side, data administrators can specialize in environments such as decision support, transaction processing, and nontraditional data such as images, text, and video. For database administration, specialization can occur by DBMS, task, and environment. Because of the complexities of learning a DBMS, DBAs typically specialize in one or a few products. Task specialization is usually divided between data modeling and performance evaluation. Environment specialization is usually divided between transaction processing and data warehouses.

In small organizations, the boundary between data administration and database administration is fluid. There may not be separate positions for data administrators and database administrators. The same people may perform duties from both positions. As organizations grow, specialization usually develops so that separate positions are created.

14.2 TOOLS OF DATABASE ADMINISTRATION

To fulfill the responsibilities mentioned in the previous section, database administrators use a variety of tools. You already have learned about tools for data modeling, logical database design, view creation, physical database design, triggers, and stored procedures. Some of the tools are SQL statements (CREATE VIEW and CREATE INDEX) while others are part of CASE tools for database development. This section presents additional tools for security, integrity, and data dictionary access and discusses management of stored procedures and triggers.

14.2.1 Security

Security involves protecting a database from unauthorized access and malicious destruction. Because of the value of data in corporate databases, there is strong motivation for unauthorized users to gain access. Competitors have strong motivation to access sensitive information about product development plans, cost-saving initiatives, and customer profiles. Lurking criminals want to steal unannounced financial results, business transactions, and sensitive customer data such as credit card numbers. Social deviants and terrorists can wreck havoc by intentionally destroying database records. With growing use of the World Wide Web to conduct business, competitors, criminals, and social deviants have even more opportunity to compromise <u>database security.</u>

Database Security protecting databases from unauthorized access and malicious destruction.

Security is a broad subject involving many disciplines. There are legal and ethical issues about who can access data and when data can be disclosed. There are network, hardware, operating system, and physical controls that augment the controls provided by DBMSs. There are also operational problems about passwords, authentication devices, and privacy enforcement. These issues are not further addressed because they are beyond the scope of DBMSs and database specialists. The remainder of this subsection emphasizes access control approaches and SQL statements for authorization rules.

For access control, DBMSs support creation and storage of authorization rules and enforcement of authorization rules when users access a database. Figure 14.4 depicts the interaction of these elements. Database administrators create <u>authorization rules</u> that define who can access which parts of a database for what operations. Enforcement of authorization rules involves authenticating the user and ensuring that authorization rules are not violated by access requests (database retrievals and modifications). Authentication occurs when a user first connects to a DBMS. Authorization rules must be checked for each access request.

The most common approach to authorization rules is known as <u>discretionary access control</u>. In discretionary access control, users are assigned access rights or privileges to specified parts of a database. For precise control, privileges are usually specified for views rather than tables or fields. Users can be given the ability to read, update, insert, and delete specified parts of a database. To simplify the maintenance of authorization rules, privileges can be assigned to groups or roles rather than individual users. Because roles are more stable than individual users, authorization rules that reference roles require less maintenance than rules referencing individual users. Users are assigned to roles and given passwords. During the database login process, the database security system authenticates users and notes the roles to which they belong.

<u>Mandatory access controls</u> are less flexible than discretionary access controls. In mandatory control approaches, each object is assigned a classification level and each user is given a clearance level. A user can access an object if the user's clearance level provides access to the classification level of the object. Typical clearance and classification levels

---

Authorization Rules define authorized users, allowable operations, and accessible parts of a database. The database security system stores authorization rules and enforces them for each database access.

Discretionary Access Control users are assigned access rights or privileges to specified parts of a database. Discretionary access control is the most common kind of security control supported by commercial DBMSs.

Mandatory Access Control a database security approach for highly sensitive and static databases. A user can access a database element if the user's clearance level provides access to the classification level of the element.

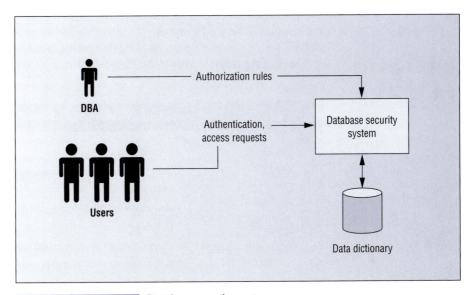

Figure 14.4   **Database security system.**

are confidential, secret, and top secret. Mandatory access control approaches primarily have been applied to highly sensitive and static databases for national defense and intelligence gathering. Because of the limited flexibility of mandatory access controls, only a few DBMSs support them. DBMSs that are used in national defense and intelligence gathering must support mandatory controls, however.

In addition to access controls, DBMSs support <u>encryption</u> of databases. Encryption involves the encoding of data to obscure their meaning. An encryption algorithm changes the original data (known as the <u>plaintext</u>). To decipher the data, the user supplies an encryption key to restore the encrypted data (known as the <u>ciphertext</u>) to its original (plaintext) format. Two of the most popular encryption algorithms are the Data Encryption Standard and the Public-Key Encryption algorithm. Because the Data Encryption Standard can be broken by massive computational power, the Public-Key Encryption algorithm has become the preferred approach.

SQL:1999 Security Statements

SQL:1999 supports discretionary authorization rules using the CREATE/DROP ROLE statements and the GRANT/REVOKE statements. To create a role, you can use the CREATE ROLE statement as demonstrated in Example 14.1. The WITH ADMIN clause means that a user assigned the role can assign the role to others. The WITH ADMIN option should be used sparingly because it provides wide latitude to the role. A role can be dropped with the DROP ROLE statement.

Example 14.1 (SQL:1999)	CREATE ROLE Statement Examples

CREATE ROLE ISFaculty;
CREATE ROLE ISAdministrator WITH ADMIN CURRENT_ROLE;
CREATE ROLE ISAdvisor;

In a GRANT statement, you specify the privileges (see Table 14.3), the object (table, column, or view), and the list of authorized users (or roles). In Example 14.2, SELECT access is given to three roles (ISFaculty, ISAdvisor, ISAdministrator) while UPDATE access is given only to the ISAdministrator. Individual users must be assigned

TABLE 14.3	Explanation of Common SQL:1999 Privileges

Privilege	Explanation
SELECT	Query the object; can be specified for individual columns
UPDATE	Modify the value; can be specified for individual columns
INSERT	Add a new row; can be specified for individual columns
DELETE	Delete a row; cannot be specified for individual columns
TRIGGER	Create a trigger on a specified table
REFERENCES	Reference columns of a given table in integrity constraints
EXECUTE	Execute the stored procedure

to roles before they can access the *ISStudentGPA* view. The GRANT statement also can be used to assign users to roles as shown in Example 14.2. To remove an access privilege, the REVOKE statement is used. At the end of Example 14.2, the SELECT privilege is removed from ISFaculty.

**Example 14.2
(SQL:1999)**

View Definition, GRANT, and REVOKE Statements

```
CREATE VIEW ISStudentGPA AS
    SELECT StdSSN, StdFirstName, StdLastName, StdGPA
      FROM Student
      WHERE StdMajor = 'IS';
--Grant privileges to roles
GRANT SELECT ON ISStudentGPA
    TO ISFaculty, ISAdvisor, ISAdministrator;
GRANT UPDATE ON ISStudentGPA.StdGPA TO ISAdministrator;
--Assign users to roles
GRANT ISFaculty TO Mannino;
GRANT ISAdvisor TO Olson;
GRANT ISAdministrator TO Smith;
REVOKE SELECT ON ISStudentGPA FROM ISFaculty RESTRICT;
```

In addition to granting the privileges in Table 14.3, a user can be authorized to pass privileges to other users using the WITH GRANT OPTION keyword. This option should be used with care because it provides wide latitude to the users assigned to the role.

Security in Oracle and Access

Oracle 9i extends the SQL:1999 security statements with the CREATE USER statement, predefined roles, and additional privileges. In SQL:1999, user creation is an implementation issue. Since Oracle does not rely on the operating system for user creation, it provides the CREATE USER statement. Oracle provides predefined roles for highly privileged users including the CONNECT role to create tables in a schema, the RESOURCE role for creating tables and application objects such as procedures, and the DBA role for managing databases. For privileges, Oracle distinguishes between system privileges (independent of object) and object privileges. Granting system privileges usually is reserved for highly secure roles because of the far-reaching nature of system privileges as shown in Table 14.4. The ORACLE object privileges are similar to the SQL:1999 privileges except that Oracle provides more objects than SQL:1999, as shown in Table 14.5.

Most DBMSs allow authorization restrictions by application objects such as forms and reports in addition to the database objects permissible in the GRANT statement. These additional security constraints are usually specified in proprietary interfaces or in application development tools, rather than in SQL. For example, Microsoft Access 2002 allows definition of authorization rules through the User and Group Permissions window as shown in Figure 14.5. Permissions for database objects (tables and stored

TABLE 14.4	Explanation of Common Oracle System Privileges

System Privilege	Explanation
CREATE X, CREATE ANY X	Create objects of kind X in one's schema;[1] CREATE ANY allows creating objects in other schemas
ALTER X, ALTER ANY X	Alter objects of kind X in one's schema; ALTER ANY X allows altering objects in other schemas
INSERT ANY, DELETE ANY, UPDATE ANY, SELECT ANY	Insert, delete, update, and select from a table in any schema
DROP X, DROP ANY X	DROP objects of kind X in one's schema; DROP ANY allows dropping of objects in other schemas
ALTER SYSTEM, ALTER DATABASE, ALTER SESSION	Issue ALTER SYSTEM commands, ALTER DATABASE commands, and ALTER SESSION commands
ANALYZE ANY	Analyze any table, index, or cluster

TABLE 14.5	Mapping between Common Oracle Privileges and Objects

	Object				
Privilege	Table	View	Sequence[2]	Procedure, Function, Package, Library, Operator, IndexType	Materialized View[3]
ALTER	X		X		
DELETE	X	X			X
EXECUTE				X	
INDEX	X				
INSERT	X	X			X
REFERENCES	X	X			
SELECT	X	X	X		X
UPDATE	X	X			X

queries) as well as application objects (forms and reports) can be specified using this window. In addition, Access SQL supports the GRANT/REVOKE statements similar to the SQL:1999 statements as well as the CREATE/DROP statements for users and groups.

---

[1] A schema is a collection of related tables and other Oracle objects that are managed as a unit.

[2] A sequence is a collection of values maintained by Oracle. Sequences typically are used for system-generated primary keys.

[3] A materialized view is stored rather than derived. Materialized views are useful in data warehouses as presented in Chapter 16.

Figure 14.5   **User and Group Permissions window in Microsoft Access 2002.**

14.2.2 Integrity Constraints

You already have seen integrity constraints presented in previous chapters. In Chapter 2, you were introduced to primary keys, foreign keys, candidate keys, and non-null constraints along with the corresponding SQL syntax. In Chapter 5, you studied cardinality constraints and generalization hierarchy constraints. In Chapter 7, you studied functional and multivalued dependencies as part of the normalization process. In addition, Chapter 8 described indexes that can be used to enforce primary and candidate key constraints efficiently. This subsection describes additional kinds of integrity constraints and the corresponding SQL syntax.

SQL Domains

In Chapter 2, standard SQL data types were defined. A data type indicates the kind of data (character, numeric, yes/no, etc.) and permissible operations (numeric operations, string operations, etc.) for columns using the data type. SQL:1999 provides a limited ability to define new data types using the CREATE DOMAIN statement. A domain can be created as a subset of a standard data type. Example 14.3 demonstrates the CREATE DOMAIN statement along with usage of the new domains in place of standard data types. The CHECK clause defines a constraint for the domain limiting the domain to a subset of the standard data type.

**Example 14.3
(SQL:1999)**   CREATE DOMAIN Statements and Usage of the Domains

```
CREATE DOMAIN StudentClass AS CHAR(2)
    CHECK ( VALUE IN ('FR', 'SO', 'JR', 'SR')   )
```

```
CREATE DOMAIN CourseUnits AS SMALLINT
    CHECK ( VALUE BETWEEN 1 AND 9 )
```

In the CREATE TABLE for the *Student* table, the domain can be referenced in the *StdClass* column.

```
StdClass   StudentClass   NOT NULL
```

In the CREATE TABLE for the *Course* table, the domain can be referenced in the *CrsUnits* column.

```
CrsUnits   CourseUnits   NOT NULL
```

SQL:1999 provides a related feature known as a distinct type. Like a domain, a distinct type is based on a primitive type. Unlike a domain, a distinct type cannot have constraints. However, the SQL specification provides improved type checking for distinct types as compared to domains. A column having a distinct type can be compared only with another column using the same distinct type. Example 14.4 demonstrates distinct type definitions and a comparison among columns based on the types.

Example 14.4 (SQL:1999)	Distinct Types and Usage of the Distinct Types

```
-- USD distinct type and usage in a table definition
CREATE DISTINCT TYPE USD AS DECIMAL(10,2);
USProdPrice   USD

CREATE DISTINCT TYPE Euro AS DECIMAL(10,2);
EuroProdPrice   Euro

-- Type error:   columns have different distinct types
USProdPrice > EuroProdPrice
```

For object-oriented databases, SQL:1999 provides user-defined types, a more powerful capability than the CREATE DOMAIN statement or the distinct type. User-defined data types can be defined with new operators and functions. In addition, user-defined data types can be defined using other user-defined data types. Chapter 18 describes user-defined data types as part of the presentation of the object-oriented features of SQL:1999.

CHECK Constraints in the CREATE TABLE Statement

When a constraint involves row conditions on columns of the same table, a CHECK constraint may be used. CHECK constraints are specified as part of the CREATE TABLE statement as shown in Example 14.5. For easier traceability, you should always name constraints. When a constraint violation occurs, most DBMSs will display the constraint name.

**Example 14.5
(SQL:1999)**

CHECK Constraint Clauses

Here is a CREATE TABLE statement with CHECK constraints for the valid GPA range and upper-class students (juniors and seniors) having a declared (non-null) major. Note that the GPA constraint could have been specified in a CREATE DOMAIN statement instead.

```
CREATE TABLE Student
(   StdSSN            CHAR(11)            NOT NULL,
    StdFirstName      VARCHAR(50)         NOT NULL,
    StdLastName       VARCHAR(50)         NOT NULL,
    StdCity           VARCHAR(50)         NOT NULL,
    StdState          CHAR(2)             NOT NULL,
    StdZip            CHAR(9)             NOT NULL,
    StdMajor          CHAR(6),
    StdClass          CHAR(6),
    StdGPA            DECIMAL(3,2),
CONSTRAINT PKStudent PRIMARY KEY (StdSSN),
CONSTRAINT ValidGPA CHECK ( StdGPA BETWEEN 0 AND 4 ),
CONSTRAINT MajorDeclared CHECK
    (   StdClass IN ('FR','SO') OR StdMajor IS NOT NULL   )   )
```

Although CHECK constraints are widely supported, most DBMSs limit the conditions inside CHECK constraints. The SQL:1999 specification allows any condition that could appear in a SELECT statement including conditions that involve SELECT statements. Most DBMSs do not permit conditions involving SELECT statements in a CHECK constraint. For example, Oracle 9i prohibits SELECT statements in CHECK constraints as well as references to columns from other tables. For these complex constraints, assertions may be used (if supported by the DBMS) or triggers if assertions are not supported.

SQL:1999 Assertions

SQL:1999 assertions are more powerful than constraints about domains, columns, primary keys, and foreign keys. Unlike CHECK constraints, assertions are not associated with a specific table. An assertion can involve a SELECT statement of arbitrary complexity. Thus, assertions can be used for constraints involving multiple tables and statistical calculations, as demonstrated in Examples 14.6 through 14.8. However, complex assertions should be used sparingly because they can be inefficient to enforce. There may be more efficient ways to enforce assertions such as through event conditions in a form and stored procedures. As a DBA, you are advised to investigate the event programming capabilities of application development tools before using complex assertions.

**Example 14.6
(SQL:1999)**

CREATE ASSERTION Statement

This assertion statement ensures that each faculty has a course load between three and nine units.

```
CREATE ASSERTION FacultyWorkLoad
  CHECK (NOT EXISTS
```

```
(   SELECT Faculty.FacSSN, OffTerm, OffYear
    FROM Faculty, Offering, Course
    WHERE Faculty.FacSSN = Offering.FacSSN
        AND Offering.CourseNo = Course.CourseNo
    GROUP BY Faculty.FacSSN, OffTerm, OffYear
    HAVING SUM(CrsUnits) < 3 OR SUM(CrsUnits) > 9   )   )
```

Example 14.7 (SQL:1999)

CREATE ASSERTION Statement

This assertion statement ensures that no two courses are offered at the same time and place. The conditions involving the *OffTime* and *OffDays* columns should be refined to check for any overlap, not just equality. Because these refinements would involve string and date functions specific to a DBMS, they are not shown.

```
CREATE ASSERTION OfferingConflict
  CHECK (NOT EXISTS
    (   SELECT O1.OfferNo
        FROM Offering O1, Offering O2
        WHERE O1.OfferNo <> O2.OfferNo
            AND O1.OffTerm = O2.OffTerm
            AND O1.OffYear = O2.OffYear
            AND O1.OffDays = O2.OffDays
            AND O1.OffTime = O2.OffTime
            AND O1.OffLocation = O2.OffLocation   )   )
```

Example 14.8 (SQL:1999)

Assertion Statement to Ensure That Full-time Students Have at Least Nine Units

```
CREATE ASSERTION FullTimeEnrollment
  CHECK (NOT EXISTS
    (   SELECT Enrollment.RegNo
        FROM Registration, Offering, Enrollment, Course
        WHERE Offering.OfferNo = Enrollment.OfferNo
            AND Offering.CourseNo = Course.CourseNo
            AND Offering.RegNo = Registration.RegNo
            AND RegStatus = 'F'
        GROUP BY Enrollment.RegNo
        HAVING SUM(CrsUnits) >= 9   )   )
```

Assertions are checked after related modification operations complete. For example, the *OfferingConflict* assertion in Example 14.7 would be checked for each insertion of an *Offering* row and for each change to one of the columns in the WHERE clause of the assertion. In some cases, an assertion should be delayed until other statements complete. The keyword DEFERRABLE can be used to allow an assertion to be tested at the end of a transaction rather than immediately. Deferred checking is an issue with transaction design discussed in Chapter 15.

Assertions are not widely supported probably because assertions overlap with triggers. An assertion is a limited kind of trigger with an implicit condition and action. Because assertions are simpler than triggers, they are usually easier to create and more efficient to execute. However, no major relational DBMS supports assertions so triggers must be used in places where assertions would be more appropriate.

14.2.3 Management of Triggers and Stored Procedures

In Chapter 11, you learned about the details of stored procedures and triggers, and you gained experience with coding stored procedures and triggers. Although a DBA writes stored procedures and triggers to help manage databases, the primary responsibilities for a DBA are to manage stored procedures and triggers, not to write them. The DBA's responsibilities include setting standards for coding practices, monitoring dependencies, and understanding trigger interactions.

For coding practices, a DBA should consider documentation standards, parameter usage, and content, as summarized in Table 14.6. Documentation standards may include naming standards, explanations of parameters, and descriptions of pre and post conditions of procedures. Parameter usage in procedures and functions should be monitored. Functions should use only input parameters. In addition, functions should not have side effects. For content, triggers should not perform integrity constraints that can be coded in declarative integrity constraints (CHECK constraints and assertions). To reduce maintenance, triggers and stored procedures should reference the data types of associated database columns. In Oracle, this practice involves anchored data types. Because most application development tools support triggers and event procedures for forms and reports, the choice between a database trigger/procedure versus an application trigger/procedure is not always clear. A DBA should participate in setting standards that provide guidance between using database triggers and procedures as opposed to application triggers and event procedures.

A stored procedure or trigger depends on the tables, views, procedures, and functions that it references as well as on access plans created by the SQL compiler. When a referenced object changes, its dependents should be recompiled. In Figure 14.6, trigger X needs recompilation if changes are made to the access plan for the UPDATE statement in the trigger body. Likewise, the procedure needs recompilation if the access plan for the SELECT statement becomes outdated. Trigger X may need recompilation if changes are made to table A or to procedure pr_LookupZ. Most DBMSs maintain dependencies to ensure that stored procedures and triggers work correctly. If a procedure or trigger uses an SQL statement, most DBMSs will automatically recompile the procedure or trigger if the associated access plan becomes obsolete.

Although most DBMSs manage dependencies, dependency maintenance by a DBMS is not absolute so a DBA should be aware of the limitations. A DBA should understand access plan obsolescence, modification of referenced objects, and deletion of referenced objects as summarized in Table 14.7. For access plans, a DBA should be aware that manual recompilation may be necessary if optimizer statistics become outdated. For remotely stored procedures and functions, a DBA can choose between timestamp and signature

TABLE 14.6	Summary of Coding Practice Concerns for a DBA

Coding Practice Area	Concerns
Documentation	Procedure and trigger naming standards; explanation of parameters; comments describing pre and post conditions
Parameter usage	Only input parameters for functions; no side effects for functions
Trigger and procedure content	Do not use triggers for standard integrity constraints; usage of anchored data types for variables; standards for application triggers and event procedures versus database triggers and procedures

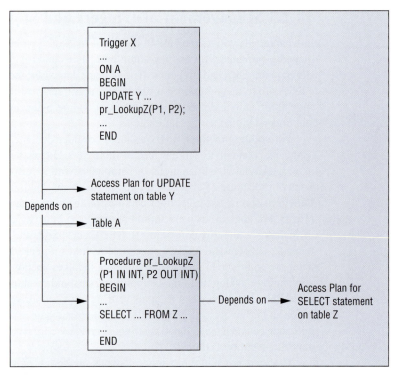

Figure 14.6 **Dependencies among database objects.**

TABLE 14.7	Summary of Dependency Concerns for a DBA

Dependency Area	Concerns
Access plan obsolescence	DBMS should automatically recompile. DBA may need to recompile when optimizer statistics become outdated.
Modification of referenced objects	DBMS should automatically recompile. DBA should choose between timestamp and signature maintenance for remote procedures and functions.
Deletion of referenced objects	DBMS marks procedure/trigger as invalid if referenced objects are deleted.

dependency maintenance. With timestamp maintenance, a DBMS will recompile a dependent object for any change in referenced objects. Timestamp maintenance may lead to excessive recompilation because many changes to referenced objects do not require recompilation of the dependent objects. Signature maintenance involves recompilation when a signature (parameter name or usage) changes. A DBA also should be aware that a DBMS will not recompile a procedure or trigger if a referenced object is deleted. The dependent procedure or trigger will be marked as invalid because recompilation is not possible.

Trigger interactions were discussed in Chapter 11 as part of trigger execution procedures. Triggers interact when one trigger fires other triggers and when triggers overlap leading to firing in arbitrary order. A DBA can use trigger analysis tools provided by

TABLE 14.8	Summary of Guidelines to Control Trigger Complexity

Guideline	Explanation
BEFORE ROW triggers	Do not use data manipulation statements in BEFORE ROW triggers to avoid firing other triggers.
UPDATE triggers	Use a list of columns for UPDATE triggers to reduce trigger overlap.
Actions on referenced rows	Be cautious about triggers on tables affected by actions on referenced rows. These triggers will fire as a result of actions on the parent tables.
Overlapping triggers	Do not depend on a specific firing order.

a DBMS or manually analyze trigger interactions if no tools are provided. A DBA should require extra testing for interacting triggers. To minimize trigger interaction, a DBA should implement the guidelines like the ones summarized in Table 14.8.

14.2.4 Data Dictionary Manipulation

Metadata data that describe other data including the source, use, value, and meaning of the data.

The data dictionary is a special database that describes individual databases and the database environment. The data dictionary contains data descriptors called <u>metadata</u> that define the source, the use, the value, and the meaning of data. DBAs typically deal with two kinds of data dictionaries to track the database environment. Each DBMS provides a data dictionary to track tables, columns, assertions, indexes, and other objects managed by the DBMS. Independent CASE tools provide a data dictionary known as the information resource dictionary that tracks a broader range of objects relating to information systems development. This subsection provides details about both kinds of data dictionaries.

Catalog Tables in SQL:1999 and Oracle

SQL:1999 contains catalog tables in the Definition_Schema as summarized in Table 14.9. The Definition_Schema contains one or more catalog tables corresponding to each object that can be created in an SQL data definition or data control statement. The base catalog tables in the Definition_Schema are not meant to be accessed in applications. For access to metadata in applications, SQL:1999 provides the Information_Schema that contains views of the base catalog tables of the Definition_Schema.

The SQL:1999 Definition_Schema and Information_Schema have few implementations because most DBMSs already had proprietary catalog tables long before the standard was released. Thus, you will need to learn the catalog tables of each DBMS with which you work. Typically, a DBMS may have hundreds of catalog tables. However, for any specific task such as managing triggers, a DBA needs to use a small number of catalog tables. Table 14.10 lists some of the most important catalog tables of Oracle.

A DBA implicitly modifies catalog tables when using data definition commands such as the CREATE TABLE statement. The DBMS uses the catalog tables to process queries, authorize users, check integrity constraints, and perform other database processing. The DBMS consults the catalog tables before performing almost every action. Thus, the integrity of the catalog tables is crucial to the operation of the DBMS. Only

TABLE 14.9	Summary of Important Catalog Tables in SQL:1999
Table	*Contents*
USERS	One row for each user
DOMAINS	One row for each domain
DOMAIN_CONSTRAINTS	One row for each domain constraint on a table
TABLES	One row for each table and view
VIEWS	One row for each view
COLUMNS	One row for each column
TABLE_CONSTRAINTS	One row for each table constraint
REFERENTIAL_CONSTRAINTS	One row for each referential constraint

TABLE 14.10	Common Catalog Tables for Oracle
Table Name	*Contents*
USER_CATALOG	Contains basic data about each table and view defined by a user.
USER_OBJECTS	Contains data about each object (functions, procedures, indexes, triggers, assertions, etc.) defined by a user. This table contains the time created and the last time changed for each object.
USER_TABLES	Contains extended data about each table such as space allocation and statistical summaries.
USER_TAB_COLUMNS	Contains basic and extended data for each column such as the column name, the table reference, the data type, and a statistical summary.
USER_VIEWS	Contains the SQL statement defining each view.

the most-authorized users should be permitted to modify the catalog tables. To improve security and reliability, the data dictionary is usually a separate database stored independently of user databases.

A DBA can query the catalog tables through proprietary interfaces and SELECT statements. Proprietary interfaces such as the Table Definition window of Microsoft Access and the DBA Studio of Oracle are easier to use than SQL but are not portable across DBMSs. SELECT statements provide more control over the information retrieved than do proprietary interfaces.

Information Resource Dictionary

Information Resource Dictionary a database of metadata that describes the entire information systems life cycle. The information resource dictionary system manages access to an IRD.

An information resource dictionary contains a much broader collection of metadata than does a data dictionary for a DBMS. An information resource dictionary (IRD) contains metadata about individual databases, computerized and human processes, configuration management, version control, human resources, and the computing environment. Conceptually, an IRD defines metadata used throughout the information systems life cycle. Both DBAs and DAs can use an IRD to manage information resources. In addition, other information systems professionals can use an IRD during selected tasks in the information systems life cycle.

| **Figure 14.7** | IRDS architecture. |

Because of its broader role, an IRD is not consulted by a DBMS to conduct operations. Rather, an <u>information resource dictionary system (IRDS)</u> manages an IRD. Many CASE tools can use the IRDS to access an IRD as depicted in Figure 14.7. CASE tools can access an IRD directly through the IRDS or indirectly through the import/export feature. The IRD has an open architecture so that CASE tools can customize and extend its conceptual schema.

There are two primary proposals for the IRD and the IRDS. The IRD and the IRDS are currently standards developed by the International Standards Organization (ISO). The implementation of the standards, however, is not widespread. Microsoft and Texas Instruments have jointly developed the Microsoft Repository, which supports many of the goals of the IRD and the IRDS although it does not conform to the standard. However, the Microsoft Repository is gaining widespread acceptance among CASE tool vendors. At this point, it appears to be the de facto standard for the IRD and the IRDS.

14.3 PROCESSES FOR DATABASE SPECIALISTS

This section describes processes conducted by data administrators and database administrators. Data administrators perform data planning as part of the information systems planning process. Both data administrators and database administrators may perform tasks in the process of selecting and evaluating DBMSs. This section presents the details of both processes.

14.3.1 Data Planning

Despite the vast sums of money spent on information technology, many organizations feel disappointed in the payoff. Many organizations have created islands of automation that support local objectives but not the global objectives for the organization. The

| **Figure 14.8** | Enterprise models developed in the information systems planning process. |

islands-of-automation approach can lead to a misalignment of the business and information technology objectives. One result of the misalignment is the difficulty in extracting the decision-making value from operational databases.

As a response to problems with islands of automation, many organizations perform a detailed planning process for information technology and systems. The planning process is known under various names such as information systems planning, business systems planning, information systems engineering, and information systems architecture. All of these approaches provide a process to achieve the following objectives:

- Evaluation of current information systems with respect to the goals and objectives of the organization.
- Determination of the scope and the timing of developing new information systems and utilization of new information technology.
- Identification of opportunities to apply information technology for competitive advantage.

Information Systems Planning the process of developing enterprise models of data, processes, and organizational roles. Information systems planning evaluates existing systems, identifies opportunities to apply information technology for competitive advantage, and plans new systems.

The <u>information systems planning</u> process involves the development of enterprise models of data, processes, and organizational roles, as depicted in Figure 14.8. In the first part of the planning process, broad models are developed. Table 14.11 shows the initial level of detail for the data, process, and organization models. Because the enterprise data model is usually more stable than the process model, it is developed first. To integrate these models, interaction models are developed as shown in Table 14.11. If additional detail is desired, the process and the data models are further expanded. These models should reflect the current information systems infrastructure as well as the planned future direction.

Data administrators play an important part in the development of information system plans. Data administrators conduct numerous interviews to develop the enterprise data model and coordinate with other planning personnel to develop the interaction models.

TABLE 14.11	**Level of Detail of Enterprise Models**

Model	Levels of Detail
Data	Subject model (initial level), entity model (detailed level)
Process	Functional areas and business processes (initial level), activity model (detailed level)
Organization	Role definitions and role relationships
Data–process interaction	Matrix and diagrams showing data requirements of processes
Process–organization interaction	Matrix and diagrams showing role responsibilities
Data–organization	Matrix and diagrams showing usage of data by roles

To improve the likelihood that plans will be accepted and used, data administrators should involve senior management. By emphasizing the decision-making potential of integrated information systems, senior management will be motivated to support the planning process.

14.3.2 Selection and Evaluation of Database Management Systems

Selection and evaluation of a DBMS can be a very important task for an organization. DBMSs provide an important part of the computing infrastructure. As organizations strive to conduct electronic commerce over the Internet and extract value from operational databases, DBMSs play an even greater role. The selection and evaluation process is important because of the impacts of a poor choice. The immediate impacts may be slow database performance and loss of the purchase price. A poorly performing information system can cause lost sales and higher costs. The longer-term impacts are high switching costs. To switch DBMSs, an organization may need to convert data, recode software, and retrain employees. The switching costs can be much larger than the original purchase price.

Selection and Evaluation Process

The selection and evaluation process involves a detailed assessment of organization needs and DBMS features. The goal of the process is to determine a small set of candidate systems that will be investigated in more detail. Because of the detailed nature of the process, a DBA performs most of the tasks. Therefore, a DBA needs a thorough knowledge of DBMSs to perform the process.

Figure 14.9 depicts the steps of the selection and evaluation process. In the first step, a DBA conducts a detailed analysis of the requirements. Because of the large number of requirements, it is helpful to group them. Table 14.12 lists major groupings of requirements while Table 14.13 shows some individual requirements in one group. Each individual requirement should be classified as essential, desirable, or optional to the requirement group. In some cases, several levels of requirements may be necessary. For individual requirements, a DBA should be able to objectively measure them in the candidate systems.

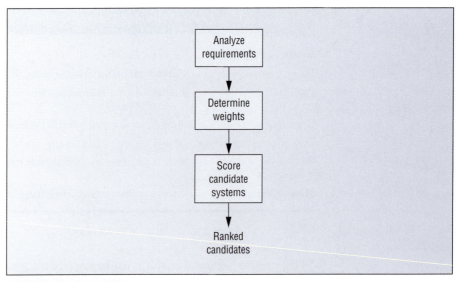

Figure 14.9 Overview of the selection and evaluation process.

TABLE 14.12	**Some Major Requirement Groups**

Category

Data definition (conceptual)

Nonprocedural retrieval

Data definition (internal)

Application development

Procedural language

Concurrency control

Recovery management

Distributed processing and data

Vendor support

Query optimization

Analytic Hierarchy Process
a decision theory technique
to evaluate problems with
multiple objectives. The
process can be used to select
and evaluate DBMSs by
allowing a systematic
assignment of weights to
requirements and scores to
features of candidate
DBMSs.

After determining the groupings, the DBA should assign weights to the major requirement groups and score candidate systems. With more than a few major requirement groups, assigning consistent weights is very difficult. The DBA needs a tool to help assign consistent weights and to score candidate systems. Unfortunately, no analytical method for weight assignment and system scoring has achieved widespread usage. To encourage the use of analytical methods for weight assignment and scoring, one promising approach is depicted.

The Analytic Hierarchy Process provides a simple approach that achieves a reasonable level of consistency. Using the Analytic Hierarchy Process, a DBA assigns weights to pairwise combinations of requirement groups. For example, a DBA should assign a weight that represents the importance of conceptual data definition as compared to non-

TABLE 14.13	Some Detailed Requirements for the Conceptual Data Definition Category

Requirement (Importance)	Explanation
Entity integrity (essential)	Declaration and enforcement of primary keys
Candidate keys (desirable)	Declaration and enforcement of candidate keys
Referential integrity (essential)	Declaration and enforcement of referential integrity
Referenced rows (desirable)	Declaration and enforcement of rules for referenced rows
Standard data types (essential)	Support for whole numbers (several sizes), floating-point numbers (several sizes), fixed-point numbers, fixed-length strings, variable-length strings, and dates (date, time, and timestamp)
User-defined data types (desirable)	Support for new data types or a menu of optional data types
User interface (optional)	Graphical user interface to augment SQL CREATE statements
General assertions (optional)	Declaration and enforcement of multitable constraints

TABLE 14.14	Interpretation of Rating Values for Pairwise Comparisons

Ranking Value of A_{ij}	Meaning
1	Requirements i and j are equally important.
3	Requirement i is slightly more important than requirement j.
5	Requirement i is significantly more important than requirement j.
7	Requirement i is very significantly more important than requirement j.
9	Requirement i is absolutely more important than requirement j.

TABLE 14.15	Sample Weights for Some Requirement Groups[4]

	Data Definition (Conceptual)	Nonprocedural Retrieval	Application Development	Concurrency Control
Data definition (conceptual)	1	1/5	1/5	1/7
Nonprocedural retrieval	5	1	1/3	1/5
Application development	5	3	1	1/3
Concurrency control	7	5	3	1

procedural retrieval. The Analytic Hierarchy Process provides a nine-point scale with interpretations shown in Table 14.14. Table 14.15 applies the scale to rank some of the requirement groups in Table 14.12. For consistency, if entry $A_{ij} = x$, then $A_{ji} = 1/x$. In addition, the diagonal elements in Table 14.15 should always be 1. Thus, it is necessary to complete only half the rankings in Table 14.15.

---

[4]The Analytic Hierarchy Process requires normalization of the weights. See the references for complete details.

Scoring candidate DBMSs can be complex because of the number of individual requirements and the need to combine individual requirements into an overall score for the requirement group. As the first part of the scoring process, a DBA should carefully investigate the features of each candidate DBMS. For each individual requirement, a binary indicator (available or not), rank, or numeric weight should be assigned.

Many ways have been proposed to combine the individual feature scores into an overall score for the requirement group. The Analytic Hierarchy Process supports pairwise comparisons among candidate DBMSs using the rating values in Table 14.14. The interpretations change slightly to reflect the comparison among candidate DBMSs rather than the importance of requirement groups. A DBA subjectively uses the individual feature scores to assign ranking values for each pairwise comparison. Other methods such as the Logic Scoring of Preferences involve a numerical combination of the individual feature weights. Because of the complexity of other methods, you should consult the chapter references for details.

Final Selection Process

Benchmark a workload to evaluate the performance of a system or product. A good benchmark should be relevant, portable, scalable, and understandable.

After the selection and evaluation process completes, the top two or three candidate DBMSs should be evaluated in more detail. Benchmarks can be used to provide a more detailed evaluation of candidate DBMSs. A benchmark is a workload to evaluate the performance of a system or product. A good benchmark should be relevant, portable, scalable, and understandable. Because developing good benchmarks requires significant expertise, most organizations should not attempt to develop a benchmark. Fortunately, the Transaction Processing Council (TPC) has developed a number of standard, domain-specific benchmarks as summarized in Table 14.16. Each benchmark was developed over an extended time period with input from a diverse group of contributors.

A DBA can use the TPC results for each benchmark to obtain reasonable estimates about the performance of a particular DBMS in a specific hardware/software environment. The TPC performance results involve total system performance, not just DBMS performance so that results are not inflated when a customer uses a DBMS in a specific hardware/software environment. To facilitate price performance trade-offs, the TPC publishes the performance measure along with price/performance for each benchmark. The price covers all cost dimensions of an entire system environment including workstations, communications equipment, system software, computer system or host, backup storage, and three years' maintenance cost. The TPC audits the benchmark results prior to publication to ensure that vendors have not manipulated the results.

TABLE 14.16	Summary of TPC Benchmarks	
Benchmark	*Description*	*Performance Measure*
TPC-C	Order entry benchmark	Transactions per minute
TPC-H	Decision support for ad hoc queries	Queries per hour
TPC-R	Decision support for business reporting	Composite queries per hour
TPC-W	Web e-commerce benchmark	Web interactions per second

To augment the published TPC results, an organization may want to evaluate a DBMS on a trial basis. Customized benchmarks can be created to gauge the efficiency of a DBMS for its intended usage. In addition, the user interface and the application development capabilities can be evaluated by building small applications.

The final phase of the selection process may involve nontechnical considerations performed by data administrators along with senior management and legal staff. Assessment of each vendor's future prospects is important because information systems can have a long life. If the underlying DBMS does not advance with the industry, it may not support future initiatives and upgrades to the information systems that use it. Because of the high fixed and variable costs (maintenance fees) of a DBMS, negotiation is often a critical element of the final selection process. The final contract terms along with one or two key advantages often make the difference in the final selection.

14.4 MANAGING DATABASE ENVIRONMENTS

DBMSs operate in several different processing environments. Data specialists must understand the environments to ensure adequate database performance and set standards and policies. This section provides an overview of the processing environments with an emphasis on the tasks performed by database administrators and data administrators. The other chapters in Part 4 provide the details of the processing environments.

14.4.1 Transaction Processing

Transaction processing involves the daily operations of an organization. Every day, organizations process large volumes of orders, payments, cash withdrawals, airline reservations, insurance claims, and other kinds of transactions. DBMSs provide essential services to perform transactions in an efficient and reliable manner. Organizations such as banks with automatic tellers, airlines with online reservation systems, and universities with online registration could not function without reliable and efficient transaction processing. With exploding interest to conduct business over the Internet, the importance of transaction processing will grow even larger.

Data specialists have many responsibilities for transaction processing, as listed in Table 14.17. Data administrators may perform planning responsibilities involving infrastructure and disaster recovery. Database administrators usually perform the more

TABLE 14.17	**Responsibilities of Database Specialists for Transaction Processing**
Area	*Responsibilities*
Transaction design	Consult about design to balance integrity and performance; educate about design issues and DBMS features
Performance monitoring	Monitor transaction performance and troubleshoot performance problems; modify resource levels to improve performance
Transaction processing infrastructure	Determine resource levels for efficiency (disk, memory, and CPU) and reliability (RAID level)
Disaster recovery	Provide contingency plans for various kinds of database failures

detailed tasks such as consulting on transaction design and monitoring performance. Because of the importance of transaction processing, database administrators often must be on call to troubleshoot problems. Chapter 15 presents the details of transaction processing for concurrency control and recovery management. After you read Chapter 15, you may want to review Table 14.17 again.

14.4.2 Data Warehouse Processing

Data warehousing involves the decision support side of databases. Because many organizations have not been able to use operational databases directly to support management decision making, the idea of a data warehouse was conceived. A data warehouse is a central database where organizationwide data are stored to facilitate decision support activities by user departments. Data from operational databases and external sources are extracted, cleaned, summarized, and then loaded into a data warehouse. Because the data warehouse contains historical data, most activity involves retrievals of highly summarized data.

Data specialists have many responsibilities for data warehouses, as listed in Table 14.18. Data administrators may perform planning responsibilities involving the data warehouse architecture and the enterprise data model. Database administrators usually perform the more detailed tasks such as performance monitoring and consulting. To support a large data warehouse, a software product separate from a DBMS may be necessary. A selection and evaluation process should be conducted to choose the most appropriate product. Chapter 16 presents the details of data warehouses. After you read Chapter 16, you may want to review Table 14.18 again.

14.4.3 Distributed Environments

DBMSs can operate in distributed environments to support both transaction processing and data warehouses. In distributed environments, DBMSs can provide the ability to distribute processing and data among computers connected by a network. For distributed processing, a DBMS may allow the distribution of functions provided by the DBMS as well as application processing to be distributed among different com-

TABLE 14.18	Responsibilities of Database Specialists for Data Warehouses
Area	*Responsibilities*
Data warehouse usage	Educate and consult about application design and DBMS features for data warehouse processing
Performance monitoring	Monitor data warehouse loading performance and troubleshoot integrity problems; modify resource levels to improve performance
Data warehouse refresh	Determine the frequency of refreshing the data warehouse and the schedule of activities to refresh the data warehouse
Data warehouse architecture	Determine architecture to support decision-making needs; select database products to support architecture; determine resource levels for efficient processing
Enterprise data model	Provide expertise about operational database content; determine conceptual data model for the data warehouse; promote data quality to support data warehouse development

TABLE 14.19	Responsibilities of Database Specialists for Distributed Environments

Area	Responsibilities
Application development	Educate and consult about impacts of distributed environment for transaction processing and data warehouses
Performance monitoring	Monitor performance and troubleshoot problems with a special emphasis on distributed environment
Distributed environment architectures	Identify goals for distributed environments; choose distributed processing and distributed database architectures to meet goals; select additional software products to support architectures
Distributed environment design	Design distributed databases; determine resource levels for efficient processing

puters in a network. For distributed data, a DBMS may allow tables to be stored and possibly replicated at different computers in a network. The ability to distribute processing and data provides the promise of improved flexibility, scalability, performance, and reliability. However, these improvements only can be obtained through careful design.

Data specialists have many responsibilities for distributed database environments, as shown in Table 14.19. Data administrators usually perform planning responsibilities involving setting goals and determining architectures. Because distributed environments do not increase functionality, they must be justified by improvements in the underlying applications. Database administrators perform more detailed tasks such as performance monitoring and distributed database design. To support distributed environments, other software products along with major extensions to a DBMS may be necessary. A selection and evaluation process should be conducted to choose the most appropriate products. Chapter 17 presents the details of distributed processing and distributed data. After you read Chapter 17, you may want to review Table 14.19 again.

14.4.4 Object Database Management

Object DBMSs support additional functionality for transaction processing and data warehouse applications. Many information systems use a richer set of data types than provided by relational DBMSs. For example, many financial databases need to manipulate time series, a data type not provided by most relational DBMSs. With the ability to convert any kind of data to a digital format, the need for new data types is even more pronounced. Business databases often need to integrate traditional data with nontraditional data based on new data types. For example, information systems for processing insurance claims must manage traditional data such as account numbers, claim amounts, and accident dates as well as nontraditional data such as images, maps, and drawings. Because of these needs, existing relational DBMSs have been extended with object capabilities and new object DBMSs have been developed.

Data specialists have many responsibilities for distributed database environments as shown in Table 14.20. Data administrators usually perform planning responsibilities involving setting goals and determining architectures. Database administrators perform more detailed tasks such as performance monitoring, consulting, and object database

TABLE 14.20	Responsibilities of Database Specialists for Object Databases

Area	Responsibilities
Application development	Educate and consult about creating new data types, inheritance for data types and tables, and other object features
Performance monitoring	Monitor performance and troubleshoot problems with new data types
Object database architectures	Identify goals for object DBMSs; choose object database architectures
Object database design	Design object databases; select data types; create new data types

design. An object DBMS can be a major extension to an existing relational DBMS or a new DBMS. A selection and evaluation process should be conducted to choose the most appropriate product. Chapter 18 presents the details of object DBMSs. After you read Chapter 18, you may want to review Table 14.20 again.

CLOSING THOUGHTS

This chapter has described the responsibilities, tools, and processes used by database specialists to manage databases and support management decision making. Many organizations provide two roles for managing information resources. Data administrators perform broad planning and policy setting, while database administrators perform detailed oversight of individual databases and DBMSs. To provide a context to understand the responsibilities of these positions, this chapter discussed the philosophy of information resource management that emphasizes information technology as a tool for processing, distributing, and integrating information throughout an organization.

This chapter described a number of tools to support database administrators. Database administrators use security rules to restrict access and integrity constraints to improve data quality. This chapter described security rules and integrity constraints along with associated SQL:1999 syntax. For triggers and stored procedures, this chapter described managerial responsibilities of DBAs to complement the coding details in Chapter 11. The data dictionary is an important tool for managing individual databases as well as integrating database development with information systems development. This chapter presented two kinds of data dictionaries: catalog tables used by DBMSs and the information resource dictionary used by CASE tools.

Database specialists need to understand two important processes to manage information technology. Data administrators participate in a detailed planning process that determines new directions for information systems development. This chapter described the data planning process as an important component of the information systems planning process. Both data administrators and database administrators participate in the selection and evaluation of DBMSs. Database administrators perform the detailed tasks while data administrators often make final selection decisions using the detailed recommendations. This chapter described the steps of the selection and evaluation process and the tasks performed by database administrators and data administrators in the process.

This chapter provides a context for the other chapters in Part 4. The other chapters provide details about different database environments including transaction processing, data warehouses, distributed environments, and object DBMSs. This chapter has emphasized the responsibilities, tools, and processes of database specialists for managing these environments. After completing the other chapters in Part 4, you are encouraged to reread this chapter to help you integrate the details with the management concepts and techniques.

REVIEW CONCEPTS

- Information resource management: management philosophy to control information resources and apply information technology to support management decision making.
- Database administrator: support position for managing individual databases and DBMSs.
- Data administrator: management position with planning and policy responsibilities for information technology.
- Discretionary access controls for assigning access rights to groups and users.
- Mandatory access controls for highly sensitive and static databases used in intelligence gathering and national defense.
- SQL CREATE/DROP ROLE statements and GRANT/REVOKE statements for discretionary authorization rules.

```
CREATE ROLE ISFaculty

GRANT SELECT ON ISStudentGPA
    TO ISFaculty, ISAdvisor, ISAdministrator

REVOKE SELECT ON ISStudentGPA FROM ISFaculty
```

- Oracle 9i system and object privileges for discretionary access control.
- SQL CREATE DOMAIN statement for data type constraints.

```
CREATE DOMAIN StudentClass AS CHAR(2)
  CHECK (VALUE IN ('FR', 'SO', 'JR', 'SR')   )
```

- SQL distinct types for improved type checking.
- SQL CREATE ASSERTION statement for complex integrity constraints.

```
CREATE ASSERTION OfferingConflict
  CHECK (NOT EXISTS
      (   SELECT O1.OfferNo
        FROM Offering O1, Offering O2
        WHERE O1.OfferNo <> O2.OfferNo
            AND O1.OffTerm = O2.OffTerm
            AND O1.OffYear = O2.OffYear
            AND O1.OffDays = O2.OffDays
            AND O1.OffTime = O2.OffTime
            AND O1.OffLocation = O2.OffLocation )   )
```

- CHECK constraints in the CREATE TABLE statement for constraints involving row conditions on columns of the same table.

```
CREATE TABLE Student
(   StdSSN          CHAR(11)          NOT NULL,
    StdFirstName    VARCHAR(50)       NOT NULL,
    StdLastName     VARCHAR(50)       NOT NULL,
    StdCity         VARCHAR(50)       NOT NULL,
```

```
StdState        CHAR(2)         NOT NULL,
StdZip          CHAR(9)         NOT NULL,
StdMajor        CHAR(6),
StdClass        CHAR(6),
StdGPA          DECIMAL(3,2),
CONSTRAINT PKStudent PRIMARY KEY (StdSSN),
CONSTRAINT ValidGPA CHECK ( StdGPA BETWEEN 0 AND 4   ),
CONSTRAINT MajorDeclared CHECK
    ( StdClass IN ('FR', 'SO') OR StdMajor IS NOT NULL   )  )
```

- Management of trigger and procedure coding practices: documentation standards, parameter usage, and content.
- Management of object dependencies: access plan obsolescence, modification of referenced objects, deletion of referenced objects.
- Controlling trigger complexity: identifying trigger interactions, minimizing trigger actions that can fire other triggers, no dependence on a specific firing order for overlapping triggers.
- Catalog tables for tracking the objects managed by a DBMS.
- Information resource dictionary for managing the information systems development process.
- Development of an enterprise data model as an important part of the information systems planning process.
- Selection and evaluation process for analyzing organization needs and DBMS features.
- Using a tool such as the Analytic Hierarchy Process for combining weights consistently in the evaluation process.
- Using standard, domain benchmark results to gauge the performance of DBMSs.
- Responsibilities of database specialists for managing transaction processing, data warehouses, distributed environments, and object DBMSs.

QUESTIONS

1. Why is it difficult to use operational databases for management decision making?
2. How must operational databases be transformed for management decision making?
3. What are the phases of the information life cycle?
4. What does it mean to integrate information life cycles?
5. What data quality dimension is important for management decision making but not for operational decision making?
6. How does knowledge management differ from information resource management?
7. What are the three pillars of knowledge management?
8. What kind of position is the data administrator?
9. What kind of position is the database administrator?

10. Which position (data administrator versus database administrator) takes a broader view of information resources?

11. What is an enterprise data model?

12. For what reasons is an enterprise data model developed?

13. What kinds of specialization are possible in large organizations for data administrators and database administrators?

14. What is discretionary access control?

15. What is mandatory access control?

16. What kind of database requires mandatory access control?

17. What are the purposes of the GRANT and REVOKE statements in SQL?

18. Why should authorization rules reference roles instead of individual users?

19. Why do authorization rules typically use views rather than tables or columns?

20. What are the two uses of the GRANT statement?

21. Why should a DBA cautiously use the WITH ADMIN clause in the CREATE ROLE statement and the WITH GRANT OPTION clause in the GRANT statement?

22. What is the difference between system privileges and object privileges in Oracle? Provide an example of a system privilege and an object privilege.

23. What other disciplines does computer security involve?

24. What is the purpose of the CREATE DOMAIN statement? Compare and contrast an SQL domain with a distinct type.

25. What additional capabilities does SQL:1999 add for user-defined types as compared to domains?

26. What is the purpose of assertions in SQL?

27. What does it mean to say that an assertion is deferrable?

28. What are alternatives to SQL assertions? Why would you use an alternative to an assertion?

29. What are the coding issues about which a DBA should be concerned?

30. How does a stored procedure or trigger depend on other database objects?

31. What are the responsibilities for a DBA for managing dependencies?

32. What is the difference between timestamp and signature dependency maintenance?

33. List at least three ways that a DBA can control trigger interactions.

34. What kind of metadata does a data dictionary contain?

35. What are catalog tables? What kind of catalog tables are managed by DBMSs?

36. What is the difference between the Information_Schema and the Definition_Schema in SQL:1999?

37. Why is it necessary to learn the catalog tables of a specific DBMS?

38. How does a DBA access catalog tables?

39. What is the purpose of an information resource dictionary?

40. What functions does an information resource dictionary system perform?

41. What are the purposes of information systems planning?

42. Why is the enterprise data model developed before the process model?

43. Why is the selection and evaluation process important for DBMSs?

44. What are some complexities in the selection and evaluation process for a complex product like a DBMS?

45. What are the steps in the selection and evaluation process?

46. How is the Analytic Hierarchy Process used in the selection and evaluation process?

47. What responsibilities does the database administrator have in the selection and evaluation process?

48. What responsibilities does the data administrator have in the selection and evaluation process?

49. What are the responsibilities of database administrators for transaction processing?

50. What are responsibilities of database administrators for managing data warehouses?

51. What are the responsibilities of database administrators for managing databases in distributed environments?

52. What are the responsibilities of database administrators for managing object databases?

53. What are the responsibilities of data administrators for transaction processing?

54. What are the responsibilities of data administrators for managing data warehouses?

55. What are the responsibilities of data administrators for managing databases in distributed environments?

56. What are the responsibilities of data administrators for managing object databases?

57. What are the characteristics of a good benchmark?

58. Why does the Transaction Processing Council publish total system performance measures rather than component measures?

59. Why does the Transaction Processing Council publish price/performance results?

60. How does the Transaction Processing Council ensure that benchmark results are relevant and reliable?

PROBLEMS

Because of the introductory nature of this chapter, there are no problems in this chapter. Problems appear at the end of the other chapters in Part 4.

REFERENCES FOR FURTHER STUDY

The book by Jay Louise Weldon (1981) remains the classic book on database administration despite its age. Davenport and Prusak (1997) and Prusak (1997) describe the concept of knowledge management and provide case studies to demonstrate its application. Specialized books such as Bowman, Emerson, and Darnovsky (1996); Cannan and Otten (1992); Date and Darwen (1997); Groff and Weinberg (1999); and Melton and Simon (2001) provide more details about the security and integrity features in SQL-92 and SQL:1999. Inmon (1986) and Martin (1982) have written detailed descriptions of information systems planning. Hackathorn and Karimi (1988) compare approaches to information systems planning. Fernandez, Summers, and Wood (1981) wrote a classic book on database security and integrity. For more details about the Analytic Hierarchy Process mentioned in Section 14.3.2, consult Saaty (1988) and Zahedi (1986). Su et al. (1987) describe the Logic Scoring of Preferences, an alternative approach to DBMS selection. The Transaction Processing Council (www.tpc.org) provides an invaluable resource about domain-specific benchmarks for DBMSs.

This appendix summarizes the SQL:1999 syntax for the CREATE/DROP ROLE statements, the GRANT/REVOKE statements, the CREATE DOMAIN statement, and the CREATE ASSERTION statement as well as the CHECK constraint clause of the CREATE TABLE statement. The conventions used in the syntax notation are identical to those used at the end of Chapter 2.

CREATE AND DROP ROLE STATEMENTS

```
CREATE ROLE RoleName
            [  WITH ADMIN UserName { CURRENT_USER  I  CURRENT_ROLE  } ]

DROP ROLE RoleName
```

GRANT AND REVOKE STATEMENTS

```
-- GRANT statement for privileges
GRANT  {  <Privilege>*  I  ALL PRIVILEGES  }  ON ObjectName
                TO UserName*  [  WITH GRANT OPTION  ]

<Privilege>:
                { SELECT  [  (ColumnName*)  ]  I
                  DELETE I
                  INSERT  [  (ColumnName*)  ]  I
                  REFERENCES  [  (ColumnName*)  ]  I
                  UPDATE  [  (ColumnName*) ]
                  USAGE I
                  TRIGGER I
                  UNDER I
                  EXECUTE  }

-- GRANT statement for roles
GRANT RoleName*
                TO UserName*  [  WITH ADMIN OPTION ]

-- REVOKE statement for privileges
REVOKE  [  GRANT OPTION FOR  ]  <Privilege>*
                ON ObjectName FROM UserName*
                [  GRANTED BY  {  CURRENT_USER  I  CURRENT_ROLE  }  ]
                {  CASCADE  I  RESTRICT  }
```

```
-- REVOKE statement for roles
REVOKE  [  ADMIN OPTION FOR  ]  RoleName*
                  FROM UserName*
                  [  GRANTED BY  {  CURRENT_USER  |  CURRENT_ROLE  }  ]
                  {  CASCADE  |  RESTRICT  }
```

CREATE DOMAIN AND DROP DOMAIN STATEMENTS

```
CREATE DOMAIN DomainName DataType
              [  CHECK (<Domain-Condition>  )  ]

<Domain-Condition>:
              {  VALUE <Comparison-Operator> Constant  |
                 VALUE BETWEEN Constant AND Constant  |
                 VALUE IN  (  Constant*  )  }

<Comparison-Operator>:
              {  =  |  <  |  >  |  <=  |  >=  |  <>  }
DROP DOMAIN DomainName { CASCADE  |  RESTRICT  }
```

CREATE ASSERTION AND DROP ASSERTION STATEMENTS

```
CREATE ASSERTION AssertionName
              CHECK  (  <Group-Condition>  )

<Group-Condition>: — initially defined in Chapter 3 and extended in Chapter 9

DROP ASSERTION AssertionName  {  CASCADE  |  RESTRICT  }
```

CHECK CONSTRAINT CLAUSE IN THE CREATE TABLE STATEMENT

```
CREATE TABLE TableName
              (  <Column-Definition>*  [  , <Table-Constraint>*  ]  )

<Column-Definition>: ColumnName DataType
              [  DEFAULT  {  DefaultValue  |  USER  |  NULL  }  ]
                 [  <Column-Constraint>  ]
```

(Continued)

```
<Column-Constraint>:  [  CONSTRAINT ConstraintName  ]
                       {  NOT NULL  |
                          <Foreign-Key-Constraint>   |  — defined in Chapter 2
                          <Uniqueness-Constraint>   |  — defined in Chapter 2
                          <Check-Constraint>  }
<Table-Constraint>:  [  CONSTRAINT ConstraintName  ]
                       {  <Primary-Key-Constraint>   |  — defined in Chapter 2
                          <Foreign-Key-Constraint>   |  — defined in Chapter 2
                          <Uniqueness-Constraint>   |  — defined in Chapter 2
                          <Check-Constraint> }

<Check-Constraint>: CHECK (  <Row-Condition>  )

<Row-Condition>: — defined in Chapter 3
```

Transaction Management

This chapter describes transaction management features to support concurrent usage of a database and recovery from failures. After this chapter, the student should have acquired the following knowledge and skills:

- Explain the ACID transaction properties and the concepts of recovery and concurrency transparency.

- Understand the role of locking to prevent interference problems among multiple users.

- Understand the role of recovery tools to deal with database failures.

- Understand transaction design issues that affect performance.

- Describe the relationship of workflow management to transaction management.

OVERVIEW

Chapter 14 presented a context for managing databases and an overview of the different processing environments for databases. You learned about the responsibilities of database specialists and the tools and processes used by database specialists. The most prevalent and important database environment is transaction processing that supports the daily operations of an organization. This chapter begins the details of Part 4 by describing how DBMSs support transaction processing.

This chapter presents a broad coverage of transaction management. Before you can understand how DBMSs support transaction processing, you need a more detailed understanding of transaction concepts. This chapter describes properties of transactions, SQL statements to define transactions, and properties of transaction processing. After learning about transaction concepts, you are ready to study concurrency control and recovery management, two major services to support transaction processing. For concurrency control, this chapter describes the objective, interference problems, and tools of concurrency control. For recovery management, this chapter describes failure types, recovery tools, and recovery processes.

Besides knowing the transaction management services provided by a DBMS, you should understand issues of transaction design. This chapter describes important issues of transaction design including hot spots, transaction boundaries, isolation levels, and integrity constraint enforcement. To broaden your background, you should understand how database transactions fit into the larger context of collaborative work. The final section describes workflow management and contrasts it with transaction management in DBMSs.

15.1 BASICS OF DATABASE TRANSACTIONS

Transaction processing involves the operating side of databases. Whereas operations management describes how physical goods are produced, transaction management describes how information goods or transactions are controlled. Transaction management, like management of physical goods, is enormously important to modern organizations. Organizations such as banks with automatic tellers, airlines with online reservation systems, and universities with online registration could not function without reliable and efficient transaction processing. Large organizations now conduct thousands of transactions per minute. With continued growth in electronic commerce, the importance of transaction processing will increase.

> **Transaction** a unit of work that should be processed reliably. DBMSs provide recovery and concurrency control services to process transactions efficiently and reliably.

In common discourse, a transaction is an interaction among two or more parties for the conduct of business such as buying a car from a dealership. Database transactions have a more precise meaning. A database <u>transaction</u> involves a collection of operations that must be processed as one unit of work. Transactions should be processed reliably so that there is no loss of data due to multiple users and system failures. To help you grasp this more precise meaning, this section presents examples of transactions and defines properties of transactions.

15.1.1 Transaction Examples

A transaction is a user-defined concept. For example, making an airline reservation may involve reservations for the departure and return. To the user, the combination of the departure and the return is a transaction, not the departure and the return separately. Most travelers do not want to depart without returning. The implication for DBMSs is that a transaction is a user-defined set of database operations. A transaction can involve any number of reads and writes to a database. To provide the flexibility of user-defined transactions, DBMSs cannot restrict transactions to only a specified number of reads and writes to a database.

An information system may have many different kinds of transactions. Table 15.1 depicts transactions of an order entry system. At any point in time, users may be conducting business with each of these transactions. For example, many customers may be placing orders while other customers check on the status of their orders.

SQL Statements to Define Transactions

To define a transaction, you can use some additional SQL statements. Figure 15.1 depicts additional SQL statements to define the prototypical automatic teller machine (ATM) transaction. The START TRANSACTION and COMMIT statements define the statements in a transaction.[1] Any other SQL statements between them are part of the

TABLE 15.1	Typical Transactions in an Order Entry System

Transaction	Description
Add order	Customer places a new order.
Update order	Customer changes details of an existing order.
Check status	Clerk reports the status of an order to customer.
Payment	Payment received from a customer.
Shipment	Goods sent to a customer.

```
START TRANSACTION
    Display greeting
    Get account number, pin, type, and amount
    SELECT account number, type, and balance
    If balance is sufficient then
        UPDATE account by posting debit
        UPDATE account by posting credit
        INSERT history record
        Display final message and issue cash
    Else
        Write error message
    End If
    On Error: ROLLBACK
COMMIT
```

Figure 15.1   Pseudocode for an ATM transaction.

---

[1]SQL: 1999 specifies the START TRANSACTION and COMMIT statements. Some DBMSs use the keyword *BEGIN* instead of *START*. Some DBMSs such as Oracle do not use a statement to explicitly start a transaction. A new transaction begins with the next SQL statement following a COMMIT statement.

transaction. Typically, a transaction involves a number of SELECT, INSERT, UPDATE, and DELETE statements. In Figure 15.1, an actual transaction would have valid SQL statements for the lines beginning with SELECT, UPDATE, and INSERT. Valid programming language statements would be substituted for lines with pseudocode such as "Display greeting."

Besides the START TRANSACTION and COMMIT statements, the ROLL-BACK statement may be used. ROLLBACK is like an undo command in a word processor. ROLLBACK causes all effects of a transaction to be removed. The database is restored to the state before the transaction was executed. One situation for issuing a ROLLBACK statement is to allow the user to cancel a transaction. The ROLLBACK statement also can be used as part of exception-handling statements such as the "On Error" line in Figure 15.1. Exception-handling statements are part of programming languages such as Java and Visual Basic. Exception handling allows unanticipated errors such as communication errors to be processed separately from the normal logic of the transaction.

As you will learn later in this chapter, transactions should be designed to have short duration. To shorten the duration of the ATM transaction, the user interaction could be placed outside of the transaction. Long-running transactions can cause excessive waiting among concurrent users of a database. However, the UPDATE and INSERT statements must remain in the same transaction because these statements are part of the same unit of work.

Other Transaction Examples

Figures 15.2 and 15.3 depict transactions for an airline reservation and product order. In both examples, the transaction consists of more than one database action (read or write).

```
START TRANSACTION
    Display greeting
    Get reservation preferences
    SELECT departure and return flight records
    If reservation is acceptable then
        UPDATE seats remaining of departure flight record
        UPDATE seats remaining of return flight record
        INSERT reservation record
        Print ticket if requested
    End If
    On Error: ROLLBACK
COMMIT
```

Figure 15.2 Pseudocode for an airline reservation transaction.

```
START TRANSACTION
    Display greeting
    Get order request
    SELECT product record
    If product is available then
        UPDATE QOH of product record
        INSERT order record
        Send message to shipping department
    End If
    On Error: ROLLBACK
COMMIT
```

Figure 15.3 Pseudocode for a product order transaction.

15.1.2 Transaction Properties

DBMSs ensure that transactions obey certain properties. The most important and widely known properties are the ACID properties (atomic, consistent, isolated, and durable) as discussed below.

- **Atomic** means that a transaction cannot be subdivided. Either all the work in the transaction is completed or nothing is done. For example, the ATM transaction will not debit an account without also crediting a corresponding account. The atomic property implies that partial changes made by a transaction must be undone if the transaction aborts.

- **Consistent** means that if applicable constraints are true before the transaction starts, the constraints will be true after the transaction terminates. For example, if a user's account is balanced before a transaction, then the account is balanced after the transaction. Otherwise, the transaction is rejected and no changes take effect.

- **Isolated** means that transactions do not interfere with each other except in allowable ways. A transaction should never overwrite changes made by another transaction. In addition, a transaction may be restricted from interfering in other ways such as not viewing the uncommitted changes made by other transactions. With this restriction, your significant other will not know that you are withdrawing money until your ATM transaction completes.

- **Durable** means that any changes resulting from a transaction are permanent. No failure will erase any changes after a transaction terminates. For example, if a bank's computer experiences a failure five minutes after a transaction completes, the results of the transaction are still recorded on the bank's database.

To ensure that transactions meet the ACID properties, DBMSs provide certain services that are transparent to database developers (programmers and analysts). In common usage, transparency means that you can see through an object, rendering its inner details invisible. For DBMSs, transparency means that the inner details of transaction services are invisible. Transparency is very important because services that ensure ACID transactions are difficult to implement. By providing these services, DBMSs improve productivity of database programmers and analysts.

DBMSs provide two services, recovery transparency and concurrency transparency, to ensure that transactions obey the ACID properties. Recovery involves actions to deal with failures such as communication errors and software crashes. Concurrency involves actions to control interference among multiple, simultaneous users of the database. The following discussion provides details about transparency for recovery and concurrency.

- **Recovery transparency** means that the DBMS automatically restores a database to a consistent state after a failure. For example, if a communication failure occurs during an ATM transaction, the effects of the transaction are automatically removed from the database. On the other hand, if the DBMS crashes three seconds after an ATM transaction completes, the details of the transaction remain permanent.

- **Concurrency transparency** means that users perceive the database as a single-user system even though there may be many simultaneous users. For example, even though many users may try to reserve a popular flight using a reservation transaction, the DBMS ensures that users do not overwrite each other's work.

Even though the inner details of concurrency and recovery are not visible to a user, these services are not free. Recovery and concurrency involve overhead that may adversely impact performance or require additional resources to reach an acceptable level of performance. The DBA must be aware of the resource implications of these services. More computing resources such as memory, disk space, and parallel processing may be useful to improve performance. For example, to reduce the time to recover from a hard-disk failure, extra hard disks known as hot spares are essential. In addition, the purchase price of a DBMS may depend on how efficiently these services can be performed. DBMSs that perform transaction processing very efficiently can be costly.

Transaction design is another reason for understanding details of concurrency control and recovery. Even if the DBA devotes adequate resources to transaction processing, poor transaction design can lead to performance problems. To achieve a satisfactory transaction design, you should have background about the details of concurrency control and recovery as well as understand transaction design principles, as discussed in the following sections.

15.2 CONCURRENCY CONTROL

Most organizations cannot function without multiuser databases. For example, airline, retail, banking, and help desk databases can have thousands of users simultaneously trying to conduct business. Multiple users can access these databases concurrently, that is, at the same time. If access was restricted to only one user at a time, little work would be accomplished and most users would take their business elsewhere. However, concurrent users cannot be permitted to interfere with each other. This section defines the objective, problems, and tools for concurrency control.

15.2.1 Objective of Concurrency Control

Transaction Throughput
the number of transactions processed per time interval. It is an important measure of transaction processing performance.

The objective of concurrency control is to maximize transaction throughput while preventing interference among multiple users. Transaction throughput, the number of transactions processed per time unit, is a measure of the amount of work performed by a DBMS. Typically, transaction throughput is reported in transactions per minute. In a high-volume environment such as order entry, DBMSs may need to process thousands of transactions per minute. From the perspective of the user, transaction throughput is related to response time. Higher transaction throughput means lower response times. Users are typically unwilling to wait more than a few seconds for completion of a transaction.

If there is no interference, the result of executing concurrent transactions is the same as executing the same transactions in some sequential order. Sequential execution means that one transaction completes before another one executes, thus ensuring no interference. Executing transactions sequentially would result in low throughput and high waiting times. Thus, DBMSs allow transactions to execute simultaneously while ensuring the results are the same as though executed sequentially.

Transactions executing simultaneously cannot interfere unless they are manipulating common data. Most concurrent transactions manipulate only small amounts of common data. For example, in an airline reservation, two users can simultaneously enter new reservation records because the reservation records are unique for each customer. However, interference can occur on the seats-remaining field of a flight table. For popular flights, many users may want to decrement the value of the seats-remaining field. It is critical that the DBMS control concurrent updating of this field in popular flight records.

Hot Spot common data that multiple users try to change. Without adequate concurrency control, users may interfere with each other on hot spots.

A <u>hot spot</u> is common data that multiple users try to change simultaneously. Essentially, a hot spot represents a scarce resource that users must queue to access. Typical hot spots are the seats-remaining for popular flights, the quantity-on-hand of popular inventory items, and the seats-taken in popular course offerings. In an ideal world, DBMSs would only track hot spots. Unfortunately, hot spots can be difficult to know in advance so DBMSs track access to all parts of a database.

Interference on hot spots can lead to lost data and poor decision making. The following sections describe interference problems and the tools to prevent them.

15.2.2 Interference Problems

There are three problems that can result because of simultaneous access to a database: (1) lost update, (2) uncommitted dependency, and (3) inconsistent retrieval. This section defines each problem and presents examples of their occurrence.

Lost Update

Lost Update a concurrency control problem in which one user's update overwrites another user's update.

Lost update is the most serious interference problem because changes to a database are inadvertently lost. In a <u>lost update,</u> one user's update overwrites another user's update, as depicted by the timeline of Figure 15.4. The timeline shows two concurrent transactions trying to update the seats remaining (SR) field of the same flight record. Assume that the value of SR is 10 before the transactions begin. After time T_2, both transactions have stored the value of 10 for SR in local buffers as a result of the read operations. After time T_4, both transactions have made changes to their local copy of SR. However, each transaction changes the value to 9, unaware of the activity of the other transaction. After time T_6, the value of SR on the database is 9. But the value after finishing both transactions should be 8, not 9! One of the changes has been lost.

Some students become confused about the lost update problem because of the actions performed on local copies of the data. The calculations at times T_3 and T_4 are performed in memory buffers specific to each transaction. Even though transaction A has changed the value of $SR,$ transaction B performs the calculation with its own local copy of SR having a value of 10. The write operation performed by transaction A is not known to transaction B unless transaction B reads the value again.

A lost update involves two or more transactions trying to change (write to) the same part of the database. As you will see in the next two problems, two transactions also can conflict if only one is changing the database.

Transaction A	Time	Transaction B
Read SR (10)	T_1	
	T_2	Read SR (10)
If $SR > 0$ then $SR = SR - 1$	T_3	
	T_4	If $SR > 0$ then $SR = SR - 1$
Write SR (9)	T_5	
	T_6	Write SR (9)

Figure 15.4   **Example lost update problem.**

Uncommitted Dependency

Uncommitted Dependency a concurrency control problem in which one transaction reads data written by another transaction before the other transaction commits. If the second transaction aborts, the first transaction may rely on data that will no longer exist.

An underlined dependency occurs when one transaction reads data written by another transaction before the other transaction commits. An uncommitted dependency is also known as a dirty read because it is caused by one transaction reading dirty (uncommitted) data. In Figure 15.5, transaction A reads the SR field, changes its local copy of the SR field, and writes the new value back to the database. Transaction B then reads the changed value. Before transaction A commits, however, an error is detected and transaction A issues a rollback. The rollback could have been issued as a result of the user canceling the transaction or as a result of a failure. The value used by transaction B is now a phantom value. The real SR value is now 10 because A's change was not permanent. Transaction B may use its value (9) to make an erroneous decision. For example, if SR's value was 1 before transaction A began, transaction B might be denied a reservation.

Because data are not permanent until a transaction commits, a conflict can occur even though only one transaction writes to the database. An uncommitted dependency involves one transaction writing and another transaction reading the same part of the database. However, an uncommitted dependency cannot cause a problem unless a rollback occurs. The other problem also involves conflicts when only one transaction writes to a database.

Problems Involving Inconsistent Retrievals

Incorrect Summary a concurrency control problem in which a transaction reads several values, but another transaction updates some of the values while the first transaction is still executing.

The last problems involve situations in which interference causes inconsistency among multiple retrievals of a subset of data. All inconsistent retrieval problems involve one transaction reading and the second transaction changing the same part of the database. The incorrect summary problem is the most significant problem involving inconsistent retrievals. An incorrect summary occurs when a transaction calculating a summary function reads some values before another transaction changes the values but reads other values after another transaction changes the values.[2] In Figure 15.6, transaction B reads SR_1

Transaction A	Time	Transaction B
Read SR (10)	T_1	
$SR = SR - 1$	T_2	
Write SR (9)	T_3	
	T_4	Read SR (9)
Rollback	T_5	

Figure 15.5 Example dirty read problem.

Transaction A	Time	Transaction B
Read SR_1 (10)	T_1	
$SR_1 = SR_1 - 1$	T_2	
Write SR_1 (9)	T_3	
	T_4	Read SR_1 (9)
	T_5	Sum = Sum + SR_1
	T_6	Read SR_2 (5)
	T_7	Sum = Sum + SR_2
Read SR_2 (5)	T_8	
$SR_2 = SR_2 - 1$	T_9	
Write SR_2 (4)	T_{10}	

Figure 15.6 Example incorrect summary problem.

[2]An incorrect summary is also known as an inconsistent analysis.

after transaction A changes the value but reads SR_2 before transaction A changes the value. For consistency, transaction B should use all the values either before or after they are changed by other transactions.

A second problem involving inconsistent retrievals is known as the phantom read problem. A <u>phantom read problem</u> occurs when a transaction executes a query with record conditions. Then, another transaction inserts or modifies data that the query would retrieve. Finally, the original transaction executes the same query again. The second query execution retrieves different records than the first execution. The new and changed records are phantom because they did not exist in the result of the first query execution.

A third problem involving inconsistent retrievals is known as the nonrepeatable read problem. A <u>nonrepeatable read problem</u> occurs when a transaction reads the same value more than one time. In between reading the data item, another transaction modifies the data item. The second retrieval contains a different value than the first retrieval because of the change made by the other transaction.

15.2.3 Concurrency Control Tools

This section describes two tools (locks and the two-phase locking protocol) used by most DBMSs to prevent the three interference problems discussed in the previous section. In addition to the two tools, the deadlock problem is presented because it can result through the use of locks. This section closes by briefly discussing optimistic concurrency control approaches that do not use locks.

Locks

Locks provide a way to prevent other users from accessing part of the database being used. Before accessing part of the database, a lock must be obtained. Other users must wait if trying to obtain a conflicting lock on the same part of the database. Table 15.2 shows conflicts for two kinds of locks. A <u>shared</u> (S) <u>lock</u> must be obtained before reading a database item, whereas an <u>exclusive</u> (X) <u>lock</u> must be obtained before writing. As shown in Table 15.2, any number of users can hold a shared lock on the same part of the database. However, only one user can hold an exclusive lock.

The concurrency control manager is the part of the DBMS responsible for managing locks. The concurrency control manager maintains a hidden table to record locks held by various transactions.[3] A lock record contains a transaction identifier, a record identifier, a kind, and a count, as explained in Table 15.3. In the simplest scheme, the kind is either

Lock a fundamental tool of concurrency control. A lock on a database item prevents other transactions from performing conflicting actions on the same item.

TABLE 15.2	Locking Conflicts	
User 1 Holds	**User 2 Requests**	
	S Lock	*X Lock*
S Lock	Lock granted	User 2 waits
X Lock	User 2 waits	User 2 waits

---

[3]The lock table is hidden from all users except the internal concurrency control manager. Under special circumstances, the database administrator can access the lock table.

TABLE 15.3	Fields in a Lock Record

Field Name	Description
Transaction identifier	Unique identifier for a transaction
Record identifier	Identifies the record to be locked
Kind	Indicates the intended usage of the locked record
Count	Number of other users holding this kind of lock

shared or exclusive, as discussed previously. Most DBMSs have other kinds of locks to improve efficiency and allow for more concurrent access. The concurrency control manager performs two operations on lock records. The <u>lock</u> operator adds a record to the lock table whereas the <u>unlock</u> operator or release operator deletes a record from the lock table.

Locking Granularity

Locking Granularity the size of the database item locked. Locking granularity is a trade-off between waiting time (amount of concurrency permitted) and overhead (number of locks held).

<u>Locking granularity</u> is one complication about locks. Granularity refers to the size of the database item locked. The previous discussion assumed that locks are held for records. Most DBMSs can hold locks for different granularities, as depicted in Figure 15.7. The entire database is the coarsest lock that can be held. If an exclusive lock is held on the entire database, no other users can access the database until the lock is released. On the other extreme, an individual field is the finest lock that can be held. Locks also can be held on parts of the database not generally seen by users. For example, locks can be held on indexes and pages (physical records).

Locking granularity is a trade-off between overhead and waiting. Holding locks at a fine level decreases waiting among users but increases system overhead because more locks must be obtained. Holding locks at a coarser level reduces the number of locks but increases the amount of waiting. In some DBMSs, the concurrency control manager tries to detect the pattern of usage and promotes locks if needed. For example, the concurrency control manager initially can grant record locks to a transaction in anticipation that only a few records will be locked. If the transaction continues to request locks, the concurrency control component can promote the record locks to a lock on the entire table.

Intent Lock a lock on a large database item (such as a table) indicating intention to lock smaller items contained in the larger item. Intent locks alleviate blocking when locking coarse items and allow efficient detection of conflicts among locks on items of varying granularity.

To alleviate the blocking caused by locking coarse items as shared or exclusive, <u>intent locks</u> usually are used. Intent locks support more concurrency on coarse items than shared or exclusive locks. Intent locks also allow efficient detection of conflicts among locks on items of varying granularity. To support read and write at lower levels of granularity, three kinds of intent locks are used: (1) intention shared when intending to read lower-level items; (2) intention exclusive when intending to write lower-level items; and (3) shared intention exclusive when intending to read and write lower-level items. For example, a transaction should request an intention shared lock on a table for which it intends to read rows of the table. The intention shared lock on the table only conflicts with exclusive locks on the table or smaller grained items.

Deadlocks

Deadlock a problem of mutual waiting that can occur when using locks. If a deadlock is not resolved, the involved transactions will wait forever.

Using locks to prevent interference problems can lead to deadlocks. A <u>deadlock</u> is a problem of mutual waiting. One transaction has a resource that a second transaction needs, and the second transaction holds a resource that the first transaction needs. Figure 15.8 depicts

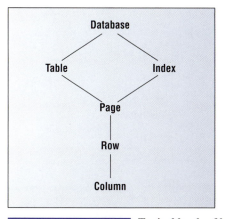

Figure 15.7 Typical levels of locking granularity.

Transaction A	Time	Transaction B
XLock SR_1	T_1	
	T_2	XLock SR_2
XLock SR_2 (wait)	T_3	
	T_4	XLock SR_1 (wait)

Figure 15.8 Example deadlock problem.

a deadlock among two transactions trying to reserve seats on a flight involving more than one leg. Transaction A acquires an exclusive lock on the first leg (say from Denver to Chicago) followed by transaction B acquiring a lock on the second leg (say from Chicago to New York). Transaction A tries to lock the second leg but is blocked because transaction B holds an exclusive lock. Likewise, transaction B must wait to obtain a lock on the first leg. Deadlocks can involve more than two transactions, but the pattern is more complex.

To control deadlocks, most DBMSs use a time-out policy. The concurrency control manager aborts (with a ROLLBACK statement) any transaction waiting for more than a specified time. Note that a time-out policy may abort transactions that are not deadlocked. The time-out interval should be set large enough so that few nondeadlocked transactions will wait that long. Deadlocks can be detected by looking for patterns of mutual waiting. Because deadlock detection can involve significant computation time, most DBMSs use a time-out policy rather than deadlock detection.

Two-Phase Locking Protocol

Definition of 2PL

1. Before reading or writing to a data item, the transaction must acquire the applicable lock to the data item.
2. Wait if a conflicting lock is held on the data item.
3. After releasing a lock, the transaction does not acquire any new locks.

To ensure that lost update problems do not occur, the concurrency control manager requires that all transactions follow the <u>Two-Phase Locking (2PL) protocol.</u> Protocol is a fancy word for a group behavior rule. A protocol binds all members of a group to behave in a specified manner. For human communication, Robert's Rules of Order require that all meeting participants follow certain rules. For data communication, protocols ensure that messages have a common format that both sender and receiver can process. For concurrency control, all transactions must follow the 2PL protocol to ensure that lost updates do not occur. Two-phase locking has three conditions as shown in the margin.

The first two conditions follow from the usage of locks as previously explained. The third condition is subtler. If new locks are acquired after releasing locks, two transactions can obtain and release locks in a pattern in which a lost update occurs.

The third condition is usually simplified so that at least exclusive locks are held until the end of the transaction. At commit time, locks of a transaction are released. Figure 15.9 graphically depicts the 2PL with the simplified third condition. At the beginning of the transaction (BOT), a transaction has no locks. A growing phase ensues in which the transaction acquires locks but never releases any locks. At the end of the transaction (EOT), the shrinking phase occurs in which all locks are released together.

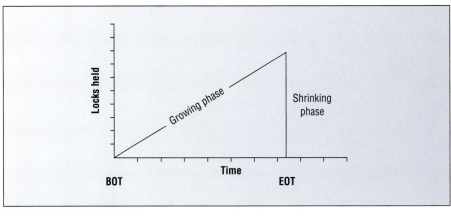

Figure 15.9	**Growing and shrinking phases of 2PL.**

Simplifying the definition of 2PL makes the protocol easier to enforce and prevents the uncommitted dependency problem. Holding locks until a transaction commits obviates the difficult problem of predicting when a transaction may release locks. Holding write locks until the end of transaction prevents the uncommitted dependency problem because changes are not exposed to other transactions until permanent (after commit). However, releasing shared locks before the end of transaction can lead to occurrences of the incorrect summary, the nonrepeatable read, and the phantom read problems. To provide control over the level of interference tolerated, the isolation level can be set as presented in Section 15.4.2.

Optimistic Approaches

The use of locks and 2PL is a pessimistic approach to concurrency control. Locking assumes that every transaction conflicts. If contention is only for relatively few hot spots, then locking may require excessive overhead.

Optimistic concurrency control approaches assume that conflicts are rare. If conflicts are rare, it is more efficient to check for conflicts rather than use locks to force waiting. In optimistic approaches, transactions are permitted to access the database without acquiring locks. Instead, the concurrency control manager checks whether a conflict has occurred. The check can be performed either just before a transaction commits or after each read and write. By reviewing the relative time of reads and writes, the concurrency control manager can determine whether a conflict has occurred. If a conflict occurs, the concurrency control manager issues a rollback and restarts the offending transaction.

Despite the appeal of optimistic approaches, most DBMSs use 2PL. Although Oracle provides a kind of optimistic concurrency control known as versioning, it does not appear to be widely used. The performance of optimistic approaches depends on the frequency of conflicts. If conflicts increase, the performance of optimistic approaches decreases. Even if conflicts are rare, optimistic approaches can have more variability because the penalty for conflicts is larger in optimistic approaches. Pessimistic approaches resolve conflicts by waiting. Optimistic approaches resolve conflicts by rolling back and restarting. Restarting a transaction may delay a transaction more than waiting for a resource to be released.

15.3 RECOVERY MANAGEMENT

Recovery management is a service to restore a database to a consistent state after a failure. This section describes the kinds of failures to prevent, the tools of recovery management, and the recovery processes that use the tools.

15.3.1 Data Storage Devices and Failure Types

From the perspective of database failures, volatility is an important characteristic of data storage devices. Main memory is <u>volatile</u> because it loses its state if power is lost. In contrast, a hard disk is <u>nonvolatile</u> because it retains its state if power is lost. This distinction is important because DBMSs cannot depend on volatile memory to recover data after failures. Even nonvolatile devices are not completely reliable. For example, certain failures make the contents of a hard disk unreadable. To achieve high reliability, DBMSs may replicate data on several kinds of nonvolatile storage media such as a hard disk, magnetic tape, and optical disk. Using a combination of nonvolatile devices improves reliability because different kinds of devices usually have independent failure rates.

Some failures affect main memory only, while others affect both volatile and nonvolatile memory. Table 15.4 shows four kinds of failures along with their effect and frequency. The first two kinds of failures affect the memory of one executing transaction. Transaction code should check for error conditions such as an invalid account number or cancellation of the transaction by the user. A program-detected failure usually leads to aborting the transaction with a specified message to the user. The SQL ROLLBACK statement can abort a transaction if an abnormal condition occurs. Recall that the ROLLBACK statement causes all changes made by the transaction to be removed from the database. Program-detected failures are usually the most common and least harmful.

Abnormal termination has an effect similar to a program-detected failure but a different cause. The transaction aborts, but the error message is often unintelligible to the user. Abnormal termination can be caused by events such as transaction time-out, communication line failure, or programming error (for example, dividing by zero). The ON ERROR statement in Figure 15.1 detects abnormal termination. A ROLLBACK statement removes any effects of the terminated transaction on the database.

The last two kinds of failures have more serious consequences but are usually far less common. A system failure is an abnormal termination of the operating system. An operating system failure affects all executing transactions. A device failure such as a disk crash affects all executing transactions and all committed transactions whose work is recorded on the disk. A device failure can take hours to recover while a system crash can take minutes.

TABLE 15.4	Failure Types, Effects, and Frequency	
Type	*Effect*	*Frequency*
Program-detected	Local (1 transaction)	Most frequent
Abnormal termination	Local (1 transaction)	Moderate frequency
System failure	Global (all active transactions)	Not frequent
Device failure	Global (all active and past transactions)	Least frequent

15.3.2 Recovery Tools

The recovery manager uses redundancy and control of the timing of database writes to restore a database after a failure. Three tools discussed in this section—transaction log, checkpoint, and database backup—are forms of redundancy. The last tool (force writing) allows the recovery manager to control when database writes are recorded. This section explains the nature of these tools, while the next section explains how these tools are used in recovery processes.

Transaction Log

Transaction Log a table that contains a history of database changes. The recovery manager uses the log table to recover from failures.

A transaction log is like a shadow following a database. Any change to the database is also recorded in the log. A typical log (Table 15.5) contains a unique log sequence number (LSN), a transaction identifier, a database action, a time, a row identifier, a column name, and values (old and new). For insert operations, the column name * denotes all columns with the new value containing an entire row of values. The old and new values are sometimes called the before and after images, respectively. If the database action is insert, the log only contains the new value. Similarly, if the database action is delete, the log only contains the old value. Besides insert, update, and delete actions, log records are created for the begin and the end of a transaction. The log is a hidden database table not available to normal users.

The recovery manager can perform two operations on the log. In an undo operation, the database reverts to a previous state by substituting the old value for whatever value is stored in the database. In a redo operation, the recovery component reestablishes a new state by substituting the new value for whatever value is stored in the database. To undo (redo) a transaction, the undo (redo) operation is applied to all log records of a specified transaction except for the start and commit records.

A log can add considerable storage overhead. In an environment of large transaction volumes, 10,000 megabytes of log records can be generated each day. Because of this large size, many organizations have both an online log stored on disk and an archive log stored on tape or optical disk. In addition to the size, the integrity of the log is crucial. Enterprise DBMSs can maintain redundant logs to provide nonstop processing in case of a log failure.

Checkpoint

Checkpoint the act of writing a checkpoint record to the log and writing log and database buffers to disk. All transaction activity ceases while a checkpoint occurs. The checkpoint interval should be chosen to balance restart time with checkpoint overhead.

The purpose of a checkpoint is to reduce the time to recover from failures. At periodic times, a checkpoint record is written to the log to record all active transactions.

TABLE 15.5	Example Transaction Log for an ATM Transaction

LSN	TransNo	Action	Time	Table	Row	Column	Old	New
1	101001	START	10:29					
2	101001	UPDATE	10:30	Acct	10001	AcctBal	100	200
3	101001	UPDATE	10:30	Acct	15147	AcctBal	500	400
4	101001	INSERT	10:32	Hist	25045	*		<1002, 500, ...>
5	101001	COMMIT	10:33					

In addition, all log buffers as well as some database buffers are written to disk. At restart time, the recovery manager relies on the checkpoint log record and knowledge of log and database page writes to reduce the amount of restart work.

The checkpoint interval is defined as the period between checkpoints. The interval can be expressed as a time (such as five minutes) or as a size parameter such as the number of committed transactions, the number of log pages, or the number of database pages. The checkpoint interval is a design parameter. A small interval reduces restart work but causes more overhead to record checkpoints. A large interval reduces checkpoint overhead but increases restart work. A typical checkpoint interval might be 10 minutes for large transaction volumes.

Recording a checkpoint may involve considerable disruption in transaction processing as all transaction activity ceases while a checkpoint occurs. No new transactions can begin, and existing transactions cannot initiate new operations during a checkpoint. The length of the disruption depends on the type of checkpoint used. In a cache-consistent checkpoint, buffer pages (log pages and some dirty database pages) remaining in memory are written to disk and then the checkpoint record is written to the log. A page is dirty if it has been changed by a transaction.

To reduce the disruption caused by cache-consistent checkpoints, some DBMSs support fuzzy checkpoints. In a fuzzy checkpoint, the recovery manager only writes the buffer pages since the previous checkpoint. Most of these pages should have already been written to disk before the checkpoint. In the checkpoint record on the log, the recovery manager notes the set of buffer pages remaining after the current checkpoint as well as all active transactions. At restart time, the recovery manager uses the two most recent fuzzy checkpoint records in the log. Thus, fuzzy checkpoints involve less overhead than cache-consistent checkpoints but may require more restart work.

Force Writing

Force Writing the ability to control when data are transferred to nonvolatile storage. This ability is fundamental to recovery management.

The ability to control when data are transferred to nonvolatile storage is known as force writing. Without the ability to control the timing of write operations to nonvolatile storage, recovery is not possible. Force writing means that the DBMS, not the operating system, controls when data are written to nonvolatile storage. Normally, when a program issues a write command, the operating system puts the data in a buffer. For efficiency, the data are not written to disk until the buffer is full. Typically, there is some small delay between arrival of data in a buffer and transferring the buffer to disk. With force writing, the operating system allows the DBMS to control when the buffer is written to disk.

The recovery manager uses force writing at checkpoint time and the end of a transaction. At checkpoint time, in addition to inserting a checkpoint record, all log and some database buffers are force written to disk. This force writing can add considerable overhead to the checkpoint process. At the end of a transaction, the recovery manager force writes any log records of a transaction remaining in memory.

Database Backup

A backup is a copy of all or part of a disk. The backup is used when the disk containing the database or log is damaged. A backup is usually made on magnetic tape because it is less expensive and more reliable than disk. Periodically, a backup should be made for both the database and the log. To save time, most backup schedules include less frequent massive backups to copy the entire contents of a disk and more frequent incremental backups to copy only the changed part.

15.3.3 Recovery Processes

The recovery process depends on the kind of failure. Recovery from a device failure is simple but can be time consuming, as listed below:

*   The database is restored from the most recent backup.
*   Then, the recovery manager applies the redo operator to all committed transactions after the backup. Because the backup may be several hours to days old, the log must be consulted to restore transactions committed after the backup.
*   The recovery process finishes by restarting incomplete transactions.

For local failures and system failures, the recovery process depends on when database changes are recorded on disk. Database changes can be recorded before the commit (immediate update) or after the commit (deferred update). The amount of work and the use of log operations (undo and redo) depend on the timing of database updates. The remainder of this section describes recovery processes for local and system failures under each scenario.

Immediate Update

Immediate Update Approach database updates are written to disk when they occur but after the corresponding log updates. To restore a database, both undo and redo operations may be needed.

In the immediate update approach, database updates are written to the disk when they occur. Database writes occur at checkpoint time and when buffers are full. However, it is essential that database writes occur after writes of the corresponding log records. This usage of the log is known as the write ahead log protocol. If log records were written after corresponding database records, recovery would not be possible if a failure occurred between the time of writing the database records and the log records. To ensure the write ahead log protocol, the recovery manager maintains a table of log sequence numbers for each database page in a buffer. A database page cannot be written to disk if its associated log sequence number is larger than the sequence number of the last log record written to disk.

Recovery from a local failure is easy because only a single transaction is affected. All log records of the transaction are found by searching the log backwards. The undo operation is then applied to each log record of the transaction. If a failure occurs during the recovery process, the undo operation is applied again. The effect of applying the undo operator multiple times is the same as applying undo one time. After completing the undo operations, the recovery manager may offer the user the chance to restart the aborted transaction.

Recovery from a system failure is more difficult because all active users are affected. To help you understand recovery from a system failure, Figure 15.10 shows the progress of a number of transactions with respect to the commit time, the most recent checkpoint, and the failure. Each transaction represents a class of transactions. For example, transaction class T1 represents transactions started and finished before the checkpoint (and the failure). No other kinds of transactions are possible.

The immediate update approach may involve both undo and redo operations, as summarized in Table 15.6. To understand the amount of work necessary, remember that log records are stable at checkpoint time and end of transaction and database changes are stable at checkpoint time. Although other database writes occur when a buffer fills, the timing of other writes is unpredictable. T1 transactions require no work because both log and database changes are stable before the failure. T2 transactions must be redone from the checkpoint because only database changes prior to the checkpoint are stable.

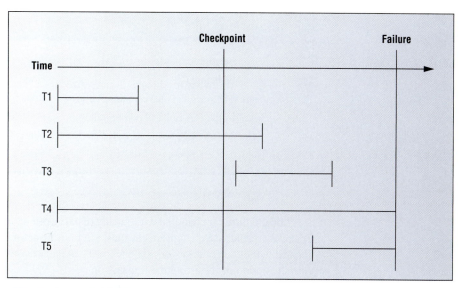

Figure 15.10   **Transaction timeline.**

	Summary of Restart Work for the Immediate Update Approach

TABLE 15.6

Class	Description	Restart Work
T1	Finished before CP	None
T2	Started before CP; finished before failure	Redo forward from the most recent checkpoint
T3	Started after CP; finished before failure	Redo forward from the most recent checkpoint
T4	Started before CP; not yet finished	Undo backwards from most recent log record
T5	Started after CP; not yet finished	Undo backwards from most recent log record

T3 transactions must be redone entirely because database changes are not guaranteed to be stable even though some changes may be recorded on disk. T4 and T5 transactions must be undone entirely because some database changes after the checkpoint may be recorded on disk.

Deferred Update

Deferred Update Approach
database updates are written only after a transaction commits. To restore a database, only redo operations are used.

In the deferred update approach, database updates are written to disk only after a transaction commits. No database writes occur at checkpoint time except for already committed transactions. The advantage of the deferred update approach is that undo operations are not necessary. However, it may be necessary to perform more redo operations than in the immediate update approach.

TABLE 15.7	Summary of Restart Work for the Deferred Update Approach	

Class	Description	Restart Work
T1	Finished before CP	None
T2	Started before CP; finished before failure	Redo forward from the first log record
T3	Started after CP; finished before failure	Redo forward from the first log record
T4	Started before CP; not yet finished	None
T5	Started after CP; not yet finished	None

Local failures are handled without any restart work in the deferred update approach. Because no database changes occur until after a transaction commits, the transaction is aborted without any undo work. The recovery manager typically would provide the user with the option of restarting the transaction.

System failures also can be handled without undo operations as depicted in Table 15.7. T4 and T5 transactions (not yet committed) do not require undo operations because no database changes are written to disk until after a transaction commits. T2 and T3 transactions (committed after the checkpoint) require redo operations because it is not known whether all database changes are stable. T2 transactions (started before the checkpoint) must be redone from the first log record rather than just from the checkpoint as in the immediate update approach. Thus, the deferred update approach requires more restart work for T2 transactions than does the immediate update approach. However, the deferred update approach requires no restart work for T4 and T5 transactions, while the immediate update approach must undo T4 and T5 transactions.

Recovery Example

Tables 15.6 and 15.7, although depicting the kind of restart work necessary, do not depict the sequence of log operations. To help you understand the log operations generated at restart time, Table 15.8 shows an example log including checkpoint records. The checkpoint action includes a list of active transactions at the time of the checkpoint. To simplify the restart process, cache consistent checkpoints are assumed.

Table 15.9 lists the log operations for the immediate update approach. The immediate update approach begins in the rollback phase. In step 1, the recovery manager adds transaction 4 to the uncommitted list and applies the undo operator to LSN 20. Likewise in step 4, the recovery manager adds transaction 3 to the uncommitted list and applies the undo operator to LSN 17. In step 5, the recovery manager adds transaction 2 to the committed list because the log record contains the COMMIT action. In step 6, the recovery manager takes no action because redo operations will be applied in the roll forward phase. In step 11, the roll backward phase ends because the START record for the last transaction on the uncommitted list has been encountered. In the roll forward phase, the recovery manager uses redo operations for each log record of active transactions.

Table 15.10 lists the log operations for the deferred update approach. The recovery manager begins by reading the log backwards like in the immediate update approach. In step 1, the recovery manager ignores log records 20 through 17 because they involve transactions that did not commit before the failure. In steps 2 and 4, the recovery manager notes that transactions 1 and 2 have committed and will need to be redone during

TABLE 15.8 Example Transaction Log

LSN	TransNo	Action	Time	Table	Row	Column	Old	New
1	1	START	10:29					
2	1	UPDATE	10:30	Acct	10	Bal	100	200
3		CKPT(1)	10:31					
4	1	UPDATE	10:32	Acct	25	Bal	500	400
5	2	START	10:33					
6	2	UPDATE	10:34	Acct	11	Bal	105	205
7	1	INSERT	10:35	Hist	101	*		<1, 400, . . .>
8	2	UPDATE	10:36	Acct	26	Bal	100	200
9	2	INSERT	10:37	Hist	102	*		<2, 200, . . .>
10	3	START	10:38					
11	3	UPDATE	10:39	Acct	10	Bal	100	200
12		CKPT(1,2,3)	10:40					
13	3	UPDATE	10:41	Acct	25	Bal	500	400
14	1	COMMIT	10:42					
15	2	UPDATE	10:43	Acct	29	Bal	200	300
16	2	COMMIT	10:44					
17	3	INSERT	10:45	Hist	103	*		<3, 400, . . .>
18	4	START	10:46					
19	4	UPDATE	10:47	Acct	10	Bal	100	200
20	4	INSERT	10:48	Hist	104	*		<3, 200, . . .>

TABLE 15.9 Restart Work Using the Immediate Update Approach

Step Number	LSN	Actions
1	20	Undo; add 4 to the uncommitted list
2	19	Undo
3	18	Remove 4 from the uncommitted list
4	17	Undo; add 3 to the uncommitted list
5	16	Add 2 to the committed list
6	15	No action
7	14	Add 1 to the committed list
8	13	Undo
9	12	Note that 3 remains uncommitted
10	11	Undo
11	10	Remove 3 from the uncommitted list
12		Roll forward phase: begin reading the log at the most recent checkpoint record (LSN = 12)
13	14	Remove 1 from the committed list
14	15	Redo
15	16	Remove 2 from the committed list; stop because the committed list is empty

TABLE 15.10		**Restart Work Using the Deferred Update Approach**

Step Number	LSN	Actions
1	20,19,18,17	No action because the transactions cannot be complete
2	16	Add 2 to the committed and incomplete lists
3	15	No action; redo during the roll forward phase
4	14	Add 1 to the committed and incomplete lists
5	13	No action because the transaction cannot be complete
6	12	Note that START records have not been found for 1 and 2
7	11,10	No action because the transaction cannot be complete
8	9,8,7,6	No action; redo during the roll forward phase
9	5	Remove 2 from the incomplete list (START record found)
10	4	No action; redo during the roll forward phase
11	3	Note that START record has not been found for 1
12	2	No action; redo during the roll forward phase
13	1	Remove 1 from the incomplete list; begin the roll forward phase
14	2	Redo
15	4	Redo
16	6	Redo
17	7	Redo
18	8	Redo
19	9	Redo
20	14	Remove 1 from the committed list
21	15	Redo
22	16	Remove 2 from the committed list; end the roll forward phase

the roll forward phase. In step 3, the recovery manager takes no action because a redo operation will be taken later during the roll forward phase. The roll backward phase continues until START records are found for all committed transactions. In the roll forward phase, the recovery manager uses redo operations for each action of transactions on the committed list. The roll forward phase ends when the recovery manager finds the COMMIT record of the last transaction on the committed list.

15.4 TRANSACTION DESIGN ISSUES

With recovery and concurrency services, it may be surprising that the transaction designer still has important design decisions. The transaction designer can be a database administrator, a programmer, or a programmer in consultation with a database administrator. The design decisions can have a significant impact on transaction processing performance. Knowledge of the details of concurrency control and recovery can make you a better transaction designer. This section describes design decisions available to transaction designers to improve performance.

15.4.1 Transaction Boundary and Hot Spots

A transaction designer develops an application to accomplish some database processing. For example, a designer may develop an application to enable a user to withdraw cash from an ATM, order a product, or register for classes. To build the application, the designer uses the transaction defining statements of SQL and the concurrency control and recovery services of the DBMS. The designer has at least several alternatives about where to use the transaction defining statements of SQL. This decision is called the <u>transaction boundary.</u>

> **Transaction Boundary** an important decision of transaction design in which an application consisting of a collection of SQL statements is divided into one or more transactions.

The transaction designer typically has the option of making one large transaction containing all SQL statements or dividing the SQL statements into multiple, smaller transactions. For example, the SQL statements in the ATM transaction can be considered one transaction, as shown in Figure 15.1. Another option is to make each SQL statement a separate transaction. When transaction boundary statements (START TRANSACTION and COMMIT) are not used, each SQL statement defaults to a separate transaction.

Trade-offs in Choosing Transaction Boundaries

When choosing a transaction's boundary, the objective is to minimize the duration of the transaction while ensuring that critical constraints are satisfied. DBMSs are designed for transactions of short duration because locking can force other transactions to wait. The duration includes not only the number of reads and writes to the database but the time spent waiting for user responses. Generally, the transaction boundary should not involve user interaction. In the ATM, airline reservation, and product order transactions (Figure 15.1, 15.2, and 15.3, respectively), the START TRANSACTION and COMMIT statements could be moved to surround just the SQL part of the pseudocode.

Duration should not compromise constraint checking. Because constraint checking must occur by the end of a transaction, it may be difficult to check some constraints if a transaction is decomposed into smaller transactions. For example, an important constraint in accounting transactions is that debits equal credits. If the SQL statements to post a debit and a credit are placed in the same transaction, then the DBMS can enforce the accounting constraint at the end of the transaction. If they are placed in separate transactions, constraint checking cannot occur until after both transactions are committed.

Hot Spots

To understand the effects of transaction boundary choices, hot spots should be identified. Recall that hot spots are common data that multiple users try to change simultaneously. If a selected transaction boundary eliminates (creates) a hot spot, it may be a good (poor) design.

Hot spots can be classified as either system independent or system dependent. <u>System-independent</u> hot spots are parts of a table that many users simultaneously may want to change. Rows, fields, and entire tables can be system-independent hot spots. For example, in the airline reservation transaction (Figure 15.2), the seats-remaining field of popular flight records is a system-independent hot spot. The seats-remaining field is a hot spot on any DBMS.

System-dependent hot spots depend on the DBMS. Usually, system-dependent hot spots involve parts of the database hidden to normal users. Pages (physical records) containing database rows or index records often can be system-dependent hot spots. For example, some DBMSs lock the next available page when inserting a record into a table. When inserting a new history record in the ATM transaction (Figure 15.1), the next available page of the history table is a system-dependent hot spot. On DBMSs that lock at the record level, there is no hot spot. There are also typically hot spots with certain commonly accessed index pages.

Example Transaction Boundary Design

To depict the transaction boundary choice, hierarchical forms provide a convenient context. A hierarchical form represents an application that reads and writes to a database. For example, the registration form of the university database (Figure 15.11) manipulates the *Registration* table in the main form and the *Enrollment* and *Offering* tables in the subform. When using the registration form to enroll in courses, a record is inserted in the *Registration* table after completing the main form. After completing each line in the subform, a record is inserted into the *Enrollment* table and the *OffSeatsRemain* column of the associated *Offering* row is updated. Although the *OffSeatsRemain* field does not appear in the subform, it must be updated after inserting each subform line.

When designing a hierarchical form, the database programmer has three reasonable choices for the transaction boundary:

1. The entire form.
2. The main form as one transaction and *all* subform lines as a second transaction.
3. The main form as one transaction and *each* subform line as separate transactions.

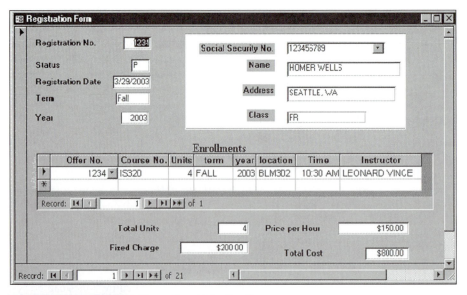

Figure 15.11 Example registration form.

The third choice is usually preferred because it provides transactions with the shortest duration. However, constraint checking may force the choice to 1 or 2. In the registration form, there are constraints that involve an entire registration such as a minimum number of hours for financial aid and prerequisites for a course. However, these constraints are not critical to check at the end of a transaction. Most universities check these constraints at a later point before the next academic period begins. Thus, choice 3 is the best choice for the transaction boundary.

There are several hot spots common to each transaction boundary choice. The *OffSeatsRemain* field in popular *Offering* rows is a system-independent hot spot in any transaction involving the subform lines. The *OffSeatsRemain* column must be updated after each enrollment. The next page in the *Enrollment* table is a system-dependent hot spot in some DBMSs. After each subform line, a row is inserted in the *Enrollment* table. If the DBMS locks the next available page rather than just the new row, all subform line transactions must obtain an exclusive lock on the next available physical record. However, if the DBMS can lock at the row level, there is no hot spot because each transaction will insert a different row.

Choice 3 provides another advantage due to reduced deadlock possibilities. In choices 1 and 2, deadlocks are possible because the transactions involve multiple course enrollments. For example, one transaction could obtain a lock on a data communications offering (IS470) and another transaction on a database offering (IS480). The first transaction may then wait for a lock on the IS480 offering, and the second transaction may wait for a lock on the IS470 offering. Choice 3 will be deadlock free if the hot spots are always obtained in the same order by every transaction. For example, if every transaction first obtains a lock on the next available page of *Enrollment* and then obtains a lock on an *Offering* row, then deadlock will not occur.

15.4.2 Isolation Levels

Two-phase locking prevents the three concurrency control problems described in Section 15.2.2 if all locks are held until the end of the transaction. However, some transactions may not need this level of concurrency control. The lost update problem is the most serious problem and should always be prevented. Some transactions may be able to tolerate conflicts caused by the uncommitted dependency and the inconsistent retrieval problems. Transactions that do not need protection from these problems can release locks sooner and achieve faster execution speed.

The <u>isolation level</u> specifies the degree to which a transaction is separated from the actions of other transactions. A transaction designer can balance concurrency control overhead with potential interference problems by specifying the appropriate isolation level.

Isolation Level defines the degree to which a transaction is separated from actions of other transactions. A transaction designer can balance concurrency control overhead with interference problems prevented by specifying the appropriate isolation level.

Table 15.11 summarizes the SQL:1999 isolation levels according to the duration and type of locks held. The serializable level prevents all concurrency control problems but involves the most overhead and waiting. To prevent concurrency control problems, predicate locks are used and all locks are long term (held until commit time). Predicate locks that reserve rows specified by conditions in the WHERE clause are essential to prevent phantom read problems. The repeatable read level uses short-term predicate locks to prevent the incorrect summary and the nonrepeatable read problems. The read committed level uses short-term shared locks to enable more concurrent access. However, it only prevents the

TABLE 15.11	Summary of Isolation Levels			
Level	*Exclusive Locks*	*Shared Locks*	*Predicate Locks*	*Problems Permitted*
Read Uncommitted	None since read-only	None	None	Only uncommitted dependencies because transactions must be read-only
Read Committed	Long-term	Short-term	None	Scholar's lost updates, incorrect summary, nonrepeatable reads
Repeatable Read	Long-term	Long-term	Short-term read, Long-term write	Phantom reads
Serializable	Long-term	Long-term	Long-term	None

uncommitted dependency problem and the traditional lost update problem. Because the read uncommitted level does not use locks, it is only appropriate for read-only access to a database.

In SQL (SQL-92 and SQL:1999), a transaction designer can specify the isolation level using the SET TRANSACTION statement, as shown in Example 15.1. The SET TRANSACTION statement is usually placed just before a START TRANSACTION statement to alter the default settings for transactions. In Example 15.1, the isolation level is set to READ COMMITTED. The other keywords are SERIALIZABLE, REPEATABLE READ, and READ UNCOMMITTED. Some DBMS vendors do not support all of these levels while other vendors support additional levels.

Example 15.1 (SQL:1999)

SET TRANSACTION Statement to Set the Isolation Level of a Transaction

SET TRANSACTION ISOLATION LEVEL READ COMMITTED
START TRANSACTION
. . .
COMMIT

In SQL:1999, SERIALIZABLE is the default isolation level. For most transactions, this level is recommended as the REPEATABLE READ level provides only a small performance improvement. The READ UNCOMMITTED level is recommended for read-only transactions that can tolerate retrieval inconsistency.

Although SQL:1999 provides SERIALIZABLE as the default level, some DBMS vendors such as Oracle and Microsoft SQL Server use READ COMMITTED as the default level. READ COMMITTED can be a dangerous default level as it permits a variation of the lost update problem known as the scholar's lost update. The word *scholar* is ironic in that the scholar's lost update problem differs only slightly from the traditional lost update problem. Figure 15.12 depicts the scholar's lost update problem. The only essential difference between the scholar's lost update problem and the traditional lost update problem is that transaction A commits before transaction B changes the common data. Thus, the scholar's lost update is a serious potential problem that should not be permitted for most transactions.

Transaction A	Time	Transaction B
Obtain S lock on *SR*	T_1	
Read *SR* (10)	T_2	
Release S lock on *SR*	T_3	
If *SR* > 0 then *SR* = *SR* −1	T_4	
	T_5	Obtain S lock on *SR*
	T_6	Read *SR* (10)
	T_7	Release S lock on *SR*
	T_8	If *SR* > 0 then *SR* = *SR* −1
Obtain X lock on *SR*	T_9	
Write *SR* (9)	T_{10}	
Commit	T_{11}	
	T_{12}	Obtain X lock on SR
	T_{13}	Write SR (9)

Figure 15.12   Example scholar's lost update problem.

15.4.3 Timing of Integrity Constraint Enforcement

Besides setting the isolation level, SQL (SQL-92 and SQL:1999) allows control of the timing of integrity constraint enforcement. By default, constraints are enforced immediately after each INSERT, UPDATE, and DELETE statement. For most constraints such as primary and foreign keys, immediate enforcement is appropriate. If a constraint is violated, the DBMS issues a rollback operation on the transaction. The rollback restores the database to a consistent state as the ACID properties ensure consistency at the end of a transaction.

For complex constraints, immediate enforcement may not be appropriate. For example, a faculty workload constraint ensures that each faculty member teaches between three and nine units each semester. If a transaction assigns an entire workload, checking the constraint should be deferred until the end of the transaction. For these kinds of complex constraints, constraint timing should be specified.

Deferred Constraint Checking enforcing integrity constraints at the end of a transaction rather than immediately after each manipulation statement. Complex constraints may benefit from deferred checking.

Constraint timing involves both constraint definition and transaction definition. SQL provides an optional constraint timing clause that applies to primary key constraints, foreign key constraints, uniqueness constraints, check constraints, and assertions. A database administrator typically uses the constraint timing clause for constraints that may need deferred checking. Constraints that never need deferred checking do not need the timing clause as the default is NOT DEFERRABLE. The timing clause defines the deferability of a constraint along with its default enforcement (deferred or immediate), as shown in Examples 15.2 and 15.3.

Example 15.2 (SQL:1999)

Timing Clause for the *FacultyWorkLoad* Assertion
The constraint is deferrable and the default enforcement is deferred.

```
CREATE ASSERTION FacultyWorkLoad
    CHECK (NOT EXISTS
```

```
(   SELECT Faculty.FacSSN, OffTerm, OffYear
    FROM Faculty, Offering, Course
    WHERE Faculty.FacSSN = Offering.FacSSN
        AND Offering.CourseNo = Course.CourseNo
    GROUP BY Faculty.FacSSN, OffTerm, OffYear
    HAVING SUM(CrsUnits) < 3 OR SUM(CrsUnits) > 9   )   )
DEFERRABLE INITIALLY DEFERRED
```

Example 15.3 (SQL:1999)

Timing Clause for the *OfferingConflict* Assertion

The constraint is deferrable and the default enforcement is immediate.

```
CREATE ASSERTION OfferingConflict
  CHECK (NOT EXISTS
    (   SELECT O1.OfferNo
        FROM Offering O1, Offering O2
        WHERE O1.OfferNo <> O2.OfferNo
            AND O1.OffTerm = O2.OffTerm
            AND O1.OffYear = O2.OffYear
            AND O1.OffDays = O2.OffDays
            AND O1.OffTime = O2.OffTime
            AND O1.OffLocation = O2.OffLocation   )   )
DEFERRABLE INITIALLY IMMEDIATE
```

For each transaction, the transaction designer may specify whether deferrable constraints are deferred or immediately enforced using the SET CONSTRAINTS statement. Normally the SET CONSTRAINTS statement is placed just after the START TRANSACTION statement as shown in Example 15.4. The SET CONSTRAINTS statement is not necessary for deferrable constraints with deferred default enforcement. For example, if the *FacultyWorkLoad* assertion is deferred, no SET CONSTRAINTS statement is necessary because its default enforcement is deferred.

Example 15.4 (SQL:1999)

SET CONSTRAINTS Statements for Several Transactions

```
START TRANSACTION
SET CONSTRAINTS FacultyWorkLoad IMMEDIATE
. . .
COMMIT

START TRANSACTION
SET CONSTRAINTS OfferingConflict DEFERRED
. . .
COMMIT
```

Implementation of the constraint timing part of SQL is highly variable. Most DBMSs do not support the constraint timing part exactly as specified in the standard. Many DBMSs have different syntax and proprietary language extensions for constraint timing.

| **Figure 15.13** | **Transaction flow with a save point.** |

15.4.4 Save Points

Some transactions have tentative actions that can be canceled by user actions or other events. For example, a user may cancel an item on an order after discovering that the item is out of stock. Because the ROLLBACK statement removes all transaction changes, it cannot be used to remove just the canceled item if the transaction involves the entire order. The transaction designer can code statements to explicitly delete the tentative parts of a transaction, but this coding can be tedious and involve excessive overhead.

SQL:1999 provides the SAVEPOINT statement to allow partial rollback of a transaction. A transaction designer uses the SAVEPOINT keyword followed by the save point name to establish an intermediate point in a transaction. To undo work since a particular save point, the ROLLBACK TO SAVEPOINT keywords can be used followed by the save point name. Figure 15.13 depicts the usage of a save point. Typically, partial rollback is used conditionally depending on a user action or an external event.

15.5 WORKFLOW MANAGEMENT

Transaction management is part of a much larger area known as workflow management. Workflow management supports business processes, both automated and human performed. In contrast, transaction management supports properties of automated database processing. This section presents workflow management to provide a broader perspective for transaction management. This section first describes workflows, a broader notion than database transactions. This section then discusses enabling technologies for workflow management showing how transaction management is an important component.

15.5.1 Characterizing Workflows

Workflow A collection of related tasks structured to accomplish a business process.

Workflows support business processes such as providing phone service, obtaining a loan, and ordering a product. Workflows consist of tasks that can be performed by computers (software and hardware), humans, or a combination. For example, in providing phone service, software determines the time of a service appointment and updates a scheduling database, while a technician inspects the phone box to determine whether a problem exists. A workflow defines the order of performing the tasks, the conditions for tasks to be performed, and the results of performing tasks. For example, providing phone service involves an initial customer contact, an optional service visit, billing, and payment collection. Each of these tasks can have conditions under which they are performed and may result in actions such as database updates and invocation of other tasks.

Many different kinds of workflows exist. Sheth, Georgakopoulos, and Hornrick (1995) classify workflows as human-oriented versus computer-oriented, as depicted in Figure 15.14. In human-oriented workflows, humans provide most of the judgment to

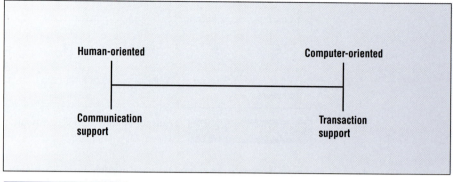

Figure 15.14   **Classification of workflow by task performance.**
(Adapted from Sheth, Georgakopoulos, and Hornrick 1995)

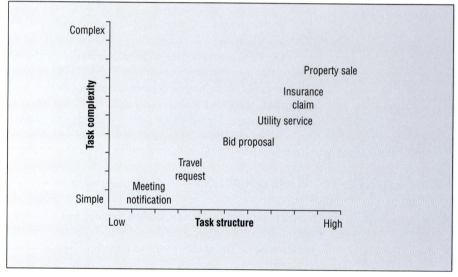

Figure 15.15   **Classification of workflow by task structure and complexity.**
(Adapted from Sheth, Georgakopoulos, and Hornrick 1995)

accomplish work. The computer has a passive role to supply data to facilitate human judgment. For example, in processing a loan, loan officers often determine the status of loans when the customer does not meet standard criteria about income and debt. Consultation with underwriters and credit personnel may be necessary. To support human-oriented workflows, electronic communication software such as e-mail, chat, and document annotation may be useful. In <u>computer-oriented</u> tasks, the computer determines the processing of work. For example, software for an ATM transaction determines whether a customer receives cash or is denied the request. To support computer-oriented workflows, transaction management is a key technology.

Another way to classify workflows is by task complexity versus task structure as depicted in Figure 15.15. <u>Task complexity</u> involves the difficulty of performing individual tasks. For example, the decision to grant a loan may involve complex reasoning using many variables. In contrast, processing a product order may involve requesting the product data from the customer. <u>Task structure</u> involves the relationships among tasks. Workflows with complex conditions have high structure. For example, processing an insurance claim may have conditions about denying the claim, litigating the claim, and investigating the claim.

15.5.2 Enabling Technologies

To support the concept of a workflow discussed in the previous section, three enabling technologies are important: (1) distributed object management; (2) workflow specification; and (3) customized transaction management. Transaction management as described in previous sections fits as part of the third technology. The remainder of this section elaborates on each technology.

Distributed Object Management

Workflows can involve many types of data in remote locations. For example, data can include photos of an insurance claim, x-rays supporting a diagnosis, and an appraisal documenting a property for a loan application. These types of data are not traditionally managed by DBMSs. A new class of DBMSs known as object DBMSs has been developed to manage diverse types of data. Chapter 18 describes this new class of DBMSs.

In addition to new types of data, the data are typically not stored at one location and may be controlled by different DBMSs. For example, to support a loan application, a loan officer uses a credit report from a credit bureau, an appraisal from a certified appraiser, and loan processing guidelines from government agencies. Accessing and controlling distributed data can be difficult. Chapter 17 describes important principles of managing distributed data. Difficulties also can arise because the data may be controlled by different systems, some of which may not support SQL.

Workflow Specification and Implementation

To support workflows, the structure of tasks must be properly represented and implemented. Representing a workflow involves identifying the tasks and specifying the relationships among tasks. A complex task can involve a hierarchy of subtasks. A complex workflow can involve many tasks with numerous relationships. Constraints, rules, and graphical notation can be used to depict the task order and completion. One use of task relationships is to define constraints among transactions. For example, workflow specification can indicate that a student should be denied financial aid unless enrolling for a minimum number of hours by a specified date.

After a workflow is specified, it must be efficiently implemented. The implementation may involve diverse hardware, software, and people. A major challenge is to make diverse components communicate efficiently. Optimizing workflows through reengineering has become an important concern in many organizations. Optimization may involve removing duplicate tasks and increasing the amount of parallel work.

A number of software systems have been developed to support workflow specification. The main function of software under the name <u>workflow management</u> is to support workflow specification and implementation.

Customized Transaction Management

The earlier sections of this chapter described how DBMSs support ACID transactions. The ACID properties are indeed important and widely supported by DBMSs. However, to support workflows, the ACID properties may not be sufficient. The following list identifies shortcomings of traditional ACID transactions for workflow management:

- Some workflows involve tasks with a long duration because of user interaction. Traditional transaction management may not work well for these conversational transactions.

- Some tasks may involve subtasks, changing the notion of atomicity. The idea of nested transactions (transactions inside transactions) has been proposed for tasks with complex structures.

- Some tasks may be performed by legacy systems that do not support the ACID properties.

- Some workflows may require tasks to be undone after they are complete. In accounting systems, it is common for compensating transactions to correct mistakes. For example, returning a defective product removes the effect of the original product order.

Some DBMSs support some of these extensions now. For example, Microsoft SQL Server provides nested transactions to support transactions that reside in procedures. Oracle provides autonomous transactions to allow interruption of a transaction by another transaction. In addition, SQL:1999 provides save points so that a ROLLBACK statement can undo only part of a transaction. This extension can reduce the amount of work lost when a long transaction fails.

To more fully support workflow management, transaction management should be customized according to workflow requirements. The transaction properties supported for a workflow should be part of the workflow specification, not hardwired into the software supporting workflow management. DBMSs supporting workflow management may need to be more flexible. DBMSs might support different kinds of transactions or even allow transaction properties to be specified. Event processing in DBMSs can be used to support some features such as compensating transactions. Most DBMSs would need a major extension to support customized transaction management.

CLOSING THOUGHTS

This chapter has described the concept of database transactions, the services provided by the DBMS to support transactions, and transaction design skills for transaction designers. A transaction is a user-defined unit of work with any number of reads and writes to a database. To define a transaction, several new SQL statements were introduced including START TRANSACTION, COMMIT, and ROLLBACK. DBMSs ensure that transactions are atomic (all or nothing), consistent (satisfy integrity constraints after completion), isolated (no interference from concurrent users), and durable (survive failures). To ensure these properties of transactions, DBMSs provide services for concurrency control (making a database seem like a single-user system) and recovery management (automatically restoring a database after a failure). These powerful services are not free as they can consume large amounts of computing resources and add to the purchase price of a DBMS.

Although the concurrency and recovery services provided by a DBMS are transparent, you should understand some details of these services. Knowledge of these services can help you allocate computing resources, select a DBMS that provides the appropriate level of transaction support, and design efficient transactions. For concurrency control, you should understand the objective, interference problems, and the two-phase locking protocol. For recovery management, you should understand the kinds of failures, the redundant storage needed for recovery, and the amount of work to restore a database after a failure.

To apply your knowledge of transaction management, this chapter demonstrated principles of transaction design. The most important choice in transaction design is the selection of a transaction boundary. The objective of choosing a transaction boundary is to minimize duration subject to the need for constraint checking. Critical constraints such as debit/credit in accounting systems may dictate that an application remain as one transaction rather than be split into smaller transactions. Other important decisions involve the isolation level, the timing of constraint enforcement, and save points for partial rollback. SQL syntax for these elements was shown in the chapter.

As a transaction designer, you should remember that transactions are only one kind of support for organizational work. Workflow management addresses issues beyond transaction management such as dependencies among transactions, different kinds of transactions, and annotation of work.

This chapter has described services of DBMSs to support transaction processing, the operating side of databases. Other chapters in Part 4 examine services to support other kinds of database processing such as data warehousing in Chapter 16. You should contrast the requirements to support transaction processing for operational decision making with the requirements to support data warehousing for tactical and strategic decision making.

REVIEW CONCEPTS

- Transactions containing a user-specified collection of database reads and writes.
- SQL statements to define transactions: START TRANSACTION, COMMIT, ROLLBACK, and SAVEPOINT.
- ACID properties of transactions: atomic, consistent, isolated, durable.
- Transparent services to hide inner details of transaction management.
- Concurrency control to support simultaneous usage of a database.
- Recovery management to restore a database to a consistent state after a failure.
- Concurrency control objective: maximizing transaction throughput while preventing interference problems.
- Interference on hot spots, common data manipulated by concurrent users.
- Effect of interference problems: lost update, uncommitted dependency, inconsistent retrieval.
- Concurrency control manager to grant, release, and analyze locks.
- Growing and shrinking phases of two-phase locking (2PL).
- Resolution of deadlocks with timeout and transaction restart.
- Optimistic concurrency control approaches when interference is rare.
- Volatile versus nonvolatile storage.
- Effect of local, system, and media failures.
- Force writing to control the timing of database writes.
- Redundant storage for recovery: log, checkpoint, backup.
- Amount of restart work in the immediate update and the deferred update recovery approaches.

- Selecting a transaction boundary to minimize duration while enforcing critical integrity constraints.
- Identifying system-independent and system-dependent hot spots in transactions.
- Isolation levels for balancing potential interference against the corresponding overhead of concurrency control.
- Potential for lost data when using the READ COMMITTED isolation level.
- Constraint timing specification to defer enforcement of integrity constraints until end of transaction.
- Save points for partial rollback of a transaction.
- Workflow management to support collaborative work.

QUESTIONS

1. What does it mean to say that a transaction is a user-defined concept? Why is it important that transactions are user-defined?

2. List transactions with which you have interacted in the last week.

3. Explain the purpose of the SQL statements START TRANSACTION, COMMIT, and ROLLBACK. How do these statements vary across DBMSs?

4. Briefly explain the meaning of the ACID properties. How do concurrency control and recovery management support the ACID properties?

5. Briefly explain the meaning of transparency as it relates to computer processing. Why is transparency important for concurrency control and recovery management?

6. What costs are associated with concurrency control and recovery management? In what role, database administrator or database programmer, would you assess these costs?

7. What is the objective of concurrency control? How is the measure used in the objective related to waiting time?

8. What is a hot spot? How are hot spots related to interference problems?

9. Discuss the consequences of each kind of interference problem. Which problem seems to be the most serious?

10. What is a lock? Briefly explain the differences between shared (S) and exclusive (X) locks?

11. What operations are performed by the lock manager?

12. What is a deadlock and how do most DBMSs handle deadlocks?

13. What is locking granularity? What are the trade-offs of holding locks at a finer level versus a coarser level of granularity?

14. What is an intent lock? Why are intent locks used on items of coarse granularity?

15. Why is the third condition of 2PL typically simplified so that locks are released at the end of a transaction?

16. What is the appeal of optimistic concurrency control approaches? Why might optimistic concurrency control approaches not be used even if they provide better expected performance?

17. Explain the difference between volatile and nonvolatile storage?

18. Explain the effects of local, system, and device failures on active and past transactions.

19. Why is force writing the most fundamental tool of recovery management?

20. What kind of redundant data is stored in a log? Why is management of the log critical to recovery?

21. What is the checkpoint interval? What is the trade-off in determining the checkpoint interval?

22. What processing occurs at checkpoint time?

23. What restart work is necessary for a media failure?

24. What restart work is necessary for local and system failures under the immediate update approach?

25. What restart work is necessary for local and system failures under the deferred update approach?

26. What is a transaction boundary? Why can an inappropriate choice for transaction boundary lead to poor performance?

27. What criteria should be used in selecting a transaction boundary?

28. Why must constraints such as the debit/credit constraint be enforced as part of a transaction rather than between transactions?

29. Explain the difference between system-independent and system-dependent hot spots. Why is it useful to identify hot spots?

30. Explain the three choices for transaction boundary of a hierarchical form.

31. How can deadlock possibility be influenced by the choice of a transaction boundary?

32. What is the purpose of the SQL isolation levels?

33. How do the isolation levels achieve more concurrent access?

34. What isolation level can be dangerous and why?

35. Provide an example of a constraint for which deferred enforcement may be appropriate.

36. What SQL statements and clauses involve constraint timing specification?

37. What is the role of the DBA in specifying constraint timing?

38. What is the role of the database programmer in specifying constraint timing?

39. What is the purpose of a save point?

40. What is a workflow and how is it related to database transactions?

41. What are the differences between human-oriented and computer-oriented workflows?

42. Provide an example of a workflow with high task complexity and another example with high task structure.

43. Discuss the enabling technologies for workflow management. What role does transaction management play in workflow management?

44. What are limitations of transaction management to support workflows?

PROBLEMS

The problems provide practice using transaction-defining SQL statements, testing your knowledge of concurrency control and recovery management, and analyzing design decisions about transaction boundaries and hot spots.

1. Identify two transactions that you have encountered recently. Define pseudocode for the transactions in the style of Figures 15.1, 15.2, and 15.3.

2. Identify hot spots in your transactions from problem 1.

3. Using a timeline, depict a lost update problem using your transactions from problem 1 if no concurrency control is used.

4. Using a timeline, depict an uncommitted dependency problem using your transactions from problem 1 if no concurrency control is used.

5. Using a timeline, depict a nonrepeatable read problem using your transactions from problem 1 if no concurrency control is used.

6. Explain whether deadlock would be a problem using your transactions from problem 1 if locking is used. If a deadlock is possible, use a timeline to demonstrate a deadlock with your transactions.

7. Use the following Accounting Database tables and the Accounting Register to answer problems 7.1 to 7.7. Comments are listed after the tables and the form.

   Account(<u>AcctNo</u>, Name, Address, Balance, LastCheckNo, StartDate)
   Entry(<u>EntryNo</u>, *AcctNo,* Date, Amount, Desc)
   Category(<u>CatNo</u>, Name, Description)
   EntryLine(*<u>EntryNo</u>, <u>CatNo</u>*, Amount, Description)

Accounting Register for Wells Fargo Credit Line

Entry No.	E101		Date:	3/11/2003
Description:	Purchases at OfficeMax		Amount:	$442.00
Invoice No.	I101			

Category	Description	Amount
Office supplies	Envelopes	25.00
Equipment	Fax machine	167.00
Computer software	MS Office upgrade	250.00

- The primary keys in the tables are underlined. The foreign keys are italicized.
- The Accounting Register records activities on an account, such as a line of credit or accounts receivable. The Accounting Register is designed for use by the accounting department of moderate-size businesses. The sample form shows one recorded entry, but a register contains all recorded entries since the opening of the account.
- The main form is used to insert a record into the *Entry* table and update the *Balance* field of the *Account* table. Accounts have a unique name (Wells Fargo Line of Credit) that appears in the title of the register. Accounts have other attributes not shown on the form: a unique number (name is also unique), start date, address, type (Receivable, Investment, Credit, etc.), and current balance.
- In the subform, the user allocates the total amount of the entry to categories. The *Category* field is a combo box. When the user clicks on the category field, the category number and name are displayed. Entering a new subform line inserts a row into the *EntryLine* table.
- The *Description* field in the subform describes a row in the *EntryLine* table rather than the *Category* table.

    7.1. What are the possible transaction boundaries for the Accounting Register form?

    7.2. Select a transaction boundary from your choices in problem 7.1. Justify your choice using the criteria defined in Section 15.4.1.

    7.3. Identify system-independent hot spots that result from concurrent usage (say, many clerks in the accounting department) of the Accounting Register. For each hot spot, explain why it is a hot spot.

    7.4. Identify system-dependent hot spots that result from concurrent usage (say many clerks in the accounting department) of the Accounting Register. You may assume that the DBMS cannot lock finer than a database page.

    7.5. Describe a lost update problem involving one of your hot spots that could occur with concurrent usage of the Accounting Register. Use a timeline to depict your example.

    7.6. Describe a dirty read situation involving one of your hot spots that could occur with concurrent usage of the Accounting Register. Use a timeline to depict your example.

    7.7. Is deadlock likely to be a problem with concurrent usage of the Accounting Register? Consider the case where locks are held until all subform lines are complete. Why or why not? If deadlock is likely, provide an example as justification. Would there still be a deadlock problem if locks were held only until completion of each line on the subform? Why or why not?

8. Use the following Patient tables and the Patient Billing Form to answer problems 8.1 to 8.4. Comments are listed after the tables and the form.

    Patient(<u>PatSSN</u>, PatName, PatCity, PatAge)
    Doctor(<u>DocNo</u>, DocName, DocSpecialty)

Bill(<u>BillNo</u>, *PatSSN,* BillDate, AdmitDate, DischargeDate)
Charge(<u>ChgNo</u>, *BillNo, ItemNo,* ChgDate, ChgQty, *DocNo*)
Item(Itemno, ItemDesc, ItemUnit, ItemRate, ItemQOH)

- The main form is used to insert a record into the *Bill* table. Fields from the *Patient* table are read-only in the main form.
- The subform can be used to insert a new row into the *Charge* table. Fields from the *Doctor* and the *Item* tables are read-only.
- When a subform line is entered, the associated item row is updated. The form field *Qty* affects the current value in the field *ItemQOH* (item quantity on hand).

    8.1.   What are the possible transaction boundaries for the Patient Billing Form?

    8.2.   Select a transaction boundary from your choices in problem 8.1. Justify your choice using the criteria defined in Section 15.4.1.

    8.3.   Identify system-independent hot spots that result from concurrent usage (say many health providers) of the Patient Billing Form. For each hot spot, explain why it is a hot spot.

    8.4.   Identify system-dependent hot spots that result from concurrent usage of the Patient Billing Form. You may assume that the DBMS cannot lock finer than a database page.

9. Use the following Airline Reservation database tables and the Flight Reservation Form to answer problems 9.1 to 9.4. Comments are listed after the tables and the form.

    Flight(<u>FlightNo</u>, *DepCityCode, ArrCityCode,* DepTime, ArrTime, FlgDays)
    FlightDate(*<u>FlightNo</u>*, <u>FlightDate</u>, RemSeats)

Reservation(<u>ResNo</u>, *CustNo,* ResDate, Amount, CrCardNo)
ReserveFlight(<u>*ResNo*</u>, <u>*FlightNo*</u>, <u>*FlightDate*</u>)
Customer(<u>CustNo</u>, CustName, CustStreet, CustCity, CustState, CustZip)
City(<u>CityCode</u>, CityName, Altitude, AirportConditions)

Flight Reservation Form

Reservation No.	R101	**Today's Date:**	8/26/2003
Credit Card No.	CC101	**Amount:**	$442.00
Customer No.	C101	**Customer Name**	Jill Horn

Flight Schedule

Flight No.	Date	Dep City	Dep Time	*Arr City*	*Arr Time*
F101	8/26/2003	DNV	10:30AM	CHG	11:45AM
F201	8/31/2003	CHG	10:00AM	DNV	1:20PM

- The primary keys in the tables are underlined. The foreign keys are italicized. Note that the combination of *ResNo, FlightNo,* and *FlightDate* is the primary key of the *ReserveFlight* table. The combination of *FlightNo* and *FlightDate* is a foreign key in the *ReserveFlight* table referring to the *FlightDate* table.

- The Flight Reservation Form is somewhat simplified as it accommodates only a single class of seating, no reserved seats, and no meals. However, commuter and low-cost airlines often have these restrictions.

- The main form is used to insert a record into the *Reservation* table. The fields from the *Customer* table are read-only.

- The subform is used to insert new rows in the *ReserveFlight* table and update the field *RemSeats* in the *FlightDate* table. The fields from the *Flight* table are read-only.

    9.1. Select a transaction boundary for the Flight Reservation Form. Justify your choice using the criteria defined in Section 15.4.1.

    9.2. Identify system-independent hot spots that result from concurrent usage (say many reservation agents) of the Flight Reservation Form. For each hot spot, explain why it is a hot spot.

    9.3. Identify system-dependent hot spots that result from concurrent usage of the Flight Reservation Form. You may assume that the DBMS cannot lock finer than a database page.

    9.4. Is deadlock likely to be a problem with concurrent usage of the Flight Reservation Form? If deadlock is likely, provide an example as justification.

10. The following timeline shows the state of transactions with respect to the most recent backup, checkpoint, and failure. Use the timeline when solving the problems in subparts of this problem.

10.1. Describe the restart work if transaction T3 is aborted (with a ROLLBACK statement) after the checkpoint but prior to the failure. Assume that the recovery manager uses the deferred update approach.

10.2. Describe the restart work if transaction T3 is aborted (with a ROLLBACK statement) after the checkpoint but prior to the failure. Assume that the recovery manager uses the immediate update approach.

10.3. Describe the restart work if a system failure occurs. Assume that the recovery manager uses the deferred update approach.

10.4. Describe the restart work if a system failure occurs. Assume that the recovery manager uses the immediate update approach.

10.5. Describe the restart work if a device failure occurs.

11. Use the World Wide Web to review transaction processing benchmarks. Why has the debit/credit benchmark been superseded by other benchmarks? How many transactions per minute are reported for various DBMSs? Inspect the code for one or more benchmark transactions. Can you identify hot spots in the transactions?

REFERENCES FOR FURTHER STUDY

This chapter, although providing a broad coverage of transaction management, has only covered the basics. Transaction management is a detailed subject for which entire books have been written. Specialized books on transaction management include Bernstein and Newcomer (1997) and Gray and Reuter (1993). Peinl, Reuter, and Sammer (1988) provide a stock-trading case study on transaction design that elaborates on the ideas presented in Section 15.4. For details about transaction processing performance, consult the home page of the Transaction Processing Performance Council (http://www.tpc.org). This group maintains many industry-standard benchmarks. For more details about workflow management, Sheth, Georgakopoulos, and Hornrick (1995) provide a good overview and numerous references. For other references, see the category "Transaction Processing" in the Web Resources section of the textbook's website.

Appendix 15.A SQL:1999 Syntax Summary

This appendix summarizes the SQL:1999 syntax for the constraint timing clause, the SET CONSTRAINTS statement, the SET TRANSACTION statement, and the save point statements discussed in the chapter. The conventions used in the syntax notation are identical to those used at the end of Chapter 2.

CONSTRAINT TIMING CLAUSE

```
CREATE TABLE TableName
                ( <Column-Definition>* [ , <Table-Constraint>* ] )

<Column-Definition>: ColumnName DataType
                [ DEFAULT { DefaultValue | USER | NULL } ]
                [ <Column-Constraint> ]

<Column-Constraint>: [ CONSTRAINT ConstraintName ]
                { NOT NULL |
                  <Foreign-Key-Constraint> | -- defined in Chapter 2
                  <Uniqueness-Constraint> | -- defined in Chapter 2
                  <Check-Constraint> } -- defined in Chapter 14
                [ <Timing-Clause> ]

<Table-Constraint>: [ CONSTRAINT ConstraintName ]
                { <Primary-Key-Constraint> | -- defined in Chapter 2
                  <Foreign-Key-Constraint> | -- defined in Chapter 2
                  <Uniqueness-Constraint> | -- defined in Chapter 2
                  <Check-Constraint> } -- defined in Chapter 14
                [ <Timing-Clause> ]

<Timing-Clause>:
                { NOT DEFERRABLE |
                  DEFERRABLE { INITIALLY IMMEDIATE |
                               INITIALLY DEFERRED } }

CREATE ASSERTION AssertionName
                CHECK ( <Group-Condition> ) [ <Timing-Clause> ]

<Group-Condition>: -- defined in Chapter 3
```

SET CONSTRAINTS STATEMENT

```
SET CONSTRAINTS  {  ALL  |  ConstraintName*  }
                 {     IMMEDIATE  |  DEFERRED  }
```

SET TRANSACTION STATEMENT

```
SET [LOCAL] TRANSACTION <Mode>*

<Mode>:  {  <Isolation-Level>  |  <Access-Mode>  |
            <Diagnostics>  }

<Isolation-Level>: ISOLATION LEVEL
                   {  SERIALIZABLE  |
                      REPEATABLE READ  |
                      READ COMMITTED  |
                      READ UNCOMMITTED  }

<Access-Mode>:  {  READ WRITE  |  READ ONLY  }

<Diagnostics>: DIAGNOSTICS SIZE Constant
```

SAVE POINT STATEMENTS

```
SAVEPOINT <SavePointName>   -- creates a save point

RELEASE <SavePointName>   -- deletes a save point

ROLLBACK TO SAVEPOINT <SavePointName>   -- rollback to a save point
```

Data Warehouse Technology and Management

This chapter provides the foundation for an emerging form of databases, called data warehouses, being used increasingly for decision support. After this chapter, the student should have acquired the following knowledge and skills:

- Explain conceptual differences between operational databases and data warehouses.

- Understand architectures to apply data warehouse technology in organizations.

- Understand the representation and manipulation of data cubes.

- Apply relational data modeling and manipulation for multidimensional data.

- Explain data quality issues and the role of extraction, transformation, and loading tools when populating a data warehouse.

- Gain insight about the complex process of refreshing a data warehouse.

OVERVIEW

Imagine a corporate executive of a national soda bottler asking the question, "What were the total diet soda sales during the past 12 months in the Northeast, and how does this number compare with the national average?" Follow-up questions may include, "What was the breakup of diet soda sales in the Northeast by state and city?" and "Is there any cyclical trend in diet soda sales over the last 10 years?" These are examples of typical decision support or business intelligence questions, asked every day by managers all over the world. Answers to these questions often require complex SQL statements that may take hours to code and execute. Furthermore, formulating some of these queries may require data from a diverse set of internal legacy systems and external market sources, involving both relational and nonrelational databases.

Decision-making questions such as those above pose new requirements on DBMSs. This chapter presents the technology and management of data warehouses to satisfy requirements of decision support. Data warehouse technology complements and extends relational database technology beyond online transaction processing and simple query capabilities such as the GROUP BY clause in SQL. In this chapter, you will learn initially about the unique requirements for data warehouse processing as opposed to the transaction processing requirements discussed in Chapter 15. Second, you will learn about the multidimensional data model and its implementation in relational databases with a special emphasis on the data warehousing features in Oracle 9i. You will learn new skills for data modeling and manipulation that complement the skills you learned in Parts 1 through 3. Finally, you will learn about maintaining a data warehouse, an important process managed by data warehouse administrators.

16.1 BASIC CONCEPTS

The type of data used for decision support purposes is conceptually different from that used in transaction processing databases. Consequently, databases that can store such data and computing architectures that can process such data are also different. This section examines these differences to provide a foundation for detailed study of technology and management issues in later sections.

16.1.1 Transaction Processing versus Decision Support

Transaction processing involves different needs in an organization than decision support. Transaction processing, as discussed in Chapter 15, allows organizations to conduct daily business in an efficient manner. Operational or production databases used in transaction processing assist with decisions such as tracking orders, resolving customer complaints, and staffing requirements. These decisions involve detailed data about business processes.

In contrast, decision support processing helps management provide medium-term and long-term direction for an organization. Management needs support for decisions about capacity planning, product development, store location, product promotion, and other needs. Historically, most organizations have assumed that operational databases can provide the data for decision support. As organizations have developed operational databases for various functions, an information gap has developed. Gradually, organizations have realized that the operational databases must be significantly transformed for decision support.

Since the early 1990s, a consensus has developed that operational databases must be transformed for decision support. Operational databases can contain inconsistencies in areas such as formats, entity identification, and units of measure that hamper usage in decision support. In addition, decision support needs a broad view that integrates business processes. Because of the different requirements, operational databases are usually separate from databases for decision support. Using a common database for both kinds of processing can significantly degrade performance and make it difficult to summarize activity across business processes.

16.1.2 Characteristics of Data Warehouses

Data Warehouse a central repository for summarized and integrated data from operational databases and external data sources.

Data warehouse, a term coined by William Inmon in 1990, refers to a central data repository where data from operational databases and other sources are integrated, cleaned, and archived to support decision making. A data warehouse provides management with convenient access to large volumes of internal and external data. Because of the potential benefits, many organizations have undertaken data warehouse projects. Return on investment from a data warehouse project can be more than 300 percent with a payback period between two and three years. To create and maintain data warehouses, the IDC division of IDG projects that the market for data warehouse tools will reach $17 billion by 2004. Further, the IDC division projects $146 billion in service revenue in 2005 for the customer relationship management market, a heavy user of data warehouse technology.

The processing requirements of decision support applications have led to four distinguishing characteristics for data warehouses, as described in the following:

- **Subject-Oriented:** A data warehouse is organized around the major business subjects or entities such as customers, orders, and products. This subject orientation contrasts to the more process orientation for transaction processing.

- **Integrated:** Operational data from multiple databases and external data sources are integrated in a data warehouse to provide a single, unified database for decision support. Consolidation of data requires consistent naming conventions, uniform data formats, and comparable measurement scales across databases and external data sources.

- **Time-Variant:** Data warehouses use time stamps to represent historical data. The time dimension is critical for identifying trends, predicting future operations, and setting operating targets. Data warehouses essentially consist of a long series of snapshots, each of which represents operational data captured at a point in time.

- **Nonvolatile:** New data in a data warehouse are appended, rather than replaced, so that historical data are preserved. The act of appending new data is known as refreshing the data warehouse. Lack of update or delete operations ensures that a data warehouse is free of update or deletion anomalies. Transaction data are transferred to a data warehouse only when most updating activity has been completed.

Table 16.1 further depicts the characteristics of data warehouses as opposed to operational databases. Transaction processing relies on operational databases with current data at the individual level, while decision support processing utilizes data warehouses with historical data at both the individual and summarized levels. Individual-level data

TABLE 16.1	Comparison of Operational Databases and Data Warehouses	
Characteristic	*Operational Database*	*Data Warehouse*
Currency	Current	Historical
Detail level	Individual	Individual and summary
Orientation	Process orientation	Subject orientation
Number of records processed	Few	Thousands
Normalization level	Mostly normalized	Frequent violations of BCNF
Update level	Volatile	Nonvolatile (refreshed)
Data model	Relational	Multidimensional (see Section 16.2)

provide flexibility for responding to a wide range of decision support needs while summarized data provide fast response to repetitive queries. For example, an order-entry transaction requires data about individual customers, orders, and inventory items, while a decision support application may use monthly sales to customers over a period of 10 years. Operational databases therefore have a process orientation (e.g., all data relevant to a particular business process), compared to a subject orientation for data warehouses (e.g., all customer data or all order data). A transaction typically updates only a few records, whereas a decision support application may query thousands to millions of records.

Data integrity and performance of transaction processing require that operational databases be highly normalized. In contrast, data warehouses are usually denormalized from Boyce-Codd Normal Form to reduce the effort to join large tables. Most data warehouse processing involves retrievals and periodic insertions of new data. These operations do not suffer from anomalies caused by a design that is not fully normalized.

Because of the different processing requirements, different data models have been developed for operational databases and data warehouses. The relational data model dominates for operational databases while the multidimensional data model dominates for data warehouses.

16.1.3 Architectures for Data Warehouses

Despite the potential benefits of a data warehouse, many data warehouse projects have failed due to poor planning. Data warehouse projects are large efforts that involve coordination among many parts of an organization. Many organizations have underestimated the time and effort to reconcile different views of a data warehouse. In addition, the sheer size of a data warehouse can lead to poor performance. An appropriate architecture can help alleviate problems with data warehouse performance and development effort.

Enterprise Data Model a conceptual data model of the data warehouse defining the structure of the data warehouse and the metadata to access operational databases and external data sources.

For most organizations, a two-tier or three-tier data warehouse architecture is appropriate. In a two-tier data warehouse architecture (Figure 16.1), operational data are transformed and then transferred to a data warehouse. To assist with the transformation process, an enterprise data model (EDM) is created. The EDM describes the structure of the data warehouse and contains the metadata required to access operational databases

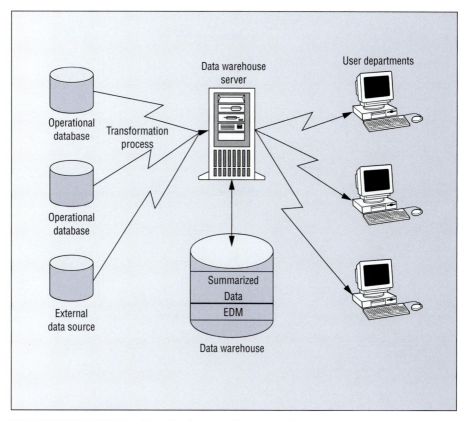

| **Figure 16.1** | **Two-tier data warehouse architecture.** |

and external data sources. The EDM may also contain details about cleaning and integrating data sources. Management uses the data warehouse directly to retrieve data for decision support.

The two-tier architecture can have performance problems for large data warehouses with data intensive applications for decision support. To alleviate these difficulties, many large organizations use a three-tier data warehouse architecture as shown in Figure 16.2. Departmental users generally need access to small portions of the data warehouse, instead of the entire warehouse. To provide them with faster access while isolating them from data needed by other user groups, smaller data warehouses called data marts are often used. Data marts act as the interface between end users and the corporate data warehouse, storing a subset of the warehouse data and refreshing those data on a periodic (e.g., weekly or monthly) basis. Generally, the data warehouse and the data marts reside on different servers to improve performance and fault tolerance. Departmental users retain control over their own data marts, while the data warehouse remains under the control of the corporate information systems staff.

Given the enterprisewide context of a data warehouse, some organizations fear that building a data warehouse may be unnecessarily delayed with lost business opportunities if too much emphasis is placed on first creating an enterprise data model. Instead, some organizations employ a bottom-up approach to data warehousing, as depicted in

Data Mart a subset or view of a data warehouse, typically at a department or functional level, that contains all data required for decision support tasks of that department.

| Figure 16.2 | **Three-tier data warehouse architecture.** |

Figure 16.3. In a <u>bottom-up data warehouse architecture</u>, data are modeled one entity at a time and stored in separate data marts. Over time, new data are synthesized, cleaned, and merged into existing data marts or built into new data marts. The set of data marts may evolve into a large data warehouse if the organization can justify the expense of building an enterprise data model.

A recent development is the emergence of <u>oper marts</u> (short for operational mart) as noted by Imhoff (2001). An oper mart is a just-in-time data mart, usually built from one operational database in anticipation of or in response to major events such as disasters and new product introductions. An oper mart supports peak demand for reporting and business analysis that accompanies a major event. After the decision support demand subsides, the oper mart may be dismantled or it may be merged into an existing data warehouse.

16.1.4 Data Mining

Data Mining the process of discovering implicit patterns in data stored in a data warehouse and using those patterns for business advantage.

Data warehouses improve the quality of decision making by consolidating and aggregating transactional data. The value of a data warehouse can be increased if hidden patterns in the data can be discovered. Data mining refers to the process of discovering implicit patterns in data and using these patterns for business advantage. Data mining facilitates the ability to detect, understand, and predict patterns.

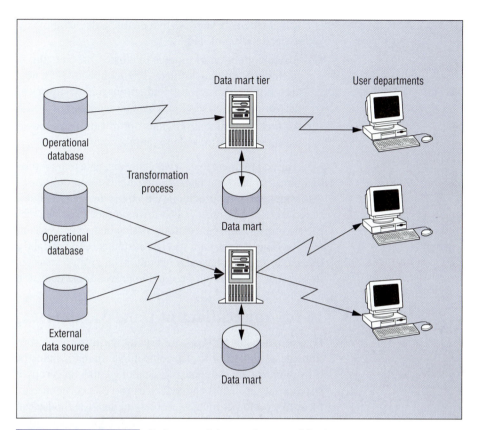

| **Figure 16.3** | **Bottom-up data warehouse architecture.** |

The most common application of data mining techniques is target marketing. Mail-order companies can increase revenues and decrease costs if they can identify likely customers and eliminate customers not likely to purchase. Data mining techniques allow decision makers to focus marketing efforts by customer demographic and psychographic data. The retail, banking, travel, and consumer goods industries also have benefited from data mining techniques. For example, the retail industry uses data mining techniques to target promotions and change the mix and the arrangement of store items.

Data mining is best considered as an adjunct to a mature data warehouse. Data mining needs more detailed data than traditional data warehouses provide. The volumes of data and the dimensionality of data can be much greater for data mining techniques than other data warehouse analysis tools. Data mining techniques thrive with clean, high-dimensional, transaction data. To support these data mining requirements, many data warehouses now store detail data at the level of the individual customer, product, and so on.

Data mining requires a collection of tools that extend beyond traditional statistical analysis tools. Traditional statistical analysis tools are not well suited to high dimensional data with a mix of numeric and categorical data. In addition, traditional statistical techniques do not scale well to large amounts of data. Data mining typically includes the following kinds of tools:

- Data access tools to extract and sample transaction data according to complex criteria from multiple-source databases.

- Data visualization tools that enable a decision maker to gain a deeper, intuitive understanding of data.
- A rich collection of models to cluster, predict, and determine association rules from large amounts of data. The models involve neural networks, genetic algorithms, decision tree induction, rule discovery algorithms, probability networks, and other expert system technologies.
- An architecture that provides optimization, client–server processing, and parallel queries to scale to large amounts of data.

As a complement to data warehousing, data mining provides insights that may elude traditional techniques. Data mining holds the promise of more effectively leveraging data warehouses by providing the ability to identify hidden relationships in the data stored there. It facilitates a data-driven discovery, using techniques such as building association rules (e.g., between advertising budget and seasonal sales), generating profiles (e.g., buying patterns for a specific customer segment), and so forth. This knowledge can be used to improve business operations in critical areas, enabling target marketing efforts, better customer service, and improved fraud detection.

16.1.5 Applications of Data Warehouses

Data warehousing projects are usually undertaken for competitive reasons: to achieve strategic advantage or to stay competitive. In many industries, a few organizations typically pioneer data warehousing technology to gain competitive advantage. Often a data warehousing project is undertaken as part of a corporate strategy to shift from a product focus to a customer focus. A successful data warehouse can help identify new markets, focus resources on profitable customers, improve retention of customers, and reduce inventory costs. After success by the pioneering organizations, other organizations quickly follow to stay competitive.

Data warehousing projects have been undertaken in a wide range of industries. A few key applications have driven the adoption of data warehousing projects as listed in Table 16.2. Highly competitive industries such as retail, insurance, airlines, and telecommunications (particularly long distance service) have invested early in data warehouse technology and projects. Less competitive industries such as regulated utilities have been slower to invest although they are increasing investments as data warehouse technology and practice mature.

16.2 MULTIDIMENSIONAL REPRESENTATION OF DATA

After understanding the unique data requirements for decision support, you are ready to learn about technology to satisfy the requirements. The multidimensional data model supports data representation and oper-

TABLE 16.2	**Data Warehousing Applications by Industry**
Industry	*Key Applications*
Airline	Yield management, route assessment
Telecommunications	Customer retention, network design
Insurance	Risk assessment, product design, fraud detection
Retail	Target marketing, supply-chain management

TABLE 16.3	**Relational Representation of Sales Data**

Product	Location	Sales
Soda	California	80
Soda	Utah	40
Soda	Arizona	70
Soda	Washington	75
Soda	Colorado	65
Diet soda	California	110
Diet soda	Utah	90
Diet soda	Arizona	55
Diet soda	Washington	85
Diet soda	Colorado	45
Lime soda	California	60
Lime soda	Utah	50
Lime soda	Arizona	60
Lime soda	Washington	45
Lime soda	Colorado	85
Orange soda	California	25
Orange soda	Utah	30
Orange soda	Arizona	35
Orange soda	Washington	45
Orange soda	Colorado	60

ations specifically tailored for decision support processing in data warehouses. This section describes the terminology and operations of the multidimensional data model.

16.2.1 Example of a Multidimensional Data Cube

Consider a company that sells soda products in different parts of the United States. In particular, the company markets four different soda products (soda, diet soda, lime soda, and orange soda) in five different states (California, Washington, Colorado, Utah, and Arizona). In order to store daily sales data for each product and each location in a relational database, you need Table 16.3, which consists of three columns (*Product, Location,* and *Sales*) and 20 rows (four instances of *Product* times five instances of *Location*).

The representation of Table 16.3 can be complex and unwieldy. First, imagine that the company wishes to add a fifth product (say, caffeine-free soda). In order to track sales by states for this new product, you need to add five rows, one each for each state. Second, note that the data in Table 16.3 represent sales data for a particular day (for example, August 10, 2003). In order to store the same data for all 365 days of 2003, you need to add a fourth column to store the sales date, and duplicate the 20 rows for each date 365 times to yield a total of 7,300 rows. By the same token, if you wish to store historic data for a period of 10 years, you need 73,000 rows. Each new row must contain the product, state, and date values.

An examination of the data in Table 16.3 reveals that the data contain two dimensions, *Product* and *Location,* and a numeric value for the unit sales. Table 16.3 therefore can be conceptually simplified by rearranging the data in a multidimensional format (Table 16.4).

The multidimensional representation is simple to understand and extend. For example, adding a fifth product category requires an additional column to the right of Table 16.4. Adding dates requires a third dimension called *Time,* resulting in a three-dimensional arrangement as shown in Figure 16.4. You can conceptually think of this three-dimensional table as a book consisting of 365 pages, each page storing sales data by product and state for a specific date of the year. In addition, the multidimensional table is more compact because the row and column labels are not duplicated as in Table 16.2.

The multidimensional representation also provides a convenient representation of summary totals. Each dimension in a cube can accommodate totals (row totals, column totals, depth totals, and overall totals) that a user can identify easily. For example, to add row totals to Table 16.4, a *Totals* column can be added with one value per row as shown

TABLE 16.4	Multidimensional Representation of Sales Data			
			Product	
Location	*Soda*	*Diet Soda*	*Lime Soda*	*Orange Soda*
California	80	110	60	25
Utah	40	90	50	30
Arizona	70	55	60	35
Washington	75	85	45	45
Colorado	65	45	85	60

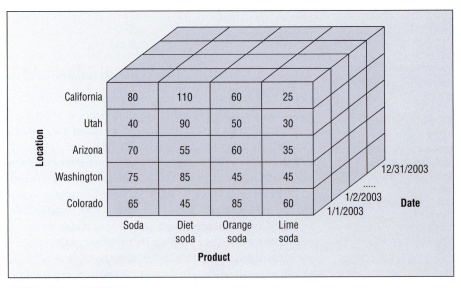

Figure 16.4 A three-dimensional data cube.

| TABLE 16.5 | Multidimensional Representation of Sales Data with Row Totals |

Location	Soda	Diet Soda	Lime Soda	Orange Soda	Totals
California	80	110	60	25	275
Utah	40	90	50	30	210
Arizona	70	55	60	35	220
Washington	75	85	45	45	250
Colorado	65	45	85	60	255

Product spans the Soda, Diet Soda, Lime Soda, Orange Soda columns.

in Table 16.5. In the relational representation as depicted in Table 16.3, totals must be added by using null values for column values. For example, to represent the total California sales for all products, the row <−, California, 275> should be added to Table 16.2 where – indicates all products.

In addition to advantages in usability, the multidimensional representation can provide increased retrieval speed. Direct storage of multidimensional data obviates the need to convert from a table representation to a multidimensional representation. However, the multidimensional representation can suffer from excessive storage because many cells can remain empty. Even with compression techniques, large multidimensional tables can consume considerably more storage space than corresponding relational tables.

In summary, a multidimensional representation provides an intuitive interface for business analysts. As the number of dimensions increases, business analysts find a multidimensional representation easy to understand and visualize as compared to a relational representation. Because the multidimensional representation matches the needs of business analysts, this representation is widely used in data warehousing even when relational tables provide physical storage.

16.2.2 Multidimensional Terminology

Data Cube a multidimensional format in which cells contain numeric data called measures organized by subjects called dimensions. A data cube is sometimes known as a hypercube because conceptually it can have an unlimited number of dimensions.

A data cube or hypercube generalizes the two-dimensional (Table 16.4) and three-dimensional (Figure 16.4) representations shown in the previous section. A data cube consists of cells containing measures (numeric values such as the unit sales amounts) and dimensions to label or group numeric data (e.g., *Product, Location,* and *Time*). Each dimension contains values known as members. For instance, the *Location* dimension has five members (California, Washington, Utah, Arizona, and Colorado) in Table 16.4. Both dimensions and measures can be stored or derived. For example, purchase date is a stored dimension with purchase year, month, and day as derived dimensions.

Dimension Details

Dimensions can have hierarchies composed of levels. For instance, the *Location* dimension may have a hierarchy composed of the levels country, state, and city. Likewise, the *Time* dimension can have a hierarchy composed of year, quarter, month, and date. Hierarchies can be used to drill down from higher levels of detail (e.g., country) to lower levels (e.g., state and city) and to roll up in the reverse direction. Although hierarchies are not essential, they allow a convenient and efficient representation. Without hierarchies, the *Location* dimension must contain the most detailed level (city). However, this representation can be difficult to compute aggregates across the dimension. Alternatively, the *Location* dimension can be divided into separate dimensions for country, state, and city resulting in a larger data cube.

For flexibility, dimensions can have multiple hierarchies. In a dimension with multiple hierarchies, usually at least one level is shared. For example, the *Location* dimension can have one hierarchy with the levels country, state, and city, and a second hierarchy with the levels country, state, and zip code. The *Time* dimension can have one hierarchy with the levels year, quarter, and date and a second hierarchy with the levels year, week, and date. Multiple hierarchies allow alternative organizations for a dimension.

Another dimension feature is the ragged hierarchy for a self-referencing relationship among members of the same level. For example, a manager dimension could have a ragged hierarchy to display relationships among managers and subordinates. An analyst manipulating a data cube may want to expand or contract the manager dimension according to the relationships among managers and subordinates.

The selection of dimensions has an influence on the sparsity of a data cube. Sparsity indicates the extent of empty cells in a data cube. Sparsity can be a problem if two or more dimensions are related. For example, if certain products are sold only in selected states, cells may be empty. If a large number of cells are empty, the data cube can waste space and be slow to process. Special compression techniques can be used to reduce the size of sparse data cubes.

Measure Details

Cells in a data cube contain measures such as the sales values in Figure 16.4. Measures support numeric operations such as simple arithmetic, statistical calculations, and simultaneous equations. A cell may contain one or more measures. For example, the number of units can be another measure for the sales data cube. The number of cells in a multidimensional cube should equal the number of records in the corresponding relational table (Table 16.4 contains 20 cells corresponding to 20 rows in Table 16.3).

Derived measures can be stored in a data cube or computed from other measures at run-time. Measures that can be derived from other measures in the same cell typically would not be stored. For example, total dollar sales can be calculated as total unit sales times the unit price measures in a cell. Summary measures derived from a collection of cells may be stored or computed depending on the number of cells and the cost of accessing the cells for the computation.

Other Data Cube Examples

As this section has indicated, data cubes can extend beyond the three-dimensional example in Figure 16.4. Table 16.6 lists common data cubes to support human resource management and financial analysis. The dimensions with slashes indicate hierarchical dimensions. The time and location dimensions are also hierarchical, but possible levels are not listed since the levels can be organization specific.

16.2.3 Time-Series Data

One kind of measure of particular interest to multidimensional databases is the time series. Time is, in fact, one of the most common dimensions in a data warehouse and is useful for capturing trends, making forecasts, and so forth. A time series provides stor-

TABLE 16.6	Data Cubes to Support Human Resource Management and Financial Analysis

Data Cube	Typical Dimensions	Typical Measures
Turnover analysis	Company/line of business/department, location, salary range, position classification, time	Head count for hires, transfers, terminations, and retirements
Employee utilization	Company/line of business/department, location, salary range, position classification, time	Full time equivalent (FTE) hours, normal FTE hours, overtime FTE hours
Asset analysis	Asset type, years in service band, time, account, company/line of business/department, location	Cost, net book value, market value
Vendor analysis	Vendor, location, account, time, business unit	Total invoice amount

age of all historic data in one cell, instead of specifying a separate time dimension. The structure of a measure becomes more complex with a time series, but the number of dimensions is reduced. A major advantage is that many statistical functions can operate directly on time-series data.

A time series is an array data type with a number of special properties as listed below. The array supports a collection of values, one for each time period. Examples of time-series measures include weekly sales amounts, daily stock closing prices, and yearly employee salaries. The following list shows typical properties for a time series:

- **Data Type:** This property denotes the kind of data stored in the data points. The data type is usually numeric such as floating point numbers, fixed decimal numbers, or integers.
- **Start Date:** This property denotes the starting date of the first data point, for example, 1/1/2004.
- **Calendar:** This property contains the calendar year appropriate for the time series, for example, 2004 fiscal year. An extensive knowledge of calendar rules, such as determining leap years and dates of holidays embedded in the calendar property, provides considerable savings in time and effort in data warehouse development.
- **Periodicity:** This property specifies the interval between data points. Periodicity can be daily, weekly, monthly, quarterly, yearly (calendar or fiscal years), hourly, 15-minute intervals, 4-4-5 accounting periods, custom periodicity, and so forth.
- **Conversion:** This property specifies how to convert unit data into aggregate data. For instance, aggregating daily sales into weekly sales requires summing daily data points, while aggregating daily stock prices into weekly prices requires an averaging operation.

16.2.4 Data Cube Operations

A number of decision support operations have been proposed for the data cube. This section discusses the most commonly used operations. A standard set of data cube operations is still under development, and not all data warehouse tools currently support all operations.

Slice

Because a data cube can contain a large number of dimensions, users often need to focus on a subset of the dimensions to gain insights. The slice operator retrieves a subset of a data cube similar to the restriction operator of relational algebra. In a slice operation, one or more dimensions are set to specific values and the remaining data cube is displayed. For example, Figure 16.5 shows the data cube resulting from the slice operation on the data cube in Figure 16.4 where Time = 1/1/2003 and the other two dimensions (*Location* and *Product*) are shown.

A variation of the slice operator allows a decision maker to summarize across members rather than to focus on just one member. The slice-summarize operator replaces one or more dimensions with summary calculations. The summary calculation often indicates the total value across members or the central tendency of the dimension such as the average or median value. For example, Figure 16.6 shows the result of a slice-summarize operation where the *Product* dimension is replaced by the sum of sales across all products. A new column called *Total Sales* can be added to store overall product sales for the entire year.

	Product			
Location	*Soda*	*Diet Soda*	*Lime Soda*	*Orange Soda*
California	80	110	60	25
Utah	40	90	50	30
Arizona	70	55	60	35
Washington	75	85	45	45
Colorado	65	45	85	60

Figure 16.5   **Example slice operation.**
(Location × Product Slice for Time = 1/1/2003)

	Time			
Location	*1/1/2003*	*1/2/2003*	. . .	*Total Sales*
California	400	670	. . .	16,250
Utah	340	190	. . .	11,107
Arizona	270	255	. . .	21,500
Washington	175	285	. . .	20,900
Colorado	165	245	. . .	21,336

Figure 16.6   **Example slice-summarize operation.**

Dice

Because individual dimensions can contain a large number of members, users need to focus on a subset of members to gain insights. The <u>dice</u> operator replaces a dimension with a subset of values of the dimension. For example, Figure 16.7 shows the result of a dicing operation to display sales for the state of Utah for January 1, 2003. Dicing typically follows a slicing operation and returns a subset of the values displayed in the preceding slice. It helps focus attention on one or more rows or columns of numbers from a slice.

Drill-Down

Users often want to navigate among the levels of hierarchical dimensions. The <u>drill-down</u> operator allows users to navigate from a more general level to a more specific level. For example, Figure 16.8 shows a drill-down operation on the state of Utah of the *Location* dimension. The plus sign by Utah indicates a drill-down operation.

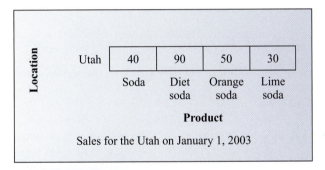

Figure 16.7   **Example dice operation.**

Location	Product			
	Soda	Diet Soda	Orange Soda	Lime Soda
California	80	110	60	25
+ Utah				
Salt Lake	20	20	10	15
Park City	5	30	10	5
Ogden	15	40	30	10
Arizona	70	55	60	35
Washington	75	85	45	45
Colorado	65	45	85	60

Figure 16.8   **Drill-down operation for the state of Utah in Figure 16.5.**

Roll-Up

Roll-up (also called drill-up) is the opposite of drill-down. <u>Roll-up</u> involves moving from a specific level to a more general level of a hierarchical dimension. For example, a decision maker may roll-up sales data from daily to quarterly level for end-of-quarter reporting needs. In the soda sales example, Figure 16.5 shows a roll-up of the state of Utah from Figure 16.7.

Pivot

The <u>pivot</u> operator supports rearrangement of the dimensions in a data cube. For example, in Figure 16.8, the position of the *Product* and the *Location* dimensions can be reversed so that *Product* appears on the rows and *Location* on the columns. The pivot operator allows a data cube to be presented in the most appealing visual order.

The pivot operator is most typically used on data cubes of more than two dimensions. On data cubes of more than two dimensions, multiple dimensions appear in the row and/or column area because more than two dimensions cannot be displayed in other ways. For example, to display a data cube with *Location, Product,* and *Time* dimensions, the *Time* dimension can be displayed in the row area inside the *Location* dimension. A pivot operation could rearrange the data cube so that the *Location* dimension displays inside the *Time* dimension.

Summary of Operators

To help you recall the data cube operators, Table 16.7 summarizes the purpose of each operator.

16.3 RELATIONAL DBMS SUPPORT FOR DATA WAREHOUSES

The multidimensional data model described in the previous section was originally implemented by special-purpose storage engines for data cubes. These multidimensional storage engines support the definition, manipulation, and optimization of large data cubes. Because of the commercial dominance of relational database technology, it was only a matter of time before relational DBMSs provided support for multidimensional data. In recent years, the major DBMS vendors have invested heavily in research and development to support multidimensional data. Because

TABLE 16.7	Summary of the Data Cube Operators	
Operator	*Purpose*	*Description*
Slice	Focus attention on a subset of dimensions	Replace a dimension with a single member value or with a summary of its measure values
Dice	Focus attention on a subset of member values	Replace a dimension with a subset of members
Drill-down	Obtain more detail about a dimension	Navigate from a more general level to a more specific level of a hierarchical dimension
Roll-up	Summarize details about a dimension	Navigate from a more specific level to a more general level of a hierarchical dimension
Pivot	Allow a data cube to be presented in a visually appealing order	Rearrange the dimensions in a data cube

of the investment level and the market power of the relational DBMS vendors, most data warehouses now use relational DBMSs, at least in part.

This section presents features of relational DBMSs to support multidimensional data. The features include data modeling approaches, dimension definitions, extensions to the GROUP BY clause, materialized views with query rewriting, and specialized storage structures and optimization techniques. To provide a specific context for the features, some examples use Oracle 9i SQL.

16.3.1 Relational Data Modeling for Multidimensional Data

Star Schema a data modeling representation for multidimensional databases. In a relational database, a star schema has a fact table in the center related to multiple dimension tables in 1-M relationships.

When using a relational database for a data warehouse, a new data modeling technique is needed to represent multidimensional data. A <u>star schema</u> is a data modeling representation of multidimensional data cubes. In a relational database, a star schema diagram looks like a star with one large central table, called the <u>fact table</u>, at the center of the star that is linked to multiple <u>dimension tables</u> in a radial manner using primary and foreign keys. The fact table stores numeric data (facts), such as sales results, while the dimension tables store descriptive data corresponding to individual dimensions of the data cube such as product, location, and time. There is a 1-M relationship from each dimension table to the fact table.

Figure 16.9 shows an ERD star schema for the sales example presented in Section 16.2. This ERD consists of four dimension entity types, *Item, Customer, Store,* and *Time,* along with one fact entity type called *Sales.* When converted to a table design, the *Sales* table has foreign keys to each dimension table (*Item, Customer, Store,* and *Time*). The *Item* entity type provides data for the *Product* dimension shown in the Section 16.2 examples, while the *Store* entity type provides data for the *Location* dimension.

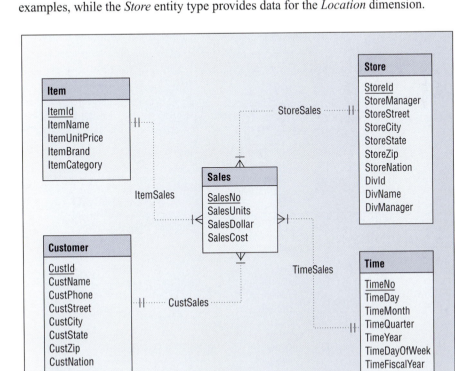

| **Figure 16.9** | ERD star schema for the store sales example. |

The store sales ERD in Figure 16.9 provides fine-grain detail for a data warehouse. The store sales ERD provides detail to the individual customer, store, and item. This level of detail is not necessary to support the sales data cubes presented in Section 16.2. However, a fine-grained level provides flexibility to support unanticipated analysis as well as data mining applications. This fine-grain level may replicate data in operational databases although the data warehouse representation may differ substantially because of the subject orientation of the data warehouse and the cleaning and integration performed on the source data.

Variations to the Star Schema

The star schema in Figure 16.9 represents only a single business process for sales tracking. Additional star schemas may be required for other processes such as shipping and purchasing. For related business processes that share some of the dimension tables, a star schema can be extended into a constellation schema with multiple fact entity types, as shown in Figure 16.10. When converted to a table design, the *Inventory* entity type be-

Constellation Schema a data modeling representation for multidimensional databases. In a relational database, a constellation schema contains multiple fact tables in the center related to dimension tables. Typically, the fact tables share some dimension tables.

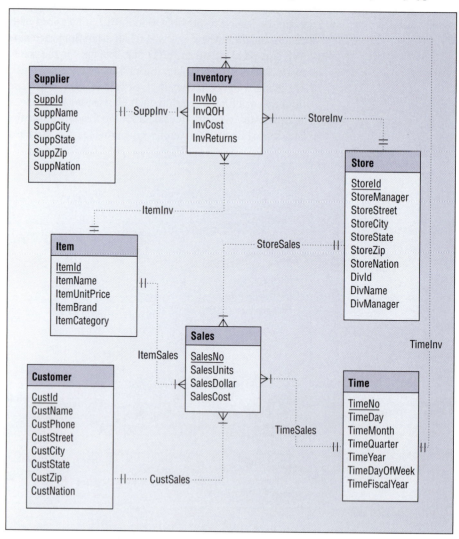

Figure 16.10   **ERD constellation schema for the sales-inventory example.**

comes a fact table and 1-M relationships become foreign keys in the fact table. The *Inventory* entity type adds a number of measures including the quantity on hand of an item, the cost of an item, and the quantity returned. All dimension tables are shared among both fact tables except for the *Supplier* and *Customer* tables.

Fact tables are usually normalized while dimension tables are often not in third normal form. For example, the *Store* entity type in Figures 16.9 and 16.10 is not in 3NF because *DivId* determines *DivName* and *DivManager*. Normalizing dimension tables to avoid storage anomalies is generally not necessary because they are usually stable and small. The nature of a data warehouse indicates that dimension tables should be designed for retrieval, not update. Retrieval performance is improved by eliminating the join operations that would be needed to combine fully normalized dimension tables.

When the dimension tables are small, denormalization provides only a small gain in retrieval performance. Thus, it is common to see small dimension tables normalized as shown in Figure 16.11. This variation is known as the snowflake schema because multiple levels of dimension tables surround the fact table. For the *Customer* and *Item* tables, full normalization may not be a good idea because these tables can contain many rows.

The star schema and its variations require 1-M relationships from the dimension tables to the fact table. The usage of 1-M relationships simplifies query formulation and supports optimization techniques discussed in Section 16.3.5. Sometimes the source data have exceptions that involve M-N relationships, not 1-M relationships. For example, if the *Sales* fact table is derived from customer invoices, some invoices may involve multiple customers such as roommates or spouses. If there is a small, fixed number of possible customers, a simple adjustment can be made to the fact or the dimension table. Multiple columns can be added to the fact or the dimension table to allow for more than one customer. For example,

Snowflake Schema a data modeling representation for multidimensional databases. In a relational database, a snowflake schema has multiple levels of dimension tables related to one or more fact tables. You should consider the snowflake schema instead of the star schema for small dimension tables that are not in 3NF.

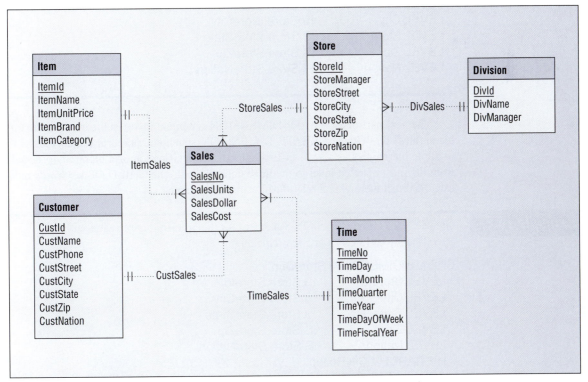

Figure 16.11   ERD snowflake schema for the store sales example.

the *Customer* table can have an additional column *SecondCustId* to identify an optional second customer on the invoice. If there can be groups of customers for an invoice, the representation is more difficult. A customer group table can be added with an associative table that connects the customer group and the *Customer* table via 1-M relationships.

16.3.2 Dimension Representation

The star schema and its variations do not provide explicit representation of hierarchical dimensions. A dimension table does not define the hierarchical relationships among the levels of a dimension. Because dimension definition is important to support data cube operations as well as optimization techniques for relational database queries, many relational DBMS vendors have created proprietary SQL extensions for dimensions. This section reviews the Oracle CREATE DIMENSION statement to indicate the types of extensions that can be found in relational DBMSs.

The Oracle CREATE DIMENSION statement supports the specification of levels, hierarchies, and constraints for a dimension. The first part of a dimension declaration involves the specification of levels. For flat (nonhierarchical) dimensions, there is only a single level in a dimension. However, most dimensions involve multiple levels as depicted in Example 16.1 for the *StoreDim* dimension. Each level corresponds to one column from the *Store* source table.

Example 16.1	Oracle CREATE DIMENSION Statement for the *StoreDim* Dimension with the Specification of Levels

```
CREATE DIMENSION StoreDim
    LEVEL StoreId      IS Store.StoreId
    LEVEL City         IS Store.StoreCity
    LEVEL State        IS Store.StoreState
    LEVEL Zip          IS Store.StoreZip
    LEVEL Nation       IS Store.StoreNation ;
```

The next part of a CREATE DIMENSION statement involves the specification of hierarchies. The Oracle CREATE DIMENSION statement supports dimensions with multiple hierarchies as shown in Example 16.2. Specification of a hierarchy proceeds from the most detailed level to the most general level. The CHILD OF keywords indicate the direct hierarchical relationships in a dimension.

Example 16.2	Oracle CREATE DIMENSION Statement for the *StoreDim* Dimension with the Specification of Levels and Hierarchies

```
CREATE DIMENSION StoreDim
    LEVEL StoreId      IS Store.StoreId
    LEVEL City         IS Store.StoreCity
    LEVEL State        IS Store.StoreState
    LEVEL Zip          IS Store.StoreZip
    LEVEL Nation       IS Store.StoreNation
    HIERARCHY CityRollup   (
      StoreId CHILD OF
      City    CHILD OF
```

```
State   CHILD OF
Nation   )
HIERARCHY ZipRollup   (
   StoreId CHILD OF
   Zip     CHILD OF
   State   CHILD OF
   Nation   );
```

The Oracle CREATE DIMENSION statement supports dimensions with levels from multiple source tables. This feature applies to normalized dimension tables in snowflake schemas. Example 16.3 augments Example 16.2 with the inclusion of an additional level (*DivId*) along with an additional hierarchy containing the new level. In the level specification, the *DivId* level references the *Division* table. In the *DivisionRollup* hierarchy, the JOIN KEY clause indicates a join between the *Store* and the *Division* tables. The JOIN KEY clause at the end of the hierarchy specification is required when a hierarchy has levels from more than one source table.

Example 16.3	Oracle CREATE DIMENSION Statement for the *StoreDim* Dimension with the Usage of Multiple Source Tables

```
CREATE DIMENSION StoreDim
   LEVEL StoreId     IS Store.StoreId
   LEVEL City        IS Store.StoreCity
   LEVEL State       IS Store.StoreState
   LEVEL Zip         IS Store.StoreZip
   LEVEL Nation      IS Store.StoreNation
   LEVEL DivId       IS Division.DivId
   HIERARCHY CityRollup   (
      StoreId  CHILD OF
      City     CHILD OF
      State    CHILD OF
      Nation   )
   HIERARCHY ZipRollup   (
      StoreId  CHILD OF
      Zip      CHILD OF
      State    CHILD OF
      Nation   )
   HIERARCHY DivisionRollup   (
      StoreId CHILD OF
      DivId
      JOIN KEY Store.DivId REFERENCES DivId   );
```

The final part of a CREATE DIMENSION statement involves the specification of constraints. The ATTRIBUTE clause defines functional dependency relationships involving dimension levels and nonsource columns in dimension tables. Example 16.4 shows ATTRIBUTE clauses for the nonsource columns in the *Division* table.

| **Example 16.4** | Oracle CREATE DIMENSION Statement for the *StoreDim* Dimension with the Usage of ATTRIBUTE Clauses for Constraints |

```
CREATE DIMENSION StoreDim
   LEVEL StoreId     IS Store.StoreId
   LEVEL City        IS Store.StoreCity
   LEVEL State       IS Store.StoreState
   LEVEL Zip         IS Store.StoreZip
   LEVEL Nation      IS Store.StoreNation
   LEVEL DivId       IS Division.DivId
   HIERARCHY CityRollup   (
     StoreId  CHILD OF
     City     CHILD OF
     State    CHILD OF
     Nation   )
   HIERARCHY ZipRollup   (
     StoreId  CHILD OF
     Zip      CHILD OF
     State    CHILD OF
     Nation   )
   HIERARCHY DivisionRollup   (
     StoreId  CHILD OF
     DivId
     JOIN KEY Store.DivId REFERENCES DivId   )
   ATTRIBUTE DivId DETERMINES Division.DivName
   ATTRIBUTE DivId DETERMINES Division.DivManager ;
```

16.3.3 Extensions to the GROUP BY Clause for Multidimensional Data

SQL:1999, the recently approved SQL standard, provides new summarization capabilities. These features are an attempt to unify the proliferation of proprietary data cube extensions, although they probably will not obviate the need for visual tools that directly support data cube operations. The new extensions involve the ability to produce summary totals (CUBE and ROLLUP operators) as well as more precise specification of the grouping columns (GROUPING SETS operator). This section describes these new parts of the GROUP BY clause using Oracle 9i as an example DBMS that implements the SQL:1999 features.

CUBE Operator

CUBE Operator an operator that augments the normal GROUP BY result with all combinations of subtotals. The CUBE operator is appropriate to summarize columns from independent dimensions rather than columns representing different levels of a single dimension.

The CUBE operator clause produces all possible subtotal combinations in addition to the normal totals shown in a GROUP BY clause. Because all possible subtotals are generated, the CUBE operator is appropriate to summarize columns from independent dimensions rather than columns representing different levels of the same dimension. For example, the CUBE operator would be appropriate to generate subtotals for all combinations of month, store state, and item brand. In contrast, a CUBE operation to show all possible subtotals of year, month, and day would have limited interest because of the hierarchy in the time dimension.

To depict the CUBE operator, Example 16.5 displays a SELECT statement with a GROUP BY clause containing just two columns. Only six rows are shown in the result so that the effect of the CUBE operator can be understood easily. With two values in the *StoreZip* column and three values in the *TimeMonth* column, the number of subtotal combinations is six (two *StoreZip* subtotals, three *TimeMonth* subtotals, and one grand total) as shown in Example 16.6. Blank values in the result represent a summary over all possible values of the column. For example, the row <80111, -, 33000> represents the total sales in the zip code 80111 over all months (- represents a do-not-care value for the month).

Example 16.5

GROUP BY Clause and Partial Result Without Subtotals

```
SELECT StoreZip, TimeMonth, SUM(SalesDollar) AS SumSales
  FROM Sales, Store, Time
  WHERE Sales.StoreId = Store.StoreId AND Sales.TimeNo = Time.TimeNo
    AND (StoreNation = 'USA' OR StoreNation = 'Canada')
    AND TimeYear = 2002
  GROUP BY StoreZip, TimeMonth;
```

StoreZip	TimeMonth	SumSales
80111	1	10000
80111	2	12000
80111	3	11000
80112	1	9000
80112	2	11000
80112	3	15000

Example 16.6 (Oracle)

GROUP BY Clause and Result with Subtotals Produced by the CUBE Operator

```
SELECT StoreZip, TimeMonth, SUM(SalesDollar) AS SumSales
  FROM Sales, Store, Time
  WHERE Sales.StoreId = Store.StoreId AND Sales.TimeNo = Time.TimeNo
    AND (StoreNation = 'USA' OR StoreNation = 'Canada')
    AND TimeYear = 2002
  GROUP BY CUBE(StoreZip, TimeMonth);
```

StoreZip	TimeMonth	SumSales
80111	1	10000
80111	2	12000
80111	3	11000
80112	1	9000
80112	2	11000
80112	3	15000
80111		33000
80112		35000
	1	19000
	2	23000
	3	26000
		68000

With more than two grouping columns, the CUBE operator becomes more difficult to understand. Examples 16.7 and 16.8 extend Examples 16.5 and 16.6 with an additional grouping column (*TimeYear*). The number of rows in the result increases from 12 rows in the result of Example 16.7 without the CUBE operator to 36 rows in the result of Example 16.8 with the CUBE operator. For three grouping columns with M, N, and P unique values, the number of subtotal rows produced by the CUBE operator is $M + N + P + M * N + M * P + N * P + 1$. Since the number of subtotal rows grows substantially with the number of grouped columns and the unique values per column, the CUBE operator should be used sparingly when there are more than three grouped columns.

Example 16.7

GROUP BY Clause with Three Grouping Columns and the Partial Result Without Subtotals

```
SELECT StoreZip, TimeMonth, TimeYear, SUM(SalesDollar) AS SumSales
  FROM Sales, Store, Time
  WHERE Sales.StoreId = Store.StoreId AND Sales.TimeNo = Time.TimeNo
    AND (StoreNation = 'USA' OR StoreNation = 'Canada')
    AND TimeYear BETWEEN 2002 AND 2003
  GROUP BY StoreZip, TimeMonth, TimeYear;
```

StoreZip	TimeMonth	TimeYear	SumSales
80111	1	2002	10000
80111	2	2002	12000
80111	3	2002	11000
80112	1	2002	9000
80112	2	2002	11000
80112	3	2002	15000
80111	1	2003	11000
80111	2	2003	13000
80111	3	2003	12000
80112	1	2003	10000
80112	2	2003	12000
80112	3	2003	16000

Example 16.8 (Oracle)

GROUP BY Clause with Three Grouping Columns and the Result with Subtotals Produced by the CUBE Operator

```
SELECT StoreZip, TimeMonth, TimeYear, SUM(SalesDollar) AS SumSales
  FROM Sales, Store, Time
  WHERE Sales.StoreId = Store.StoreId AND Sales.TimeNo = Time.TimeNo
    AND (StoreNation = 'USA' OR StoreNation = 'Canada')
    AND TimeYear BETWEEN 2002 AND 2003
  GROUP BY CUBE(StoreZip, TimeMonth, TimeYear);
```

StoreZip	TimeMonth	TimeYear	SumSales
80111	1	2002	10000
80111	2	2002	12000
80111	3	2002	11000
80112	1	2002	9000
80112	2	2002	11000
80112	3	2002	15000
80111	1	2003	11000
80111	2	2003	13000
80111	3	2003	12000
80112	1	2003	10000
80112	2	2003	12000
80112	3	2003	16000
80111	1		21000
80111	2		25000
80111	3		23000
80112	1		19000
80112	2		22000
80112	3		31000
80111		2002	33000
80111		2003	36000
80112		2002	35000
80112		2003	38000
	1	2002	19000
	2	2002	23000
	3	2002	26000
	1	2003	21000
	2	2003	25000
	3	2003	28000
80111			69000
80112			73000
	1		40000
	2		48000
	3		54000
		2002	68000
		2003	74000
			142000

The CUBE operator is not a primitive operator. The result of a CUBE operation can be produced using a number of SELECT statements connected by the UNION operator, as shown in Example 16.9. The additional SELECT statements generate subtotals for each combination of grouped columns. With two grouped columns, three additional SELECT statements are needed to generate the subtotals. With N grouped columns, $2^N - 1$ additional SELECT statements are needed. Obviously, the CUBE operator is much easier to write than a large number of additional SELECT statements.

Example 16.9

Rewrite Example 16.6 without Using the CUBE Operator

In each additional SELECT statement, a default value (0 for numeric columns and ' ' for text columns) replaces the column in which totals are not generated.

```
SELECT StoreZip, TimeMonth, SUM(SalesDollar) AS SumSales
  FROM Sales, Store, Time
  WHERE Sales.StoreId = Store.StoreId AND Sales.TimeNo = Time.TimeNo
    AND (StoreNation = 'USA' OR StoreNation = 'Canada')
    AND TimeYear = 2002
  GROUP BY StoreZip, TimeMonth
  UNION
SELECT StoreZip, 0, SUM(SalesDollar) AS SumSales
  FROM Sales, Store, Time
  WHERE Sales.StoreId = Store.StoreId AND Sales.TimeNo = Time.TimeNo
    AND (StoreNation = 'USA' OR StoreNation = 'Canada')
    AND TimeYear = 2002
  GROUP BY StoreZip
  UNION
SELECT ' ', TimeMonth, SUM(SalesDollar) AS SumSales
  FROM Sales, Store, Time
  WHERE Sales.StoreId = Store.StoreId AND Sales.TimeNo = Time.TimeNo
    AND (StoreNation = 'USA' OR StoreNation = 'Canada')
    AND TimeYear = 2002
  GROUP BY TimeMonth
  UNION
SELECT ' ', 0, SUM(SalesDollar) AS SumSales
  FROM Sales, Store, Time
  WHERE Sales.StoreId = Store.StoreId AND Sales.TimeNo = Time.TimeNo
    AND (StoreNation = 'USA' OR StoreNation = 'Canada')
    AND TimeYear = 2002;
```

ROLLUP Operator

ROLLUP Operator an operator that augments the normal GROUP BY result with a partial set of subtotals. The ROLLUP operator is appropriate to summarize levels from a dimension hierarchy.

The SQL ROLLUP operator provides a similar capability to the roll-up operator for data cubes. The roll-up operator for data cubes produces totals for more general parts of a dimension hierarchy. The SQL ROLLUP operator produces subtotals for each ordered subset of grouped columns to simulate the effects of the roll-up operator for data cubes. For example, the SQL operation ROLLUP(TimeYear, TimeQuarter, TimeMonth, TimeDay) produces subtotals for the column subsets *<TimeYear, TimeQuarter, TimeMonth>*, *<TimeYear, TimeQuarter>*, *<TimeYear>* as well as the grand total. As this example implies, the order of columns in a ROLLUP operation is significant.

As the previous paragraph indicates, the ROLLUP operator produces only a partial set of subtotals for the columns in a GROUP BY clause. Examples 16.10 and 16.11 demonstrate the ROLLUP operator in order to contrast it with the CUBE operator of Example 16.6. Note that Example 16.10 contains three subtotal rows compared to six subtotal rows in Example 16.6 with the CUBE operator. In Example 16.11, subtotals are produced for the values in the column combinations *<StoreZip, TimeMonth>*, *<StoreZip>*, and the grand total. In Example 16.8 with the CUBE operator, subtotals are also produced for the values in the column combinations *<StoreZip, TimeYear>*, *<TimeMonth, TimeYear>*, *<TimeMonth>*, and *<TimeYear>*. Thus, the ROLLUP operator produces far fewer subtotal rows compared to the CUBE operator as the number of grouped columns and unique values per column increases.

| *Example 16.10* *(Oracle)* | GROUP BY Clause and Result with Subtotals Produced by the ROLLUP Operator |

GROUP BY Clause and Result with Subtotals Produced by the ROLLUP Operator
This example should be compared with Example 16.6 to understand the difference between the CUBE and ROLLUP operators.

```
SELECT StoreZip, TimeMonth, SUM(SalesDollar) AS SumSales
  FROM Sales, Store, Time
  WHERE Sales.StoreId = Store.StoreId AND Sales.TimeNo = Time.TimeNo
    AND (StoreNation = 'USA' OR StoreNation = 'Canada')
    AND TimeYear = 2002
  GROUP BY ROLLUP(StoreZip, TimeMonth);
```

StoreZip	TimeMonth	SumSales
80111	1	10000
80111	2	12000
80111	3	11000
80112	1	9000
80112	2	11000
80112	3	15000
80111		33000
80112		35000
		68000

Example 16.11 (Oracle)

GROUP BY Clause with Three Grouping Columns and the Result with Subtotals Produced by the ROLLUP Operator
This example should be compared with Example 16.8 to understand the difference between the CUBE and ROLLUP operators.

```
SELECT StoreZip, TimeMonth, TimeYear, SUM(SalesDollar) AS SumSales
  FROM Sales, Store, Time
  WHERE Sales.StoreId = Store.StoreId AND Sales.TimeNo = Time.TimeNo
    AND (StoreNation = 'USA' OR StoreNation = 'Canada')
    AND TimeYear BETWEEN 2002 AND 2003
  GROUP BY ROLLUP(StoreZip, TimeMonth, TimeYear);
```

StoreZip	TimeMonth	TimeYear	SumSales
80111	1	2002	10000
80111	2	2002	12000
80111	3	2002	11000
80112	1	2002	9000
80112	2	2002	11000
80112	3	2002	15000
80111	1	2003	11000
80111	2	2003	13000
80111	3	2003	12000
80112	1	2003	10000
80112	2	2003	12000
80112	3	2003	16000
80111	1		21000
80111	2		25000
80111	3		23000
80112	1		19000
80112	2		22000
80112	3		31000
80111			69000
80112			73000
			142000

Like the CUBE operator, the ROLLUP operator is not a primitive operator. The result of a ROLLUP operation can be produced using a number of SELECT statements connected by the UNION operator as shown in Example 16.12. The additional SELECT statements generate subtotals for each ordered subset of grouped columns. With three grouped columns, three additional SELECT statements are needed to generate the subtotals. With N grouped columns, N additional SELECT statements are needed. Obviously, the ROLLUP operator is much easier to write than a large number of additional SELECT statements.

Example 16.12

Rewrite of Example 16.11 Without Using the ROLLUP Operator
In each additional SELECT statement, a default value (0 for numeric columns and ' ' for text columns) replaces the column in which totals are not generated.

```
SELECT StoreZip, TimeMonth, TimeYear, SUM(SalesDollar) AS SumSales
 FROM Sales, Store, Time
 WHERE Sales.StoreId = Store.StoreId AND Sales.TimeNo = Time.TimeNo
    AND (StoreNation = 'USA' OR StoreNation = 'Canada')
    AND TimeYear BETWEEN 2002 AND 2003
 GROUP BY StoreZip, TimeMonth, TimeYear
 UNION
SELECT StoreZip, TimeMonth, 0, SUM(SalesDollar) AS SumSales
 FROM Sales, Store, Time
 WHERE Sales.StoreId = Store.StoreId AND Sales.TimeNo = Time.TimeNo
    AND (StoreNation = 'USA' OR StoreNation = 'Canada')
```

```
        AND TimeYear BETWEEN 2002 AND 2003
  GROUP BY StoreZip, TimeMonth
UNION
SELECT StoreZip, 0, 0, SUM(SalesDollar) AS SumSales
  FROM Sales, Store, Time
  WHERE Sales.StoreId = Store.StoreId AND Sales.TimeNo = Time.TimeNo
      AND (StoreNation = 'USA' OR StoreNation = 'Canada')
      AND TimeYear BETWEEN 2002 AND 2003
  GROUP BY StoreZip
UNION
SELECT ' ', 0, 0, SUM(SalesDollar) AS SumSales
  FROM Sales, Store, Time
  WHERE Sales.StoreId = Store.StoreId AND Sales.TimeNo = Time.TimeNo
      AND (StoreNation = 'USA' OR StoreNation = 'Canada')
      AND TimeYear BETWEEN 2002 AND 2003;
```

GROUPING SETS Operator

GROUPING SETS

Operator an operator in the GROUP BY clause that requires explicit specification of column combinations. The GROUPING SETS operator is appropriate when precise control over grouping and subtotals is required.

For more flexibility than is provided by the CUBE and ROLLUP operators, you can use the GROUPING SETS operator. When you use the GROUPING SETS operator, you explicitly specify the combinations of columns for which you need totals. In contrast, the specification of subtotals is implicit in the CUBE and ROLLUP operators. The GROUPING SETS operator is appropriate when precise control over grouping is needed. If explicit control is not required, the CUBE and ROLLUP operators provide more succinct specification.

To depict the GROUPING SETS operator, the previous examples are recast using the GROUPING SETS operator. In Example 16.13, the GROUPING SETS operator involves subtotals for the *StoreZip* and *TimeMonth* columns along with the grand total denoted by the empty parentheses. The subset (*StoreZip, TimeMonth*) also must be specified because all column combinations must be explicitly specified, even the normal grouping without the GROUPING SETS operator. Example 16.14 contains eight column combinations to provide the same result as Example 16.8 with the CUBE of three columns. Example 16.15 contains three column combinations to provide the same result as Example 16.11 with the ROLLUP of three columns.

Example 16.13 (Oracle)

GROUP BY Clause Using the GROUPING SETS Operator
This example produces the same result as Example 16.6.

```
SELECT StoreZip, TimeMonth, SUM(SalesDollar) AS SumSales
  FROM Sales, Store, Time
  WHERE Sales.StoreId = Store.StoreId AND Sales.TimeNo = Time.TimeNo
      AND (StoreNation = 'USA' OR StoreNation = 'Canada')
      AND TimeYear = 2002
  GROUP BY GROUPING SETS((StoreZip, TimeMonth), StoreZip,
        TimeMonth, ());
```

Example 16.14 (Oracle)	GROUP BY Clause Using the GROUPING SETS Operator

This example produces the same result as Example 16.8.

```
SELECT StoreZip, TimeMonth, TimeYear, SUM(SalesDollar) AS SumSales
  FROM Sales, Store, Time
  WHERE Sales.StoreId = Store.StoreId AND Sales.TimeNo = Time.TimeNo
    AND (StoreNation = 'USA' OR StoreNation = 'Canada')
    AND TimeYear BETWEEN 2002 AND 2003
  GROUP BY GROUPING SETS ( ( StoreZip, TimeMonth, TimeYear),
      (StoreZip,TimeMonth), (StoreZip, TimeYear),
      (TimeMonth, TimeYear), StoreZip, TimeMonth, TimeYear, () );
```

Example 16.15 (Oracle)	GROUP BY Clause Using the GROUPING SETS Operator

This example produces the same result as Example 16.11.

```
SELECT StoreZip, TimeMonth, TimeYear, SUM(SalesDollar) AS SumSales
  FROM Sales, Store, Time
  WHERE Sales.StoreId = Store.StoreId AND Sales.TimeNo = Time.TimeNo
    AND (StoreNation = 'USA' OR StoreNation = 'Canada')
    AND TimeYear BETWEEN 2002 AND 2003
  GROUP BY GROUPING SETS ( (StoreZip, TimeMonth, TimeYear),
      (StoreZip,TimeMonth), StoreZip, ()   );
```

Example 16.16 depicts a situation in which the GROUPING SETS operator is preferred to the CUBE operator. Because the *TimeYear* and *TimeMonth* columns are from the same dimension hierarchy, a full cube usually is not warranted. Instead, the GROUPING SETS operator can be used to specify the column combinations from which subtotals are needed. Subtotals involving *TimeMonth* without *TimeYear* are excluded in Example 16.16 but are included in a full CUBE operation.

Example 16.16 (Oracle)	GROUP BY Clause Using the GROUPING SETS Operator to Indicate the Column Combinations from Which Subtotals Are Needed

```
SELECT StoreZip, TimeMonth, TimeYear, SUM(SalesDollar) AS SumSales
  FROM Sales, Store, Time
  WHERE Sales.StoreId = Store.StoreId AND Sales.TimeNo = Time.TimeNo
    AND (StoreNation = 'USA' OR StoreNation = 'Canada')
    AND TimeYear BETWEEN 2002 AND 2003
  GROUP BY GROUPING SETS( (StoreZip, TimeYear, TimeMonth),
      (StoreZip, TimeYear), (TimeMonth, TimeYear),
      StoreZip, TimeYear, ()   );
```

Variations of the CUBE, ROLLUP, and GROUPING SETS Operators

The CUBE, ROLLUP, and GROUPING SETS operators can be combined to provide the appropriate mix of explicit grouping specifications with the GROUPING SETS operator along with subtotals provided by the ROLLUP and the CUBE operators. This list provides some of the possible variations when using these operators.

- A partial CUBE can be done to produce subtotals for a subset of independent dimensions. For example, the clause GROUP BY TimeMonth, CUBE(ItemBrand, StoreState) produces totals on the column subsets <*TimeMonth, ItemBrand, StoreState*>, <*TimeMonth, ItemBrand*>, <*TimeMonth, StoreState*>, and <*TimeMonth*>.
- A partial ROLLUP can be done to produce subtotals for a subset of columns from the same dimension hierarchy. For example, the clause GROUP BY ItemBrand, ROLLUP(TimeYear, TimeMonth, TimeDay) produces totals on the column subsets <*ItemBrand, TimeYear, TimeMonth, TimeDay*>, <*ItemBrand, TimeYear, TimeMonth*>, <*ItemBrand, TimeYear*>, and <*ItemBrand*>.
- Composite columns can be used with the CUBE or ROLLUP operators to skip some subtotals. For example, the clause GROUP BY ROLLUP(TimeYear, (TimeQuarter, TimeMonth), TimeDay) produces totals on the column subsets <*TimeYear, TimeQuarter, TimeMonth, TimeDay*>, <*TimeYear, TimeQuarter, TimeMonth*>, <*TimeYear*>, and < >. The composite column <*TimeQuarter, TimeMonth*> is treated as a single column in the ROLLUP operation.
- CUBE and ROLLUP operations can be included in a GROUPING SETS operation. For example, the clause GROUP BY GROUPING SETS(ItemBrand, ROLLUP(TimeYear, TimeMonth), StoreState) produces totals on the column subsets <*ItemBrand*>, <*StoreState*>, <*TimeYear, TimeMonth*>, <*TimeYear*>, and < >. The nested ROLLUP operation creates subtotals on the column subsets <*TimeYear, TimeMonth*>, <*TimeYear*>, and < >.

Other Extensions for Decision Support

In addition to the GROUP BY extensions, a number of new aggregate functions can be used in the SELECT statement. Some of the typical extensions are listed below:

- Ranking functions support requests for the top or the bottom percentage of results.
- Ratio functions simplify the formulation of queries that compare individual values to group totals.
- Functions for moving totals and averages allow smoothing of data for time-series analysis. The OLAP extension in SQL:1999 provides the WINDOW clause to specify moving averages.

16.3.4 Materialized Views and Query Rewriting

Materialized View a stored view that must be periodically synchronized with its source data. Materialized views support storage of summarized data for fast query response.

To support queries involving large fact tables, relational DBMSs provide materialized views. A materialized view is a stored view that must be periodically synchronized with its source data. Materialized views are attractive in data warehouses because the source data are stable except for periodic refreshments that can usually be performed during nonpeak times. In contrast, nonmaterialized views dominate operational database processing because the refresh cost can be high. Along with materialized views, most relational DBMSs support automatic substitution of materialized views for source tables in a process known as query rewriting. This section depicts materialized views using the Oracle 9i syntax and provides examples of the query rewriting process.

Materialized Views in Oracle 9i

Specification of a materialized view in Oracle 9i involves elements of base table specification and the mapping specification of traditional views along with the specification of materialization properties. Since a materialized view is stored, most of the storage properties for base tables can also be specified for materialized views. Since the storage properties are not the focus here, they will not be depicted. The mapping specification is the same for views as for materialized views. A SELECT statement provides the mapping necessary to populate a materialized view. The materialization properties include the method of refresh (incremental or complete), the timing of refresh (on demand or on commit), and the build timing (immediate or deferred). Oracle has a number of restrictions on the types of materialized views that can be incrementally refreshed so incremental refreshment will not be discussed here.

Examples 16.17 to 16.19 depict the syntax of the CREATE MATERIALIZED VIEW statement. These statements appear similar to CREATE VIEW statements except for the materialization clauses. The build timing is immediate in Examples 16.17 and 16.19, while the build timing is deferred (on demand) in Example 16.18. The refresh method is complete and the refresh timing is on demand in all three materialized views. The SELECT statement following the AS keyword provides the mapping to populate a materialized view.

Example 16.17 (Oracle)	Materialized View Containing Sales for All Countries for Years after 2000 Grouped by State and Year

```
CREATE MATERIALIZED VIEW MV1
BUILD IMMEDIATE
REFRESH COMPLETE ON DEMAND
ENABLE QUERY REWRITE AS
SELECT StoreState, TimeYear, SUM(SalesDollar) AS SUMDollar1
  FROM Sales, Store, Time
  WHERE Sales.StoreId = Store.StoreId AND Sales.TimeNo = Time.TimeNo
    AND TimeYear > 2000
  GROUP BY StoreState, TimeYear;
```

Example 16.18 (Oracle)	Materialized View Containing USA Sales in All Years Grouped by State, Year, and Month

```
CREATE MATERIALIZED VIEW MV2
BUILD DEFERRED
REFRESH COMPLETE ON DEMAND
ENABLE QUERY REWRITE AS
SELECT StoreState, TimeYear, TimeMonth,
        SUM(SalesDollar) AS SUMDollar2
  FROM Sales, Store, Time
  WHERE Sales.StoreId = Store.StoreId AND Sales.TimeNo = Time.TimeNo
    AND StoreNation = 'USA'
  GROUP BY StoreState, TimeYear, TimeMonth;
```

Example 16.19 (Oracle)	Materialized View Containing Canadian Sales before 2001 Grouped by City, Year, and Month

```
CREATE MATERIALIZED VIEW MV3
BUILD IMMEDIATE
REFRESH COMPLETE ON DEMAND
ENABLE QUERY REWRITE AS
SELECT StoreCity, TimeYear, TimeMonth,
        SUM(SalesDollar) AS SUMDollar3
 FROM Sales, Store, Time
 WHERE Sales.StoreId = Store.StoreId AND Sales.TimeNo = Time.TimeNo
    AND StoreNation = 'Canada'
    AND TimeYear <= 2000
 GROUP  BY StoreCity, TimeYear, TimeMonth;
```

Query Rewriting

Query Rewriting a
substitution process in which
a materialized view replaces
references to fact and
dimension tables in a query.
In addition to the
substitution, the query
optimizer evaluates whether
the substitution will improve
performance over the original
query.

The query rewriting process for materialized views reverses the query modification process for traditional views. The query modification process substitutes base tables for views in queries that reference views so that materialization of the views is not needed. In contrast, the query rewrite process substitutes materialized views for base tables to avoid accessing large fact and dimension tables. In the original data warehouse queries, users reference the fact and dimension tables.

Overall, query rewriting is more complex than query modification because query rewriting involves a more complex substitution process and requires the optimizer to evaluate costs. In both processes, the DBMS—not the user—performs the substitution process. In the query rewriting process, the query optimizer must evaluate whether the substitution will improve performance over the original query. In the query modification process, the query optimizer does not compare the cost of the modified query to the original query because modification usually provides substantial cost savings.

Example 16.20 presents an example data warehouse query and the rewritten query to depict the query rewriting process. Since *MV*1 includes sales data for all countries in years greater than 2000, it can be used in place of the *Sales* and the *Store* tables. Grouping is not necessary in the rewritten query because grouping already is performed in *MV*1.

Example 16.20	Data Warehouse Query and Rewritten Query Using the *MV*1 Materialized View

```
-- Data warehouse query
SELECT StoreState, TimeYear, SUM(SalesDollar)
 FROM Sales, Store, Time
 WHERE Sales.StoreId = Store.StoreId AND Sales.TimeNo = Time.TimeNo
    AND StoreNation IN ('USA','Canada')
    AND TimeYear = 2002
 GROUP BY StoreState, TimeYear;
```

```
-- Query Rewrite: replace Sales and Time tables with MV1
SELECT DISTINCT MV1.StoreState, TimeYear, SumDollar1
FROM MV1, Store
WHERE MV1.StoreState = Store.StoreState
AND TimeYear = 2002
AND StoreNation IN ('USA','Canada');
```

Example 16.21 presents a more complex example of query rewriting involving three parts combined using the UNION operator. The first query block retrieves the total sales in USA or Canada from 2001 to 2003. The second query block retrieves the USA store sales in 2000. The third query block retrieves Canadian store sales in 2000. The GROUP BY clauses are necessary in the second and third query blocks because the underlying materialized views perform aggregation on a finer level of detail than the query requires. In the third query block, the condition on *StoreNation* is needed because some cities can have identical names in both countries.

Example 16.21

Data Warehouse Query and Rewritten Query Using the *MV*1, *MV*2, and *MV*3 Materialized Views

```
-- Data warehouse query
SELECT StoreState, TimeYear, SUM(SalesDollar)
  FROM Sales, Store, Time
  WHERE Sales.StoreId = Store.StoreId AND Sales.TimeNo = Time.TimeNo
    AND StoreNation IN ('USA','Canada')
    AND TimeYear BETWEEN 2000 and 2003
  GROUP BY StoreState, TimeYear;

-- Query Rewrite
SELECT DISTINCT MV1.StoreState, TimeYear, SumDollar1 AS StoreSales
FROM MV1, Store
WHERE MV1.StoreState = Store.StoreState
    AND TimeYear <= 2003
    AND StoreNation IN ('USA','Canada')
UNION
SELECT StoreState, TimeYear, SUM(SumDollar2) as StoreSales
FROM MV2
WHERE MV1.StoreState = Store.StoreState
    AND TimeYear = 2000
GROUP BY StoreState, TimeYear
UNION
SELECT DISTINCT StoreState, TimeYear, SUM(SumDollar3) as StoreSales
FROM MV3, Store
WHERE MV3.StoreCity = Store.StoreCity
    AND TimeYear = 2000 AND StoreNation = 'Canada'
GROUP BY StoreState, TimeYear;
```

These examples indicate the range of query rewriting possibilities rather than capabilities of actual DBMSs. Most enterprise DBMSs support query rewriting but the range of query rewriting supported varies. Because of the complexity and the proprietary nature of query rewrite algorithms, the details of query rewriting algorithms are beyond the scope of this textbook.

16.3.5 Storage and Optimization Technologies

Several storage technologies have been developed to provide multidimensional data capabilities. The storage technologies support <u>On Line Analytic Processing (OLAP)</u>, a generic name applied to decision support capabilities for data cubes. This section describes the features of OLAP storage technologies with an emphasis on current market trends.

MOLAP (Multidimensional OLAP)

MOLAP a storage engine that directly stores and manipulates data cubes. MOLAP engines generally offer the best query performance but place limits on the size of data cubes.

Originally, vendors of decision support software developed a storage architecture that directly manipulates data cubes. This storage architecture, known as <u>MOLAP</u>, for Multidimensional OLAP, was the only choice as a storage technology for data warehouses until the mid-1990s. At the current time, MOLAP has been eclipsed as the primary storage architecture for data warehouses, but it still is an important technology for summary data cubes and small data warehouses and data marts.

MOLAP storage engines directly manipulate stored data cubes. The storage engines of MOLAP systems are optimized for the unique characteristics of multidimensional data such as sparsity and complex aggregation across thousands of cells. Because data cubes are precomputed, MOLAP query performance is generally better than competing approaches that use relational database storage. Even with techniques to deal with sparsity, MOLAP engines can be overwhelmed by the size of data cubes. A fully calculated data cube may expand many times as compared to the raw input data. This data explosion problem limits the size of data cubes that MOLAP engines can manipulate.

ROLAP (Relational OLAP)

ROLAP relational DBMS extensions to support multidimensional data. ROLAP engines support a variety of storage and optimization techniques for summary data retrieval.

Because of the potential market size and growth of data warehouse processing, vendors of relational DBMSs have extended their products with additional features to support operations and storage structures for multidimensional data. These product extensions are collectively known as <u>ROLAP</u>, for Relational OLAP. Given the growing size of data warehouses and the intensive research and development by relational DBMS vendors, it was only a matter of time before ROLAP became the dominant storage engine for data warehouses.

In the ROLAP approach, relational databases store multidimensional data using the star schema or its variations, as described in Section 16.3.1. Data cubes are dynamically constructed from fact and dimension tables as well as from materialized views. Typically, only a subset of a data cube must be constructed as specified in a user's query. Extensions to SQL as described in Section 16.3.3 allow users to manipulate the dimensions and measures in virtual data cubes.

ROLAP engines incorporate a variety of storage and optimization techniques for summary data retrieval. This list explains the most prominent techniques:

- **Bitmap join indexes** (see Chapter 8 for details) are particularly useful for columns in dimension tables with few values such as *CustState*. A bitmap join index provides a precomputed join from the values of a dimension table to the rows of a fact table. To support snowflake schemas, some DBMS vendors support bitmap join indexes for dimension tables related to other dimension tables. For example, a bitmap index for the *Division.DivManager* column has an index record that contains a bitmap for related rows of the *Store* table and a second bitmap for rows of the *Sales* table related to matching rows of the *Store* table.

- **Star join query optimization** uses bitmap join indexes on dimension tables to reduce the number of rows in a fact table to retrieve. A star join involves a fact table joined with one or more dimension tables. Star join optimization involves three phases. In the first phase, the bitmap join indexes on each dimension table are combined using the union operator for conditions connected by the OR operator and the intersection operator for conditions connected by the AND operator. In the second phase, the bitmaps resulting from the first phase are combined using the intersection operator. In the third phase, the rows of the fact table are retrieved using the bitmap resulting from the second phase. Star join optimization can result in substantially reduced execution time as compared to traditional join algorithms that combine two tables at a time.

- **Query rewriting using materialized views** can eliminate the need to access large fact and dimension tables. If materialized views are large, they can be indexed to improve retrieval performance. Query rewriting uses the query optimizer to evaluate the benefit of using materialized views as compared to the fact and dimension tables.

- **Summary storage advisors** determine the best set of materialized views that should be created and maintained for a given query workload. For consistency with other components, the summary advisor is integrated with the query rewriting component and the query optimizer.

- **Partitioning, striping, and parallel query execution** provide opportunities to reduce the execution time of data warehouse queries. The choices must be carefully studied so that the use of partitioning and striping support the desired level of parallel query execution.

Despite the intensive research and development on ROLAP storage and optimization techniques, MOLAP engines still provide faster query response time. However, MOLAP storage suffers from limitations in data cube size so that ROLAP storage is preferred for fine-grained data warehouses. In addition, the difference in response time has narrowed so that ROLAP storage may involve only a slight performance penalty if ROLAP storage and optimization techniques are properly utilized.

HOLAP a storage engine for data warehouses that combines ROLAP and MOLAP storage engines. HOLAP involves both relational and multidimensional data storage as well as combining data from both relational and multidimensional sources for data cube operations.

HOLAP (Hybrid OLAP)

Because of the trade-offs between MOLAP and ROLAP, a third technology known as HOLAP—for Hybrid OLAP—has been developed to combine ROLAP and MOLAP. HOLAP allows a data warehouse to be divided between relational storage of fact and dimension tables and multidimensional storage of summary data cubes. When an OLAP query is submitted, the HOLAP system can combine data from the ROLAP managed data and the MOLAP managed data.

Despite the appeal of HOLAP, it has potential disadvantages that may limit its use. First, HOLAP can be more complex than either ROLAP or MOLAP, especially if a DBMS vendor does not provide full HOLAP support. To fully support HOLAP, a DBMS vendor must provide both MOLAP and ROLAP engines as well as tools to combine both storage engines in the design and operation of a data warehouse. Second, there is considerable overlap in functionality between the storage and optimization techniques in ROLAP and MOLAP engines. It is not clear whether the ROLAP storage and optimization techniques should be discarded or used in addition to the MOLAP techniques. Third, because the difference in response time has narrowed between ROLAP and MOLAP, the combination of MOLAP and ROLAP may not provide significant performance improvement to justify the added complexity.

16.4 POPULATING A DATA WAREHOUSE

Although data warehouses largely contain replicated data, populating a data warehouse is much more difficult than simply copying from data sources. Populating a data warehouse is a process of matching decision support needs to the realities of available data. To fulfill decision support needs, data warehouses use data from many internal and external sources. Reconciling the differences among data sources is a significant challenge especially considering that source systems typically cannot be changed. As its data sources change, a data warehouse should be refreshed in a timely manner to support decision making. Because data sources change at different rates, the determination of the time and content to refresh can be a significant challenge. Because of these challenges, populating a data warehouse is perhaps the most significant activity in the development of a data warehouse.

This section presents several important aspects of populating a data warehouse. The first part describes the kinds of data sources available for populating a data warehouse. The second part describes the workflow for maintaining a data warehouse. The final part discusses the problem of determining the frequency of refreshment and the content to refresh.

16.4.1 Sources of Data

Accessing source data presents challenges in dealing with a variety of formats and constraints on source systems. External source systems usually cannot be changed. Internal source systems may or may not be changeable to accommodate the requirements of a data warehouse. Even if a source system can be changed, budget constraints may allow only minor changes. Source data may be stored in legacy format or modern format. Legacy format generally precludes retrieval using nonprocedural languages such as SQL. Modern format means that the source data can be accessed as a relational database or as Web pages. Unless stored with formal meta data, Web pages can be difficult to parse and will be nonstandard across websites.

Change data from source systems provide the basis to update a data warehouse. Change data comprise new source data (insertions) and modifications to existing source data (updates and deletions). Further, change data can affect fact tables and/or dimension tables. The most common change data involve insertions of new facts. Insertions of new dimensions and modifications of dimensions are less common but are still important to capture.

Depending on the characteristics of the source system, change data can be described as cooperative, logged, queryable, or snapshot. <u>Cooperative change data</u> involve notification from the source system about changes. The notification typically occurs at transaction completion time using a trigger. Cooperative change data can be input immediately into a data warehouse or placed in a queue for later input possibly with other changes. Because cooperative change data involve modifications to both a source system and the data warehouse, it is the least common format for change data.

<u>Logged change data</u> involve file that record changes or other user activity. For example, a transaction log contains every change made by a transaction, and a Web log contains page access histories (called clickstreams) by website visitors. Logged change data usually involve no changes to a source system as logs are readily available for most source systems. However, logs can contain large amounts of irrelevant data. In addition, derivation of the relevant data needed for the data warehouse can require matching related log records, a resource-intensive task. Logged change data are used most commonly for the customer relation subset of a data warehouse.

As its name implies, <u>queryable change data</u> come directly from a data source via a query. Queryable change data require timestamping in the data source. Since few data sources contain timestamps for all data, queryable change data usually are augmented with other kinds of change data. Queryable change data are most applicable for fact tables using fields such as order date, shipment date, and hire date that are stored in operational data sources.

<u>Snapshot change data</u> involve periodic dumps of source data. To derive change data, a difference operation uses the two most recent snapshots. The result of a difference operation is called a delta. Snapshots are the most common form of change data because of applicability. Snapshots are the only form of change data without requirements on a source system. Because computing a snapshot can be resource intensive, there may be constraints about the time and frequency of retrieving a snapshot.

16.4.2 Workflow for Maintaining a Data Warehouse

Maintaining a data warehouse involves a variety of tasks that manipulate change data from source systems. Figure 16.12 presents a generic workflow that organizes the tasks. The preparation phase manipulates change data from individual source systems. Extraction involves the retrieval of data from an individual source system. Transportation involves movement of the extracted data to a staging area. Cleaning involves a variety of tasks to standardize and improve the quality of the extracted data. Auditing involves recording results of the cleaning process, performing completeness and reasonableness checks, and handling exceptions.

The integration phase involves merging the separate, cleaned sources into one source. Merging can involve the removal of inconsistencies among the source data. Auditing involves recording results of the merging process, performing completeness and reasonableness checks, and handling exceptions.

The update phase involves propagating the integrated change data to various parts of the data warehouse including fact and dimension tables, materialized views, stored data cubes, and data marts. After propagation, notification can be sent to user groups and administrators.

The preparation and integration phases should resolve data quality problems as summarized in Table 16.8. Data from legacy systems are typically dirty, meaning that they may not conform to each other or to organizationwide data quality standards. If

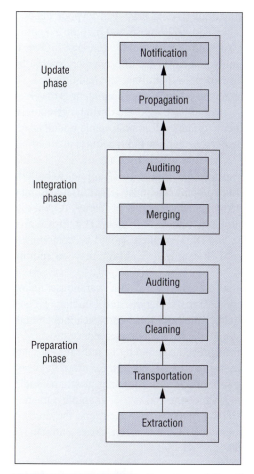

| **Figure 16.12** | Generic workflow for data warehouse maintenance. |

| **TABLE 16.8** | **Typical Data Quality Problems** |

Multiple identifiers: some data sources may use different primary keys for the same entity such as different customer numbers

Multiple names: the same field may be represented using different field names

Different units: measures and dimensions may have different units and granularities

Missing values: data may not exist in some databases; to compensate for missing values, different default values may be used across data sources

Orphaned transactions: some transactions may be missing important parts such as an order without a customer

Multipurpose fields: some databases may combine data into one field such as different components of an address

Conflicting data: some data sources may have conflicting data such as different customer addresses

Different update times: some data sources may perform updates at different intervals directly implemented, dirty data may lead to poor decision making. To resolve data quality problems, the auditing task should include exception handling. Exceptions can be noted in a log file and then manually addressed. Over time, exceptions should decrease as data quality standards are improved on internal data sources.

In addition to exception handling, the auditing task should include completeness checks and reasonableness checks. A completeness check counts the number of reporting units to ensure that all have reported during a given period. A reasonableness check determines whether key facts fall in reasonable bounds and are a reasonable extrapolation of previous history. Exceptions may require reconciliation by business analysts before propagation to the data warehouse.

The generic workflow in Figure 16.12 applies to both the initial loading and the periodic refreshment of a data warehouse. The initial loading often requires a long period of data cleaning to resolve data quality problems. A goal of initial loading is to discover the data quality problems and resolve them. The refresh process typically varies among data sources. The workflow process should be customized to fit the requirements of each data source. For example, auditing may be minimized for high-quality data sources.

To support the complexity of data warehouse maintenance, software products known as Extraction, Transformation, and Loading (ETL) tools have been developed. These tools, available from both third-party vendors and DBMS vendors, eliminate the need to write custom code for many maintenance tasks. Most ETL tools use rule specifications rather than procedural coding to indicate logic and actions. Some ETL tools can generate code that can be customized for more flexibility. In addition to ETL tools, some DBMS vendors provide data loading programs and proprietary SQL extensions that support some maintenance tasks. For example, Oracle 9i supports the SQL Loader program as well as the MERGE statement and the multiple-table INSERT statement. ETL tools and proprietary SQL extensions are essential to reduce the effort to implement the workflow tasks.

16.4.3 Optimizing the Refresh Process

Refreshing a data warehouse is a complex process that involves the management of time differences between the updating of data sources and the updating of the related data warehouse objects (tables, materialized views, data cubes, data marts). In Figure 16.13, valid time lag is the difference between the occurrence of an event in the real world (valid time) and the storage of the event in an operational database (transaction time). Load time lag is the difference between transaction time and the storage of the event in a data warehouse (load time). For internal data sources, there may be some control over valid time lag. For external data sources, there is usually no control over valid time lag. Thus, a data warehouse administrator has most control over load time lag.

Figure 16.13 implies that data sources can change independently leading to different change rates for fact tables and dimension tables. Fact tables generally record completed events such as orders, shipments, and purchases with links to related dimensions. For example, inserting a row in the *Sales* table requires foreign keys that reference the *Customer, Store, Time,* and *Item* tables. However, updates and insertions to the related dimension tables may occur at different times than the fact events. For example, a customer may move or an item may change in price at different times than orders, shipments, or inventory purchases. As a result of the different change rates, a data warehouse administrator should manage the load time lag separately for dimension tables and fact tables.

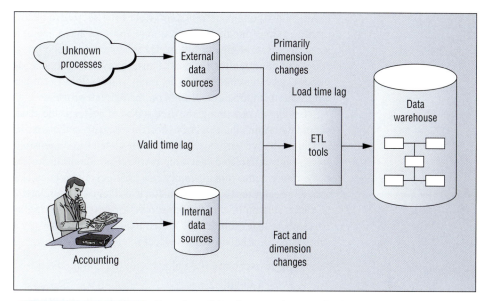

Figure 16.13   Overview of the data warehouse refresh process.

The primary objective in managing the refresh process is to determine the refresh frequency for each data source. The optimal refresh frequency maximizes the net refresh benefit defined as the value of data timeliness minus the cost of refresh. The value of data timeliness depends on the sensitivity of decision making to the currency of the data. Some decisions are very time sensitive such as inventory decisions. Organizations along a supply chain attempt to minimize inventory carrying costs by stocking goods as close as possible to the time needed. Other decisions are not so time sensitive. For example, the decision to close a poor performing store would typically be done using data over a long period of time.

Fisher and Berndt (2001) have proposed a method to measure the value of data timeliness. They defined a measure of the error rate of a data warehouse with respect to a given workload of queries. To determine the error rate, the data volatility of queries and dimensions is estimated. Even if a data warehouse stores individual level data, most queries will involve aggregations, not retrieval of the individual level data. For example, most queries on the store sales schema would involve the item brand or category, not the individual items. Given an assessment of the error rate, the value of data timeliness can be assessed using the frequency or other weighting for data warehouse queries.

The cost to refresh a data warehouse includes both computer and human resources. Computer resources are necessary for all tasks in the maintenance workflow. Human resources may be necessary in the auditing tasks during the preparation and integration phases. The level of data quality in source data also affects the level of human resources required. The development effort to use ETL tools and write custom software is not part of the refresh cost unless there is ongoing development cost with each refresh. An important distinction involves the fixed cost and the variable cost of refreshment. Large fixed cost encourages less frequent refresh because the fixed cost occurs with each refresh. Fixed cost may include startup and shutdown effort as well as resource rental.

Along with balancing the value of timeliness against the cost of refresh, the data warehouse administrator should consider constraints on the refresh process. To support online updates, both the source system and the data warehouse must cooperate. However, constraints on either the data warehouse (online updating impacts query performance) or a source system (not cost effective to change the source system) may restrict online updating. Source systems may have accessibility constraints that restrict access to nonpeak hours. Data warehouse users may demand refreshes in response to unanticipated events. Thus, the data warehouse administrator should determine a refresh schedule for all data sources that optimizes the net refresh benefit while satisfying the constraints on the refresh process.

Besides determining the frequency of refresh, the data warehouse administrator should determine the level of historical integrity in the data warehouse. The level of historical integrity is primarily an issue for updates to dimension tables. When a dimension row is updated, related fact table rows are no longer historically accurate. For example, if the city column of a customer row changes, the related sales rows are no longer historically accurate. To preserve historical integrity, the related sales rows should point to an older version of the customer row. Without underlying support for historical databases, there is no simple way to maintain historical integrity. Kimball (April 1996) presents three alternatives for historical integrity:

- **Type I:** overwrite old values with the changed data. This method provides no historical integrity.
- **Type II:** use version numbers to augment the primary key of dimension tables. For each change to a dimension row, insert a row in the dimension table with a larger version number. For example, to handle the change to the city column, there is a new row in the *Customer* table with the same customer number but a larger version number than the previous row.
- **Type III:** use columns to maintain a fixed history. For example, to maintain a history of the current city and the two previous city changes, three city columns can be stored in the *Customer* table along with associated date columns to record the date changed.

CLOSING THOUGHTS

This chapter provided an introduction to the concepts and practice of data warehousing. The chapter began by examining conceptual differences between relational databases, traditionally used for transaction processing, and multidimensional databases, suggested for the new generation of decision support applications. The unique characteristics of decision support data were outlined, followed by a discussion of data warehouse architectures, data marts, and data mining.

Data warehouses can be implemented using the multidimensional data model, the relational model, or a combination of both models. For the multidimensional data model, the chapter presented the terminology associated with data cubes and the operators to manipulate data cubes. For the relational data model, the chapter presented data modeling techniques (the star schema and its variations), SQL extensions in the GROUP BY clause for querying dimensional data, materialized views, and storage technologies. The storage technologies support data warehouses using both relational and data cube storage engines.

Irrespective of the data model and storage architecture, populating a data warehouse is a difficult process that must be carefully managed. The chapter presented the kinds of data sources used in populating a data warehouse, a generic workflow describing the tasks involved in maintaining a data warehouse, and design issues to consider in the refresh process. The chapter advocated the usage of ETL tools to reduce the amount of custom code to implement procedures that populate a data warehouse.

REVIEW CONCEPTS

- Data needs for transaction processing versus decision support applications.
- Characteristics of a data warehouse: subject-oriented, integrated, time-variant, and nonvolatile.
- Architectures for deploying a data warehouse: two-tier, three-tier, bottom-up.
- Multidimensional data cube: dimensions, measures, hierarchies, time-series data type.
- Multidimensional operators: slice, dice, drill-down, roll-up, pivot.
- Star schema: fact table and related dimension tables.
- Variations of the star schema: snowflake schema (multiple dimension levels) and constellation schema (multiple fact tables).
- Extensions of the GROUP BY clause for subtotal calculation: CUBE, ROLLUP, and GROUPING SETS operators.
- Materialized views and query rewriting for storage and manipulation of summary data.
- Multidimensional storage architectures: ROLAP, MOLAP, and HOLAP.
- Kinds of change data used to populate a data warehouse: cooperative, logged, queryable, and snapshot.
- Phases in the workflow for maintaining a data warehouse: preparation, integration, and propagation.
- Importance of ETL (extraction, transformation, loading) to reduce the coding in procedures to populate a data warehouse.
- Determining the refresh frequency for a data warehouse: balancing the frequency of refresh against the cost of refresh.
- Maintaining historical integrity between fact and dimension tables.

QUESTIONS

1. Why are operational databases not particularly suited for decision support applications?

2. How is a data warehouse different from a data mart?

3. When is the three-tier data warehouse architecture more appropriate than the two-tier data warehouse architecture?

4. What are the components of an enterprise data model?

5. What are some causes for failures in data warehouse projects?

6. Does a bottom-up data warehouse architecture use an enterprise data model?

7. What is an oper mart?

8. What are the advantages of multidimensional representation over relational representation for data used for decision support?

9. Explain why a dimension may have multiple hierarchies.

10. What are the advantages of using time-series data in a cell instead of time as a dimension?

11. How is slicing a data cube different from dicing?

12. What are the differences between drilling down a data cube and slicing or dicing it?

13. How is a pivot operation useful for multidimensional databases?

14. Explain the significance of sparsity in a data cube.

15. What is a star schema?

16. What are the differences between fact tables and dimension tables?

17. How does a snowflake schema differ from a star schema?

18. What is a constellation schema?

19. What is the purpose of the Oracle CREATE DIMENSION statement?

20. What is the purpose of the SQL CUBE operator?

21. What is the purpose of the SQL ROLLUP operator?

22. What is the purpose of the SQL GROUPING SETS operator?

23. Briefly list some of the variations of the CUBE, ROLLUP, and GROUPING SETS operators.

24. Why are materialized views important for data warehouses but not important for operational databases?

25. What materialization properties does Oracle 9i provide for materialized views?

26. Compare and contrast query rewriting for materialized views to query modification for traditional (nonmaterialized) views.

27. Explain the significance of indexing fact and dimension tables in a data warehouse.

28. What are the pros and cons of a MOLAP storage engine?

29. What are the pros and cons of a ROLAP storage engine?

30. What are the pros and cons of a HOLAP storage engine?

31. List some storage and optimization techniques in ROLAP engines.

32. What are cooperative change data?

33. What are logged change data?

34. What are queryable change data?

35. What are snapshot change data?

36. Briefly describe the phases of data warehouse maintenance.

37. List common data quality problems that should be resolved by the preparation and integration phases.

38. What is the benefit of using ETL tools in data warehouse maintenance?

39. What is valid time lag?

40. What is load time lag?

41. What is the primary objective in managing the refresh process for a data warehouse?

42. What are three alternatives for preserving historical integrity in a data warehouse?

PROBLEMS

Part 1: Automobile Insurance Problems

Part 1 provides practice with data cube definition and operations as well as star schemas. The questions in Part 1 involve the database that follows used by an automobile insurance provider to support policy transactions (create and maintain customer policies) and claims transactions (claims made by other parties). The policy transactions utilize the tables *Item, Agent, InsuredParty, Policy, InsuredAuto,* and *PolicyItem,* while the claims transactions use the tables *InsuredParty, Claimant, ThirdParty, Policy, InsuredAuto,* and *Claim.* The nine tables in this database are shown, along with the primary keys (shown in bold font) and the foreign keys (shown in italics). For each table, assume the field formats of your own choice.

Table: Item

ItemNo	ItemDesc	ItemMinCoverage	ItemMaxCoverage

Primary key: ItemNo
Foreign keys: None

Table: Agent

AgentNo	AgentName	AgentPhone	AgentDept	AgentType	AgentRegion

Primary key: AgentNo
Foreign keys: None

Table: InsuredParty

IPSSN	IPDrivLicNo	IPState	IPName	IPPhone	IPAddr	IPDOB	IPCity	IPZip	IPRiskCat

Primary key: IPSSN
Foreign keys: none
IPDOB is the insured party's date of birth

Table: Claimant

ClmtNo	ClmtName	ClmtPhone	ClmtInsComp	ClmtPolNo	ClmtAddr	ClmtCity	ClmtState	ClmtZip

Primary key: ClmtNo
Foreign keys: None

Table: ThirdParty

TPSSN	TPName	TPPhone	TPDesc	TPAddr	TPCity	TPState	TPZip

Primary key: TPSSN
Foreign keys: None

Table: Policy

PolNo	PolBegDate	PolEndDate	*IPSSN*	*AgentNo*	PolPremium	PolEffDate

Primary key: PolNo
Foreign keys: IPSSN, AgentNo

Table: InsuredAuto

IAVIN	IALicPlateNo	IAState	IAMake	IAModel	IAYear	IAAirBags	*IADriverSSN*	*PolNo*

Primary key: IPVIN
Foreign keys: IADriverSSN (refers to InsuredParty), PolNo

Table: PolicyItem

IAVIN	*ItemNo*	PICoverage	PIPremium	PIComments

Primary key: IAVIN, ItemNo
Foreign keys: IAVIN, ItemNo

Table: Claim

ClaimNo	ClaimAmount	ClaimEstimate	ClaimDesc	ClaimDate	*IAVIN*	*ClmtNo*	*TPSSN*

Primary key: ClaimNo
Foreign keys: IAVIN, ClmtNo, TPSSN

1. Identify dimensions and measures in a data cube for automobile policy analysis.

2. Draw a star or snowflake schema to support the dimensions and measures in the data cube from problem 1. You may want to use denormalization to reduce the number of dimension tables and the relationships among dimension tables.

3. Identify dimensions and measures in a data cube for claims analysis.

4. Draw a star or snowflake schema to support the dimensions and measures in the data cube from problem 3. You may want to use denormalization to reduce the number of dimension tables and the relationships among dimension tables.

5. In the policy schema, how can the data be divided between a production database and a data warehouse? What should be the finest-level grain in a data cube?

6. Identify hierarchies in the dimensions in the data cube for the policy transaction.

7. In the claims schema, how can the data be divided between a production database and a data warehouse? What should be the finest-level grain in a data cube?

8. Identify hierarchies in the dimensions in the data cube for the claims analysis.

9. Describe the data cube resulting from the operation to slice the policy data cube by a certain agent.

10. Describe the data cube resulting from the operation to dice the data cube result of the slice operation in problem 9 by insured parties having zip codes in a specified state.

11. Begin with a data cube with four dimensions (*InsuredParty*, *InsuredAuto*, *Item*, and *Agent*) and one measure (policy amount) in the cells. From this data cube, describe the operation to generate a new data cube with three dimensions (*InsuredParty*, *Item*, and *Agent*) and one measure (average auto policy amount).

12. Identify dimension levels and hierarchies within the *Agent* table. You do not need to use the Oracle CREATE DIMENSION statement.

13. Identify dimension levels and hierarchies within the *InsuredParty* table. You do not need to use the Oracle CREATE DIMENSION statement.

14. Identify dimension levels and hierarchies within the *InsuredAuto* table. You do not need to use the Oracle CREATE DIMENSION statement.

15. Is it necessary to have a time dimension table for the automobile insurance data warehouse? Please justify your answer and explain how time is represented if not in a separate dimension table.

Part 2: Store Sales Problems

Part 2 provides practice with relational database manipulation of multidimensional data. The questions in Part 2 involve the store sales snowflake schema used in Section 16.3. For your reference, Figure 16.P1 displays the ERD for the store sales snowflake schema. To support the usage of Oracle 9i with these problems, the student section of the textbook's website contains Oracle CREATE TABLE statements and sample data for the tables of the store sales schema.

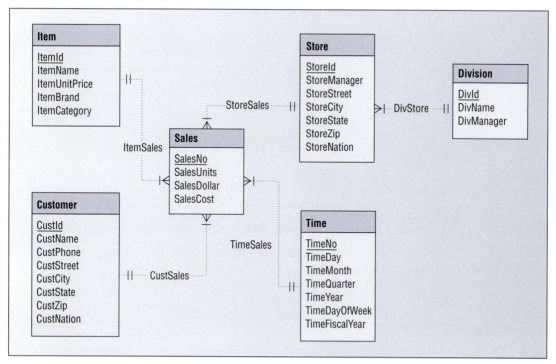

Figure 16.P1   ERD snowflake schema for the store sales example.

1. Write a SELECT statement to summarize sales by store state, year, and item brand. The result should compute the SUM of the dollar sales for the years 2002 and 2003. The result should include full totals for every combination of grouped fields.

2. Write a SELECT statement to summarize sales by year, quarter, and month. The result should compute the SUM of the dollar sales for the years 2002 and 2003. The result should include partial totals in order of the grouped fields (year, quarter, and month).

3. Write a SELECT statement to summarize sales by store state, month, and year. The result should compute the SUM of the dollar sales for the years 2002 and 2003. The result should include partial totals in order of the grouped fields (year and month). Do not use the GROUPING SETS operator in your SQL statement.

4. Rewrite the SQL statement solution for problem 1 without using the CUBE, ROLLUP, or GROUPING SETS operators. To reduce your time, you can write the first few query blocks and then indicate the pattern to rewrite the remaining query blocks. In rewriting the queries, you may use two single quotes (with nothing inside) as the default text value and 0 as the default numeric value.

5. Rewrite the SQL statement solution for problem 2 without using the CUBE, ROLLUP, or GROUPING SETS operators. In rewriting the queries, you may use two single quotes (with nothing inside) as the default text value and 0 as the default numeric value.

6. Rewrite the SQL statement solution for problem 3 without using the CUBE, ROLLUP, or GROUPING SETS operators. In rewriting the queries, you can use two single quotes (with nothing inside) as the default text value and 0 as the default numeric value.

7. Rewrite the SQL statement solution for problem 3 using the GROUPING SETS operator instead of the ROLLUP operator.

8. Write an Oracle CREATE DIMENSION statement for a customer dimension consisting of the customer identifier, the city, the state, the zip, and the country. Define two hierarchies grouping the customer identifier with the city, the state, and the nation and the customer identifier with the zip, the state, and the nation.

9. Write an Oracle CREATE DIMENSION statement for a time dimension consisting of the time identifier, the day, the month, the quarter, the year, the fiscal year, and the day of the week. Define three hierarchies grouping the time identifier, the day, the month, the quarter, and the year, the time identifier and the fiscal year, and the time identifier and the day of the week.

10. Write an Oracle CREATE MATERIALIZED VIEW statement to support the store sales schema. The materialized view should include the sum of the dollar sales and the sum of the cost of sales. The materialized view should summarize the measures by the store identifier, the item identifier, and the time number. The materialized view should include sales in the year 2002.

11. Write an Oracle CREATE MATERIALIZED VIEW statement to support the store sales schema. The materialized view should include the sum of the dollar sales and the sum of the cost of sales. The materialized view should summarize the measures by the store identifier, the item identifier, and the time number. The materialized view should include sales in the year 2003.

12. Rewrite the SQL statement solution for problem 1 using the materialized views in problems 10 and 11. You should ignore the CUBE operator in the solution for problem 1. Your SELECT statement should reference the materialized views as well as base tables if needed.

13. Rewrite the SQL statement solution for problem 1 using the materialized views in problems 10 and 11. Your SELECT statement should reference the materialized views as well as base tables if needed. You should think carefully about how to handle the CUBE operator in your rewritten query.

14. Rewrite the SQL statement solution for problem 3 using the materialized views in problems 10 and 11. You should ignore the ROLLUP operator in the solution for problem 3. Your SELECT statement should reference the materialized views as well as base tables if needed.

15. Rewrite the SQL statement solution for problem 3 using the materialized views in problems 10 and 11. Your SELECT statement should reference the materialized views as well as base tables if needed. You should think carefully about how to handle the ROLLUP operator in your rewritten query.

REFERENCES FOR FURTHER STUDY

Although this chapter provided a detailed introduction about data warehouses, you may want to augment this chapter with specialized material due to the importance and the scope of the subject. Devlin (1997); Kimball (2002); and Inmon (1996), the father of data warehousing, have written widely read books on data warehouses. To elaborate on specific details in the chapter, you should consult Bouzeghoub et al. (1999) and Fisher and Berndt (2001) about the refresh process and Imhoff (2001) about oper marts. For details about Oracle 9i data warehousing features, you should consult the online documentation in the Oracle Technology Network Site (http://otn.oracle.com). The *Communications of the ACM* devoted an entire issue (September 1998) to data warehousing. See the bibliography entries for Bontempo and Zagelow; Claudio, Sigal, Gardner, Sutter, and Scott; and Watson and Haley. The *Journal of Data Warehousing* from the Data Warehousing Institute (http://www.dw-institute.com) and the *DM Review* (http://www.dmreview.com) provide timely articles on data warehousing trends, vendors, and issues. You also can find additional information in websites under the topics "Data Warehouses" and "Data Mining" in the Web Resources section of the textbook's website.

Client–Server Processing and Distributed Databases

LEARNING OBJECTIVES

This chapter describes how database management systems utilize computer networks and remote computers to support client–server processing and distributed databases. After this chapter, the student should have acquired the following knowledge and skills:

■ List reasons for distributed processing and distributed data.

■ Describe two-tier, three-tier, and multiple-tier client–server database architectures.

■ Compare and contrast approaches for Web database connectivity.

■ Describe differences between technology for tightly integrated and loosely integrated distributed databases.

■ Compare the different kinds of distributed database transparency.

■ Understand the nature of query processing and transaction processing for distributed databases.

OVERVIEW

Chapters 15 and 16 described database processing for transactions and decision support. As both chapters explained, transaction and decision support processing are vital to modern organizations. In this chapter, you will learn how computer networks, remote computers, and remote data storage can improve reliability and performance for both kinds of processing.

This chapter explains how DBMSs utilize computer networks, remote computers, and remote data storage. Before understanding the details, you should understand the motivation for utilizing these resources. This chapter discusses the pros and cons of both distributed processing and distributed data. After grasping the motivation, you are ready to learn how DBMSs allow work to be distributed among computers in a client–server manner. This chapter describes client–server architectures and the use of the architectures for Web database connectivity. Distributing data in addition to distributing processing allows more flexibility but also involves more complexity. To depict the trade-off between flexibility and complexity, this chapter explains distributed database architectures, levels of transparency for distributed data, and distributed database processing for queries and transactions.

17.1 OVERVIEW OF DISTRIBUTED PROCESSING AND DISTRIBUTED DATA

To understand the issues, it is easier to separate distributed processing from distributed data. Both areas have distinct architectures, design problems, and processing technologies. After learning them separately, you can understand how to combine them. This section begins your study by discussing the historical development and motivations behind distributed processing and data.

17.1.1 Evolution of Distributed Processing and Distributed Data

The technologies available for distributed processing and data have evolved from previous technologies. Even in the early days of computing, there was widespread recognition of the need to share resources across a network. <u>Timesharing</u> was a popular way to share resources in the 1970s. In a timesharing network, computer terminals are connected to a mainframe computer (see Figure 17.1). Computing time is shared among users typing on character-based terminals. Timesharing networks support only small amounts of data transmitted between a mainframe computer and terminals. Thus, graphical interfaces were not feasible given the data transmission limitations and the limited intelligence of the terminals.

The advent of personal computers and local area networks spurred changes in distributed processing in the 1980s. Local area networks support high-speed data transfer while personal computers support rich graphical interfaces. Thus, larger amounts of data can be transmitted and computer graphics can be supported by a personal computer, not a mainframe computer. File sharing and remote procedure calls augmented timesharing. In <u>file sharing</u> [Figure 17.2(a)], a personal computer requests a file from another computer on a network. In a <u>remote procedure call</u> [Figure 17.2(b)], a personal computer invokes a stored procedure on another computer in a network. File sharing and remote procedure calls are simple ways to share processing and data in a network.

Because of limitations with file sharing and remote procedure calls, distributed processing and distributed data evolved again in the 1990s. Recall that Chapter 1 (Section 1.4.2) introduced the idea of the client–server approach for utilizing computer

Figure 17.1   Timesharing network.

Figure 17.2   Resource sharing with a network of personal computers.

networks, remote computers, and remote data. A <u>client</u> is a program that makes requests to a server. The <u>server</u> performs the request and communicates the result to the client.

The client–server approach supports the use of remote computing resources. In Figure 17.3(a), different computers contain the client and the server software. In this arrangement, processing power is spread among various computers that are connected by a network. In Figure 17.3(b), both the processing resources and the data resources are dispersed across multiple locations or sites. The processing capabilities of a server computer can range from a workstation to a powerful mainframe. The client–server approach

(a) Distributed processing only

Client

Client

Client

Server

Database

(b) Distributed processing and data

Server

Server

Client

Client

Client

Client

Database

Database

| **Figure 17.3** | Using the client–server approach with distributed processing and data. |

provides the flexibility to use the capacity that matches the task. The client and the server software can even be deployed on the same computer if the task requirements do not require separate computers.

Distributed DBMSs and the client–server approach provide more flexibility than file sharing and remote procedure calls. For sharing data, <u>distributed DBMSs</u> allow subsets of a table to be distributed among computers in a network. Users submit queries instead of requests for entire files. As you will see in the second half of this chapter, the distributed DBMS assumes the burden of locating and assembling data when requested. For sharing processing, the client–server approach can distribute work among any number of computers in a network. When requesting work, a client can submit a request and continue (asynchronous) instead of waiting for the remote procedure to finish (synchronous). In addition, the client–server approach supports more intelligence in a message than in a procedure call.

17.1.2 Motivation for Distributed Processing

Distributed processing with the client–server approach offers a number of advantages related to flexibility, scalability, and interoperability. <u>Flexibility</u> refers to the ease of maintaining and adapting a system. Maintenance costs often dominate the cost of initially developing an information system because of long life and system revisions. The client–server approach promotes flexibility because volatile sections of code can be isolated from more stable sections. For example, user interface code can be separated from the business rules and the data access code. If a new interface is deployed, other parts of the code remain unchanged. In addition, the client–server approach is ideally suited for object-oriented programming to support reusability. Chapter 18 describes object-oriented databases and programming.

The client–server approach supports scalable growth of hardware and software capacity. Scalability refers to the ability to add and remove capacity in small units. Vertical scalability refers to the ability to add capacity on the server side. For example, work from an overloaded server may be moved to a new server to alleviate a bottleneck or handle new demand from additional workstations. The new server can have just the level of additional computing capacity necessary. Horizontal scalability refers to the ability to add capacity on the client side through additional workstations and movement of work between clients and servers. For example, work can be moved from clients to a server to allow the use of inexpensive client hardware (thin clients). Work also can move in the opposite direction (from server to client) to alleviate server processing loads and take advantage of client computing capabilities.

Scalable growth also can lead to improved performance. For example, adding middleware can reduce contention problems caused by many users accessing a database. The next section describes middleware that can efficiently manage many simultaneous users accessing a database. In addition, specialized servers can be employed to handle work that would otherwise slow all users. For example, multimedia servers can handle requests for images, thus freeing other servers from this time-consuming task.

Client–server systems based on open standards support interoperability. Interoperability refers to the ability of two or more systems to exchange and use software and data. Open standards promote a marketplace of suppliers, leading to lower costs and higher quality. Software components in the marketplace are interoperable if they conform to the standards. The most heavily standardized area is the Internet, where client–server databases are becoming increasingly important, as discussed in Section 17.3.

Despite the advantages of distributed processing, some significant pitfalls may occur. Developing client–server software may be more complex because of architectural choices. A client–server architecture specifies an arrangement of components and a division of processing among the components. Section 17.2 presents several possible architectures for client–server database processing. The choice of an inappropriate architecture can lead to poor performance and maintenance problems. In addition to architectural issues, the designer may face a difficult decision about building a client–server database on proprietary methods versus open standards. Proprietary methods allow easier resolution of problems because one vendor is responsible for all problems. Proprietary methods also may have better performance because they are not as general as open standards. In the long run, proprietary methods can be expensive and inflexible, however. If a vendor does not grow with the industry, a client–server database may become outdated and expensive to upgrade.

17.1.3 Motivation for Distributed Data

Distributed data offer a number of advantages related to data control, communication costs, and performance. Distributing a database allows the location of data to match an organization's structure. For example, parts of a customer table can be located close to customer processing centers. Decisions about sharing and maintaining data

TABLE 17.1	Summary of Distributed Processing and Data	
	Distributed Processing	*Distributed Data*
Advantages	Flexibility, interoperability, scalability	Local control of data, improved performance, reduced communication costs, increased reliability
Disadvantages	High complexity, high development cost, possible interoperability problems	High complexity, additional security concerns

can be set locally to provide control closer to the data usage. Often, local employees and management understand issues related to data better than management at remote locations.

Distributed data can lead to lower communication costs and improved performance. Data should be located so that 80 percent of the requests are local. Local requests incur little or no communication costs and delays compared to remote requests. Increased data availability also can lead to improved performance. Data are more available because there is no single computer responsible for controlling access. In addition, data can be replicated so that they are available at more than one site.

Despite the advantages of distributed data, some significant pitfalls may occur. Distributed database design issues are very difficult. A poor design can lead to higher communication costs and poor performance. Distributed database design is difficult because of the lack of tools, the number of choices, and the relationships among choices. Distributed transaction processing can add considerable overhead, especially for replicated data. Distributed data involve more security concerns because many sites can manage data. Each site must be properly protected from unauthorized access.

17.1.4 Summary of Advantages and Disadvantages

Before moving forward, you should take a moment to compare distributed processing and distributed data. Table 17.1 summarizes the advantages and the disadvantages of distributed processing and distributed data as separate technologies. To gain maximum leverage, the technologies can be combined. At this time, distributed processing with the client–server approach is the more mature and widely deployed technology. As distributed database technology matures and gains acceptance, organizations will deploy both technologies.

17.2 CLIENT–SERVER DATABASE ARCHITECTURES

Client–Server Architecture an arrangement of components (clients and servers) among computers connected by a network. A client–server architecture supports efficient processing of messages (requests for service) between clients and servers.

The design of a client–server database affects the advantages and the disadvantages cited in the previous section. A good design tends to magnify advantages and reduce disadvantages relative to an organization's requirements. A poor design may exacerbate disadvantages and diminish advantages. Proper design of a client–server database may make the difference between success and failure of an information system project. To help you achieve good designs, this section discusses design issues of client–server databases and describes how these issues are addressed in various architectures.

17.2.1 Design Issues

Two design issues, division of processing and process management, affect the design of a client–server database. Division of processing refers to the allocation of tasks to clients and servers. Process management involves interoperability among clients and servers and efficient processing of messages between clients and servers. Software for process management is known as middleware because of its mediating role. This section describes these issues so that you will understand how various architectures address them in the next section.

Division of Processing

In a typical client–server database, there are a number of tasks that can be performed locally on a client or remotely on a server. The following list briefly describes these tasks:

- **Presentation:** code to maintain the graphical user interface. The presentation code displays objects, monitors events, and responds to events. Events include user-initiated actions with the mouse and the keyboard as well as external events initiated by timers and other users.
- **Validation:** code to ensure the consistency of the database and user inputs. Validation logic often is expressed as integrity rules that are stored in a database.
- **Business logic:** code to perform business functions such as payroll calculations, eligibility requirements, and interest calculations. Business logic may change as the regulatory and the competitive environments change.
- **Workflow:** code to ensure completion of business processes. Workflow code may route forms, send messages about a deadline, and notify users when a business process is completed.
- **Data access:** code to extract data to answer queries and modify a database. Data access code consists of SQL statements and translation code that is usually part of the DBMS. If multiple databases are involved, some translation code may reside in software separate from a DBMS.

Parts of these tasks can be divided between clients and servers. For example, some validation can be performed on a PC client and some can be performed on a database server. Thus, there is a lot of flexibility about how processing tasks can be divided. Section 17.2.2 describes several popular ways to divide processing tasks.

Middleware

Interoperability is an important function of <u>middleware</u>. Clients and servers can exist on platforms with different hardware, operating systems, DBMSs, and programming languages. Figure 17.4 depicts middleware allowing clients and servers to communicate without regard to the underlying platforms of the clients and the servers. The middleware enables a client and a server to communicate without knowledge of each other's platform.

Efficient message control is another important function of middleware. In a typical client–server environment, there are many clients communicating with a few servers. A server can become overloaded just managing the messages that it receives rather than

Middleware a software component in a client–server architecture that performs process management. Middleware allows servers to efficiently process messages from a large number of clients. In addition, middleware can allow clients and servers to communicate across heterogeneous platforms. To handle large processing loads, middleware often is located on a dedicated computer.

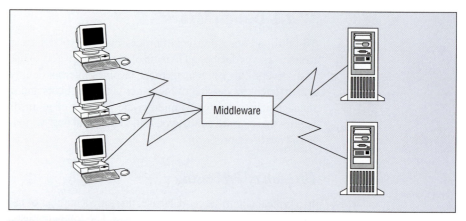

| **Figure 17.4** | **Client–server computing with middleware.** |

completing the requests. Middleware frees servers to concentrate on completing requests rather than managing requests. Middleware can perform queuing, scheduling, and routing of messages allowing clients and servers to perform work at different speeds and times.

Based on the functions of interoperability and message control, several kinds of middleware are commercially available, as described in the following list:

- **Transaction-processing monitors** are the oldest kind of middleware. Traditionally, transaction-processing monitors relieve the operating system of managing database processes. A transaction-processing monitor can switch control among processes much faster than an operating system. In this role, a transaction processing monitor receives transactions, schedules them, and manages them to completion. Recently, transaction-processing monitors have taken additional tasks such as updating multiple databases in a single transaction.

- **Message-oriented middleware** maintains a queue of messages. A client process can place a message on a queue and a server process can remove a message from a queue. Message-oriented middleware differs from transaction processing monitors primarily in the intelligence of the messages. Transaction-processing monitors provide built-in intelligence but use simple messages. In contrast, message-oriented middleware provides much less built-in intelligence but supports more complex messages.

- **Object-request brokers** provide a high level of interoperability and message intelligence. To use an object-request broker, messages must be encoded in a standard interface description language. An object-request broker resolves platform differences between a client and a server. In addition, a client can communicate with a server without knowing the location of the server.

- **Data access middleware** provides a uniform interface to relational and nonrelational data using SQL. Requests to access data from a DBMS are sent to a data access driver rather than directly to the DBMS. The data access driver converts the SQL statement into the SQL supported by the DBMS and then routes the request to the DBMS. The data access driver adds another layer of overhead between an application and a DBMS. However, the data access driver supports independence between an application and the

| **Figure 17.5** | **Two-tier architecture.** |

proprietary SQL supported by a DBMS vendor. The two leading data access middleware are the Open Database Connectivity (ODBC) supported by Microsoft and the Java Database Connectivity (JDBC) supported by Oracle.

17.2.2 Description of Architectures

The design issues are addressed in a number of architectures. For each architecture, this section describes typical division of processing, message management approaches, and trade-offs among architectures.

Two-Tier Architecture

Two-Tier Architecture a client–server architecture in which a PC client and a database server interact directly to request and transfer data. The PC client contains the user interface code, the server contains the data access logic, and the PC client and the server share the validation and business logic.

The two-tier architecture features a PC client and a database server as shown in Figure 17.5. The PC client contains the presentation code and SQL statements for data access. The database server processes the SQL statements and sends query results back to the PC client. In addition, the database server performs process management functions. The validation and business logic code can be split between the PC client and the database server. The PC client can invoke stored procedures on the database server for business logic and validation. Typically, much of the business logic code resides on the client. PC clients in a two-tier architecture are sometimes called "fat clients" because of the large amount of business logic they contain.

The two-tier architecture is a good approach for systems with stable requirements and a moderate number of clients. On the positive side, the two-tier architecture is the simplest to implement due to the number of good commercial development environments. On the negative side, software maintenance can be difficult because PC clients contain a mix of presentation, validation, and business logic code. To make a significant change in business logic, code must be modified on many PC clients. In addition, utilizing new technology may be difficult because two-tier architectures often rely on proprietary software rather than open standards. To lessen reliance on a particular database server, the PC client can connect to intermediate database drivers such as the Open Database Connectivity (ODBC) drivers instead of directly to a database server. The intermediate database drivers then communicate with the database server.

Performance can be poor when a large number of clients submit requests because the database server may be overwhelmed with managing messages. Several sources report that two-tier architectures are limited to about 100 simultaneous clients. With a larger number of simultaneous clients, a three-tier architecture may be necessary. In addition, connecting to intermediate drivers rather than directly to a database server can slow performance.

Three-Tier Architecture

Three-Tier Architecture a client–server architecture with three layers: a PC client, a backend database server, and either a middleware or an application server.

To improve performance, the <u>three-tier architecture</u> adds another server layer as depicted in Figure 17.6. One way to improve performance is to add a middleware server [Figure 17.6(a)] to handle process management. The middleware usually consists of a transaction-processing monitor or message-oriented middleware. A transaction-processing monitor may support more simultaneous connections than message-oriented middleware. However, message-oriented middleware provides more flexibility in the kinds of messages supported. A second way to improve performance is to add an application server for specific kinds of processing such as report writing. In either approach, the additional server software can reside on a separate computer, as depicted in Figure 17.6. Alternatively, the additional server software can be distributed between the database server and PC clients.

Figure 17.6 **Three-tier architecture.**

Although the three-tier architecture addresses performance degradations of the two-tier architecture, it does not address division-of-processing concerns. The PC clients and the database server still contain the same division of code although the tasks of the database server are reduced. Multiple-tier architectures provide more flexibility on division of processing.

Multiple-Tier Architecture

Multiple-Tier Architecture a client–server architecture with more than three layers: a PC client, a backend database server, an intervening middleware server, and application servers. The application servers perform business logic and manage specialized kinds of data such as images.

To improve performance and provide flexible division of processing, <u>multiple-tier architectures</u> support additional layers of servers, as depicted in Figure 17.7. The application servers can be invoked from PC clients, middleware, and database servers. The additional server layers provide a finer division of processing than a two- or a three-tier architecture. In addition, the additional server layers can also improve performance because both middleware and application servers can be deployed.

Software buses provide a flexible and standard approach for multiple-tier architectures, as shown in Figure 17.8. A software bus resolves differences among server and client platforms. Software units of code or objects can be located on any server, even replicated on multiple servers to improve reliability. PC clients can request objects without knowing the platform, location, or implementation details of the object. Currently, there are three candidates for software buses: the Common Object Request Broker Architecture (CORBA) of the Object Management Group, the Common Language Runtime of Microsoft, and the Enterprise Java Beans of Sun Microsystems. All three approaches operate over the Internet and corporate intranets, as described in the next section.

Beyond software buses, frameworks support the integration of business components, services, customers, and partners. Software buses are important building blocks for frameworks. Frameworks also use many other technologies to support the implementation of complex business processes. Corresponding to the three candidates for

| **Figure 17.7** | **Multiple-tier architecture.** |

Figure 17.8   **Multiple-tier architecture with software bus.**

software buses are three candidates for frameworks: the Enterprise Collaboration Architecture of the Object Management Group, the .NET of Microsoft, and the J2EE of Sun Microsystems.

The multiple-tier architecture, especially with the generality and power of software buses and frameworks, is the most general client–server architecture. It can be the most difficult to implement because of its generality especially when using open standards. However, a good design and implementation of a multiple-tier architecture can provide the most benefits in terms of scalability, interoperability, and flexibility.

17.3 WEB DATABASE CONNECTIVITY

Web Database Connectivity client–server architectures that allow a Web page to query and update remote databases managed by servers on the Internet.

As the Internet has become wildly popular, so has the need for accessing databases through World Wide Web (WWW or Web) pages. Internet commerce depends heavily on database access for websites devoted to book sales, travel reservations, and software distribution. Web database connectivity allows a database to be manipulated through a Web page. A user may use a Web form to change a database or view a report generated from a database. This section discusses a number of approaches to deploy client–server databases through the Web. Before discussing these approaches, brief tutorials about the Internet and the World Wide Web are provided.

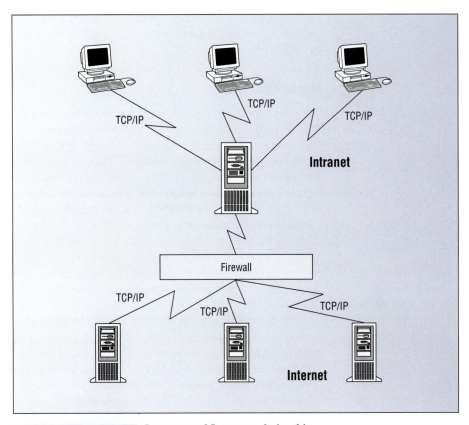

| **Figure 17.9** | **Intranet and Internet relationship.** |

17.3.1 Internet Basics

The Internet provides resource sharing among thousands of networks. For this reason it is called a "network of networks." To provide resource sharing among different kinds of computers, operating systems, and communication equipment, the Internet uses standard protocols. A <u>protocol</u> is a fancy word for a rule about group behavior or interaction. The Internet uses the Transmission Control Protocol (TCP) and the Internet Protocol (IP) to communicate among networks. Collectively, these protocols are known as TCP/IP. The TCP splits messages into fixed-length units called datagrams or packets, reassembles them at the other end, resends lost datagrams, and rearranges them in the right order. The IP routes individual datagrams among networks. Routing can be a complex task because of incompatibilities among networks, many possible routes, and the changing status of routes. To facilitate routing, each computer on the Internet has a unique numeric address known as an IP address.

In addition to Internet usage, the TCP/IP protocols are used for private networks known as intranets. An <u>intranet</u> is a collection of computers and communication devices using the TCP/IP protocol. However, for security reasons, computers in an intranet are usually not accessible from computers on the Internet. The combination of the Internet with accessible intranet computers is known as the extranet. For added security, an intranet can be protected from outside access by a firewall, as depicted in Figure 17.9.

Client–server database access is necessary in intranets for internal computing needs. In contrast, client–server database access in the Internet is usually for outside parties such as customers and suppliers.

World Wide Web

The most popular application on the Internet is the World Wide Web (WWW). Using the WWW, you can browse pages located on any computer on the Internet. Another set of standards provides the foundation for the WWW. The Hypertext Transfer Protocol (HTTP) establishes a session between a browser and a Web server. During the session, the browser and the server interact to send and receive files containing Web pages. Each page has a unique address known as a Uniform Resource Locator (URL). The first part of an URL specifies the protocol of a service. The second part of an URL specifies a computer on the Internet containing the file. Communication devices such as routers and gateways translate the second part into a numeric IP address. The third part of an URL specifies a path to a file containing the page. For example, in the URL http://www.microsoft.com/products/default.html, <u>http</u> indicates the service, www.microsoft.com indicates the computer, and products/default.html indicates the directory and the filename of the page.

The browser and the server work together to send and receive pages. Web pages are written in a language called the <u>HyperText Markup Language (HTML)</u>. A browser displays pages on a PC by interpreting HTML code in the file sent by a server. Part of the HTML code can contain hyperlinks or requests for other pages. When a user clicks on a hyperlink, the browser sends a request to a server to retrieve the page, as depicted in Figure 17.10. The server locates the file containing the page and sends it to the requesting browser. The user then sees the requested page after the browser interprets the HTML code in the file.

To access databases, additional servers and interactions augment the browser (client) and Web server actions of Figure 17.10. Since a Web server mediates almost all requests from a browser, the architectures would seem to fit at least the three-tier architecture. A Web server does not provide the same services as database middleware, discussed in Section 17.2.1, however. Although a Web server can invoke a database server,

Figure 17.10 **Web page request cycle.**

the Web server does not provide the process management services of database middle-ware. Therefore, this book does not consider a Web server as database middleware un-less it is augmented with additional process management capabilities. The next sections describe the role of Web servers in two-tier, three-tier, and multiple-tier architectures for Web database interconnectivity.

XML

HTML has a number of limitations that have become more pronounced as the Web has grown explosively. In HTML, the content, the structure, and the formatting of a page are mixed together. This mixture makes it difficult to search Web pages, display Web pages in customized formats for different devices, and standardize the content of Web pages. To support the rapid growth of the Web, the ability to search, display, and standardize Web pages must improve.

These limitations have led to the development of the eXtensible Markup Language (XML), a meta language for Web documents. XML was designed as a simple language to support the specification of other languages (that is, a meta language). The simple idea behind XML has evolved into a collection of languages that provide a clean separation between the content, the structure, and the formatting of a document. The content of a document is specified as an XML document. To standardize the structure of a document, the XML Schema language has been developed.[1] A schema describes the structure of a document including field names, data types, constraints, and field nesting. In this sense, an XML schema is similar to a view with a definition but no mapping. To specify the formatting of a document, the eXtensible Style Language (XSL) was developed. XSL supports transformation of XML documents into HTML and other display languages. An XML document can reference a schema to specify the structure of the document and a style sheet to specify its formatting. Validating XML parsers can ensure that an XML document conforms to the rules specified in its associated schema.

In terms of the Web page request cycle of Figure 17.10, the server and/or the browser may be capable of processing XML and XSL in addition to HTML. If the browser contains XML and XSL processors, the server can send XML and XSL to the browser instead of HTML. The browser then can transform the XML and XSL into HTML and then display the HTML. If the browser does not contain XML and XSL processors, the server can process the XML and the XSL and send HTML to the browser. At this time, the major browsers contain XML and XSL processors, although server processing of XML is still common because older browser versions do not support XML processing.

Because XML and its derivative languages have become the medium for data interchange on the Web, most major DBMSs support storage, parsing, and querying of XML documents. DBMSs provide an efficient tool to store and retrieve large collections of XML documents. Most enterprise DBMSs support query languages for XML data. The World Wide Web Consortium is currently developing an XML language known as XQuery for retrieval of XML documents. Most DBMS vendors will support XQuery after its specification is accepted.

---

[1]The older approach to standard document structure was known as Document Type Definitions (DTDs). Schemas have a number of significant advantages to DTDs so usage of DTDs may eventually disappear.

17.3.2 Common Gateway Interface

Common Gateway Interface (CGI) an interface that allows a Web server to invoke an external program on the same computer. CGI was the earliest and still is the most universal way to achieve Web database connectivity.

The Common Gateway Interface (CGI) allows a Web server to communicate with an external program. The Web server can pass parameters to the external program. The external program uses the parameters to produce output that is sent back to the browser. Usually, the output contains HTML/XML so that the browser can display it properly. The CGI approach is portable across most Web servers, although the external program may not be portable. The external program can be written in a compiled language like C or an interpreted language like PERL.

The CGI provides several ways to facilitate database connectivity, as depicted in Figure 17.11. In the straight CGI approach, the external program sends SQL statements to the database server and encodes the results in HTML or XML format. In the hybrid CGI approach, the external program sends SQL statements to a partner program that interacts with a database server. The hybrid CGI approach usually provides better performance because the partner program manages database connections among multiple CGI processes. In effect, the partner program performs some middleware functions.

The hybrid CGI approach, although more efficient than the straight CGI approach, may not scale to many simultaneous users. A more efficient approach is to add additional process management functions in the Web server so that the Web server directly communicates with the database server. The next section describes several approaches to direct communication between a Web server and a database server.

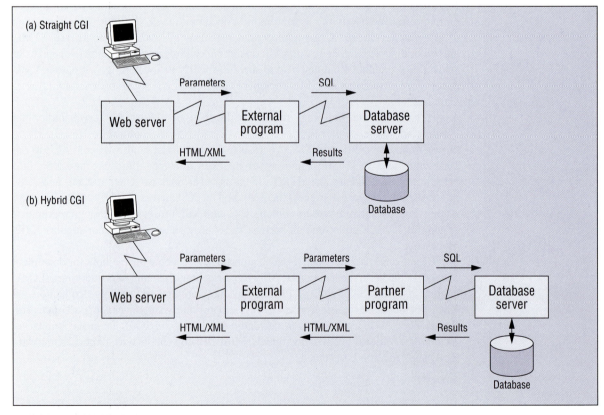

Figure 17.11 CGI approaches to Web database connectivity.

17.3.3 Server-Side Connectivity

Server-Side Connectivity
an approach to Web database connectivity in which a browser communicates with a database server without invoking an external program. Although server-side connectivity is more scalable than the Common Gateway Interface, it requires a specialized Web server or a separate middleware server.

Server-side connectivity bypasses the external program needed with the CGI approaches. The Web server directly communicates with the database server without invoking an external program. However, an extended Web server (Figure 17.12) or plugin module may be needed to provide the direct connection between the Web server and the database server. The extended Web server supports tasks such as management of simultaneous users, support for transactions that span Web pages, and message queuing.

To utilize server-side connectivity, the programmer writes SQL statements and associated database-processing logic in a Web page or external file. To insulate the client from the database logic, the database code can execute stored procedures on the database server. The database code is enclosed in special symbols to indicate that it executes on the server, not the client. For example, Microsoft provides server-side technology known as Active Server Pages. In an Active Server Page, code surrounded by the special characters <% and %> executes on the server, not the client. Database code can be used in an Active Server Page to query and update remote databases. After the database server processes the request, the Web server sends the database results back to the browser as HTML or XML. Other technologies such as Java Server Pages and PHP pages operate similarly to Active Server Pages.

A limitation of server database connectivity is the need for a specialized Web server or a plugin to a Web server. A middleware server can eliminate the need for a specialized Web server, as depicted in Figure 17.13. The middleware contains a listener component that routes database requests to the middleware server. The middleware server provides transaction management and message queuing services.

The server-side approaches provide robust services for transaction processing as well as a software bus for utilizing remote objects. The specialized Web servers and the middleware servers can support hundreds to thousands of simultaneous users. The software bus built into specialized Web servers and middleware servers provides transparent access to objects distributed across the Internet. The software bus fulfills the promise of a multiple-tier architecture for Web database connectivity.

Figure 17.12   **Server-side connectivity approach.**

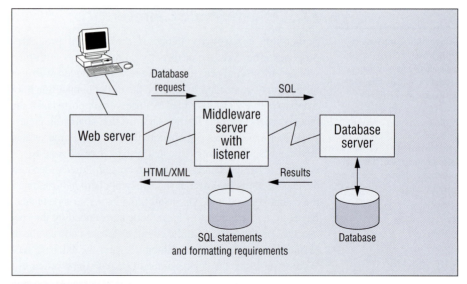

| **Figure 17.13** | **Server-side connectivity with a middleware server.** |

Client-Side Connectivity a style of computing on the World Wide Web in which client computing capacity can be more fully utilized without storing code on the client. Client-side connectivity can enhance database connectivity by providing a more customized interface than permitted by HTML and by allowing data buffering by the client.

17.3.4 Client-Side Connectivity

Although server-side connectivity supports a multiple-tier architecture, it does not fully exploit client computing capabilities. In the server-side approaches, the browser is limited to interpretation of XML and HTML. Even with the scripting capabilities supported by most Web browsers, client computing capabilities can be underutilized. The client-side approaches utilize available computing capabilities without storing the code on the client.

Figure 17.14 depicts two approaches to enhance client interfaces for database processing. Java is a language intended for embedded applications. A Java applet is a special kind of program that executes inside a virtual machine located in a Web browser. The virtual machine prevents an applet from damaging the resources of a PC. A Web server sends a Java applet to a requesting Web browser inside a PC client. After receiving the applet, the Web browser executes it to produce specified effects on the browser.

ActiveX® differs from Java in that an ActiveX object is a binary file that can be executed directly on a PC client.[2] No virtual machine is used for ActiveX objects. Like Java applets, a Web server sends an ActiveX object as a result of a request by a PC client. Unlike Java applets, ActiveX objects can execute inside a browser or as separate processes.

The client-side approaches can be integrated with the server-side approaches described in the previous section. This combination provides the advantages of a multiple-tier client–server architecture with a customized interface on a PC client. PC clients remain thin because the customization code (Java applets and ActiveX objects) resides on a remote server. In addition, PC clients can execute remote code on other servers through Java or ActiveX code.

---

[2]ActiveX is part of the Microsoft Component Object Model (COM). ActiveX objects or controls involve user interaction. Other kinds of COM objects involve processing only, not user interaction.

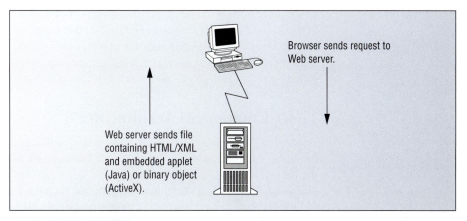

Browser sends request to
Web server.

Web server sends file
containing HTML/XML
and embedded applet
(Java) or binary object
(ActiveX).

| **Figure 17.14** | **Web page request cycle with client-side connectivity.** |

TABLE 17.2	Summary of Web Connectivity Approaches

Approach	Architecture	Example Product	Comments
Straight CGI	Two-tier	Apache Web server with external PERL program	Inexpensive; portability only limited by external program; limited scalability
Hybrid CGI	Two-tier	Apache Web server with Cold Fusion server extensions	More expensive than straight CGI; portability depends on partner program; scalable to modest loads
Extended Web server (server-side connectivity)	Three-tier and multiple-tier	Internet Information Server with Microsoft Transaction Server	Expensive; Web server dependent; highly scalable
Middleware server (server-side connectivity)	Three-tier and multiple-tier	Oracle Application Server	Expensive; Web server independent; highly scalable
Client-side connectivity	Two- and multiple-tier	Microsoft Remote Data Service	Customized client interface; efficient data buffering; usually works with server-side connectivity approaches

17.3.5 Summary of Web Database Connectivity Approaches

To help you compare and contrast database connectivity approaches, Table 17.2 provides a convenient summary. For websites attracting a modest number of hits, the CGI approaches work well. For large commercial sites, the server-side connectivity approaches are needed. The middleware-server approach works well with existing Web servers. The extended–Web server approach may require a commitment to a specific Web server and operating system.

17.4 ARCHITECTURES FOR DISTRIBUTED DATABASE MANAGEMENT SYSTEMS

Distributed DBMSs are more complex than DBMSs to support client–server processing. To support client–server processing, the most important extension is middleware for process management. Middleware, although complex, is often a separate product from the DBMS. To support distributed database processing, fundamental extensions to a DBMS are necessary. Underlying the extensions are a different component architecture that manages distributed database requests and a different schema architecture that provides additional layers of data description. This section describes the component architecture and schema architecture to provide a foundation for more details about distributed database processing in following sections.

17.4.1 Component Architecture

Distributed DBMSs support global requests that use data stored at more than one site. A site is any computer with a unique network address such as an IP address. Sites are often geographically distributed, although the definition supports sites located in close proximity. Global requests include queries that combine data from more than one site and transactions that update data at more than one site. If all requests require only data from one site, distributed database processing capabilities are not required.

To depict global requests, you need to begin with a distributed database. Distributed databases are potentially useful for organizations that operate in multiple locations. Figure 17.15 depicts a distributed database for an electronic retail company. The company performs customer processing at Boise and Tulsa and manages warehouses at Seattle and Denver. The distribution of the database follows the geographical locations of the business. The *Customer, Order,* and *OrderLine* tables (customer-order data) are split between

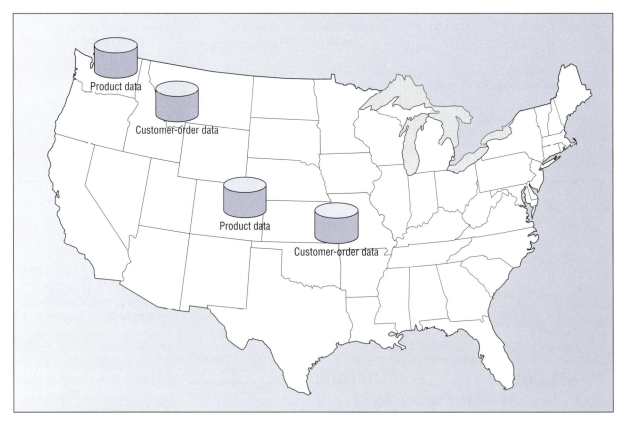

Figure 17.15   **Distribution of order-entry data.**

Boise and Tulsa, while the *Product* and *Inventory* tables (product data) are split between Seattle and Denver. An example of a global query is to check both warehouse sites for sufficient quantity of a product to satisfy a shipment invoice. An example of a global transaction is an order-entry form that inserts records into the *Order* and *OrderLine* tables at one location and updates the *Product* table at the closest warehouse site.

To support global queries and transactions, distributed DBMSs contain additional components as compared to traditional, nondistributed DBMSs. Figure 17.16 depicts a possible arrangement of the components of a distributed DBMS. Each server with access to the distributed database is known as a site. If a site contains a database, a local data manager (LDM) controls it. The local data managers provide complete features of a DBMS as described in other chapters. The distributed data manager (DDM) optimizes query execution across sites, coordinates concurrency control and recovery across sites, and controls access to remote data. In performing these tasks, the DDM uses the global dictionary (GD) to locate parts of the database. The GD can be distributed to various sites similar to the way that data are distributed. Because of the complexity of the distributed database manager, Section 17.6 presents more details about distributed query processing and transaction processing.

In the component architecture, the local database managers can be homogeneous or heterogeneous. A distributed DBMS with homogeneous local DBMSs is <u>tightly integrated</u>. The distributed database manager can call internal components and access the internal state of local data managers. The tight integration allows the distributed DBMS to efficiently support both distributed queries and transactions. However, the homogeneity requirement precludes integration of existing databases.

A distributed DBMS with heterogeneous local data managers is <u>loosely integrated</u>. The distributed database manager acts as middleware to coordinate local data managers. SQL often provides the interface between the distributed data manager and the local data managers. The loose integration supports data sharing among legacy systems and independent organizations. However, the loosely integrated approach may not be able to support transaction processing in a reliable and efficient manner.

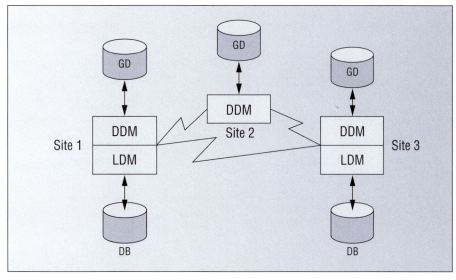

Figure 17.16   **Component architecture of a distributed DBMS.**

17.4.2 Schema Architectures

To accommodate distribution of data, additional layers of data description are necessary. However, there is no widely accepted schema architecture for distributed databases like the widely accepted <u>Three Schema Architecture</u> for traditional DBMSs. This section depicts possible schema architectures for tightly integrated distributed DBMSs and loosely integrated distributed DBMSs. The architectures provide a reference about the kinds of data description necessary and the compartmentalization of the data description.

The schema architecture for a tightly integrated distributed DBMS contains additional layers for fragmentation and allocation as depicted in Figure 17.17. The fragmentation schema contains the definition of each fragment while the allocation schema contains the location of each fragment. A fragment can be defined as a vertical subset (project operation), a horizontal subset (restrict operation), or a mixed fragment (combination of project and restrict operations). A fragment is allocated to one site but sometimes to multiple sites. If the distributed DBMS supports replication, a fragment can be allocated to multiple sites. In some distributed DBMSs that support replication, one copy of a fragment is considered the primary copy and the other copies are secondary. Only the primary copy is guaranteed to be current.

The schema architecture for a loosely integrated distributed DBMS supports more autonomy of local database sites in addition to data sharing. Each site contains the traditional three schema levels, as depicted in Figure 17.18. To support data sharing, the distributed DBMS provides a local mapping schema for each site. The local mapping

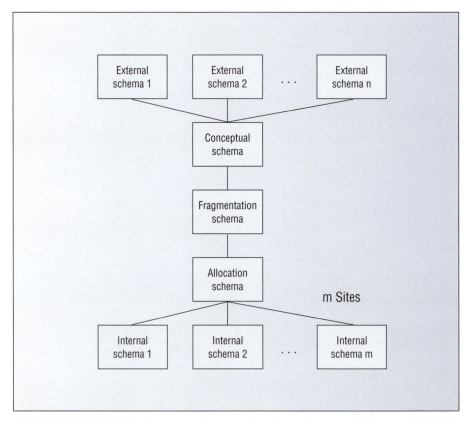

Figure 17.17   **Schema architecture for a tightly integrated distributed DBMS.**

schemas describe the exportable data at a site and provide conversion rules to translate data from a local format into a global format. The global conceptual schema depicts all of the kinds of data and relationships that can be used in global requests. Some distributed DBMSs do not have a global conceptual schema. Instead, global external schemas provide views of shared data in a common format.

There can be many differences among the local data formats. Local sites may use different DBMSs, each with a different set of data types. The data models of the local DBMSs can be different, especially if legacy systems are being integrated. Legacy systems might use file interfaces and navigational data models (network and hierarchical) that do not support SQL. Even if local sites support a common SQL standard, there can be many differences such as different data types, scales, units of measure, and codes. The local mapping schemas resolve these differences by providing conversion rules that transform data from a local format into a global format.

The tightly integrated and loosely integrated architectures represent two extreme possibilities. Many variations between these two architectures have been proposed and implemented. For example, to provide additional local autonomy but more efficiency for global requests, a loosely integrated system can require that all local sites support a common SQL interface. The tightly and loosely integrated approaches also can be combined. Networks of tightly integrated distributed databases can be loosely integrated to share selective data in global requests. In this case, the loosely integrated distributed DBMS acts as a gateway between tightly integrated distributed databases.

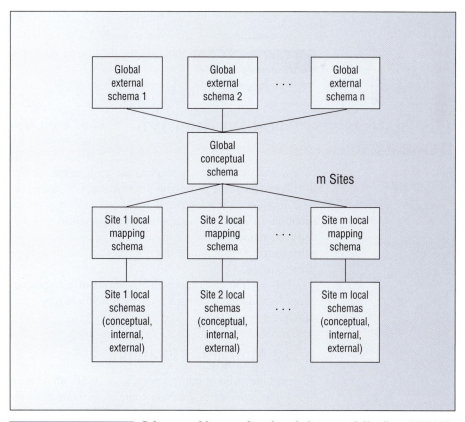

Figure 17.18   **Schema architecture for a loosely integrated distributed DBMS.**

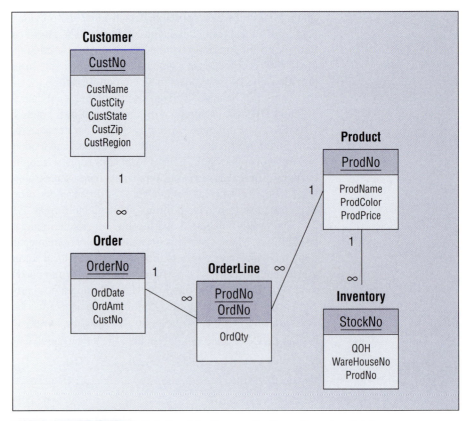

Figure 17.19   Relationship diagram for the order entry database.

17.5 TRANSPARENCY FOR DISTRIBUTED DATABASE PROCESSING

Recall from Chapter 15 that transparency refers to the visibility (visible or hidden) of internal details of a service. In transaction processing, concurrency and recovery services are transparent, or hidden from database users. In distributed database processing, transparency is related to data independence. If database distribution is transparent, users can write queries with no knowledge of the distribution. In addition, distribution changes will not cause changes to existing queries and transactions. If the database distribution is not transparent, users must reference some distribution details in queries and distribution changes can lead to changes in existing queries.

This section describes common levels of transparency and provides examples of query formulation with each level. Before discussing transparency levels, a motivating example is presented.

17.5.1 Motivating Example

To depict the levels of transparency, more details about the order-entry database are provided. The order-entry database contains five tables, as shown in the relationship diagram of Figure 17.19. You may assume that customers are located in two regions (East and West) and products are stored in two warehouses (1: Denver, 2: Seattle).

TABLE 17.3	Fragments Based on the *CustRegion* Field[3]

```
CREATE FRAGMENT Western-Customers AS
   SELECT * FROM Customer WHERE CustRegion = 'West'

CREATE FRAGMENT Western-Orders AS
   SELECT Order.* FROM Order, Customer
      WHERE Order.CustNo = Customer.CustNo AND CustRegion = 'West'

CREATE FRAGMENT Western-OrderLines AS
   SELECT OrderLine.* FROM Customer, OrderLine, Order
      WHERE OrderLine.OrdNo = Order.OrdNo
         AND Order.CustNo = Customer.CustNo AND CustRegion = 'West'

CREATE FRAGMENT Eastern-Customers AS
   SELECT * FROM Customer WHERE CustRegion = 'East'

CREATE FRAGMENT Eastern-Orders AS
   SELECT Order.* FROM Order, Customer
      WHERE Order.CustNo = Customer.CustNo AND CustRegion = 'East'

CREATE FRAGMENT Eastern-OrderLines AS
   SELECT OrderLine.* FROM Customer, OrderLine, Order
      WHERE OrderLine.OrdNo = Order.OrdNo
         AND Order.CustNo = Customer.CustNo AND CustRegion = 'East'
```

One collection of fragments can be defined using the customer region field as shown in Table 17.3. The *Western-Customers* fragment consists of customers with a region equal to West. There are two related fragments: the *Western-Orders* fragment, consisting of orders for western customers and the *Western-OrderLines* fragment, consisting of order lines matching western orders. Similar fragments are defined for rows involving eastern customers.

Semi-Join an operator of relational algebra that is especially useful for distributed database processing. A semi-join is half of a join: the rows of one table that match with at least one row of another table. Only the rows of the first table appear in the result.

The order and order line fragments are derived from a customer fragment using the semi-join operator. A <u>semi-join</u> is half of a join: the rows of one table that match the rows of another table. For example, a semi-join operation defines the *Western-Orders* fragment as the rows of the *Order* table matching customer rows with a region of West. A fragment defined with a semi-join operation is sometimes called a derived horizontal fragment. Because some fragments should have rows related to other fragments, the semi-join operator is important for defining fragments.

Warehouse fragments are defined using the *WareHouseNo* field as shown in Table 17.4. In the fragment definitions, warehouse number 1 is assumed to be located in Denver and warehouse number 2 in Seattle. The *Product* table is not fragmented because the entire table is replicated at multiple sites.

Fragmentation can be more complex than described in the order-entry database. There can be many additional fragments to accommodate a business structure. For example, if there are additional customer processing centers and warehouses, additional fragments can be defined. In addition, vertical fragments can be defined as projection operations in addition to the horizontal fragments using restriction and semi-join operations. A fragment can even be defined as a combination of projection, selection, and

---

[3]The syntax in Table 17.3 is not official SQL syntax.

TABLE 17.4	Fragments Based on the *WareHouseNo* Field

```
CREATE FRAGMENT Denver-Inventory AS
   SELECT * FROM Inventory WHERE WareHouseNo = 1

CREATE FRAGMENT Seattle-Inventory AS
   SELECT * FROM Inventory WHERE WareHouseNo = 2
```

TABLE 17.5	Allocation of Fragments of the Order-Entry Database

Fragments	Site
Western-Customers, Western-Orders, Western-OrderLines	Boise
Eastern-Customers, Eastern-Orders, Eastern-OrderLines	Tulsa
Denver-Inventory, Product	Denver
Seattle-Inventory, Product	Seattle

semi-join operations. The only restriction is that the fragments must be disjoint. Disjointness means that horizontal fragments do not contain common rows and vertical fragments do not contain common columns except for the primary key.

After fragments are defined, they are allocated to sites. Fragments are sometimes defined based on where they should be allocated. The allocation of order-entry fragments follows this approach, as shown in Table 17.5. The Boise site contains the western customer fragments, while the Tulsa site contains the eastern customer fragments. Similarly, the inventory fragments are split between the Denver and the Seattle sites. The *Product* table is replicated at the Denver and the Seattle sites because each warehouse stocks every product.

In practice, the design and the allocation of fragments are much more difficult than depicted here. Designing and allocating fragments is similar to index selection. Data about the frequency of queries, the frequency of parameter values in queries, and the behavior of the global query optimizer are needed. In addition, data about the frequency of originating sites for each query are needed. The originating site for a query is the site in which the query is stored. Just as for index selection, optimization models and tools can aid decision making about fragment design and allocation. The details of the optimization models and the tools are beyond the scope of this book. The references at the end of the chapter provide details about fragment design and allocation.

17.5.2 Fragmentation Transparency

Fragmentation Transparency a level of independence in distributed DBMSs in which queries can be formulated without knowledge of fragments.

Fragmentation transparency provides the highest level of data independence. Users formulate queries and transactions without knowledge of fragments, locations, or local formats. If fragments, locations, or local formats change, queries and transactions are not affected. In essence, users perceive the distributed database as a centralized database. Fragmentation transparency involves the least work for users but the most work for distributed DBMSs.

TABLE 17.6	Representative Requests Using the Order-Entry Database

Find Order
```
SELECT * FROM Order, Customer
    WHERE Order.CustNo = $X
        AND Order.CustNo = Customer.CustNo
```

Find Product Availability
```
SELECT * FROM Inventory
    WHERE ProdNo = $X
```

Update Inventory
```
UPDATE Inventory SET QOH = QOH − 1
    WHERE ProdNo = $X AND WareHouseNo = $Y
```

Customer Move
```
UPDATE Customer SET CustRegion = $X
    WHERE CustNo = $Y
```

To contrast the transparency levels, Table 17.6 lists some representative queries and transactions that use the order entry database. In these queries, the parameters $X and $Y are used rather than individual values. With fragmentation transparency, queries and transactions can be submitted without change regardless of the fragmentation of the database.

17.5.3 Location Transparency

Location Transparency a level of independence in distributed DBMSs in which queries can be formulated without knowledge of locations. However, knowledge of fragments is necessary.

Location transparency provides a lesser level of data independence than fragmentation transparency. Users need to reference fragments in formulating queries and transactions. However, knowledge of locations and local formats is not necessary. Even though site knowledge is not necessary, users are indirectly aware of a database's distribution because many fragments are allocated to a single site. Users may make an association between fragments and sites.

Location transparency involves more work in formulating requests as shown in Table 17.7. In the "find" queries, the union operator collects rows from all fragments. The Update Inventory query involves about the same amount of coding. The user substitutes a fragment name in place of the condition on *WareHouseNo* because this condition defines the fragment.

In the Customer Move request, much more coding is necessary. An update operation cannot be used because the field to update defines the fragment. Instead, rows must be inserted in the new fragments and deleted from the old fragments. For the customer fragment, the SELECT . . . INTO statement stores field values in variables that are used in the subsequent INSERT statement. The deletions are performed in the stated order if referenced rows must be deleted last. If deletions cascade, only one DELETE statement on the *Western-Customers* fragment is necessary.

The SQL statements for the first two requests do not reveal the number of union operations that may be required. With two fragments, only one union operation is necessary. With *n* fragments, $n - 1$ union operations are necessary, however.

To some extent, views can shield users from some of the fragment details. For example, using a view defined with union operations would obviate the need to write the union operations in the query. However, views may not simplify manipulation statements.

TABLE 17.7	Requests Written with Location Transparency

Find Order
```
SELECT * FROM Western-Orders, Western-Customers
    WHERE Western-Orders.CustNo = $X
        AND Western-Orders.CustNo = Western-Customers.CustNo
UNION
SELECT * FROM Eastern-Orders, Eastern-Customers
    WHERE Eastern-Orders.CustNo = $X
        AND Eastern-Orders.Custno = Eastern-Customers.CustNo
```

Find Product Availability
```
SELECT * FROM Denver-Inventory
    WHERE ProdNo = $X
UNION
SELECT * FROM Seattle-Inventory
    WHERE ProdNo = $X
```

Update Inventory (Denver)
```
UPDATE Denver-Inventory SET QOH = QOH − 1
    WHERE ProdNo = $X
```

Customer Move (West to East)
```
SELECT CustName, CustCity, CustState, CustZip
    INTO $CustName, $CustCity, $CustState, $CustZip
    FROM Western-Customers WHERE CustNo = $Y

INSERT INTO Eastern-Customers
 (CustNo, CustName, CustCity, CustState, CustZip, CustRegion)
 VALUES ($Y, $CustName, $CustCity, $CustState, $CustZip, 'East')

INSERT INTO Eastern-Orders
 SELECT * FROM Western-Orders WHERE CustNo = $Y

INSERT INTO Eastern-OrderLines
 SELECT * FROM Western-OrderLines
  WHERE OrdNo IN
   (SELECT OrdNo FROM Western-Orders WHERE CustNo = $Y)

DELETE FROM Western-OrderLines
    WHERE OrdNo IN
       (SELECT OrdNo FROM Western-Orders WHERE CustNo = $Y)

DELETE Western-Orders WHERE CustNo = $Y

DELETE Western-Customers WHERE CustNo = $Y
```

If the DBMS does not support fragmentation transparency, it seems unlikely that updatable views could span sites. Thus, the user would still have to write the SQL statements for the Customer Move request.

17.5.4 Local Mapping Transparency

Local Mapping Transparency a level of independence in distributed DBMSs in which queries can be formulated without knowledge of local formats. However, knowledge of fragments and fragment allocations (locations) is necessary.

Local mapping transparency provides a lesser level of data independence than location transparency. Users need to reference fragments at sites in formulating queries and transactions. However, knowledge of local formats is not necessary. If sites differ in formats as in loosely integrated distributed databases, local mapping transparency still relieves the user of considerable work.

TABLE 17.8	Requests Written with Local Mapping Transparency

Find Order
```
SELECT *
  FROM Western-Orders@Boise, Western-Customers@Boise
    WHERE Western-Orders@Boise.CustNo = $X
      AND Western-Orders@Boise.CustNo =
          Western-Customers@Boise.CustNo
UNION
  SELECT *
    FROM Eastern-Orders@Tulsa, Eastern-Customers@Tulsa
    WHERE Eastern-Orders@Tulsa.CustNo = $X
      AND Eastern-Orders@Tulsa.CustNo =
          Eastern-Customers@Tulsa.CustNo
```

Find Product Availability
```
SELECT * FROM Denver-Inventory@Denver
  WHERE ProdNo = $X
UNION
SELECT * FROM Seattle-Inventory@Seattle
  WHERE ProdNo = $X
```

Update Inventory (Denver)
```
UPDATE Denver-Inventory@Denver SET QOH = QOH − 1
  WHERE ProdNo = $X
```

Customer Move (West to East)
```
SELECT CustName, CustCity, CustState, CustZip
  INTO $CustName, $Custcity, $CustState, $CustZip
  FROM Western-Customers@Boise WHERE CustNo = $Y

INSERT INTO Eastern-Customers@Tulsa
 (CustNo, CustName, CustCity, CustState, CustZip, CustRegion)
 VALUES ($Y, $CustName, $CustCity, $CustState, $CustZip, 'East')

INSERT INTO Eastern-Orders@Tulsa
 SELECT * FROM Western-Orders@Boise WHERE CustNo = $Y

INSERT INTO Eastern-OrderLines@Tulsa
 SELECT * FROM Western-OrderLines@Boise
   WHERE OrdNo IN
    (SELECT OrdNo FROM Western-Orders@Boise
      WHERE CustNo = $Y)

DELETE FROM Western-OrderLines@Boise
   WHERE OrdNo IN
    (SELECT OrdNo FROM Western-Orders@Boise
      WHERE CustNo = $Y)

DELETE Western-Orders@Boise WHERE CustNo = $Y

DELETE Western-Customers@Boise WHERE CustNo = $Y
```

Location transparency may not involve much additional coding effort from that shown in Table 17.8. The only changes between Tables 17.7 and 17.8 are the addition of the site names in Table 17.8. If fragments are replicated, additional coding is necessary in transactions. For example, if a new product is added, two INSERT statements (one for each site) are necessary with local mapping transparency. With location transparency, only one INSERT statement is necessary. The amount of additional coding depends on the amount of replication.

From the discussion in this section, you may assume falsely that fragmentation transparency is preferred to the other levels of transparency. Fragmentation transparency provides the highest level of data independence but is the most complex to implement. Many distributed DBMSs cannot achieve this level of data independence. In addition, fragmentation transparency may encourage excessive resource consumption because users do not perceive the underlying distributed database processing. With location and local mapping transparency, users perceive the underlying distributed database processing at least to some extent. The amount and complexity of distributed database processing can be considerable, as described in the next section.

17.6 DISTRIBUTED DATABASE PROCESSING

Just as distributed data can add complexity for query formulation, it adds considerable complexity to query processing and transaction processing. Distributed database processing involves movement of data, remote processing, and site coordination that are absent from centralized database processing. Although the details of distributed database processing can be hidden from programmers and users, performance implications sometimes cannot be hidden. This section presents details about distributed query processing and distributed transaction processing to make you aware of complexities that can affect performance.

17.6.1 Distributed Query Processing

Distributed query processing is more complex than centralized query processing for several reasons. Distributed query processing involves both local (intrasite) and global (intersite) optimization. Global optimization involves data movement and site selection decisions that are absent in centralized query processing. For example, to perform a join of distributed fragments, one fragment can be moved, both fragments can be moved to a third site, or just the join values of one fragment can be moved. If the fragments are replicated, then a site for each fragment must be chosen.

Distributed query processing is also more complex because multiple optimization objectives exist. In a centralized environment, minimizing resource (input–output and processing) usage is consistent with minimizing response time. In a distributed environment, minimizing resources may conflict with minimizing response time because of parallel processing opportunities. Parallel processing can reduce response time but increase the overall amount of resources consumed (input–output, processing, and communication). In addition, the weighting of communication costs versus local costs (input–output and processing) depends on network characteristics. For wide area networks, communication costs can dominate local costs. For local area networks, communication costs are more equally weighted with local costs.

The increased complexity makes optimization of distributed queries even more important than optimization of centralized queries. Because distributed query processing involves both local and global optimization, there are many more possible access plans for a distributed query than a corresponding centralized query. Variance in performance among distributed access plans can be quite large. The choice of a bad access plan can lead to extremely poor performance. In addition, distributed access plans sometimes need to adjust for site conditions. If a site is unavailable or overloaded, a distributed access plan should dynamically choose another site. Thus, some of the optimization process may need to be performed dynamically (during run-time) rather than statically (during compile time).

TABLE 17.9	Statistics for the Query and the Network

Record length is 1,000 bits for each table.

The customer has 5 orders in the specified date range.

Each order contains on the average 5 products.

The customer has 3 orders in the specified date range and color.

There are 200 'red' products.

There are 10,000 orders, 50,000 order lines, and 1,000 products in the fragments.

Fragment allocation is given in Table 17.6.

Delay per Message is 0.1 second.

Data Rate is 100,000 bits per second.

To depict the importance of distributed query optimization, access plans for a sample query are presented. To simplify the presentation, a wide area network with relatively slow communication times is used. Only communication times (*CT*) are shown for each access plan. Communication time consists of a fixed message delay (*MD*) and a variable transmission time (*TT*). Each record is transmitted as a separate message.

$CT = MD + TT$

MD = Number of messages * Delay per message

TT = Number of bits/Data rate

Global Query: List the order number, order date, product number, product name, product price, and order quantity for eastern orders with a specified customer number, date range, and product color. Table 17.9 lists statistics for the query and the network.

SELECT * EO.OrdNo, OrdDate, P.ProdNo, QtyOrd, ProdName, ProdPrice
　　FROM Eastern-Orders EO, Eastern-Orderlines EOL, Product P
　　WHERE EO.CustNo = $X AND EO.OrdNo = EOL.OrdNo AND P.Color = 'Red'
　　　AND EOL.ProdNo = P.ProdNo and OrdDate BETWEEN $Y AND $Z

1. Move the *Product* table to the Tulsa site where the query is processed.
   $CT = 1,000 * 0.1 + (1,000 * 1,000)\,/100,000 = 110$ seconds
2. Restrict the *Product* table at the Denver site, then move the result to Tulsa where the remainder of the query is processed.
   $CT = 200 * 0.1 + (200 * 1,000)\,/100,000 = 22$ seconds
3. Perform join and restrictions of *Eastern-Orders* and *Eastern-OrderLines* fragments at the Tulsa site. Move the result to the Denver site to join with the *Product* table.
   $CT = 25 * 0.1 + (25 * 2,000)\,/100,000 = 3$ seconds
4. Restrict the *Product* table at the Denver site. Move only the resulting product numbers (32 bits) to Tulsa. Perform joins and restrictions at Tulsa. Move the results back to Denver to combine with the *Product* table.
   CT (Denver to Tulsa) $= 200 * 0.1 + (200 * 32)\,/100,000 = 20.064$ seconds
   CT (Tulsa to Denver) $= 15 * 0.1 + (15 * 2,000)\,/100,000 = 1.8$ seconds
   $CT = CT$ (Denver to Tulsa) $+ CT$ (Tulsa to Denver) $= 21.864$ seconds

These access plans show a wide variance in communication times. Even more variance would be shown if the order fragments were moved from Tulsa to Denver. The third access plan dominates the others because of its low message delay. Additional analysis of the local processing costs would be necessary to determine the best access plan.

17.6.2 Distributed Transaction Processing

Distributed transaction processing follows the principles described in Chapter 15. Transactions obey the ACID properties and the distributed DBMS provides concurrency and recovery transparency. However, a distributed environment makes the implementation of the principles more difficult. Independently operating sites must be coordinated. In addition, new kinds of failures exist because of the communication network. To deal with these complexities, new protocols are necessary. This section presents an introduction to the problems and solutions of distributed concurrency control and commit processing.

Distributed Concurrency Control

Distributed concurrency control can involve more overhead than centralized concurrency control because local sites must be coordinated through messages over a communication network. The simplest scheme involves centralized coordination, as depicted in Figure 17.20. At the beginning of a transaction, the coordinating site is chosen and the transaction is divided into subtransactions performed at other sites. Each site hosting a subtransaction submits lock and release requests to the coordinating site using the normal two-phase locking rules.

Centralized coordination involves the fewest messages and the simplest deadlock detection. However, reliance on a centralized coordinator may make transaction processing less reliable. To alleviate reliance on a centralized site, lock management can be

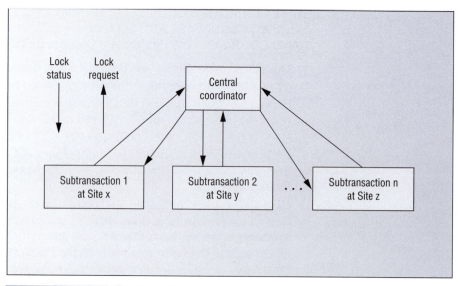

Figure 17.20 **Centralized concurrency control.**

distributed among sites. The price for higher reliability is more message overhead and more complex deadlock detection. The number of messages can be twice as much in the distributed coordination scheme as compared to the centralized coordination scheme.

With both centralized and distributed coordination, replicated data are a problem. Updating replicated data involves extra overhead because a write lock must be obtained on all copies before any copy is updated. Obtaining write locks on multiple copies can cause delays and even rollbacks if a copy is not available.

Primary Copy Protocol a protocol for concurrency control of distributed transactions. Each replicated fragment is designated as either the primary copy or a secondary copy. During distributed transaction processing, only the primary copy is guaranteed to be current at the end of a transaction. Updates may be propagated to secondary copies after end of transaction.

To reduce overhead with locking multiple copies, the primary copy protocol can be used. In the primary copy protocol, one copy of each replicated fragment is designated as the primary copy, while the other copies are secondary. Write locks are necessary only for the primary copy. After a transaction updates the primary copy, updates are propagated to the secondary copies. However, secondary copies may not be updated until after the transaction commits. The primary copy protocol provides improved performance but at the cost of noncurrent secondary copies. Because reduced overhead is often more important than current secondary copies, many distributed DBMSs use the primary copy protocol.

Distributed Commit Processing

Distributed DBMSs must contend with failures of communication links and sites, failures that do not affect centralized DBMSs. Detecting failures involves coordination among sites. If a link or site fails, any transaction involving the site must be aborted. In addition, the site should be avoided in future transactions until the failure is resolved.

Failures can be more complex than just a single site or communication link. A number of sites and links can fail simultaneously leaving a network partitioned. In a partitioned network, different partitions (collections of sites) cannot communicate although sites in the same partition can communicate. The transaction manager must ensure that different parts of a partitioned network act in unison. It should not be possible for sites in one partition to decide to commit a transaction but sites in another partition to decide not to commit a transaction. All sites must either commit or abort.

Two-Phase Commit Protocol (2PC) a rule to ensure that distributed transactions are atomic. 2PC uses a voting and a decision phase to coordinate commits of local transactions.

The most widely known protocol for distributed commit processing is the two-phase commit protocol.[4] For each transaction, one site is chosen as the coordinator and the transaction is divided into subtransactions performed at other participant sites. The coordinator and the participant sites interact in a voting phase and a decision phase. At the end of both phases, each participant site has acted in unison to either commit or abort its subtransaction.

The voting and decision phases require actions on both the coordinator and the participant sites as depicted in Figure 17.21. In the decision phase, the coordinator sends a message to each participant asking if it is ready to commit. Before responding, each participant forces all updates to disk when the local transaction work finishes. If no failure occurs, a participant writes a ready-commit record and sends a ready vote to the coordinator. At this point, a participant has an uncertain status because the coordinator may later request the participant to abort.

---

[4]Do not confuse two-phase commit with two-phase locking. The two-phase commit protocol is used only for distributed transaction processing. Two-phase locking can be used for centralized and distributed concurrency control.

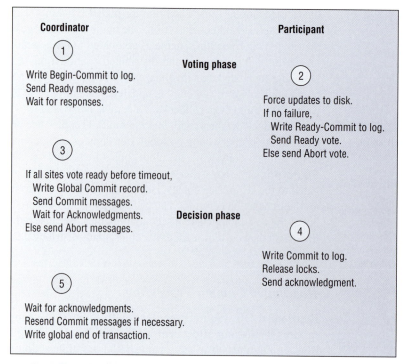

Figure 17.21   **Two-phase commit processing for coordinator and participants.**

The decision phase begins when the coordinator either receives votes from each participant or a timeout occurs. If a timeout occurs or at least one participant sends an abort vote, the coordinator aborts the entire transaction by sending abort messages to each participant. Each participant then performs a rollback of its changes.

If all participants vote ready, the coordinator writes the global commit record and asks each participant to commit its subtransaction. Each participant writes a commit record, releases locks, and sends an acknowledgment to the coordinator. When the coordinator receives acknowledgment from all participants, the coordinator writes the global end-of-transaction record. If a failure occurs in either the voting or the decision phase, the coordinator sends an abort message to all participating sites.

In practice, the two-phase commit protocol presented in Figure 17.21 is just the basic protocol. Other complications such as a failure during recovery and timeouts complicate the protocol. In addition, modifications to the basic protocol can reduce the number of messages needed to enforce the protocol. Because these extensions are beyond the scope of this book, you should consult the references at the end of the chapter for more details.

The two-phase commit protocol can use a centralized or a distributed coordinator. The trade-offs are similar to centralized versus distributed coordination for concurrency control. Centralized coordination is simpler than distributed coordination but can be less reliable.

The two-phase commit protocol does not handle any conceivable kind of failure. For example, the two-phase commit protocol may not work correctly if log records are lost. There is no known protocol guaranteeing that all sites act in unison to commit or abort in the presence of arbitrary failures. Because the two-phase commit protocol efficiently handles common kinds of failures, it is widely used in distributed transaction processing.

CLOSING THOUGHTS

This chapter has described the motivation, the architectures, and the services of DBMSs that support distributed processing and distributed data. Utilizing distributed processing and data can significantly improve DBMS services but at the cost of new design challenges. Distributed processing can improve scalability, interoperability, and flexibility while distributed data can improve data control, communication costs, and system performance. To realize these benefits, significant challenges caused by the complexity of distributed processing and data must be overcome.

Choosing an appropriate architecture is one way to overcome additional complexity. This chapter described several client–server architectures to utilize distributed processing. The two-tier, three-tier, and multiple-tier architectures provide alternatives among cost, complexity, and benefit levels. Implementing a client–server architecture on the Internet can provide additional advantages because the open standards of the Internet promote a competitive marketplace. This chapter described several architectures that support Web database connectivity.

This chapter also described architectures and processing for distributed DBMSs. Architectures for distributed DBMSs differ in the integration of the local databases. Tightly integrated systems provide both query and transaction services but require uniformity in the local DBMSs. Loosely integrated systems support data sharing among a mix of modern and legacy DBMSs. An important part of the data architecture is the level of data independence. This chapter described several levels of data independence that differ by the level of data distribution knowledge required to formulate global requests. To provide an introductory understanding to the complexity of distributed database processing, this chapter described distributed query processing and transaction processing. Both services involve complex issues not present in centralized DBMSs.

REVIEW CONCEPTS

- Timesharing, file sharing, and remote procedure calls as early forms of distributed processing and distributed data.
- Motivations for distributed processing: scalability, interoperability, and flexibility.
- Motivations for distributed data: increased local control, reduced communication costs, and improved performance.
- Design issues in distributed processing: division of processing and process management.
- Kinds of code to distribute between a client and a server.
- Process management tasks performed by database middleware.
- Differences between transaction-processing monitors, message-oriented middleware, and software buses.
- Characteristics of two-tier, three-tier, and multiple-tier architectures.
- Characteristics of CGI, extended server, and middleware server approaches for Web database connectivity.
- Role of client-side processing in Web database connectivity.
- Global queries and transactions.
- Role of the local database manager, the distributed database manager, and the global dictionary in the component architecture of a distributed DBMS.
- Schema architectures for tightly integrated and loosely integrated distributed DBMSs.

- Relationship of distributed database transparency levels and data independence.
- Kinds of fragmentation: horizontal, vertical, and derived horizontal.
- Complexity of fragment design and allocation.
- Query formulation for fragmentation transparency, location transparency, and local mapping transparency.
- Performance measures and objectives for distributed query processing.
- Use of two-phase locking for distributed concurrency control.
- Use of the primary copy protocol to reduce update overhead with replicated data.
- Additional kinds of failures in a distributed database environment.
- Two-phase commit protocol for ensuring atomic commit of participant sites in a distributed transaction.
- Trade-offs between centralized and distributed coordination for distributed concurrency control and recovery.

QUESTIONS

1. What is the role of clients and servers in distributed processing?

2. Briefly define the terms *flexibility, interoperability,* and *scalability.* How does distributed processing support interoperability, flexibility, and scalability?

3. Discuss some of the pitfalls of developing client–server systems.

4. How can a distributed database improve data control?

5. How can a distributed database reduce communication costs and improve performance?

6. Discuss some of the pitfalls when developing distributed databases.

7. Discuss why distributed processing is more mature and more widely implemented than distributed databases.

8. Why are division of processing and process management important in client–server architectures?

9. Explain how two-tier architectures address division of processing and process management.

10. Explain how three-tier architectures address division of processing and process management.

11. Explain how multiple-tier architectures address division of processing and process management.

12. What is a thin client? How does a thin client relate to division of processing in client–server architectures?

13. List some reasons for choosing a two-tier architecture.

14. List some reasons for choosing a three-tier architecture.

15. List some reasons for choosing a multiple-tier architecture.

16. What is a software bus? How does a software bus differ from other kinds of middleware such as a transaction-processing monitor and message-oriented middleware?

17. Is a Web server middleware? Explain why or why not.

18. Why was XML developed?

19. What is the relationship of XML to the XML Schema Language and the eXtensible Style Language (XSL)?

20. Why do most major DBMSs support XML?

21. Why is there widespread interest in database connectivity over the Internet and intranets?

22. What is the Common Gateway Interface (CGI) and how is it used for Web database connectivity?

23. List some reasons to use an extended Web server for Web database connectivity.

24. List some reasons to use a middleware server for Web database connectivity instead of an extended Web server.

25. How does client-side connectivity enhance server-side processing for database connectivity?

26. What is a global request?

27. How does the integration level of the distributed DBMS affect the component architecture?

28. When is a tightly integrated distributed DBMS appropriate? When is a loosely integrated distributed DBMS appropriate?

29. Discuss the differences in the schema architecture for tightly and loosely integrated distributed DBMSs.

30. How is distributed database transparency related to data independence?

31. Is a higher level of distribution transparency always preferred? Briefly explain why or why not.

32. What is a derived horizontal fragment and why is it useful? What is the relationship of the semi-join operator and derived horizontal fragmentation?

33. What is the larger difference in query formulation: (1) fragmentation transparency to location transparency or (2) location transparency to local mapping transparency? Justify your answer.

34. Why is fragment design and allocation a complex task?

35. Why is global query optimization important?

36. What are differences between global and local optimization in distributed query processing?

37. Why are there multiple objectives in distributed query processing? Which objective seems to be more important?

38. What are the components of performance measures for distributed query processing? What factors influence how these components can be combined into a performance measure?

39. How does two-phase locking for distributed databases differ from two phase locking for centralized databases?

40. Why is the primary copy protocol widely used?

41. What kinds of additional failures occur in a distributed database environment? How can these failures be detected?

42. What is the difference between the voting and the decision phases of the two-phase commit protocol?

43. Discuss the trade-offs between centralized and distributed coordination in distributed concurrency control and recovery.

PROBLEMS

The problems provide practice with defining fragments, formulating queries at various transparency levels, and defining strategies for distributed query processing. The questions use the revised university database tables that follow. This database is similar to the database used in Chapter 3 except for the additional campus columns in the *Student, Offering,* and *Faculty* tables.

Student(StdNo, StdName, StdCampus, StdCity, StdState, StdZip, StdMajor, StdYear)

Course(CourseNo, CrsDesc, CrsCredits)

Offering(OfferNo, CourseNo, OffCampus, OffTerm, OffYear, OffLocation, OffTime, OffDays, FacNo)
  FOREIGN KEY CourseNo REFERENCES Course
  FOREIGN KEY FacNo REFERENCES Faculty

Enrollment(OfferNo, StdNo, EnrGrade)
  FOREIGN KEY OfferNo REFERENCES Offering
  FOREIGN KEY StdNo REFERENCES Student

Faculty(FacNo, FacName, FacCampus, FacDept, FacPhone, FacSalary, FacRank)

1. Write SQL SELECT statements to define two horizontal fragments as students who attend (1) the Boulder campus and (2) the Denver campus.

2. Write SQL SELECT statements to define two horizontal fragments as faculty who teach at (1) the Boulder campus and (2) the Denver campus.

3. Write SQL SELECT statements to define two horizontal fragments as offerings given at (1) the Boulder campus and (2) the Denver campus.

4. Write SQL SELECT statements to define two derived horizontal fragments as enrollments associated with offerings given at (1) the Boulder campus and (2) the Denver campus.

5. Write a SELECT statement to list the information systems courses offered in spring quarter 2004. Information systems courses contain the string "IS" in the course description. Include the course number, the description, the offer number, and the time in the result. Assume fragmentation transparency in your formulation.

6. Write a SELECT statement to list the information systems courses offered in spring quarter 2004. Information systems courses contain the string "IS" in the course description. Include the course number, the description, the offer number, and the time in the result. Assume location transparency in your formulation.

7. Write a SELECT statement to list the information systems courses offered in spring quarter 2004. Information systems courses contain the string "IS" in the course description. Include the course number, the description, the offer number, and the time in the result. Assume local mapping transparency in your formulation. The *Offering* fragments are allocated to the Boulder and the Denver sites. The *Course* table is replicated at both sites.

8. Move offering number O1 from the Boulder to the Denver campus. In addition to moving the offering between campuses, change its location to Plaza 112. Assume fragmentation transparency in your formulation.

9. Move offering number O1 from the Boulder to the Denver campus. In addition to moving the offering between campuses, change its location to Plaza 112. Assume location transparency in your formulation.

10. Move offering number O1 from the Boulder to the Denver campus. In addition to moving the offering between campuses, change its location to Plaza 112. Assume local mapping transparency in your formulation.

11. For the following query, compute communication time (CT) for the distributed access plans listed below. Use the formulas in Section 17.6.1 and the query and network statistics (Table 17.10) in your calculations.

```
SELECT Course.CourseNo, CrsDesc, OfferNo, OffTime, FacName
  FROM BoulderOfferings BOF, Course, DenverFaculty DF
  WHERE Course.CourseNo = BOF.Course AND OffTerm = 'Spring'
    AND OffYear = 2004 AND DF.FacNo = BF.FacNo
    AND FacDept = 'Information Systems'
```

TABLE 17.10	Statistics for Problem 11

Record length is 1,000 bits for each table.

32 bits for *FacNo*.

20 information systems faculty.

5,000 spring 2004 offerings.

10 spring 2004 Boulder offerings taught by Denver faculty.

4,000 courses, 20,000 offerings, and 2,000 faculty in the fragments.

Course table is replicated at both the Denver and the Boulder sites.

BoulderOfferings fragment is located at the Boulder site.

DenverFaculty fragment is located at the Denver site.

Delay per message is 0.1 second.

Data rate is 100,000 bits per second.

11.1 Move the entire *DenverFaculty* fragment to the Boulder site and perform the query.

11.2 Move the entire *BoulderOfferings* fragment to the Denver site and perform the query.

11.3 Move the restricted *BoulderOfferings* fragment to the Denver site and perform the query.

11.4 Move the restricted *DenverFaculty* fragment to the Boulder site and perform the query.

11.5 Restrict the *DenverFaculty* fragment and move the join values (*FacNo*) to the Boulder site. Join the *FacNo* values with the *Course* table and the *BoulderOfferings* fragment at the Boulder site. Move the result back to the Denver site to join with the *DenverFaculty* fragment.

12. Investigate the client–server computing options of a major DBMS. Identify the tools provided by the database vendor to develop two-tier, three-tier, and multiple-tier architectures with and without the Internet.

REFERENCES FOR FURTHER STUDY

This chapter, although providing a broad coverage of distributed processing and data, has only covered the basics. Specialized books on distributed database management include the classic by Ceri and Pelagatti (1984) and the more recent book by Ozsu and Valduriez (1991). The book by Ceri and Pelagatti has a well-written chapter on distributed database design. Date (1990) presents 12 objectives for distributed systems with the most emphasis on distributed DBMSs. Bernstein (1996) provides a detailed presentation of the role of middleware in client–server architectures. There are many trade books and magazines that cover client–server databases and Web database connectivity. Orfali, Harkey, and Edwards (1996) provide a detailed, practical guide to client–server computing including much material on client server databases. Many practical articles about client–server and distributed databases can be found in the *DBAZine* (http://www.dbazine.com) and the *Database Advisor* (http://www.advisor.com). Some good websites on client–server computing are the CGI Resource Index (http://www.cgi-resources.com), the Object Management Group (http://www.omg.org), and the Software Engineering Institute's description of client–server computing (http://www.sei.cmu.edu/str/descriptions/clientserver.html).

Object Database Management Systems

LEARNING OBJECTIVES

This chapter describes extensions to DBMSs to support complex data and operations. After this chapter, the student should have acquired the following knowledge and skills:

■   List business reasons for using object database technology.

■   Define the principles of object-oriented computing.

■   Compare and contrast architectures for object database management.

■   Understand features in SQL:1999 for defining and manipulating user-defined types, typed tables, and subtable families.

■   Understand features in Oracle 9i for defining and manipulating user-defined types and typed tables.

OVERVIEW

Chapter 17 described client–server processing to utilize remote processing capabilities and computer networks. An increasing amount of client–server processing involves complex data and operations that DBMSs do not support. In many cases, client–server processing can be improved if new kinds of data and operations are more closely integrated with traditional data. In this chapter, you will learn about extensions to DBMSs for objects, combinations of complex data and operations.

This chapter provides a broad introduction to object DBMSs. You will learn first about the business reasons to extend database technology. This chapter discusses the increasing use of complex data and the mismatch between DBMSs and programming languages as the driving forces behind object database technology. After grasping the motivation, you are ready to learn about object technology and its impact on DBMSs. You will learn about the principles of object-oriented computing and DBMS architectures to support these principles. This chapter presents inheritance, encapsulation, and polymorphism as the underlying principles of object technology. To support these principles, this chapter presents five architectures for object DBMSs. The last part of this chapter presents object support in SQL:1999, the emerging standard for object relational DBMSs, and Oracle 9i, a significant implementation of the SQL:1999 standard. You will learn about data definition and data manipulation features for object databases.

18.1 MOTIVATION FOR OBJECT DATABASE MANAGEMENT

This section discusses two forces driving the demand for object database management. After a discussion of these forces, example applications are presented to depict the need for object database management.

18.1.1 Complex Data

Most relational DBMSs support only a few data types. Built-in data types supported in SQL include whole numbers, real numbers, fixed-precision numbers (currency), dates, times, and text. These data types are sufficient for many business applications, or at least significant parts of many applications. Many business databases contain fields for names, prices, addresses, and transaction dates that readily conform to the standard data types.

Advances in hardware and software capability have enabled complex data to be captured and manipulated in a digital format. Almost any kind of complex data such as images, audio, video, maps, and three-dimensional graphics can be digitally stored. For example, an image can be represented as a two-dimensional array of pixels (picture elements) where each pixel contains a numeric property representing its color or shade of gray. Digital storage is usually cheaper and more reliable than traditional means such as paper, film, or slides. In addition, digital storage allows easier retrieval and manipulation. For example, you can retrieve digital images by content and similarity to other images. Digital images can be manipulated in an image editor with operations such as cropping, texturing, and color tuning.

The ability to store and manipulate complex data does not by itself drive the demand for object database technology. Rather, the need to store large amounts of complex data and integrate complex data with simple data drives the demand for object database technology. Many business applications require large amounts of complex data. For example, insurance claims processing and medical records can involve large amounts of image data. Storing images in separate files becomes tedious for a large collection of images.

The ability to retrieve complex and simple data simultaneously is becoming important in many business applications. For example, to review a patient's condition, a physician may request X rays along with vital statistics. Without integration, two separate programs are required to display the data: an image editor to display the X rays and a DBMS to retrieve the vital statistics. The ability to retrieve both images and vital statistics in a single query is a large improvement. Besides retrieving complex data, new operations also may be necessary. For example, a physician may want to compare the similarity of a patient's X rays with X rays that show abnormalities.

18.1.2 Type System Mismatch

Increasingly, software written in a procedural language needs to access a database. Procedural languages support customized interfaces for data entry forms and reports, operations beyond the capability of SQL, and batch processing. For example, writing a computer program is often necessary to operate on self-referencing data such as a parts hierarchy. Embedded SQL is often used to access a database from within a computer program. After executing an embedded SQL statement, database fields are stored in program variables that can be manipulated further.

A mismatch between the data types in a relational DBMS and the data types of a programming language makes software more complex and difficult to develop. For example, payroll processing can involve many kinds of benefits, deductions, and compensation arrangements. A relational database may have one representation for benefits, deductions, and compensation arrangements while a programming language may have a rather different representation. Before coding the complex calculations, the data must be transformed from the relational database representation (tables) into the programming language representation (records or objects). After the calculations, the data must be transformed back into the relational database representation.

This data type mismatch is even more pronounced for complex data. Programming languages usually have richer type systems than DBMSs. For example, relational databases provide a tedious representation of geometric shapes in a building's floor plan. Objects such as points, lines, and polygons may be represented as one text field or as several numeric fields such as *X* and *Y* coordinates for points. In contrast, a programming language may have custom data types for points, lines, and polygons. There may be considerable coding to transform between the relational database representation and the programming language representation.

In addition, a relational DBMS cannot perform elementary operations on complex data. Thus, a computer program must be written instead of using a query language. For example, a complex program must be written to compute the similarity between two images. The program will probably contain 10 to 100 times the amount of code found in a query. In addition, the program must transform between the database and the programming language representations.

18.1.3 Application Examples

This section depicts several applications that involve a mix of simple and complex data as well as ad hoc queries. These applications have features increasingly found in many business applications. As you will see, object DBMSs support the requirements of these kinds of applications.

Dental Office Support

Dental offices use a mix of simple and complex data to make appointments, generate bills, and conduct examinations. Setting appointments requires a calendar with time blocks for service providers (dentists and hygienists). In conducting examinations, service providers use dental charts (graphic of mouth with each tooth identified), X rays, patient facts, and dental histories. After an examination, bill preparation uses the list of services in the examination and patient insurance data. Queries that involve both complex and simple data include showing a dental chart with recent dental problems highlighted and comparing X rays for symptoms of gum loss.

Real Estate Listing Service

Real estate listing services increasingly use complex data to facilitate customer searches. A real estate listing includes a mix of simple and complex data. The simple data include numerous facts about homes such as the number of bedrooms, the square feet, and the listing price. Complex data include photographs of homes, floor plans, video tours, and area maps. Queries can involve a mix of simple and complex data. Customers want to see homes in a specified neighborhood with selected features. Some customers may want to see homes with the closest match to a set of ideal features where the customer assigns a weight to each feature. After selecting a set of homes, a customer wants to explore the appearance, the floor plan, and the facts about the homes.

Auto Insurance Claims

Auto insurance companies use complex data to settle claims. Analyzing claims involves complex data such as photographs, accident reports, and witness statements as well as simple data such as driver and vehicle descriptions. Settling claims involves a map showing service providers as well as service provider rates and service history. Queries for accident data and a list of service providers in close proximity to a customer involve both simple and complex data.

18.2 OBJECT-ORIENTED PRINCIPLES

To provide a foundation to understand the architectures and features of object DBMSs, this section presents three fundamental principles of object-oriented computing. After presenting the principles, this section discusses their impact on object DBMSs and object-oriented programming languages.

18.2.1 Encapsulation

An object is a combination of data and procedures. The data are sometimes referred to as variables and the procedures as methods. Each object has a unique identifier that never changes unless the object is destroyed. Object identifiers are not visible to users. In contrast, primary keys in relational databases are visible.

Classes contain collections of objects. A class definition consists of a collection of variables and methods. The variables are sometimes called instance variables to distinguish them from variables that apply to the entire class (called class variables). Example 18.1 shows the class *Point* with two variables (*x* and *y* denoting the Cartesian coordinates) and two methods (*Distance* and *Equals*).[1] Each variable has an associated data type. Each method has an interface and an implementation. The interface shows the in-

---

[1] The examples in this section conform to the Object Definition Language (ODL) standard defined by the Object Database Management Group.

puts and the outputs of the method. The implementation shows the detailed coding. For brevity, implementations are not shown in the examples. Example 18.2 depicts a more business-oriented example.

Example 18.1

Partial *Point* Class

```
CLASS Point   {
//  VARIABLES:
    ATTRIBUTE Real X; // X coordinate
    ATTRIBUTE Real Y; // Y coordinate
// METHODS:
    Float Distance(IN Point aPoint);
        // Computes the Distance between 2 points
    Boolean Equals (IN Point aPoint);
        // Determines if two Points have the same coordinates
} ;
```

Example 18.2

Partial *Bond* Class

```
CLASS Bond   {
// VARIABLES:
    ATTRIBUTE Float IntRate; // Interest Rate
    ATTRIBUTE Date Maturity; // Maturity Date
// METHODS:
    Float Yield();
// Computes the Bond's Yield
} ;
```

Encapsulation objects can be accessed only through their interfaces.

Encapsulation means that objects can be accessed only through their interfaces. The internal details (variable definitions and method implementations) are not accessible. For example, you can use the *Distance* and the *Equals* methods only to manipulate *Point* objects. To use the *Distance* method, you supply two *Point* objects. The first *Point* object is implicit in the interface because *Distance* is a method of *Point*. To make *Point* objects more usable, there should be additional methods for creating points, destroying points, and moving points.

Encapsulation provides two benefits for managing software complexity. First, a class is a larger unit of reusability than a procedure. In many cases, classes can be reused rather than just individual procedures. More complex classes can be defined using simpler classes. Examples 18.3 and 18.4 depict classes that use the *Point* and the *Bond* classes defined in Examples 18.1 and 18.2. The new classes (*Rectangle* and *Portfolio*) do not need to recode the variables and methods of the *Point* and the *Bond* classes, respectively.

Example 18.3

Rectangle Class Using the *Point* Class

```
CLASS Rectangle   {
// VARIABLES:
    ATTRIBUTE Point UpperLeftCorner; // Upper Left Point
    ATTRIBUTE Point LowerRightCorner; // Lower Right Point
```

```
// METHODS:
  Float Area();
    // Computes the Area of the Rectangle
  Float Length ();
    // Computes the Length
  Float Height ();
    // Computes the Height
};
```

Example 18.4 — *Portfolio* Class Using the *Bond* Class

```
CLASS Portfolio   {
// VARIABLES:
  ATTRIBUTE Set<Bond> BondHoldings; // set of Bonds
  ATTRIBUTE Set<Stock> StockHoldings; // Set of Stocks
// METHODS:
  Float PortfolioReturn();
// Computes the portfolio's Return
};
```

As a second benefit, encapsulation provides a form of data independence. Because internal details of objects are hidden, changes to the internal details can be made without changing the code that uses the objects. Recall from Chapter 1 that data independence promotes reduced software maintenance costs.

18.2.2 Inheritance

Inheritance sharing of data and code among similar classes (classes and subclasses).

Chapter 5 presented classification and inheritance for the Entity Relationship Model. These concepts are similar in object-oriented models except that inheritance applies to both data and procedures. Chapter 5 described inheritance only for attributes of an entity type. Examples 18.5 and 18.6 present classes that inherit from the *Point* and the *Bond* classes. Figure 18.1 depicts a graphical representation of the inheritance relationships. A color point is a point with color. Likewise a corporate bond is a bond with an issuing company and an investment rating. In the subclasses (a child class that inherits from a parent class), the variables and the methods of the parent classes are not repeated. When using the subclasses, the methods in the parent classes can be used.

Example 18.5 — *ColorPoint* Example (Subclass of *Point*)

```
CLASS ColorPoint EXTENDS Point   {
// VARIABLES:
  ATTRIBUTE Integer Color; // Integer value denoting a color
// METHODS:
  Integer Brighten(IN Real Intensity);
    // Computes a new color that is brighter
};
```

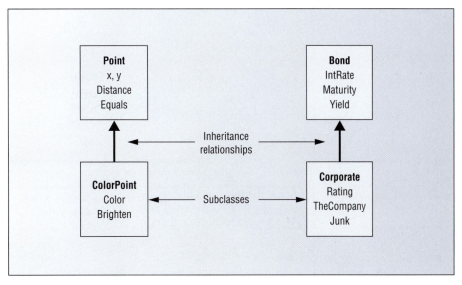

Figure 18.1   Class hierarchies with the *ColorPoint* and the *Corporate* subclasses.

Example 18.6   *Corporate* Bond Example (Subclass of *Bond*)

```
CLASS Corporate EXTENDS Bond   {
// VARIABLES:
  RELATIONSHIP Company TheCompany; // Company issuing the Bond
  ATTRIBUTE String Rating; // Moody's Rating
// METHODS:
  Boolean Junk();
// TRUE if the bond's rating means low quality
};
```

As discussed in Chapter 5, inheritance can extend to multiple levels. For example, if *Investment* is the parent class of *Bond,* the *Corporate* class inherits from both *Investment* and *Bond.* Inheritance also can extend to multiple parents. Figure 18.2 depicts an investment class hierarchy with multiple inheritance. A convertible security is a bond that becomes a stock if the bondholder chooses. The conversion price and the conversion ratio determine whether a bondholder should convert. The *Convertible* class inherits directly from the *Stock* and the *Bond* classes. Multiple inheritance can be problematic because of conflicts. In Figure 18.2, the *Yield* method can be inherited from either *Stock* or *Bond.* There are various schemes for resolving inheritance conflicts. Ultimately, the database designer must decide on the class from which to inherit.

Inheritance provides an improved organization of software and incremental reusability. The graphical class organization depicts similarity among classes. Programmers can reduce their time to search for similar code by using the graphical class organization. After finding a similar class, database designers and programmers can incrementally add more features (variables and methods). The only new coding is only for the new features, not the existing features.

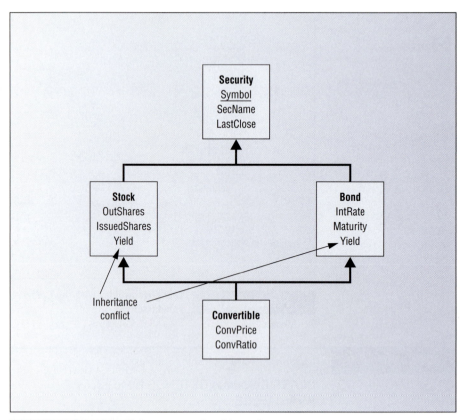

Figure 18.2   **Investment class hierarchy.**

18.2.3 Polymorphism

Polymorphism ability of a computing system to choose among multiple implementations of a method.

Polymorphism literally means "of many forms." In object-oriented computing, polymorphism permits a method to have multiple implementations. A method implementation in a subclass can override the method implementation in a parent class. Some methods must be overridden because the meaning of the method changes for a subclass. For example, the *Equals* method in class *ColorPoint* compares the coordinates and the color whereas the method implementation in the *Point* class only compares the coordinates. In contrast, the *Area* method has a more efficient implementation for the *Rectangle* class than for the parent *Polygon* class. As another example, the *Yield* method (Figure 18.2) must be overridden in the *Convertible* subclass to combine the calculations in the parent *Stock* and *Bond* classes.

Requesting a method execution involves sending a message to an object. A message contains a method name and parameters, similar to a procedure call. One of the parameters is the object that receives the message. The receiver object decides the action to take. If the object's class contains the method, it is executed. Otherwise, the object forwards the message to its parent class for execution. In Figure 18.3, a *ColorPoint* object receives a message requesting a distance calculation. Since the *ColorPoint* class does not contain an implementation of the *Distance* method, the message is sent to the parent class, *Point*. The *Point* class executes the method because it contains an implementation of the *Distance* method.

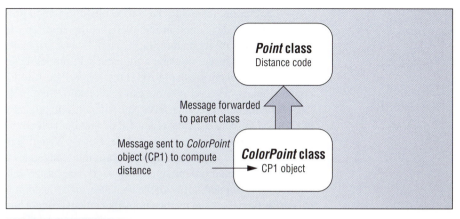

| **Figure 18.3** | Processing a message. |

Because object-oriented computing involves messages, client–server processing and object-oriented computing are closely related. Clients and servers are often objects communicating through messages. Client–server processing allows objects to be located on different computers.

In processing a message, the object DBMS assumes responsibility for choosing the appropriate implementation of a method. Associating or <u>binding</u> a message to a method implementation can be done statically when code is compiled or dynamically when code is executed. Static binding is more efficient but dynamic binding can be more flexible. Dynamic binding is sometimes called "late" binding because it happens just before code execution.

Along with binding, a DBMS ensures that objects and methods are compatible. This function is known as type checking. <u>Strong type checking</u> ensures that there are no incompatibility errors in code. For example, strong type checking prevents computing an area for a point object because the *Area* method applies to polygons not points. Because complex expressions can involve many methods and objects, strong type checking is an important kind of consistency check in object-oriented computing.

Polymorphism supports fewer, more reusable methods. Because a method can have multiple implementations, the number of method names is reduced. A user needs to know only the method name and the interface, not the appropriate implementation to use. For example, a user only needs to know that the *Area* method applies to polygons, not the appropriate implementation for a rectangle. The DBMS assumes responsibility for finding the appropriate implementation.

Polymorphism also supports incremental modification of code. In coding another implementation of a method for a subclass, much of the code for the method's implementation in the parent class often can be used. For example, to code the redefinition of the *Equals* method in the *ColorPoint* class, another equality condition (for the color of a point) should be added to the conditions to test the *x* and *y* coordinates.

Strong Type Checking the ability to ensure that programming code contains no incompatibility errors. Strong type checking is an important kind of error checking for object-oriented coding.

18.2.4 Programming Languages versus DBMSs

These principles apply to both object-oriented programming languages and object DBMSs. However, the application of the principles varies somewhat between programming languages and DBMSs.

Programming languages have used object-oriented principles for many years. Simula, a language developed in the 1960s, is the first reported object-oriented programming language. As its name implies, Simula was originally developed as a simulation language. Objects and messages are natural in modeling simulations. Smalltalk, a language developed during the 1970s at the Xerox Palo Alto Research Center, was the first popular object-oriented programming language. Smalltalk originally emphasized objects for graphical user interfaces. Inheritance among classes for windows and controls is a natural fit. Since the development of Smalltalk, there have been many other object-oriented programming languages. Java, C++, Visual Basic, and C# are some of the most widely used object-oriented programming languages today.

Object-oriented programming languages emphasize software maintenance and code reusability. To support software maintenance, encapsulation is strictly enforced. The internal details (variables and method implementations) cannot be referenced. In addition, some languages support restrictions on accessing methods. To support reusability, some languages support additional kinds of inheritance to share code. Reuse of code can extend to collections of classes, classes with data type parameters, and redefined code in a subclass.

Object DBMSs are more recent than object-oriented programming languages. Research and development of object DBMSs began in the 1980s. By the early 1990s, there were a number of commercial object DBMSs. In addition, there was considerable work on extending relational DBMSs with new object features. The next section describes a number of architectures for object DBMSs.

Because early object DBMSs began as extensions of object-oriented programming languages, query language support did not exist. Instead, early object DBMSs provided support for persistent data that last longer than the execution of a program. Large amounts of persistent data could be accessed although in a procedural manner. The early object DBMSs were designed to support applications with large amounts of complex data such as computer-aided design.

Most object DBMSs now support nonprocedural data access. Some of the object-oriented principles are relaxed to accommodate this emphasis. Encapsulation usually is relaxed so that an object's data can be referenced in a query. Database security features provide access to object features rather than public/private distinctions employed in object-oriented programming languages. Inheritance mechanisms usually are simpler because it is assumed that most coding is through a query language, not a procedural language. In addition, most object DBMSs now provide query optimization and transaction processing capabilities.

18.3 ARCHITECTURES FOR OBJECT DATABASE MANAGEMENT

Although adding object-oriented features to a DBMS is a good idea, there is no widespread agreement about what features to add and how features should be added. Some approaches provide small extensions that leave most of the object-oriented processing outside of a DBMS. Other approaches involve a complete rewrite of a DBMS to accommodate objects. The marketplace probably will support a variety of approaches because of the different requirements among customers. This section describes several object database management architectures along with their strengths and weaknesses.

Large Object Architecture storage of large objects (binary or text) in a database along with external software to manipulate large objects. The BLOB (binary large object) and CLOB (character large object) data types are used to store fields with large objects.
....

18.3.1 Large Objects and External Software

The earliest approach to add objects to relational databases was to use large objects with external software. Complex data are stored in a field as a binary or text large object. For example, an image uses the BLOB (binary large object) data type while a large text doc-

External software for
manipulating complex data

SQL statements

Simple and
complex data

Database server

Simple
data

Complex
data

Relational database

Figure 18.4   **Large object architecture.**

ument uses the <u>CLOB (character large object)</u> data type. As depicted in Figure 18.4, large objects usually are stored separately from other data in a table. A query can retrieve but not display large objects. Software external to the DBMS displays and manipulates large objects. External software includes ActiveX® controls, Java applets, and Web browser plug-ins.

The large object approach is simple to implement and universal. Only small changes to a DBMS are required. All kinds of complex data can be stored. In addition, a large market for third-party software may be available for prominent kinds of complex data. For example, many third-party tools have been implemented for popular image formats.

Despite some advantages, the large object approach suffers from serious performance drawbacks. Because the DBMS does not understand the structure and the operations of complex data, no optimization is possible. Data cannot be filtered using characteristics of large objects. No indexes can be used to select records using characteristics of large objects. Because large objects are stored separately from other data, additional disk accesses may be necessary. The order of the large objects may not coincide with the order of other table data.

18.3.2 Specialized Media Servers

Specialized Media Server Architecture the use of a dedicated server to manage complex data outside of a database. Programmers use an application programming interface to access complex data.

In the <u>specialized media server architecture,</u> complex data reside outside of a DBMS as depicted in Figure 18.5. A separate server may be dedicated to manipulating a single kind of complex data such as video or images. Programmers use an application programming interface (API) to access complex data through a media server. The API provides a set of procedures to retrieve, update, and transform a specific kind of complex data. To simultaneously manipulate simple data and complex data, program code contains a mix of embedded SQL and API calls to the media server.

Specialized media servers provide better performance than the large object approach but sacrifice some flexibility. Dedicated servers and highly specialized APIs provide good performance for specific kinds of complex data. Because an API is

| Figure 18.5 | Specialized media server architecture. |

provided rather than a query language, the range of operations may be limited though. For example, a video server may support fast streaming of video but not searching by content.

When combining simple and complex data, the specialized server approach may perform poorly. A query optimizer cannot jointly optimize retrieval of simple and complex data because the DBMS is not aware of complex data. In addition, a media server may not provide indexing techniques for search conditions. Transaction processing is limited to simple data because specialized media servers do not typically support transaction processing.

18.3.3 Object Database Middleware

Object Database Middleware the use of middleware to manage complex data possibly stored outside of a database along with traditional data stored in a database.

Object database middleware circumvents problems with media servers by simulating object features. Clients no longer directly access media servers as shown in Figure 18.6. Instead, clients send SQL statements to middleware, which makes API calls to media servers and sends SQL statements to database servers. The SQL statements can combine traditional operations on simple data with specialized operations on complex data. Object database middleware relieves the user of knowing a separate API for each media server. In addition, object database middleware provides location independence because users do not need to know where complex data reside.

Object middleware provides a way to integrate complex data stored on PCs and remote servers with relational databases. Without object middleware, some of the complex data could not be combined easily with simple data. Even if an architecture that integrates more tightly with the DBMS is desired, the object middleware approach can be used for complex data that users do not want to store in a database.

Object middleware can suffer performance problems because of a lack of integration with a DBMS. Combining complex and simple data suffers the same performance problems as with specialized media servers. The DBMS cannot optimize requests that simultaneously combine simple and complex data. Middleware can provide transaction

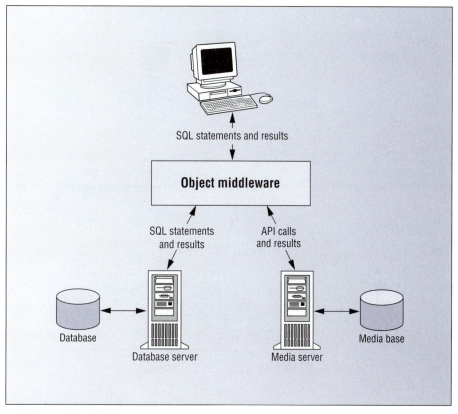

SQL statements and results

Object middleware

SQL statements
and results

API calls
and results

Database

Database server

Media server

Media base

| Figure 18.6 | **Object middleware approach.** |

processing that combines simple and complex data. However, transaction performance can be slow because two-phase commit and distributed concurrency control techniques must be used.

18.3.4 Object Relational Database Management Systems for User-Defined Types

The first three approaches involve little or no change to a DBMS but provide only limited query and optimization capabilities. With larger changes to a DBMS, more query and optimization capabilities are possible.

Object Relational DBMS a relational DBMS extended with an object query processor for user-defined data types. SQL:1999 provides the standard for object relational DBMSs.

To provide additional query capabilities, <u>object relational DBMSs</u> support user-defined types and functions. Almost any kind of complex data can be added as a user-defined type. Image data, spatial data, time series, and video are just a few of the possible data types. For each user-defined type, a collection of functions can be defined. These functions can be used in SQL statements, not just in programming language code. Inheritance and polymorphism apply to user-defined data types. To improve performance, specialized storage structures can be used when accessing complex data. For example, multidimensional Btrees can be provided for accessing spatial data.

Although user-defined types are the most salient feature of object relational databases, there are a number of other prominent object features including subtable families (generalization hierarchies for tables), the array data type, and the row data type.

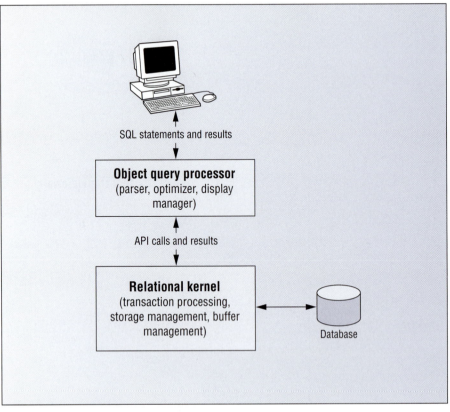

Figure 18.7	**Component architecture for object relational DBMSs.**

Section 18.4 presents examples of user-defined types and these other object features in SQL:1999, the standard for object relational DBMSs. Section 18.5 presents the object features in Oracle 9i, a significant implementation of the SQL:1999 standard.

User-defined types involve a table-driven architecture as depicted in Figure 18.7. The object query processor uses table-driven code for user-defined types. The parser decomposes references to expressions involving user-defined types and functions. The display manager controls the presentation of simple and complex data. The optimizer searches for storage structures that can be used to optimize expressions containing user-defined types and functions. The relational kernel comprises transaction processing, storage management, and buffer management. It provides the engine used by the object query processor. Little or no changes are necessary to the relational kernel.

Object relational DBMSs provide good integration of complex data, but reliability may be a concern. The integration of simple and complex data involves considerable changes to the parser, display manager, and optimizer. However, the base of code in the kernel remains relatively stable. Reliability can be compromised in the implementations of user-defined functions and storage structures. DBMS vendors, third-party vendors, and in-house developers can provide user-defined types, which can be complex and difficult to implement. Implementation errors can affect the integrity of both simple and complex data. In addition, third-party data types can be subject to viruses.

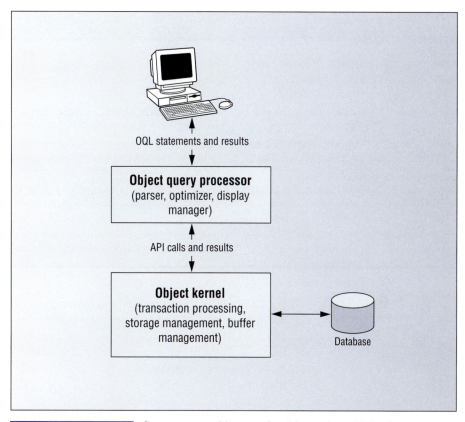

OQL statements and results

Object query processor
(parser, optimizer, display manager)

API calls and results

Object kernel
(transaction processing, storage management, buffer management)

Database

| Figure 18.8 | **Component architecture for object-oriented DBMSs.** |

18.3.5 Object-Oriented Database Management Systems

Some experts have argued that more fundamental changes to a DBMS are needed to support objects. Both the data model and the kernel must be changed to accommodate objects. This conviction has driven a number of start-up software companies to implement a new class of object DBMSs, as depicted in Figure 18.8. The software companies have banded together to form the Object Database Management Group (ODMG). The ODMG has proposed an object definition language (ODL) and an object query language (OQL). These languages are the counterpart of SQL for object-oriented DBMSs.

Despite some important advantages of object-oriented DBMSs, they continue to occupy a market niche. Most of the products are used in applications where ad hoc query, query optimization, and transaction processing are not important. Instead, the products emphasize support for complex data in large software systems. Most of the object-oriented DBMSs began as extended programming languages with support for persistent objects (i.e., objects that exist after a program terminates). Gradually, the object-oriented DBMSs have provided ad hoc query, query optimization, and efficient transaction support. Still, questions remain about the ability of object-oriented DBMSs to provide high performance for traditional business applications. As object kernel technology matures, these concerns should cease. However, gaining significant market share against the established market-leading relational products will be difficult.

Object-Oriented DBMS a new kind of DBMS designed especially for objects. Object-oriented DBMSs have an object query processor and an object kernel. The Object Data Management Group provides the standard for object-oriented DBMSs.

TABLE 18.1	**Summary of Architectures**	
Architecture	*Example Products*	*Comments*
Large objects	Most SQL-92 DBMSs	Storage of any kind of data; uncertain performance; limited query language support
Media servers	Oracle 7.3 with text and spatial data servers	No query language support; uncertain performance when combining simple and complex data; good performance on complex data
Object database middleware	Microsoft Universal Data Access and OLE DB	Ability to combine distributed and diverse data sources; flexible service levels for data sources; uncertain performance when combining and updating simple and complex data
Object relational (SQL:1999)	IBM Unidata Data Blades, IBM DB2 Extenders, Oracle 9i	Good performance with specialized storage structures; good query language support; some type mismatch with programming languages
Object-oriented (ODMG)	ObjectStore, UniSQL, O2, Versant, Gemstone	Good query language support; uncertain performance for traditional applications; good type match with programming languages

The ODMG and SQL standards groups have recognized the need for a unified standard. In a few years, a unified standard may emerge that allows portability between SQL:1999 and ODMG-compliant DBMSs. Even when this unification occurs, considerable time may elapse before most products support the unified standard. Both ODMG and SQL:1999 are very large standards. Most DBMS vendors will support only a subset of the standards.

18.3.6 Summary of Object Database Architectures

To help you remember the architectures for object DBMSs, Table 18.1 provides a convenient summary. All of the architectures fulfill a certain market niche. The simpler architectures (large objects and media servers) should become less popular over time. The struggle for dominance among the other three architectures may not be decided for some time. The object database middleware architecture will likely coexist with the other architectures to handle complex data stored outside of a database.

18.4 OBJECT DATABASE FEATURES IN SQL:1999

To clarify object database concepts, this section provides examples using SQL:1999, the object relational database language.[2] The SQL:1999 standard includes a core language part and a number of packages, as summarized in Table 18.2. The SQL:1999 standard is quite large as it consists of five documents totaling more than 2,100 pages. Since the adoption of the SQL:1999 standard, a number of other packages are currently under development, including temporal database support, management of external data, SQL bindings for the Java language, and XML features.

The SQL:1999 standard provides two levels of conformance. Minimal conformance includes all core features in the SQL/Framework and the SQL/Foundation documents as well as one binding style (the module binding style or the embedded SQL binding style)

---

[2]SQL:1999 was formerly known as SQL3. The name was changed with a four-digit year designation to support year 2000 naming conventions.

TABLE 18.2	Overview of the SQL:1999 Packages

SQL:1999 Package	Scope
Core	SQL environment, SQL implementation, tables, views, predefined data types, SQL statements, conformance specifications
Persistent stored modules	Computational completeness, stored modules, function overloading
Call-level interface	Call-level interface for SQL
Enhanced datetime facilities	Time zone specification, interval data type
Enhanced integrity management	Assertions, triggers, constraint management
OLAP facilities	Cube and roll-up operators, row and table constructors, FULL JOIN and INTERSECT operators
Basic object support	User-defined data types, single inheritance, reference types, arrays
Enhanced object support	Path expressions, subtable definition, subtable search, subtypes

for a host programming language. Enhanced conformance involves support for one or more SQL packages in addition to the minimal conformance requirements. Because of the lack of testing suites and independent certification, the conformance level of a specific DBMS is difficult to determine.

Because SQL-92 is a dominant standard now, this author anticipates that SQL:1999 will become the dominant standard for object database management. Because of the size and scope of the standard, vendors may take several years to adopt its most popular parts. Over time, major vendors will be forced to adhere to most of the SQL:1999 standard due to market pressures. At the time this chapter was written (March 2002), user-defined types and functions were the most widely implemented part of the SQL:1999 standard for object relational databases.

This section presents examples from the Basic Object Support and Enhanced Object Support packages. These examples use the real estate database discussed in Section 18.1. This section extends the real estate database with residential properties, owners, and agents.

18.4.1 User-Defined Types

One of the most fundamental extensions in SQL:1999 is the user-defined type for bundling data and procedures together. User-defined types support the definition of new structured data types as well as the refinement of the standard data types. A structured data type has a collection of attributes and methods. In SQL-92, the CREATE DOMAIN statement supports refinements to standard data types but not the definition of new structured types.

Example 18.7 shows the *Point* type to contrast with the ODMG notation shown in Example 18.1. Some differences are apparent, such as the keywords (TYPE versus CLASS) and the order of specification (the field name before the data type). The first part of a user-defined type contains the attribute definitions. The double hyphen denotes a comment. For methods, the first parameter is implicit like the ODMG notation. For example, the *Distance* method lists only one *Point* parameter because the other *Point* parameter is implicit. In SQL:1999, methods only use input parameters and should return values. The body of methods is not shown in the CREATE TYPE statement but rather in the CREATE METHOD statement. The keywords NOT FINAL mean that subtypes can be defined. The keyword INSTANTIABLE means that instances of the type can be created.[3]

Example 18.7   *Point* Type in SQL:1999

```
CREATE TYPE Point AS
(   X FLOAT,  -- X coordinate
    Y FLOAT   ) -- Y coordinate
  METHOD Distance(P2 Point) RETURNS FLOAT,
     -- Computes the distance between 2 points
  METHOD Equals (P2 Point) RETURNS BOOLEAN
     -- Determines if 2 points are equivalent
NOT FINAL
INSTANTIABLE;
```

As stated in the previous paragraph, SQL:1999 methods are somewhat limited in that they must return single values and only use input parameters. In addition, the first parameter of a method is implicitly an instance of the type in which it is associated. SQL:1999 provides functions and procedures that do not have the restrictions of methods. Because functions and procedures are not associated with a specific type, SQL:1999 provides separate definition statements (CREATE FUNCTION and CREATE PROCEDURE). Procedures can use input, output, and input–output parameters whereas functions only use input parameters.

Example 18.8 shows the *ColorPoint* type, a subtype of *Point*. The UNDER keyword indicates the parent type. Because SQL:1999 does not support multiple inheritance, only a single type name can follow the UNDER keyword. In the method definitions, the OVERRIDING keyword indicates that the method overrides the definition in a parent type.

Example 18.8   *ColorPoint* Type

```
CREATE TYPE ColorPoint UNDER Point AS
(Color INTEGER )
  METHOD Brighten (Intensity INTEGER) RETURNS INTEGER,
     -- Increases color intensity
  OVERRIDING METHOD Equals (CP2 ColorPoint)
        RETURNS BOOLEAN
     -- Determines if 2 ColorPoints are equivalent
     FINAL;
```

---

[3]The keywords NOT INSTANTIABLE mean that the type is abstract without instances. Abstract types contain data and code but no instances. Abstract types have been found to enhance code sharing in object-oriented programming.

Besides the explicit methods listed in the CREATE TYPE statement, user-defined types have implicit methods that can be used in SQL statements and stored procedures, as shown below:

- **Constructor method:** creates an empty instance of the type. The constructor method has the same name as the data type. For example, Point() is the constructor method for the *Point* type.
- **Observer methods:** retrieve values from attributes. Each observer method uses the same name as its associated attribute. For example, X() is the observer method for the *X* attribute of the *Point* type.
- **Mutator methods:** change values stored in attributes. Each mutator method uses the same name as its associated attribute with one parameter for the value. For example, X(45.0) changes the value of the *X* attribute.

SQL:1999 features the ARRAY collection type to support types with more than one value such as time series and geometric shapes. Arrays can store any data type except other arrays. Example 18.9 uses an ARRAY to define a polygon type with a maximum of 10 corners. The number following the ARRAY keyword indicates the maximum size of the array.

Example 18.9   *Polygon* Type Using an ARRAY

```
CREATE TYPE Polygon AS
  (Corners Point ARRAY[10], -- Array of Corner Points
   Color INTEGER )
  METHOD Area() RETURNS FLOAT,
   -- Computes the area
  METHOD Scale (Factor FLOAT) RETURNS Polygon
   -- Computes a new polygon scaled by factor
NOT FINAL;
```

User-defined types are integrated into the heart of SQL:1999. User-defined types can be used as data types for columns in tables, passed as parameters, and returned as values. User-defined methods can be used in expressions in the SELECT, the WHERE, and the HAVING clauses.

18.4.2 Table Definitions and Subtable Families

SQL:1999 supports two styles of table definitions. The traditional SQL-92 style uses foreign keys to link two tables. Example 18.10 depicts the *Property* table using a foreign key to reference the agent representing the property. The view column uses the binary large object (BLOB) type. If a user-defined type for JPEG images is available, it would be a better choice than the BLOB type.

Example 18.10   *Agent* and *Property* Tables Using the Traditional SQL-92 Definition Style

```
CREATE TABLE Agent
(AgentNo  INTEGER,
 Name     VARCHAR(30),
```

```
Street     VARCHAR(50),
City       VARCHAR(30),
State      CHAR(2),
Zip        CHAR(9),
Phone      CHAR(13),
Email      VARCHAR(50),
CONSTRAINT AgentPK PRIMARY KEY(AgentNo)   );

CREATE TABLE Property
(PropNo   INTEGER,
 Street    VARCHAR(50),
 City      VARCHAR(30),
 State     CHAR(2),
 Zip       CHAR(9),
 SqFt      INTEGER,
 View      BLOB,
 AgentNo   INTEGER,
 Location Point,
 CONSTRAINT PropertyPK PRIMARY KEY(PropNo),
 CONSTRAINT AgentFK FOREIGN KEY(AgentNo) REFERENCES Agent );
```

SQL:1999 supports the row type constructor to allow rows of a table to be stored as variables, used as parameters, and returned by functions. A row type is a sequence of name/value pairs. One use of a row type is to collect related columns together so that they can be stored as a variable or passed as a parameter. Example 18.11 depicts the *Property* table using a row type for the address columns (*Street, City, State,* and *Zip*).

Example 18.11   Revised *Property* Table Definition with a Row Type

```
CREATE TABLE Property
(PropNo    INTEGER,
 Address    ROW   (Street    VARCHAR(50),
                   City      VARCHAR(30),
                   State     CHAR(2),
                   Zip       CHAR(9) ),
 SqFt      INTEGER,
 View      BLOB,
 AgentNo   INTEGER,
 Location Point,
 CONSTRAINT PropertyPK PRIMARY KEY(PropNo),
 CONSTRAINT AgentFK FOREIGN KEY(AgentNo) REFERENCES Agent );
```

SQL:1999 provides an alternative style of table definition known as <u>typed tables</u> to support object identifiers and object references. With typed tables, a table definition references a user-defined type rather than providing its own list of columns. Example 18.12 depicts the *AgentType* user-defined type and the *Agent* table referring to *AgentType*. In addition, the *AddressType* (a named structured type) is used in place of the unnamed ROW type in Example 18.11. The REF clause defines an object identifier for the table. The SYSTEM GENERATED keywords indicate that the object identifiers are generated by the DBMS, not the user application (USER GENERATED keywords).

Example 18.12   Definition of *AddressType* and *AgentType* Followed by the Typed *Agent* Table Based on *AgentType*

```
CREATE TYPE AddressType AS
 (Street    VARCHAR(50),
  City      VARCHAR(30),
  State     CHAR(2),
  Zip       CHAR(9)   )
NOT FINAL;

CREATE TYPE AgentType AS
(AgentNo  INTEGER,
 Name     VARCHAR(30),
 Address  AddressType,
 Phone    CHAR(13),
 Email    VARCHAR(50) )
 NOT FINAL;

CREATE TABLE Agent OF AgentType
(REF IS AgentOld SYSTEM GENERATED,
 CONSTRAINT AgentPK PRIMARY KEY(AgentNo) );
```

Other tables can reference tables based on user-defined types. Object references provide an alternative to value references of foreign keys. Example 18.13 depicts a definition of the *PropertyType* table with a reference to the *AgentType*. The SCOPE clause limits a reference to the rows of a table rather than objects of the type.

Example 18.13   Definition of the *PropertyType* with a Reference to the *Agent* Table and the Typed *Property* Table

```
CREATE TYPE PropertyType AS
(PropNo   INTEGER,
 Address  AddressType,
 SqFt     INTEGER,
 View     BLOB,
 Location Point,
 AgentRef REF(AgentType) SCOPE Agent   )
 NOT FINAL;

CREATE TABLE Property
(REF IS PropertyOld SYSTEM GENERATED,
 CONSTRAINT PropertyPK PRIMARY KEY(PropNo)   ) ;
```

As these examples demonstrate, SQL:1999 provides a variety of ways to define tables (typed versus untyped tables, references versus traditional foreign keys, ROW types versus columns versus named structured types). For training of application programmers, consistent usage of table definition styles is important. A reasonable rule of thumb is to use the traditional table definitions (untyped tables with unstructured columns and foreign keys) or typed tables with named structured types and reference types. Mixing table definition styles can burden application programmers because the definition style influences the coding used in retrieval and manipulation statements.

Inheritance applies to tables in a similar way as it applies to user-defined types. A table can be declared as a subtable of another table. A subtable inherits the columns of its parent tables. SQL:1999 limits inheritance for tables to single inheritance. A potentially confusing part of table inheritance involves type inheritance. Tables involved in subtable relationships must be typed tables with the associated types also participating in subtype relationships as demonstrated in Example 18.14. Note that the REF clauses and primary key constraints are inherited from the *Property* table so they are not specified for the *Residential* and the *Industrial* tables.

Example 18.14   Subtypes and Subtables for Residential and Industrial Properties

```
CREATE TYPE ResidentialType UNDER PropertyType
(BedRooms  INTEGER,
 BathRooms  INTEGER,
 Assessments DECIMAL(9,2) ARRAY[6] )
NOT FINAL
INSTANTIABLE;


CREATE TABLE Residential OF ResidentialType UNDER Property;


CREATE TYPE IndustrialType UNDER PropertyType
(Zoning VARCHAR(20),
 AccessDesc VARCHAR(20),
 RailAvailable BOOLEAN,
 Parking VARCHAR(10) )
NOT FINAL
INSTANTIABLE;


CREATE TABLE Industrial OF IndustrialType UNDER Property;
```

Set inclusion determines the relationship of rows of a table to rows in its subtables. Every row in a subtable is also a row in each of its ancestor (direct parents and indirect parents) tables. Each row of a parent table corresponds to at most one row in direct subtables. This set inclusion relationship extends to an entire subtable family, including the root table and all subtables directly or indirectly under the root table. For example, a subtable family includes security as the root; bond and stock, under investment; and corporate, municipal, and federal, under bond. The root of a subtable family is known as the maximal table. Security is the maximal table in this example.

Data manipulation operations on a row in a subtable family affect related rows in parent tables and subtables. The following is a brief description of side effects when manipulating rows in subtable families.

- If a row is inserted into a subtable, then a corresponding row (with the same values for inherited columns) is inserted into each parent table. The insert cascades upward in the subtable family until it reaches the maximal table.
- If a column is updated in a parent table, then the column is also updated in all direct and indirect subtables that inherit the column.
- If an inherited column is updated in a subtable, then the column is changed in the corresponding rows of direct and indirect parent tables. The update cascade stops in the parent table in which the column is defined, not inherited.
- If a row in a subtable family is deleted, then every corresponding row in both parent and subtables is also deleted.

18.4.3 Manipulating Complex Objects and Subtable Families

The richer data definition capabilities of SQL:1999 lead to new features when using row type columns and reference type columns in data manipulation and data retrieval statements. When inserting data into a table with a row type column, the keyword ROW must be used as demonstrated in Example 18.15. If a column uses a user-defined type instead of the ROW type, the type name must be used as depicted in Example 18.16.

Example 18.15

Using the ROW Keyword When Inserting a Row in a Table with a Row Type Column
This example assumes that the *Address* column of the *AgentType* type was defined with the ROW type.

```
INSERT INTO Agent
(AgentNo, Name, Address, Email, Phone)
VALUES (999999, 'Sue Smith',
        ROW('123 Any Street', 'Denver', 'CO', '80217'),
        'sue.smith@anyisp.com', '13031234567')
```

Example 18.16

Using the Type Name When Inserting Two Rows in a Table with a Structured Type Column
This example corresponds to the *AgentType* type defined in Example 18.12.

```
INSERT INTO Agent
(AgentNo, Name, Address, Email, Phone)
VALUES (999999, 'Sue Smith',
        AddressType('123 Any Street', 'Denver', 'CO', '80217'),
        'sue.smith@anyisp.com', '13031234567');

INSERT INTO Agent
(AgentNo, Name, Address, Email, Phone)
VALUES (999998, 'John Smith',
        AddressType('123 Big Street', 'Boulder', 'CO', '80217'),
        'john.smith@anyisp.com', '13034567123');
```

When inserting data into a table with a reference type column, the object identifier can be obtained with a SELECT statement. If object identifiers for a referenced table are user-generated (such as primary key values), a SELECT statement may not be necessary. Even with user-generated object identifiers, a SELECT statement may be necessary if the object identifier is not known when the row is inserted. Example 18.17 demonstrates a SELECT statement to retrieve the object identifier (*AgentOID*) from the related row of the *Agent* table. In the SELECT statement, the other values to insert are constant values. For the *Assessments* column, the constant value is an array of values denoted by the ARRAY keyword along with the square brackets that surround the array element values.

Example 18.17   Using a SELECT Statement to Retrieve the Object Identifier of the Related *Agent* Row

```
INSERT INTO Residential
(PropNo, Address, SqFt, AgentRef, BedRooms, BathRooms, Assessments)
SELECT 999999, AddressType('123 Any Street', 'Denver', 'CO', '80217'),
          2000, AgentOID, 3, 2, ARRAY[190000, 200000]
FROM Agent
WHERE AgentNo = 999999;
```

Example 18.17 also demonstrates several aspects about subtypes and subtables. First, the INSERT statement can reference the columns in both types because of the subtype relationship involving *ResidentialType* and *PropertyType*. Second, inserting a row into the *Residential* table automatically inserts a row into the *Property* table because of the subtable relationship between the *Residential* and the *Property* tables.

Reference columns can be updated using a SELECT statement in a manner similar to that used in Example 18.17. Example 18.18 demonstrates an UPDATE statement using a SELECT statement to retrieve the object identifier of the related agent.

Example 18.18   Using a SELECT Statement to Retrieve the Object Identifier of the Related *Agent* Row

```
UPDATE Residential
     SET AgentRef =
        (   SELECT AgentOID FROM Agent WHERE AgentNo = 999998 )
     WHERE PropNo = 999999;
```

Path expressions using the dot operator and the dereference operator provide an alternative to the traditional value-based joins in SQL-92. Example 18.19 depicts the use of the dot and the dereference operators in path expressions. For columns with a row or user-defined type, you should use the dot operator in path expressions. The expression Address.City references the city component of the *Address* row column. For columns with a reference type, you should use the dereference operator (->) in path expressions. The expression AgentRef->Name retrieves the *Name* column of the related *Agent* row. The dereference operator (->) must be used instead of the dot operator because the column *AgentRef* has the type REF(AgentType). The distinction between dot and dereference operators is one of the more confusing aspects of SQL:1999. Other object-oriented languages such as the ODMG query language and Java do not have this distinction.

Example 18.19 SELECT Statement with Path Expressions and the Dereference Operator

```
SELECT PropNo, P.Address.City, P.AgentRef->Address.City
   FROM Property P
   WHERE AgentRef->Name = 'John Smith'
```

Sometimes there is a need to test membership in a specific table without being a member of other subtables. Example 18.20 retrieves industrial properties where the square feet column is greater than 3,000. The FROM clause restricts the scope to rows whose most specific type is the *IndustrialType*. Thus, Example 18.20 does not retrieve any rows of the *Residential* table, a subtable of the *Property* table.

Example 18.20 Using ONLY to Restrict the Range of a Table in a Subtable Family

```
SELECT PropNo, Address, Location
   FROM ONLY (Industrial)
   WHERE Sqft > 3000
```

18.5 OBJECT DATABASE FEATURES IN ORACLE 9i

The most widely implemented part of the SQL:1999 object packages is the user-defined type. The major relational DBMS vendors including IBM and Oracle have implemented user-defined types that provide similar features as the SQL:1999 standard. User-defined types are important for storage and manipulation of complex data in business databases.

Beyond user-defined types, the object features in the SQL:1999 standard have not been implemented by the major DBMS vendors except for Oracle. Although Oracle 9i does not claim enhanced SQL:1999 conformance, it supports most of the features of the SQL:1999 object packages as well as some additional object features. This section presents the most important object features of Oracle 9i using the examples from the previous section. Even if you do not use Oracle 9i, you can gain insight about the complexity of the SQL:1999 object features and the difficulty of ensuring enhanced conformance with the SQL:1999 standard.

18.5.1 Defining User-Defined Types and Typed Tables in Oracle 9i

Oracle 9i supports user-defined types with a syntax close to the SQL:1999 syntax. As depicted in Example 18.21, most of the differences are cosmetic such as the different placement of the parentheses, the reserved word RETURN instead of RETURNS in SQL:1999, and the reserved word OBJECT for root-level types. Differences in methods are more significant. Oracle 9i supports functions and procedures as methods compared to only method functions in SQL:1999. Thus, the *Print* procedure in Example 18.21 is not used in Example 18.7 because SQL:1999 does not support method procedures.[4] In

---

[4]The Application Development Guide for Oracle 9i provides an example using empty parentheses for procedures without parameters (Print()). However, the Oracle SQL compiler displays an error message when the parentheses are included. Thus, the Print procedure is declared without parentheses.

addition, Oracle 9i supports order methods for direct object to object comparisons, map methods for indirect object comparisons, and static methods for global operations that do not need to reference the data of an object instance.

Example 18.21

Point Type in Oracle 9i
This example corresponds to Example 18.7 for SQL:1999.

```
CREATE TYPE Point AS OBJECT
(   x FLOAT(15),
    y FLOAT(15),
  MEMBER FUNCTION Distance(P2 Point) RETURN NUMBER,
    -- Computes the distance between 2 points
  MEMBER FUNCTION Equals (P2 Point) RETURN BOOLEAN,
    -- Determines if 2 points are equivalent
  MEMBER PROCEDURE Print )
NOT FINAL
INSTANTIABLE;
```

Oracle 9i supports inheritance for user-defined types similarly to SQL:1999. An important difference involves the overriding of methods. In Oracle 9i, overriding methods have the same name and signature in the parent type and subtype. A signature consists of the method's name and the number, types, and order of the parameters. If two methods have different signatures, there is no overriding as both methods exist in the subtype. As in SQL:1999, the OVERRIDING keyword should be used when overriding a method. In Example 18.22, there is no overriding as the *Equals* method in *ColorPoint* has a different signature than the *Equals* method in *Point*. The *Equals* method in *ColorPoint* uses a *ColorPoint* argument whereas the *Equals* method in *Point* uses a *Point* argument. However, the *Print* method in *ColorPoint* overrides the *Print* method in *Point* as both methods have the same signature.

Example 18.22

ColorPoint Type in Oracle 9i
This example corresponds to Example 18.8 for SQL:1999.

```
CREATE TYPE ColorPoint UNDER Point
(Color INTEGER,
  MEMBER FUNCTION Brighten (Intensity INTEGER) RETURN INTEGER,
    -- Increases color intensity
MEMBER FUNCTION Equals (CP2 ColorPoint) RETURN BOOLEAN,
    -- Determines if 2 ColorPoints are equivalent
    -- Overriding is not used because the two Equals methods
    -- have different signatures.
OVERRIDING MEMBER PROCEDURE Print )
NOT FINAL
INSTANTIABLE;
```

Oracle 9i supports row types and typed tables similarly to SQL:1999, as depicted in Example 18.23. Like SQL:1999, Oracle 9i supports the ROW type and user-defined types for structuring subsets of columns. For example, in *AgentType,* the address attribute could use the ROW type instead of the user-defined *AddressType.* For the CREATE TABLE statement, Oracle 9i specifies object identifiers differently than SQL:1999. In Oracle 9i, the OBJECT IDENTIFIER clause defines an object identifier as system-generated or user-generated. System-generated object identifiers do not have a name as SQL:1999 provides. However, Oracle provides functions to manipulate system-generated object identifiers so a column name is not necessary.

Example 18.23	Oracle 9i Definition of *AddressType* and *AgentType* Followed by the Typed *Agent* Table Based on *AgentType*

This example corresponds to Example 18.12 for SQL:1999.

```
CREATE TYPE AddressType AS OBJECT
(   Street    VARCHAR(50),
    City      VARCHAR(30),
    State     CHAR(2),
    Zip       CHAR(9)   )
NOT FINAL;


CREATE TYPE AgentType AS OBJECT
(AgentNo  INTEGER,
 Name     VARCHAR(30),
 Address  AddressType,
 Phone    CHAR(13),
 Email    VARCHAR(50) )
NOT FINAL;


CREATE TABLE Agent OF AgentType
(   CONSTRAINT AgentPK PRIMARY KEY(AgentNo)   )
    OBJECT IDENTIFIER IS SYSTEM GENERATED ;
```

Oracle 9i supports reference types for columns similarly to SQL:1999 as depicted in Example 18.24. The usage of the SCOPE clause is somewhat different in Oracle 9i, however. In Oracle 9i, the SCOPE clause cannot be used in a user-defined type as it can in SQL:1999. To compensate, you can define a referential integrity constraint to limit the scope of a reference as shown for the *Property* table in Example 18.24.

Example 18.24	Oracle 9i Definition of the *PropertyType* with a Reference to the *Agent* Table and the Typed *Property* Table

This example corresponds to Example 18.13 for SQL:1999.

```
CREATE TYPE PropertyType AS OBJECT
(PropNo   INTEGER,
 Address  AddressType,
 SqFt     INTEGER,
```

```
AgentRef REF AgentType,
Location Point )
NOT FINAL
INSTANTIABLE;

CREATE TABLE Property OF PropertyType
 (   CONSTRAINT PropertyPK PRIMARY KEY(PropNo),
     CONSTRAINT AgentRefFK FOREIGN KEY(AgentRef) REFERENCES
         Agent   )
   OBJECT IDENTIFIER IS SYSTEM GENERATED ;
```

Example 18.25 shows the user-defined types for residential and industrial properties along with the table definitions. The constraint and object identifier clauses are repeated in the *Residential* and *Industrial* tables because Oracle 9i does not support subtables.

Example 18.25

CREATE TYPE and CREATE TABLE Statements for Residential and Industrial Properties
This example corresponds to Example 18.14 for SQL:1999.

```
CREATE TYPE AssessType AS VARRAY(6) OF DECIMAL(9,2);

CREATE TYPE ResidentialType UNDER PropertyType
(BedRooms  INTEGER,
 BathRooms  INTEGER,
 Assessments AssessType   )
NOT FINAL
INSTANTIABLE;

CREATE TABLE Residential OF ResidentialType
  (CONSTRAINT ResidentialPK PRIMARY KEY(PropNo),
   CONSTRAINT AgentRefFK1 FOREIGN KEY(AgentRef) REFERENCES
       Agent   )
   OBJECT IDENTIFIER IS SYSTEM GENERATED ;

CREATE TYPE IndustrialType UNDER PropertyType
(Zoning VARCHAR(20),
 AccessDesc VARCHAR(20),
 RailAvailable CHAR(1),
 Parking VARCHAR(10) )
NOT FINAL
INSTANTIABLE;

CREATE TABLE Industrial OF IndustrialType
(CONSTRAINT IndustrialPK PRIMARY KEY(PropNo),
 CONSTRAINT AgentRefFK2 FOREIGN KEY(AgentRef) REFERENCES
     Agent   )
 OBJECT IDENTIFIER IS SYSTEM GENERATED ;
```

Example 18.25 also shows differences between the declaration of array columns in Oracle 9i and SQL:1999. In Oracle 9i, the VARRAY constructor cannot be used directly with columns of a table or attributes of a user-defined type. Instead, the VARRAY constructor must be used in a separate user-defined type as shown in the *AssessType* type in Example 18.25. In addition, Oracle 9i uses parentheses for the array size instead of the square brackets used in SQL:1999.

18.5.2 Using Typed Tables in Oracle 9i

We begin this section with manipulation statements to insert and modify objects in the typed tables. Example 18.26 demonstrates an INSERT statement using a type name for the structured *Address* column. If the *Address* column was defined with the ROW type constructor, the Oracle 9i syntax would be identical to Example 18.15 with the ROW keyword replacing *AddressType*.

Example 18.26

Inserting Two Rows into the Typed *Agent* Table
This example corresponds to Example 18.16 for SQL:1999.

```
INSERT INTO Agent
(AgentNo, Name, Address, Email, Phone)
VALUES (999999, 'Sue Smith',
        AddressType('123 Any Street', 'Denver', 'CO', '80217'),
          'sue.smith@anyisp.com', '13031234567');


INSERT INTO Agent
(AgentNo, Name, Address, Email, Phone)
VALUES (999998, 'John Smith',
        AddressType('123 Big Street', 'Boulder', 'CO', '80217'),
          'john.smith@anysip.com', '13034567123');
```

Because Oracle 9i does not support subtables, additional manipulation statements are used to simulate set inclusion among subtables. In Example 18.27, INSERT statements are used for both the parent table and subtable. Ideally, triggers could be defined to hide the additional manipulation statements.

Example 18.27

INSERT Statements to Add an Object into the *Property* and the *Residential* Tables
This example corresponds to Example 18.17 for SQL:1999.

```
INSERT INTO Residential
(PropNo, Address, SqFt, AgentRef, BedRooms, BathRooms, Assessments)
SELECT 999999, AddressType('123 Any Street', 'Denver', 'CO', '80217'),
        2000, REF(A), 3, 2, AssessType(190000, 200000)
FROM Agent A
WHERE AgentNo = 999999;

-- This INSERT statement maintains set inclusion between the Property
-- and the Residential tables.
INSERT INTO Property
(PropNo, Address, SqFt, AgentRef)
```

```
SELECT 999999, AddressType('123 Any Street', 'Denver', 'CO', '80217'),
       2000, REF(A)
FROM Agent A
WHERE AgentNo = 999999;
```

Example 18.27 also demonstrates the REF function to obtain a system-generated object identifier. When using the REF function, you must use a correlation variable (table alias) as the parameter. You cannot use the table name instead of the correlation variable. The REF statement also can be used in UPDATE statements as demonstrated in Example 18.28.

Example 18.28   Using a SELECT Statement with the REF Function to Retrieve the Object Identifier of the Related *Agent* Row

This example corresponds to Example 18.18 for SQL:1999.

```
UPDATE Residential
    SET AgentRef =
    (   SELECT REF(A) FROM Agent A WHERE AgentNo = 999998 )
    WHERE PropNo = 999999;

-- This UPDATE statement maintains consistency between the Property
-- and the Residential tables.
UPDATE Property
    SET AgentRef =
    (   SELECT REF(A) FROM Agent A WHERE AgentNo = 999998 )
    WHERE PropNo = 999999;
```

Oracle 9i supports path expressions containing the dot operator and the DEREF function. The DEREF function can also be used in SQL:1999 in place of the -> operator. The DEREF function uses an object identifier as a parameter as shown in Example 18.29. When using columns that have an object type such as *Address,* a correlation variable must be used.

Example 18.29   Oracle 9i SELECT Statement with Path Expressions Containing the Dot Operator and the DEREF Function

This example corresponds to Example 18.19 for SQL:1999.

```
SELECT PropNo, P.Address.City, DEREF(AgentRef).Address.City
FROM Property P
WHERE DEREF(AgentRef).Name = 'John Smith';
```

Although Oracle 9i supports the DEREF function, it does not seem necessary to use it. The dot operator can be used in path expressions even when a column has a reference type as shown in Example 18.30. Note that a correlation variable is necessary when using REF columns in a path expression with the dot operator.

Example 18.30   Oracle 9i SELECT Statement with Path Expressions Containing the Dot Operator Instead of the DEREF Function
This example corresponds to Example 18.19 for SQL:1999.

```
SELECT PropNo, P.Address.City, P.AgentRef.Address.City
 FROM Property P
 WHERE P.AgentRef.Name = 'John Smith';
```

Like SQL:1999, Oracle 9i supports the ONLY keyword in the FROM clause. However, the ONLY keyword applies to views not tables in Oracle 9i. Thus, Example 18.20 will not work in Oracle 9i unless object views are used instead of tables.

The VALUE function takes a correlation variable as a parameter and returns instances of the object table associated with the correlation variable. Thus, the VALUE function can be used to retrieve all columns from typed tables instead of using the * for untyped tables, as shown in Example 18.31. However, Oracle 9i provides an error message for the statement in Example 18.31 because the VALUE function does not work on tables based on nonfinal types. The SELECT statement in Example 18.32 works correctly because *AgentType1* lacks the NOT FINAL clause.

Example 18.31   Using the VALUE Function to Retrieve All Columns from a Typed Table
Note that this statement causes an error in Oracle 9i because *AgentType* is not final.

```
SELECT VALUE(A) FROM Agent A;
```

Example 18.32   Using the VALUE Function to Retrieve All Columns from a Table Based on a Final Type

```
CREATE TYPE AgentType1 AS OBJECT
(AgentNo  INTEGER,
 Name      VARCHAR(30),
 Phone     CHAR(10),
 Email     VARCHAR(50)   );

CREATE TABLE Agent1 OF AgentType1
(   CONSTRAINT Agent1PK PRIMARY KEY(AgentNo)   )
    OBJECT IDENTIFIER IS SYSTEM GENERATED ;
INSERT INTO Agent1
(AgentNo, Name, Email, Phone)
VALUES (999998, 'John Smith',
         'john.smith@anyisp.com', '13037894567');

SELECT VALUE(A) FROM Agent1 A;
```

18.5.3 Other Object Features in Oracle 9i

Oracle 9i provides object features beyond SQL:1999. Type substitutability and hierarchical views may substitute for the lack of subtables. Nested tables provide nonnormalized data storage and retrieval.

The Oracle 9i documentation suggests the use of type substitutability to manage extents of parent tables and related subtables. Type substitutability means that a column or row defined to be of type X can contain instances of X and any of its subtypes. When using type substitutability to support subtables, user-defined types are defined with the subtype relationships, but only one typed table (the root table) is defined. All manipulation operations are performed on the root table using type substitution to simulate the set inclusion relationships. However, the syntax for performing manipulation operations when reference types are involved is not clear because there does not appear to be a way to specify the order of columns when using a type name. In addition, the Oracle 9i documentation does not clearly state that type substitutability can provide management of set inclusion relationships as specified in the SQL:1999 standard. For more details about type substitutability, you should consult the Oracle 9i online documentation.

The Oracle 9i documentation also suggests the use of hierarchical views to manage extents of parent tables and related subtables. Hierarchical views use the UNDER keyword just like type hierarchies. Unlike subtable families, several storage models are possible to store the hierarchical views. The database administrator must choose the best storage model and ensure that users understand how to use the hierarchical views in retrieval and manipulation statements. Thus, although hierarchical views may be useful, they do not provide a satisfactory substitute for subtables.

Oracle 9i provides extensive support for nested tables using the TABLE type constructor. For flexibility, multiple levels of nesting can be used. In the opinion of the author, nested tables will have limited uses in traditional business databases. There are no guidelines about when or how to use nested tables in business databases. Nested tables may be more useful in engineering applications such as computer-aided design.

CLOSING THOUGHTS

This chapter has described the motivation, principles, and architectures of object DBMSs. Object database technology is driven by demands to integrate complex and simple data and software productivity problems due to type mismatches between DBMSs and programming languages. Three principles of object-oriented computing, encapsulation, inheritance, and polymorphism, guide the development of object DBMSs. Encapsulation, the hiding of implementation details, supports data independence. Encapsulation is often relaxed for DBMSs to allow ad hoc queries. Inheritance, the sharing of code and data, supports software reusability. Polymorphism, the allowance of multiple implementations for procedures, permits incremental modification and a smaller vocabulary of procedures.

Because of the variety of ways to implement the object-oriented principles and the difficulty of implementation, a number of object DBMS architectures are commercially available. This chapter described five architectures and discussed their advantages and disadvantages. The first two architectures do not fully support the object-oriented principles as they involve simple schemes to store large objects and invoke specialized servers outside of a DBMS. The last three architectures provide different paths to implement the object-oriented principles. The architectures differ primarily on the level of integration with a DBMS. Object database middleware involves the least integration with a DBMS but provides the widest scope of complex data. Object relational DBMSs contain an object query processor on top of a relational kernel. Object-oriented DBMSs contain both an object query processor and an object kernel. The marketplace has not yet decided on the superiority of the latter three architectures.

To provide a more concrete view of object databases, this chapter presented the object database definition and manipulation features of SQL:1999, the revision of SQL-92. SQL:1999 supports user-defined types to accommodate new kinds of complex data.

Expressions in queries can reference columns based on user-defined types and the methods of user-defined types. SQL:1999 supports inheritance and polymorphism for user-defined types as well as set inclusion relationships for subtable families. Because SQL:1999 is a complex extension of SQL-92, there are few DBMSs that support enhanced conformance of the standard. Object relational features of Oracle 9i were presented to demonstrate the implementation of many SQL:1999 object features although Oracle 9i does not claim enhanced conformance of the SQL:1999 object packages.

REVIEW CONCEPTS

- Examples of complex data that can be stored in digital format.
- Use of complex data as a motivation for object database technology.
- Type mismatches as a motivation for object database technology.
- Encapsulation as a kind of data independence.
- Relaxing encapsulation to support ad hoc queries.
- Inheritance as a way to share code and data.
- Polymorphism to reduce the vocabulary of procedures and allow incremental sharing of code.
- Difference between static and dynamic binding.
- Strong type checking to eliminate incompatibility errors in expressions.
- Reasons for marketplace support for a variety of object database management architectures.
- Level of integration with a DBMS for each object database management architecture.
- Characteristics of each object database management architecture.
- Reasons for the existence of two standards for object database management.
- User-defined types in SQL:1999 for defining complex data and operations.
- Subtable families in SQL:1999: inheritance and set inclusion.
- Relationship of subtable families and user-defined types.
- Use of the SQL:1999 row type and reference type in object tables.
- Use of path expressions and the dereference operator (>) in SQL:1999 SELECT statements.
- Referencing subtables in SELECT statements.
- Defining and using user-defined types and typed tables in Oracle 9i.

QUESTIONS

1. How does the use of complex data drive the need for object database technology?

2. What problems are caused by mismatches between the types provided by a DBMS and a programming language?

3. Present an example application that uses both simple and complex data. Use a different application than discussed in Section 18.1.3.

4. Define encapsulation. How does encapsulation support the goal of data independence?

5. How do object DBMSs relax encapsulation? Why is encapsulation relaxed? What is the role of database security control as a substitute for encapsulation?

6. Define inheritance. What are the benefits of inheritance?

7. Define polymorphism. What are the benefits of polymorphism?

8. What is strong type checking? Why is strong type checking important?

9. What is the difference between static and dynamic binding?

10. Which implementation of object-oriented principles occurred first: object-oriented programming languages or object DBMSs?

11. Compare the emphasis in object-oriented programming languages to object DBMSs.

12. Discuss the reasons that multiple object DBMS architectures have been developed.

13. Discuss the benefits and limitations of storing large objects in the database. Why is external software needed when large objects are stored in a database?

14. Discuss the benefits and the limitations of using specialized media servers.

15. Discuss the benefits and the limitations of using object database middleware. Why does object database middleware support the broadest range of complex data?

16. Discuss the benefits and the limitations of using an object relational DBMS. What changes are made to the query processor of a relational DBMS to convert it into an object relational DBMS?

17. Discuss the benefits and the limitations of using an object-oriented DBMS. How does an object-oriented DBMS differ from an object-relational DBMS?

18. Why have object-oriented DBMSs occupied a market niche compared to relational DBMSs?

19. Which object DBMS architecture do you think will dominate in five years?

20. What is a persistent object? What is the difference between a persistent object and a temporary object?

21. Why are there two standard languages for object DBMSs?

22. What are the components of a user-defined type in SQL:1999?

23. What are the differences between SQL:1999 methods, functions, and procedures?

24. How are SQL:1999 user-defined types used in table definitions and expressions?

25. What is a row type? How are row types used in SQL:1999 table definitions?

26. Explain the differences in encapsulation for user-defined types versus typed tables in SQL:1999.

27. What is a typed table?

28. How do you define a subtable?

29. Discuss the relationship of subtable families and set inclusion.

30. What side effects occur when a row is inserted in a subtable?

31. What side effects occur when a subtable row is updated?

32. What side effects occur when a subtable row is deleted?

33. What is the difference between a foreign key and a reference?

34. When should you use a SELECT statement as part of an INSERT statement when adding objects to a typed table?

35. What is the difference in notation between combining tables that are linked by a foreign key versus a column with a reference type?

36. What is a path expression? When do you use a path expression?

37. When do you need to use the dereference operator (>) in a path expression?

38. What is the purpose of the ONLY keyword in a SQL:1999 SELECT statement?

39. Compare and contrast methods in SQL:1999 with methods in Oracle 9i.

40. What are criteria for overriding a method in Oracle 9i?

41. What is the most significant limitation for object databases in Oracle 9i as compared to SQL:1999?

42. Briefly discuss the importance of object features in Oracle 9i that are not part of SQL:1999.

43. What is minimal conformance for SQL:1999?

44. What is enhanced conformance for SQL:1999?

45. Briefly discuss the state of conformance testing for SQL:1999.

PROBLEMS

The problems provide practice with using SQL:1999 and Oracle 9i to define user-defined types and typed tables as well as to use typed tables. Problems 1 to 16 involve SQL:1999 while problems 17 to 32 involve Oracle 9i.

1. Using SQL:1999, define a user-defined type for a time series. The variables of a time series include an array of floating point values (maximum of 365), the begin date, the duration (maximum number of data points in the time series), the calendar type (personal or business), and the period (day, week, month, or year). Define methods as listed in Table 18.P1. You need to define the parameters for the methods, not the code to implement the methods. The *TimeSeries* parameter refers to the implicit *TimeSeries* object.

TABLE 18.P1	**List of Methods for the TimeSeries Type**	
Name	*Parameters*	*Result*
WeeklyAvg	TimeSeries	TimeSeries
MonthlyAvg	TimeSeries	TimeSeries
YearlyAvg	TimeSeries	TimeSeries
MovingAvg	TimeSeries, Start Date, Number of Values	Float
RetrieveRange	TimeSeries, Start Date, Number of Values	TimeSeries

2. Using SQL:1999, define a security type and a typed security table. A security has fields for the unique symbol, the security name, and a time series of closing prices. Both the *Security* type and table have no parent.

3. Using SQL:1999, define a stock type and a typed stock table. A stock has fields for the number of issued shares, the number of outstanding shares, and the time series of closing prices. The *Stock* table inherits from the *Security* table, and the *Stock* type inherits from the *Security* type.

4. Using SQL:1999, define a bond type and a typed bond table. A bond has fields for the interest rate and the maturity date. The *Bond* table inherits from the *Security* table, and the *Bond* type inherits from the *Security* type.

5. Using SQL:1999, define a customer type and a typed customer table. A customer has fields for the unique customer number, the name, the address, the phone, and the e-mail address. The address field is a row type with fields for street, city, state, and zip. The phone field is a row type with fields for country code, area code, and local number. You should define types for the address and phone so that the types can be reused. Both the *Customer* type and table have no parent.

6. Using SQL:1999, define a portfolio holding type and a typed portfolio holding table. A holding has fields for the customer (reference data type), the security (reference data type), and the shares held. The primary key of the *Holding* table is a combination of the *CustNo* field of the related customer and the *Symbol* field of the related security. Define referential integrity or SCOPE constraints to limit the range of the customer reference and the security reference. Both the *Holding* type and table have no parent.

7. Using SQL:1999, insert an object into the typed *Stock* table for Microsoft common stock.

8. Using SQL:1999, insert an object into the typed *Stock* table for Dell Corporation common stock.

9. Using SQL:1999, insert an object into the typed *Stock* table for IBM common stock. Enter a value in the closing prices (time series type) column by specifying the array of values, the period, the calendar type, the begin date, and the duration.

10. Using SQL:1999, insert an object into the typed *Customer* table. Use 999999 as the customer number, John Smith as the customer name, and Denver as the city.

11. Using SQL:1999, insert an object into the typed *Customer* table. Use 999998 as the customer number, Sue Smith as the customer name, and Boulder as the city.

12. Using SQL:1999, insert an object into the typed *Holding* table. Connect the holding object to the Microsoft *Security* object and the Sue Smith *Customer* object. Use 200 as the number of shares held.

13. Using SQL:1999, insert an object into the typed *Holding* table. Connect the holding object to the IBM *Security* object and the Sue Smith *Customer* object. Use 100 as the number of shares held.

14. Using SQL:1999, update the customer reference column of the *Holding* object from problem 12 to the John Smith *Customer* object.

15. Using SQL:1999, write a SELECT statement to list the securities held by Denver customers. Only list the securities with more than 100 shares held. Include the customer name, the symbol, and the shares held in the result.

16. Using SQL:1999, write a SELECT statement to list the customer name, security symbol, and the number of shares held for each stock held by Denver customers.

17. Using Oracle 9i, define a user-defined type for a time series. The variables of a time series include an array of floating point values (maximum of 365), the begin date, the duration (maximum number of data points in the time series), the calendar type (personal or business), and the period (day, week, month, or year). Define methods as previously listed in Table 18.P1. You need to define the parameters for the methods, not the code to implement the methods. The *TimeSeries* parameter refers to the implicit *TimeSeries* object.

18. Using Oracle 9i, define a security type and a typed security table. A security has fields for the unique symbol, the security name, and a time series of closing prices. Both the *Security* type and table have no parent.

19. Using Oracle 9i, define a stock type and a typed stock table. A stock has fields for the number of issued shares, the number of outstanding shares, and the time series of closing prices. The *Stock* table inherits from the *Security* table, and the *Stock* type inherits from the *Security* type.

20. Using Oracle 9i, define a bond type and a typed bond table. A bond has fields for the interest rate and the maturity date. The *Bond* table inherits from the *Security* table, and the *Bond* type inherits from the *Security* type.

21. Using Oracle 9i, define a customer type and a typed customer table. A customer has fields for the unique customer number, the name, the address, the phone, and the e-mail address. The address field is a row type with fields for street, city, state, and zip. The phone field is a row type with fields for country code, area code, and local number. You can define types for the address and phone so that the types can be reused. Both the *Customer* type and table have no parent.

22. Using Oracle 9i, define a portfolio holding type and a typed portfolio holding table. A holding has fields for the customer (reference data type), the security (reference data type), and the shares held. The primary key of the *Holding* table is a combination of the *CustNo* field of the related customer and the *Symbol* field of the related security. Define referential integrity or SCOPE constraints to limit the range of the customer reference and the security reference. Both the *Holding* type and table have no parent.

23. Using Oracle 9i, insert an object into the typed *Stock* table for Microsoft common stock. To manage subtables, you should also insert the same object into the typed *Security* table.

24. Using Oracle 9i, insert an object into the typed *Stock* table for Dell Corporation common stock. To manage subtables, you should also insert the same object into the typed *Security* table.

25. Using Oracle 9i, insert an object into the typed *Stock* table for IBM common stock. To manage subtables, you should also insert the same object into the typed *Security* table. Enter a value in the closing prices (time-series type) column by specifying the array of values, the period, the calendar type, the begin date, and the duration.

26. Using Oracle 9i, insert an object into the typed *Customer* table. Use 999999 as the customer number, John Smith as the customer name, and Denver as the city.

27. Using Oracle 9i, insert an object into the typed *Customer* table. Use 999998 as the customer number, Sue Smith as the customer name, and Boulder as the city.

28. Using Oracle 9i, insert an object into the typed *Holding* table. Connect the holding object to the Microsoft *Security* object and the Sue Smith *Customer* object. Use 200 as the number of shares held.

29. Using Oracle 9i, insert an object into the typed *Holding* table. Connect the holding object to the IBM *Security* object and the Sue Smith *Customer* object. Use 100 as the number of shares held.

30. Using Oracle 9i, update the customer reference column of the *Holding* object from problem 28 to the John Smith *Customer* object.

31. Using Oracle 9i, write a SELECT statement to list the securities held by Denver customers. Only list the securities with more than 100 shares held. Include the customer name, the symbol, and the shares held in the result.

32. Using Oracle 9i, write a SELECT statement to list the customer name, security symbol, and the number of shares held for each stock held by Denver customers.

REFERENCES FOR FURTHER STUDY

This chapter has only introduced a very broad and deep subject. For more details, you are encouraged to consult specialized books, articles, and websites. The most definitive sources about SQL:1999 are the standards documents (available at the *TechStreet* site www.techstreet.com) developed by the National Committee on Information Technology Standards (NCITS) Technical Committee H2 on Databases of the American National Standards Institute (ANSI). Because the standards documents are rather difficult to read, you may prefer the books by Gulutzan and Pelzer (1999) and Melton and Simon (2001). Additional books on object database management include Stonebraker and Moore (1996) on object relational DBMSs and Cattell and Barry (1997) on the object data management standard.

More recent trade articles, application development advice, and documentation can be found at websites. The *Intelligent Enterprise* magazine (http://www.iemagazine.com), the *Advisor.com* site (http://www.advisor.com), the *DBAZine* site (www.dbazine.com), and the DevX help site (www.devx.com/gethelp) have practical advice about object database development issues. Some good websites on object database standards include the Object Data Management Group (http://www.odmg.org) and the Object Information Management Technical Committee (http://www.objs.com/x3h7/h7home.htm). The major DBMS vendors also provide a wealth of information about their respective object DBMSs. For more details about the object relational features of Oracle 9i, you should consult the *Oracle 9i SQL Reference Manual* and the *Oracle9i Application Developer's Guide: Object-Relational Features* that are available through the Oracle Technology Network site (otn.oracle.com).

GLOSSARY

A

Access Plan a tree that encodes decisions about file structures to access individual tables, the order of joining tables, and the algorithm to join tables. Access plans are generated by the optimization component to implement queries submitted by users.

ACID Properties transaction properties supported by DBMSs. ACID is an acronym for atomic, consistent, isolated, and durable. Atomic means all or nothing. Consistent means that a database does not violate integrity constraints before or after a transaction commits. Isolated means that other transactions cannot see the updates made by a transaction until after the transaction terminates. Durable means that the effects of a transaction are permanent after committing even if a failure occurs.

Actions on Referenced Rows possible actions in response to the deletion of a referenced row or the update of the primary key of a referenced row. The possible actions are restrict (do not permit the action on the referenced row), cascade (perform the same action on the related rows), nullify (set the foreign key of related rows to null), and default (set the foreign key of related rows to a default value). See also referenced rows.

Aggregate Function a summary or statistical function. The standard aggregate functions in SQL are MIN, MAX, COUNT, SUM, and AVG.

Analyst/Programmer an information system professional who is responsible for collecting requirements, designing applications, and implementing information systems. An analyst/programmer may create and use external views to develop forms, reports, and other parts of an information system.

Analytic Hierarchy Process a decision theory technique to evaluate problems with multiple objectives. The Analytic Hierarchy Process can be used to select and evaluate DBMSs by allowing a systematic assignment of weights to requirements and scores to features of candidate DBMSs.

ANSI American National Standards Institute, one of the groups responsible for SQL standards.

Application Profile a statistical summary of the forms, reports, and queries that access a database. Application profiles are an important input of the physical database design phase because they are used to predict demand for the database.

Assertion the most general kind of integrity constraint supported in SQL:1999. An assertion can involve a SELECT statement of arbitrary complexity. The CREATE ASSERTION statement defines assertions in SQL:1999.

Associative Entity Type a weak entity type that depends on two or more entity types for its primary key. In the Crow's Foot ERD notation, associative entity types represent M-way relationships.

Attribute a property of an entity type or relationship. Each attribute has a data type defining allowable values and operations. Attribute is synonymous with field and column.

Authorization Rules define authorized users, allowable operations, and accessible parts of a database. The database security system stores authorization rules and enforces them for each database access. Also known as security constraints.

B

Benchmark a workload to evaluate the performance of a system or product. A good benchmark should be relevant, portable, scalable, and understandable.

BETWEEN-AND Operator a shortcut operator to test a numeric or date column against a range of values. The BETWEEN-AND operator returns true if the column is greater than or equal to the first value and less than or equal to the second value.

Binary Large Object (BLOB) a data type for fields containing large binary data such as images. BLOB data can be retrieved but not displayed. The BLOB data type provides a simple way to extend a DBMS with object features. See also the Large Object Architecture.

Binding in query optimization, binding refers to associating an access plan with an SQL statement. In object-oriented computing, binding refers to associating a method name with its implementation. Binding can be static (decided at compile-time) or dynamic (decided at run-time). Static binding is more efficient but sometimes less flexible than dynamic binding. See also Access Plan and Message.

Bitmap Index a secondary file structure consisting of a column value and a bitmap. A bitmap contains one bit position for each row of a referenced table. A bitmap column index references the rows containing the column value. A bitmap join index references the rows of a child table that join with rows of the parent table containing the column. Bitmap indices work well for stable columns with few values typical of tables in a data warehouse. See also Star Join.

Bottom-Up Data Warehouse Architecture an architecture for a data warehouse in which data marts are built for user departments. If a need for an enterprise data model emerges, the data marts will evolve to a data warehouse. See also Two-Tier Data Warehouse Architecture and Three-Tier Data Warehouse Architecture.

Boyce-Codd Normal Form (BCNF) a table is in BCNF if every determinant is a candidate key. BCNF is a revised definition for 3NF.

Btree File a popular file structure supported by most DBMSs because it provides good performance on both key search as well as sequential search. A Btree file is a balanced, multiway tree. The most popular variation of the Btree is the B+tree, in which all keys are redundantly stored in the leaf nodes. The B+tree provides improved performance on sequential and range searches. A Btree can be used as a primary or secondary file structure.

Buffer an area in main memory containing physical database records transferred from disk.

C

Call-Level Interface (CLI) a language style for integrating a programming language with a nonprocedural language such as SQL. A CLI includes a set of procedures and a set of type definitions for manipulating the results of SQL statements in computer programs. The most widely used CLIs, the Open Database Connectivity

(ODBC) supported by Microsoft and the Java Database Connectivity (JDBC) supported by Oracle, are compatible with the SQL:1999 CLI.

Candidate Key a minimal superkey. A superkey is minimal if removing any columns makes it no longer unique.

Cardinality a constraint on the number of entities participating in a relationship. In an entity relationship diagram, the minimum and maximum number of entities are specified for both directions of a relationship.

CASE Tool a tool to facilitate database and information systems development. CASE tools support features for drawing, analysis, prototyping, and data dictionary. CASE is an acronym for computer-aided software engineering.

Character Large Object (CLOB) a data type for columns containing large text data such as documents and Web pages. The CLOB data type provides a simple way to extend a DBMS with object features. See also the Large Object Architecture.

Checkpoint the act of writing a checkpoint record to the log and force writing log and database buffers to disk. The checkpoint record in the log contains the list of active transactions. All transaction activity must cease while a checkpoint occurs. The checkpoint interval should be chosen to balance restart time with checkpoint overhead.

Class a collection of objects. A class definition includes variables for object data and methods for object procedures.

Client a program that submits requests to a server such as accessing or updating a database.

Client–Server Architecture an arrangement of components (clients and servers) among computers connected by a network. The client–server architecture supports efficient processing of messages (requests for service) between clients and servers.

Client-Side Connectivity a style of computing on the World Wide Web in which client computing capacity can be more fully utilized without storing code on the client. Client-side connectivity can enhance database connectivity by providing a more customized interface than permitted by HTML and by allowing data buffering by the client.

Clustering Index an index in which the order of the data records is close to the index order. A clustering index can be organized as a primary index or a secondary file structure. See also Index Selection, Nonclustering Index, Primary File Structure, and Secondary File Structure.

Collision a condition involving insertions to a hash file. A collision occurs when two or more records hash to the same location. For each record, a hash function transforms the key value into an address. See also hash file.

Column a field or attribute in a table. Each column has a data type defining allowable values and operations. Column is synonymous with field and attribute.

Combined Primary Key a combination of columns (more than one) designated as the primary key. Also known as a composite primary key.

Common Gateway Interface (CGI) an interface that allows a Web server to invoke an external program. CGI was the earliest and still is the most universal way to achieve Web database connectivity.

Completeness Constraint a constraint about generalization hierarchies. A completeness constraint means that every entity in a supertype has a related entity in one of the subtypes. In other words, the union of the set of entities in the subtypes equals the set of entities in the supertype.

Conceptual Evaluation Process the sequence of operations and intermediate tables used to derive the result of a SELECT statement. The evaluation process is conceptual because most SQL compilers will take many shortcuts to produce the result. The conceptual evaluation process may help you gain an initial understanding of the SELECT statement as well as help you to understand more difficult problems.

Conceptual Schema a data description that covers all entities and relationships in a database. The conceptual schema is concerned with the meaning of the database, not its physical implementation. See also Schema, Internal Schema, External View, and Three Schema Architecture.

Concurrency Transparency a service provided by a DBMS so that users perceive a database as a single-user system even though there may be many simultaneous users. The concurrency control manager is the component of a DBMS responsible for concurrency transparency.

Constellation Schema a data modeling representation for multidimensional databases. In a relational database, a constellation schema contains multiple fact tables in the center related to dimension tables. Typically the fact tables share some dimension tables. See also Snowflake Schema, Star Schema, Fact Table, and Dimension Table.

Cooperative Change Data data obtained from a source system for refreshing a data warehouse. Cooperative change data involve notification from a source system typically at transaction completion time using a trigger. See also Logged Change Data, Snapshot Change Data, and Queryable Change Data.

Cross Product Style a way to formulate joins in a SELECT statement. The cross product style lists the tables in the FROM clause and the join conditions in the WHERE clause.

CUBE Operator an operator that augments the normal GROUP BY result with all combinations of subtotals. The SQL:1999 standard provides the CUBE operator as an extension of the GROUP BY clause to support multidimensional data. The CUBE operator is appropriate to summarize columns from multiple dimensions rather than columns representing different levels of a single dimension.

Cursor a construct in a database programming language that allows storage and iteration through a set of records returned by a SELECT statement. A cursor is similar to a dynamic array in which the array size is determined by the size of the query result. A database programming language provides statements or procedures to declare cursors, open and close cursors, position cursors, and retrieve values from cursors.

D

Data Access Middleware provide a uniform interface to relational and nonrelational data using SQL. Requests to access data from a DBMS are sent to a data access driver rather than directly to the DBMS. The data access driver converts the SQL statement into the SQL supported by the DBMS and then routes the request to the DBMS. The two leading data access middleware are the Open Database Connectivity (ODBC) supported by Microsoft and the Java Database Connectivity (JDBC) supported by Oracle.

Data Administrator (DA) a management position that performs planning and policy setting for the information resources of an entire organization.

Data Cube a multidimensional format in which cells contain numeric data called measures organized by subjects called dimensions. A data cube is sometimes known as a hypercube because conceptually it can have an unlimited number of dimensions.

Data Dictionary a special database that describes individual databases and the database environment. The data dictionary contains data descriptors called metadata that define the source, the use, the value, and the meaning of data. See also Metadata.

Data Independence a database should have an identity separate from the applications (computer programs, forms, and reports) that use it. The separate identity allows the database definition to be changed without affecting related applications.

Data Mart a subset or view of a data warehouse, typically at a department or functional level, that contains all the data required for decision support tasks of that department. In addition, a data mart insulates departmental users from data used by other departments. In some organizations, a data mart is a small data warehouse rather than a view of a larger data warehouse.

Data Mining the process of discovering implicit patterns in data stored in a data warehouse and using those patterns for business advantage such as predicting future trends.

Data Model a graphical model depicting the structure of a database. A data model contains entity types and relationships among entity types. See also Environment Interaction Model and Process Model.

Data Type defines a set of values and permissible operations on the values. Each column of a table is associated with a data type.

Data Warehouse a central repository for summarized and integrated data from operational databases and external data sources.

Database a collection of persistent data that can be shared and interrelated.

Database Administrator (DBA) a support position that specializes in managing individual databases and DBMSs.

Database Management System (DBMS) a collection of components that support data acquisition, dissemination, maintenance, retrieval, and formatting. An enterprise DBMS supports databases that are critical to an organization. A desktop DBMS supports databases for small workgroups and small businesses. An embedded DBMS is part of a larger system such as a device or application. Embedded DBMSs provide limited features but have low memory, processing, and storage requirements.

Database Programming Language a procedural language with an interface to one or more DBMSs. The interface allows a program to combine procedural statements with nonprocedural database access. See also Call-Level Interface and Statement-Level Interface.

Database Security protecting databases from unauthorized access and malicious destruction.

Datasheet a way to display a table in which the column names appear in the first row and the body in the other rows. Datasheet is a Microsoft Access term.

Deadlock a problem of mutual waiting that can occur when using locks. If a deadlock is not resolved, the involved transactions will wait forever.

Deferred Constraint Checking enforcing integrity constraints at the end of a transaction rather than immediately after each manipulation statement. Complex constraints may benefit from deferred checking.

Deferred Update Approach an approach used by a recovery manager to record database changes on disk. In this approach, database updates are written only after a transaction commits. To restore a database, only redo operations are used.

Denormalization combining tables so that they are easier to query. Denormalization is the opposite of normalization. Denormalization can be useful to improve query performance or to ignore a dependency that does not cause significant storage anomalies.

Desktop DBMS supports database used by work teams and small businesses. Desktop DBMSs are designed to run on personal computers and small servers. See also Enterprise DBMS and Embedded DBMS.

Detail Line the innermost (most nested) line on a hierarchical report.

Determinant the column(s) appearing on the left-hand side of a functional dependency. Alternatively known as an LHS for left-hand side.

Dice a data cube operator in which a dimension is replaced by a subset of its values. See also Slice.

Difference an operator of relational algebra that combines rows from two tables. The difference operator extracts rows that belong to the first table only. Both tables must be union compatible to use the difference operator.

Dimension a label or subject that organizes numeric data in a data cube. A dimension contains values known as members such as a location dimension having members for countries. Dimensions may be organized in hierarchies composed of levels to support the data cube operations of drill-down and roll-up. A dimension hierarchy may be ragged showing relationships among members of the same dimension level.

Dimension Table a table in a star schema or snowflake schema that stores dimensions or subjects used to aggregate facts.

Discretionary Access Control users are assigned access rights or privileges to specified parts of a database. Discretionary access control is the most common kind of security control supported by commercial DBMSs.

Disjointness Constraint a constraint about generalization hierarchies. A disjointness constraint means that the subtypes do not share any common entities. In other words, the intersection of the sets of entities in the subtypes is empty.

Distributed DBMS a collection of components that supports requests for data residing on multiple sites. A distributed DBMS finds remote data, optimizes global requests, and coordinates transactions at multiple sites. Also known as a distributed database management system (DDBMS).

Distributed Processing allows geographically dispersed computers to cooperate when providing data access and other services. See also Client–Server Architecture.

Divide an operator of relational algebra that combines rows from two tables. The divide operator produces a table in which the values of a column from one input table are associated with all the values from a column of the second table.

Drill-Down a data cube operator that supports navigation from a more general level of a dimension to a more specific level of a dimension. See also Roll-Up.

E

Embedded DBMS resides in a larger system, either an application or a device such as a Personal Digital Assistant or smart card. Embedded DBMSs provide limited transaction processing features but have low memory, processing, and storage requirements. See also Desktop DBMS and Enterprise DBMS.

Embedded SQL using SQL inside a host programming language such as COBOL or Visual Basic. Additional SQL statements that can be used only in a programming language cause other SQL statements to be executed and use database results inside the program. See also Standalone SQL.

Encapsulation a principle of object-oriented computing in which an object can be accessed only through its interface. The internal details (variables and method implementations) cannot be accessed. Encapsulation supports lower software maintenance costs.

Encryption involves the encoding of data to obscure their meaning. An encryption algorithm changes the original data (known as the plaintext). To decipher the data, the user supplies an encryption key to restore the encrypted data (known as the ciphertext) to its original (plaintext) format.

Enterprise Data Model (EDM) a conceptual data model of an organization. An enterprise data model can be used for data planning (what databases to develop) and decision support (how to integrate and clean existing databases).

Enterprise DBMS a conceptual data model of an organization. An enterprise data model can be used for data planning (what databases to develop) and decision support (how to integrate and clean existing databases).

Entity a cluster of data usually about a single topic that can be accessed together. An entity can denote a person, place, event, or thing.

Entity Integrity a constraint involving primary keys. No two rows of a table can contain the same value for the primary key. In addition, no row can contain a null value for any columns of a primary key.

Entity Type a collection of entities (persons, places, events, or things) of interest in an application, represented by a rectangle in an entity relationship diagram.

Environment Interaction Model a graphical model showing the relationships between events and processes. An event such as the passage of time or an action from the environment can trigger a process to start or stop.

Equi-join a join operator where the join condition involves equality. See also Join and Natural Join.

ETL Tools software tools for extraction, transformation, and loading of change data from data sources to a data warehouse. ETL tools eliminate the need to write custom coding for many data warehouse maintenance tasks.

Exact String Matching searching for one string value using the equality comparison operator. *See also* Inexact String Matching.

Exclusive Lock a lock that prevents other users from accessing a database item. Exclusive locks conflict with all other kinds of locks (shared, other exclusive locks, and intent). An exclusive lock indicates that a user will change the value of a database item. Also known as an X lock.

Existence Dependency an entity that cannot exist unless another related entity exists. A mandatory relationship produces an existence dependency. See also Mandatory Relationship.

Explicit PL/SQL Cursor a cursor that can be used in procedures written in PL/SQL, the database programming language of Oracle. An explicit cursor is declared with the CURSOR statement in the DECLARE section. Explicit cursors are usually manipulated by the OPEN, CLOSE, and FETCH statements. Explicit cursors can be referenced anyplace inside the BEGIN section. See also Cursor and Implicit PL/SQL Cursor.

Expression a combination of constants, column names, functions, and operators that produces a value. In conditions and result columns, expressions can be used in any place that column names appear.

Extended Cross Product an operator of relational algebra that combines two tables. The extended cross product (product for short) operator builds a table from two tables consisting of all possible combinations of rows, one from each of the two input tables.

External View a description of derived data appropriate for a given user group. Also known as external schema and view. See also Schema and Three Schema Architecture.

F

Fact Table a table in a star schema or snowflake schema that stores numeric values of relevance to a decision maker. See also Star Schema and Snowflake Schema.

File a collection of data on a permanent storage device such as a hard disk. The data or physical records on the file are organized to support efficient processing. Files are part of the internal schema of a database.

File Sharing a method to share data over a computer network in which a personal computer requests a file from another computer on the network.

First Generation Database Technology proprietary file structures and program interfaces that supported sequential and random searching. However, the user was required to write a computer program to access data. First generation database technology was largely developed during the 1960s.

Force Writing the ability to control when data are transferred to nonvolatile storage. This ability is fundamental to recovery management. Force writing typically occurs at end of transaction and checkpoint time.

Foreign Key a column or combination of columns in which the values must match those of a candidate key. A foreign key must have the same data type as its associated candidate key. In the CREATE TABLE statement of SQL:1999, a foreign key must be associated with a primary key rather than merely a candidate key.

Form a document used in a business process, formatted to provide a convenient way to enter and edit data. A form is designed to support a business task such as processing an order, registering for classes, or making an airline reservation.

Form Entity Type in the form analysis process, the form entity type is derived from the primary key of the form. The form entity type should be placed in the center of the ERD.

Form Structure a hierarchy depicting the relationship among form fields. A group of form fields is known as a node. Most forms have a simple structure with a parent node (main form) and a child node (subform).

Forward Engineering the ability to generate definitions for a target database management system from an ERD and data dictionary properties. See also CASE Tool and Reverse Engineering.

Fourth Generation Database Technology extends the boundaries of database technology to unconventional data and the Internet. Fourth generation systems can store and manipulate unconventional data types such as images, videos, maps, sounds, and animations as well as provide Web access to databases. Fourth generation database technology was largely commercialized during the 1990s.

Fourth Normal Form (4NF) a table is in 4NF if it does not contain any nontrivial MVDs. A nontrivial MVD is an MVD that is not also an FD.

Fragment a subset of a table that is allocated to sites. Fragments can be horizontal subsets (restrict operator), vertical subsets (project operator), derived horizontal subsets (semi-join operator), and combinations of these kinds of fragments. See also Semi-Join Operator, Fragmentation Transparency, Location Transparency, and Local Mapping Transparency.

Fragmentation Transparency a level of independence in distributed DBMSs in which queries can be formulated without knowledge of fragments. See Location Transparency and Local Mapping Transparency.

Full Outer Join an outer join that produces the matching rows of the join part as well as the nonmatching rows from both tables.

Functional Dependency (FD) a constraint about two or more columns of a table. X determines Y ($X \rightarrow Y$) if there exists at most one value of Y for every value of X. A functional dependency is like a primary key because if X and Y are placed in a separate table, X is the primary key.

G

Generalization Hierarchy a collection of entity types arranged in a hierarchical structure to show similarity in attributes. Each subtype or child entity represents a subset of its supertype or parent entity. See also Supertype and Subtype.

Group Condition a comparison involving an aggregate function such as SUM or COUNT. Group conditions cannot be evaluated until after the GROUP BY clause is evaluated.

GROUPING SETS Operator an operator in the GROUP BY clause that requires explicit specification of column combinations. The GROUPING SETS operator is appropriate when precise control over grouping is required. The SQL:1999 standard provides the GROUPING SETS operator as an extension of the GROUP BY clause to support multidimensional data.

H

Hash File a specialized file structure that supports search by key. Hash files transform a key value into an address to provide fast access. Hash files may have poor performance for sequential access. A hash file may be static (requires periodic reorganization) or dynamic (does not require periodic reorganization). A hash structure may be used as a primary or a secondary file structure.

Hash Join a join algorithm that uses an internal hash file for each table. The hash join algorithm can be used only for equi-joins. The hash join performs better than sort merge when the tables are not sorted or indexes do not exist. See also Sort Merge.

Hierarchical Form a formatted window for data entry and display using a fixed (main form) and variable (subform) part. One record is shown in the main form and multiple, related records are shown in the subform.

Hierarchical Report a formatted display of a query using indentation to show grouping and sorting. Also known as a control break report.

Histogram a two-dimensional graph where the x-axis represents column ranges and the y-axis represents the number of rows containing the range of values. Histograms support more detailed distribution data than the uniform value assumption. Histograms are part of a table profile.

HOLAP an acronym for Hybrid On-Line Analytical Processing. HOLAP is an implementation approach that combines the MOLAP and the ROLAP storage engines. HOLAP involves both relational and multidimensional data storage as well as combining data from both relational and multidimensional sources for data cube operations. See also MOLAP and ROLAP.

Homonym in view integration, a group of words that have the same sound and often the same spelling but have different meanings. Homonyms arise because of context of usage. See also Synonym.

Hot Spot common data that multiple users try to change simultaneously. Without adequate concurrency control, users may interfere with each other on hot spots. A system-independent hot spot does not depend on the details of a particular concurrency control manager. Typically, system-independent hot spots involve fields or rows in a database. A system-dependent hot spot depends on the details of the concurrency control manager, especially the locking granularity.

Hybrid Join a join algorithm that combines the sort merge and nested loops algorithms. The outer table must be sorted or have a join column index. The inner table must have an index on the join column. This algorithm can only be used for equi-joins. The hybrid join performs better than the sort merge when the inner table has a nonclustering index on the join column. See also Nested Loops and Sort Merge.

HyperText Markup Language (HTML) the language in which most Web documents are written. HTML combines the structure, the content, and the layout of a document. See also XML and XSL.

I

Identification Dependency involves a weak entity and one or more identifying relationships. See also Weak Entity and Identifying Relationship.

Identifying Relationship a relationship that provides a component of the primary key to a weak entity. See also Weak Entity and Identification Dependency.

Immediate Update Approach an approach used by a recovery manager to record database changes on disk. In this approach, database updates are written to the disk when they occur but after the corresponding log updates. To restore a database, both undo and redo operations may be needed. See also Deferred Update Approach and Write Ahead Log Protocol.

Implicit PL/SQL Cursor a cursor that can be used in procedures written in PL/SQL, the database programming language of Oracle. An implicit cursor is neither explicitly declared nor explicitly opened. Instead a special version of the FOR statement declares, opens, iterates, and closes a locally named SELECT statement. An implicit cursor cannot be referenced outside of the FOR statement in which it is declared. See also Cursor and Explicit PL/SQL Cursor.

Incorrect Summary a concurrency control problem in which a transaction reads several values, but another transaction updates some of the values while the first transaction is still executing. Also known as an inconsistent analysis.

Incremental Integration an approach to view integration where a partially integrated ERD is merged with the next view. To integrate n views, there are $n - 1$ integration steps.

Index a secondary file structure that provides an alternative path to the data. Indexes typically contain only key values, not the other fields in a logical record. Indexes may be organized as Btrees, hash structures, or bitmap structures. See also Btree File, Hash File, and Bitmap Index.

Index Selection for each table, select at most one clustering index and zero or more nonclustering indexes. In a clustering index, the order of the data records is close to the index order. In a nonclustering index, the order of the data records is unrelated to the index order. Index selection is an important subproblem of physical database design. Index selection usually chooses Btree indexes. Other kinds of indexes (hash and bitmap) also can be considered.

Indirect User users who access a database through reports or data extracts rather than through their own initiative. See also Parametric User and Power User.

Inexact String Matching searching for a pattern of strings rather than just one string. In SQL, inexact matching uses the LIKE operator and pattern-matching characters.

Information Life Cycle the stages of information transformation in an organization. Typical stages of an information life cycle include acquisition, storage, protection, processing, formatting, dissemination, and usage.

Information Resource Dictionary (IRD) a database of metadata that describes the entire information systems life cycle. The information resource dictionary system manages access to an IRD. Also known as the repository.

Information Resource Management a broad management philosophy that seeks to use information technology as a tool for processing, distributing, and integrating information throughout an organization.

Information System a system that accepts data from its environment, processes the data, and produces output data for decision making. An information system consists of people, procedures, input data, output data, databases, software, and hardware.

Information Systems Planning the process of developing enterprise models of data, processes, and organizational roles. Information systems planning evaluates existing systems, identifies opportunities to apply information technology for competitive advantage, and plans new systems. Also known as business systems planning, information systems engineering, and information systems architecture.

Inheritance a data modeling feature that supports sharing of attributes between a supertype and a subtype. Subtypes inherit attributes from their supertypes. In SQL:1999, inheritance applies to both user-defined types and subtable families. Inheritance supports sharing of code and data among similar objects.

Integration Strategy a mix of incremental and parallel approaches to integrate a set of views. The views are divided into subsets. For each subset of views, incremental integration is used. Parallel integration is usually applied to the ERDs resulting from integrating the view subsets.

Intent Lock a lock on a large database item (such as a table) indicating intention to lock smaller items contained in the larger item. Intent locks alleviate blocking when locking coarse items and allow efficient detection of conflicts among locks on items of varying granularity.

Internal Schema a description of the physical implementation of a database. See also Schema, Conceptual Schema, External View, and Three Schema Architecture.

Internet a global "network of networks" that is built from standard protocols.

Interrelated a fundamental characteristic of databases. Interrelated means that data stored as separate units can be connected to provide a whole picture. To support the interrelated characteristic, databases contain clusters of data known as entities and relationships connecting entities.

Intersection an operator of relational algebra that combines rows from two tables. The intersection operator finds rows that are common to both tables. Both tables must be union compatible to use the intersection operator.

Intranet a collection of computers and communication devices using the TCP/IP protocol. For security reasons, computers in an intranet are usually not accessible from computers on the Internet.

ISO International Standards Organization, one of the groups responsible for SQL standards.

Isolation Level defines the degree to which a transaction is separated from actions of other transactions. A transaction designer can balance concurrency control overhead with interference problems prevented by specifying the appropriate isolation level.

J

Join an operator of relational algebra used to combine rows from two tables. The join operator produces a table containing rows that match on a condition involving a column from each input table. See also Equi-join and Natural Join.

Join Algorithm an algorithm to implement the join operator. A query optimization component selects the least cost join algorithm for each join operation in a query. The common join algorithms are nested loops, sort merge, hybrid join, hash join, and star join.

Join Operator Style a way to formulate joins in a SELECT statement. The join operator style lists join operations in the FROM clause using the INNER JOIN and ON keywords.

K

Key Preserving Table an Oracle term for the updatable table in a join view. A join view preserves a table if every candidate key of the table can be a candidate key of the join result table. This means that the rows of an updatable join view can be mapped in a 1-1 manner with each key preserved table. In a join involving a 1-M relationship, the child table could be key preserved because each child row is associated with at most one parent row.

Knowledge Management applying information technology with human information processing capabilities and organization processes to support rapid adaptation to change.

L

Large Object Architecture an architecture for object databases in which large objects (binary or text) are stored in a database along with external software to manipulate large objects.

Law of Transitivity a rule that states if an object A is related to an object B and B is related to C, then one can conclude that A is related to C. Functional dependencies obey the law of transitivity. See also Functional Dependency and Transitive Dependency.

Load Time the time when a data warehouse is updated.

Load Time Lag the difference between transaction time and load time. Determining the load time lag is an important part of managing the refresh of a data warehouse. See also Valid Time Lag.

Local Mapping Transparency a level of independence in distributed DBMSs in which queries can be formulated without knowledge of local formats. However, knowledge of fragments and fragment allocations is necessary. See also Fragment, Fragmentation Transparency, and Location Transparency.

Location Transparency a level of independence in distributed DBMSs in which queries can be formulated without knowledge of locations. However, knowledge of fragments is necessary. See also Fragment, Fragmentation Transparency, and Local Mapping Transparency.

Lock a fundamental tool of concurrency control. A lock on a database item prevents other transactions from performing conflicting actions on the same item. See also Exclusive Lock, Intent Lock, and Shared Lock.

Locking Granularity the size of the database item locked. Locking granularity is a trade-off between waiting time (amount of concurrency permitted) and overhead (number of locks held).

Logged Change Data data obtained from a source system for refreshing a data warehouse. Logged change data involve files that record changes or other user activity such as Web logs or transaction logs. See also Cooperative Change Data, Snapshot Change Data, and Queryable Change Data.

Logical Expression an expression resulting in a true or false (Boolean) value. Logical expressions can involve comparisons and the logical operators (AND, OR, NOT, etc.).

Lost Update a concurrency control problem in which one user's update overwrites another user's update.

M

Main Form the fixed part of a hierarchical form. The main form shows one record at a time.

Mandatory Access Control a database security approach for highly sensitive and static databases. In mandatory control approaches, each object is assigned a classification level and each user is given a clearance level. A user can access a database element if the user's clearance level provides access to the classification level of the element.

Mandatory Relationship a relationship with a minimum cardinality of one or more. A mandatory relationship produces an existence dependency on the entity type associated with the minimum cardinality of one. See also Optional Relationship and Existence Dependency.

Many-to-Many (M-N) Relationship in the Entity Relationship Model, a relationship in which objects of each entity type can be related to many objects of the other entity type. M-N relationships have maximum cardinalities of more than one in each direction. In the Relational Model, two 1-M relationships and a linking or associative table represent an M-N relationship. See also One-to-Many Relationship and Relationship.

Materialized View a stored view that must be periodically synchronized with its source data. Relational DBMSs provide materialized views with summarized data for fast query response. See also Query Rewriting and View.

Message a request to invoke a method on an object. When an object receives a message, it looks for an implementation in its own class. If an implementation cannot be found, the message is sent to the object's parent class. See also Binding.

Message-Oriented Middleware maintain a queue of messages. A client process can place a message on a queue and a server can remove a message from a queue. Message-oriented middleware support complex messages among clients and servers.

Metadata data that describe other data including the source, use, value, and meaning of the data. See also Data Dictionary.

Middleware a software component in a client–server architecture that performs process management. Middleware allows servers to process messages efficiently from a large number of clients. In addition, middleware can allow clients and servers to communicate across heterogeneous platforms. Prominent kinds of database middleware include transaction-processing monitors, message-oriented middleware, and object-request brokers.

Modification Anomaly an unexpected side effect that occurs when changing the data in a table with excessive redundancies.

MOLAP an acronym for Multidimensional On-Line Analytical Processing. MOLAP is a storage engine that directly stores and manipulates data cubes. MOLAP engines generally offer the best query performance but suffer from limitations in the size of data cubes supported.

Multiple-Tier Architecture a client–server architecture with more than three layers: a PC client, a backend database server, an intervening middleware server, and application servers. The application servers perform business logic and manage specialized kinds of data such as images. See also Two-Tier Architecture and Three-Tier Architecture.

Multivalued Dependency (MVD) a constraint involving three columns. The MVD $A \rightarrow\rightarrow B \mid C$ (read A multidetermines B or C) means that (1) a given A value is associated with a collection of B and C values; and (2) B and C are independent given the relationships between A and B and A and C. All FDs are also MVDs, but not all MVDs are FDs. An MVD is nontrivial if it is also not an FD. See also Relationship Independence and Functional Dependency.

M-way (Multiway) Relationship a relationship involving more than two entity types. In some ERD notations such as the Crow's Foot, an M-way relationship is represented as an associative entity type.

N

Name Qualification preceding a column name with its table name. The column name alone is an abbreviation. If the same column name occurs in two tables in an SQL statement, the column name must be qualified with its table name. The combination of the table name and column name must be unique across all tables in a database.

Natural Join a variation of the join operator of relational algebra. In a natural join, the matching condition is equality (equi-join), one of the matching columns is discarded in the result table, and the join columns have the same unqualified names. See also Equi-join and Join.

Nested Loops a join algorithm that uses an outer table and an inner table. The nested loops algorithm is the most general join algorithm as it can be used to evaluate all join operations, not just equi-joins. The nested loops algorithm performs well when there are few rows in the outer table or when all pages of the inner table fit into memory. An index on a foreign key join column allows efficient usage of the nested loops algorithm when there are restrictive conditions on the parent table. See also Hash Join and Sort Merge.

Nested Query a query inside a query. In an SQL SELECT statement, a SELECT statement can be part of conditions in the HAVING and WHERE clauses. See Type I and Type II Nested Query for two variations. Also known as a subquery and an inner query.

Node Key a field(s) in a node of a form structure with unique values. The key of the root node is unique among all form instances. The key of a child node is unique within its parent node.

Nonclustering Index an index in which the order of the data records is not related to the index order. A nonclustering index is always a secondary file structure. See also Index Selection, Clustering Index, and Secondary File Structure.

Nonmatching Row a row that does not combine with a row from a second table to satisfy a join condition. The row will not be in the result of the join operation, but it will be in the result of an outer join operation.

Nonprocedural Database Language a language such as SQL that allows you to specify what part of a database to access rather than to code a complex procedure. Nonprocedural languages do not include looping statements.

Nonrepeatable Read a concurrency control problem in which a transaction reads the same value more than one time. In between reading the data item, another transaction modifies the data item.

Nontrivial MVD an MVD that is not also an FD. By definition, every FD is an MVD. However, not all MVDs are FDs. MVDs in which a column is associated with more than one value of two columns is a nontrivial MVD.

Normal Form a rule about allowable dependencies.

Normalization the process of removing redundancies from tables so that the tables are easier to change. To normalize a table, list the functional dependencies and make tables that satisfy a normal form, usually third normal form (3NF) or Boyce-Codd normal form (BCNF).

Null Value a special value that represents the absence of an actual value. A null value can mean that the actual value is unknown or does not apply to the given row.

O

Object an instance of a class in object-oriented computing. An object has a unique identifier that is invisible and nonchangeable.

Object Database Middleware an architecture for object databases in which middleware manages complex data possibly stored outside of a database along with traditional data stored in a database.

Object-Oriented DBMS a new kind of DBMS designed especially for objects. Object-oriented DBMSs have an object query processor and an object kernel. The Object Data Management Group provides the standard for object-oriented DBMSs.

Object Relational DBMS a relational DBMS extended with an object query processor for user-defined data types. SQL:1999 provides the standard for object relational DBMSs.

Object-Request Broker a kind of middleware that provides a high level of interoperability and message intelligence. To use an object-request broker, messages must be encoded in a standard interface description language. An object-request broker resolves platform differences between a client and a server and allows communication without knowing the location of the server.

OLAP (Online Analytical Processing) general name of technology to support multidimensional databases. OLAP technology encompasses the multidimensional data model and implementation approaches.

One-Sided Outer Join an outer join that produces the matching rows (the join part) as well as the nonmatching rows from only one of the tables, the designated input table.

One-to-Many (1-M) Relationship in the Entity Relationship Model, a relationship in which the maximum cardinality is 1 in one direction and M in the other direction. In the Relational Data Model, a referential integrity constraint usually indicates a 1-M relationship. See also Relationship and Many-to-Many Relationship.

One-to-Many (1-M) Updatable Query a type of updatable view in Microsoft Access involving one or more 1-M relationships.

Oper (Operational) Mart a just-in-time data mart usually built from one operational database in anticipation or in response to major events such as disasters and new product introductions. An oper mart supports peak demand for reporting and business analysis that accompanies a major event. See also Data Mart.

Operational Database a database to support the daily functions of an organization. Operational databases directly support major functions such as order processing, manufacturing, accounts payable, and product distribution.

Optimistic Concurrency Control a concurrency control approach in which transactions are permitted to access a database without acquiring locks. Instead, the concurrency control manager checks whether a conflict has occurred. The check can be performed either just before a transaction commits or after each read and write. By reviewing the relative time of reads and writes, the concurrency control manager can determine whether a conflict has occurred. If a conflict occurs, the concurrency control manager issues a rollback and restarts the offending transaction.

Optional Relationship a relationship with a minimum cardinality of zero. An optional relationship means that entities can be stored without participation in the relationship. See also Mandatory Relationship.

Outer Join an operator of relational algebra that combines two tables. In an outer join, the matching and nonmatching rows are retained in the result. See One-Sided and Full Outer Join for two variations of this operator.

Overlapping Triggers two or more triggers with the same timing, granularity, and applicable table. The triggers overlap if an SQL statement causes both triggers to fire. You should not depend on a particular firing order for overlapping triggers. See also Trigger and Trigger Execution Procedure.

P

Package a PL/SQL unit of modularity. Packages support a larger unit of modularity than procedures or functions. A package may contain procedures, functions, exceptions, variables, constants, types, and cursors. By grouping related objects together, a package provides easier reuse than individual procedures and functions.

Parallel Integration an approach to view integration where all views are integrated in one step. To integrate n views, there are n view design steps and one integration step. The view design steps may be performed in parallel by separate design teams.

Parametric User someone who uses a database by requesting existing forms or reports using parameters, input values that change from usage to usage. See also Indirect User and Power User.

Persistent a fundamental characteristic of databases. Persistent means that data have a lifetime longer than the execution of a computer program. To be persistent, data must reside on stable storage such as magnetic disk.

Phantom Read Problem a concurrency control problem in which a transaction executes a query with record conditions but another transaction inserts new rows or modifies existing rows while the first transaction is still executing. The first transaction then rexecutes the original query again, but the results are different than the results for the first execution. The new rows are phantom because they did not exist for the first execution of the query.

Physical Record collection of bytes that are transferred between volatile storage in main memory and stable storage on a disk. The number of physical record accesses is an important measure of database performance.

Pivot a data cube operator in which the dimensions in a data cube are rearranged. See also Data Cube.

Polymorphism a principle of object-oriented computing in which a computing system has the ability to choose among multiple implementations of a method. The appropriate implementation is chosen by the system (object DBMS or object-oriented programming language). Polymorphism permits a smaller vocabulary of procedures and incremental sharing of code.

Power User someone who uses a database by submitting unplanned or ad hoc requests for data. Power users should have a good understanding of nonprocedural access. See also Indirect User and Parametric User.

Primary Copy Protocol a protocol for concurrency control of distributed transactions. Each replicated fragment is designated as either the primary copy or a secondary copy. During distributed transaction processing, only the primary copy is guaranteed to be current at the end of a transaction. Updates may be propagated to secondary copies after the end of a transaction.

Primary File Structure a file structure storing both key data and nonkey data. Sequential files can only be file structures. Hash structures and Btrees can be primary or secondary file structures. See also Secondary File Structure.

Primary Key a specially designated candidate key. The primary key for a table cannot contain null values.

Procedural Language Interface a method to combine a nonprocedural language such as SQL with a programming language such as COBOL or Visual Basic. Embedded SQL is an example of a procedural language interface.

Process Model a graphical model showing the relationships between processes. A process can provide input data used by other processes or use output data of other processes. The well-known data flow diagram is an example of a process model.

Project an operator of relational algebra. A project operation retrieves a subset of specified columns of the input table. Duplicate rows are eliminated in the result if present.

Prototype a fast implementation of an application in an information system. Prototypes can demonstrate forms, reports, and menus to enable feedback from users.

Q

Query request to extract useful data. Query formulation involves translating a problem into a language (such as an SQL SELECT statement) understood by a DBMS.

Query Binding the process of associating a query with an access plan. Some DBMSs rebind automatically if a query changes or the database changes (file structures, table profiles, data types, etc.).

Query Rewriting a substitution process in which a materialized view replaces references to fact and dimension tables in a query. In addition to the substitution, the query optimizer evaluates whether the substitution will improve performance over the original query. See also Materialized View.

Queryable Change Data data obtained from a source system for refreshing a data warehouse. Since queryable change data come directly from a data source via a query, the data source must have timestamps. See also Cooperative Change Data, Logged Change Data, and Snapshot Change Data.

R

RAID (Redundant Arrays of Independent Disks) a collection of disks (a disk array) that operates as a single disk. RAID storage supports parallel read and write operations with high reliability.

RAID-1 an architecture for RAID storage in which redundant arrays of disks provide high reliability and performance but with large storage overhead. RAID-1 uses disk mirroring to achieve high performance and reliability.

RAID-5 an architecture for RAID storage in which randomly located error-correcting pages provide high reliability without excessive storage overhead. RAID-5 uses striping to achieve good performance and reliability without excessive storage overhead.

Read-Only View a view that can be used in SELECT statements but not in UPDATE, INSERT, and DELETE statements. All views are at least read-only.

Recovery Transparency a service provided by a DBMS to automatically restore a database to a consistent state after a failure. The recovery manager is the component of a DBMS responsible for recovery transparency.

Referenced Row a row of a parent table having a primary key value that is identical to the foreign key values of rows in a child table. See also Actions on Referenced Rows.

Referential Integrity an integrity constraint involving a candidate key in one table with the related foreign key of another table. Only two kinds of values can be stored in a foreign key: (1) a value matching a candidate key value in some row of the table containing the associated candidate key or (2) a null value. See also Primary Key, Candidate Key, and Foreign Key.

Relation synonymous with table. A term typically used in academic research about databases.

Relational Algebra a set of operators to manipulate relational databases. Each operator uses one or two tables as input and produces a new table as output.

Relational Data Model using tables, matching values for connections among tables, and table operators to represent a collection of data.

Relational DBMS a system that uses the Relational Data Model to manage collections of data.

Relationship in the Entity Relationship Model, a relationship is a named association among entity types. In the Relational model, a relationship is a connection among tables shown by column values in one table that match column values in another table. Referential integrity constraints and foreign keys indicate relationships in the Relational Model. See also One-to-Many Relationship, Many-to-Many Relationship, and Referential Integrity.

Relationship Cycle a collection of relationships arranged in a loop starting and ending with the same entity type. You should examine relationship cycles to determine whether a relationship can be derived from other relationships.

Relationship Equivalence a rule about the equivalence between 1-M and M-N relationships. An M-N relationship can be replaced by an associative entity type and two identifying 1-M relationships. See also Associative Entity Type and Identifying Relationship.

Relationship Independence a relationship that can be derived from two independent relationships.

Remote Procedure Call a method to share processing resources over a computer network in which a personal computer invokes a stored procedure on another computer in the network.

Report a stylized presentation of data appropriate to a selected audience. Reports enhance the appearance of data that are displayed or printed. See also Hierarchical Report.

Restrict an operator of relational algebra. A restrict operation retrieves a subset of rows that satisfy a given condition.

Reverse Engineering the ability to extract definitions from a target database management system and use the definitions to create an ERD and data dictionary properties. See also CASE Tool and Forward Engineering.

ROLAP an acronym for Relational On-Line Analytical Processing. ROLAP involves relational DBMS extensions to support multidimensional data. ROLAP engines support a variety of storage and optimization techniques for summary data retrieval.

Roll-Up a data cube operator that supports navigation from a more specific level of a dimension to a more general level of a dimension. The roll-up operator requires a hierarchical dimension. See also Drill-Down.

ROLLUP Operator an operator in the GROUP BY clause that augments the normal GROUP BY result with a partial set of subtotals. The SQL:1999 standard provides the CUBE operator as an extension of the GROUP BY clause to support multidimensional data. The ROLLUP operator is appropriate to summarize columns from the same dimension hierarchy.

Row Condition a comparison not involving an aggregate function. Row conditions are evaluated in the WHERE clause.

Rules about Referenced Rows rules that describe actions on related rows when a row in a primary key table (the referenced row) is deleted or its primary key is updated.

S

Save Point an intermediate point in a transaction in which a rollback may occur. Save points are supported by proprietary SQL extensions and by the SQL:1999 standard.

Schema a definition of the conceptual, external, or internal parts of a database. At the conceptual level, a schema is a diagram depicting the entities and relationships in a database. See also Three Schema Architecture, External View, Conceptual Schema, and Internal Schema.

Schema Mapping describes how a schema at a higher level is derived from a schema at a lower level. A mapping provides the knowledge to convert a request from a higher schema representation to a lower schema representation. See also Three Schema Architecture and Schema.

Second Generation Database Technology the first true DBMSs that managed multiple entity types and relationships. However, to obtain access to data, a computer program still had to be written. Second generation database technology was largely developed during the 1970s.

Second Normal Form (2NF) a table is in 2NF if every nonkey column is dependent on the whole key, not part of the key.

Secondary File Structure a file structure storing key data along with pointers to the nonkey data. Bitmap indexes can be secondary file structures only. Hash structures and Btrees may be primary or secondary file structures. See also Primary File Structure.

Self-Join a join between a table and itself (two copies of the same table). Typically, a self-join is used to query self-referencing relationships.

Self-Referencing Relationship a relationship involving the same table or entity type. Self-referencing relationships represent associations among members of the same set. Also known as a unary, reflexive, or recursive relationship.

Semi-Join Operator an operator of relational algebra that is especially useful for distributed database processing. A semi-join is half of a join: the rows of one table that match with at least one row of another table.

Sequential File a simple file organization in which records are stored in insertion order by key value. Sequential files are simple to maintain and provide good performance for processing large numbers of records.

Server a program that processes requests on behalf of a client. A database server may interpret SQL statements, locate data, update tables, check integrity rules, and return data back to clients.

Server-Side Connectivity an approach to Web database connectivity in which a browser communicates with a database server without invoking an external program. Although server-side connectivity is more scalable than the Common Gateway Interface, it requires a specialized Web server or a separate middleware server.

Shared a fundamental characteristic of databases. Shared means that a database can have multiple uses and users. A large database can have hundreds of functions that use it as well as thousands of users simultaneously accessing it.

Shared Lock a lock that allows some users to read a database item but prevents these users from changing the value of a database item. Shared locks conflict with exclusive locks but not other shared locks. A shared lock indicates that a user will read but not change the value of a database item. Also known as an S lock.

Simple Synthesis Procedure a set of steps to produce tables in BCNF using a collection of functional dependencies. The simple synthesis procedure is limited to simple dependency structures.

Slice a data cube operator in which a dimension is replaced by a single member value or with a summary of its member values. See also Dice.

Snapshot Change Data data obtained from a source system for refreshing a data warehouse. Snapshot change data involve periodic dumps of source data. To derive change data, a difference operation uses the two most recent snapshots. See also Cooperative Change Data, Logged Change Data, and Queryable Change Data.

Snowflake Schema a data modeling representation for multidimensional databases. In a relational database, a snowflake schema has multiple levels of dimension tables related to one or more fact tables. You should use the snowflake schema instead of the star schema for small dimension tables that are not in third normal form. See also Star Schema, Constellation Schema, Fact Table, and Dimension Table.

Sort Merge a join algorithm that requires both tables to be sorted on the join column. The sort merge algorithm can be used only for equi-joins. The sort merge algorithm performs well if the sort cost is small or if a clustered join index exists. See also Hash Join and Nested Loops.

Sparsity the extent of empty cells in a data cube. If a large number of cells are empty, the data cube can waste space and be slow to process. Special compression techniques can be used to reduce the size of sparse data cubes. Sparsity can be a problem if two or more dimensions are related such as products and regions where products are sold. See also Data Cube.

Specialized Media Server Architecture an architecture for object databases in which a dedicated server manages complex data outside of a database. Programmers use an application programming interface to access complex data.

SQL an acronym for the Structured Query Language. SQL is an industry-standard database language that includes statements for database definition (such as the CREATE TABLE statement), database manipulation (such as the SELECT statement), and database control (such as the GRANT statement). SQL began as a proprietary language developed by IBM. SQL is now a widely supported international standard for databases.

SQL:1999 the new standard of the Structured Query Language. SQL:1999 supports numerous extensions beyond SQL-92. An important extension is support for object relational databases. The SQL:1999 standard is so large that it may not be fully implemented for a number of years.

Standalone SQL using a specialized editor that submits SQL statements directly to the DBMS and displays the results returned from the DBMS. See also Embedded SQL.

Star Join a join algorithm that combines two or more tables in which there is one child table related to multiple parent tables in 1-M relationships. Each parent table must have a bitmap join index. The star join is the best join algorithm when there are highly selective conditions on the parent tables. The star join algorithm is widely used to optimize data warehouse queries. See also Bitmap Index.

Star Schema a data modeling representation for multidimensional databases. In a relational database, a star schema has a fact table in the center related to dimension tables. See also Snowflake Schema, Constellation Schema, Fact Table, and Dimension Table.

Statement-Level Interface a language style for integrating a programming language with a nonprocedural language such as SQL. A statement-level interface involves changes to the syntax of a host programming language to accommodate embedded SQL statements. SQL:1999 specifies statements to establish database connections, execute SQL statements, use the results of an SQL statement, associate programming variables with database columns, handle exceptions in SQL statements, and manipulate database descriptors.

Storage Area Network (SAN) a specialized high-speed network that connects storage devices and servers. The goal of SAN technology is to integrate different types of storage subsystems into a single system and to eliminate the potential bottleneck of a single server controlling storage devices. A SAN is complementary to RAID disk storage.

Stored Procedure a collection of statements that are managed by a DBMS. Stored procedures extend the capabilities of SQL. Most DBMSs provide a proprietary language in which to write stored procedures.

Stripe the set of physical records that can be read or written in parallel in RAID storage. Normally, a stripe contains a set of adjacent physical records.

Striping a technique for allocating physical records in RAID storage so that parallel read and write operations are possible.

Strong Type Checking the ability to ensure that expressions contain no incompatibility errors. Strong type checking is an important kind of error checking for object-oriented coding.

Subform the variable or repeating part of a hierarchical form. The subform can show multiple records at a time.

Subquery see Nested Query.

Subtype a child entity type in a generalization hierarchy. A subtype represents a more specialized entity type than its supertype.

Summarize an operator of relational algebra that compresses the rows of a table. A summarize operation produces a table with rows that summarize the rows of the input table. Aggregate functions are used to summarize the rows of the input table.

Superkey a column or combination of columns containing unique values for each row. The combination of every column in a table is always a superkey because rows in a table must be unique.

Supertype a parent entity type in a generalization hierarchy. A supertype represents a more general entity type than its subtypes.

Synonym in view integration, a group of words that are spelled differently but have the same meaning. Synonyms often occur because different parts of an organization may use different vocabulary to describe the same things. See also Homonym.

System a set of related components that work together to accomplish some objectives.

T

Table a named, two-dimensional arrangement of data. A table consists of a heading part and a body part.

Table Body synonymous with the rows of a table.

Table Heading consists of the table name, the column names, and a data type for each column.

Table Profile a statistical summary of the rows, columns, and participating relationships of a table. Table profiles are an important input of the physical database design phase because they are used to predict the fraction of a table accessed in a query.

Ternary Relationship a relationship involving three entity types. In some ERD notations such as the Crow's Foot notation, a ternary relationship is represented as an associative entity type with three 1-M relationships.

Third Generation Database Technology relational DBMSs incorporating nonprocedural access, optimization technology, and transaction processing capabilities. Third generation database technology was largely commercialized during the 1980s.

Third Normal Form (3NF) a table is in 3NF if it is in 2NF and every nonkey column is dependent only on the key.

Three Schema Architecture an architecture for compartmentalizing database descriptions. The Three Schema Architecture contains the external or user level, the conceptual level, and the internal or physical level. The Three Schema Architecture was proposed as a way to achieve data independence.

Three-Tier Architecture a client–server architecture with three layers: a PC client, a backend database server, and either a middleware or an application server. See also Two-Tier Architecture and Multiple-Tier Architecture.

Three-Tier Data Warehouse Architecture an architecture for a data warehouse in which user departments access data marts rather than the data warehouse. An extraction process involving the data warehouses periodically refreshes the data marts. See also Two-Tier Data Warehouse Architecture and Bottom-Up Data Warehouse Architecture.

Timesharing a computer network in which computer terminals are connected to a mainframe computer. Timesharing supports only small amounts of data transmitted between a mainframe computer and terminals.

Traditional Set Operators the union, intersection, and difference operators of relational algebra.

Transaction a unit of work that should be processed reliably. DBMSs provide recovery and concurrency control services to process transactions efficiently and reliably.

Transaction Boundary an important decision of transaction design in which an application consisting of a collection of SQL statements is divided into one or more transactions. Transaction boundary decisions can affect (positively or negatively) transaction throughput.

Transaction Log a table that contains a history of database changes. The recovery manager uses the log to recover from failures.

Transaction Processing reliable and efficient processing of large volumes of repetitive work. DBMSs ensure that simultaneous users do not interfere with each other and that failures do not cause lost work. See also Transaction.

Transaction Processing Council (TPC) an organization that develops standard, domain-specific benchmarks and publishes the results. The TPC has developed benchmarks for order entry transaction processing, ad hoc decision support queries, business reporting decision support, and Web ecommerce transaction processing. See also Benchmark.

Transaction-Processing Monitor an early and still important kind of database middleware. A transaction-processing monitor receives transactions, schedules them, and manages them to completion. Transaction-processing monitors also may support updating multiple databases in a single transaction.

Transaction Throughput the number of transactions processed per time interval. It is a measure of transaction processing performance. Typically, transaction throughput is reported in transactions per minute.

Transaction Time the time when an operational data source is updated.

Transitive Dependency a functional dependency derived by the law of transitivity. Transitive FDs should not be recorded as input to the normalization process. See also Functional Dependency and Law of Transitivity.

Trigger a rule that is stored and executed by a DBMS. Because a trigger involves an event, a condition, and a sequence of actions, it also is known as an event-condition-action rule. Triggers were not part of SQL-92, although many vendors provided extensions for them. Triggers are part of SQL:1999. See also Overlapping Triggers.

Trigger Execution Procedure specifies the order of execution among various kinds of triggers, integrity constraints, and database manipulation statements. Trigger execution procedures can be complex because the actions of a trigger may fire other triggers. See also Overlapping Triggers.

Two-Phase Commit Protocol (2PC) a rule to ensure that distributed transactions are atomic. 2PC uses a voting and a decision phase to coordinate commits of local transactions.

Two-Phase Locking Protocol (2PL) a rule to ensure that concurrent transactions do not interfere with each other. 2PL requires that locks are used before reading or writing a database item, a transaction waits if a conflicting lock is held on a data item, and locks are not released until new locks are no longer needed. To simplify implementation, most DBMSs hold at least exclusive locks until a transaction commits.

Two-Tier Architecture a client–server architecture in which a PC client and a database server interact directly to request and transfer data. The PC client contains the user interface code, the server contains the data access logic, and the PC client and the server share the validation and business logic. See also Three-Tier Architecture and Multiple-Tier Architecture.

Two-Tier Data Warehouse Architecture an architecture for a data warehouse in which user departments directly use the data warehouse rather than smaller data marts. See also Three-Tier Data Warehouse Architecture and Bottom-Up Data Warehouse Architecture.

Type I Nested Query a nested query in which the inner query does not reference any tables used in the outer query. Type I nested queries can be used for some join problems and some difference problems.

Type II Nested Query a nested query in which the inner query references a table used in the outer query. Type II nested queries can be used for difference problems but should be avoided for join problems.

U

Uncommitted Dependency a concurrency control problem in which one transaction reads data written by another transaction before the other transaction commits. If the second transaction aborts, the first transaction has read phantom data that will no longer exist. Also known as a dirty read.

Uniform Value Assumption assuming that each column value is equally likely (has the same number of rows). The uniform value assumption allows compact representation of a distribution, but it can lead to large estimation errors that lead to poor choices in query optimization and index selection.

Union an operator of relational algebra that combines rows from two tables. The result of a union operation has all the rows from either table. Both tables must be union compatible to use the union operator.

Union Compatibility a requirement for the union, intersection, and difference operators of relational algebra. Union compatibility requires that both tables have the same number of columns and each corresponding column have the same data type.

Updatable View a view that can be used in SELECT statements as well as UPDATE, INSERT, and DELETE statements. When modifying the rows of an updatable view, the DBMS translates the view modifications into modifications to rows of the base tables.

V

Valid Time the time when an event occurs.

Valid Time Lag the difference between the occurrence of an event in the real world (valid time) and the storage of the event in an operational database (transaction time). See also Valid Time, Load Time Lag, and Transaction Time.

View virtual or derived table. A view is derived from base or physical tables using a query. See also Materialized View.

View Materialization a method to process a query on a view by executing the query directly on the stored view. The stored view can be materialized on demand (when the view query is submitted) or periodically rebuilt from the base tables. For data warehouses, materialization is the preferred strategy for processing view queries.

View Modification a method to process a query on a view involving the execution of only one query. A query using a view is translated into a query using base tables by replacing references to the view with its definition. For transaction databases, view modification is the preferred strategy for processing view queries.

Volatile Storage storage that loses its state when the power is disconnected. Main memory is typically volatile. Nonvolatile storage does not lose its state when power is disconnected. A hard disk is an example of nonvolatile storage.

W

Waterfall Model a reference framework for information systems development. The waterfall model consists of iteration among analysis, design, and implementation.

Weak Entity an entity type that borrows part or all of its primary key from another entity type. A weak entity is also existent dependent. See also Identification Dependency and Identifying Relationship.

Web Database Connectivity client–server architectures that allow a Web page to query and update remote databases managed by servers on the Internet.

WITH CHECK OPTION a clause in the CREATE VIEW statement that can be used to prevent updates with side effects. If the WITH CHECK OPTION is specified, INSERT or UPDATE statements that violate a view's WHERE clause are rejected.

Workflow a collection of related tasks structured to accomplish a business process.

World Wide Web (WWW) a collection of pages that can be viewed over the Internet. In the WWW, a browser displays pages sent by a Web server. The WWW is the most popular application on the Internet.

Write Ahead Log Protocol in the immediate update recovery process, log records must be written to stable storage before database records.

X

XML (eXtensible Markup Language) a simple language that supports the specification of other languages. XML has evolved into a collection of languages that separate the content, structure, and formatting of documents on the World Wide Web. The XML Schema Language, an important member of the XML language family, supports standardization of the structure of XML documents.

XSL (eXtensible Style Language) a language for defining the format of documents on the World Wide Web. XSL supports the transformation of XML documents into HTML and other layout languages. XSL allows device-dependent layout of Web documents.

BIBLIOGRAPHY

Batini, C., Ceri, S., and Navathe, S. *Conceptual Database Design,* Redwood City, CA, Benjamin/Cummings, 1992.

Batra, D. "A Method for Easing Normalization of User Views," *Journal of Management Information Systems* 14, 1 (Summer 1997), 215–233.

Bernstein, P. "Middleware: A Model for Distributed Services," *Communications of the ACM* 39, 2 (February 1996), 86–97.

Bernstein, P. "Repositories and Object-Oriented Databases," in *Proceedings of BTW 97,* Ulm, Germany, Springer-Verlag, (1997), pp. 34–46 (reprinted in *ACM SIGMOD Record* 27 (1), March 1998).

Bernstein, P., and Dayal, U. "An Overview of Repository Technology," in *Proceedings of the 20th Conference on Very Large Data Bases,* San Francisco, CA, Morgan Kaufmann, August 1994, pp. 705–713.

Bernstein, P., and Newcomer, E. *Principles of Transaction Processing,* San Francisco, CA, Morgan Kaufmann, 1997.

Bontempo, C., and Zagelow, G. "The IBM Data Warehouse Architecture," *Communications of the ACM* 41, 9 (September 1998), 38–41.

Booch, G., Jacobson, I., and Rumbaugh, J. *The Unified Modeling Language User Guide,* Reading, MA, Addison-Wesley, 1998.

Bouzeghoub, M., Fabret, F., and Matulovic-Broque, M. "Modeling Data Warehouse Refreshment Process as a Workflow Application," in *Proceedings of the International Workshop on Design and Management of Data Warehouses,* Heidelberg, Germany (June 1999).

Bowman, J., Emerson, S., and Darnovsky, M. *The Practical SQL Handbook,* Reading, MA, Addison-Wesley, 1996.

Cannan, S., and Otten, G. *SQL: The Standard Handbook,* Berkshire, England, McGraw-Hill Europe, November 1992.

Carlis, J., and Maguire, J. *Mastering Data Modeling,* Reading, MA, Addison-Wesley, 2001.

Cattell, R., and Barry, D. *The Object Database Standard: ODMG 2.0,* San Francisco, CA, Morgan Kaufmann, November 1997.

Celko, J. *Joe Celko's SQL Puzzles & Answers,* San Francisco, CA, Morgan Kaufmann, 1997.

Ceri, S., and Pelagatti, G. *Distributed Databases: Principles and Systems,* New York, NY, McGraw-Hill, 1984.

Chaudhuri, S. "An Overview of Query Optimization in Relational Systems," in *Proceedings of the ACM Symposium on Principles of Database Systems,* Seattle, WA, 1998, pp. 34–43.

Chaudhuri, S., and Narasayya, V. "An Efficient, Cost-Driven Index Selection Tool for Microsoft SQL Server," in *Proceedings of the 23rd VLDB Conference,* Athens, Greece, 1997, pp. 146–155.

Chaudhuri, S., and Narasayya, V. "Automating Statistics Management for Query Optimizers," *IEEE Transactions on Knowledge and Data Engineering* 13, 1 (January/February 2001), 7–28.

Choobineh, J., Mannino, M., Konsynski, B., and Nunamaker, J. "An Expert Database Design System Based on Analysis of Forms," *IEEE Trans. Software Engineering* 14, 2 (February 1988), 242–253.

Choobineh, J., Mannino, M., and Tseng, V. "A Form-Based Approach for Database Analysis and Design," *Communications of the ACM* 35, 2 (February 1992), 108–120.

Claudio, C. "Health Care Management," *Communications of the ACM* 41, 9 (September 1998), 58–61.

Codd, T. "A Relational Model for Large Shared Data Banks," *Communications of the ACM* 13, 6 (June 1970).

Date, C. "What Is a Distributed Database System," in *Relational Database Writings 1985–1989,* C. J. Date (ed.), Reading, MA, Addison-Wesley, 1990.

Date, C. *An Introduction to Database Systems,* 6th Ed., Reading, MA, Addison-Wesley, 1995.

Date, C., and Darwen, H. *A Guide to the SQL Standard,* Reading, MA, Addison-Wesley, 1997.

Davenport, T., and Prusak, L. *Working Knowledge: How Organizations Manage What They Know,* Boston, MA, Harvard Business School Press, 1997.

Davis, J. "Universal Servers: Part 1 and Part 2," *DBMS Online,* June and July 1997, http://www.dbmsmag.com/9706d13.html.

Davydov, M. "Capitalizing on Information Assets," *Database Programming and Design* 6, February 1993, 34–41.

Devlin, B. *Data Warehouse: From Architecture to Implementation,* Reading, MA, Addison Wesley Longman, 1997.

Elmasri, R., and Navathe, S. *Fundamentals of Database Systems,* 4th Ed., Redwood City, CA, Addison-Wesley, 2002.

Ensor, D., and Stevenson, D. *Oracle Design,* Sebastopol, CA, O'Reilly and Associates, 1997.

Fagin, R. "A Normal Form for Relational Databases That Is Based on Domains and Keys," *ACM Transactions on Database Systems* 6, 3 (September 1981), 387–415.

Fernandez, E., Summers, R., and Wood, C. *Database Security and Integrity,* Reading, MA, Addison-Wesley, 1981.

Finkelstein, S., Schkolnick, M., and Tiberio, T. "Physical Database Design for Relational Databases," *ACM Transactions on Database Systems* 13, 1 (March 1988), 91–128.

Fisher, J., and Berndt, D. "Creating False Memories: Temporal Reconstruction Errors in Data Warehouses," in *Proceedings Workshop on Technologies and Systems (WITS 2001),* New Orleans, December 2001.

Fowler, M., and Scott, K. *UML Distilled,* Reading, MA, Addison-Wesley, 1997.

Gardner, S. "Building the Data Warehouse," *Communications of the ACM* 41, 9 (September 1998), 52–57.

Gibson, M., Hughes, C., and Remington, W. "Tracking the Trade-Offs with Inverted Lists," *Database Programming and Design* 2, 1 (January 1989), 28–34.

Gillette, R., Muench, D., and Tabaka, J. *Physical Database Design for Sybase SQL Server,* Englewood Cliffs, NJ, Prentice Hall, 1996.

Graefe, G. "Options for Physical Database Design," *ACM SIGMOD Record* 22, 3 (September 1993), 76–83.

Gray, J., and Reuter, A. *Transaction Processing: Concepts and Techniques,* San Francisco, CA, Morgan Kaufmann, 1993.

Groff, J., and Weinberg, P. *SQL: The Complete Reference,* New York, NY, Osborne McGraw-Hill, 1999.

Guimaraes, T. "Information Resources Management: Improving the Focus," *Information Resources Management Journal* 1, Fall 1988, 10–21.

Gulutzan, P., and Pelzer, T. *SQL-99 Complete, Really,* Lawrence, KS, R & D Books, 1999.

Hackathorn, R., and Karimi, J. "A Framework for Comparing Information Engineering Methods," *MIS Quarterly* 12, 2 (June 1988), 203–219.

Hawryszkiewycz, I. *Database Analysis and Design,* New York, NY, SRA, 1984.

Imhoff, C. "Intelligent Solutions: Oper Marts: An Evolution in the Operational Data Store," *DM Review* 11, 9 (September 2001), 16–18.

Inmon, W. *Information Systems Architecture,* New York, NY, John Wiley & Sons, 1986.

Inmon, W. *Building the Data Warehouse,* 2nd Ed., New York, NY, John Wiley & Sons, 1996.

Jarke, M., and Koch, J. "Query Optimization in Database Systems," *ACM Computing Surveys* 16, 2 (June 1984), 111–152.

Kent, W. "A Simple Guide to the Five Normal Forms in Relational Database Theory," *Communications of the ACM* 26, 2 (February 1983), 120–125.

Kimball, R. "Dealing with Dirty Data," *DBMS* 9, 10 (September 1996), 55–62.

Kimball, R. "Slowly Changing Dimensions," *DBMS* 9, 4 (April 1996), 18–22.

Kimball, R. *The Data Warehouse Toolkit,* 2d Ed., New York, NY, John Wiley & Sons, 2002.

Mannino, M., Chu, P., and Sager, T. "Statistical Profile Estimation in Database Systems," *ACM Computing Surveys* 20, 3 (September 1988), 191–221.

Martin, J. *Strategic Data-Planning Methodologies,* Englewood Cliffs, NJ, Prentice Hall, 1982.

Melton, J., and Simon, A. *Understanding the New SQL: A Complete Guide,* San Fransisco, CA, Morgan Kaufmann, 1992.

Melton, J., and Simon, A. *SQL:1999 Understanding Relational Language Components,* San Fransisco, CA, Morgan Kaufmann, 2001.

Muller, R. *Database Design for Smarties: Using UML for Data Modeling,* San Francisco, CA, Morgan Kaufmann, February 1999.

Nelson, M., and DeMichiel, L. "Recent Trade-Offs in SQL3," *ACM SIGMOD Record* 23, 4 (December 1994), 84–89.

Nijssen, G., and Halpin, T. *Conceptual Schema and Relational Database Design,* Sydney, Prentice Hall of Australia, 1989.

Orfali, R., Harkey, D., and Edwards, J. *The Essential Client/Server Survival Guide,* 2nd Ed., New York, John Wiley & Sons, 1996.

Ozsu, T., and Valduriez, P. *Principles of Distributed Database Systems,* Englewood Cliffs, NJ, Prentice Hall, 1991.

Park, C., Kim, M., and Lee, Y. "Finding an Efficient Rewriting of OLAP Queries Using Materialized Views in Data Warehouses," *Decision Support Systems* 32, 12 (2002), 379–399.

Peinl, P., Reuter, A., and Sammer, H. "High Contention in a Stock Trading Database: A Case Study," in *Proceedings of the ACM SIGMOD Conference,* Chicago, IL, May 1988, pp. 260–268.

Prusak, L. (ed.) *Knowledge in Organizations,* Boston, MA, Butterworth-Heinemann, 1997.

Redman, T. *Data Quality: Management and Technology,* New York, Bantam Books, 1992.

Rodgers, U. "Denormalization: Why, What, and How?" *Database Programming and Design* 2, 12 (December 1989), 46–53.

Saaty, T. *The Analytic Hierarchy Process,* New York, McGraw-Hill, 1988.

Schumacher, R. "Oracle Performance Strategies," *DBMS* 10, (1994), 89–93.

Scott, J. "Warehousing Over the Web," *Communications of the ACM* 41, 9 (September 1998), 64–65.

Sheth, A., Georgakopoulos, D., and Hornrick, M. "An Overview of Workflow Management: From Process Modeling to Workflow Automation Infrastructure," *Distributed and Parallel Databases* 3 (1995), 119–153, Kluwer Academic Publishers.

Sigal, M. "A Common Sense Development Strategy," *Communications of the ACM* 41, 9 (September 1998), 42–48.

Stonebraker, M., with Moore, D. *Object Relational DBMSs: The Next Great Wave,* San Francisco, CA, Morgan Kaufmann, 1996.

Strong, D., Lee, Y., and Wang, R. "10 Potholes in the Road to Information Quality," *IEEE Computer* 30, 8 (August 1997), 38–46.

Su, S., Dujmovic, J., Batory, D., Navathe, S., and Elnicki, R. "A Cost–Benefit Decision Model: Analysis, Comparison, and Selection of Data Management Systems," *ACM Transactions on Database Systems* 12, 3 (September 1987), 472–520.

Sutter, J. "Project-Based Warehouses," *Communications of the ACM* 41, 9 (September 1998), 49–51.

Teorey, T. *Database Modeling and Design,* 3rd Ed., San Francisco, CA, Morgan Kaufmann, 1999.

Teorey, T., and Fry, J. *Design of Database Structures,* Englewood Cliffs, NJ, Prentice Hall, 1982.

Ullman, J. *Principles of Database and Knowledge Base Systems,* Volume I, Rockville, MD, Computer Science Press, 1988.

Viehman, P. "24 Ways to Improve Database Performance," *Database Programming and Design* 7 (February 1994), 32–41.

Watson, H., and Haley, B. "Managerial Considerations," *Communications of the ACM* 41, 9 (September 1998), 32–37.

Watson, R. *Data Management: An Organizational Perspective,* New York, John Wiley and Sons, 1996.

Weldon, J. *Data Base Administration,* New York, Plenum Press, 1981.

Whitten, J., and Bentley, L. *Systems Analysis and Design Methods,* New York, Irwin/McGraw-Hill, 2001.

Zahedi, F. "The Analytic Hierarchy Process: A Survey of the Method and Its Applications," *Interfaces* 16, 4 (1986), 96–108.

INDEX